Cambridge Preparation for the TOEFL® Test

JOLENE GEAR

Consultant
JOHN HASKELL

CAMBRIDGE
UNIVERSITY PRESS

Published by the Press Syndicate of the University of Cambridge
The Pitt Building, Trumpington Street, Cambridge CB2 1RP
40 West 20th Street, New York, NY 10011-4211, USA
10 Stamford Road, Oakleigh, Melbourne 3166, Australia

First published 1993
Second printing 1994

Printed in the United States of America

Library of Congress Cataloging-in-Publication Data

Gear, Jolene.
Cambridge preparation for the TOEFL test / Jolene Gear;
consultant, John Haskell.
p.   cm.
Includes index.
ISBN 0-521-36745-X (pbk.)
1. Test of English as a Foreign Language – Study guides.
2. English language – Textbooks for foreign speakers. 3. English
language – Examinations – Study guides. I. Title.
PE1128.G35   1993
428.2'4'076 – dc20   92-46239
                                                                      CIP

A catalog record for this book is available from the British Library

ISBN 0-521-36745-X   Book
ISBN 0-521-36539-2   Cassette Set
ISBN 0-521-42191-8   Book/Cassette Set Package

Book design: McNally Graphic Design
Layouts and text composition: Leon Bolognese & Associates, Inc.

ACKNOWLEDGMENTS

I would like to thank the many people who made the publication of this book possible. My deepest appreciation goes to my husband, Robert Gear, who contributed numerous items and assisted in researching, proofreading, piloting, and revising throughout the preparation of the manuscript. I am also indebted to Sandra Graham and her colleagues at Cambridge University Press for the advice, patience, understanding, and professionalism that they demonstrated throughout the process of bringing this manuscript into print.

Also, my gratitude goes to John Haskell, my ETS consultant, who read and commented on the early drafts of this manuscript; Ahmed Gomaa and my colleagues at the University of Kuwait for initial piloting and suggestions; Ted Quock at Simul Academy, Tokyo, Japan, for his helpful comments in the pilot study; and those teachers and students from the following institutions who took part in field-testing the book and cassettes:

American Language and Culture Institute – CSU, California, USA
Cambridge Centre for Languages, Cambridge, England
CES Inc., New York, USA
Ecole Centrale de Lyon, France
Ecole des Cadres, Paris, France
ESARC–ESSIGE, St. Clément, France
D. B. Hood Community School, Toronto, Canada
Istituto Americano, Florence, Italy
ISMRA, Caen, France
Kyoto YMCA English School, Japan
Mohawk College, Hamilton, Canada
Nichibei Kaiwa Gakuin, Tokyo, Japan
San José State University, California, USA
Sankei International College, Toyko, Japan
Sheridan College, Mississauga, Canada
Simul Academy, Tokyo Japan
Temple University, Tokyo, Japan
Trident College, Hiroshima, Japan
Université Paris-Dauphiné, France
University of Arkansas at Little Rock, USA
University of California Extension – Davis, USA
University of Florida, USA
University of Washington, USA
Vincennes University, Indiana, USA

Finally, a special word of thanks goes to my father-in-law, William Gear, who helped me meet deadlines by providing a word processor, office space, and financial support when we were unable to return to our positions at the University of Kuwait owing to circumstances in the Gulf.

CONTENTS

TO THE USER

About the book

Cambridge Preparation for the TOEFL® Test helps you build the skills necessary to answer the questions on the TOEFL successfully. Also, it thoroughly familiarizes you with the TOEFL format and suggests test-taking strategies to help you improve your TOEFL scores.

The book and its accompanying cassettes may be used for self-study or as a classroom text for TOEFL preparation courses. You may also wish to use the text to review or refresh your English language skills.

Important features of this book

- An **introduction** that explains what the TOEFL is and other information that you need to know about the test.

- A comprehensive **table of contents** in which the entries identify the contents of each exercise in the text.

- **A Diagnostic Test**, which helps you to pinpoint your weaknesses in English and which directs you to the exercises that will help you strengthen those areas.

- Test-taking **strategies** for each of the four sections of the TOEFL – Listening Comprehension, Structure and Written Expression, Vocabulary and Reading Comprehension, and the Test of Written English.

- **Exercises** that isolate and gradually build upon specific skills needed for success on the TOEFL.

- Several short **mini-tests** in each section which use the TOEFL format and which allow you to check your mastery of a particular set of skills.

- A complete TOEFL-format **section test** at the end of the Listening Comprehension, Structure and Written Expression, and Vocabulary and Reading Comprehension sections. Each of these tests covers the material of its corresponding section and indicates whether you have mastered the skills in that section.

- Two full-length **Practice Tests**, which give you further practice with the TOEFL format and test-taking strategies. The Practice Tests' answer keys direct you to the exercises that will help you strengthen those areas which are causing you difficulties.

- An explanatory **Answer Key**, which gives reasons for correct and incorrect answers for many exercises and tests.

- **Cassettes** that include all the Listening Comprehension exercises and Listening Comprehension test material in the text. Like the actual TOEFL, many different native American English speakers have been used in the recording to give you the opportunity to hear a wide selection of voices.

- **Transcripts** of all the Listening Comprehension exercises and Listening Comprehension test materials on the cassettes. The transcripts aid you in checking your answers further by allowing you to compare your responses with what was actually stated.

- An **index** that allows you to easily locate exercises that work on specific skills (e.g., making inferences) or grammar points (e.g., subject-verb agreement).

- **Extended practices**, which provide additional work in many skill areas.

- **Cross-references**, which indicate the pages where explanations, transcripts, or other related exercises can be found.

How to use *Cambridge Preparation for the TOEFL Test*

1. Complete the full-length, TOEFL-format Diagnostic Test on page 6. The Diagnostic Test will highlight areas that you need to concentrate on the most, thus saving you from spending time studying material you already know.

2. When you have completed the Diagnostic Test, check your answers using the Answer Key starting on page 422. For every wrong answer you gave, the Answer Key will direct you to exercises that will build the skills you need in order to answer that type of question correctly.

3. Read the strategies at the beginning of the Listening Comprehension, Structure and Written Expression, Vocabulary and Reading Comprehension, and the Test of Written English sections.

4. Work through the exercises that concentrate on the skills you need to develop. Take the mini-tests as you proceed through a section to check your progress.

5. When you have finished all the necessary exercises in a particular section, take the test at the end of that section to verify your progress in mastering the skills. For example, once you have worked through the Listening Comprehension exercises, take the Listening Comprehension TOEFL Test at the end of the Listening Comprehension section.

6. Take the two full-length, TOEFL-format Practice Tests. You may want to take one halfway through your course of study to confirm your progress and then take the other as a final check before taking the TOEFL.

7. When you have completed a Practice Test, check your answers using the Answer Key. For every wrong answer you gave, the Answer Key will direct you to exercises that will build the skills you need in order to answer that type of question correctly.

Note: It is probably not necessary for you to do every exercise in this book in preparation for the TOEFL, so concentrate on the exercises covering your weaknesses as indicated by the Diagnostic Test and the Practice Tests. Moreover, it is not necessary for you to complete all the items within an exercise. If you discover that the exercise is too easy for you, go on to an exercise that will be more challenging.

TO THE TEACHER

- The Diagnostic Test will show you the areas that your students need to concentrate on the most. Don't feel that every exercise, or all items within an exercise, must be completed.

- When students are doing the TOEFL-format exercises/tests, provide the same test conditions that the students will experience during the actual tests (e.g., use answer sheets, play the cassettes without pauses, allow only one section to be worked on during the time alloted).

- In skills-building exercises, pause the cassette after each question if students need more time to answer. Gradually reduce the pauses until the students can answer the questions in the amount of time allowed on the TOEFL.

- Use the exercises in all sections to build skills in other areas.

    There may be many unfamiliar words, which would be useful to learn, in sections other than the Vocabulary section. Help students to identify which of the words are useful and which may never be encountered again.

    Making inferences, drawing conclusions, and identifying topics are important skills to acquire for success in both listening and reading comprehension.

    An understanding of the grammatical structure of a sentence is important for determining the meaning of a Listening Comprehension item.

    The format of the Listening Comprehension talks, the Reading Comprehension passages, and the TWE essays is similar; that is, they all begin with an introduction that includes the topic, continue with ideas which support the topic, and end with a conclusion.

- Useful homework assignments can be made outside of the book (e.g., watching an English movie, listening to an English radio program, interviewing a native English speaker, reading an English newspaper or magazine article). Stress to the students that all English language experience is useful in studying for the TOEFL.

- In class, focus on areas that the Diagnostic Test has indicated most students are having trouble understanding. Homework assignments can be individualized so that each student can focus on his or her specific areas of difficulties.

- It is more important to thoroughly know the fundamental structures found on every test (e.g., articles, simple subject and verb agreement) than to spend too much time concentrating on more complex structures (e.g., subjunctives) that may not occur on any particular test.

INTRODUCTION TO THE TOEFL

Reasons for taking the TOEFL

The Test of English as a Foreign Language (TOEFL) is an examiniation used to evaluate a nonnative English speaker's proficiency in the English language. Many North American colleges and universities, as well as a large number of institutions, agencies, and programs, ask for official TOEFL score reports. An acceptable score on the TOEFL depends on the specific requirements of the particular institution or agency involved.

To be admitted to a North American college or university, you will probably need a score of 475 to 550. Although some colleges accept students with a low score (under 450), usually those students are required to enroll in remedial classes or in ESL classes as part of their course of study. Other colleges and universities require a high score (600 or above). This score is frequently required for students who wish to work at the graduate level. A few colleges and universities don't require nonnative English-speaking students to take the TOEFL. They may, however, have their own English proficiency exam which students are required to take upon arrival. Because these exams test the same skills as the TOEFL, preparing yourself for the TOEFL is a good way to prepare for any English proficiency exam.

Information about the TOEFL

The *Bulletin of Information for TOEFL/TWE and TSE* is available from the Eductional Testing Service (ETS) in Princeton, New Jersey, USA. This *Bulletin* includes the necessary registration forms and the instructions for completing the forms, as well as information concerning methods of payment and special services. You must register in advance using the registration form and envelope provided in the *Bulletin*. You cannot register at the center on the test date. To receive a copy of the *Bulletin*, write to:

TOEFL/TSE Services
P.O. Box 6151
Princeton, NJ 08541-6151
USA

You should register in advance of the given deadlines to ensure a place because the test centers have limited seating and may fill up early. Tests are administered on Fridays and Saturdays, and you can register for either day. Check the bulletin to confirm that the center(s) in your area will be open on the date(s) you select.

Some colleges and universities require their propsective students to take the Test of Written English (TWE). This test is administered with the TOEFL five times a year. Be sure you have requested a date when a Test of Written English is included if the institution you wish to attend requires that score.

Some universities also require their prospective students to take the Test of Spoken English (TSE). If you intend to register for this test on the same day as the TOEFL test, you can use the same registration form. However, if you decide not to take the TOEFL and TSE on the same day, you must register separately for each test date.

Test scores are sent to the test taker and to any colleges and universities you have indicated on the registration form. Most colleges accept only the official score report received directly from ETS.

Before the test date, you will receive an admission ticket. If you have not received your ticket within two weeks of the test date, you should contact TOEFL/TSE Services at the numbers given in the Bulletin. Attached to your admission ticket will be a TOEFL photo file record. You must sign the form and attach a recent photograph of yourself showing you as you will look on the day of the test. You will be required to present this record at the test center.

To be admitted to the test center, you must show your admission ticket, the TOEFL photo file record, and the form of identification printed on your admission ticket (e.g., your passport). In addition to your admission ticket and identification documents, you should bring a watch, a good eraser, and several sharpened #2 or HB black lead pencils. Do not bring paper, recording devices, cameras, dictionaries, and so on.

Plan on being at the test center for at least 3 1/2 hours. The total time for taking the TOEFL is under 3 hours; the TWE takes approximately 30 minutes. Remember that in addition to the actual test-taking time, time is needed for checking identification, going over the instructions, and filling out the personal information sheet.

You may not change your test date or cancel your registration. You may, however, receive a partial credit for test dates missed if you request one within 60 days of the original test date. Check the *Bulletin* for details.

You can take the TOEFL as many times as you wish. However, colleges and universities usually consider only the most recent score. ETS keeps records of scores for 2 years. You will probably have to take the TOEFL again if your score report is more than 2 years old.

TOEFL format

Table 1 gives the general outline for the Institutional Testing Program (ITP). This TOEFL is used by institutions and businesses. It is administered only to students in English programs that have made special arrangements with ETS. The scores from the ITP are usually not considered valid for university admission requirements.

The TOEFL tests administered on Fridays and Saturdays usually have the same format and length.

TABLE 1   TOEFL Format

Section	Number of items	Time
Listening Comprehension		
Part A similar statement identification	20	
Part B questions over short conversations	15	
Part C questions over mini-talks	15	
Total	50	30–40 minutes
Structure and Written Expression		
Identifying correct completion	15	
Identifying incorrect words or phrases	25	
Total	40	25 minutes
Vocabulary and Reading Comprehension		
Identify synonyms	30	
Reading passages	30	
Total	60	45 minutes
Test of Written English*		
One essay, 250–300 words	1	30 minutes

*The Test of Written English is given five times a year.

Scoring information

Sections 1, 2, and 3

The score you receive on the TOEFL is not the percentage of correct answers. Statistical procedures are used to convert the correct-answer score into a score that equates the scores for people of equal ability. In other words, if a particular test is more difficult, the converted score reflects the same English ability that the taker's score on an easier version would reflect.

For a general idea of your total score, use Table 2 to convert your Practice Test scores into a TOEFL score. Note: This may not be the exact score you will receive on the TOEFL.

TABLE 2

Correct answer score	Converted scores		
	Section 1	Section 2	Section 3
60			66–67
57–59			64–65
54–56			62–63
51–53			60–61
48–50	65–68		58–59
45–47	61–64		56–57
42–44	58–60		54–55
39–41	56–57	65–68	51–53
36–38	54–55	62–64	49–50
33–35	52–53	58–61	47–48
30–32	50–51	54–57	45–46
27–29	48–49	51–53	43–44
24–26	46–47	48–50	40–42
21–23	44–45	45–47	38–39
18–20	42–43	42–44	35–37
15–17	40–41	39–41	33–34
12–14	38–39	36–38	31–32
9–11	35–37	33–35	29–30
6–8	31–34	29–32	26–28
3–5	28–30	24–28	24–25
0–2	25–27	20–23	21–23

Use Table 3 to determine your scores for Practice Tests 1 and 2 in this book.

TABLE 3

	Test 1		Test 2	
	Correct answer score	Converted score	Correct answer score	Converted score
Section 1	_____	_____ – _____	_____	_____ – _____
Section 2	_____	_____ – _____	_____	_____ – _____
Section 3	_____	_____ – _____	_____	_____ – _____
Total of converted score		_____ _____		_____ _____
Multiply by 10		_____ _____		_____ _____
Divided by 3		_____ _____		_____ _____
TOEFL score		_____ – _____		_____ – _____

Example for calculating your score

If you had 40 correct in Section 1, 30 correct in Section 2, and 35 correct in Section 3, enter those numbers in the "Correct answer score " column in Table 3. Now find "40" (the number of correct answers for Section 1) in the "Correct answer score" column in Table 2, and look across to the converted scores in the "Section 1" column: "56–57." Write "56" and "57" on the "Converted score" lines in Table 3. Do the same for the correct answer scores for Sections 2 and 3. Add the converted scores, multiply them by 10 and then divide that number by 3. Round off to the nearest number. Your TOEFL score will be between these two numbers. Table 4 shows a worked-out example.

TABLE 4

	Test 1	
	Correct answer score	**Converted score**
Section 1 ·	40	56 – 57
Section 2	30	54 – 57
Section 3	35	47 – 48
Total of converted score		157 162
Multiply by 10		1570 1620
Divided by 3		523.3 540
TOEFL score		523 – 540

Your total score will be between 523 and 540.

Essay score

The TWE is scored on a scale from 1 to 6. A score of 6 shows strong writing abilities, 5 average writing abilities, and 4 minimal writing abilities. A score of 3, 2, or 1 shows a lack of writing technique.

Your essay is read by two ETS evaluators. Each one gives your essay a score. The two scores are averaged to produce your final TWE score. This TWE score does not affect your total TOEFL score.

For the two practice TOEFL essays in this book, you should ask an experienced English language writing teacher for an opinion of your essay.

How to take the TOEFL successfully

Preparing for the TOEFL

1. If you do not have a sound basic knowledge of English, it is best to take English language courses before taking a TOEFL preparation course. TOEFL preparation materials are designed to prepare you for the test. They are not designed to teach you English.

2. Begin your TOEFL studies as soon as you decide to take the exam. It will not be useful to try to learn everything the week before the exam date.

3. Study on a regular basis. Thoroughly learning a small amount of information daily is better than insufficiently or inaccurately learning a large amount of information at one sitting.

4. All English practice is helpful. Listening to a movie or radio program in English is good for building your listening comprehension skills. Reading English newspaper or magazine articles will improve your reading comprehension skills. Systematically add new words to your vocabulary. Even though these activities are not directly related to the TOEFL test, they will help you.

5. Work carefully through the exercises in *Cambridge Preparation for the TOEFL Test* that were indicated by the Diagnostic Test as your weak areas. Once you have mastered the skills in your weak areas, you may want to skim other exercises to improve your stronger skills even further. However, it is best to concentrate the most effort on your weak areas.

Studying for the TOEFL

1. Practice budgeting your time. The TOEFL is taken under time limit pressures. Learn to use your time wisely so that you can complete each section.

2. Identify your problem areas. Concentrate on those areas, but review other areas as well.

3. Know your goal. Write to the administration office of the college or university of your choice, and ask for their entrance requirements. They will confirm what TOEFL score is required for admission.

4. Check yourself on the Practice Tests to discover if you usually change correct answers to incorrect answers when unsure of an item. If you *do* change correct answers to incorrect answers, you will want to stay with your first choice when you take the TOEFL.

Taking the test

1. The test center staff will tell you where to sit. You can ask for the volume of the cassette to be adjusted at the beginning of the test administration, but remember that it is unlikely that all test takers will be pleased.

2. Listen to the instructions carefully. The cassette will explain how to complete the personal data sheet and how to mark your answer sheet. It is important that you follow these instructions.

3. If you need to erase, do so thoroughly using a clean eraser.

4. Work quickly through the easy items. Be sure to skip a space on the answer sheet when you skip a difficult item. After you answer the easy items, return to the ones you skipped.

5. If you finish one of the sections early, do not work on any other section of the test. This is not permitted. If you are caught working on the wrong section, your test will be invalidated.

6. Be prepared for changes. Occasionally a TOEFL test has more items to answer in a longer period of time or a change in format.

7. Answer all questions; however, do not waste time on difficult items. If you think one of two answers is correct, choose one and go on. If you just don't know, then you should guess. You are not penalized for guessing, and your guess may be correct.

8. If you see that the time is almost finished and you can't read and answer all the remaining items, choose A, B, C, or D as your *guess letter* and quickly answer the items with that one letter. You are more likely to get some correct answers if you use one letter than if you use them all.

DIAGNOSTIC
• TEST •

Before you use this book, take the following Diagnostic Test. Its format is the same as that of the TOEFL.

Take this test as if you were taking an actual TOEFL test. If you are unsure of TOEFL procedures, read the instructions on pages 1 and 2 in the Introduction to this book.

Before you take the test, make the following preparations:

1. Arrange to have a quiet room where you will not be disturbed for the duration of the test. The entire test will take approximately 2 hours.
2. Bring the following items: a cassette player, the cassette which contains the Diagnostic Test, two pencils with erasers, and a timing device such as an alarm clock or timer.
3. Tear the answer sheet for the Diagnostic Test out of this book. You will find it on page 543.

When you have completed the test, check your answers against the Answer Key starting on page 422. If you marked a wrong answer, the Answer Key will tell you which exercises in the book will help you improve in that area. For example, you may see:

(See Exercises L4–L6.)

These are the exercises you should do for further practice.

If you use the book in this way, you will identify the areas where you may be weak and need practice. After you have completed the exercises that focus on these areas, you may want to review other material in the book.

Now start the recording and go on to the next page to begin the Diagnostic Test.

GO ON TO THE NEXT PAGE →

SECTION 1
LISTENING COMPREHENSION

In this section of the test, you will have an opportunity to demonstrate your ability to understand spoken English. There are three parts to this section, with special directions for each part. Do not read ahead or turn the pages while the directions are being read. Do not take notes or write in your workbook at any time.

Part A

Directions: For each question in Part A, you will hear a short sentence. Each sentence will be spoken just once. The sentences you hear will not be written out for you.

After you hear a sentence, read the four choices in your workbook, marked (A), (B), (C), and (D), and decide which one is closest in meaning to the sentence you heard. Then, on your answer sheet, find the number of the question and fill in the space that corresponds to the letter of the answer you have chosen. Fill in the space completely so that the letter inside the oval cannot be seen.

Listen to an example.

On the recording, you hear: *The new observatory is nothing less than outstanding.*

In your workbook, you read: (A) The new observatory is excellent.
                            (B) There is nothing outstanding to observe.
                            (C) You must stand outside to make the observance.
                            (D) His new observations are more outstanding than usual.

Sample Answer
● Ⓑ Ⓒ Ⓓ

The woman said, "The new observatory is nothing less than outstanding." Sentence (A), "The new observatory is excellent," is closest in meaning to what the woman said. Therefore, the correct choice is (A).

NOW WE WILL BEGIN PART A WITH QUESTION 1.

GO ON TO THE NEXT PAGE

1. (A) Tom's part in the play included mime.
   (B) Tom pointed to an ice drink.
   (C) It was kind of Tom to do what he did.
   (D) Tom waved his hand as he parted.

2. (A) We shipped her the gift.
   (B) We broke what was in the package.
   (C) We arranged to go away.
   (D) We shared the cost of the gift.

3. (A) Sue is good at convincing people to help.
   (B) Sue has knocked on people's doors for money.
   (C) Sue gets snacks for people who don't have the time and money.
   (D) Sue cashes checks for people who have time to wait.

4. (A) Mark can't stand driving.
   (B) Mark only drives on Friday nights.
   (C) Mark only drives on weekdays.
   (D) Mark doesn't drive on Friday nights.

5. (A) Although Janet seldom watches TV, this week she has watched it nightly.
   (B) Janet doesn't usually watch TV during the day but likes to watch it at night.
   (C) Janet has watched certain weekly TV programs every night for years.
   (D) Janet usually watches TV on the weekend but never on weekday nights.

6. (A) It has been 50 years since Bill began to play the piano.
   (B) After 15 years of playing the piano, Bill still plays it.
   (C) Bill used to play the piano, but hasn't played it for 15 years.
   (D) Bill has played the piano since he was 15 years old.

7. (A) Peter and I don't go to the optician's very often.
   (B) Peter and I don't usually agree on who to vote for.
   (C) Peter and I usually don't look each other in the eye during our discussions.
   (D) Peter and I only see each other at election times.

8. (A) Tuna fish costs twice as much as before.
   (B) The cost of tuna fish goes up two or three times a year.
   (C) The cost of tuna fish has gone up twice in the last three years.
   (D) During the last three years, rice has cost half as much as tuna fish.

9. (A) I do better in botany.
   (B) I do better in zoology.
   (C) I do as well in zoology as in botany.
   (D) Botany is easy but zoology is not.

10. (A) Write to me or call me.
    (B) Keep away from me.
    (C) Take care of yourself.
    (D) Don't be gone too long.

11. (A) You went to the rally, didn't you?
    (B) I couldn't believe you went to the rally.
    (C) It doesn't seem possible that you weren't at the rally.
    (D) Your going to the rally seems unbelievable.

GO ON TO THE NEXT PAGE

12. (A) I would like some jam from the cupboard, if I weren't so full.
    (B) This cupboard is so full, I can't find the jam.
    (C) The cupboard wasn't full, so I was able to find the jam.
    (D) The cupboard was so full, I found the door jammed.

13. (A) Carmen is bored with serving the boat club directors.
    (B) Carmen brought the chalkboard in to the directors of the boat club.
    (C) Carmen is a waitress on board the ship called *Directors*.
    (D) Carmen is one of the directors of the boat club.

14. (A) Dan's leave-taking surprised us.
    (B) That Dan asked us to make a speech was not true.
    (C) The way Dan waltzes amazes us.
    (D) We did not know what to say when Dan wrongly accused us.

15. (A) Diane and Barbara haven't been friends for a long time.
    (B) Diane and Barbara haven't met each other's friends since they were children.
    (C) Even though Diane and Barbara are longtime friends, they don't get together very often.
    (D) Even though Diane and Barbara are longtime friends, their children don't like each other.

16. (A) The children fell asleep in the car.
    (B) The children couldn't sit still after the trip.
    (C) The children had a rest after the long drive.
    (D) The children were arrested after the long journey.

17. (A) That was a narrow escape!
    (B) Why did he close off the hallway?
    (C) Liz just called you.
    (D) Was that shout nearby?

18. (A) Sam caught the ice the waitress dropped.
    (B) Sam eyed the waitress.
    (C) Sam got the waitress's attention.
    (D) Sam looked for the waitress.

19. (A) Does Alice have trouble writing at night?
    (B) How can Alice write for that paper nightly?
    (C) I never know what Alice will write about.
    (D) I don't know how Alice wrote that paper in one night.

20. (A) The professor talked more than four hours.
    (B) The professor's previous lectures were shorter.
    (C) The professor's class usually lasts more than an hour.
    (D) The professor's lecture hall was farther away than the classroom.

GO ON TO THE NEXT PAGE

Part B

Directions: In Part B you will hear short conversations between two people. After each conversation, a third person will ask a question about what was said. You will hear each conversation and question about it only one time. After you hear a conversation and the question about it, read the four possible answers in your workbook and decide which one is the best answer to the question you heard. Then, on your answer sheet, find the number of the question and fill in the space that corresponds to the letter of the answer you have chosen.

Listen to an example.

On the recording, you hear: (First Man)   *I think I'll have the curtains changed.*
                          (Woman)   *They are a bit worn.*

                          (Second Man) *What does the woman mean?*

In your workbook, you read: (A) She thinks every bit of change is important.
                           (B) She wants to wear them.
                           (C) She thinks they've been worn enough.
                           (D) She thinks they are in bad condition.

Sample Answer

You learn from the conversation that the woman thinks the curtains are worn. The best answer to the question "What does the woman mean?" is (D), "She thinks they are in bad condition." Therefore, the correct choice is (D).

NOW WE WILL BEGIN PART B WITH THE FIRST CONVERSATION.

21. (A) He has a brother.
    (B) He's related to the man by marriage.
    (C) He's a lawyer.
    (D) He's married to the woman.

22. (A) There will be a large turnout.
    (B) She has someone to testify on her behalf.
    (C) There was an accident.
    (D) She'll recount a witty incident.

23. (A) At the traffic lights.
    (B) At the stop sign.
    (C) At the library.
    (D) At the dead end.

24. (A) She wants the man to explore a cave with the club.
    (B) She thinks it's a bad time of year to see the grotto.
    (C) She wants to know why the man doesn't become a member of the club.
    (D) She thinks the man has a good reason for joining them.

25. (A) He finished repairing the furniture more than five years ago.
    (B) He has taken the least time of anyone to finish.
    (C) He began to repair furniture more than five years ago.
    (D) He will be restoring furniture for at least five more years.

26. (A) She doesn't understand that his father needs the car.
    (B) They don't have to go to the movies tonight.
    (C) It's fine with her to take a bus.
    (D) They could go to an earlier movie, then return the car to his father.

27. (A) Peter is a professional carpenter.
    (B) A professor designed the cabinets.
    (C) A carpenter built the cabinets.
    (D) Peter had a small cabin built.

28. (A) He doesn't want the woman to drive.
    (B) He agrees that the fog could be dangerous.
    (C) He wants her to pull over to the other side of the street.
    (D) He doesn't want to continue driving in the fog.

29. (A) They need to buy some gasoline.
    (B) They should ask directions.
    (C) They need to check their headlights and taillights.
    (D) They should pull off the road.

30. (A) Buy a hat.
    (B) Visit a friend.
    (C) Buy a drink.
    (D) Get a haircut.

31. (A) At the library.
    (B) On a boat.
    (C) In a car.
    (D) In a restaurant.

GO ON TO THE NEXT PAGE

32. (A) Works with plants.
    (B) Runs a beauty shop.
    (C) Teaches in a nursery school.
    (D) Gives advice in a law firm.

33. (A) Its size.
    (B) Its color.
    (C) Its cost.
    (D) Its style.

34. (A) She is surprised he didn't finish.
    (B) She is surprised he took so long to finish.
    (C) She is surprised the exam was so easy.
    (D) She is surprised the exam took hardly any time at all.

35. (A) He was ill.
    (B) He was embarrassed.
    (C) He was confused.
    (D) He was envious.

GO ON TO THE NEXT PAGE

Part C

Directions: In this part of the test, you will hear longer conversations and talks. After each conversation or talk, you will be asked some questions. You will hear the talks and conversations and the questions about them only <u>one</u> time. They will <u>not</u> be written out for you.

After you hear a question, read the four possible answers in your workbook and decide which <u>one</u> is the best answer to the question you heard. Then, on your answer sheet, find the number of the question and fill in the space that corresponds to the letter of the answer you have chosen. Answer all questions on the basis of what is <u>stated</u> or <u>implied</u> by the speakers in the talk or conversation.

Here is an example.

On the recording, you hear: *Listen to a conversation between a professor and a student.*

(Woman)	*Would you please type this paper? I can't read your handwriting.*
(First Man)	*I'm sorry, Professor Mills. I don't have a typewriter, and besides, I can't type.*
(Woman)	*Well, rewrite it then, but be sure to make it clear.*

Now listen to a sample question.

(Second Man) *What does the professor want the man to do?*

In your workbook, you read: (A) Buy a typewriter.
(B) Read his handwriting.
(C) Clear the papers away.
(D) Rewrite the paper.

Sample Answer

The best answer to the question "What does the professor want the man to do?" is (D), "Rewrite the paper." Therefore, the correct choice is (D).

Remember, you are not allowed to take notes or write in your workbook.

NOW WE WILL BEGIN PART C.

36. (A) Facts about saffron.
    (B) How important saffron is.
    (C) How saffron is produced.
    (D) The cost of saffron.

37. (A) It is produced in Spain.
    (B) The finest variety comes from La Mancha.
    (C) It is the world's most prized foodstuff.
    (D) It is obtained from the *Crocus sativus*.

38. (A) India and Iran.
    (B) Saudi Arabia and Bahrain.
    (C) The United States and Italy.
    (D) Middle Eastern countries and France.

39. (A) Saudi Arabia.
    (B) Bahrain.
    (C) Spain.
    (D) India.

40. (A) In an art history classroom.
    (B) In an art museum.
    (C) In an art supplies shop.
    (D) In an artist's workshop.

41. (A) Sells paintings.
    (B) Steals Rembrandts.
    (C) Buys stolen pictures.
    (D) Gives tours in a museum.

42. (A) For 3 years.
    (B) For 4 years.
    (C) For 5 years.
    (D) For 20 years.

43. (A) It is a Rembrandt.
    (B) It is worth $5 million.
    (C) It is easily recognized.
    (D) It is 9 by 11 inches.

44. (A) At the hotel reception desk.
    (B) At the lost and found office.
    (C) At the Chicago airport.
    (D) At a train depot.

45. (A) He flies Transcontinental planes.
    (B) He takes baggage claim tickets.
    (C) He fills out identification tags.
    (D) He helps people recover missing items.

46. (A) Straps.
    (B) A black suitcase.
    (C) Identification.
    (D) Baggage claim tickets.

47. (A) Fill out the form.
    (B) Cover the luggage.
    (C) Search for the name and address.
    (D) Contact the woman.

48. (A) The wall is designed with elements of real cliffs.
    (B) The natural rocks are embedded into the cliffs.
    (C) The sculpted concete blocks are varied.
    (D) The cliffs are challenging.

49. (A) A wall was constructed.
    (B) A festival took place.
    (C) An outdoor education course was offered.
    (D) A variety of cliff elements were found.

50. (A) The United States.
    (B) 100 students from fifteen universities.
    (C) The outdoor education department.
    (D) The nation's intercollegiate campus.

THIS IS THE END OF THE LISTENING COMPREHENSION SECTION OF THE DIAGNOSTIC TEST.

THE NEXT PART OF THE TEST IS SECTION 2. TURN TO THE
DIRECTIONS FOR SECTION 2 IN YOUR WORKBOOK,
READ THEM, AND BEGIN WORK.
DO NOT READ OR WORK ON ANY OTHER SECTION OF THE TEST.

SECTION 2
STRUCTURE AND WRITTEN EXPRESSION

Time – 25 minutes

This section is designed to measure your ability to recognize language that is appropriate for standard written English. There are two types of questions in this section, with special directions for each type.

Directions: Questions 1–15 are incomplete sentences. Beneath each sentence you will see four words or phrases marked (A), (B), (C), and (D). Choose the one word or phrase that best completes the sentence. Then, on your answer sheet, find the number of the question and fill in the space that corresponds to the letter of the answer you have chosen. Fill in the space so that the letter inside the oval cannot be seen.

Example   John Le Carré ----- for his novels concerning espionage.
(A) famous
(B) has fame
(C) is famous
(D) famed for

Sample Answer
Ⓐ Ⓑ ● Ⓓ

The sentence should read, "John Le Carré is famous for his novels concerning espionage." Therefore, you should choose answer (C).

After you read the directions, begin work on the questions.

1. Blood flow ----- by the heart.
   (A) which is controlled
   (B) being controlled
   (C) controlled
   (D) is controlled

2. ----- D. J. Stanford decided to devote his free time to anthropological study.
   (A) He was fifteen
   (B) His age was fifteen
   (C) When he was fifteen
   (D) The age of fifteen

3. Not all birds -----.
   (A) fly
   (B) flying
   (C) to fly
   (D) flown

4. The construction kits consist of small interlocking parts that can be -----.
   (A) together they are fitted
   (B) that when fitted together
   (C) fitted together
   (D) together are fitted

5. The man who managed ----- the documents is now a national hero.
   (A) obtain
   (B) obtaining
   (C) to obtain
   (D) obtained

6. The western part of Oregon generally receives more rain than ----- the eastern part.
   (A) does
   (B) in it does
   (C) it does in
   (D) in

7. ----- porpoises and dolphins, whales are mammals.
   (A) As
   (B) Also
   (C) Like
   (D) When

8. In the eighteenth century ----- as meeting places by literary figures.
   (A) coffeehouses were used
   (B) coffeehouses which were used
   (C) even though coffeehouses were
   (D) there were coffeehouses

9. The Romans used central heating systems very much like -----.
   (A) those of today
   (B) today's do
   (C) those they do
   (D) the systems which are now

GO ON TO THE NEXT PAGE

10. The surface of the moon was shaped by meteorites whose impact ----- craters of all sizes.
    (A) form
    (B) forming
    (C) formed
    (D) are forming

11. ----- living in Birmingham, England, that the American writer Washington Irving wrote *Rip Van Winkle*.
    (A) It was
    (B) There he was
    (C) It was while
    (D) While he was

12. ----- lack of success and financial reward, Vincent van Gogh persevered with his painting.
    (A) Because of his
    (B) Despite his
    (C) His
    (D) Although his

13. ----- censored in his native Ireland and elsewhere, influenced a generation of writers.
    (A) James Joyce's *Ulysses*, was
    (B) James Joyce's *Ulysses*,
    (C) James Joyce wrote *Ulysses*,
    (D) That James Joyce wrote *Ulysses*,

14. ----- known as "Stonehenge" has never been determined.
    (A) Who built the stone circle
    (B) The stone circle
    (C) That the stone circle
    (D) There is the stone circle

15. Certain Paleolithic artifacts are given special terms -----.
    (A) which indicating their location of discovery
    (B) whose locations are indicating their discovery
    (C) what the location of their discovery is
    (D) indicating the location of their discovery

Directions: In questions 16–40 each sentence has four underlined words or phrases. The four underlined parts of the sentence are marked (A), (B), (C), and (D). Identify the one underlined word or phrase that must be changed in order for the sentence to be correct. Then on your answer sheet, find the number of the question and fill in the space that corresponds to the letter of the answer you have chosen.

Example The balloonists who remained aloft in the air radioed the control center.
                     A   B   C   D

Sample Answer
(A) (B) ● (D)

The sentence should read, "The balloonists who remained aloft radioed the control center." Therefore, you should choose answer (C).

After you read the directions, begin work on the questions.

16. The spacecraft is traveling 50 times as faster than the speed of a pistol bullet.
    A   B   C D

17. The traveler can to reach some of the villages along the Amazon only by riverboat.
                        A   B   C   D

18. Natural predators, disturbing from tourists, and pollution have all contributed to the
                              A   B   C
    decline of the California Condor.
       D

GO ON TO THE NEXT PAGE

19. Today the number of people which enjoy winter sports is almost double that of
             A   B   C   D
    twenty years ago.

20. The Soay sheep, the old breed of sheep in existence, has changed little since
                      A   B   C   D
    3500 B.C.

21. *Voyager 2* is a spacecraft which has greatly expanded ours knowledge of the solar
                           A   B   C   D
    system.

22. Dolphins, whales, and many others sea creatures use highly sophisticated
                        A   B   C
    navigation systems.
                D

23. The smallest things in the universe are, paradoxically, be explored by the largest
           A   B   C   D
    machines.

24. Fiber is a important element in nutrition, and it aids in protecting the digestive tract
            A   B   C
    as well.
    D

25. Copper is a metal which is easy worked and which mixes well with other metals to
                     A   B   C   D
    form alloys.

26. The pilgrims twice encircle the tomb two times in solemn procession.
        A   B   C   D

27. The Bactrian, nor Asian camel, can be identified by its two humps.
                A   B   C   D

28. First European settlers of Australia left the city of Portsmouth in May 1787.
       A   B   C   D

29. Scurvy, caused by the lack of vitamin C, could kill the most of a ship's crew on a
                 A   B   C
    long voyage.
           D

30. The term "Punchinello" refer to a clown in Italian puppet shows.
         A   B   C   D

GO ON TO THE NEXT PAGE

31. Symptoms of multiple sclerosis may be eased by injecting a solution consisted of
    <u>Symptoms</u>   <u>may be eased</u>   <u>a</u> solution <u>consisted</u> of
        A   B   C   D
    snake venom.

32. The rupture of the Mareb Dam in ancient Yemen brought it about the collapse of
        <u>rupture</u>   <u>brought</u> <u>it</u> about the <u>collapse</u> of
            A   B   C   D
    many small kingdoms.

33. The tiger's cunning, strength, and agile have earned it a legendary reputation.
                                        <u>agile</u> <u>have earned</u> <u>it</u> a <u>legendary</u> reputation.
                                          A   B   C   D

34. Uranus is the alone planet in the solar system which is tipped on its side.
                    <u>alone</u> planet <u>in the</u> solar system <u>which</u> is tipped on <u>its</u> side.
                      A   B   C   D

35. Most critics agree that William Shakespeare was the greater writer in the English
    <u>Most</u> critics <u>that</u>   <u>greater</u> writer <u>in the</u> English
      A   B   C   D
    language.

36. Much nutritionists argue that people's intake of fat should be reduced.
    <u>Much</u> nutritionists <u>argue</u>   should be <u>reduced</u>.
      A   B   D
                                        C

37. The refracting telescope contains lenses that magnify the image which reaches its.
                              <u>contains</u> lenses <u>that</u> <u>magnify</u> the image which reaches <u>its</u>.
                                 A   B   C   D

38. In some societies hired people cook, clean, take care after the children, and do the
                        <u>hired</u> people <u>cook</u>, clean, take care <u>after</u> the children, and <u>do</u> the
                          A   B   C   D
    yard work.

39. Many American novelists, such as Gore Vidal, resides in other countries.
    <u>Many</u>   <u>such as</u>   <u>resides</u> <u>in</u> other countries.
      A   B   C   D

40. Some paper dolls, which were once relatively cheap, are previously considered
                      <u>which</u> were once <u>relatively</u> cheap, are <u>previously</u> considered
                        A   B   C
    valuable collectors' items.
                        <u>items</u>.
                          D

THIS IS THE END OF SECTION 2 OF THE DIAGNOSTIC TEST.

IF YOU FINISH BEFORE TIME IS UP, CHECK YOUR WORK
ON SECTION 2 ONLY.
DO NOT READ OR WORK ON ANY OTHER SECTION OF THE TEST.

SECTION 3
VOCABULARY AND READING COMPREHENSION

Time – 45 minutes

This section is designed to measure your comprehension of standard written English. There are two types of questions in this section, with special directions for each type.

Directions: In questions 1–30 each sentence has an underlined word or phrase. Below each sentence are four other words or phrases, marked (A), (B), (C), and (D). You are to choose the one word or phrase that best keeps the meaning of the original sentence if it is substituted for the underlined word or phrase. Then, on your answer sheet, find the number of the question and fill in the space that corresponds to the letter you have chosen. Fill in the space so that the letter inside the oval cannot be seen.

Example   Many women have made a <u>mark on</u> American art since the early 1800s.

Sample Answer

   (A) target for
   (B) dedication to
   (C) contribution to
   (D) degree of

The best answer is (C) because "Many women have made a contribution to American art since the early 1800s" is closest in meaning to the original sentence. Therefore, you should choose answer (C).

After you read the directions, begin work on the questions.

1. Savannah, Georgia, was founded in 1733 as a <u>refuge</u> for persecuted Protestants from Europe.
 (A) home
 (B) sanctuary
 (C) prison
 (D) compound

2. The Vietnam Memorial in Washington, D.C., <u>commemorates</u> the 58,000 Americans who died or remain missing in Vietnam.
 (A) values
 (B) honors
 (C) indicates
 (D) memorizes

3. The eleven Bass Islands are <u>clustered</u> together at the western end of Lake Erie.
 (A) thrown
 (B) mixed
 (C) grouped
 (D) constructed

4. The Bighorn Mountain sheep is a <u>shy</u> animal, rarely sighted by human beings.
 (A) crafty
 (B) deadly
 (C) timid
 (D) swift

5. In the 1870s, the German archaeologist Heinrich Schliemann <u>found</u> the legendary ruins of Troy.
 (A) made
 (B) created
 (C) started
 (D) discovered

6. In the ninth century, Norway was still divided into numerous <u>petty</u> kingdoms.
 (A) insignificant
 (B) conflicting
 (C) collective
 (D) subordinate

7. In 1985, José Cubero became the second Spanish matador to be <u>slain</u> by a bull in less than a year.
 (A) beaten
 (B) fought
 (C) charged
 (D) killed

8. The Mafia organization observes a <u>rigid</u> code of secrecy.
 (A) reliant
 (B) strict
 (C) violent
 (D) direct

GO ON TO THE NEXT PAGE ➤

9. Wild Bill Hickok was reputedly shot dead while holding a poker hand of aces and eights.
   (A) ideally
   (B) surely
   (C) theoretically
   (D) supposedly

10. A devastating earthquake destroyed San Francisco in the early 1900s.
    (A) ruined
    (B) restored
    (C) erased
    (D) dismantled

11. Despite expensive public education campaigns, heart disease still kills a tremendous number of people.
    (A) huge
    (B) predictable
    (C) memorable
    (D) growing

12. Corn from Iowa is used primarily for animal feed rather than food for human consumption.
    (A) finally
    (B) mainly
    (C) usually
    (D) completely

13. The great astronomer Galileo is the only contemporary figure mentioned in Milton's epic *Paradise Lost*.
    (A) distinguished
    (B) assigned
    (C) named
    (D) signified

14. Contact with poison ivy can make a person ill enough to warrant hospitalization.
    (A) justify
    (B) stress
    (C) oblige
    (D) urge

15. William Tyndale was publicly executed in 1536 for making what his enemies considered a false translation of the Bible.
    (A) an incorrect
    (B) an imaginary
    (C) an illusory
    (D) an approximate

16. Today, between 600 and 900 grizzly bears survive in the lower 48 states.
    (A) meander
    (B) persist
    (C) ramble
    (D) pursue

17. Buddha's first sermon is believed to have been delivered at Sarnath near Varanasi, India.
    (A) released
    (B) demanded
    (C) introduced
    (D) given

18. The sacred ibis of ancient Egypt still inhabits parts of Africa.
    (A) saintly
    (B) secular
    (C) holy
    (D) grave

19. Enlightenment thought had a profound influence on the formation of the American Constitution.
    (A) professional
    (B) deep
    (C) intensive
    (D) vast

20. Before settlement, the Great Lakes borderland was covered extensively with evergreen forests.
    (A) externally
    (B) widely
    (C) generally
    (D) wholly

21. The fame of Edgar Allan Poe rests on his short stories as well as his poetry.
    (A) position
    (B) merit
    (C) credit
    (D) reputation

22. The largest living tortoise is the giant tortoise, which lives in the Galápagos Islands.
    (A) current
    (B) real
    (C) present
    (D) existing

GO ON TO THE NEXT PAGE

23. A prehistoric figurine of exceptional importance has recently been unearthed in Cyprus.
    (A) evolved
    (B) excavated
    (C) elicited
    (D) separated

24. Galaxies consist of roughly a hundred million stars.
    (A) integrate
    (B) fulfill
    (C) number
    (D) contain

25. Falconry was once a leisure-time activity of the European nobility.
    (A) post
    (B) function
    (C) prosperity
    (D) pursuit

26. The largest concentration of lemmings is found in the mountains of central Norway.
    (A) accumulation
    (B) mingling
    (C) unity
    (D) dispersal

27. Hollywood film producers regularly budget tens of millions of dollars for a film.
    (A) allocate
    (B) scatter
    (C) spread
    (D) distribute

28. Paul Bunyan and Pecos Bill are two of the well-known characters in popular North American tales.
    (A) lies
    (B) jokes
    (C) history books
    (D) stories

29. The gigantic ice sculptures in the Minnesota Winter Festival are very impressive.
    (A) frigid
    (B) heavy
    (C) awesome
    (D) enormous

30. The prickly pear anchors itself on rocky, barren slopes and grows to about 3 meters high.
    (A) dissects
    (B) restrains
    (C) supports
    (D) secures

Directions: In the rest of this section you will read several passages. Each one is followed by several questions about it. For questions 31–60, you are to choose the best answer, (A), (B), (C), or (D), to each question. Then, on your answer sheet, find the number of the question and fill in the space that corresponds to the letter of the answer you have chosen.

Answer all questions following a passage on the basis of what is stated or implied in that passage.

Read the following passage.

The horse has played a little-known but very important role in the field of medicine. Horses were injected with toxins of diseases until their blood built up immunities. Then a serum was made from their blood. Serums to fight both diphtheria and tetanus were developed in this way.

Example According to the passage, horses were given
    (A) poisons from illnesses
    (B) immunities to diseases
    (C) diphtheria and tetanus serums
    (D) medicines to fight toxins

Sample Answer
● (B) (C) (D)

The passage states that " horses were injected with toxins of diseases." Therefore, you should choose answer (A).

After you read the directions, begin work on the questions.

GO ON TO THE NEXT PAGE

Questions 31–37

1   A few scientists are dedicated to researching mysterious unclassified beasts
2   which other scientists refuse to believe exist. While these cryptozoologists keep an
3   open mind about their object of study, they are quick to point to cases in which the
4   skeptics were proved mistaken. For example, the pygmy hippopotamus, once
5   claimed to be extinct, was found to exist in East Africa. The giant squid was
6   dismissed as the product of an overactive imagination until a specimen was washed
7   up on a beach in 1873.
8   One of the most intriguing mysteries being investigated by cryptozoologists is
9   "Bigfoot," a large hairy humanoid creature which many people claim to have seen
10 in parts of North America. In 1967, a film of Bigfoot was actually taken by an
11 amateur photographer. Some scientists are convinced of Bigfoot's existence, while
12 others argue that Bigfoot is just an elaborate hoax.
13 The Loch Ness monster provokes similar disagreements among researchers. In
14 this case some scientists argue that while some creature may have been seen, it is
15 probably a type of whale which penetrates the loch when the river Ness floods.
16 The Yeti of the Himalayas may be the most fascinating undiscovered creature.
17 Many climbers claim to have seen the Yeti or its footprints, and local inhabitants of
18 the mountains are convinced of its existence. Such well-known mysteries as the
19 Yeti and less well-known mysteries as the Congo dinosaur and the Queensland tiger
20 will no doubt be the source of much speculation for years to come.

31. A cryptozoologist would probably show most
    interest in
    (A) an elephant
    (B) a lizard
    (C) human beings
    (D) a giant octopus

32. Which of these statements is NOT true?
    (A) Bigfoot has been discovered in North America.
    (B) Mountain climbers claim to have seen the Yeti.
    (C) The Loch Ness monster may be a whale.
    (D) The pygmy hippopotamus exists.

33. The giant squid became a classified creature when
    (A) it was dismissed as having been imagined
    (B) one was washed up on the shore
    (C) one was found in East Africa
    (D) it was filmed to sell products

34. The main topic of the passage is
    (A) wild animals
    (B) false beliefs
    (C) unclassified creatures
    (D) cryptozoologists

35. The author discusses the pygmy hippopotamus to
    show that creatures which many people believe do
    not exist
    (A) live in Africa
    (B) are extinct
    (C) are fascinating
    (D) may exist

36. What is the tone of this passage?
    (A) disbelieving
    (B) instructive
    (C) humorous
    (D) sarcastic

37. According to the passage, the existence of the Yeti
    is
    (A) a well-established fact
    (B) less well-known than the Congo dinosaur
    (C) considered certain by Himalayan inhabitants
    (D) proved by its footprints

GO ON TO THE NEXT PAGE

Questions 38–44

1   People who suffer from excessive drowsiness during the daytime may be
2   victims of a condition known as "narcolepsy." While most people may feel sleepy
3   while watching TV or after eating a meal, narcoleptics may fall asleep at unusual
4   or embarrassing times. They may doze while eating, talking, taking a shower, or
5   even driving a car. Victims can be affected in one of two ways. Most narcoleptics
6   have several sleeping spells during each day with alert periods in between.
7   A minority of others feel drowsy almost all the time and are alert for only brief
8   intervals.
9   There are no reliable data showing how many people have narcolepsy. Some
10   estimates put the number as high as 300,000 in the United States alone. The cause
11   of this illness has not been identified, although recent research suggests that the
12   problem may stem from an immune system reacting abnormally to the brain's
13   chemical processes. There is currently no cure for narcolepsy, so sufferers of this
14   condition can only have their symptoms treated through a combination of
15   counseling and drugs.

38. According to the passage, it can be said that
    (A) most people are narcoleptics sometimes
    (B) narcoleptics are drug addicts
    (C) narcolepsy is a very rare condition
    (D) the number of narcoleptics is unknown

39. Narcolepsy is a condition in which people
    (A) doze after eating a meal
    (B) have unusual brain chemistry
    (C) only sleep in the day
    (D) doze at unusual times

40. The passage implies that narcolepsy
    (A) is an imaginary problem
    (B) can be a serious disorder
    (C) is easily cured
    (D) is really laziness

41. The cause of narcolepsy may be related to
    (A) brain chemistry
    (B) sleeping
    (C) watching television
    (D) drugs

42. Which of the following statements about narcolepsy is NOT true?
    (A) Doctors treat symptoms rather than causes.
    (B) The causes of narcolepsy have not been found yet.
    (C) Narcolepsy affects people in two basic ways.
    (D) Researchers know how many people suffer from this problem.

43. A person is most likely to be narcoleptic if he or she falls asleep while
    (A) watching a movie
    (B) eating at a restaurant
    (C) lying on the beach
    (D) taking a long car trip

44. The main topic of this passage is
    (A) aspects of narcolepsy
    (B) causes of narcolepsy
    (C) treatment of narcolepsy
    (D) development of narcolepsy

GO ON TO THE NEXT PAGE

Questions 45–51

1   According to airline industry statistics, almost 90% of airline accidents are survivable
2 or partially survivable. But passengers can increase their chances of survival by learning
3 and following certain tips. Experts say that you should read and listen to safety
4 instructions before takeoff and ask questions if you have uncertainties. You should fasten
5 your seat belt low on your hips and as tightly as possible. Of course, you should also
6 know how the release mechanism of your belt operates. During takeoffs and landings you
7 are advised to keep your feet flat on the floor. Before takeoff you should locate the
8 nearest exit and an alternative exit and count the rows of seats between you and the exits
9 so that you can find them in the dark if necessary.
10   In the event that you are forewarned of a possible accident, you should put your hands
11 on your ankles and keep your head down until the plane comes to a complete stop. If
12 smoke is present in the cabin, you should keep your head low and cover your face with
13 napkins, towels, or clothing. If possible, wet these for added protection against smoke
14 inhalation. To evacuate as quickly as possible, follow crew commands and do not take
15 personal belongings with you. Do not jump on escape slides before they are fully
16 inflated, and when you jump, do so with your arms and legs extended in front of you.
17 When you get to the ground, you should move away from the plane as quickly as
18 possible, and never smoke near the wreckage.

45. What is the main topic of the passage?
(A) airline industry accident statistics
(B) procedures for evacuating aircraft
(C) guidelines for increasing aircraft passenger survival
(D) safety instructions in air travel

46. It can be inferred from the passage that people are more likely to survive fires in aircrafts if they
(A) keep their heads low
(B) wear a safety belt
(C) don't smoke in or near a plane
(D) read airline safety statistics

47. According to the passage, which exits should an airline passenger locate before takeoff?
(A) the ones that can be found in the dark
(B) the two closest to the passenger's seat
(C) the nearest exit
(D) the ones with counted rows of seats between them

48. What is the main purpose of the passage?
(A) to satisfy travelers
(B) to sell airline tickets
(C) to provide safety advice
(D) to give statistical evidence

49. According to the passage, airline travelers should keep their feet flat on the floor
(A) throughout the flight
(B) during takeoffs and landings
(C) especially during landings
(D) only if an accident is possible

50. Travelers are urged by experts to read and listen to safety instructions
(A) in an emergency
(B) before locating the exits
(C) if smoke is in the cabin
(D) before takeoff

51. Which of the following are airline passengers advised NOT to do?
(A) locate the nearest exit
(B) ask questions about safety
(C) fasten their seat belts before takeoff
(D) carry personal belongings in an emergency

GO ON TO THE NEXT PAGE

Questions 52–58

1   Many researchers believe that apes can communicate with human beings.
2   Investigations made at several laboratories in the United States and elsewhere
3   indicate that chimpanzees and gorillas are capable of understanding language and
4   using linguistic responses at the level of a four-year-old child. Washoe, an adult
5   chimpanzee who was raised as if she were a deaf child, can translate words she
6   hears into American Sign Language. Koko, a 400-pound lowland gorilla, is
7   claimed to have understood a poem written about her. Tests of Koko's auditory
8   comprehension show that she is able to make discriminations between such words
9   as "funny," "money," and "bunny."
10   The scientists at the forefront of this research admit that their work has been
11 severely criticized. The skeptics in general claim that apes' language behavior is
12 merely imitative. For this behavior to be called "language," it must also be
13 communicative. The proponents of ape language counter that those who deny the
14 validity of this research have never worked with apes. They point out that new
15 fields of investigation always create controversy. They add that subhuman primates
16 have not been taught to speak, however, because the outer layer of their brain
17 hemispheres is not sufficiently refined.

52. According to the passage, ape language researchers say that apes can
(A) understand spoken language
(B) speak
(C) think
(D) write poetry

53. Washoe is
(A) a four-year-old child
(B) a deaf gorilla
(C) a scientist
(D) a chimpanzee that uses signs

54. According to the passage, ape-human communication is
(A) accepted by scientists
(B) rejected by researchers
(C) treated skeptically by some scientists
(D) unquestioned

55. It may be inferred from the passage that
(A) only gorillas and chimpanzees are primates
(B) only human beings are primates
(C) all animals except apes are primates
(D) humans and other apes are primates

56. Which one of the following statements is NOT true according to the passage?
(A) Gorillas can speak.
(B) Chimpanzees can use sign language.
(C) A gorilla has understood a poem.
(D) Ape communication is a controversial topic.

57. In line 13, the word "proponents" refers to
(A) people who believe that apes communicate
(B) skeptics who have criticized the research
(C) tests that indicate auditory discrimination
(D) apes that have learned to communicate

58. What is the tone of the passage?
(A) ironic
(B) disbelieving
(C) instructive
(D) judgmental

GO ON TO THE NEXT PAGE

Questions 59 and 60

Choose the statement that is the closest restatement of the first sentence.

59. In order to develop to full potential, a baby needs to be physically able to respond to the environment.
    (A) Full physical potential is needed in order for a baby to be able to respond to the environment.
    (B) It is necessary for a baby to be able to physically respond to the environment for it to develop its full potential.
    (C) A physically able baby needs to develop its full potential in order to respond to its environment.
    (D) Response to the environment of physically able babies needs to be developed to its full potential.

60. There are up to 600 butterfly species worldwide known collectively as "swallowtails."
    (A) The "swallowtail" species has as many as six hundred butterflies worldwide.
    (B) Six hundred collections of butterfly species known as "swallowtails" exist worldwide.
    (C) Worldwide, as many as 600 species of butterflies called "swallowtails" exist.
    (D) Collectively known as the "swallowtail" species, there are up to 600 butterflies worldwide.

THIS IS THE END OF SECTION 3 OF THE DIAGNOSTIC TEST.

IF YOU FINISH BEFORE TIME IS UP, CHECK YOUR WORK
ON SECTION 3 ONLY.
DO NOT READ OR WORK ON ANY OTHER SECTION OF THE TEST.

SECTION
·1·
LISTENING COMPREHENSION

Read the directions to each exercise. When you understand what to do, start the recording. You will hear the exercise title and then question number one. The directions and the example are <u>not</u> on the recording.

Start the recording when you see the 🔲

Stop or pause the recording when you see the 🔲 symbol and the word **STOP** or **PAUSE.**

PART A   SHORT SENTENCES

For each item in Part A of the Listening Comprehension section of the TOEFL, you will hear a short sentence. You must listen carefully because each sentence is spoken only one time. After you hear the sentence, you must choose from four sentences in your test book the one that is closest in meaning to the sentence you heard. You will have 15 seconds to make your choice and fill in the space on your answer sheet. There are 20 items in Part A.

STRATEGIES TO USE FOR LISTENING COMPREHENSION, PART A

1. Concentrate on the statement.

Focus all your attention on the statement you are listening to. Do not try to read answers at the same time you are listening. Do not work on previous items when the statement is being spoken. Do not think about other items.

2. Listen for meaning.

A wrong answer may confuse you by having words that sound similar to (or the same as) those in the spoken statement. Look at these examples.

(A) The **moss** is on the wall.
(B) The **moth** is on the wall.

"Moss" and "moth" may be confused because they are similar in sound.

(C) We **rode** in the boat.
(D) We **rowed** the boat.

"Rode" and "rowed" may be confused because they are pronounced the same but have different meanings.

(E) Can Bob ever play tennis!
(F) Can Bob ever play tennis?

The two sentences are the same in wording, but the first is an exclamation that means "Bob plays tennis very well." The second sentence is a simple question that means "Does Bob ever get a chance to play tennis?"

3. Listen for vocabulary.

A wrong answer may confuse you by using the same words in a different way.

(A) Jill **overcooked** *Tony's* dinner.
(B) Jill **cooked** the dinner **over** at *Tony's*.

The words in bold do not mean the same. "Overcooked" means "cooked too long," and "cooked over at Tony's" means "made at Tony's house." The meaning of the italicized words might also be confused. "Tony's" in the first sentence refers to "Tony's dinner," and "Tony's" in the second sentence means "Tony's house."

(C) Betty **slipped out** during Conrad's speech.
(D) Betty **slipped up** during Conrad's speech.

Be aware of expressions or word combinations that are similar but have differences. For example, in (C) and (D) the expressions in bold do not mean the same. "Slipped out" means "left quietly and quickly," and "slipped up" means "made a mistake."

4. Listen for structure.

A wrong answer may confuse you by being slightly different in the word order or in the words used.

(A) Never have I been so worried.
(B) I have never been worried.

Although both of these statements include a negative adverb and the same subject and verb, they do not mean the same. The first sentence means "I have never been this worried before." The second sentence means "Nothing has ever worried me."

(C) Sue does better in math than science.
(D) Sue does better in math and science.

Although both sentences make a comparison, they do not have the same meaning. The first sentence compares how well Sue does in math with how well she does in science (she does not do as well in science as she does in math). The second sentence compares how well Sue does in both math *and* science with how well she does in other, unnamed, courses.

5. Choose the best answer.

Remember that the best answer restates the original statement. That means the correct answer will say the same thing but *in different words*.

6. Know what works for you.

If you are uncertain which answer is correct, you can do one of two things:

(A) Use your intuition (instincts).
(B) Guess.

Sometimes you do not know the answer but have an unexplained feeling that one of the answers is correct. You have no other reason to believe it is correct. This is your *intuition*. Test your intuition while working through the mini-tests in this book by marking items that you answered intuitively. If your intuition is usually correct, trust it when you take the TOEFL.

Sometimes students answer intuitively and then change their answers. Check yourself while working through the mini-tests in this book. Do you frequently change right answers to wrong ones, or are your changes usually correct? If your first answer is usually the correct one, don't change your answers on the TOEFL.

Remember that wrong answers will not count against you. If you don't know an answer and have no feeling about which of the four choices may be correct, use a *guess letter*. A guess letter is one letter (A, B, C, or D) that you can use to answer all items you don't know. You are more likely to get some correct answers if you use one letter consistently than if you use all letters randomly.

7. Use every second wisely.

Don't lose time thinking about something you don't know. Answer the question, and then prepare yourself to concentrate on the next item.

PRACTICE WITH SOUNDS

Many items are difficult because of sound or word confusions. Use Listening Exercises L1–L6 to develop the following skills:

1. Understanding words that sound similar
2. Understanding intonation
3. Understanding words that sound the same as other words but have different meanings
4. Understanding the correct meaning of words that have several different meanings

(For additional practice with these skills, see Exercises L20–L24 and L57.)

Exercise L1   *Identifying the correct sound*

Read the following pairs of sentences. Then listen to the spoken sentence. Circle the letter of the sentence with the same meaning as the sentence you heard.

Example   You will hear: *I saw the pear.*

You will read: (A) I saw the fruit.
(B) I saw the animal.

You should circle (A) because a "pear" is a "fruit."

START

1. (A) Did you see the boat?
   (B) Did you see the animal?

2. (A) He gave me something to ring.
   (B) He gave me something to pay.

3. (A) I didn't have any idea.
   (B) I didn't have any paste.

4. (A) The army officer was sitting at his desk.
   (B) The city official was sitting at his desk.

5. (A) Where did she put the object to cook in?
   (B) Where did she put the object to write with?

6. (A) John bought something to drink from.
   (B) John bought something to wear on his head.

7. (A) Can you help me color this belt?
   (B) Can you help me fasten this belt?

8. (A) Please put the animal in the garage.
   (B) Please put the little wagon in the garage.

🔲 **STOP**

Answers to Exercise L1 are on page 427.

Exercise L2   **Recognizing questions and statements**

Sometimes intonation determines the meaning of a sentence. Listen to the spoken sentence. Write "Q" if you heard a question and "S" if you heard a statement.

Example   You will hear: *What a good book!*

You will write: _S_

You should write "S" because the sentence is a declaration and not a question.

🔲 **START**

1. _____   5. _____

2. _____   6. _____

3. _____   7. _____

4. _____   8. _____

🔲 **STOP**

Answers to Exercise L2 are on page 427.

Exercise L3   **Identifying words that are pronounced the same but have different meanings**

The following pairs of words are pronounced the same but have different meanings. Listen to the spoken sentence and circle the word you heard in the sentence.

Example   You will hear: *Put the book here.*

You will read: (here)   hear

You should circle "here" because the word you heard refers to location.

🔲 **START**

1. right	write	5. heir	air
2. feet	feat	6. fore	four
3. weight	wait	7. weigh	way
4. hour	our	8. fare	fair

🔲 **STOP**

Answers to Exercise L3 are on page 427.

Exercise L4 **Identifying which meaning is correct**

Read the following list of words and the four possible meanings for each. Listen to the spoken sentence and circle the letter of the meaning that is used in the sentence you heard.

Example You will hear: *He runs a small business.*

You will read: runs
       (A) meet
       (B) moves quickly
       (C) operates
       (D) elapses

You should circle (C) because "runs" means "operates" in the spoken sentence.

START

1. exhaust
   (A) deprive of strength
   (B) use up completely
   (C) fumes from an engine
   (D) say all there is about something

2. simple
   (A) easy
   (B) plain
   (C) innocent
   (D) feebleminded

3. board
   (A) piece of wood
   (B) get on a transportation vehicle
   (C) meals supplied on a regular basis
   (D) group of people controlling a business

4. fast
   (A) abstinence from eating
   (B) quickly
   (C) firmly attached
   (D) unfading

5. kid
   (A) baby goat
   (B) young child
   (C) tease
   (D) leather

6. beat
   (A) route
   (B) rhythm
   (C) hit
   (D) defeat

7. common
   (A) ordinary
   (B) ill-bred
   (C) general
   (D) shared

8. class
   (A) division
   (B) distinction
   (C) social grouping
   (D) group of learners

STOP

Extended practice: Make your own sentences using each of the meanings for these eight words.

Answers to Exercise L4 are on page 427.

Exercise L5 **Identifying multiple meanings in sentences**

In your book is a list of words and one of their meanings. For each word you will hear two sentences. Write the letter of the sentence that uses the meaning given in your book.

Example You will hear: (A) *The house needs a new coat of paint.*
                  (B) *Ted's family has a coat of arms.*

You will read: _A_ coat = thin layer

You should write "A" in the space because "coat" means "a thin layer" in that sentence.

⏏ START

1. _____   light = be known

2. _____   strike = attack

3. _____   box = fight

4. _____   space = region beyond Earth's atmosphere

5. _____   note = to take notice of

6. _____   shower = a party

7. _____   spring = to jump suddenly

8. _____   exercise = make use of   ⏹ STOP

Answers to Exercise L5 are on page 427.

Exercise L6   ***Matching words in sentences***

In your book is a list of sentence with an underlined word in each. You will hear two spoken sentences. Write the letter of the sentence that uses the underlined word in the same way as the sentence in your book.

Example   You will hear: (A) *Peter's dog heels very well on command.*
                              (B) *The horse kicked up its heels as it crossed the pasture.*

              You will read: _B_ I've got painful blisters on my heels.

You should write "B" in the space because "heels" in the sentence "The horse kicked up its heels as it crossed the pasture," has the same meaning as "heels" in the sentence "I've got painful blisters on my heels."

⏏ START

1. _____   The llamas were sure-footed along the steep pass.

2. _____   Mr. Turner is a just man and can give you good advice.

3. _____   Jane bought the flower from the stall on the other side of the street.

4. _____   Ron caused the canoe to tip over.

5. _____   The children have been taught to file out calmly during the fire drills.

6. _____   The incorrect answers have a check by them.

7. _____   The banks are always closed on holidays.

8. _____   Martha attached a swing to the branch of the tree in the backyard.   ⏹ STOP

Answers to Exercise L6 are on page 428.

PRACTICE WITH TIME, QUANTITY, AND COMPARISONS

Many items are difficult because of confusions in time, quantity, or comparisons. Use Listening Exercises L7 and L8 to develop your skills in understanding the meanings of certain time, quantity, and comparison statements. Study the following examples. (For additional practice, see Exercises L26 and L27.)

1. Time

Mary said she **would be finished** within the week.   (Mary will be finished sometime during the week.)

Although the tense "would be finished" may appear to be an action occurring in the past, it was Mary's statement concerning an action in the future that was said in the past.

2. Quantity

I want **no more and no less** than you have.   (I want an equal amount.)

The quantity "no more and no less" means an equal amount.

3. Comparisons

Tom **isn't much taller** than Jane.   (Tom is taller than Jane, but not by very much.)

The comparison "not much taller" means that the difference in height is small.

Exercise L7   ***Listening for time, quantity, and comparison***

Listen to the spoken sentences. Circle the letter of the sentence that is true based on the information you heard.

TIME

Example   You will hear: *I will have graduated before I'm married.*

You will read: (A) I'm married.
(B) I'm not married.

The tense "will have graduated" refers to a future action. The graduation will take place sometime in the future, and then the marriage will take place sometime after that. Therefore, you should circle (B) because the speaker is not married yet.

 START

1. (A) You're coming tomorrow.
   (B) You're telling me tomorrow.

2. (A) Jane should arrive around 1:45.
   (B) Jane should arrive after 2:00.

3. (A) Connie's father is in the hospital.
   (B) Connie's father was in the hospital.

4. (A) Jeff is leaving next week.
   (B) Jeff is leaving in two weeks' time.

5. (A) Tom stopped studying at midnight.
   (B) Tom started studying at midnight.

PAUSE

QUANTITY

Example   You will hear: *The work load has doubled.*

You will read: (A) There is twice as much work to do.
(B) There is half as much work to do.

The term "double" means "two times the amount" or "twice as much." Therefore, you should circle (A) because the amount of work is two times as much as it was.

START

6. (A) Alice needs about two credits to graduate.
   (B) Alice doesn't need more credits to graduate.

7. (A) Dick sold one dictionary.
   (B) Dick didn't sell any dictionaries.

8. (A) Professor Merrill has written thirty or more articles on art history.
   (B) Professor Merrill has not written more than thirty articles on art history.

9. (A) The coin collection is more valuable.
   (B) The coin collection is less valuable.

10. (A) Twelve eggs are needed to make the cake.
    (B) Six eggs are needed to make the cake.

PAUSE

COMPARISONS

Example   You will hear: *The fog is heavier than usual tonight.*

You will read: (A) The fog is usually heavier than it is tonight.
(B) There is more fog tonight than there usually is.

The comparison is between the amount of fog tonight and the usual amount of fog. You should circle (B) because tonight the fog is heavier than it usually is.

START

11. (A) I haven't eaten any cookies.
    (B) I have eaten as many cookies as you.

12. (A) The other staff members don't have as many responsibilities as Tim.
    (B) The other staff members have as many responsibilities as Tim.

13. (A) The bus is more expensive than the train.
    (B) The train is more expensive than the bus.

14. (A) Frank's salary is higher than Emma's.
    (B) Emma's salary is higher than Frank's.

15. (A) Irene makes fewer mistakes when she types quickly than when she types slowly.
    (B) Irene makes more mistakes when she types quickly than when she types slowly.

Answers to Exercise L7 are on page 428.   **STOP**

Exercise L8   ***More practice with time, quantity, and comparisons***

Listen to the spoken statement. Circle the letter of the sentence that is true based on the information you heard.

Example   You will hear: *The more Ned studies his geology lessons, the worse he does on the quizzes.*

You will read: (A) Ned is doing well in geology.
(B) Ned isn't doing well in geology.

You should circle (B) because Ned has been doing poorer on his geology quizzes since he's begun studying more.

 START

1. (A) Tom has touched the cake before.
   (B) Tom hasn't touched the cake before.

2. (A) It's too late to tell me tomorrow.
   (B) It's too late to tell me after tomorrow.

3. (A) Steve has taken more hours than Linda.
   (B) Steve and Linda have taken the same number of hours.

4. (A) We expected more members to come.
   (B) We expected fewer members to come.

5. (A) Jane didn't buy enough food.
   (B) Jane bought too much food.

6. (A) I shouldn't have the lead.
   (B) I should have the lead.

7. (A) Carol doesn't like that class.
   (B) Carol likes that class.

8. (A) The music started before we arrived.
   (B) The music started after we arrived.

9. (A) After the new regulation goes into effect, extensions will be given.
   (B) After the new regulation goes into effect, extensions will not be given.

10. (A) I'll buy fewer than twelve file folders.
    (B) I'll buy twelve or more file folders.

 STOP

Answers to Exercise L8 are on page 428.

PRACTICE WITH IDIOMS AND PHRASAL VERBS

1. Idioms

An idiom is a group of words that together have a different meaning from the individual words.

Examples   **shoot one's mouth off**   (talk too much)
Ted shot his mouth off at the meeting, and no one else had a chance to speak.   (Ted talked so much that no one else could speak.)

hard up   (lack money)
I'm sorry I can't lend you $10, because I'm really hard up this month. (I have very little money this month.)

Remember: The meaning of an idiom cannot be figured out by putting together the meanings of the individual words. Instead, the group of words as a whole has a special meaning, which you need to learn.

2. Phrasal verbs

A phrasal verb (also called a two-word verb or three-word verb) is a verb + preposition (e.g., "take after") or a verb + an adverb (e.g., "take apart") that together have a special meaning. Phrasal verbs can also be three words (e.g., "take out on").

Examples   Sue **takes after** her father.   (Sue resembles her father.)

I'll have to **take apart** the engine to fix it.   (I'll have to separate the engine into its different parts in order to fix it.)

He was angry about failing the exam and **took** it **out on** his friend.   (He showed his disappointment at failing the exam by being angry with his friend.)

Idioms and phrasal verbs are seen frequently on the TOEFL. Misinterpreting their meaning may lead to the wrong choice of answer. Use Listening Exercises L9–L11 to develop your skills in identifying the correct meaning of these phrases. (For additional practice, see Exercises L28–L30.)

Exercise L9   **Understanding idiomatic expressions**

Listen to the spoken statements. Circle the letter of the sentence that is true based on the sentence you heard.

Example   You will hear: *He caught the drift of the conversation.*

You will read: (A) He got sick.
    (B) He understood.

You should circle (B) because the idiom "caught the drift" means "understood."

▶ **START**

1. (A) Marsha has to swim regularly.
   (B) Marsha swims as much as she wants.

2. (A) Jim was very worried.
   (B) No one besides Jim was worried.

3. (A) Bob was angry.
   (B) Bob was a pilot.

4. (A) Ann will visit me.
   (B) Ann will bid me good-bye.

5. (A) Gordon has fragile health.
   (B) Gordon likes ball games.

6. (A) I'll take care of that problem later.
   (B) I'll pay the toll to cross the bridge.

7. (A) Sue got into everything.
   (B) Sue didn't help at all.

8. (A) Janet was ahead of everyone at camp.
   (B) Janet has the idea to go camping.

9. (A) The movie is frightening.
   (B) The movie is boring.

10. (A) My grandfather is young for his age.
    (B) My grandfather is rather old.

Answers to Exercise L9 are on page 428.

▶ **STOP**

Exercise L10   ***Identifying the correct idiom or phrasal verb***

Listen to the spoken statement. Circle the letter of the expression that could be substituted in the spoken statement.

Example   You will hear: *I don't let anyone treat me unfairly.*

You will read: (A) take after me
(B) push me around
(C) push my luck
(D) run into me

You should circle (B) because "push me around" means the same as "treat me unfairly."

▭ **START**

1. (A) put up with the idea
   (B) put the idea together
   (C) put the idea across
   (D) put away the idea

2. (A) see the light
   (B) see the light at the end of the tunnel
   (C) light up
   (D) go out like a light

3. (A) was in over his head
   (B) was head over heels in love
   (C) lost his head
   (D) had a big head

4. (A) footing the bills
   (B) on his toes
   (C) pulling my leg
   (D) underfoot

5. (A) come rain or shine
   (B) for a rain check
   (C) at the end of the rainbow
   (D) for a rainy day

6. (A) put that bicycle together
   (B) put that bicycle aside
   (C) put that bicycle down
   (D) put that bicycle out

7. (A) laying into good workers
   (B) laying off good workers
   (C) laying the blame on good workers
   (D) laying their eyes on good workers

8. (A) test the waters
   (B) be a test case
   (C) be put to the test
   (D) stand the test of time

9. (A) held it against her son
   (B) held onto her son
   (C) got hold of her son
   (D) held her son up

10. (A) give me a run for my money
    (B) make my blood run cold
    (C) run me ragged
    (D) put me in the running

Answers to Exercise L10 are on page 428.

▭ **STOP**

Exercise L11   ***Identifying the correct meaning of expressions***

Listen to the spoken statement. Circle the letter of the sentence that is true based on the information you heard.

Example   You will hear: *The professor would have let the student stay late to complete the exam, but he finished ahead of time.*

You will read: (A) The student stayed late in order to finish the exam.
(B) The professor made the student stay after class because he didn't arrive on time.
(C) The student was ahead of the professor in meeting the deadline to finish the test.
(D) The student completed the test early.

You should circle letter (D) because if the student finished "ahead of time," he completed the test early.

START

1. (A) Jeff and Mike gradually became friends.
   (B) Jeff and Mike became less friendly over the years.
   (C) Even when young, Jeff and Mike weren't friends.
   (D) As boys, Jeff and Mike liked each other.

2. (A) Sue and Mary had an accident in the parking lot.
   (B) Sue and Mary jogged together at the mall.
   (C) Sue happened to meet Mary at the mall.
   (D) Sue ran into the mall to see Mary.

3. (A) Since John is doing the best, he'll win.
   (B) John has the best chance of winning.
   (C) Although John is trying very hard, he won't win.
   (D) John can't stand metal.

4. (A) Bess works out by going jogging.
   (B) Bess will run all the way to work.
   (C) Eventually everything will turn out well.
   (D) Long runs are the best way to get a good workout.

5. (A) Rebecca did all right on her entrance exams.
   (B) Rebecca passed the entrance on the right.
   (C) Rebecca did everything correctly.
   (D) Rebecca immediately let her parents know about the test.

6. (A) Max told Pete to lock the door on time.
   (B) Max has frequently told Pete to lock the door.
   (C) Max waited for Pete to lock the door.
   (D) Pete always locks the door for Max.

7. (A) Ellen could hold Amy's coat and gloves in the other hand.
   (B) Amy needs new gloves rather than a coat.
   (C) Ellen handed Amy a new coat and gloves.
   (D) Ellen has difficulty in getting clothes for Amy.

8. (A) Bill didn't take the test because of the time.
   (B) Bill didn't take the test, although he wasn't late.
   (C) Bill checked the test out for a short time.
   (D) Bill used his identification card to take the test.

STOP

Answers to Exercise L11 are on page 429.

CHECK YOUR PROGRESS

Check your progress in the areas covered in Exercises L1–L11 by completing the following mini-test. This exercise uses the same format as Part A of the Listening Comprehension section on the TOEFL.

START

Exercise L12   *Mini-test*

Directions: For each question you will hear a short sentence. Each sentence will be spoken just once. The sentences you hear will <u>not</u> be written out for you. Therefore, you must listen carefully to understand what the speaker says.

After you hear a sentence, read the four choices in your book, marked (A), (B), (C), and (D), and decide which <u>one</u> is closest in meaning to the sentence you heard. Then circle the letter that corresponds to the answer you have chosen.

Listen to an example.

On the recording, you hear: *If you can't finish this research, please let me know no later than Wednesday.*

In your workbook, you read: (A) Tell me by Wednesday if you're unable to finish.
          (B) Please help me find the ladder.
          (C) You'll need more than a liter of varnish.
          (D) Don't tell me about the research until after Wednesday.

The woman said, "If you can't finish this research, please let me know no later than Wednesday." Sentence (A), "Tell me by Wednesday if you're unable to finish," is closest in meaning to what the woman said. Therefore, the correct choice is (A).

1. (A) Although Mary doesn't like her job, she's good at it.
   (B) Mary dislikes how much work she has to do.
   (C) Mary dislikes her homework as much as her job.
   (D) If Mary liked her work, she would do a better job.

2. (A) Peter is a good cook.
   (B) Can Peter bake?
   (C) Is it possible for Peter to do the baking?
   (D) Does Peter know how to make candy?

3. (A) Do you want me to watch your little brother?
   (B) Tell me if you want me to make him stop.
   (C) Tell me if he needs to be careful.
   (D) Let me know when you can take care of my brother.

4. (A) How much might I earn?
   (B) Where do I turn?
   (C) When should I return?
   (D) When can I have a chance?

5. (A) Jim wants at least twenty-five guests.
   (B) Bob wants as many guests as possible listed.
   (C) Bob doesn't want more than twenty-five people to be invited.
   (D) Jim wants to invite as many guests as Bob.

6. (A) The night train bothered me.
   (B) I can't sleep at night on trains.
   (C) The downpour woke me up in the night.
   (D) I slept through the rainstorm.

7. (A) Did you make plane reservations?
   (B) Have you got the book about airplane trips?
   (C) Have you seen the fight?
   (D) Did you highlight the book?

8. (A) David likes more than two spoonfuls of sugar in his tea.
   (B) David doesn't like sugar in his tea.
   (C) David uses the most sugar in his tea.
   (D) David never has more than two spoonfuls of sugar in his tea.

9. (A) Peggy knows a lot of people in the cafeteria.
   (B) Peggy and her friends drink malts in the cafeteria.
   (C) Everyone complains about the food in the cafeteria.
   (D) Peggy criticizes everyone in the cafeteria.

10. (A) That's my iced tea.
    (B) Mice bite.
    (C) I like icing.
    (D) There's a pain in my eyes.

11. (A) The board members can attend the conference for free.
    (B) Those participating in the conference must pay for their own meals.
    (C) There aren't any chalkboards for the conference.
    (D) The conference notice isn't included on the bulletin board.

12. (A) Roger forgot some of his belongings when he rushed out.
    (B) Roger was very worried about his umbrella and scarf.
    (C) Roger left his umbrella and scarf for Murray to use.
    (D) Roger can't do without his umbrella and scarf.

13. (A) Dan is going to eat beef.
    (B) Dan is going to have leftovers for dinner.
    (C) Dan invited Beth to his house to eat.
    (D) Dan is going to Beth's house for dinner.

14. (A) Rick put two volumes into the library book drop.
    (B) Rick returned two library books.
    (C) It took Rick several hours to walk to the library.
    (D) Rick worked a couple of hours at the library.

15. (A) Ron's got fleas.
    (B) Ron has to send the card.
    (C) Ron's pet has a flea problem.
    (D) Ron's cap is made of fleece.

16. (A) I went to Dawn's house four times.
    (B) Dawn put her head out to see me.
    (C) It wasn't yet sunrise when I left.
    (D) I was yawning as I left.

17. (A) Jill forgot her food on the bus.
    (B) Jill left to catch the bus.
    (C) Jill laughed too much on the bus.
    (D) Jill didn't bring her meal onto the bus.

18. (A) The students were given half the questionnaire.
    (B) A handful of students were asked the question.
    (C) Only six students answered the question.
    (D) The students turned in the questionnaire at 12:30.

19. (A) Ted's frightened to eat over at Pat's.
    (B) Ted's worried about putting on weight.
    (C) Ted eats too much when he's afraid.
    (D) Ted doesn't like fattening foods.

20. (A) We always took the bus in the past.
    (B) It took too much time to go by bus.
    (C) Usually we all were on time for the bus.
    (D) We spent a lot of time on buses.

🔈 STOP

Answers to Exercise L12 are on page 430.

PRACTICE WITH VARIOUS STRUCTURES

The following structures occur with some frequency on the TOEFL. Use Listening Exercises L13–L18 to develop your skills in understanding the meaning of these structures. Study the following examples. (For additional practice, see Exercises L32–L37.)

1. Verbs that show the idea that someone or something caused ("get," "make," "have"), requested ("ask"), or permitted ("let") something to happen

CAUSE

Andy **got** Bill to do the work.   (Bill did the work because Andy either persuaded or paid him to do it.)

The teacher **made** Susan rewrite the essay.   (Susan rewrote the essay because her teacher required her to do so.)

Mary **had** Tim get a haircut.   (Mary asked Tim to get a haircut, and he did.)

I **got** my flat tire fixed.   (I caused my flat tire to be fixed by
I **had** my flat tire fixed.   asking/paying someone to do it.)

REQUEST

Jack **asked** Marvin to bring a hammer.   (If Marvin brought the hammer, it was because Jack asked him to bring it. It was Martin's choice whether or not to do this.)

PERMISSION

I **let** Becky have the cake.   (Becky had the cake because I told her she could have it.)

2. Words that express a negative meaning

Sue **seldom** does her homework.   (Sue doesn't do her homework very often.)

Rick **neither** jogs **nor** swims.   (Rick doesn't jog and he doesn't swim.)

Robin **didn't work** quickly.   (Robin worked slowly.)

It is **unlikely** that Tom brought the game.   (Tom probably didn't bring the game.)

3. Modals; can, could, had better, may, might, must, ought to, shall, should, will, would (special auxiliary verbs which indicate a speaker's attitude or mood about what is being said)

Ms. Jones **can** do the typing.   (I think Ms. Jones is able to do the typing.)

Can I give the report now?   (I want permission to give the report now.)

Jane **could** buy the television.   (I think Jane is able to buy the television.)

Could you close the door?   (A polite request meaning I want you to close the door.)

Mr. Smith **may** come to the opening.   (I think it is possible that Mr. Smith will come to the opening.)

Lee **might** have written down the assignment.   (I think it is possible that Lee wrote down the assignment.)

Ann **must** have gone to the fair.   (I think that Ann has gone to the fair.)

Frank **should** have been at the concert.   (Frank wasn't at the concert, but it was advisable for him to be there.)

Should you have any trouble, call me.   (If you have trouble, call me.)

Will you please speak quietly?   (A polite request meaning I want you to speak quietly.)

4. Conditional sentences (which indicate a possible situation and its consequences)

If it rains, we will go to the shopping mall.   (There might be rain. In that case, we are going to go to the mall.)

If he had bought the book, I would have read it.   (He hasn't bought the book. Therefore, I haven't read it.)

If they had followed my advice, they wouldn't have had that problem.   (They didn't follow my advice. Therefore, they had that problem.)

Had we gone at 4:00, we would have missed seeing Rob.   (We stayed and, therefore, we did see Rob.)

5. Ways of expressing causes and results

We left **because** the noise was bothersome.   (The bothersome noise caused us to leave. Our leaving was a result of the noise's being bothersome.)

Joan was **so** happy she hugged everyone.   (Joan's happiness caused her to hug everyone. Her hugging everyone was the result of her happiness.)

It was **such** an extraordinary movie that we watched it twice.   (Our watching the movie twice was a result of the movie's being extraordinary.)

Now that Fred has a part-time job, he will have the money to buy that car.   (Fred's having the money to buy the car is a result of his getting a job.)

It was difficult to drive **due to** the fog.   (The fog made it difficult to drive.)

After the bypass was built, the traffic passing through the city center was more manageable.   (The traffic's being more manageable in the city center is a result of the bypass's being built.)

6. Reflexive pronouns (used to indicate that the person doing the action is the same as the person receiving the action; also used for emphasis)

I bought **myself** a new watch.   (I was the person who bought the watch, and I was the person who received the watch.)

Jack cut **himself** while shaving.   (Jack was the person who did the cutting, and Jack was the person who got cut.)

Linda painted the picture **herself**.   (Linda's painting the picture without help from anyone else is being emphasized.)

7. Verb + infinitive (e.g., "stopped to rest") or verb + gerund ("stopped resting")

Chris **stopped to buy** some matches.   (Chris stopped somewhere and bought some matches there.)

Chris **stopped buying** matches.   (Chris doesn't buy matches anymore.)

Liz **remembered to bring** the chairs.   (Liz didn't forget to bring the chairs. She brought them.)

Liz **remembered bringing** the chairs.   (Liz knows that she brought the chairs because she remembers having done so.)

8. "Used to" (a habitual action in the past) versus "be used to" (be accustomed to)

Dick **used to** jog in the mornings.   (Dick regularly went jogging in the mornings. This is no longer his habit.)

Susan **is used to** singing on stage.   (Susan is accustomed to singing on stage.)

9. "Was to have" (was supposed to)

I **was to have done** the assignment.   (I was given the assignment to do, but I didn't do it.)

I **was supposed to have done** the assignment.   (I was given the assignment to do, but I didn't do it.)

Exercise L13   **Understanding causatives**

Listen to the spoken statement, followed by a question. Circle the letter of the correct answer.

Example   You will hear: *Tom will advise Nick to buy that car.*
                      Who might buy a car?

You will read: (A) Tom
                        (B)) Nick

You should circle (B) because Nick might buy the car that Tom recommends.

1. (A) Mrs. Jones
   (B) Bob

2. (A) Kathy
   (B) John

3. (A) Vicky
   (B) Ann

4. (A) Mary
   (B) Dan

5. (A) Nancy's
   (B) Jeff's

6. (A) Debbie
   (B) Jim

7. (A) Ellen's
   (B) Fred's

8. (A) Sue
   (B) Don

9. (A) Liz
   (B) Ms. Nelson

10. (A) Mr. Jones
    (B) Tom

 STOP

Answers to Exercise L13 are on page 432.

Exercise L14   **Understanding negative meaning**

Listen to the spoken statement. Circle the letter of the sentence that is implied in the statement you heard.

Example   You will hear: *Never have so many people been unemployed.*

You will read: ((A)) There is a lot of unemployment.
                        (B) There is little unemployment.

You should circle (A) because the statement "Never have so many people been unemployed," suggests that "many people are unemployed."

▶ START

1. (A) I usually catch the 7:45 train.
   (B) I never catch the 7:45 train.

2. (A) Motivation is often the reason for success.
   (B) Experience is often the reason for success.

3. (A) No one came to class.
   (B) One student was absent.

4. (A) My suggestions usually aren't taken seriously.
   (B) My suggestions usually are taken seriously.

5. (A) There isn't enough bread.
   (B) There is just enough bread.

6. (A) I haven't read anything.
   (B) I have read something.

7. (A) The car was nice looking.
   (B) The car was bad looking.

8. (A) Rita's never invited Sarah.
   (B) Rita's always invited Sarah.

9. (A) Ben's friends should call after 11:00.
   (B) Ben's friends shouldn't call after 11:00.

10. (A) It's amazing that Dan finished on time.
    (B) It's not surprising that Dan finished on time.

 STOP

Answers to Exercise L14 are on page 432.

Exercise L15   Understanding modals

Listen to the spoken statement. Circle the letter of the sentence that is closer in meaning to or implied in the statement you heard.

Example   You will hear: *Jane should have stayed in bed after her operation.*

You will read: (A) Jane stayed in bed.
              (B) Jane didn't stay in bed.

You should circle (B) because "should have stayed" means "Jane didn't stay in bed."

 START

1. (A) Sam is probably out of town.
   (B) Sam is probably in town.

2. (A) We won't meet once a week.
   (B) We will meet once a week.

3. (A) Lynn studies more now.
   (B) Lynn doesn't study more now.

4. (A) Ben heard the talk.
   (B) Ben didn't hear the talk.

5. (A) Ricky prefers the beach.
   (B) Ricky prefers the park.

6. (A) Please call tomorrow.
   (B) Please don't call tomorrow.

7. (A) It was necessary for Jill to go back to the dorm.
   (B) Jill most likely went back to the dorm.

8. (A) I know John got the job.
   (B) I don't know if John got the job.

9. (A) Sharon has already left.
   (B) Sharon hasn't left yet.

10. (A) We don't see each other enough.
    (B) We see each other too much.

 STOP

Answers to Exercise L15 are on page 432.

Exercise L16   **Identifying conditions**

Listen to the spoken statement. Circle the letter of the sentence that is closer in meaning to or implied in the statement you heard.

Example   You will hear: *If you have a boarding pass, please get in line.*

You will read: (A) You must stand in line if you have a pass.
                (B) You must stand in line if you don't have a pass.

START

1. (A) Sarah got a raise.
   (B) Sarah didn't get a raise.

2. (A) William goes to the movies on rainy Fridays.
   (B) William doesn't go to the movies on rainy Fridays.

3. (A) She will buy the car.
   (B) She might buy the car.

4. (A) Mary's mother was in Spain.
   (B) Mary's mother wasn't in Spain.

5. (A) Sam quit his job.
   (B) Sam didn't quit his job.

6. (A) She bought the dress.
   (B) She didn't buy the dress.

7. (A) I gain weight easily.
   (B) I don't gain weight easily.

8. (A) I have cash.
   (B) I don't have cash.

9. (A) I drank a lot of coffee.
   (B) I didn't drink a lot of coffee.

10. (A) Ted will bring sandwiches.
    (B) Ted might bring sandwiches.

STOP

Answers to Exercise L16 are on page 432.

Exercise L17   **Identifying causes and results**

Listen to the spoken statement. Write "C" in the space if the phrase in your book contains the cause, and write "R" if it contains the result.

Example   You will hear: *I had to work late last night because I had to finish that report.*

You will read: _C_ I had to finish that report.

You should write "C" in the space because "I had to finish that report" is the cause of "I had to work late."

[▭▭] **START**

1. _____ it was such a boring lecture

2. _____ everyone was at the lake

3. _____ Mike has a car

4. _____ Bob burned his tongue

5. _____ you take notes

6. _____ I need to cash this check

7. _____ Paul didn't finish it

8. _____ you are a math major

9. _____ we stayed at home and watched TV

10. _____ the instructor didn't come

[▭▭] **STOP**

Answers to Exercise L17 are on page 432.

Exercise L18 **Understanding other structures**

Listen to the spoken statement. Circle the letter of the sentence that is true based on the statement you heard.

Example You will hear: *Mary painted the picture herself.*

You will read: (A) Mary made the picture.
(B) The picture is of Mary.

You should circle (A) because "Mary painted the picture herself" means "Mary did it alone with no help."

[▭▭] **START**

1. (A) Professor Silva still smokes.
   (B) Professor Silva has quit smoking many times.

2. (A) Bill still skis.
   (B) Bill no longer skis.

3. (A) I don't jog before breakfast anymore.
   (B) I have the habit of jogging before breakfast.

4. (A) Sue knows she gave the plants some water.
   (B) Sue didn't forget to give the plants some water.

5. (A) Carol had her photograph taken.
   (B) Carol snapped the picture.

6. (A) Barbara is accustomed to working in art.
   (B) Barbara doesn't work for an art dealer now.

7. (A) Mark left the lights on.
   (B) Mark turned the lights off.

8. (A) Alison lit a match.
   (B) Alison doesn't light matches anymore.

[▭▭] **STOP**

Answers to Exercise L18 are on page 432.

CHECK YOUR PROGRESS

Check your progress in the areas covered in Exercises L13–L18 by completing the following mini-test. This exercise uses the same format as Part A of the Listening Comprehension section on the TOEFL.

START

Exercise L19   **Mini-test**

Directions: For each question you will hear a short sentence. Each sentence will be spoken just once. The sentences you hear will <u>not</u> be written out for you.

After you hear a sentence, read the four choices in your book, marked (A), (B), (C), and (D), and decide which <u>one</u> is closest in meaning to the sentence you heard. Then circle the letter that corresponds to the answer you have chosen.

Listen to an example.

On the recording, you hear: *I couldn't have done a better job than Sam.*

In your workbook, you read: (A) I couldn't do the job and neither could Sam.
(B) I did a better job than Sam did.
(C) Sam did a job that l couldn't have done so well.
(D) Sam couldn't do the job that I did.

The man said, "I couldn't have done a better job than Sam." Sentence (C), "Sam did a job that I couldn't have done so well," is closest in meaning to what the man said. Therefore, the correct choice is (C).

1. (A) Ted didn't want to marry Ann.
    (B) Ted married Ann even though she was ugly.
    (C) Had Ted married Ann she'd have been beautiful.
    (D) Ted married Ann because she was beautiful.

2. (A) Julie can't remember if she signed the paper.
    (B) Julie forgot to signal to the man in uniform.
    (C) Julie didn't remember the sign about applications.
    (D) Julie didn't put her name on the form.

3. (A) Mr. Roberts gave Andy's newsletter to Sue.
    (B) Sue got the newsletter from Andy.
    (C) Andy gave Mr. Roberts Sue's newsletter.
    (D) Sue gave Mr. Roberts the newsletter.

4. (A) The test should have been taken months ago.
    (B) The test you took was probably harder than any other.
    (C) You must take the most difficult exam.
    (D) You should have taken the most difficult exam.

5. (A) Jim hit the grape juice with a mop.
    (B) Jim knocked over the mop and grape juice.
    (C) Jim didn't clean up the juice he spilled.
    (D) Jim picked up the mop and knocked over the juice.

6. (A) David has never had a serious problem.
    (B) David hardly ever makes it to his classes.
    (C) David has never been more serious about attending classes
    (D) David's physical condition does not keep him from classes.

7. (A) Kim called us to go on a picnic.
    (B) The picnic was canceled due to the weather.
    (C) Kim decided it was a good day for an outing.
    (D) Kim wanted the outing on a cloudy day.

8. (A) Please sign your name on the line.
    (B) Go ahead, if you've been given a seat number.
    (C) Are you going to sign up on time?
    (D) Please, let's sit in the grandstand.

9. (A) The professor left the testing center.
   (B) The student wasn't permitted into the center.
   (C) The student left the center to get his card.
   (D) The professor forgot the student's card at the center.

10. (A) Donna found a good job after finishing art school.
    (B) Donna hopes to get a job at the gallery.
    (C) Donna's been promised a job at the Art Academy.
    (D) Donna's job at the gallery will pay for her schooling.

11. (A) Will's report was on cross-country skiing.
    (B) The ski club has reported that snow is needed.
    (C) The report on skiing was correct.
    (D) Snow has been forecast.

12. (A) Mrs. Davis's son told her he didn't like dogs.
    (B) Mrs. Davis's son's dog has strayed away from home.
    (C) Mrs. Davis wants her son to stay away from strange dogs.
    (D) Mrs. Davis told her son that he should get a pet dog.

13. (A) Do you want to place an ad in the newspaper?
    (B) Could you buy the newspaper for me?
    (C) Did you see the classified ads in the newspaper?
    (D) May I read the classified ads from your newspaper?

14. (A) Marie gave Rick's speech.
    (B) Rick gave Marie his speech.
    (C) Rick got a speech for Marie.
    (D) Marie wrote the speech for Rick.

15. (A) Nancy used to dance a lot.
    (B) Nancy is accustomed to dancing less.
    (C) Nancy doesn't find it difficult to dance.
    (D) Nancy isn't dancing as much as she used to.

16. (A) There's no way you can finish in time.
    (B) Jerry will never help you finish.
    (C) With Jerry's help, you can finish.
    (D) You can help Jerry finish on time.

17. (A) Amy should first discuss the report with the committee.
    (B) Amy must submit the report for a check.
    (C) The committee must check Amy's submitted report.
    (D) The committee must report on Amy's check.

18. (A) Let me finish making this phone call.
    (B) Could you please leave while I make this phone call?
    (C) Please phone me before you go to the bus stop.
    (D) We can leave as soon as I use the telephone.

19. (A) Rebecca must swim laps until she's worn out.
    (B) Rebecca was probably tired from all her swimming.
    (C) Rebecca always swims laps until she's exhausted.
    (D) Rebecca exhausted all the other lap swimmers.

20. (A) Even with the door closed, the music was too loud.
    (B) Simon couldn't get the door closed.
    (C) The music couldn't be heard through the closed door.
    (D) Simon was trying to hear the music.

▭ **STOP**

Answers to Exercise L19 are on page 432.

PART B   SHORT CONVERSATIONS

In Part B of the Listening Comprehension section of the TOEFL, you will hear short conversations. After each conversation, you will hear a question about what was said. You must listen carefully, because you will hear the conversation and question only one time. Then you must choose the correct answer to the question from four sentences in your test book. You will have 15 seconds to make your choice and fill in the space on your answer sheet. There are 15 questions in Part B.

STRATEGIES TO USE FOR LISTENING COMPREHENSION, PART B

1. Concentrate on the conversation.

Focus all your attention on the conversation you are listening to. Each speaker speaks only once in a short conversation. Do not try to read answers at the same time you are listening. Do not work on previous items when the conversation is being spoken. Do not think about other items.

2. Listen for meaning.

The wrong answers may be similar to information heard in the conversation either in sound, vocabulary, structure, or meaning, but they do not answer the question. For examples of these kinds of confusions, see pages 27–28, strategies 2–4.

3. Concentrate on who, what, and where.

Many of the questions concern what the speakers are doing, what the speaker's job or profession is, and where the conversation is taking place. Concentrate on these details. Look at this example:

(First Man)   *I think I'll order the Diner's Special of hash browns, eggs, and a choice of sausages or bacon.*
(Woman)   *I'm not that hungry. I'll just have coffee and toast.*
(Second Man) *Where does this conversation most probably take place?*

In this conversation, we can infer from the following clues that the people are in a restaurant: (1) The man wants to "order" a meal. (2) The "Diner's Special" is probably the name of a meal particular to the restaurant.

4. Concentrate on the context.

The first speaker often sets the context, and the question often relates to how the second speaker responds. Look at this example:

(First Man)   *I've just locked my car keys in the trunk.*
(Woman)   *Don't worry. I've got mine.*
(Second Man) *Why isn't the woman concerned?*

In this conversation, the man sets the context – he's locked his keys in the car. The woman's response indicates that she is not concerned about the incident because she has a set of keys to the car as well.

5. Know what works for you.

If you are uncertain which answer is correct, you can do one of two things:

(A) Use your intuition (instincts).
(B) Guess.

(See Part A, item 6, page 28.)

6. Use every second wisely.

Don't lose time thinking about something you don't know. Answer each question. Then prepare yourself to concentrate on the following conversation and question.

PRACTICE WITH SOUNDS

Many items are difficult because of sound or word confusions. Use Listening Exercises L20–L24 to develop the following skills.

1. Understanding words that sound similar
2. Understanding words that sound the same as other words but have different meanings
3. Understanding the correct meaning of words that have several different meanings

(For additional practice in these areas, see Exercises L1–L6 and Exercise L57.)

Exercise L20 **Identifying words that are pronounced the same but have different meanings**

The following pairs of words are pronounced the same but have different meanings. Listen to the spoken conversation and circle the word you heard in the conversation.

Example   You will hear: (Man)   *Where shall I put this vase?*
(Woman) *Right here on the table.*

You will read: (here)   hear

You should circle "here" because the conversation refers to location.

▶ **START**

1. dye   die   3. won   one   5. hole   whole   ■ **STOP**
2. breaks   brakes   4. lone   loan

Answers to Exercise L20 are on page 434.

Exercise L21 **Identifying the meaning of the word in the conversation**

In your book are the definitions of two words which are pronounced the same but spelled differently. Listen to the word, followed by a short conversation. Circle the letter of the definition of the word as it's used in the conversation you heard.

Example   You will hear: *tow*

   (Man)   *My car broke down on Grand Avenue during rush hour.*
   (Woman)   *I bet it was expensive to get a tow.*

   You will read: (A) a pull
                  (B) an appendage of the foot

You should circle (A) because "a pull" is the definition of "a tow" used in the conversation. ("A toe" is an appendage of the foot.)

START

1. (A) encounter
   (B) animal flesh

2. (A) exchange of goods for money
   (B) sheet of canvas used to catch the wind

3. (A) people who work on a ship or plane
   (B) trip on a ship

4. (A) seven days
   (B) fatigued

5. (A) letters
   (B) man

STOP

Answers to Exercise L21 are on page 434.

Exercise L22   **Identifying which meaning is correct**

Read the following list of words and the four possible definitions for each. Listen to the spoken conversation and circle the letter of the meaning that is used in the conversation.

Example   You will hear: (Man)   *How often do you go skiing?*
                              (Woman) *About three times a month.*

   You will read: times
                  (A) occasions
                  (B) multiply
                  (C) durations
                  (D) tempos

You should circle (A) because "times" in the conversation means "occasions."

START

1. degree
   (A) step
   (B) academic qualification
   (C) angle
   (D) level of heat

2. major
   (A) army officer
   (B) musical scale
   (C) more important
   (D) a university student's specialization

3. spring
   (A) time of year
   (B) stream
   (C) leap
   (D) coil

4. volume
   (A) loudness
   (B) large mass
   (C) amount of space
   (D) one of a set of books

5. sound
   (A) noise
   (B) healthy
   (C) dependable
   (D) body of water

STOP

Answers to Exercise L22 are on page 434.

Extended practice: Make your own sentences using each of the meanings.

Exercise L23   ***Identifying multiple meanings in conversations***

In your book is a list of words and one of their meanings. Listen to the two spoken conversations. Write the letter of the conversation that uses the meaning given in your book.

Example   You will hear: (A) (Woman) *Can you lend me five dollars?*
                               (Man)   *Are you short of money again?*
                           (B) (Woman) *Why does this light keep going off?*
                               (Man)   *There's a short in it.*

You will read: _B_ short = fault in electrical wiring

You should write "B" in the space because "short" means "a fault in the electrical wiring" in conversation (B).

⏸ **START**

1. _____ stroke = a single movement that is repeated

2. _____ hot = spicy

3. _____ mount = get on

4. _____ blow = hit

5. _____ cast = throw

6. _____ cross = annoyed   ⏹ **STOP**

Answers to Exercise L23 are on page 434.

Exercise L24   ***Matching words in conversations***

In your book is a list of conversations with an underlined word in each. Listen to two spoken conversations and identify the one that uses the underlined word in the same way as the conversation in your book. You may want to pause the recording between conversations.

Example   You will hear: (A) (Woman) *How was your tennis <u>match</u>?*
                               (Man)   *We won!*
                           (B) (Man)   *Mary's shoes and hat don't <u>match</u>.*
                               (Woman) *I think they look fine.*

You will read: _B_ (Man)   Would these curtains <u>match</u> our carpet?
                         (Woman) Why don't you ask for a sample to take home?

You should write "B" in the space because "match" in the conversation (B) means the same as "match" in the conversation in your book.

⏸ **START**

1. _____ (Man)   Do you prefer bridge or canasta?
              (Woman) Actually, I don't care for <u>card</u> games in general.

2. _____ (Man)   How do you make such a <u>rich</u> fruitcake?
              (Woman) I use lots of butter and eggs.

3. _____ (Man)   A baked potato is better for your <u>body</u> than fried potatoes.
              (Woman) I don't care. I prefer fried potatoes.

4. _____ (Man)   How many application <u>forms</u> did you receive today?
            (Woman) Six. But none of the applicants is qualified for the job.

5. _____ (Man)   I sure am tired of studying.
            (Woman) Me too. We could use a <u>break</u> after midterm exams.   ▭ **STOP**

Answers to Exercise L24 are on page 434.

CHECK YOUR PROGRESS

Check your progress in the areas covered in Exercises L20–L24 by completing the
following mini-test. This exercise uses the same format as Part B of the Listening
Comprehension section on the TOEFL.

 START

Exercise L25   **Mini-test**

<u>Directions</u>: In Part B you will hear short conversations between two people. After each
conversation, a third person will ask a question about what was said. You will hear each
conversation and question about it only <u>one</u> time.

After you hear a conversation and the question about it, read the four possible answers in
your book and decide which <u>one</u> is the best answer to the question you heard. Then circle
the letter that corresponds to the answer you have chosen.

Listen to an example.

On the recording, you hear: (First Man)   *Nick broke the window pane while cleaning*
                                                           it.
                                         (Woman)   *Did he hurt himself?*
                                         (Second Man) *What did Nick do?*

In your workbook, you read: (A) He hurt himself.
                                          (B) He cleaned the wound.
                                          (C) He broke the glass.
                                          (D) He got soaked.

You learn from the conversation that Nick broke the window pane while he was cleaning
it. The best answer to the question "What did Nick do?" is (C), "He broke the glass."
Therefore, the correct choice is (C).

1. (A) If the woman means to take the tea.   3. (A) Missing a trip.
   (B) If the woman's going to take a plane.   (B) Booking a flight.
   (C) If the woman wants something in her drink.   (C) Returning in a month.
   (D) If the tea is too plain.   (D) Keeping a book.

2. (A) Judy and David's house.   4. (A) Deciding what to put on.
   (B) Arguing.   (B) Buying pants by check.
   (C) Little things.   (C) Matching the paints.
   (D) Boxing.   (D) Painting stripes.

5. (A) He'll be gone for a week.
    (B) He doesn't have much strength.
    (C) His timing is bad.
    (D) He's been sick four times.

6. (A) Sleeping in class.
    (B) Listening to the professor.
    (C) Boring his classmates.
    (D) Wandering around the classroom.

7. (A) Go to space.
    (B) Return to class.
    (C) Take his glass.
    (D) Carry the pack.

8. (A) Join the group.
    (B) Lend him money.
    (C) Clean the engine.
    (D) Change the parts.

9. (A) Play with her daughter.
    (B) Act in the theater.
    (C) Eat a roll.
    (D) Play a game.

10. (A) An extra tire.
    (B) A stopped-up drain.
    (C) A bathroom plug.
    (D) An odor.

11. (A) Play pool.
    (B) Take a cab.
    (C) Cool the car.
    (D) Go swimming.

12. (A) Go climbing.
    (B) Take the airplane.
    (C) Use the steps.
    (D) Fly too often.

13. (A) A place to go shopping.
    (B) Taking a class photo.
    (C) Framing a painting.
    (D) Buying some glass.

14. (A) They are ordering two steaks.
    (B) They are collecting the essays.
    (C) They are trying to prove what was stated.
    (D) They are looking for errors in a paper.

15. (A) He'd parked his truck in a bad place.
    (B) He'd driven his truck around the block.
    (C) He'd put his truck in reverse.
    (D) He'd packed the blocks in the truck.

 STOP

Answers to Exercise L25 are on page 434.

PRACTICE WITH TIME, QUANTITY, AND COMPARISONS

Many items are difficult because of confusions in time, quantity, or comparisons. Use Listening Exercises L26 and L27 to develop your skills in understanding the meanings of certain time, quantity, and comparison statements. Study the examples in Part A, page 33. (For additional practice, see Exercises L7 and L8.)

Exercise L26   *Listening for time, quantity, and comparisons*

Listen to the spoken conversation. Circle the letter of the sentence that is true based on the information you heard.

TIME

Example   You will hear: (Man)   *Are you going to the library today?*
                              (Woman) *Not until after lunch.*

You will read: (A) The woman is going to the library later.
               (B) The woman isn't going to the library today.

You should circle (A) because the woman means that she is not going to the library now but that she is going to the library after lunch.

START

1. (A) It's been less than three years since the woman saw Mary.
   (B) It's been more than three years since the woman saw Mary.

2. (A) The woman told Tom about the book he ordered.
   (B) The woman will tell Tom about the book he ordered.

3. (A) The dog show is next week.
   (B) The dog show is the week after next.

4. (A) Mr. Green's grocery closes at 9:00 on Fridays.
   (B) Mr. Green's grocery doesn't open until 9:00 on Fridays.

5. (A) The man stopped taking lessons six years ago.
   (B) The man has been taking lessons for six years.

PAUSE

QUANTITY

Example   You will hear: (Man)   *How often does* The New Adventure *magazine come out?*
                              (Woman) *Bimonthly.*

You will read: (A) *The New Adventure* magazine comes out every month.
               (B) *The New Adventure* magazine comes out two times a month.

You should circle (B) because "bi" means twice (two times) and the magazine comes out bimonthly.

START

6. (A) The man bought one cassette tape.
   (B) The man bought a few cassette tapes.

7. (A) Sam's completed more than 60 credit hours.
   (B) Sam's completed less than 60 credit hours.

8. (A) The people don't understand an example.
   (B) The people don't understand two examples.

9. (A) A few students couldn't get loans.
   (B) A lot of students couldn't get loans.

10. (A) The woman has one brother.
    (B) The woman has two brothers.

PAUSE

COMPARISONS

Example   You will hear: (Man)   *Are the roads icy tonight?*
                              (Woman) *Yes, but no more than last night.*

You will read: (A) The roads were more icy last night.
               (B) The roads are just as icy tonight.

You should circle (B). The woman's statement means that the roads tonight are just as icy as they were last night.

▭ **START**

11. (A) The man is having more difficulty with geology than calculus.
    (B) The man is having more difficulty with calculus than geology.

12. (A) The woman would prefer a big box.
    (B) The woman would prefer a better box.

13. (A) The people agree that schedules should be more flexible.
    (B) The people agree that there should be fewer working hours.

14. (A) The woman intended to write half as much as she did.
    (B) The woman intended to write more than what she did.

15. (A) Interstate 90 is faster.
    (B) Interstate 90 is more interesting.   ▭ **STOP**

Answers to Exercise L26 are on page 435.

Exercise L27   **Understanding the meaning in expressions of time, quantity, and comparisons**

Listen to the spoken conversation. Circle the letter of the sentence that is true based on the information you heard.

Example   You will hear: (Man)   *Are you still going to Aspen?*
                             (Woman)   *I don't know. The more we discuss the trip, the less we agree on it.*

You will read: (A) They agree on the trip.
               (B) They don't agree on the trip.

You should circle (B) because the more they discuss the trip, the more they do not agree on it ("the less we agree on it").

▭ **START**

1. (A) She doesn't want more chairs.
   (B) She wants more chairs.

2. (A) He didn't buy as many books last semester as this semester.
   (B) He bought more books last semester than this semester.

3. (A) He spent less than two hours on his speech preparation.
   (B) He spent more than two hours on his speech preparation.

4. (A) He bought candy.
   (B) He didn't buy candy.

5. (A) The last day is a week away.
   (B) The last day is more than a week away.

6. (A) Approximately 3,000 students were working before.
   (B) Approximately 750 students were working before.   ▭ **STOP**

Answers to Exercise L27 are on page 436.

PRACTICE WITH IDIOMS AND PHRASAL VERBS

Misinterpreting the meaning of an idiomatic expression or phrasal verb may lead to the wrong choice of answer. Use Listening Exercises L28–L30 to develop your skills in identifying the correct meaning of these expressions. Study the examples in Part A (pages 35–36). For additional practice, see Exercises L9–L11.

Exercise L28   ***Understanding idiomatic expressions***

Listen to the spoken conversation. After each conversation, you will hear a question. Circle the letter of the sentence that answers the question correctly.

Example   You will hear: (Woman)   *This class will be a breeze.*
                                  (First Man)   *I agree.*

                                  (Second Man) *What does the woman mean?*

You will read: (A) The class work will be easy.
                     (B) The classroom will be windy.

You should circle (A) because the idiom "be a breeze" means "be easy."

1. (A) Tom didn't meet her.
   (B) Tom stood on her toes.

2. (A) The woman wants to break the bottle open.
   (B) The woman wants to try opening the bottle herself.

3. (A) There was an explosion in the chemistry classroom.
   (B) The chemistry teacher became very angry.

4. (A) The man will register for the music course.
   (B) The man won't register for the music course.

5. (A) The woman might know Cindy.
   (B) The woman doesn't know Cindy.

6. (A) The man had to run to the registration office.
   (B) The man had difficulty with the registration personnel.

 STOP

Answers to Exercise L28 are on page 436.

Exercise L29   ***Identifying the correct expressions***

Listen to the spoken conversation. Circle the letter of the sentence containing the idiom or phrasal verb that could be substituted in the conversation.

Example   You will hear: (Man)   *Did the professor collect the assignment?*
                                  (Woman)   *No. But I gave him mine anyway.*

You will read: (A) But I handed in mine anyway.
                     (B) But I gave him a hand anyway.
                     (C) But I went hand in hand with him anyway.
                     (D) But I put my hands on it anyway.

You should circle (A) because the idiom "handed in" could have been used instead of "gave him."

▭ START

1. (A) Because I have fallen behind.
   (B) Because I have fallen asleep.
   (C) Because I have fallen in love.
   (D) Because I have fallen apart.

2. (A) He always weighs his words.
   (B) He always gains weight.
   (C) He always throws his weight around.
   (D) He always pulls his weight.

3. (A) Yes, I had a night out.
   (B) Yes, I made a night of it.
   (C) Yes, I turned day into night.
   (D) Yes, I had a bad night.

4. (A) She may, on the off chance.
   (B) She stands a good chance.
   (C) She may chance upon it.
   (D) She may chance it.

5. (A) The professor called it a day.
   (B) The professor called a halt to it.
   (C) The professor called my bluff.
   (D) The professor called attention to it.

6. (A) Janet and Mike were turning the other cheek.
   (B) Janet and Mike were speaking tongue in cheek.
   (C) Janet and Mike were dancing cheek to cheek.
   (D) Janet and Mike were being cheeky.

7. (A) You just saw the last of it.
   (B) You were seeing things.
   (C) You saw your way clear to do it.
   (D) You saw the daylight.

8. (A) Don't let her throw cold water on it.
   (B) Don't let her throw a party.
   (C) Don't let her throw in the towel.
   (D) Don't let her throw it away.

9. (A) You might as well.
   (B) You will come off well.
   (C) You should leave well enough alone.
   (D) It's just as well.

10. (A) I was sent on a wild goose chase.
    (B) I sowed my wild oats.
    (C) I was wild about it.
    (D) It spread like wildfire.

▭ STOP

Answers to Exercise L29 are on page 436.

Exercise L30 ***Identifying the correct meaning of expressions***

You will hear a spoken conversation. After each conversation you will hear a question. Circle the letter of the answer that is true based on the conversation you heard.

Example You will hear: (Woman) *Why did your flight take so long?*
(First Man) *There was a four-hour layover in Chicago for refueling.*
(Second Man) *What reason does the man give the woman?*

You will read: (A) The flight personnel were discharged.
(B) They spent the night in Chicago.
(C) The plane needed fuel.
(D) There was fog over Chicago.

You should circle (C) because if there was a "layover" (a stop) for refueling, it was because the plane needed fuel.

START

1. (A) Keep the laundry.
   (B) Wash the truck.
   (C) Write or call.
   (D) Be certain about it.

2. (A) She wants to toss stones in the park.
   (B) She's afraid of someone throwing rocks at them.
   (C) She thinks the park is close enough to walk to.
   (D) She doesn't want to drive over the stony roads.

3. (A) He has to get things organized.
   (B) He likes to get a good seat in the stands.
   (C) He gets upset about standing in long lines.
   (D) He has to help put the TV sets in the recording studio.

4. (A) He is working for a packaging company.
   (B) He has become engrossed in his work.
   (C) He has just completed a job assignment.
   (D) He had to cover for a co-worker.

5. (A) The woman made an ethical mistake.
   (B) The woman got a point wrong on the exam.
   (C) The woman missed a very good speech.
   (D) The woman didn't understand the lecture.

6. (A) The doctor told her to run in order to lose weight.
   (B) She ran so quickly to the doctor's office that she arrived panting.
   (C) She discovered how to lose weight in a brochure at the doctor's.
   (D) The doctor was cross with her for not exercising and watching her diet.

7. (A) Rebecca won't return his watch.
   (B) Rebecca won't tell him the time.
   (C) Rebecca won't tell him when the play starts.
   (D) Rebecca won't speak to him at all.

8. (A) Mary votes well.
   (B) Mary can do a good job.
   (C) Mary takes what she can.
   (D) Mary takes elections seriously.

9. (A) Set up his own business.
   (B) Pay attention to his own affairs.
   (C) Take care of the business.
   (D) Guess what's on her mind.

10. (A) He doesn't have the approval to begin.
    (B) He is ahead of the committee on the project.
    (C) The head of the committee is going away.
    (D) He has to turn in the project ahead of time.

 STOP

Answers to Exercise L30 are on page 437.

CHECK YOUR PROGRESS

Check your progress in the areas covered in Exercises L26–L30 by completing the following mini-test. This exercise uses the same format as Part B of the Listening Comprehension section on the TOEFL.

 START

Exercise L31   *Mini-test*

Directions: You will hear short conversations between two people. After each conversation, a third person will ask a question about what was said. You will hear each conversation and the question about it only one time.

After you hear a conversation and the question about it, read the four possible answers in your book and decide which <u>one</u> is the best answer to the question you heard. Then circle the letter that corresponds to the answer you have chosen.

Listen to an example.

On the recording, you hear: (Man)   *Have you followed up on Michael's recommendations?*

(First Woman)   *Sally has. And her report looks very promising.*

(Second Woman) *What did Sally do?*

In your workbook, you read: (A) Followed Michael.
(B) Promised a report.
(C) Recommended Michael.
(D) Submitted a report.

You infer from the conversation that Sally wrote a report concerning the recommendations she "followed up on." The best answer to the question "What did Sally do?" is (D), "Submitted a report." Therefore, the correct choice is (D).

1. (A) The woman should close her eyes.
   (B) The woman should get some sleep.
   (C) The woman should turn off the light.
   (D) The woman should close up her house.

2. (A) Pack up a dinner for the party.
   (B) Return to the party after dinner.
   (C) Not go to the dinner party.
   (D) Have dinner in the backyard.

3. (A) The man seems unconcerned about his grade.
   (B) The man has not studied hard enough.
   (C) The man has broken the lamp in the sociology class.
   (D) The man did not write darkly enough on the score sheet.

4. (A) The reasons to brush up on driving skills.
   (B) The reasons he was in a hurry.
   (C) The reasons not to talk about it.
   (D) The reasons the accident occurred.

5. (A) He's not working as hard as he should.
   (B) He's been napping at work.
   (C) His job is to sleep.
   (D) He's depressed about his work.

6. (A) They are put on TV.
   (B) They are screamed at.
   (C) They eat ice cream.
   (D) They are disqualified.

7. (A) Ted lets the yokes sink to the bottom.
   (B) Ted understands after he thinks about things.
   (C) Ted doesn't realize the eggs stink.
   (D) Ted takes time to wash in the basin.

8. (A) Ate very quickly.
   (B) Baked cookies.
   (C) Did little work.
   (D) Worked in shorts.

9. (A) Neil usually feels sticky after class.
   (B) Neil usually meets Rick after class.
   (C) Neil is usually stuck up after class.
   (D) Neil usually stays after class.

10. (A) Simplified his course.
    (B) Watered his horse the required amount.
    (C) Required a change of courses.
    (D) Dropped his course requirements.

11. (A) He returned the class papers.
    (B) He lost consciousness.
    (C) He passed everyone in the course.
    (D) He taught the course in the past.

12. (A) She fell on the road across from the fish market.
    (B) An interesting building tumbled.
    (C) She found the store by accident.
    (D) The fish market is a hop away.

13. (A) He's taken up smoking.
    (B) He's worn out from smoking.
    (C) He's given up smoking.
    (D) He swears by smoking.

14. (A) The man didn't want the tags.
    (B) The man didn't get along with Cindy.
    (C) The man didn't price the books.
    (D) The man didn't want them to come.

15. (A) It needs to be cleaned.
    (B) It needs to be made smaller.
    (C) It needs to be returned.
    (D) It needs to be mended.

 STOP

Answers to Exercise L31 are on page 437.

PRACTICE WITH VARIOUS STRUCTURES

Certain structures occur with some frequency on the TOEFL. Study examples of these structures in Part A (pages 41–43). Then use Listening Exercises L32–L37 to develop your skills in understanding the meaning of these structures. (For additional practice, see Exercises L13–L18.)

Exercise L32   ***Understanding causatives***

Listen to the spoken conversation. Circle the letter of the correct answer.

Example   You will hear: (First Man)   *Is Ron or Vicky giving the introductory speech?*

                         (Woman)   *Since Ron isn't available that evening, I asked Vicky.*

                  (Second Man) *Who will give the speech?*

      You will read: (A) Ron
                    (B) Vicky

You should circle (B) because according to the conversation Vicky was asked to give the introductory speech.

 START

1. (A) a professional
   (B) her sister

2. (A) Joe
   (B) Fred

3. (A) Mike
   (B) Tom

4. (A) Ms. Jones
   (B) Dr. Welsh

5. (A) her mother
   (B) her father

6. (A) Rebecca
   (B) Barbara

7. (A) Mary
   (B) Alex

8. (A) Sue
   (B) Jane

 STOP

Answers to Exercise L32 are on page 439.

Exercise L33   ***Understanding negative meaning***

Listen to the spoken conversation. Circle the letter of the sentence that is true based on the conversation you heard.

Example   You will hear: (Man)   *I've never had such a bad headache.*
                         (Woman)   *Maybe you should see a doctor about it.*

You will read: (A) The man has never had a headache.
(B) The man has never had a headache as bad as this one.

You should circle (B) because according to the conversation the man has a bad headache.

🔲 **START**

1. (A) The man had some trouble with the exercises.
   (B) The man had a lot of trouble with the exercises.

2. (A) The man doesn't know the right people.
   (B) The man doesn't know the right things.

3. (A) The woman saw more than one blouse that she liked.
   (B) The woman saw no blouses that she liked.

4. (A) Mark is tense about the test.
   (B) Mark isn't tense about the test.

5. (A) There was enough equipment.
   (B) There wasn't enough equipment.

6. (A) Beth isn't pretty.
   (B) Beth is pretty.

7. (A) Robert has trouble pleasing his parents.
   (B) Robert rarely tries so hard to please his parents.

8. (A) Steve is ambitious.
   (B) Steve isn't ambitious.

🔲 **STOP**

Answers to Exercise L33 are on page 439.

Exercise L34   **Understanding modals**

Listen to the spoken conversation. Circle the letter of the sentence that is true based on the conversation you heard.

Example   You will hear: (Man)   *Joyce must have dropped the class.*
(Woman) *I don't think so. She's been very ill recently.*

You will read: (A) Joyce has dropped the class.
(B) Joyce is sick.

You should circle (B) because according to the conversation Joyce has been ill.

🔲 **START**

1. (A) The woman used to take long walks.
   (B) The woman is used to taking long walks.

2. (A) The man is going to finish the report.
   (B) The man is going to the cafeteria.

3. (A) The woman will be attending the ceremony.
   (B) The woman may not be attending the ceremony.

4. (A) Jim probably called a plumber.
   (B) Jim probably didn't call a plumber.

5. (A) The soccer match was probably exciting.
   (B) The soccer match probably wasn't exciting.

6. (A) The woman thinks she'll have Professor Roth for Biology.
   (B) The woman doesn't think she'll have Professor Roth for biology.

7. (A) The woman has been married for 10 years.
   (B) The woman hasn't been married for 10 years yet.

8. (A) Henry may be learning how to ski.
   (B) Henry isn't learning how to ski.

▭ **STOP**

Answers to Exercise L34 are on page 439.

Exercise L35   *Identifying conditions*

Listen to the spoken conversation. Circle the letter of the sentence that is true based on the conversation you heard.

Example   You will hear: (Woman)   *Would you mind if I didn't come?*
                            (Man)   *No. Of course not.*

You will read: (A) The woman isn't going with the man.
                (B) The woman didn't go with the man.

You should circle (A) because in the conversation the woman is asking the man to excuse her from going.

▭ **START**

1. (A) The woman studied a lot for the test.
   (B) The woman didn't study a lot for the test.

2. (A) The man didn't meet Helen Martin.
   (B) The man met Helen Martin.

3. (A) Sue's on probation.
   (B) Sue isn't on probation.

4. (A) Marion didn't attend the march.
   (B) Marion attended the march.

5. (A) Marvin went with Larry.
   (B) Marvin didn't go with Larry.

6. (A) The experiment may not work.
   (B) The experiment does not work.

7. (A) Peggy told Bruce to leave her alone.
   (B) Peggy didn't tell Bruce to leave her alone.

8. (A) The man has taken a walk.
   (B) The man hasn't taken a walk.

▭ **STOP**

Answers to Exercise L35 are on page 439.

Exercise L36   *Identifying causes and results*

Listen to the spoken conversation. Write "C" in the space if the phrase in your book contains the cause, and write "R" if it contains the result.

Example 1   You will hear: (Woman) *I had such a bad day that I came home and yelled at my roommate.*
                         (Man)   *So that's why she's so upset.*

            You will read: ___R___   she's so upset

You should write an "R" in the space because the roommate is upset as a result of the woman's yelling at her.

Example 2   You will hear: (Man)   *Now that Pat is married, we hardly see her.*
                       (Woman) *You can't expect her to continue the life of a single woman.*

            You will read: ___C___   Pat is married

You should write a "C" in the space because Pat's marriage is the cause of the speaker's not seeing her very often.

▶ **START**

1. _____ the movie at the Student Union is free

2. _____ I do my own cooking

3. _____ Monday is a national holiday

4. _____ I skipped class

5. _____ I went into the office

6. _____ we had to decline

7. _____ my parents are going to call tonight

8. _____ the coffee is ready

■ **STOP**

Answers to Exercise L36 are on page 439.

Exercise L37   ***Understanding other structures***

Listen to the spoken conversation. Circle the letter of the sentence that is true based on the conversation you heard.

Example   You will hear: (Man)   *Bruce was to have brought extra chairs.*
                      (Woman) *Don't worry. We can do without them.*

            You will read: (A) Bruce brought chairs.
                           (B) Bruce didn't bring chairs.

You should circle (B) because the use of "was to have" means that Bruce was supposed to bring the chairs but didn't.

▶ **START**

1. (A) Mary bought some jam.
   (B) Mary doesn't buy jam anymore.

2. (A) Ralph has signed the contract.
   (B) Ralph hasn't signed the contract yet.

3. (A) Chris remembered that he didn't lock the door.
   (B) Chris remembered he wasn't supposed to lock the door.

4. (A) The man has applied for a loan.
   (B) The man hasn't applied for a loan.

5. (A) Ms. Stevenson has the habit of working late.
   (B) Ms. Stevenson doesn't work late anymore.

6. (A) The woman has turned in the report.
   (B) The woman hasn't turned in the report.

7. (A) John didn't get the tickets.
   (B) John doesn't remember that he got the tickets.

8. (A) Pamela told herself the date and time.
   (B) It was Pamela who told the woman the date and time.   ▭ **STOP**

Answers to Exercise L37 are on page 439.

CHECK YOUR PROGRESS

Check your progress in the areas covered in Exercises L32–L37 by completing the following mini-test. This exercise uses the same format as Part B of the Listening Comprehension section on the TOEFL.

▭ **START**

Exercise L38   Mini-test

Directions: You will hear short conversations between two people. After each conversation, a third person will ask a question about what was said. You will hear each conversation and the question about it only <u>one</u> time.

After you hear a conversation and the question about it, read the four possible answers in your book and decide which <u>one</u> is the best answer to the question you heard. Then circle the letter that corresponds to the answer you have chosen.

Listen to an example.

On the recording, you hear: (First Man)   *Lee wanted Mary to tell Ann about his accident.*

(Woman)   *Mary is good at breaking bad news.*

(Second Man) *What happened to Lee?*

In your workbook, you read: (A) He was told the news.
(B) He had an accident.
(C) He got a lucky break.
(D) He broke his back.

You learn from the conversation that Lee had an accident. The best answer to the question "What happened to Lee?" is (B), "He had an accident." Therefore, the correct choice is (B).

1. (A) When he gets a car, he will offer the woman a ride.
   (B) If he is going to campus, he will get a car.
   (C) Whether he has a car or not, he will take her.
   (D) If they are going at the same time, he will take her.

2. (A) He passed the exam.
   (B) He must not have passed the exam.
   (C) He didn't pass the exam.
   (D) He did very well on the exam.

3. (A) She is in the hospital.
   (B) She wants Tom to give her the card.
   (C) She won't be able to visit Tom.
   (D) She needs to make a get-well card.

4. (A) He likes sports.
   (B) He wants to be contrary.
   (C) He prefers his older brother.
   (D) He enjoys reading.

5. (A) She's going to quit taking her class next month.
   (B) Mary's quit her class for a month.
   (C) She quit Mary's class in order to take aerobics.
   (D) She's postponed her class for a month.

6. (A) He is surprised with the results.
   (B) He wouldn't go over the statistics.
   (C) He doesn't believe the computations.
   (D) He hasn't looked at the results.

7. (A) The man can't write reports very well.
   (B) The woman may have difficulty reading the man's handwriting.
   (C) It is impossible to write a report so quickly.
   (D) It is impossible to type a report so quickly.

8. (A) Bob wouldn't trust him to use his recorder.
   (B) Bob wouldn't want him to record the lecture.
   (C) Bob hasn't used his new cassette recorder yet.
   (D) Bob wouldn't bet on the new recorder.

9. (A) Only Dan.
   (B) The department head.
   (C) Maria.
   (D) Dan and Maria.

10. (A) The mall.
    (B) The street bazaar.
    (C) Downtown.
    (D) The town hall.

11. (A) Andrew and Joan are avoiding each other.
    (B) Andrew and Joan don't like to walk together.
    (C) Andrew and Joan argue whenever they go walking.
    (D) Andrew and Joan go for walks whenever they argue.

12. (A) Roger probably forgot to come.
    (B) Roger is usually early.
    (C) Roger is always on time.
    (D) Roger will come later.

13. (A) Nancy couldn't sell her car.
    (B) Nancy wouldn't sell her car.
    (C) There was nothing wrong with Nancy's car.
    (D) Nancy sold her car easily.

14. (A) She had to finish by Monday.
    (B) She finished last Monday.
    (C) She finishes on Monday.
    (D) She finished by Monday.

15. (A) Have a talk.
    (B) Go to the library.
    (C) Study something.
    (D) Try to get a book.

 STOP

Answers to Exercise L38 are on page 439.

PRACTICE WITH UNDERSTANDING MEANING FROM CONTEXT

You can guess the meaning of a statement by thinking about the context of a conversation.

For example:

(Woman) *Would you like to go to the Barnacle for dinner tonight?*
(Man)   *I'm never eating there again!*

From the conversation we can guess that the Barnacle is a restaurant and that the man doesn't like eating there (perhaps he doesn't like the food there, or maybe the service isn't good). We can also assume that the man is not accepting the woman's invitation.

Use Listening Exercises L39 and L40 to develop your skills in deriving meaning through context.

Exercise L39   ***Identifying what people are doing***

Listen to the spoken conversation. Identify what the two people in the conversation are doing.

Example   You will hear: (Man)   *Shall we go to the amusement park or the beach?*
                        (Woman) *It's up to you.*

You will read: The man is   The woman is
              (A) suggesting some options   (C) letting the man decide
              (B) giving an opinion   (D) declining his offer

You should circle (A) because the man has suggested either going to the amusement park or going to the beach. You should circle (C) because the woman's remark means that it is for him to decide.

▶ **START**

1. The man is   The woman is
   (A) expressing uncertainty   (C) asking for permission
   (B) extending an invitation   (D) accepting an offer

2. The woman is   The man is
   (A) gossiping   (C) expressing doubt
   (B) complaining   (D) giving encouragement

3. The man is
   (A) giving an excuse
   (B) breaking a date

   The woman is
   (C) thanking the man
   (D) expressing sympathy

4. The man is
   (A) expressing disappointment
   (B) arranging an appointment

   The woman is
   (C) suggesting a time
   (D) organizing a trip

5. The woman is
   (A) explaining a situation
   (B) asking for help

   The man is
   (C) making a joke
   (D) asking for a choice

6. The man is
   (A) asking for an opinion
   (B) making a hypothesis

   The woman is
   (C) agreeing
   (D) refusing politely

7. The man is
   (A) causing an argument
   (B) expressing confusion

   The woman is
   (C) advising
   (D) elaborating

8. The man is
   (A) stating a problem
   (B) expressing thanks

   The woman is
   (C) paying a compliment
   (D) giving a suggestion

 STOP

Answers to Exercise L39 are on page 440.

Exercise L40   *Understanding responses*

Listen to the spoken conversation. Circle the letter of the sentence that is true based on the conversation you heard.

Example   You will hear: (Man)   *I think I'm catching a cold.*
                        (Woman) *Maybe you should take some vitamin C.*

You will read: (A) The woman is making a suggestion.
                      (B) The woman is making an offer.

You should circle (A) because the woman is suggesting that the man take some vitamin C for his cold.

START

1. (A) The woman thinks the man is a good writer.
   (B) The woman thinks the man is being boastful.

2. (A) The woman is ill.
   (B) The woman is complaining.

3. (A) The man is accepting an invitation.
   (B) The man is rejecting an invitation.

4. (A) The man agrees.
   (B) The man doesn't agree.

5. (A) The man is accepting dessert.
   (B) The man is declining dessert.

6. (A) The woman agrees to the request.
   (B) The woman does not agree to the request.

7. (A) The woman is criticizing the man.
   (B) The woman is disagreeing with the man.

8. (A) The woman is offering the man some cookies.
   (B) The woman is refusing some help.

 STOP

Answers to Exercise L40 are on page 441.

PRACTICE WITH REMEMBERING DETAILS

In a conversation, several details may be mentioned which could be confused. Various places, names, times, etc., may be included, and the question will concern one of these details in particular. Do not read the answers before you listen to the conversation. This may lead to your confusing the details. Concentrate on the conversation. The details are remembered more easily in context. Look at the following example.

1. Concentrate on the conversation.

You will hear: (Man)   *Are you going to London via New York or Washington, D.C.?*
                (Woman) *I have a nonstop flight from Chicago.*

The man's question sets the context: The woman is going to London. The man wants to know if she will pass through New York or Washington, D.C. She responds that she has a nonstop flight from Chicago. Therefore, she will go directly from Chicago (the starting point) to London (the arrival point).

2. Concentrate on the question.

You will hear: (Second Man) *Where is the woman going?*

3. Read the answers.

You will read: (A) London
               (B) New York
               (C) Washington, D.C.
               (D) Chicago

You heard all four locations mentioned in the conversation. Because you have concentrated on the details in context, you are more likely to answer the item quickly and correctly. You would mark answer (A) and then prepare yourself for the next conversation.

Use Listening Exercises L41–L46 to develop your skills in remembering details. (For additional practice, see Exercises L60–L66.)

Exercise L41   **Getting all the facts**

Listen to the spoken conversation. Each conversation includes several details. Circle the letter of any detail that is mentioned in the conversation. There is more than one answer for each conversation.

Example   You will hear: (Man)   *Flight 204 departs at 11:15.*
                            (Woman) *Do you have a flight that leaves after 1:30?*

You will read: (A) 1:30
               (B) 1:13
               (C) 11:15
               (D) 11:50

You should circle (A) and (C) because these are details mentioned in the conversation.

▣ START

1. (A) tennis shoes
   (B) climbing boots
   (C) sandals
   (D) high heels

2. (A) cheese
   (B) coffee
   (C) crackers
   (D) soup

3. (A) the plane
   (B) the concourse
   (C) the check-in desk
   (D) the gate

4. (A) 1982
   (B) 1983
   (C) 1984
   (D) 1985

5. (A) shopping mall
   (B) health club
   (C) flower shop
   (D) photographer's

▣ STOP

Answers to Exercise L41 are on page 441.

Exercise L42   Identifying who

Sometimes you hear several names mentioned in a conversation. Listen to the spoken conversation. Answer the question that follows the conversation by circling the letter of the correct name.

Example   You will hear: (Woman)   *Did Bruce or Steve study at Michigan State University?*

(First Man)   *Ron did. Bruce and Steve studied at Indiana.*

(Second Man) *Who studied at Michigan State University?*

You will read: (A) Bruce
(B) Steve
Ⓒ Ron

▣ START

1. (A) Cathy
   (B) Sue
   (C) Jim

2. (A) Robert's
   (B) Ted's
   (C) Frank's

3. (A) Mary
   (B) John
   (C) Sara

4. (A) Max
   (B) Ned
   (C) Ben

5. (A) Donna
   (B) Jackie
   (C) Liz

▣ STOP

Answers to Exercise L42 are on page 441.

Exercise L43   Identifying where

Sometimes you hear several places mentioned in a conversation. Listen to the spoken conversation. Answer the question that follows the conversation by circling the letter of the correct place.

Example   You will hear: (First Man)   *Is the University of Wyoming in Cheyenne or Casper?*

(Woman)   *Neither. It's in Laramie.*

(Second Man) *Where is the University of Wyoming?*

You will read: (A) Cheyenne
(B) Casper
(C) Laramie

▶ **START**

1. (A) France
   (B) Spain
   (C) Italy

2. (A) the boxing match
   (B) the football game
   (C) the movies

3. (A) the dry cleaner's
   (B) the clinic
   (C) the bookstore

4. (A) Texas
   (B) Boston
   (C) New York

5. (A) at the stop sign
   (B) at the school
   (C) at the light

■ **STOP**

Answers to Exercise L43 are on page 441.

Exercise L44   ***Identifying what***

Sometimes you hear several activities mentioned in a conversation. Listen to the spoken conversation. Answer the question that follows the conversation by circling the letter of the correct activity.

Example   You will hear: (First Man)   *After the movie, let's go for a snack.*

(Woman)   *That's a good idea. But before the movie I want to buy a gift for my nephew.*

(Second Man) *What will they do first?*

You will read: (A) go to the movies
(B) eat a snack
(C) buy a present

▶ **START**

1. (A) reading a novel
   (B) reciting poetry
   (C) writing short stories

2. (A) go mountain climbing
   (B) go skiing
   (C) go rafting

3. (A) attend parties
   (B) read
   (C) listen to music

4. (A) a documentary
   (B) a golf tournament
   (C) a movie

5. (A) pay the bill
   (B) get the car
   (C) wait for the woman

■ **STOP**

Answers to Exercise L44 are on page 441.

Exercise L45   **Identifying when**

Sometimes you hear several times mentioned in a conversation. Listen to the spoken conversation, which may mention days, months, years, or time. Answer the question that follows the conversation by circling the letter of the correct time.

Example   You will hear: (First Man) *What is your schedule like?*

   (Woman) *I have classes from 9:00 to 12:00 on Monday, Wednesday, and Friday, and a Tuesday and Thursday class at 11:30.*

   (Second Man) *What time is the class on Tuesday?*

You will read: (A) 9:00
   (B) 12:00
   (C) 11:30

[►] **START**

1. (A) Thursday
   (B) Friday
   (C) Saturday

2. (A) 8:30
   (B) 6:15
   (C) 6:30

3. (A) after 10:00 A.M.
   (B) after 11:45 A.M.
   (C) after 4:30 P.M.

4. (A) morning
   (B) afternoon
   (C) evening

5. (A) the day before yesterday
   (B) last night
   (C) this morning

[►] **STOP**

Answers to Exercise L45 are on page 441.

Exercise L46   **Identifying how much and how many**

Sometimes you hear different quantities mentioned in a conversation. Listen to the spoken conversation. Answer the question that follows the conversation by circling the letter of the correct amount.

Example   You will hear: (Woman) *The blue sheets cost $37.60 and the green ones cost $16.45.*

   (First Man) *Well, here are some flowered ones on sale for only $15.50.*

   (Second Man) *How much are the green sheets?*

You will read: (A) $37.60
   (B) $16.45
   (C) $15.50

[►] **START**

1. (A) $26.53
   (B) $24.49
   (C) $2.04

2. (A) fewer than twelve
   (B) a dozen
   (C) twenty-four

3. (A) three
   (B) fifteen
   (C) six

4. (A) 50 percent
   (B) more than 25 percent
   (C) 6 percent

5. (A) $49.95
   (B) $96.99
   (C) $6.00

🔊 **STOP**

Answers to Exercise L46 are on page 441.

PRACTICE WITH MAKING INFERENCES FROM VOCABULARY CLUES

Many items require you to answer questions concerning what people are doing, what their professions are, or where the conversation takes place. These details are not given. You must figure out these answers by using the vocabulary clues in the conversations.

Look at the following example.

You will hear: (Woman)   *I enjoy waiting for the nibble and the fight, but I don't like putting the worm on the hook.*

   (First Man)   *You don't have to use worms for bait. You could use flies or even cheese.*

   (Second Man) *What are the people discussing?*

You will read: (A) gardening
   (B) flying
   (C) fighting
   (D) fishing

In the conversation, the word "fishing" is never used. You can conclude that this is what the people are discussing through the use of words concerning fishing. A fish nibbles on the bait. When the fish is hooked, it fights to get off the line. One must put bait (something to attract the fish) on the hook (a bent piece of metal for catching things). Worms, cheese, and flies are all types of bait that can be used for catching fish.

Use Listening Exercises L47–L49 to develop your inference skills. (For additional practice, see Exercises L67–L69.)

Exercise L47   *Inferring activities through vocabulary*

Listen to the spoken conversation. Answer the question that follows the conversation by circling the letter of the correct activity.

Example   You will hear: (First Man)   *Jeff needs a hammer, wood, and nails to build those cabinets.*

   (Woman)   *He's really good around the house, isn't he?*

   (Second Man) *What is Jeff going to do?*

You will read: (A) mechanics
   (B) carpentry
   (C) store keeping
   (D) banking

You should circle (B) because building cabinets is carpentry work. Other vocabulary clues that help identify the activity are "hammer," "wood," and "nails."

START

1. (A) watching TV
   (B) playing cards
   (C) dancing
   (D) going to a party

2. (A) to drive a car
   (B) to fix bicycles
   (C) to play golf
   (D) to dance ballroom dances

3. (A) eating at an expensive restaurant
   (B) playing a game
   (C) landing an airplane
   (D) paying their rent

4. (A) cutting the grass
   (B) painting a wall
   (C) cooking a meal
   (D) planting flowers

5. (A) take a shower
   (B) water the lawn
   (C) clean the living room
   (D) wash the car

STOP

Answers to Exercise L47 are on page 441.

Exercise L48   ***Inferring professions through vocabulary***

Listen to the spoken conversation. Answer the question that follows the conversation by circling the letter of the correct job.

Example   You will hear: (First Man)   *Open wide so I can see that back molar.*
   (Woman)   *I hope it can be filled instead of pulled.*
   (Second Man) *What is the man's job?*

   You will read: (A) doctor
   (B) wrecker
   (C) dentist
   (D) service station attendant

You should circle (C) because a dentist would be doing the kind of work that is being discussed in the conversation. Vocabulary clues are "open wide," "back molar," "filled," and "pulled."

START

1. (A) baker
   (B) actress
   (C) veterinarian
   (D) waitress

2. (A) office clerk
   (B) secretary
   (C) librarian
   (D) biologist

3. (A) supermarket clerk
   (B) factory worker
   (C) teacher
   (D) theater manager

4. (A) plumber
   (B) actor
   (C) pilot
   (D) thief

5. (A) shoe salesperson
   (B) mechanic
   (C) seamstress
   (D) car dealer

STOP

Answers to Exercise L48 are on page 441.

Exercise L49   *Inferring locations through vocabulary*

Listen to the spoken conversation. Answer the question that follows the conversation by circling the letter of the correct place.

Example   You will hear: (Woman)   *The window is open to take bets now. Which horse are you betting on?*

(FirstMan)   *The black one. I always win when my money's on the darkest animal.*

(Second Man) *Where does this conversation take place?*

You will read: (A) a bank
(B) a racetrack
(C) a blacksmith's
(D) a drive-in restaurant

You should circle (B) because the people in the conversation are talking about placing bets on horses at the betting window.

▶ **START**

1. (A) student loan office
   (B) bank
   (C) supermarket
   (D) laundromat

2. (A) the beach
   (B) the airport
   (C) the grocery store
   (D) the pharmacy

3. (A) a travel agency
   (B) a car rental agency
   (C) an insurance agency
   (D) a gas station

4. (A) at a hospital
   (B) at the scene of an accident
   (C) at a fire station
   (D) at a police station

5. (A) at a swimming pool
   (B) at a golf course
   (C) at a tennis court
   (D) at an ice-skating rink

■ **STOP**

Answers to Exercise L49 are on page 441.

PRACTICE WITH DRAWING CONCLUSIONS

Based on the information given in the conversation, you sometimes have to come to a logical conclusion.

Look at the following example.

You will hear: (First Man)   *I had my heart set on going to Vienna with the choir.*
(Woman)   *Keep practicing and you'll pass the audition next year.*

(Second Man) *How does the man probably feel?*

You will read: (A) encouraged
(B) heartened
(C) disappointed
(D) exuberant

In the conversation, the man states that he had his heart set on going to Vienna (he wanted to go very much). The woman's response indicates that he isn't going. She is attempting to encourage him by pointing out that there is another trip next year, so he will have another chance to go. Since he wanted to go so much but cannot go, we can draw the conclusion that he is very disappointed. He would be neither exuberant (in high spirits) nor heartened (encouraged) about a failure to achieve his goal.

Use Listening Exercises L50–L51 to develop your skills in drawing conclusions. (For additional practice, see Exercise L70.)

Exercise L50   *Identifying feelings, attitudes, and personality traits*

Listen to the spoken conversation. Circle the letter of the best answer to the question that follows the conversation.

Example   You will hear: (First Man) *I wish I could pole vault as well as Joe can.*
                                  (Woman)   *He seems to have wings, doesn't he?*
                                  (Second Man) *How does the man feel?*

You will read: (A) critical
              (B) angry
              (C) content
              (D) envious

You should circle (D) because the man is expressing a desire to do as well as Joe. This desire shows his feelings of envy, as he cannot do as well as Joe. He has not criticized or shown any anger about Joe's abilities. If he felt content, he would not be wishing to be like Joe.

START

1. (A) elated
   (B) depressed
   (C) bored
   (D) energetic

2. (A) terrified
   (B) desperate
   (C) enthusiastic
   (D) discouraged

3. (A) He is cautious.
   (B) He is doubtful.
   (C) He is defiant.
   (D) Be is objective.

4. (A) confident
   (B) insecure
   (C) interested
   (D) devious

5. (A) subjective
   (B) defensive
   (C) indecisive
   (D) inquisitive

6. (A) sincere
   (B) lazy
   (C) selfish
   (D) boring

7. (A) irascible
   (B) sensitive
   (C) obstinate
   (D) efficient

8. (A) She hates them.
   (B) They frighten her.
   (C) They make her sick.
   (D) She thinks they're aloof.

Answers to Exercise L50 are on page 441.

STOP

Exercise L51   *Drawing conclusions*

Listen to the spoken conversation. Circle the letter of the answer that is probably true.

Example   You will hear: (Man)   *Are you coming for a walk with me?*
                                  (Woman) *I really have my hands full with this typing.*

You will read: (A) She probably will go with the man.
(B) She probably won't go with the man.

You should circle (B) because you can conclude that she won't go with the man because she has so much typing to do.

 START

1. (A) The people probably will go get something to drink.
   (B) The people probably won't go get something to drink.

2. (A) The woman probably drank the milk.
   (B) The woman probably broke the glass.

3. (A) The man is probably good at math.
   (B) The man probably has trouble with math.

4. (A) Chris is probably doing poorly in his studies.
   (B) Chris is probably doing well in his studies.

5. (A) The man probably will invite Tim.
   (B) The man probably won't invite Tim.

6. (A) The party probably will be over.
   (B) The party probably won't be over.

7. (A) The man probably has sales experience.
   (B) The man probably doesn't have sales experience.

8. (A) The woman probably wouldn't like what he wrote.
   (B) The man probably didn't write anything.

STOP

Answers to Exercise L51 are on page 442.

CHECK YOUR PROGRESS

Check your progress in the areas covered in Exercises L39–L51 by completing the following mini-test. This exercise uses the same format as Part B of the Listening Comprehension section on the TOEFL.

START

Exercise L52   Mini-test

Directions: You will hear short conversations between two people. After each conversation, a third person will ask a question about what was said. You will hear each conversation and the question about it only <u>one</u> time.

After you hear a conversation and the question about it, read the four possible answers in your book and decide which <u>one</u> is the best answer to the question you heard. Then circle the letter that corresponds to the answer you have chosen.

Listen to an example.

On the recording, you hear: (Man)   *Where did you put the leftover pizza?*
                            (First Woman)   *I threw it out.*
                            (Second Woman) *What can we say about the woman?*

In your workbook, you read: (A) She left the pizza out.

              (B) She got sick.

              (C) She doesn't like cold pizza.

              (D) She forgot the pizza.

You learn from the conversation that the woman threw out the leftover (cold) pizza. The best answer to the question "What can we say about the woman?" is (C), "She doesn't like cold pizza." Therefore, the correct choice is (C).

1. (A) She's afraid to eat out.
   (B) She's frightened she may have an accident.
   (C) She's busy this evening.
   (D) She'll go out after she's reported the incident.

2. (A) Bank teller.
   (B) Flight attendant.
   (C) Engineer.
   (D) Ticket seller.

3. (A) Boston.
   (B) Washington, D.C.
   (C) New Orleans.
   (D) Denver.

4. (A) 8:15.
   (B) 8:50.
   (C) 10:30.
   (D) 12:00.

5. (A) $20.95.
   (B) $19.88.
   (C) $29.95.
   (D) $59.90.

6. (A) The children don't enjoy taking the bus.
   (B) The mother can't get the children to their lesson by bus.
   (C) The father does the maintenance work on the car.
   (D) They are a one-car family.

7. (A) Horseback riding.
   (B) Camping.
   (C) Skiing.
   (D) Sailing.

8. (A) At a bookstore.
   (B) At a bank.
   (C) At a library.
   (D) At a gift shop.

9. (A) Seeing a film.
   (B) Going to the theater.
   (C) Viewing TV.
   (D) Attending a football game.

10. (A) He never studies for exams.
    (B) He only studies occasionally.
    (C) He's going to study next week.
    (D) He only studies in the library.

11. (A) There is little to worry about.
    (B) The interview is important to him.
    (C) The event will be short.
    (D) He's never had an interview before.

12. (A) Ordering a book.
    (B) Tearing up a catalog.
    (C) Blanking out the numbered spaces.
    (D) Buying shoes by mail.

13. (A) The man hasn't seen Lynn's dog.
    (B) Lynn hasn't seen the man's dog.
    (C) Lynn's dog and cat don't get along.
    (D) The man hasn't seen the new cat.

14. (A) She forgot about the book.
    (B) She hoped to keep the book.
    (C) She already returned the book.
    (D) She won't lend the man any more books.

15. (A) She's unappreciative.
    (B) She causes a lot of trouble.
    (C) She wastes people's time.
    (D) She's very helpful.

 STOP

Answers to Exercise L52 are on page 442.

PART C   SHORT TALKS AND CONVERSATIONS

In Part C of the Listening Comprehension section of the TOEFL, you will hear several short talks and conversations. Each passage begins with a spoken statement identifying the question numbers that correspond to it and a statement that sets the context. For example, you will hear: "Questions 38–41. Listen to a talk given by a college math instructor."

The conversation or talk begins immediately following these statements. You must focus your attention and concentrate carefully on the conversation or talk because you will hear it only one time and taking notes is not permitted. After each selection you will hear three or four questions about what was said. These are spoken only one time. You will have 15 seconds to choose from four possible answers in your test book and fill in the space on your answer sheet. There are a total of 15 questions in Part C.

STRATEGIES TO USE FOR LISTENING COMPREHENSION, PART C

1. Concentrate on the passage.

Focus all your attention on the conversation or talk you are listening to. Do not try to read answer choices at the same time you are listening. Remember that all the information in the answer choices may be mentioned in the passage. You do not want to get the choices confused with what is actually stated. Do not work on previous items when the conversation or talk is being spoken, and do not think about other items.

2. Concentrate on who, what, and where.

Many of the questions concern what the people are talking about (the topic of the conversation), who the person is (what his or her job or profession is), and where the conversation is taking place. Concentrate on the details and clues that reveal this information.

3. Concentrate on the context and content.

The first speaker of a conversation often gives the context, and the first sentence of a talk usually gives the topic. The language in the conversations is less formal, while the language in the talks is more formal and frequently concerns an academic topic. It is not necessary to have previous knowledge of the subject matter discussed in the talks. All the information needed to answer the questions is included within the talks. Try to remember the details in context so as not to get confused.

4. Concentrate on the question.

All correct and incorrect answers include details mentioned in the passage. An incorrect answer may contain information that is true according to the passage but which does not answer the question. Sometimes an incorrect answer contains information that has been stated in a way that changes its meaning and, therefore, does not answer the question. Keep the question in your mind as you read the four choices.

5. Know what works for you.

If you are uncertain which answer is correct, you can do one of two things:

(A) Use your intuition (instincts).
(B) Guess.

(See Part A, item 6, page 28.)

6. Use every second wisely.

Don't lose time thinking about something you don't know. Answer each question quickly, and then prepare yourself to listen carefully to the next question.

PRACTICE WITH TOPICS

Immediate identification of the topic will help you to anticipate the information you will hear and need to retain to answer the questions. Use Listening Exercises L53–L56 to develop your skills in identifying the topic and what follows.

Exercise L53   **Predicting the topic from the first statement**

Listen to the spoken statement. Predict the topic to be discussed and write your prediction in the space provided.

Example 1   You will hear: *I attended Professor Brown's talk on Balzac last night.*

You will write: Balzac or Professor Brown's talk

(because the conversation will probably continue with a discussion about the talk)

Example 2   You will hear: *The molecular structure of synthetic vitamins is the same*
                                  as that of natural vitamins.

              You will write: vitamins
                               _____

                               (because the lecture will probably continue with more
                               information about vitamins)

▶️ **START**

1. _____

2. _____

3. _____

4. _____

5. _____   ◼️ **STOP**

Answers to Exercise L53 are on page 443.

Exercise L54   ***Identifying the topic from the first statement***

Listen to the first statement of the conversation or talk. Circle the letter of the answer that
states the topic.

Example   You will hear: *I met Lucy's cousin, the famous circus juggler, at Dale's party*
                               last night.

           You will read: (A) the famous circus
                          (B) Lucy's party
                          (C) a performer
                          (D) a smuggler

You should circle (C) because the speaker will probably continue discussing the person
she met: the cousin who is a circus performer.

▶️ **START**

1. (A) uses of acupuncture in the West
   (B) China in recent years
   (C) the practice of acupuncture
   (D) ancient cures of arthritis

2. (A) fabric
   (B) muscles
   (C) millimeters
   (D) lengths

3. (A) hardware
   (B) stores
   (C) metal
   (D) shelves

4. (A) the skiing techniques
   (B) the skiing in the Alps
   (C) the skiing last week
   (D) the skiing competition

5. (A) communications technology
   (B) challenges in communication
   (C) educational satellites
   (D) educational possibilities

◼️ **STOP**

Answers to Exercise L54 are on page 443.

Exercise L55   ***Determining if the topic is stated in the first sentence of a passage***

Sometimes the topic is not stated at the beginning of the passage. Listen to the conversation or talk. Write "yes" in the blank if the topic can be identified in the first sentence. Write "no" if it cannot.

Example   You will hear: (Woman) *While I'm here, I'd like to visit the museum.*

          (Man)   *That's a good idea. The museum is having a special exhibition on fish rubbings.*

          (Woman) *Fish rubbings? What are they? Touching a horrible slimy fish?*

          (Man)   *No. It's an ancient art form in which fish are used to make prints.*

          (Woman) *Where was this art form practiced?*

          (Man)   *I'm not sure. I think both in the Far East and by some Indians in America.*

          You will write: *no*

The conversation is mainly about "fish rubbings," which is mentioned by the second speaker. You should write "no" in the space because the topic is not mentioned in the first sentence of the conversation.

▶️ **START**

1. _____   4. _____

2. _____   5. _____

3. _____   ⏹️ **STOP**

Answers to Exercise L55 are on page 444.

Exercise L56   ***Predicting what will logically follow the topic sentence***

Following the flow of ideas will help you remember what the the speaker said and anticipate the questions that will be asked. Listen to the spoken statement. Predict the next statement.

Example   You will hear: *Mary has bought a pet snake.*

          You will read: (A) She hates reptiles.

                      (B) She got it at the pet shop on the corner.

                      (C) She has a new car.

                      (D) The puppies are on sale for as much as 50% off.

You should circle (B) because the place where she bought the snake is most closely related to the topic sentence.

▶️ **START**

1. (A) It dates back to the late Iron Age.
   (B) The oldest one is the Uffigton White Horse.
   (C) The horse was carved in chalk.
   (D) Old pottery is frequently in the shape of animals.

2. (Second Person)
  (A) Yes. Go up to Personnel on the second floor, to your right.
  (B) Yes. We can exchange the tablecloth.
  (C) Oh, the last secretary was always complaining.
  (D) No. But I have to work overtime occasionally.

3. (Second Person)
  (A) I like turkey sandwiches.
  (B) I think a piece of strawberry pie would be too much.
  (C) We can leave the dishes until the morning.
  (D) I couldn't bear to eat another thing.

4. (A) Goethe tried painting and drawing in Italy.
  (B) Goethe discovered the principle of the primitive plant in Rome.
  (C) Goethe set out for Italy in the autumn of 1786.
  (D) There was a large colony of German artists in Rome.

5. (Second Person)
  (A) My term paper is due before 4:00 this afternoon.
  (B) My temperature's down, but my glands are still swollen.
  (C) You could bring a couple of packages of lemon drops.
  (D) You'd better stay in bed for the rest of the day.

 STOP

Answers to Exercise L56 are on page 444.

PRACTICE WITH MULTIPLE MEANINGS

Sometimes listeners miss important details or major ideas because they are confused by a less frequently used meaning of a common word. Use Listening Exercise L57 to develop your skills in determining the correct meaning of a word in a sentence. (For additional practice, see Exercises L4–L6 and Exercises L22–L24.)

Exercise L57   *Multiple meanings*

Write a definition of the given word in the first blank. Complete all 10 items. Then listen carefully to the statement. In the second blank, write the meaning of the word according to the way it is used in the statement you heard.

Example   You will read: *landed*   (A) _____

                                  (B) _____

        You will write: (A) _____ *to arrive somewhere* _____

        You will hear: *The landed aristocrat paid many people very little to plant the crops on his fields.*

        You will write: (B) _____ *propertied* _____

In the first space, you may also have written "touch down" as in "the plane landed smoothly," "obtain" as in "he landed the perfect job," or "propertied" as in "the landed classes controlled the economy." In the second space, you should write "propertied" because this is the meaning that "landed" has in the sentence you heard.

WRITE, then **START**

1. stones   (A) _____

            (B) _____

2. pilot   (A) _____

            (B) _____

3. log   (A) _____

            (B) _____

4. spell   (A) _____

            (B) _____

5. deal   (A) _____

            (B) _____

6. spotted   (A) _____

            (B) _____

7. storm   (A) _____

            (B) _____

8. course   (A) _____

            (B) _____

Answers to Exercise L57 are on page 444.   **STOP**

PRACTICE WITH REFERENTS

Instead of repeating words or complete phrases in a sentence or talk, speakers use pronouns and shorter phrases called "referents." Referents refer back to a previously mentioned word or phrase, or they anticipate a word or phrase to be mentioned. To follow a conversation or talk, it is necessary to understand the referents. Use Listening Exercises L58 and L59 to develop your skills in understanding referents. (For additional practice in referents, see Exercise R2.)

Exercise L58   *Understanding referents in a statement*

Listen to the spoken statement. In the space, write the word or phrase the referent refers to.

Example   You will hear: *Vaslav Nijinsky, one of a famous company of dancers brought to Paris and London before World War I, was in some respects the most remarkable of them all.*

           You will read: them   *dancers* _____

You should write "dancers" in the space because "them" refers back to the dancers that Nijinsky was with.

[▣▣] **START**

1. they _____

2. those _____

3. some _____

4. they _____

5. their _____

Answers to Exercise L58 are on page 444.   [▣▣] **STOP**

Exercise L59   ***Understanding referents in a passage***

Listen to the complete spoken passage for each item. Pause the recording while you write in the space the word or phrase the referents refer to. After you have completed all the items, listen to the recording a second time to check your answers.

Example   You will hear: *The Browns' house was in such bad condition that they hired a carpenter, who did an excellent job of fixing it up.*

You will read: (A) they the Browns _____

(B) who a carpenter _____

(C) it   the Browns' house _____

[▣▣] **START**

1. (A) them _____

(B) these problems _____

(C) their _____

[▣▣] **PAUSE**

2. (A) it _____

(B) that _____

(C) one _____

[▣▣] **PAUSE**

3. (A) it _____

(B) they _____

(C) that _____

[▣▣] **PAUSE**

4. (A) this climb _____

   (B) it _____

   (C) these _____

▭ PAUSE

5. (A) there _____

   (B) her _____

   (C) one _____

Answers to Exercise L59 are on page 444.　　　　**▭ STOP**

PRACTICE WITH REMEMBERING DETAILS

Many details that you need to remember are given in the conversations and talks. Sometimes these details are stated in different words. Use Listening Exercises L60–L66 to develop your skills in remembering and recognizing details. (For additional practice, see Exercises L41–L46.)

Exercise L60　　*Understanding restatements*

You will hear a statement. Circle the letter of the answer that gives the same information as the spoken statement.

Example　You will hear: *Minute as atoms are, they consist of still tinier particles.*

        You will read: (A) Atoms are made up of even smaller particles.
               (B) Small particles consist of minute atoms.

You should circle (A) because it gives the same information in different words.

▭ START

1. (A) In Homer's time, the people used many old words from the Kárpathos dialect.
   (B) The people in Kárpathos use many words that were used in Homer's time.

2. (A) In 1783, a Frenchman made the first manned flight in a hot-air balloon.
   (B) In 1783, a Frenchman made a 25-minute flight in the first hot-air balloon.

3. (A) The Aztec word for "beautiful bird" is "quetzal," which means "tail feather."
   (B) The Aztec word for "tail feather" is the name given to a beautiful bird – the quetzal.

4. (A) Centers were established to relieve those people stricken by the drought.
   (B) The drought-stricken areas set up many relief centers.

5. (A) The human past has been revolutionized by our concept of recently discovered fossils.
   (B) Our concept of the human past has been revolutionized by recently discovered fossils.

Answers to Exercise L60 are on page 444.   **STOP**

Exercise L61   ***Getting all the facts***

For each item, circle the letters of the answers that contain information from the spoken conversation or talk.

Example   You will hear: (Man)   *Have you decided to follow the coast or take the interstate to Portland?*
                          (Woman) *I think I'll follow the coast and stop for a picnic along one of the beaches at Newport.*
                          (Man)   *That's a good idea.*
                          (Woman) *And coming back, I'll take the interstate through Salem and stop there to see a cousin.*

You will read: (A) Portland
               (B) New York
               (C) Newport
               (D) Salem

You should circle (A), (C), and (D) because these places were all mentioned in the conversation.

 START

1. (A) purchasing a bicycle
   (B) riding a bicycle
   (C) servicing a bicycle
   (D) maintaining a bicycle

2. (A) a suburb
   (B) a district
   (C) a city
   (D) a garden

3. (A) humans
   (B) animals
   (C) dinosaurs
   (D) platycarpus

4. (A) frescoes
   (B) treasures
   (C) sculptures
   (D) statues

5. (A) test takers
   (B) examiners
   (C) detectives
   (D) manufacturers

STOP

Answers to Exercise L61 are on page 444.

Exercise L62   ***Identifying who***

Sometimes you will hear several names mentioned in a conversation or talk. Listen to the conversation or talk. Answer the question that follows by circling the letter of the correct name.

Example   You will hear: (First Man) *Joan, why don't you invite Liz to the picnic.*
                          (Woman)   *That's a good idea. I could ask her to bring her roommate too. What is her name?*

(First Man)   *I think it's Elaine, but I'm not sure.*
(Woman)   *Vicky will know. I'll ask her.*
(Second Man) *Who does the man suggest be invited?*

You will read: (A) Joan
(B) Liz
(C) Vicky

▶ **START**

1. (A) Carl
   (B) Angela
   (C) Terry

2. (A) Agatha Christie
   (B) Vanessa Redgrave
   (C) Dustin Hoffman

3. (A) Buffalo Bill
   (B) Annie Oakley
   (C) Chief Sitting Bull

4. (A) William Krell
   (B) Scott Joplin
   (C) John Philip Sousa ■ **STOP**

Answers to Exercise L62 are on page 444.

Exercise L63   *Identifying where*

Sometimes you will hear several places mentioned in a conversation or talk. Listen to each conversation or talk. Answer the question that follows by circling the letter of the correct place.

Example   You will hear: (First Man) *I've never been to Scandinavia, so I've decided to spend the summer there.*
(Woman) *That will be expensive, won't it?*
(First Man) *Not really. My grandfather is from a small Swedish town near the Norwegian border. He still has a sister there.*
(Woman) *Will you stay with her?*
(First Man) *For some of the time. The expensive part will be my stay in Denmark. I don't know anyone there.*
(Second Man) *Where is the man's grandfather from?*

You will read: (A) Sweden
(B) Norway
(C) Denmark

▶ **START**

1. (A) California
   (B) Arizona
   (C) Alaska

2. (A) the club
   (B) the theater
   (C) the office

3. (A) the stage
   (B) the concert hall
   (C) the exhibition hall

4. (A) England
   (B) Scotland
   (C) China ■ **STOP**

Answers to Exercise L63 are on page 444.

Exercise L64   ***Identifying what***

Sometimes you will hear several activities mentioned in a conversation or talk. Listen to the conversation or talk. Answer the question that follows by circling the letter of the correct activity.

Example   You will hear: (First Man)   *What did you do over the summer, Donna?*
                              (Woman)   *Mostly I helped my father in his dress shop.*
                              (First Man) *I can't imagine you selling dresses.*
                              (Woman)   *I didn't. I helped him with the bookkeeping.*
                                            Also, I put price tags on the new clothes and
                                            designed the window displays.

                              (Second Man) *What didn't Donna do?*

        You will read: (A) sell dresses
                       (B) keep accounts
                       (C) design window displays

START

1. (A) have birthdays
   (B) paste checkout sheets
   (C) see new books

2. (A) buy a cassette
   (B) pick up her lenses
   (C) take a fencing class

3. (A) dance folk dances
   (B) draw pictures
   (C) write down dance movements

4. (A) emigrated to the New World
   (B) found a passage to India
   (C) discovered Virginia

Answers to Exercise L64 are on page 444.   **STOP**

Exercise L65   ***Identifying when***

Sometimes you will hear several times mentioned in a conversation or talk. Listen to the conversation or talk which may mention days, months, years, or time. Answer the question that follows by circling the letter of the correct time.

Example   You will hear: (First Man)   *Why hasn't Frank come yet? He told me he'd*
                                            be here the first thing in the morning.
                              (Woman)   *I'm sorry. Didn't I tell you he called and said*
                                            he couldn't make it until this afternoon?
                              (First Man) *No, you didn't. What time did he say he'd be*
                                            here?
                              (Woman)   *About 4:00.*
                              (First Man) *Four o'clock! That means we'll be working*
                                            on this report until midnight.

                              (Second Man) *When will Frank come to the people's house?*

        You will read: (A) in the morning
                       (B) in the afternoon
                       (C) at midnight

START

1. (A) 9:00
   (B) 10:00
   (C) 2:00

2. (A) Thursday
   (B) Friday
   (C) Saturday

3. (A) 1642
   (B) 1832
   (C) 1946

4. (A) in the winter
   (B) in the summer
   (C) in the spring

 STOP

Answers to Exercise L65 are on page 444.

Exercise L66 **Identifying how much and how many**

Sometimes you will hear several quantities or numbers mentioned in a conversation or talk. Listen to the conversation or talk. Answer the question that follows by circling the letter of the correct quantity or number.

Example You will hear:
(Woman)	*How long will you be gone?*
(First Man)	*About three weeks.*
(Woman)	*What are your plans?*
(First Man)	*We'll spend a week at Lake Tahoe, three or four days in San Francisco and about four days in Los Angeles.*
(Woman)	*What about the rest of your vacation?*
(First Man)	*Well, we'll be on the road several days and then when we get home we want to spend a couple of days resting up from our trip.*
(Second Man)	*How many days will the man be at Lake Tahoe?*

You will read: (A) 3
(B) 7
(C) 4

START

1. (A) 20
   (B) 12
   (C) 24

2. (A) $60.00
   (B) $25.00
   (C) $45.00

3. (A) 198
   (B) 110
   (C) 171

4. (A) millions
   (B) thousands
   (C) one-third of them

 STOP

Answers to Exercise L66 are on page 444.

PRACTICE WITH MAKING INFERENCES FROM VOCABULARY CLUES

Many items require you to answer questions concerning what people are doing, what their professions are, or where the conversation takes place. These details are not given. You must make inferences by using clues from the vocabulary in the conversation. In other words, you must decide what is true on the basis of the information you are given. Study the example in Part B, page 74.

Use Listening Exercises L67–L69 to develop your inference skills. (For additional practice, see Exercises L47–L49.)

Exercise L67   *Inferring activities through vocabulary*

Listen to the spoken conversation, which contains vocabulary corresponding to an activity. Answer the question that follows the conversation by circling the letter of the correct activity.

Example   You will hear: (First Man)   *What shall I do now?*
                               (Woman)   *Can you heat the water while I chop the onions?*
                               (First Man)   *How much water should I put in?*
                               (Woman)   *Enough to cover the potatoes.*
                               (First Man)   *Should I add any spices?*
                               (Woman)   *Not yet. Wait until after I put the beef in the pot.*

                               (Second Man) *What are the people doing?*

              You will read: (A) digging potatoes
                             (B) butchering a cow
                             (C) planting beets
                             (D) cooking a meal

You should circle (D) because "chopping onions," "heating enough water to cover the potatoes," "adding spices," and "putting the beef into the pot" are all activities that relate to cooking. Therefore, you can infer that the people are cooking a meal.

START

1. (A) riflery
   (B) bullfighting
   (C) archery
   (D) bowling

2. (A) fixing a car
   (B) running an engine
   (C) changing the oil
   (D) looking for a toolbox

3. (A) borrowing cigarettes
   (B) looking for a light
   (C) throwing away the trash
   (D) carrying matches

4. (A) playing a game
   (B) getting lost
   (C) visiting royalty
   (D) walking at night

STOP

Answers to Exercise L67 are on page 444.

Exercise L68   *Inferring professions through vocabulary*

Listen to the spoken conversation, which contains vocabulary corresponding to a profession. Answer the question that follows the conversation by circling the letter of the correct profession.

Example   You will hear: (Woman)   *Are you ready?*
                               (First Man)   *Just about. I want to comb my hair.*
                               (Woman)   *Okay. When you're ready, take a seat here.*
                               (First Man)   *Like this?*
                               (Woman)   *Fine. Now move your head to the left and up. Perfect. Keep your eyes focused on me and smile. That's it!*
                               (First Man)   *Can we take another shot? I'm sure I blinked.*

                               (Second Man) *What is the woman's job?*

You will read: (A) photographer
(B) sculptor
(C) painter
(D) hairstylist

You should circle (A) because the man is "posing," the woman wants him "to smile and focus his eyes on her," and then the man wants her "to take another shot because he blinked."

 START

1. (A) a nurse
   (B) a lifeguard
   (C) an ambulance driver
   (D) a teacher

2. (A) a beautician
   (B) a gardener
   (C) a plumber
   (D) a carpet salesperson

3. (A) a bill collector
   (B) a businesswoman
   (C) an accountant
   (D) a telephone operator

4. (A) rides bicycles
   (B) practices football
   (C) restores old instruments
   (D) plays an organ

STOP

Answers to Exercise L68 are on page 444.

Exercise L69   **Inferring locations through vocabulary**

Listen to the spoken conversation, which contains vocabulary corresponding to a place. Answer the question that follows the conversation by circling the letter of the correct location.

Example   You will hear: (First Man)   *The band is very good tonight. Would you like to dance?*

(Woman)   *I'm sorry, I can't.*

(First Man)   *If you don't know the steps, I can show you.*

(Woman)   *It's not that. I twisted my ankle on my way in and it still hurts.*

(First Man)   *Would you like me to take you to the hospital for X rays?*

(Woman)   *That's very kind of you. But the waiter is bringing an ice pack, and besides, I'm enjoying the music.*

(Second Man)   *Where does this conversation take place?*

You will read: (A) in a concert hall
(B) at a parade
(C) at a hospital
(D) in a nightclub

You should circle (D) because a nightclub would be a place where people "dance," "listen to music," and "waiters attend tables."

START

1. (A) at a student cafeteria
   (B) at a supermarket
   (C) at a restaurant
   (D) at the man's mother's house

2. (A) at a campground
   (B) at a police station
   (C) at a fire watchtower
   (D) at a radio station

3. (A) at Jim's Wrecker Service
   (B) on Elm Street
   (C) at a police station
   (D) in a Subaru car

4. (A) at a dress shop
   (B) at a tailor's
   (C) at a bridal shop
   (D) at a jewelry store

🔲 **STOP**

Answers to Exercise L69 are on page 445.

PRACTICE WITH DRAWING CONCLUSIONS

Based on the information given in a conversation or talk, you sometimes have to come to a logical conclusion. Study the example in Part B, page 76.

Use Listening Exercise L70 to develop your skills in drawing conclusions. (For additional practice, see Exercises L50 and L51.)

Exercise L70   *Inferring feelings, attitudes, and personality traits*

Listen to the spoken conversation. Answer the question that follows the conversation by circling the letter of the correct response.

Example   You will hear: (Woman)   *We just returned from a fantastic camping trip in the mountains.*
(First Man)   *I should take my family camping sometime.*
(Woman)   *You really should. It's great to get away from all the noise in the city.*
(First Man)   *Not to mention the pollution.*
(Woman)   *That's right. We had so much fun hiking in the day and singing around the campfire at night.*
(Second Man)   *How does the woman feel?*

You will read: (A) enthusiastic
(B) careful
(C) regretful
(D) permissive

You should circle (A) because the woman is showing enthusiasm about her trip by describing it as "fantastic," saying "it's great to get away," and telling the man that they had "so much fun."

🔲 **START**

1. (A) hindered
   (B) distressed
   (C) envious
   (D) generous

2. (A) ashamed
   (B) anxious
   (C) annoyed
   (D) pleased

3. (A) lifted the woman's spirits
   (B) made the woman feel guilty
   (C) depressed the woman
   (D) ridiculed the woman

4. (A) squeamish
   (B) courageous
   (C) quarrelsome
   (D) refined

5. (A) He's a good sport.
   (B) He's a braggart.
   (C) He's a great sportsman.
   (D) He's a bully.

🔲 **STOP**

Answers to Exercise L70 are on page 445.

PRACTICE WITH PUTTING IT ALL TOGETHER

Throughout the exercises in Part C, you have been listening for specific items in conversations and talks. It is important to understand these items in context. Use Listening Exercises L71–L73 to develop your skills in understanding complete conversations and talks.

Exercise L71   *Remembering details*

For each item, listen to the complete conversation or talk. Pause the recording while you write the main answers to the three Wh-questions. Some questions have more than one possible answer. Try to write at least one answer to each question.

Example   You will hear: *John and Mary worked in a big department store. They saved their money until they were able to set up a little shop of their own.*

You will read: (A) Who?   John and Mary
(B) Where?   a big department store
(C) What?   a shop of their own

You should write "John and Mary" in the space asking "Who?" because they are the people discussed in the passage. Write "a big department store" in the space asking "Where?" because this is where they worked. Write "a shop of their own" or "money" in the space asking "What?" because a shop is what they want to have and money is what they are saving.

▱ **START**

1. (A) Who? _____

   (B) When? _____

   (C) What? _____

▱ **PAUSE**

2. (A) Where? _____

   (B) When? _____

   (C) What? _____

▱ **PAUSE**

3. (A) When? _____

   (B) Where? _____

   (C) Why? _____

▱ **PAUSE**

4. (A) Who? _____

   (B) What? _____

   (C) How often? _____

 PAUSE

5. (A) What? _____

   (B) Who? _____

   (C) Why? _____

 PAUSE

6. (A) When? _____

   (B) What? _____

   (C) Where? _____

Answers to Exercise L71 are on page 445.   **STOP**

Exercise L72   *Focusing on details*

For each item, listen to the complete conversation or talk. Pause the recording while you read the questions and circle the letters of the questions that can be answered from the information you heard.

Example   You will hear: *Sue went shopping for her mother's birthday present. She bought a pair of tan slacks and a green sweater. Then she had lunch at a new restaurant on Fourth Avenue.*

        You will read: (A) Who went shopping?
                    (B) Where did she buy the clothes?
                    (C) What color was the sweater?
                    (D) What time did she return?

You should circle (A) and (C) because the passage states that "Sue went shopping and bought a green sweater." The information needed to answer questions (B) and (D) is not given in the passage, so you should not circle these letters.

 START

1. (A) Where does this conversation take place?
   (B) Where did the woman see the show?
   (C) What was the name of the motorcycle team?
   (D) How old were the children?
   (E) What doesn't interest the man?
   (F) Where did the man go last evening?

 PAUSE

2. (A) What is the main topic of the talk?
   (B) Which bird has the longest wingspan?
   (C) According to the speaker, how much does the female bustard weigh?
   (D) What is another name for the condor?
   (E) How much area do the South American vulture's wings cover?
   (F) Where does the albatross live?

▢ PAUSE

3. (A) Where does the conversation take place?
   (B) What did the man learn to do?
   (C) When did the man take his course?
   (D) When did the woman go to New Mexico?
   (E) What can be inferred about the temperatures inside adobe structures?
   (F) According to the man, where can you build mud houses?

▢ PAUSE

4. (A) Where does this conversation take place?
   (B) What is the woman's job?
   (C) How often do the people go diving?
   (D) How far are the people from the shore?
   (E) Who owns all the equipment?
   (F) When are the divers going to ascend?

▢ PAUSE

5. (A) What is the main idea of this talk?
   (B) In what season does fox hunting take place?
   (C) Where does fox hunting take place?
   (D) Who wants to stop fox hunting?
   (E) How many foxes are killed each year in the hunts?
   (F) How often does fox hunting take place?

▢ STOP

Answers to Exercise L72 are on page 445.

Exercise L73   **Writing details**

For each item, listen to the complete conversation or talk. Pause the recording while you read the questions and write the answers for those that can be answered using the information you hear. Some answers can be inferred. Not all the questions can be answered.

Example   You will hear: *All evening both adults and children were entranced by the magician's skillful tricks of illusion.*

You will read: (A) Who watched the magician?
adults and children

(B) Where did the magician perform?

(C) What did the magician do?
tricks

(D) When did the magician perform?
in the evening

The information needed to answer question (B) is not given in the talk, so you should leave (B) blank.

🔲 START

1. (A) Where will the exhibition take place?

   _____

   (B) Who will give the lectures?

   _____

   (C) How long will the exhibition be at the Metropolitan Museum of Art?

   _____

   (D) What time is the Turkish singing to be held?

   _____

   (E) Which day is the gallery open from 12:00 to 5:00?

   _____

   (F) How many lectures will be presented?

   _____

🔲 PAUSE

2. (A) What is the talk about?

   _____

   (B) What is one of the mentioned causes of speech disorders?

   _____

   (C) At what age do most speech disorders start?

   _____

   (D) What can be inferred about a deaf person?

   _____

   (E) When is the best time to seek help for a disorder?

   _____

   (F) Who helps people with disorders of communication?

   _____

🔲 PAUSE

3. (A) What is the main idea of the talk?

   _____

(B) Where does the talk take place?

_____

(C) Which language predominates in the United States?

_____

(D) What other English-speaking countries are mentioned as having an official language?

_____

(E) When did Louisiana make French and English official state languages?

_____

(F) How many languages are recognized in the United States Constitution?

_____

🔲 **PAUSE**

4. (A) Where does this conversation take place?

_____

(B) What is the man's job?

_____

(C) How tall did the woman grow?

_____

(D) What did the woman have as a child?

_____

(E) What does the man want to know about smoking?

_____

(F) How many colds did the woman have last year?

_____

🔲 **PAUSE**

5. (A) Where does this conversation take place?

_____

(B) What does the man do?

_____

(C) When does the new semester begin?

_____

(D) What days of the week does the batik class take place?

_____

(E) In which college can it be inferred that the woman studies?

_____

(F) According to the conversation, what is batik?

_____

Answers to Exercise L73 are on page 445. **STOP**

Extended practice: Answer the questions in Exercise L72 in the same way as in Exercise L73.

CHECK YOUR PROGRESS

Check your progress in the areas covered in Exercises L53–L73 by completing the following mini-test. This exercise uses the same format as Part C of the Listening Comprehension section on the TOEFL.

 START

Exercise L74   ***Mini-test***

Directions: You will hear conversations and talks. After each conversation or talk, you will be asked some questions. You will hear the conversations and talks and the questions about them only <u>one</u> time. They will not be written out for you.

After you hear a question, read the four possible answers in your workbook and decide which <u>one</u> is the best answer to the question you heard. Then circle the letter of the answer you have chosen. Answer all questions on the basis of what is <u>stated</u> or <u>implied</u> by the speakers in the talk or conversation.

Here is an example.

On the recording, you hear: *Listen to a conversation between two friends.*

(Woman)	*The way David was going on about that terrible virus, I thought that Mary was deathly ill.*
(First Man)	*What was the matter with her?*
(Woman)	*It wasn't her at all. He was talking about her computer.*
(First Man)	*Oh no, that is serious. I hope that program they lent me wasn't contaminated.*
(Woman)	*Contaminated? Now you're talking nonsense too.*
(First Man)	*No, I'm not. Did David say whether they have a vaccine yet?*
(Woman)	*A vaccine? For a computer? I don't believe it!*

Now listen to a sample question.

(Second Man) *What doesn't the woman believe?*

In your workbook, you read: (A) That her friend is seriously ill.
(B) That the illness is contagious.
(C) That the man is being serious
(D) That the vaccine is safe.

The best answer to the question "What doesn't the woman believe?" is (C), "That the man is being serious." Therefore, the correct choice is (C).

Remember you are not allowed to take notes or write in your workbook.

1. (A) He eats too many carbohydrates.
   (B) He wants to be a vegetarian.
   (C) He doesn't like to broil his steaks.
   (D) He needs to lose weight.

2. (A) Eliminate starches.
   (B) Eat fewer fatty foods.
   (C) Drink a large amount of milk.
   (D) Eat only vegetables.

3. (A) They contain too much fat and not enough protein.
   (B) They provide important carbohydrates.
   (C) They need to be cooked differently.
   (D) They should be eaten with vegetables and milk.

4. (A) The stoneworkers.
   (B) The gargoyles.
   (C) The spirits.
   (D) The cathedral.

5. (A) They frighten away bad spirits.
   (B) They give walls protection.
   (C) They collect water in their mouths.
   (D) They are caricatures of friends.

6. (A) Because they spit out water.
   (B) Because they represent the artists' friends.
   (C) Because they frighten stoneworkers.
   (D) Because they are put on cathedrals.

7. (A) He wonders if the gargoyles are friends.
   (B) He wonders if the stoneworkers are friends.
   (C) He wonders if the stoneworkers' friends were ugly.
   (D) He wonders if the stoneworkers' friends got angry.

8. (A) Tropical butterflies' habitats.
   (B) Pest control.
   (C) Ecological balance research.
   (D) A butterfly sanctuary and breeding center.

9. (A) Pollution.
   (B) Industrialization.
   (C) Diseases.
   (D) Research.

10. (A) Studies into tropical butterflies' habitat.
    (B) The breeding of Malaysian butterflies.
    (C) The providing of a butterfly sanctuary.
    (D) The marketing of Malaysian butterflies.

11. (A) How the ecological balance would be affected.
    (B) How much pollution and industrialization destroys butterflies' habitats.
    (C) How many butterflies are being driven away by population growth.
    (D) How diseases attack caterpillars.

12. (A) Shadows.
    (B) Profiles.
    (C) Shades.
    (D) Curiosities.

13. (A) Ivory.
    (B) Plastic.
    (C) Porcelain.
    (D) Glass.

14. (A) The artist who invented shadow portraits.
    (B) The man who paid $6,000 for a shadow painting.
    (C) The finance minister who didn't spend money.
    (D) The man whose profile was the most infamous.

15. (A) They were inexpensive.
    (B) They were mistaken for junk.
    (C) They were curiosities.
    (D) They were from the eighteenth century.

 STOP

Answers to Exercise L74 are on page 445.

START

Exercise L75   Listening Comprehension Practice Test

When you have completed the exercises from Part A, Part B, and Part C as recommended by the Diagnostic Test, test your skills by taking this final TOEFL Listening Comprehension Practice Test. This test includes Listening Comprehension Part A, Part B, and Part C. Maintain the same test conditions that would be experienced during the actual TOEFL test. Tear out and use the answer sheet on page 545 and play the recording without pausing.

Answers to Exercise L75 are on page 446. The transcript for this exercise starts on page 534.

SECTION 1
LISTENING COMPREHENSION

In this section of the test, you will have an opportunity to demonstrate your ability to understand spoken English. There are three parts to this section, with special directions for each part. Do not read ahead or turn the pages while the directions are being read. Do not take notes or write in your workbook at anytime.

Part A

Directions: For each question in Part A, you will hear a short sentence. Each sentence will be spoken just once. The sentences you hear will not be written out for you.

After you hear a sentence, read the four choices in your workbook, marked (A), (B), (C), and (D), and decide which one is closest in meaning to the sentence you heard. Then, on your answer sheet, find the number of the question and fill in the space that corresponds to the letter of the answer you have chosen. Fill in the space completely so that the letter inside the oval cannot be seen.

Listen to an example.

On the recording, you hear: *The new observatory is nothing less than outstanding.*

In your workbook, you read: (A) The new observatory is excellent.
(B) There is nothing outstanding to observe.
(C) You must stand outside to make the observance.
(D) His new observations are more outstanding than usual.

Sample Answer
● Ⓑ Ⓒ Ⓓ

The man said, "The new observatory is nothing less than outstanding." Sentence (A), "The new observatory is excellent," is closest in meaning to what the man said. Therefore, the correct choice is (A).

NOW WE WILL BEGIN PART A WITH QUESTION 1.

1. (A) The testing ended last week.
   (B) We haven't had an exam in over a week.
   (C) We'll be finished taking the tests in two weeks.
   (D) The testing will take over two weeks.

2. (A) My car has a dent.
   (B) He wrecked his car.
   (C) It was a casual incident.
   (D) The accident wasn't my fault.

3. (A) Robert gets put out by Judy's gloating.
   (B) Judy had a wavy permanent put in her hair.
   (C) Robert tolerates a lot of complaining.
   (D) Judy was panting and waving.

4. (A) Sue enrolled in an intensive German language course.
   (B) Sue had a bad accident in Germany.
   (C) Sue booked a trip to Germany.
   (D) Sue met a German in her math course.

5. (A) Maria likes gravy on salad.
   (B) Maria got the gravy confused with the dressing.
   (C) Maria messed up the salad dressing.
   (D) Maria mixed the salad with the gravy spoon.

6. (A) Mr. Simmons is walking down the lane to his house.
   (B) Mr. Simmons doesn't like to stay at home on rainy days.
   (C) The drains at Mr. Simmons' house aren't working.
   (D) Mr. Simmons works at home when it rains.

7. (A) Rebecca didn't board flight 219.
   (B) Rebecca didn't miss the connection.
   (C) Rebecca boarded flight 219.
   (D) Rebecca must have boarded connecting flight 219.

8. (A) Virginia hasn't called the electrician recently.
   (B) Virginia still has that used electric stove.
   (C) Virginia is more accustomed to using gas ranges.
   (D) Virginia doesn't use much electricity.

9. (A) Lisa married Sam for his money.
   (B) Lisa wouldn't marry Sam because he's fat.
   (C) Sam is not rich enough to buy Lisa's factory.
   (D) Lisa should have married Sam because he is rich.

10. (A) Mark took some pictures of Indians in New York.
    (B) Mark arrived in New York, then went to Indiana.
    (C) Mark traveled from Indiana to New York.
    (D) After arriving in New York, Mark tripped and fell.

11. (A) Nancy asked Ann to fix the car.
    (B) Nancy and Ann discussed repairing the car.
    (C) Nancy and Ann spoke to the mechanic.
    (D) Nancy and Ann wanted the car repainted.

GO ON TO THE NEXT PAGE

12. (A) Margaret was sorry that Mrs. Morris lost her necklace.
    (B) Margaret should say she's sorry for losing the necklace.
    (C) Margaret made a better apology than Mrs. Morris did.
    (D) Margaret apologized to Mrs. Morris for the lost necklace.

13. (A) Nicky couldn't contact the weather bureau.
    (B) Nicky checked the weather forecast.
    (C) Nicky didn't get any information about the check.
    (D) Nicky's going to have a good checkup.

14. (A) David brought the late students in to see Fred.
    (B) Fred was upset because David mentioned the late students.
    (C) Fred was angry because students were brought in late.
    (D) David was angry with Fred because the students were late.

15. (A) Martha wants to be left alone tonight.
    (B) Martha wants to eat only dessert tonight.
    (C) Martha wants a special sweet tonight.
    (D) Martha doesn't care if there's no dessert tonight.

16. (A) How would you like going to a new restaurant?
    (B) How would you like to go to the Roadside Cafe?
    (C) Would you get my change from the Roadside Cafe?
    (D) Has the Roadside Cafe changed location?

17. (A) I can't pay my debt yet.
    (B) I want the money you borrowed by next week.
    (C) I can't lend you the money until next week.
    (D) Could you return my money by next week?

18. (A) Kim doesn't cook American food.
    (B) Kim thinks American food is objectionable.
    (C) Kim thinks American fast food is all right.
    (D) The object of fast food is to get a quick meal.

19. (A) Jason moved backwards, not forward, in the line.
    (B) Jason knows his part extremely well.
    (C) Jason lined up with his back toward the memorial.
    (D) Jason moved behind the line.

20. (A) Lee is probably cold.
    (B) Lee is probably sick.
    (C) Lee probably got caught.
    (D) Lee probably caught the cod.

GO ON TO THE NEXT PAGE

Part B

Directions: In Part B you will hear short conversations between two people. After each conversation, a third person will ask a question about what was said. You will hear each conversation and question about it only one time. After you hear a conversation and the question about it, read the four possible answers in your workbook and decide which one is the best answer to the question you heard. Then, on your answer sheet, find the number of the question and fill in the space that corresponds to the letter of the answer you have chosen.

Listen to an example.

On the recording, you hear: (Man)   *I think I'll have the curtains changed.*
                            (First Woman)   *They are a bit worn.*

                            (Second Woman) *What does the woman mean?*

In your workbook, you read: (A) She thinks every bit of change is important.   **Sample Answer**
                            (B) She wants to wear them.
                            (C) She thinks they've been worn enough.
                            (D) She thinks they are in bad condition.

You learn from the conversation that the woman thinks the curtains are worn. The best answer to the question "What does the woman mean?" is (D), "She thinks they are in bad condition." Therefore, the correct choice is (D).

NOW WE WILL BEGIN PART B WITH THE FIRST CONVERSATION.

21. (A) Peter couldn't work because he injured his arm.
    (B) Peter really didn't want to help.
    (C) The woman hurt Peter.
    (D) The woman had to take Peter to the hospital.

22. (A) Fitting a suit.
    (B) Painting a picture.
    (C) Repairing an appliance.
    (D) Working a jigsaw puzzle.

23. (A) His class will finish in a minute.
    (B) He thinks classes will end too soon.
    (C) He would like classes to be over sooner.
    (D) He thinks the week after next is very early.

24. (A) She was too tired to drive.
    (B) She sat in her car to rest.
    (C) She had two flat tires.
    (D) She bought an extra set.

25. (A) Elected the student-body president.
    (B) Promised to help with housing troubles.
    (C) Caused the students to have difficulties with rent.
    (D) Assisted students having trouble finding living accommodations.

26. (A) Plants make him sick.
    (B) He does Barbara's gardening.
    (C) He's very energetic about yard work.
    (D) Barbara has him trim the bushes.

27. (A) She has problems with math.
    (B) She doesn't mind failing.
    (C) She's good at solving math problems.
    (D) She doesn't take care in her work.

28. (A) Because the woman wants to film the deer.
    (B) Because the woman can't take the picture.
    (C) Because he was slow in giving the woman the camera.
    (D) Because he forgot to buy film.

29. (A) He read the textbooks.
    (B) He did his homework.
    (C) He went to the review.
    (D) He failed the test.

30. (A) The man should stop thinking.
    (B) The man should be more careful when he drives.
    (C) Carol goes to the same places on purpose.
    (D) Carol stops her car when being followed closely.

31. (A) He could meet her halfway.
    (B) He could lend her the money.
    (C) They could take part of the journey.
    (D) They could share the cost.

GO ON TO THE NEXT PAGE

32. (A) In a basket-weaving class.
    (B) At a ball game.
    (C) At a courthouse.
    (D) Along a mountain pass.

33. (A) It will be the first time a president listens to her perform.
    (B) She has never played in a concert.
    (C) She has never been anxious about performing.
    (D) The president has never played her music.

34. (A) Sells cars.
    (B) Repairs engines.
    (C) Collects scrap metal.
    (D) Installs car radios.

35. (A) There is more traffic than usual.
    (B) There is less traffic than usual.
    (C) There is the same amount of traffic as usual.
    (D) Every day the amount of traffic increases.

GO ON TO THE NEXT PAGE

Part C

Directions: In this part of the test, you will hear longer conversations and talks. After each conversation or talk, you will be asked some questions. You will hear the talks and conversations and the questions about them only <u>one</u> time. They will <u>not</u> be written out for you.

After you hear a question, read the four possible answers in your workbook and decide which <u>one</u> is the best answer to the question you heard. Then, on your answer sheet, find the number of the question and fill in the space that corresponds to the letter of the answer you have chosen. Answer all questions on the basis of what is <u>stated</u> or <u>implied</u> by the speakers in the talk or conversation.

Here is an example.

On the recording, you hear: *Listen to a conversation between a professor and a student.*

(First Woman)   *Would you please type this paper? I can't read your handwriting.*

(Man)   *I'm sorry, Professor Mills. I don't have a typewriter, and besides, I can't type.*

(First Woman)   *Well, rewrite it then, but be sure to make it clear.*

Now listen to a sample question.

(Second Woman) *What does the professor want the man to do?*

In your workbook, you read: (A) Buy a typewriter.
(B) Read his handwriting.
(C) Clear the papers away.
(D) Rewrite the paper.

Sample Answer

The best answer to the question "What does the professor want the man to do?" is (D), "Rewrite the paper." Therefore, the correct choice is (D).

Remember, you are not allowed to take notes or write in your workbook.

NOW WE WILL BEGIN PART C.

36. (A) At a circus.
    (B) At a concert.
    (C) At a parade.
    (D) On a float.

37. (A) New Orleans.
    (B) Birmingham.
    (C) France.
    (D) the Caribbean.

38. (A) Drive to Birmingham.
    (B) Return to the Mardi Gras.
    (C) Listen to music.
    (D) Give the woman a bracelet.

39. (A) They are clowns.
    (B) They are musicians.
    (C) They are dancers.
    (D) They are spectators.

40. (A) An act of defiance.
    (B) A social event.
    (C) A group of Indians.
    (D) A cargo of tea.

41. (A) During the American War of Independence.
    (B) In 1773.
    (C) When Americans began drinking coffee.
    (D) At night.

42. (A) Because Americans were drinking coffee.
    (B) Because the tea was too highly taxed.
    (C) Because the colonists were taxed without being represented.
    (D) Because Indians were revolting against the invasion of Europeans.

43. (A) The British rulers.
    (B) King George III.
    (C) Indians.
    (D) Prominent citizens.

44. (A) In England.
    (B) In India.
    (C) Overboard a ship.
    (D) In Boston.

45. (A) Rachel.
    (B) Betty and Peter.
    (C) Rachel's mother.
    (D) Betty's cousin.

46. (A) Signed for a package.
    (B) Conducted research in biology.
    (C) Wrote to her mother.
    (D) Opened a parcel.

GO ON TO THE NEXT PAGE

47. (A) They were a gift.
    (B) They were being studied.
    (C) They were very interesting.
    (D) They were ordered.

48. (A) A way of training nursing students.
    (B) A computer system that makes critical decisions.
    (C) Diagnosis of chronic pulmonary disease.
    (D) Emergency room procedures.

49. (A) Students can practice on elderly patients.
    (B) Students can learn how to use a stethoscope.
    (C) Students can get grades.
    (D) Students can make critical decisions.

50. (A) Its ability to grade students.
    (B) Its ability to simulate body parts.
    (C) Its ability to take students through emergency situations.
    (D) Its ability to show elderly people.

THIS IS THE END OF THE LISTENING COMPREHENSION PRACTICE TEST.

SECTION
·2·

STRUCTURE AND WRITTEN EXPRESSION

Section 2 of the TOEFL, Structure and Written Expression, uses two types of questions. Questions 1–15 are incomplete sentences. You must decide which of four choices best completes the sentence. Although all four answers may be grammatically correct independently of the incomplete sentences, only one is grammatically correct in the context of the sentence. Therefore, you should spend your time analyzing the type of structure needed to make a grammatically correct sentence. There are 15 items to complete. Spend no more than 40 seconds on each item.

In questions 16–40, each sentence has four words or phrases underlined and labeled (A), (B), (C), and (D). One of those four items is incorrect. You must decide which one is incorrect and mark its corresponding letter on your answer sheet. The error is always one of the underlined words or phrases. Therefore, you should spend your time analyzing parts of the sentence. You do not need to correct the error, so move quickly on to the next item. There are 25 items to complete. Spend no more than 40 seconds on each item.

STRATEGIES TO USE FOR STRUCTURE AND WRITTEN EXPRESSION

1. Remember that you are looking for standard written English.

The language and topics in this section will be more formal than the conversational language used in the Listening Comprehension section. The topics frequently relate to academic subjects. You do not have to know about these subjects to answer the items correctly.

2. Remember to change tactics.

In questions 1–15, you are looking for one correct answer to complete the sentence. In questions 16–40, you are looking for the one answer that is wrong. Remember to change from looking for *correct* answers to looking for *incorrect* answers.

3. Know what works for you.

If you are uncertain which answer is correct, you can do one of two things:

  (A) Use your intuition (instincts).
  (B) Guess.

Sometimes you do not know the answer but have an unexplained feeling that one of the answers is correct. You have no other reason to believe it is correct. This is your *intuition*. Test your intuition while working through the TOEFL mini-tests in this book by marking items that you answered intuitively. If your intuition is usually correct, trust it when you take the TOEFL.

Sometimes students answer intuitively and then change their answers. Check yourself while working through the TOEFL mini-tests in this book. Do you frequently change right answers to wrong ones, or are your changes usually correct? If your first answer is usually the correct one, don't change your answers on the TOEFL.

Remember that wrong answers will not count against you. If you don't know an answer and have no feeling about which of the four choices may be correct, use a *guess letter*. A guess letter is one letter (A, B, C, or D) that you can use to answer all items you don't know. You are more likely to get some correct answers if you use one letter consistently than if you use all letters randomly.

4. Answer every item.

If you do not know the answer, do not leave a blank space. Answer it using your intuition or a guess letter. Mark the item you are unsure of in the test booklet. If you have time, you can go back and think about the marked items. If you change any answer, be sure you thoroughly erase your first answer.

5. Use every second wisely.

Don't lose time thinking about something you don't know. Answer the question, and go on to the next item.

STRATEGIES TO USE FOR QUESTIONS 1–15

1. Read the incomplete sentence first.

Examine the sentence and decide what is needed to complete it.

2. Read all choices.

Once you have decided what is needed to complete the sentence, read all the choices. More than one of the choices may contain the structure you are looking for. Examine those choices to determine which one completes the sentence correctly.

3. Use your time wisely.

Do not look for mistakes within the answers. Usually all answers are grammatically correct by themselves. However, only one answer is correct when it is placed in the sentence.

STRATEGIES TO USE FOR QUESTIONS 16–40

1. Read the complete sentence.

If you can't identify the incorrect word or phrase after you read the sentence, look at each underlined word. Think about its position in the sentence and what may be incorrect about it.

2. Remember that the error will always be underlined.

Do not look for errors in the other parts of the sentence. Look at the rest of the sentence for clues to help you find the error.

3. Do not correct the sentence.

You do not have to correct the sentence. Therefore, do not lose time thinking about how to correct it. Go on to the next item.

PRACTICE WITH NOUNS

Ask yourself these questions when checking nouns.

1. What kind of noun is it? Is it count or noncount?

A *count noun* refers to people or things that can be counted. You can put a number before this kind of noun. If the noun refers to one person or thing, it needs to be in the singular form. If it refers to more than one person or thing, it needs to be in the plural form.

    one desk   one book   three desks   fifty books

A *noncount noun* refers to general things such as qualities, substances, or topics. They cannot be counted and have only a singular form.

    food   air   money   intelligence

Noncount nouns can become count nouns when they are used to indicate types:

    the wines of California
    the fruits of the Northwest

2. Is there a quantifier with the noun that can be used to identify the nature of the noun?

A *quantifier* is a word that indicates an amount or quantity.

(A) Some quantifiers are used with both plural count nouns and noncount nouns.

    all   any   enough   a lot of   plenty of
    more   most   some   lots of

Examples   I have **enough** money to buy the watch. (noncount)
                 I have **enough** sandwiches for everyone. (count)

(B) Some quantifiers are used only with noncount nouns.

    a little   much

Examples   There's **a little** milk.
                 There's not **much** sugar.

(C) Some quantifiers are used only with plural count nouns.

    both   many   a few   several

Examples   I took **both** apples.
                 We saw **several** movies.

(D) Some quantifiers are used only with singular count nouns.

    another   each   every

Examples   Joe wanted **another** piece of pie.
                 Every child in the contest received a ribbon.

3. Is the form of the noun correct?

Noncount nouns only have a singular form. Most count nouns have a singular form and a plural form. The plural form for most nouns has an *-s* or *-es* ending. However, there are other singular and plural patterns.

(A) Some nouns form their plurals with a vowel change or an ending change.

Singular	Plural
foot	feet
goose	geese
tooth	teeth
mouse	mice
louse	lice
man	men
woman	women

(B) Some nouns form their plurals by changing a consonant before adding *-s* or *-es*.

Singular	Plural
wolf	wolves
leaf	leaves
wife	wives
knife	knives

(C) Some nouns form their plurals by adding an ending.

Singular	Plural
child	children
ox	oxen

(D) Some nouns have the same plural and singular form. These nouns frequently refer to animals or fish. However, there are exceptions.

bison	fish	series	offspring
deer	salmon	species	spacecraft
sheep	trout	corps	

Example   One **fish** is on the plate.
Two **fish** are in the pan.

(E) When a noun is used as an adjective, it takes a singular form.

We are leaving for two **weeks**.   (noun)
We are going on a two-**week** vacation.   (adjective)

(F) *Collective nouns* refer to an entire group. When a collective noun indicates a period of time, a sum of money, or a measurement, it takes a singular verb.

Two weeks is enough time to finish the contract.
Ten dollars is all I have.
Seven pounds is an average weight for a newborn.

(G) Some nouns end in *-s* but are actually singular and take singular verbs.

Academic subjects: mathematics, politics, physics, economics, civics, statistics
Physics is Professor Brown's specialty.

Diseases: measles, mumps, herpes
Measles is usually contracted during childhood.

4. Is the noun used in a noun position?

Nouns are used in the following positions:

As subjects   An **engineer** designed the bridge.

As complements   My sister is an **engineer**.

As objects   I gave the **engineer** your message.
Eric lent the book to the **engineer**.
Jan walked past the **engineer**.

5. Is the correct form of the word used?

The form of a word depends on its position in the sentence. (See Practice with Word Forms on page 161.) Notice how the word "invitation" changes form.

Noun form   The **invitation** to Jerry's wedding has arrived.
Verb form   Susan **invited** us to dinner on Sunday.
Adjective form   The hot chocolate looked very **inviting**.
Adverb form   The man smiled **invitingly** as he opened the door.

Use Exercises S1–S5 to develop your skills in identifying nouns.

Exercise S1   *Identifying count and noncount nouns*

Write "C" if the underlined noun is a count noun, and "N" if it is a noncount noun.

Examples   _N_   I studied mathematics with Professor Crane.
           _C_   We caught three fish for dinner.

You should write "N" in the first blank because "mathematics" is a noncount noun. You should write "C" in the second blank because "fish" is a count noun in this sentence.

1. _____ Rayon was mixed with cotton to strengthen the fabric.

2. _____ The glass in the window was cracked.

3. _____ Forty children are in Bobby's class.

4. _____ The news concerning the election was very positive.

5. _____ Thomas dropped a pin on the carpet.

6. _____ The knowledge gained from the experience was invaluable.

7. _____ There is a hair on your jacket.

8. _____ Linda likes exotic fruits.

Extended practice: Some of the underlined nouns in these sentences can be either count or noncount. Identify those nouns and write your own sentences using them in both ways.

Answers to Exercise S1 are on page 447.

Exercise S2   **Reviewing plural and singular forms**

Write the correct form of the plural or singular word.

Examples	**Singular**	**Plural**
	foot	*feet*
	ox	oxen

Singular	**Plural**
1. person	_____
2. _____	lives
3. _____	series
4. _____	teeth
5. _____	children
6. man	_____
7. _____	sheep
8. leaf	_____
9. mouse	_____
10. goose	_____

Answers to Exercise S2 are on page 447.

Exercise S3   **Locating and checking plurals and singulars**

Some of the following sentences contain a noun error. Circle the incorrect nouns.

Example   One of the (philosopher) came to the meeting last evening.

You should circle "philosopher" because there must be more than one in a group of philosophers for one of them to come to the meeting.

1. Ultrasound bounces sound wave off the internal structure of the body.
2. Public lands in many parts of the West may be overgrazed as cattle, sheep, and wildlives compete for forage.
3. A landslide at a mining site uncovered a brownish yellow stone which yielded 650 gram of gold.
4. Lorenzo Ruiz, the first Filipino saints, was born about 1600 in Binondo to a Chinese father and a Tagala mother.
5. America was discovered and inhabited thousands of years before the Europeans arrived.
6. For two century, Madrid's Plaza Mayor has served as the city's chief forum.
7. Putting radio collars on bears helps scientists to gather important informations concerning the bears' movements.

8. Many of the old attitudes and values may be disappearing, along with the families that supported them.

Extended practice: Correct the nouns that you have identified as incorrect.

Answers to Exercise S3 are on page 447.

Exercise S4   ***Checking noun form***

Write the correct form of the underlined noun. Some underlined nouns are correct.

Example   The <u>exploration</u> was a big, good-natured man.

      explorer

You should write "explorer" in the space because this is the noun form that is used for people (see item 5 on page 116).

1. The <u>furnishings</u> of the house provide an insight into the social and domestic life on the estate.

2. A new <u>colonization</u> was established in Hawaii.

3. The <u>disturb</u> caused the seal to move her pups.

4. The <u>existence</u> of methane in the atmosphere is what gives Uranus its blue-green color.

5. The <u>freeze</u> killed all the new leaves on the trees.

6. The <u>landing</u> of the troops took place under the cover of night.

7. The <u>import</u> of children's play is reflected in their behavior.

8. Inside the forest, the <u>active</u> is constant.

9. The earliest <u>arrive</u> had to endure the discomfort of wading across the river.

10. When the Red Cross brought food, the <u>situate</u> was mercifully improved.

Answers to Exercise S4 are on page 447.

Exercise S5 **Checking nouns**

Look at the underlined nouns in each sentence. Circle the noun that is incorrect.

Example The <u>knowledge</u> was passed from one <u>generation</u> to another ⟨generations⟩ over the <u>centuries</u>.

You should circle "generations" because the word "another" is used only with singular nouns (see 2D on page 114).

1. During the ten <u>years</u> he was a <u>politic</u>, his <u>policies</u> changed drastically.
2. Joe insisted that his <u>success</u> was due to <u>motivated</u> rather than <u>brilliance</u>.
3. Scientists have managed to clone that kind of protein <u>genes</u>, but only as an <u>exercise</u> in basic <u>research</u>.
4. The most renowned of America's <u>metalworker</u>, Samuel Yellin, designed the <u>ironwork</u> for the New York Federal Reserve <u>Bank</u>.
5. The <u>childrens</u> were counting the <u>toys</u> and <u>candy</u> they had collected during the <u>festivities</u>.
6. On the <u>outskirts</u> of the <u>town</u>, <u>wolf</u> are frequently seen slinking through the <u>shadows</u>.
7. The police <u>officer</u> gave some <u>advices</u> on crime <u>prevention</u> at the community <u>meeting</u>.
8. One <u>series</u> of grammar <u>book</u> that was used in the experimental <u>class</u> was written by the <u>students</u> themselves.

Extended practice: Write the correct form of the nouns you have circled.

Answers to Exercise S5 are on page 447.

PRACTICE WITH ARTICLES AND DEMONSTRATIVES

Ask yourself these questions when checking articles ("a," "an," "the") and demonstratives ("this," "these," "that," "those").

1. Is the indefinite article ("a" or "an") used correctly?

(A) "A" is used before a consonant sound and "an" is used before a vowel sound.

(B) The letter "u" can have a consonant *or* vowel sound:

a university BUT an umbrella

(C) The letter "h" is sometimes not pronounced:

a horse BUT an hour

2. Should an indefinite article be used?

Use "a" or "an":

(A) before singular count nouns when the noun is mentioned for the first time.

I see **a house**.

(B) when the singular form is used to make a general statement about all people or things of that type.

A concert pianist spends many hours practicing.   (All concert pianists spend many hours practicing.)

(C) in expressions of price, speed, and ratio.

     60 miles **an** hour   four times **a** day

"A" or "an" are not used:

(D) before plural nouns.

     Flowers were growing along the river bank.

(E) before noncount nouns.

     I wanted advice.

3. Should the definite article ("the") be used?

"The" is used:

(A) before a noun that has already been mentioned:

     I saw a man. **The** man was wearing a hat.

or when it is clear in the situation which thing or person is referred to:

     The books on the shelf are first editions.
     I went to **the** bank. (a particular bank)

(B) before a singular noun that refers to a species or group.

     The tiger lives in Asia.   (Tigers, as a species, live in Asia.)

(C) before adjectives used as nouns.

     The children collected money to donate to the institution for **the** deaf.
     ("the deaf" = deaf people)

(D) when there is only one of something.

     The sun shone down on the earth.
     This is **the** best horse in the race.

(E) before a body part in a prepositional phrase that belongs to the object in the sentence:

     Someone hit me on **the** head.   ("Me" is the object, and it is my head that was hit.)

or a body part in a prepositional phrase that belongs to the subject of a passive sentence

     I was hit on **the** head.   ("I" is the subject of the passive sentence, and it is my head that was hit.)

Note: A possessive pronoun, rather than the article "the," is usually used with body parts.

     I hit **my** head.   ("I" is neither the object of this sentence nor the subject of a passive sentence. Therefore, a possessive pronoun is used.)

Some proper names use "the" and some don't.

(F) "The" is usually used with canals, deserts, forests, oceans, rivers, seas, and *plural* islands, lakes, and mountains.

     the Suez Canal   the Black Forest
     the Hawaiian Islands   the Atlantic Ocean

"The" is not used with planets and *singular* islands, lakes, mountains, and parks.

     Central Park   Lake Michigan
     Fiji Island   Mount Rushmore

(G) "The" is used when the name of a country or state includes the word "of," the type of government, or a plural form.

> the Republic of Ireland
> the United Kingdom
> the Philippines

(H) "The" is *not* used with:

the names of other countries and states:

> Japan   Brazil   Germany

the names of continents:

> Africa   Asia   Europe

the names of cities:

> Chicago   Mexico City   Hong Kong

4. Which article, if any, should be used?

(A) The expression "*a* number of " means "several" or "many" and takes a plural verb. The expression "*the* number of" refers to the group and takes a singular verb.

> **A large number** of tourists *get* lost because of that sign.
> **The number of** lost tourists *has* increased recently.

(B) The following nouns do not always take an article:

> prison   school   college
> church   bed   home
> court   jail   sea

Look at how the meaning changes:

Example   bed

No article: Jack went to bed.   (= Jack went to sleep. "Bed" refers to the general idea of sleep.)

With "the":   Jack went to **the** bed.   (Jack walked over to a particular bed. The bed is referred to as a specific object.)

With "a":   Jack bought **a** bed.   (Jack purchased an object called a bed.)

(C) Articles are not used with possessive pronouns ("my," "your," etc.) or demonstratives ("this," "that," "these," and "those").

> Where is **my** coat?
> **That** watch is broken.

(D) Noncount nouns are used without an article to refer to something in general. Sometimes an article is used to show a specific meaning.

> People all over the world want **peace**.   (= peace in general)
> The **peace** was broken by a group of passing children.   ("The peace" refers to peace at a specific time and place.)

> The imparting of **knowledge** was the job of the elders in the community. (= knowledge in general)
> I have a **knowledge** of computers.   (= a specific type of knowledge)

5. Are the demonstratives ("this," "that," "these," and "those") used correctly?

(A) The demonstrative adjectives and pronouns are for objects nearby the speaker:

   this (singular)   these (plural)

and for objects far away from the speaker:

   that (singular)   those (plural)

(B) Demonstratives are the only adjectives that agree in number with their nouns.

   That hat is nice.
   Those hats are nice.

(C) When there is the idea of selection, the pronoun "one" (or "ones") often follows the demonstrative.

   I want a book. I'll get this (one).

If the demonstrative is followed by an adjective, "one" (or "ones") *must* be used:

   I want a book. I'll get this **big** one.

Use Exercises S6–S10 to develop your skills in identifying articles and demonstratives.

Exercise S6   *Identifying the need for articles*

Write the correct article ("a," "an," or "the"). If no article is needed, write Ø.

Example   There was a documentary about __the__ United Arab Emirates on TV last
               night.

You should write "the" in the blank because the name of the country includes its type of government.

1. The old woman made a special tea with _____ herb that smelled of oranges.

2. Through his telescope we could see what looked like canals on _____ Mars.

3. The children were released from _____ school early last Friday because of a teachers' conference.

4. Robin Hood supposedly stole from _____ rich.

5. _____ untold number of people perished while attempting to cross Death Valley.

6. Albert is _____ only actor that I know personally.

7. An antelope can reach speeds of 60 miles _____ hour.

Answers to Exercise S6 are on page 448.

Exercise S7   *Checking articles*

If the underlined article is used incorrectly, cross it out and write the correct article.

Example   A̶ island in the Pacific Ocean was used for the experiment.   __An__

1. Countless tourists will be thronging to the Greek islands. _____

2. The tomato originated in Central America. _____

3. The steam engine was developed in an eighteenth century. _____

4. A hour passed before the rescue ship arrived. _____

5. The Russia has a very diverse culture. _____

6. A university education was one of the requirements for the position. _____

7. The doctor refrained from giving him a advice. _____

Answers to Exercise S7 are on page 448.

Exercise S8   *Checking demonstratives*

Circle the letter of the demonstrative that completes the sentence.

Example   ----- books are the ones I bought at the auction.
   (A) This
   (B) These

You should circle letter (B) because the demonstrative must agree in number with its noun. The plural "these" is used with the plural noun "books."

1. I was shocked by ----- news.
   (A) that
   (B) those

2. The last reliable sighting of ----- bird was in 1952.
   (A) this
   (B) these

3. ----- species of deer is almost extinct.
   (A) That
   (B) Those

4. I know ----- boy over there.
   (A) this
   (B) that

5. ----- fish tastes best when baked in butter.
   (A) This
   (B) These

6. ----- physics courses offered at the university are very elementary.
   (A) That
   (B) Those

7. Only in the park are ----- buffalo protected.
   (A) that
   (B) those

8. ----- two rings here on my little finger belonged to my great-grandmother.
   (A) Those
   (B) These

Answers to Exercise S8 are on page 448.

Exercise S9   **Correcting articles and demonstratives**

Correct any sentence that contains an error in the underlined phrase.

Examples   He is going to school.   Elderly sometimes need special care.

                                                                    The eldlerly

The first sentence is correct. For the second sentence you should write "The" before the word "elderly" because "the" is needed when an adjective is used without its noun. "The elderly" means "elderly people."

1. The brick house is the nicer of the two.

5. The general always listened to advice from his staff.

2. Staff evaluation procedures are completed at least twice the year.

6. Since beginning of the age of computers, technological advances have increased ten fold.

3. For a first time ever, the developed market-economy countries drew up a document covering international policies.

7. Jackson Pollock's freer techniques raised painting to new levels of the improvisation.

4. Postwar women had more opportunities to find the work than they had had in the prewar days.

8. The boy took his sister by the hand.

Answers to Exercise S9 are on page 448.

Exercise S10   **Locating and checking articles and demonstratives**

Underline all the articles and demonstratives in the following sentences. Then circle any that have been used incorrectly.

Example   (A)lemon originated in (the) China and spread south to the Malaysian islands and west to India.

You should underline and circle "A" before "lemon" (see 3B, page 120) and "the" before "China" (see 3H, page 121). You should underline "the" before "Malaysian" (see 3F, page 120).

1. That dissertations have to be completed within a four-year time limit.

2. The good Dr. Sneider began his first year at Arizona State University after having been appointed a associate professor.

3. At a height of the tourist season, the small seaside community boasts a population of 15,000.

4. Since the beginning the research, Dr. Ahmedi has collected 70 different kinds of plant rocks.

5. In a famous book by Daniel Defoe, the hero, Robinson Crusoe, spent 20 years on a island.

6. Those child's computer was installed with added features for the blind.

7. The tourists on the bus witnessed the beauty of the Mount Rushmore.

8. The kangaroo travels at speeds up to 20 miles the hour by jumping on the powerful hind legs.

Answers to Exercise S10 are on page 448.

PRACTICE WITH PRONOUNS

Ask yourself these questions when checking pronouns.

1. Is the pronoun in its correct form?

Subject Pronoun	Object Pronoun	Possessive Adjective	Possessive Pronoun	Reflexive Pronoun
I	me	my	mine	myself
you	you	your	yours	yourself
he	him	his	his	himself
she	her	her	hers	herself
it	it	its	its	itself
we	us	our	ours	ourselves
you	you	your	yours	yourselves
they	them	their	theirs	themselves

Examples   When you see the African lions in the park, you see them in their true environment.

Both pronouns "you" are in the subject position. The pronoun "them" is the object pronoun and refers to the lions. The pronoun "their" is in the possessive form because the environment discussed in the sentence is that of the lions.

2. Is a possessive pronoun used to refer to parts of the body?

Possessive pronouns are usually used with reference to parts of the body.
[For exceptions, see Practice with Articles and Demonstratives, 3E, page 120.]

Examples   She put the shawl over **her** shoulder.
She lifted the boy and put the shawl over **his** shoulder.

3. Does the pronoun agree with the word it refers to?

Example   The little girl put on **her** hat.

If the hat belongs to the girl, the possessive pronoun must agree with the word "girl."

4. Is it clear which word the pronoun refers to?

Example   When onion vapors reach your nose, they irritate the membranes in your nostrils, and **they** in turn irritate the tear ducts in your eyes.

It is unclear whether "they" refers to vapors, membranes, or nostrils.

Use Structure Exercises S11–S15 to develop your skills with pronouns.

Exercise S11   Locating pronouns

Circle the pronouns in the following sentences.

Example   When the boy grabbed the lizard, (its) tail broke off in (his) hand.

1. In 1978, Maxie Anderson and his two partners made the first crossing of the Atlantic in their hot-air balloon.
2. When Caesar and his troops invaded Britain, they anchored their transports above what they erroneously thought was the high tidemark.
3. As the bare mountains turned green, the people found themselves looking forward to spring.
4. The dialect that is spoken in Olimbos is so old that many of its words date back to the time of Homer.
5. The girl picked a wild rose and held it against her face.
6. The island itself didn't become accessible to us until the late 1940s.
7. In 1804 Joseph-Marie Jacquard introduced a punch-card mechanism that permitted weavers to control their looms single-handedly.
8. The deceiving look of a sinkhole is part of its danger as well as its fascination.

Answers to Exercise S11 are on page 448.

Exercise S12   Checking pronoun form

If the underlined pronoun is incorrect, write its correct form.

Example   We prepared the supper by <u>ourself</u>.

     ourselves

"Our" refers to more than one person. Therefore, "self" should be in the plural form.

1. The forest rangers tranquilized the grizzly bears and attached radios to <u>them</u> necks.

_____

2. While tide pools can survive natural assaults, <u>their</u> are defenseless against humans.

_____

3. You and your brother need to take time to prepare <u>yourself</u> for the long journey.

_____

4. The larvae metamorphose into miniature versions of <u>their</u> adult form.

_____

5. These minute insects – twenty of <u>they</u> could fit on a pinhead – drift on wind currents.

_____

6. Most of the families made <u>theirselves</u> a home of packing crates and sheet metal.

_____

7. <u>His</u> is a future dictated by poverty and hardship.

_____

8. It took <u>their</u> days to reach the lower regions in the winter.

_____

Answers to Exercise S12 are on page 448.

Exercise S13   *Identifying referents*

Write the word that the underlined pronoun refers to.

Example   He put the roast on the table and began to eat it.

it _____roast_____

The pronoun "it" refers to "roast."

1. Vikings buried their chief with his boat, complete with his supplies.

   their _____   his _____   his _____

2. Creatures cannot exist without membranes to hold them together.

   them _____

3. People thought the symbol had mystical powers, so they wore it as a good luck charm.

   they _____   it _____

4. There are no restrictions on debates in the English House of Lords, so if its members think something is important, they will talk it through until they are satisfied.

   its _____   they _____

   it _____   they _____

5. The dean expressed his support for setting up a private university provided it was supervised by the Department of Education.

   his _____   it _____

6. This was the place where the Roman ship had sunk with its cargo of stone.

   This _____   its _____

7. To pass his time away in jail, Charles d'Orléans smuggled out rhyming love letters to his wife, and this may have been the beginning of the custom of sending Valentine cards to loved ones.

   his _____   his _____   this _____

8. During a drying time of six to eight weeks, the nutmeg shrinks away from its hard seed coat until the kernels rattle in their shells when shaken.

   its _____   their _____

Answers to Exercise S13 are on page 448.

Exercise S14   *Checking for referent-pronoun agreement*

If the underlined pronoun does not agree with the word it refers to, write the correct pronoun.

Example   The dog bit themselves on the tail.

_____itself_____

1. The importance of this archaeological site is that they reveals a whole civilization.

   _____

2. We know the risks and we are quite happy to take us.

   _____

3. The ancient Tayronas distinguished themselves as craftsmen working in gold, clay, and stone.

_____

4. The gun was beautifully engraved, making their value close to $20,000.

_____

5. Local conservationists describe the park as one of the only places where people can park their cars and walk right to the water and see whales and dolphins.

_____

6. When trawling for crab, he took several books so that he could study it during the long hours.

_____

7. Colonel Shelly led Jim and Terry to the campsite themselves.

_____

8. So numerous are the family's properties that the duchess cannot name it all.

_____

> Answers to Exercise S14 are on page 449.

Exercise S15 **Checking for clarity**

If the underlined pronoun in each sentence has a clear referent, circle the referent (the word it refers to). If the referent is not clear, put a question mark over all possible referents.

        ?   ?

Example   Mary is not bringing her daughter because she is sick.

It is unclear who is sick: Mary or her daughter.

1. There are records of Dutch travelers, among others, carrying batik to the West.

2. The process is time consuming, but the result is so satisfying that one feels it is well worth the effort.

3. To understand ancient Egypt, Dr. Malcolm has studied its hieroglyphics and tried to interpret them.

4. One of the by-products of growing older is the tendency of one's idols to fall from their pedestals.

5. The seals basking on the ice showed little interest as the marine biologists drove out to where they usually dive.

6. Toxic waste from industry may linger in the environment for decades before it becomes safe.

7. Because the ice crystals from which they form are usually hexagonal, snowflakes often have six-sided shapes.

8. People's needs are not being met, and resources are being degraded because they are wasted and mismanaged, not because they are scarce.

9. Fog can be predicted by keeping track of the dew point and ambient temperature and marking them on a graph.

10. Botanists are so worried that the pollution problem may be irreversible in many areas that they are organizing their own monitoring programs.

Answers to Exercise S15 are on page 449.

CHECK YOUR PROGRESS

Check your progress in the areas covered in Exercises S1–S15 by completing the following mini-test. This exercise uses the same format as questions 16–40 of the Structure and Written Expression section on the TOEFL.

Exercise S16   **Mini-test**   *(Time – 15 minutes)*

Directions: In questions 1–25 each sentence has four underlined words or phrases. The four underlined parts of the sentence are marked (A), (B), (C), and (D). Identify the <u>one</u> underlined word or phrase that must be changed in order for the sentence to be correct. Then circle the letter that corresponds to the answer you have chosen.

Example   A trade center since <u>antiquity</u>, Catalonia <u>itself</u> has often been ruled by
       A   B   C
    <u>outsider</u>.
      Ⓓ

You should circle D in your book because the underlined noun "outsider" should be in plural form. (The article "an" would have been included if there had been only one outsider who ruled Catalonia.) The sentence should read, "A trade center since antiquity, Catalonia itself has often been ruled by outsiders."

1. Crickets rub <u>the</u> legs <u>together</u> to make <u>their</u> chirping <u>sound</u>.
                A   B   C   D

2. <u>Progressive</u> for <u>its</u> time, Constantinople offered free medical services and <u>care</u> for <u>a</u>
     A   B   C   D
    destitute.

3. A pack of five <u>wolfs</u> <u>encircled</u> and killed the <u>moose</u>.
    <u>A</u>   B   C   D

4. Divers earn <u>them</u> living by retrieving money <u>thrown</u> into <u>the</u> river by <u>pilgrims</u>.
             A   B   C   D

5. Conservationists <u>hope</u> that <u>someday</u> captive wildlife <u>populations</u> will be
                   A   B   C
    reestablished in <u>a</u> wild.
                  D

6. The institute encouraged the <u>participations</u> of teachers by providing <u>them</u> with travel
    A   B   C
    expenses and <u>lodging</u>.
                 D

7. <u>Dogs</u> that are <u>trained</u> to lead <u>a</u> blind must be <u>loyal</u>, intelligent, and calm.
    A   B   C   D

8. <u>The</u> sale of pet <u>turtles</u> was banned because of the disease risk <u>they</u> posed to young
    A   B   C
<u>child</u>.
   D

9. <u>Inevitably</u> scholars disagree on <u>an</u> authenticity of many objects whose <u>origins</u> are
    A   B   C
<u>unknown</u>.
   D

10. Three species of <u>the</u> fruit <u>bat</u> have been found <u>to have</u> a primatelike visual <u>systems</u>.
                   A   B   C   D

11. Although Emily Dickinson wrote some of <u>the</u> most haunting lines of American
                                                    A
<u>poetry</u>, only seven of her poems <u>were</u> published during <u>their</u> lifetime.
   B   C   D

12. Many <u>Chineses</u> connect <u>the</u> word "happiness" with the symbols for <u>white</u>, silk, and
           A   B   C
<u>tree</u>.
   D

13. Oil <u>strikes</u> on the North Slope in <u>the</u> Alaska provided the fuel to drive <u>its</u> economic
      A   B   C
<u>growth</u>.
   D

14. <u>Totem</u> poles provide eloquent <u>records</u> of a tribe's <u>lineage</u> and <u>his</u> history.
     A   B   C   D

15. The local hot <u>springs</u> now serve as a bathhouse for <u>them</u> tranquil little <u>town</u>.
             A   B   C   D

16. Sitka was the <u>capital</u> of Russian America, and <u>the</u> town still holds <u>a</u> legacies of <u>its</u>
             A   B   C   D
Russian founders.

17. The <u>scars</u> of <u>the</u> earthquake remain in the naked <u>rock</u>, and stunted trees mark
     A   B   C
<u>their</u> fault line.
   D

18. Special elastic <u>ligament</u> allow <u>the</u> whale's <u>jaws</u> to accommodate <u>its</u> wide-angle bites.
                A   B   C   D

19. Barcelona was a <u>stronghold</u> of <u>an</u> anti-Franco Republican forces during the Spanish
                A   B   C
civil <u>war</u>.
   D

20. When the <u>limestone</u> just below <u>the</u> ground surface dissolves, the <u>lands</u> collapses and
              A   B   C
    <u>forms</u> ponds.
     D

21. Small Australian <u>fishes</u> called galaxiids feed on algae and mosses <u>that</u> grow in <u>the</u>
              A   B   C
    warm <u>waters</u>.
        D

22. Solon H. Borglum's <u>sculptures</u> of horses show <u>he</u> to be <u>one</u> of the finest equestrian
                  A   B   C
    <u>artists</u> in the history of art.
     D

23. Aeronautical <u>historian</u> have concluded that <u>the</u> Frenchman Clement Ader made a
               A   B
    short <u>leap</u> but never a sustained <u>flight</u>.
        C   D

24. Dr. August Raspet was <u>a</u> researcher and designer of <u>sailplanes</u> and <u>inventors</u> of the
                       A   B   C
    flying <u>bicycle</u>.
       D

25. As conscripted <u>craftsman</u> under Swedish <u>rule</u>, Finns introduced <u>the</u> log <u>cabin</u> to
             A   B   C   D
    America.

Answers to Exercise S16 are on page 449.

PRACTICE WITH SUBJECTS

Ask yourself these questions when checking subjects.

1. Does the sentence contain a subject?

All complete sentences contain a subject. Exception: the command form, in which the subject is understood. (For example, "Do your homework.")

(A) The subject may consist of one or more nouns:

> **Birds** fly.
> **Birds and bats** fly.

(B) The subject may consist of a *phrase* (a group of words that includes the subject noun and words that modify it):

> _____ **SUBJECT PHRASE** _____
> The first Persian **carpet** I bought was very expensive.

The subject noun is "carpet." In general, the entire subject phrase can be replaced by a pronoun. In this case:

> **It** was very expensive.

(C) Various structures may be used for subjects.

Noun	The **clover** smells sweet.
Pronoun	**It is** a new bookcase.
Clause (contains noun + verb)	**What they found** surprised me.
Gerund (-ing forms)	**Swimming** is good exercise.
Gerund phrase	**Working ten years in the mine** was enough.
Infinitive (to + verb)	**To sleep in** is a luxury.
Infinitive phrase	**To be able to read** is very important.

(D) Several different clause structures can be used for subjects.

Wh- structures:

Where we go depends on the job opportunities.

Yes/no structures:

Whether it rains or not doesn't matter.

"The fact that" structures ("the fact" is frequently omitted in these structures):

The fact that he survived the accident is a miracle.
That he survived the accident is a miracle.

2. Is there an unnecessary subject pronoun?

A subject noun or phrase and the pronoun that could replace it cannot be used in the same sentence.

Correct	**A ball** is a toy.	**A ball and a bat** are in the yard.
	It is a toy.	**They** are in the yard.
Incorrect	**A ball** it is a toy.	
	A ball and a bat they are in the yard.	

3. Does the subject agree with the verb?

Examples

    S   V
Susie is working.

    ____S____   V
Susie, Bill, and Albert are working.

The subject (S) and the verb (V) must agree in person and number. Note the following subject-verb agreement rules.

(A) A prepositional phrase does not affect the verb.

    S   V
The houses **on that street** are for sale.

    S   V
The house **with the broken steps** is for sale.

(B) The following expressions do not affect the verb.

accompanied by	as well as
along with	in addition to
among	together with

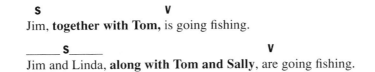

Jim, **together with Tom,** is going fishing.

<u>   S   </u>   V
Jim and Linda, **along with Tom and Sally,** are going fishing.

(C) Subjects joined by "and" or "both . . . and . . ." take a plural verb.

Both Jill **and** Lydia *are* leaving town.

(D) When "several," "many," "both," and "few" are used as pronouns, they take a plural verb.

Several *have* already left the party.

(E) When the following phrases are used, the verb agrees with the subject that is closer to the verb in the sentence.

either . . . or
neither . . . nor
not only . . . but also

Neither my sister **nor** my brothers *want* to work in an office.
Neither my brothers **nor** my sister *wants* to work in an office.

(F) The expression "a number of" (meaning "several") is plural. The expression "the number of" is singular.

A number of items *have* been deleted.
The number of deleted items *is* small.

(G) When a word indicating nationality refers to a language, it is singular. When it refers to the people, it is plural.

Japanese *was* a difficult language for me to learn.
The Japanese *are* very inventive people.

(H) When clauses, infinitives, or gerunds are used as subjects, they usually take a singular verb.

What it takes *is* lots of courage.
To fly in space *is* her dream.
Learning a new skill *is* very satisfying.

Some gerunds can take a plural form. These gerunds use a plural verb.

Their findings suggest that the fire was caused by an arsonist.

4. Have "it" and "there" been used correctly?

(A) Sometimes a speaker wants to focus on the type of information that is expressed by an adjective. Since an adjective (ADJ) cannot be used in a subject position, the word "it" is used as the subject:

S   V   ADJ
It was windy and the rain beat down.

Sometimes a speaker wants to emphasize a noun and its relative clause. The speaker uses "it" in the subject position followed by the verb "be":

S   V   <u>   CLAUSE   </u>
It was Tom who broke the window.

Sometimes a speaker wants to say that something exists, or wants to mention the presence of something. The word "there" is used as the subject, and the verb agrees with the noun or noun phrase (N PHR):

```
      S    V    N PHR
```
There were six men in the boat.

(B) "It" can be used to refer to a previously stated topic. "It" can also be used to fill the subject position [see 4(A)].

It was warm in the house and I was afraid the milk might spoil, so I put **it** into the refrigerator.

The first "it" is used as the subject. The second "it" refers to the milk.

(C) "There" can be an adverb which tells where something is. "There" can also be used to fill the subject position [see 4(A)].

There are three bottles of orange juice over **there** by the sink.

The first "there" is used to fill the subject position and indicates that three bottles exist. The second "there" is an adverb which indicates where the bottles are.

Use Exercises S17–S23 to develop your skills in identifying and using subjects.

Exercise S17   *Focusing on subjects*

Underline the complete subject of the sentence and circle the subject noun (the noun that agrees with the verb).

Examples   Port cities are often the distribution centers for a country.

The beautiful, large, green parrots with the tuft of red plumage on their heads are on sale.

1. Until the mid-1950s, fishermen thought the eagles' gorging during annual salmon runs depleted stocks.

2. Sam, along with other students, plans on protesting the change in academic requirements.

3. Pictured on the one-dollar stamp is St. John's Cathedral.

4. Birds, mammals, reptiles, and fish that are not hunted, fished, or trapped need protection too.

5. Since nitrogen is a characteristic and relatively constant component of protein, scientists can measure protein by measuring nitrogen.

6. Far too many preservation programs in too many states rely on unstable voluntary donations.

7. When a tornado sweeps through a city, it causes a narrow band of total destruction.

8. Pesticide residues in livestock are largely the result of pesticide contamination in the general environment.

Answers to Exercise S17 are on page 451.

Exercise S18   **Locating subjects**

Underline the complete subjects of the following sentences.

Example   Running is my favorite kind of exercise.

1. How wildlife has adapted to life along the road systems is the topic of the lecture.

2. To be among 200-foot-high towering rocks is an exhilarating experience.

3. Very early in the experiment, isolating the insects became necessary.

4. What was decided during the meeting has been well documented.

5. Whispering in class not only prevents the whisperers from understanding the lesson, but also bothers those who are trying to hear the class lecture.

6. To create and produce new combinations of line and color takes a real flair.

7. What caused the most damage to Michelangelo's works in the Sistine Chapel was a gluelike substance spread over the frescoes early in the sixteenth century.

8. Rolling dice, buying property, and accumulating play money is what seems to be the attraction of many board games.

Answers to Exercise S18 are on page 451.

Exercise S19   *Checking subject-verb agreement*

Write "C" (correct) if the subject agrees with the verb. Write "I" (incorrect) if the subject does not agree with the verb.

Examples   _C_   An important goal was to increase tourism.

_I_   The houses is open to the public.

In the first sentence, the subject "goal" agrees with the verb "was." In the second sentence, the subject "houses," does not agree with the verb "is."

1. _____ Deer are frequently seen in the meadow at dusk.

2. _____ Physics are my favorite subject.

3. _____ Neither her sons nor her daughter plays the piano.

4. _____ Nowadays, crossing Puget Sound in ferries are fast and convenient.

5. _____ Each river and ravine create an obstacle in the cross-country race.

6. _____ The president, together with his cabinet members, are meeting the African Trade Delegation.

7. _____ Two weeks is plenty of time to finish the course.

8. _____ A lion and a lioness from Kenya is arriving at the Metropolitan Zoo today.

Extended practice: Correct the sentences in the preceding exercise that have subject-verb errors.

Answers to Exercise S19 are on page 451.

Exercise S20 ***Choosing the correct subject***

All of the following statements need a subject. Circle the letter of the correct subject from the four possible choices.

Example ----- are becoming endangered because their natural habitat is being lost.
(A) That animals
(B) Animals
(C) To be animals
(D) Being animals

You should circle (B) because the sentence needs a simple subject that agrees with the plural verb.

1. ----- takes eight years after sowing.
   (A) The nutmeg yields fruit
   (B) That the nutmeg yields fruit
   (C) For the nutmeg to yield fruit
   (D) To the nutmeg's yielding fruit

2. ----- has been used as a perfume for centuries.
   (A) To use lavender
   (B) That the lavender
   (C) Lavender
   (D) For the lavender

3. ----- shortens and thickens the muscles on either side of the jaw.
   (A) The teeth clenching
   (B) Clenching the teeth
   (C) That clenching the teeth
   (D) The teeth clenched

4. Even though 26 percent of Californian residents do not speak English in their homes, only ----- do not speak English at all.
   (A) that 6 percent of them
   (B) those of the 6 percent
   (C) to the 6 percent of them
   (D) 6 percent of them

5. ----- started as a modern sport in India at the same time that it did in Europe.
   (A) To ski
   (B) That skiing
   (C) Ski
   (D) Skiing

6. ----- was caused by a cow's kicking over a lantern has been told to American schoolchildren for several generations.
   (A) That the Great Chicago Fire
   (B) The Great Chicago Fire
   (C) To burn in the Great Chicago Fire
   (D) Burning in the Great Chicago Fire

7. ----- are effective means of communication.
   (A) Theater, music, dance, folk tales, and puppetry
   (B) That theater, music, dance, folk tales, and puppetry
   (C) To use theater, music, dance, folk tales, and puppetry
   (D) Using theater, music, dance, folk tales, and puppetry

8. When China's dramatic economic reforms began to encourage private enterprise, ----- began to set up a variety of businesses immediately.
   (A) that entrepreneurs
   (B) to be an entrepreneur
   (C) entrepreneur
   (D) entrepreneurs

9. ----- are worthy of protection moved English Heritage historians into action against developers.
   (A) Some buildings in and around Fleet Street
   (B) That some buildings in and around Fleet Street
   (C) Some buildings that are in and around Fleet Street
   (D) To build in and around Fleet Street

10. ----- makes the mountain patrol team's job interesting and fulfilling.
    (A) Climbers and trekkers in distress are assisted
    (B) Assisting climbers and trekkers in distress
    (C) Assistance is given to climbers and trekkers that are in distress
    (D) Climbers and trekkers in distress

Answers to Exercise S20 are on page 451.

Exercise S21   Understanding "it"

If the underlined "it" refers to another word in the passage, write the word it refers to. If the underlined "it" does not refer to another word in the passage, write its accompanying adjective.

Examples   I went into the dark house. It was very difficult to see anything.

difficult

I started a fire in the fireplace. It was burning slowly.

fire

In the first passage, "it" does not refer to another word; therefore, you should write the accompanying adjective "difficult" in the blank. In the second passage, "it" refers to the noun "fire"; therefore, you should write "fire" in the blank.

1. The castle of Neuschwanstein is one of many fanciful castles Ludwig II of Bavaria had built. It was to be the ultimate castle for a private kingdom.

2. Ross Island, rich in scenic beauty with old buildings and monuments of historical value, was a British headquarters. It is now a tourist attraction.

3. The gorilla is essentially a peaceful creature. It is true that the gorilla will fight, but only in life threatening situations.

4. Noticing strange animal behavior might be a way to predict future earthquakes. It is believed that animals can sense environmental disturbances up to several days before the onset of a tremor.

5. A video firm is investing substantial sums in the filming of a classic Russian opera. It is hoped that this will help popularize opera.

6. Coronary heart disease is sometimes referred to as the twentieth-century epidemic. It has been responsible for a third of all deaths among males and a quarter of all deaths among females in the USA.

7. Some people think chiropractors are quacks. But it cannot be disputed that many have gained benefits from chiropractic treatment.

8. Stuttering is a communication disorder involving the rate and rhythm of speech. It may have psychological or environmental causes.

Answers to Exercise S21 are on page 452.

Exercise S22   Understanding "there"

If the underlined "there" refers to the existence of something, write what exists. If the underlined "there" is used to refer to a place, write the name of the place.

Examples   I can see the books there on the table.

table

There were six literature books and two history books.

six literature books and two history books

In the first sentence, "there" refers to a place, the table. In the second sentence, "there" refers to the existence of two dictionaries and two history books.

1. At present, 12 northern white rhinos live in the wild and 15 in captivity. There are no females in the West and those in Eastern Europe are getting too old for breeding.

   _____

2. During the Second World War, water in England was rationed due to a shortage. In the bathtubs at Buckingham Palace there were lines marking the limit allowed.

   _____

3. A rare foal was recently born at Cricket St. Thomas Wildlife Park. There they breed the smallest miniature ponies in the world.

   _____

4. When telephones were first invented, many business owners refused to have them installed in their offices. There were messenger services that they believed to be more efficient.

   _____

5. It is not uncommon for Americans to retire to homes in the southern states. There they find the climate more to their satisfaction.

   _____

6. Not only have poetry sales almost doubled in the past three years, but there has also been a renaissance in writing.

   _____

7. In Europe, water companies keep live trout in special troughs to monitor water pollution. Special sensors there can detect high levels of pollution through the trout's gill movements.

   _____

8. The world's largest optical telescope has been officially opened in Australia. There scientists will make measurements of stars in the Milky Way galaxy at a far higher resolution than is possible with any other instrument.

   _____

Answers to Exercise S22 are on page 452.

Exercise S23   *Checking "there" and "it"*

Circle the letter of the one word or phrase that completes the sentence.

Example   ----- two kinds of decorative art.
      (A) It is
      (B) There are
      (C) There
      (D) It

You should circle (B) because "there are" indicates the existence of two kinds of decorative art. The verb "is" in (A) does not agree with the plural "two kinds," and the answers in (C) and (D) do not include a verb to complete the sentence.

1. ----- not until the invention of the camera that artists correctly painted horses racing.
   (A) There was
   (B) It was
   (C) There
   (D) It

2. Once a crocodile has seized an animal, ----- drags the prey beneath the surface of the water.
   (A) it
   (B) it is
   (C) there
   (D) there is

3. Our feeling for beauty is inspired by the harmonious arrangement of order and disorder as ----- occurs in nature.
   (A) it is
   (B) there
   (C) there is
   (D) it

4. ----- nutrition and adult literacy classes for the program's workers.
   (A) There
   (B) There are
   (C) It is
   (D) It

5. In the city center ----- noisy market stalls set in a maze of winding alleys.
   (A) it
   (B) it is
   (C) there
   (D) there are

6. In America, ----- a growing demand for Indonesian food.
   (A) there is
   (B) it is
   (C) it
   (D) there

7. -----, in the center of old Sanaa, many of the city's houses, some ten centuries old, will collapse if restoration isn't started soon.
   (A) There are
   (B) It is
   (C) There
   (D) It

8. Nowadays people in most countries use money because ----- impossible to carry on trade in the modern world without it.
   (A) it
   (B) there
   (C) there is
   (D) it is

> *Answers to Exercise S23 are on page 452.*

CHECK YOUR PROGRESS

Check your progress in using the identification skills you have been practicing in Exercises S17–S23. Exercise S24 is a mini-test which uses the same format as questions 1–15 of the Structure and Written Expression section on the TOEFL.

Then check your progress in the error identification skills you have been practicing in Exercises S1–S24 by completing Exercise S25. This mini-test uses the same format as questions 16–40 of the Structure and Written Expression section on the TOEFL.

Exercise S24   **Mini-test**   *(Time – 10 minutes)*

Directions: Questions 1–15 are incomplete sentences. Beneath each sentence you will see four words or phrases marked (A), (B), (C), and (D). Choose the <u>one</u> word or phrase that best completes the sentence. Then circle the letter that corresponds to the answer you have chosen.

Example   ----- of unexplored places has led humans to make space flights.
      (A) Challenge
      (B) The challenge
      (C) Challenging
      (D) To challenge

You should circle (B) because there are specific challenges that have led humans to make space flights. Those challenges are of unexplored places.

1. ----- are phosphorescent in the dark
   surprises many people.
   (A) That certain species of centipedes
   (B) Certain species of centipedes
   (C) There are certain species of centipedes
   (D) It is certain species of centipedes

2. ----- from the leaves of the rare weeping
   tree even though the sky may be cloudless.
   (A) Great drops of water dripping
   (B) Great drops of water drip
   (C) Water dripping in great drops
   (D) That great drops of water are dripping

3. ----- with strong flippers, seals gracefully
   glide through the sea.
   (A) Paddle and steer
   (B) It is paddling and steering
   (C) That they paddle and steer
   (D) Paddling and steering

4. ----- is a tiny sea animal that looks like
   shrimp.
   (A) It is the krill
   (B) The krill
   (C) There is the krill
   (D) That the krill

5. -----, which is a traditional Valencian dish,
   is made of rice, chicken, and seafood.
   (A) It is paella
   (B) Paella
   (C) Paella is
   (D) There is paella

6. ----- from horseback is a valid form of pest
   control has come under attack.
   (A) That the hunting of foxes
   (B) The hunting of foxes
   (C) It is the hunting of foxes
   (D) There is fox hunting

7. ----- by its previous owner explains why no
   one has searched for it.
   (A) Having cursed the treasure
   (B) The treasure has been cursed
   (C) It was the curse of the treasure
   (D) The treasure's having been cursed

8. ----- that produced the famous Crab
   nebula, which is a favorite among
   astronomers.
   (A) That it was a supernova
   (B) It was a supernova
   (C) A supernova
   (D) There a supernova

9. ----- unnecessary red tape and promote
   research were the main objectives of the
   committee.
   (A) To circumvent
   (B) That to circumvent
   (C) The circumvention of
   (D) Circumventing

10. ----- mixed with a base such as egg yolk
    was the exclusive medium for painting
    panels in the Middle Ages.
    (A) Finely ground pigments
    (B) It is a finely ground pigment
    (C) A finely ground pigment
    (D) That a finely ground pigment

11. ----- toward animated cartoons with
    war-related topics has come under
    criticism from such groups as the National
    Coalition Against Television Violence.
    (A) It is the trend
    (B) Trends
    (C) That the trend
    (D) The trend

12. Today ----- the single largest organized
    industry in India.
    (A) the cotton textile industry is
    (B) it is the cotton textile industry
    (C) the cotton textile industry
    (D) there is the cotton textile industry

13. ----- of the "Rubaiyat of Omar Khayyam"
    earned Edward Fitzgerald fame.
    (A) It is translating
    (B) His translation
    (C) Its being translated
    (D) In his translation

14. When we put on thick woolen clothing,
    ----- in the woolen loops that protects us
    from the cold.
    (A) it is the air
    (B) that the air
    (C) the air
    (D) there is the air

15. ----- in the frozen wastes of Antarctica
    takes special equipment.
    (A) Survive
    (B) It is survival
    (C) That survival
    (D) To survive

Answers to Exercise S24 are on page 453.

Exercise S25   **Mini-test**   *(Time – 15 minutes)*

Directions: In questions 1–25 each sentence has four underlined words or phrases. The four underlined parts of the sentence are marked (A), (B), (C), and (D). Identify the <u>one</u> underlined word or phrase that must be changed in order for the sentence to be correct. Then circle the letter that corresponds to the answer you have chosen.

Example   As road <u>traffic</u> increases, elevated <u>highways</u> are built to help solve <u>the</u>
               A   B   C
        problem of traffic <u>jam</u>.
                 Ⓓ

You should circle (D) in your book because the underlined word "jam" should be plural (it refers to traffic jams in general, not a specific traffic jam).

1. <u>Ironworking</u> probably spread to <u>a</u> rest of Africa <u>via</u> the Meroitic <u>civilization</u>.
      A   B   C   D

2. <u>Physicists</u> <u>is</u> a fascinating course <u>of</u> study <u>to follow</u>.
      A   B   C   D

3. In the <u>novel</u>, everyone <u>they</u> encounter <u>try</u> to thwart <u>their</u> efforts.
         A   B   C   D

4. The treasures <u>of</u> the ancient world <u>they</u> <u>never</u> cease to <u>amaze</u> us.
           A   B   C   D

5. <u>Every</u> recruits was <u>given</u> a uniform, <u>supplies</u>, and <u>training</u>.
      A   B   C   D

6. The jury <u>took</u> a long <u>times</u> to reach <u>an</u> agreement <u>among</u> themselves.
        A   B   C   D

7. <u>Some</u> of the most <u>famous</u> Middle Eastern newspapers, *The Pyramids,* was
      A   B
    established <u>in</u> Egypt <u>in</u> 1875.
         C   D

8. The <u>illustrated</u> and photographs of fish and corals <u>of</u> the Great Barrier Reef <u>are</u>
         A   B   C   D
    extraordinary.

9. <u>The number</u> of battles were <u>fought</u> <u>between</u> the <u>fleets</u> of Nelson and Napoleon.
     A   B   C   D

10. Included in <u>this</u> series <u>are</u> "The Enchanted Horse," <u>among</u> other famous <u>children's</u>
           A   B   C   D
    stories.

11. The ships now <u>lying</u> at the bottom of Abukir Bay <u>was</u> rumored to be <u>carrying</u>
             A   B   C
    treasures taken <u>from</u> Malta.
               D

12. <u>A</u> military installations that they <u>have</u> concealed underground will <u>be used only</u> in
A   B   C
an extreme <u>emergency</u>.
D

13. All <u>them</u> who share a common <u>interest</u> in music are <u>brought</u> together <u>by</u> the Music
A   B   C   D
Guild.

14. Trade relations between Egypt and Africa <u>began</u> in 1460 B.C. <u>when</u> Queen
A   B
Hatshepsut sent <u>hers</u> ships to the country of Punt, <u>today's</u> Somalia.
C   D

15. Planning, rehearsing, reading <u>aloud</u>, and <u>interpret</u> parts <u>from</u> famous dramas will
A   B   C
<u>be included</u> in the City Readers Theater sessions.
D

16. Ever since the <u>early</u> Greeks began the serious <u>contemplation</u> of natural things, <u>there</u>
A   B   C
have existed two different emphases in thinking about <u>universe</u>.
D

17. That the museum includes <u>displays</u> of the papyrus-making process <u>are</u> yet another
A   B   C
reason for not missing <u>it</u>.
D

18. The Freedom of Information Act, <u>passed</u> by the U.S. Congress in 1966, <u>gives</u> U.S.
A   B
<u>citizen</u> the right of <u>access</u> to public records.
C   D

19. The <u>beautiful</u> of Cyprus, with <u>its</u> pine-covered mountains, sandy beaches, historical
A   B
monuments, and <u>picturesque</u> villages, <u>is</u> legendary.
C   D

20. <u>The</u> seemingly endless attacks of mosquitoes, <u>fly</u>, and other pests can <u>ruin</u> an
A   B   C
otherwise enjoyable <u>outing</u> in the woods.
D

21. <u>Much</u> university-educated people managed to avoid <u>being</u> conscripted <u>into</u> the army
A   B   C
at the outbreak <u>of</u> the war.
D

22. The <u>anthropologist</u> is <u>interested</u> not in the <u>actions</u> of an individual, but in the social
A   B   C
<u>significant</u> of these actions.
D

23. The very obvious differences <u>among</u> the various <u>cultures</u> discussed <u>is</u> at most
                               A   B   C

   <u>skin-deep</u>.
    D

24. Having lived <u>there</u> for long <u>period</u>, the French writer Stendhal <u>knew</u> Italy <u>well</u>.
            A   B   C   D

25. <u>As soon as</u> they were <u>seated</u>, the <u>man</u> began to whisper among <u>themselves</u>.
    A   B   C   D

Answers to Exercise S25 are on page 453.

PRACTICE WITH VERBS

Ask yourself these questions when checking verbs.

1. Does the sentence contain a verb?

The verb may consist of a single word, or a main verb and one or more auxiliary words (aux-words).

(A) A verb can indicate a state of being (what the subject is) or location.

> Betty **is** intelligent.
> Robin and Donald **are** doctors.
> Mickey **is** at work.

(B) A verb can indicate what the subject is like or becomes.

> That child **seems** frightened.
> The book **had become** obsolete.

(C) A verb can indicate an action (what the subject is doing).

> The students **will finish** in time.
> My neighbor **has bought** a new car.

2. Does the verb agree with the subject?

Verbs must agree in number and person with the subject. (See agreement rules in Practice with Subjects, 3, page 132.)

3. Is the verb tense correct?

Verbs indicate a point in time or period of time in the past, present, or future.

Tense	Used for	Example sentences
SIMPLE PRESENT	(A) a present state of affairs	(A) My sister **lives** in Washington.
	(B) a general fact	(B) The sun **rises** in the east.
	(C) habitual actions	(C) I **listen** to the radio in the mornings.
	(D) future timetables	(D) My flight **leaves** at 10:00.

Tense	Used for	Example sentences
PRESENT CONTINUOUS	(A) a specific action that is occurring (B) a general activity that takes place over a period of time (C) future arrangements	(A) Andrew **is watching** TV (right now). (B) My sister **is living** in Washington. Sue's condition **is improving.** These days, **I'm taking** it easy. (C) **I'm inviting** Emma to the party on Friday.
SIMPLE PAST	(A) an action that began and ended at a particular time in the past (B) an action that occurred over a period of time but was completed in the past (C) an activity that took place regularly in the past.	(A) The mail **came** early this morning. (B) Dad **worked** in advertising for ten years. (C) We **jogged** every morning before class.
PAST CONTINUOUS	(A) interrupted actions (B) a continuous state or repeated action in the past (C) events planned in the past	(A) I **was sewing** when the telephone rang. While I **was sewing**, the telephone rang. (B) She **was looking** very ill. I **was meeting** lots of people at that time. (C) Nancy **was leaving** for Chicago but had to make a last-minute connection.
FUTURE (*going to*)	(A) expressing a future intent based on a decision made in the past (B) predicting an event that is likely to happen in the future (C) predicting an event that is likely to happen based on the present conditions	(A) Jim **is going** to bring his sister tonight. (B) You**'re going** to pass the test. Don't worry. (C) I don't feel well. **I'm going** to faint.
FUTURE (*will*)	(A) making a decision at the time of speaking (B) predicting an event that is likely to happen in the future. (C) indicating willingness to do something	(A) **I'll call** you after lunch. (B) You **will pass** the test. Don't worry. (C) If I don't feel better soon, I **will go** to the doctor.

Tense	Used for	Example sentences
FUTURE CONTINUOUS	(A) an action that will be ongoing at a particular time in the future (B) future actions which have already been decided	(A) At noon tomorrow, **I'll be taking** the children to their piano lessons. (B) **I'll be wearing** my black evening dress to the dinner.
PRESENT PERFECT	(A) an action that happened at an unspecified time (B) an action that has recently occurred (C) an action that began in the past and continues up to the present (often used with "for" or "since") (D) an action that happened repeatedly before now	(A) She **has** never **climbed** a mountain. I'm sorry. I **have forgotten** your name. (B) **He's** just **gone** to sleep. (C) Jacky **has lived** in Maine all her life. **I've been** here since Monday. He's **known** her for two weeks. (D) We **have flown** across the Pacific four times. **I've failed** my driver's test twice.
PRESENT PERFECT CONTINUOUS	(A) an action that began in the past and has just recently ended (B) an action that began in the past and continues in the present (C) an action repeated over a period of time in the past and continuing in the present (D) a general action recently in progress (no particular time is mentioned)	(A) **Have** you **been raking** the lawn? There's grass all over your pant legs. (B) Laura **has been studying** for two hours. (C) Simon **has been smoking** since he was thirteen. (D) **I've been thinking** about going to college next year.
PAST PERFECT	(A) a past action that occurred before another past action (B) an action that was expected to occur in the past	(A) Tom **had left** hours before we got there. (B) I **had hoped** to know about the job before now.
PAST PERFECT CONTINUOUS	(A) an action that occurred before another past action (B) an action that was expected to occur in the past	(A) They **had been playing** tennis before the storm broke. His eyes hurt because he **had been reading** for eight hours. (B) I **had been expecting** his change in attitude.

Tense	Used for	Example sentences
FUTURE PERFECT	(A) an action that will be completed before a particular time in the future	(A) By next July, my parents **will have been married** for fifty years.
FUTURE PERFECT CONTINUOUS	(A) emphasizing the length of time that has occurred before a specific time in the future	(A) By May, my father **will have been working** at the same job for thirty years.

4. Are the modals used correctly?

Modals are always followed by the base form of a verb. They indicate mood or attitude.

can	had better	may	must	shall	will
could	have to	might	ought to	should	would

We **can** leave after 2:30. (= We are able to leave . . .)

We **could** leave after 2:30. (This is a possibility.)
may
might

We **had better** leave after 2:30. (This is advisable.)
ought to
should

We **must**   leave in the morning. (This is a necessity.)
have to

We **shall** leave in the morning. (This is an intention.)
will

We **would** leave every morning at 8:30. (This is a past habit.)

Modals have many meanings. Here are some special meanings you should know.

Must
I'm completely lost. I **must** have taken a wrong turn at the traffic light.
That man **must** be the new president.

In these sentences "must" is used to show that an assumption is being made. When the assumption concerns a past action, it is always followed by "have."

Cannot/Could Not
You **can't** be hungry. We just ate!
He **couldn't** have taken the book. I had it with me.

In these sentences "cannot" and "couldn't have" indicate impossibility.

5. Is the sentence passive or active?

An active sentence focuses on the person or thing doing the action. A passive sentence focuses on the person or thing affected by the action.

Examples   The tower was built at the turn of the century.   (Someone built the tower.)
Rebecca had been given the assignment.   (Someone gave the assignment to Rebecca.)

The passive voice is formed by the verb "be" in the appropriate tense followed by the past participle of the verb.

Examples

	Active	**Passive**
Present	My brother **washes** our car every weekend.	Our car **is washed** every weekend.
Present continuous	My brother **is washing** our car.	Our car **is being washed.**
Simple past	My brother **washed** our car yesterday.	Our car **was washed** yesterday.
Past perfect	My brother **had** just **washed** our car before it rained.	Our car **had** just **been washed** before it rained.

6. Is the verb in the correct word order?

(A) The following aux-words (helping words) are used in Yes/No questions and *Wh-* questions.

AUX-WORDS					
Present	**Past**	**Present**	**Past**	**Present**	**Past**
will can may must	would could might	have/has do/does	had did	is/am/are shall	was/were should

Examples   Where **did** Al buy his camera?
Should I mention the problems involved?

(B) The negative is formed by adding the word "not" or the ending "n't" after the first aux-word.

> I **cannot** go home.
> We **had not** gone to the shop.
> They **aren't** going with us.

(C) The verbs "do," "have," and "will" should not be confused with the aux-words "do," "have," and "will."

Verbs	**Aux-words**
I **do** my homework right after class.	**Do** you take the bus?
The Adamses **have** an electric typewriter.	They **have** worked for us for many years.
My grandfather **willed** us his fortune.	I **will** bring my suit to the convention.

7. Is the verb in the correct form?

(A) Verbs may be confused with the forms of other words. Notice how the word "mechanize" changes form.

Verb form	The owners are going to **mechanize** the factory.
Noun form	The **mechanization** of the factory will take place in the near future.
Adjective form	**Mechanical** devices will be installed to do the work.
Adverb form	They are going to hire **mechanically** minded personnel.

(B) Verb forms may be confused with other verb forms.

Although the regular past tense uses an -ed ending, there are many irregular forms in English. It is important to know the past forms and past participle forms of irregular verbs for the TOEFL.

> I walk**ed** to the library. (regular)
> I **came** back by bus. (irregular)

8. Are infinitives used correctly?

An infinitive is a verbal formed with "to" and the base form of the verb. It can be used as a noun, an adverb, or adjective.

> **To eat** is a necessity. (noun)
> I came home **to change**. (adverb)
> He always has money **to spend**. (adjective)

(A) The following verbs can be followed by an infinitive:

afford	consent	hope	prepare	swear
agree	decide	intend	pretend	threaten
appear	demand	learn	promise	tend
arrange	deserve	manage	refuse	try
ask	desire	mean	regret	volunteer
attempt	expect	need	seem	wait
beg	fail	offer	struggle	want
care	forget	plan	strive	wish
claim	hesitate			

Examples   We *agreed* **to go** to the movies.
Emma couldn't *afford* **to buy** the ring.
Terry *volunteered* **to work** on the committee.

(B) The following adjectives can be followed by an infinitive:

anxious	difficult	hard	ready
boring	eager	pleased	strange
common	easy	prepared	usual
dangerous	good		

Examples   I am *anxious* **to hear** from him.
We were *ready* **to leave** in a hurry.
It is *dangerous* **to smoke** near gasoline.

(C) The following verbs can be followed by a noun or pronoun and an infinitive:

advise	convince	force	order	teach
allow	dare	hire	permit	tell
ask	encourage	instruct	persuade	urge
beg	expect	invite	remind	want
cause	forbid	need	require	warn
challenge				

Examples   He *advised* **me to buy** a newer car.
I *persuaded* **my father to lend** me the money.
They *hired* **Sam to trim** the trees.

9. Are gerunds used correctly?

A gerund is formed by adding *-ing* to the base form of the verb. It is used as a noun.

Examples   **Swimming** is healthy for you. (subject)
You should try **studying** more. (object)
He was suspected of **cheating**. (object of the preposition)

(A) The following verbs can be followed by a gerund:

admit	deny	postpone	resist
advise	discuss	practice	resume
anticipate	enjoy	quit	risk
appreciate	finish	recall	suggest
avoid	keep	recommend	tolerate
can't help	mention	regret	try
consider	mind	report	understand
delay	miss	resent	

Examples   We *appreciated* his **giving** us the car.
I *finished* **writing** the report.
Lou *enjoys* **playing** tennis on weekends.

(B) Some two-word verbs can be followed by gerunds.

aid in	depend on	put off
approve of	give up	rely on
be better off	insist on	succeed in
call for	keep on	think about
confess to	look forward to	think of
count on	object to	worry about

Examples   You can *count on* his **being** there.
I *keep on* **forgetting** her name.
Sam *confessed to* **eating** all the cookies.

(C) Some adjectives + prepositions can be followed by gerunds.

accustomed to	intent on
afraid of	interested in
capable of	successful in
fond of	tired of

Examples   Sue is *accustomed to* **working** long hours.
Edward is *interested in* **becoming** an artist.
I am *afraid of* **catching** another cold.

(D) Some nouns + prepositions can be followed by gerunds.

choice of	method of/for
excuse for	possibility of
intention of	reason for

Examples   I have no *intention of* **driving** to Nevada.
Sean had a good *excuse for* **arriving** late.
There is a *possibility of* **flying** to Cyprus.

10. Are the infinitives and gerunds interchangeable?

(A) Some verbs can be followed by either an infinitive or gerund without a difference in meaning.

begin	dread	love
can't stand	hate	prefer
continue	like	start

Examples   I *hate* **to go** shopping.
I *hate* **going** shopping.

(B) Some verbs can be followed by either an infinitive or gerund, but there is a difference in meaning.

forget	remember	stop

Examples   I *stopped* **to buy** tomatoes.
(I stopped at the store and bought tomatoes.)

I *stopped* **buying** tomatoes.
(I no longer buy tomatoes.)

11. Are adjectives that are formed from verbs used correctly?

The adjective takes the present participle form when describing the "actor" and the past participle form when describing the "receiver."

Examples

The teacher	bores	the student.
(the actor)	(the action)	(the acted upon)

The teacher is do**ing** the action. Therefore, the teacher is bor**ing**.

The **boring** teacher put the student to sleep.

The student is act**ed** upon. Therefore, the student is bor**ed**.

The **bored** student was sleeping in class.

Other verbs used as adjectives:

amaze	depress	exhaust	satisfy
amuse	disgust	fascinate	shock
annoy	embarrass	frighten	terrify
astonish	excite	horrify	worry
confuse			

Use Exercises S26–S32 to develop your skills in identifying and using verbs on the TOEFL.

Exercise S26   ***Focusing on verbs***

Underline the complete verb in the independent clause. (See page 176 for clause information.)

Example   The unassembled and conveniently packed furniture <u>can be carried</u> home by customers.

You should underline "can be carried" because this is the verb (passive voice).

1. The actors bounce onto the stage, toss each other into the air, and roll on the mats.

2. The heavy swells and stiff winds of the Indian Ocean caused problems for the inexperienced crew.

3. The temperature dropped down to –30 degrees Fahrenheit, and a gale-force wind blew snow across the fields.

4. It would have been easier for the team to postpone the game than to continue in the rain.

5. Fingerprints might have proved that the suspect was at the scene of the crime.

6. Her father was a renowned historian, and her mother wrote children's stories.

7. The robots grasp, fasten, and paint the parts that are too dangerous for humans to handle.

8. What can be done for the refugees is being financed through government funds.

Answers to Exercise S26 are on page 454.

Exercise S27   **Recognizing the passive and active voices**

Write "A" if the sentence is in the active voice and "P" if the sentence is in the passive voice.

Examples   *A*   Flanders borders the sea and is mostly flat plain with sandy beaches.

P   When the Eiffel Tower was first built, it was considered a monstrosity.

1. _____ The traffic situation had become so difficult that the authorities decided to change the roads in the downtown area to one-way.

2. _____ Almost a century after his death, Horatio Alger Jr. is still associated with hardworking poor boys achieving success.

3. _____ As a result of the deforestation, irrigation ditches are in danger of silting up and the plains are vulnerable to flooding.

4. _____ The men who had put on at least 15 pounds since graduation lived longer than those who had gained less.

5. _____ J. Paul Getty, once the richest American, was buried near the Getty Museum in Malibu.

6. _____ The committee's members had finished discussing the issue by the time the vice president arrived.

7. _____ Fast food restaurants have been established in almost every country in the world.

8. _____ The spacecraft was designed, built, and equipped under the supervision of scientists from ten nations.

Answers to Exercise S27 are on page 454.

Exercise S28   *Checking verb tense*

If the underlined verb tense is incorrect, write the correct tense in the blank.

Example   Yesterday Sam <u>will be seen</u> on a bicycle.

was seen

1. The people <u>were resettled</u> outside the park boundaries.

_____

2. Suburbs <u>harbor</u> an extraordinary variety of birds, insects, plants, and animals since the urban sprawl began.

_____

3. Aerial photography <u>will</u> recently and unexpectedly <u>revealed</u> many historical sites.

_____

4. Electricity using superconductivity <u>can travel</u> farther with greater efficiency.

_____

5. Navigational errors <u>have been</u> now almost a thing of the past.

_____

6. Today neurochips <u>are being designed</u> for processing many tracks at once.

_____

7. In the future we <u>may have been measuring</u> movements on Earth's crust that are undetectable today.

_____

8. Mice with disorders similar to human diseases <u>have been grown</u> from genetically engineered mouse cells.

_____

Answers to Exercise S28 are on page 454.

Exercise S29   *Checking subject-verb agreement*

Write "C" (correct) if the verb agrees with the subject. Write "I" (incorrect) if the verb does not agree with the subject.

Example   ___I___   They was going to the movies.

1. _____   The difference between the living conditions in the countryside and in towns has been eliminated.

2. _____   A reorganization of the brain cells occurs during adolescence.

3. _____   The radiation levels from a computer display terminal is well below presently accepted standards of exposure.

4. _____   The tropical fish were transferred to another department.

5. _____   Mathematics are important for those students studying physics.

6. _____   Pollution together with water erosion is taking its toll on the buildings.

7. _____   A picnic in the park and a visit to the National Museum is planned for the tour group.

8. _____ That species of butterfly are commonly seen in many parts of North and South America.

Answers to Exercise S29 are on page 455.

Exercise S30 **Checking verb form**

If the underlined verb in the following sentences is incorrect, write the correct form.

Example Yesterday I <u>beginned</u> a new book.
began

You should write "began" in the space because the past tense of "begin" is irregular.

1. The word "comet" <u>comes</u> from the Greek adjective *kometes*, which means "wearing long hair."

   _____

2. The mythical hero Orpheus once <u>haunted</u> the pine forests of the legendary Rhodopes.

   _____

3. Alpine meadows <u>be</u> a tranquil sight.

   _____

4. The guide <u>speaked</u> of the fortress's glorious past.

   _____

5. The content of fluorine in mineral water <u>mades</u> it an excellent prophylactic agent against tooth decay.

   _____

6. The exiles <u>longed</u> to return to their native land.

   _____

7. Construction on the street network <u>begun</u> in 1989.

   _____

8. International, political, and cultural forums <u>are holded</u> throughout the year at the new convention center.

   _____

9. At the foot of the Tetons <u>lies</u> the oldest mountain resort in Wyoming.

   _____

10. The main street of the village <u>dates</u> back to the fourth century B.C.

   _____

Answers to Exercise S30 are on page 455.

Exercise S31 **Checking infinitive and gerunds**

Circle the letter of the word or phrase that correctly completes the sentence.

Example Would you consider ----- that car if it had better mileage statistics?
(A) to buy
(B) buying

1. The environmentalists hope ----- the forest to its former condition.
   (A) to restore
   (B) restoring

2. Some of the old members were persuaded ----- on the club constitution.
   (A) to work
   (B) working

3. The lynx carefully avoided ----- near the trap.
   (A) to go
   (B) going

4. You should postpone ----- the manager until we hear the outcome of tomorrow's meeting.
   (A) to see
   (B) seeing

5. In the lecture the professor mentioned ----- to Africa to collect a rare species of butterfly.
   (A) to travel
   (B) traveling

6. Alexander Pushkin managed ----- great stories despite being surrounded by spies and censored by the tsar.
   (A) to write
   (B) writing

7. I contemplated ----- Austria for my vacation but decided against it.
   (A) to visit
   (B) visiting

8. The delegates discussed ----- the annual conference in New York City.
   (A) to have
   (B) having

Answers to Exercise S31 are on page 455.

Exercise S32   *Completing the sentence*

Circle the letter of the verb that correctly completes the sentence.

Example   The girl, smiling broadly, ----- the podium.
   (A) approaching
   (B) approached
   (C) approach
   (D) had been approached

1. In 1970, the Canadian scientist George Kell ----- that warm water freezes more quickly than cold water.
   (A) proved
   (B) proving
   (C) proves
   (D) prove

2. The rebuilding of the Inca capital Cuzco was ----- in the 1460s.
   (A) begun
   (B) beginning
   (C) began
   (D) begin

3. Only through diplomatic means can a formal agreement be -----.
   (A) reach
   (B) to reach
   (C) reaching
   (D) reached

4. People have been ----- exorcists with increasing frequency over the last three years.
   (A) summoned
   (B) summoning
   (C) summons
   (D) summon

5. The film processing company has ----- a means of developing the 62-year-old film that might solve the mystery.
   (A) devising
   (B) devised
   (C) been devised
   (D) devise

6. Platinum ----- a rare and valuable metal, white in color, and next to silver and gold, the easiest to shape.
   (A) is
   (B) was
   (C) has been
   (D) be

7. A great deal of thought has ----- into the designing of a concert hall.
   (A) went
   (B) going
   (C) to go
   (D) been gone

8. The healthful properties of fiber have ----- for years.
   (A) known
   (B) be knowing
   (C) knew
   (D) been known

9. The vessel that sank may ----- the gold and jewels from the dowry of Catherine of Aragon.
(A) carry
(B) be carried
(C) have to carry
(D) have been carrying

10. Galileo ----- his first telescope in 1609.
(A) builds
(B) built
(C) building
(D) were built

Answers to Exercise S32 are on page 455.

PRACTICE WITH SUBJECT/AUX-WORD INVERSIONS

The order of the subject and the auxiliary word (aux-word) or verb can be changed in various situations. Ask yourself these questions when checking changes in word order.

1. Has the word order been changed to make a question?

(A) In a statement, the subject is followed by the verb.

S AUX V
She has seen the Grand Canyon.

___S___ V
The boxes are on the table.

(B) In a question, the subject follows the aux-word or verb.

AUX S V
Have you seen the Grand Canyon?

V ___S___
Where are the boxes?

(C) An aux-word is used in a question except when the main verb is "be." An aux-word can be understood or used in a statement.

Do you live in a small town?   ("Do" is the aux-word.)
I live in a small town.   ("Do" is understood.)
I do live in a small town.   ("Do" can be used in statements for emphasis.)

2. Has the word order been changed to avoid repetition?

Examples

Jane works at Spencer Motors, and Bill works at Spencer Motors.
Jane works at Spencer Motors and **so does Bill.**

Jane isn't working on Saturday, and Bill isn't working on Saturday.
Jane isn't working on Saturday and **neither is Bill.**

3. Has the word order been changed because the statement begins with a prepositional phrase of location?

Example

_____S_____ V
Austin, Texas, lies at the edge of the Hill Country.

V _____S_____
At the edge of the Hill Country **lies Austin, Texas.**

4. Has the word order been changed because the conditional "if" has been omitted?

Example   **If I had gone** to the post office, I would have bought stamps.
           Had I gone to the post office, I would have bought stamps.

5. Has the word order been changed because the statement begins with a negative word or phrase?

These words and phrases are followed by a change in word order when they begin a sentence or an independent clause:

hardly ever	on no account
neither	only
never	only by
no sooner . . . than	only in this way
nor	only then
not often	rarely
not once	scarcely
not only . . . as well	scarcely . . . when
not only . . . but also	seldom
not until	so
nowhere	under no circumstances

Examples

     S   V
Mary *not only* **works** at the post office *but* she *also* works at the grocery store.

        AUX   S   V
Not only **does Mary work** at the post office, *but* she *also* works at the grocery store.

     S   V
Max *never* **bought** another motorcycle again.

        AUX   S   V
Never again **did Max buy** another motorcycle.

               S   AUX   V
Mark won't like that bread, and **he won't like** that cheese.

               AUX S   V
Mark won't like that bread *nor* **will he like** that cheese.

Use Exercises S33–S36 to develop your skills in identifying word order changes you may encounter on the TOEFL.

Exercise S33   ***Identifying words and phrases that cause a change in word order***

Underline the word or phrase in each sentence that causes a change in word order.

Example   <u>Seldom</u> does Amanda buy a newspaper.

You should underline "seldom" because it has a negative meaning, which causes a change in word order when it comes at the beginning of a sentence or independent clause.

1. Rarely are people given permission to return to homes contaminated during a toxic waste accident.

2. On no account should the photocopy machines in the office be used for personal materials.

3. Only if I had known the difference would I have bought the more expensive camera.

4. Not until next year will the new tax change take place.

5. Not only was he driving too fast, but recklessly as well.

6. No sooner had the administration announced the policy change than the students began their protest.

7. Nowhere had the explorers been met with more hospitality than in the Nepalese village.

8. So incredible were explorer John Colter's descriptions of the Yellowstone area that people didn't believe in its existence.

Answers to Exercise S33 are on page 456.

Exercise S34   ***Locating inversions***

Underline the subject, aux-word, and verb that have been inverted in each sentence.

                                    AUX   **S**   **V**

Example   Only once a day <u>does Mildred leave</u> the house.

1. Had the drought not lowered the reservoir, the ancient village would not have been discovered.

2. Under no circumstances should the staff members' telephone numbers be given out.

3. Coffee contains caffeine, and so does tea.

4. Not until you've had a medical checkup should you start the exercise program.

5. Only when the institute is given funding will they be able to continue their research.

6. The letter was not mailed in time, and neither was the package.

7. Should an emergency arise, call 911.

8. On the island remains the only representation of the Indians' handicraft.

Answers to Exercise S34 are on page 456.

Exercise S35   ***Correcting word order***

Rewrite the sentence if the word order is incorrect.

Example   Not often a Rembrandt is stolen.
           Not often is a Rembrandt stolen.

1. In either case, we must report the accident to the police.

2. Not only before exercising one should stretch but after exercising as well.

3. North of Winona, Minnesota, lies Lake City, which is considered the official "birthplace" of waterskiing.

_____

4. Driving through downtown Houston during rush hour is difficult, as is parking there.

_____

5. A dry, cold climate is not suitable for beautiful skin, and neither a hot climate is.

_____

6. Only in 1865 were antiseptics first used.

_____

7. Not only swallows build their nests inside farm buildings, but do sparrows as well.

_____

8. Should you be bitten or stung by a venomous creature, you must call an ambulance immediately.

_____

Answers to Exercise S35 are on page 456.

Exercise S36   *Completing the sentence*

Circle the letter of the answer that correctly completes the sentence.

Example   ----- has the work been so easy.
  (A) Only by
  (B) Never

1. ----- after years of planning did the project get underway.
   (A) Seldom
   (B) Only

2. ----- should the expense of the new bridge be considered a problem.
   (A) Scarcely
   (B) Nor

3. ----- had the restaurant opened than people were flocking to eat there.
   (A) No sooner
   (B) Nowhere

4. ----- should a young child be allowed to play with fireworks without parental supervision.
   (A) Under no circumstances
   (B) No sooner than

5. ----- have playing cards been used for card games but also for fortune-telling.
   (A) Not as much
   (B) Not only

6. ----- will the emperor penguin leave its nest before the chick hatches.
   (A) Not once
   (B) Not until

7. ----- intensive research can a vaccine for the virus be found.
   (A) Only when
   (B) Only through

8. ----- are the autumn colors so splendid as in New England.
   (A) Only
   (B) Nowhere

Answers to Exercise S36 are on page 456.

CHECK YOUR PROGRESS

Check your progress in using the skills you have been practicing in Exercises S26–S36 by completing the following mini-test. This exercise uses the same format as questions 1–15 of the Structure and Written Expression section on the TOEFL.

Exercise S37   *Mini-test*   *(Time – 10 minutes)*

Directions: Questions 1–15 are incomplete sentences. Beneath each sentence you will see four words or phrases marked (A), (B), (C), and (D). Choose the <u>one</u> word or phrase that best completes the sentence. Then circle the letter that corresponds to the answer you have chosen.

Example   Samuel Pepys's *Diary* ----- eyewitness descriptions of the Great Plague and the Fire of London.
    (A) was contained
    (B) has been containing
    (C) contains
    (D) is containing

You should circle (C), "contains," which is a verb in the simple present tense. Since the book continues to exist, it still contains this information.

1. Potatoes and onions ----- from sprouting by a new technology using radiation.
    (A) are preventing
    (B) prevention is
    (C) are prevented
    (D) prevented

2. Only if ----- will proper labeling be essential.
    (A) the law is changed
    (B) is changed the law
    (C) is the law changed
    (D) the law being changed

3. The sulky, a horsedrawn carriage, ----- to have been invented in the early nineteenth century by an English physician.
    (A) believed
    (B) was believing
    (C) is believed
    (D) is believing

4. ----- a herd of horses on Assateague Island.
    (A) The pirate Blackbeard reputedly left
    (B) The pirate Blackbeard reputedly leaving
    (C) Had the pirate Blackbeard reputedly left
    (D) No sooner did the pirate Blackbeard reputedly leave

5. Lack of exercise and high-fat diets have ----- to be factors in heart attacks.
    (A) long been known
    (B) been long known
    (C) known been long
    (D) long known been

6. ----- the water clear but also prevent the river from overflowing.
    (A) Not only the hippo's eating habits keep
    (B) Keep not only the hippo's eating habits
    (C) The hippo's eating habits not only keep
    (D) Not only keep the hippo's eating habits

7. Not until 1865 ----- the first antiseptic treatment on a compound fracture.
   (A) when Joseph Lister tried
   (B) when did Joseph Lister try
   (C) did Joseph Lister try
   (D) that Joseph Lister tried

8. At each end of the tube -----, one which gathers light and one which magnifies the image.
   (A) are two lenses there
   (B) two lenses are
   (C) are two lenses
   (D) two lenses are there

9. When ----- into the Colorado wilderness, no one could have predicted how popular the animal would become.
   (A) llamas first bring
   (B) were llamas first brought
   (C) first bringing llamas
   (D) llamas were first brought

10. Centuries ago, ----- known source of frankincense and myrrh was Yemen.
    (A) not only
    (B) the only
    (C) only
    (D) only the

11. Noise pollution generally receives less attention than ----- air pollution.
    (A) does
    (B) it does
    (C) over
    (D) it does over

12. During the investigations, those questioned included ----- top officials, but also the minor employees who carried out the orders.
    (A) when
    (B) both
    (C) without
    (D) not only

13. Putrefaction ----- by bacteria and not by a chemical process.
    (A) to be caused
    (B) causing
    (C) caused
    (D) is caused

14. West of Newport -----, one of the many mansions surrounded by acres of gardens.
    (A) where the Aston stately home stands
    (B) the stately home stands of Aston
    (C) the stately home of Aston stands
    (D) stands the stately Aston home

15. In the Sonora desert, the daytime temperatures ----- to 50 degrees Celsius.
    (A) rise
    (B) rising
    (C) to rise
    (D) risen

Answers to Exercise S37 are on page 456.

PRACTICE WITH WORD FORMS

Ask yourself these questions when checking word forms.

1. Is the word a noun, a verb, an adjective, or an adverb?

A word may have one or more related forms. Notice how the word "decide" changes form.

Nouns	The **decision** was made months ago.
Verbs	We **decided** to move to a larger house.
Adjectives	His **decisive** action brought order to the meeting.
Adverbs	She acted very **decisively**.

2. Is the word in its correct position?

(A) Nouns are in the following positions (see Practice with Nouns, 5, page 116):

As subjects	The **doctor** came immediately.
As complements	My mother is a **doctor**.
As objects	We saw the **doctor**.
	The nurse gave the file to the **doctor**.
	The nurse stood beside the **doctor**.

(B) Verbs are used to express the action of the subject (see Practice with Verbs, 7, page 147).

> Linda **ran** all the way to the bus stop.
> Paul **rented** a tuxedo.

(C) Adjectives are words that modify (describe) the noun.

Adjectives have only one form, which is used with singular and plural nouns.

> The **heavy** book was difficult for the **little** boy to carry.
> The **old** man was carrying a **brown paper** sack.

To check if a word is an adjective, the question "what kind of" can be asked.

> I was **sad** because I lost my **lace** handkerchief.

"What kind of person was I?" – sad. "What kind of handkerchief was it?" – lace. Therefore, "sad" and "lace" are adjectives.

(D) Adverbs modify verbs, adverbs, and adjectives.

>   **V**   **ADV**
> The soldier fought **bravely**.

>   **ADV** **ADJ**
> I am **very** fond of toffee.

>   **ADV** **ADV**
> Jack ran very **swiftly**.

To check if a word is an adverb, the questions "how," "when," "where," and "how often" can be asked.

> The boy skipped **happily** along the road.

"How did the boy skip?" – happily. Therefore, "happily" is an adverb.

> I went **outside**.

"Where did I go?" – outside. Therefore, "outside" is an adverb.

Adverbs can be used in many different positions in the sentence.

Frequently I eat out.
I **frequently** eat out.
I eat out **frequently**.

Most adverbs are formed by adding *-ly* to the adjective form.

Examples

ADJ	ADJ
He was a **brave** soldier.	She is a **competent** truck driver.
ADV	**ADV**
He fought **bravely**.	She drives trucks **competently**.

Some adverbs and adjectives have the same form.

deep	hard	late	low
early	high	leisurely	much
far	kindly	little	near
fast			

The adverb forms "highly," "lowly," "deeply," "nearly," "hardly," and "lately" exist, but they have different meanings than the adverb form without *-ly*.

Examples

ADV
The seagull soared **high** above the rocks. (*"Where* did the seagull fly?" – A long way above the rocks.)

ADV
The people spoke **highly** of their governor. (*"How* did the people speak?" – Favorably, or with praise.)

The adverbs "warmly," "hotly," "coolly," "coldly," "presently," "shortly," "scarcely," and "barely" have different meanings than their adjective forms.

Examples

ADJ
It was a **hot** day.   (The temperature was high.)

ADV
They debated the issue **hotly**.   (They showed strong emotions during the debate.)

3. Do the word endings (suffixes) help identify the word forms?

The employ**er**'s enthusi**asm** infect**ed** all the employ**ees**.

-er, -or, and *-ee* are endings used for people.
-ism and *-asm* are endings used for nouns.
-ed is an ending for verbs and adjectives.

Look at the chart on page 163 for endings that can help you identify word forms.

Nouns	Verbs	Adjectives	Adverbs
-acy (-cy)			
-age			
-al		-al (-ial, -ical)	
-ance (-ence)			
-ant (-ent)		-ant (-ent)	
-ate	-ate	-ate	
-ation			
-dom			
-ee			
-eer			
-en	-en	-en	
-er, (-or)			
-ese		-ese	
-ess (-tress)			
-ful		-ful	
-hood			
-ian (-an)		-ian	
-ia			
-ic (-ics)		-ic	
-id			
-ide			
-in (-ine)			
-ing	-ing	-ing	
-ion			
-ism			
-ist			
-ite			
-ity			
-let (-lette)			
-ling			
-ment			
-ness			
-ocracy			
-ry (-ary, -ery)			
-ship			
-ster			
-tive			
-y (-ie)			
	-ed	-y	
	-er	-ed	
	-ify	-er	
	-ize		
		-able (-ible)	
		-ile	
		-ish	
		-ive (-ative, -itive)	
		-less	
		-like	
		-ly	-ly
		-ous (-eous, -ious)	
			-wards
			-wise

Use Exercises S38–S43 to develop your skills in identifying the correct word forms and their positions.

Exercise S38 **Identifying suffixes**

Identify the following as a noun (N), a verb (V), an adjective (ADJ), or an adverb (ADV) by the word ending.

Example ___N___ department

You should write "N" in the space because the ending -ment indicates a noun.

1. _____ perfectionist
2. _____ energetic
3. _____ childhood
4. _____ fantasize
5. _____ graceful
6. _____ eagerly
7. _____ allowance
8. _____ suitable

9. _____ ability
10. _____ hasten
11. _____ sponsorship
12. _____ jovial
13. _____ commemorate
14. _____ publicly
15. _____ happiness

Answers to Exercise S38 are on page 457.

Exercise S39 **Identifying functions**

Identify the underlined word as a noun (N), a verb (V), an adjective (ADJ), or an adverb (ADV). Use word endings as clues.

Example ___N___ <u>Anger</u> was voiced against the installation of nuclear missiles.

1. _____ The Portuguese used to trade <u>extensively</u> with Bahrain in centuries past.

2. _____ Confirmation of the <u>successful</u> maneuvers of *Voyager 2* was not expected for several hours.

3. _____ The censorship committee <u>threatened</u> to take action against five publishing companies.

4. _____ The number of children per <u>household</u> has been steadily declining.

5. _____ From the <u>practical</u> point of view, one map system is as good as another.

6. _____ Marie Curie was the first <u>scientist</u> to win two Nobel Prizes in science.

7. _____ The entire business has been <u>computerized</u> for over two years.

8. _____ The streets of desert towns were <u>purposely</u> made narrow to provide the maximum amount of shade.

9. _____ There were two courtyards in the house, one for reception and the other for <u>private</u> use.

10. _____ The book is well illustrated and appears to be <u>extremely</u> comprehensive.

Extended practice: Write the other forms for the underlined words and use them in sentences.

Answers to Exercise S39 are on page 457.

Exercise S40 **Checking noun forms**

If the underlined word is not in noun form, write the noun form.

Example The <u>explore</u> lasted six months and brought the team into many dangerous situations.

exploration

1. Not even death is beyond the realm of <u>commercialism</u>.

2. The <u>restore</u> of the old fort was completed over a year ago.

3. In 1975, the Ames test implicated <u>peroxide</u> in hair dyes as a cancer agent.

4. The worshipers find <u>tranquil</u> in the great cool room.

5. Their insomnia was not caused by the high altitude but by the <u>exciting</u>.

6. The introduction of new <u>various</u> of apples and other crops has increased farm yield.

7. Transport has been the major <u>impede</u> to development in the area.

8. <u>Smoke</u> that escapes from a burning cigarette can be dangerous for bystanders.

9. <u>Immigrated</u> from a wide variety of countries have given the United States cultural diversity.

10. Low <u>employee</u> among the young is being blamed for the rise in vandalism.

Answers to Exercise S40 are on page 457.

Exercise S41 **Checking verb forms**

If the underlined word is not in verb form, write the verb form.

1. Roaches <u>tolerant</u> and even thrive in climatic extremes.

2. Many farmers <u>fertilize</u> their crops with fish emulsion and cattle manure.

3. Each year bees <u>pollinate</u> about three billion dollars' worth of bee-dependent crops.

4. Thirty centuries ago Phoenicians were the first to <u>establishment</u> colonies on the coast of modern-day Tunisia.

5. The container, which was <u>fashioned</u> from a skull, is for ceremonial offerings.

6. The painting <u>symbols</u> the impermanence of the body.

7. The old man <u>explanation</u> his life as one of the nine monks in the monastery.

8. The lake provides recreation for the multitudes who <u>patronize</u> the tourist facilities.

9. Many cultures still dramatically <u>verbal</u> their pasts in song.

_____

10. Bold steps have <u>improved</u> the economy.

_____

Answers to Exercise S41 are on page 457.

Exercise S42   Checking adjective forms

If the underlined word is not in adjective form, write the adjective form.

1. Our previous supervisor had better <u>organizational</u> skills.

_____

2. Ranchers joined with state and federal governments in a <u>cooperate</u> control program.

_____

3. In the theocracy that evolved in Tibet, religious and <u>administrative</u> power centered in one person.

_____

4. The Musin-Puskin collection features many rare and unknown works of <u>historically</u> interest.

_____

5. The sacred mountain draws pilgrims who offer thanks for the bountiful and <u>beauty</u> land.

_____

6. Butch Cassidy was an outlaw <u>fame</u> for robbing trains.

_____

7. The <u>deerlike</u> figures found in the Grand Canyon were made from willow shoots and have been dated as far back as 2100 B.C.

_____

8. The lands are available to people only for <u>tradition</u> purposes.

_____

9. Techniques such as <u>aerial</u> stereographic photography yield most of the detail on a map.

_____

10. The <u>bury</u> place of the Macedonian king was unplundered.

_____

Answers to Exercise S42 are on page 457.

Exercise S43   Checking adverb forms

If the underlined word is not in adverb form, write the adverb form.

1. Pesticides are necessary to maintain high crop yields in a world with a decreasing acreage of arable land and a <u>steadily</u> expanding population.

_____

2. Millions of dollars are donated <u>year</u> to the Red Cross to aid people in disaster-struck areas.

_____

3. Scientists can observe a chemical's effect in rats and reasonable expect a like effect in humans.

_____

4. In communes. the land and products are collective owned.

_____

5. The mildly paranoid person may lead a relatively normal life.

_____

6. In early American colonial settlements secular education was virtual nonexistent.

_____

7. While undeniable appealing, burros have also been destructive.

_____

8. The anthropologist unearthed rows of large stones, clearly the foundation of another building.

_____

9. Because of his family ties, he frequent came back to the town.

_____

10. The departure appears to have taken place hastily.

_____

Answers to Exercise S43 are on page 457.

PRACTICE WITH WORD CHOICES

The following words are frequently seen on the TOEFL Test.

    and, or, but
    either . . . or, neither . . . nor, both . . . and
    so, as, such as
    too, enough, so
    many, much, few, little
    like, alike, unlike
    another, the others, other, others

Ask yourself the following questions when you encounter these words.

1. Have the words "and," "or," and "but" been used correctly?

(A) "And" joins two or more words, phrases, or clauses of similar value or equal importance.

    We went swimming **and** boating.
    We looked in the house **and** around the yard for the lost necklace.
    We booked the flight, **and** we picked up the tickets the same day.

When "and" joins two equal subjects, the verb must be plural.

    Swimming **and** boating *are* fun.

(B) "Or" joins two or more words, phrases, or clauses that contain the idea of a choice.

    We could go swimming **or** boating.
    We could look in the house **or** around the yard for the lost necklace.
    We could book the flight now, **or** we could wait until tomorrow.

(C) "But" shows a contrast between two or more words, phrases, or clauses.

> We went swimming **but** not boating.
> We didn't look in the house **but** around the yard for the lost necklace.
> We booked the flight, **but** we haven't picked up the tickets.

2. Have the words "either . . . or," "neither . . . nor," and "both . . . and" been used correctly?

(A) "Either" is used with "or" to express alternatives.

> We can **either** go to the park **or** stay home and watch TV.

(B) "Neither" is used with "nor" to express negative alternatives.

> He **neither** called **nor** came to visit me. (He didn't call, and he didn't visit me.)

(C) "Both" is used with "and" to combine two words, phrases, or clauses.

> He had **both** the time **and** the patience to be a good parent.

3. Have the words "so," "as," and "such as" been used correctly?

(A) "So" can connect two independent clauses. It means "therefore" or "as a result."

> She was hungry, **so** she ate early.

(B) "As" can be used to introduce an adverb clause. It can mean "while," "like," "because," "the way," or "since."

> **As** I understood it, Max was the winner. ("The way I understood it . . . ")
> It began to snow **as** I was walking. ("It began to snow while I was walking.")

(C) "Such as" is used to introduce examples.

> He likes to wear casual clothes, **such as** a T-shirt and blue jeans.

4. Have the words "too," "enough," and "so" been used correctly?

(A) "Too" means more than necessary. It precedes an adjective or adverb.

> The food was **too** cold to eat.
> He ran **too** slowly to win the race.

(B) "Enough" means a sufficient amount or number. It follows an adjective or adverb.

> The day was warm **enough** for a picnic.
> The girl swam fast **enough** to save her friend.

(C) "So" can be used in adverb clauses of cause/result before adverbs and adjectives. (The use of "that" in the examples below is optional.)

> The rain fell **so** hard (that) the river overflowed.
> The boy ate **so** many cookies (that) he got a stomachache.

5. Have the words "many," "much," "few," and "little" been used correctly?

(A) "Many" and "few" are used with count nouns.

> **Few** cities are as crowded as Tokyo.

(B) "Much" and "little" are used with noncount nouns.

> They have made **little** progress on the contract.

6. Have the words "like," "alike," and "unlike" been used correctly?

(A) When "like" is a preposition followed by an object, it means "similar."

Like my father, I am an architect.   ("My father is a architect, and I am one too.")

(B) "Unlike" is a preposition followed by an object and means "not similar."

Unlike my mother, her mother has a full-time job.   ("Her mother has a full-time job, but my mother does not.")

(C) "Alike" can be an adverb meaning "equally" or an adjective meaning "similar."

As an adverb   The tuition increase was opposed by students and teachers **alike**.
As an adjective   My brother and sister are **alike** in many ways.

7. Have the words "another," "the others," "other," and "others" been used correctly?

(A) "Another" + a singular noun means "one more."

I want **another** peach.
I want **another** one.

(B) "The other" + a singular noun means "the last of the group being discussed."

We bought three peaches. My brother and I each ate one. We left **the other** peach on the table.

(C) "The other" + a plural noun means "the rest of the group."

This peach is rotten, but **the other** peaches in the box are good.

(D) "The other" + a noncount noun means "all the rest."

We put the oranges in a bowl and stored **the other** fruit in the refrigerator.

(E) "Other" + a plural noun means "more of the group being discussed."

There are **other** peaches in the box.

(F) "Other" + a noncount noun means "more of the group."

There is **other** fruit besides peaches in the box.

8. Have any of the following words been used incorrectly?

able/enable
accept/except
after/afterwards
amounts/number/quantity
aside/beside/besides
big/great
do/make
live/life/alive
people/person
rather/rather than
separate/apart
some/somewhat

Check your dictionary to find the differences in the preceding list. Add more words as you find them in your studies.

Use Exercises S44–S51 to develop your skills in identifying the correct word choice.

Exercise S44   *Checking "and," "or," and "but"*

If the underlined word is used incorrectly, write the correction in the space.

Example   Alexander likes both apples or bananas.   ___and___

1. All but one of the fourteen colossal heads were toppled by earthquakes. _____

2. The eggs are boiled or then peeled. _____

3. New types of tomatoes have been developed that can resist high but low
   temperatures. _____

4. Istanbul is a city that spans two world cultures – the oriental and the
   occidental. _____

5. A fir tree or pine tree is most commonly used for Christmas trees. _____

6. The land provides people not only with food and clothing, and houses and buildings
   as well. _____

7. The new sports center will provide more opportunities for students but teachers alike.
   _____

8. What we saw was not a unique experience and an event of significance. _____

Answers to Exercise S44 are on page 457.

Exercise S45   *Checking "either . . . or," "neither . . . nor," and "both . . . and"*

If the underlined word is used incorrectly, write the correction in the space.

1. Antiochus I claimed descent from both Alexander the Great and the Persian monarch
   King Darius. _____

2. Neither the Mormon Trail or the Oregon Trail was easy to follow. _____

3. Goats provide both milk for cheese or wool for clothing. _____

4. When search parties failed to find the missing heir, Michael Rockefeller, authorities
   declared that he had both drowned or been eaten by sharks. _____

5. People think of voodoo as either an obscure ritual nor pure superstition.
   _____

6. In 1927, critics gave bad reviews to Buster Keaton's film *The General,* which is now
   regarded as both a classic or the best work of a cinematic genius. _____

7. The new park will have neither a marina and an aquarium. _____

8. The head of the Water Department said that either solar ponds nor desalination plants
   could provide all the needed water. _____

Answers to Exercise S45 are on page 457.

Exercise S46   ***Checking "so," "as," and "such as"***

If the underlined word or words are used incorrectly, write the correction in the space.

1. There are remains of Rajput art and architecture, <u>as</u> the cusped arches and traces of painting on the ceiling. _____

2. <u>As</u> Einstein suggested 70 years ago, space can vibrate. _____

3. Supernovas occur only once every few decades, <u>so</u> an instrument sensitive enough to detect such events is needed. _____

4. <u>Such as</u> rockets zoom around in space, technicians track their progress on computer terminals._____

5. Organisms respond to stimuli <u>so</u> pressure, light, and temperature. _____

6. During the American Revolution, people took part in subversive actions, <u>such as</u> the Boston Tea Party. _____

7. The hormone androvine acts <u>so</u> a painkiller and is six times as strong as morphine. _____

8. During a stroke, the blood flow to the heart is blocked <u>such as</u> the cells of the heart muscle die from the lack of oxygen. _____

Answers to Exercise S46 are on page 457.

Exercise S47   ***Checking "too," "enough," and "so"***

If the underlined word is used incorrectly, write the correction in the space.

1. The West was <u>so</u> dry, the wood shrank on the wagons. _____

2. The grip of the Venus-flytrap is <u>too</u> tight that an insect cannot escape from the leaf. _____

3. The revival of the ancient art of tapestry making has provided <u>too</u> jobs in the village for everyone. _____

4. The seven-gated city wall was once wide <u>so</u> to admit donkeys and carts. _____

5. The students were <u>too</u> eager to use the computers that they skipped their lunch break. _____

6. According to some ecologists, not <u>enough</u> is being done to save the whale from extinction. _____

7. Unfortunately <u>enough</u> many of the buildings have collapsed because of lack of maintenance. _____

8. If the eggs become <u>enough</u> warm, the chicks will not hatch. _____

Answers to Exercise S47 are on page 457.

Exercise S48   ***Checking "many," "much," "few," and "little"***

If the underlined word is used incorrectly, write the correction in the space.

1. Intergalactic adventures are what <u>many</u> of today's animation consists of.

   _____

2. <u>Little</u> scientists doubt the existence of an ozone hole over the polar regions.

   _____

3. Yachting attracts <u>many</u> of the world's most famous and wealthy people.

   _____

4. There are adult literacy classes for the workers, <u>much</u> of whom never graduated from

   high school. _____

5. The rhinoceros has <u>few</u> natural enemies. _____

6. The shark will eat anything from <u>little</u> fish to tin cans. _____

7. Heavy fines and jail sentences have made <u>few</u> difference in preventing antelope

   poaching. _____

8. Tropical fish and song birds give <u>many</u> pleasure to people who need to relax.

   _____

Answers to Exercise S48 are on page 457.

Exercise S49   ***Checking "like," "alike," and "unlike"***

If the underlined word is used incorrectly, write the correction in the space.

1. The Cannes Film Festival exists, <u>like</u> most film festivals, for the purpose of

   awarding prizes. _____

2. Identical twins are <u>like</u> in many ways and are often difficult to tell apart.

   _____

3. The harpsichord is a keyboard instrument <u>alike</u> the piano. _____

4. The Topkapi palace encompasses the forms of grand monuments and of vernacular

   styles <u>like</u>. _____

5. Occasionally dolphins, <u>like</u> whales, get stranded on beaches. _____

6. <u>Like</u> automobiles, which use a four-stroke engine, motorcycles use a two-stroke

   engine. _____

7. Many sailing techniques of today and those of centuries past are <u>alike</u>. _____

8. <u>Unlike</u> the coyote, which hunts in packs, the fox prefers to hunt alone. _____

Answers to Exercise S49 are on page 457.

Exercise S50   ***Checking "another," "the others," "other," and "others"***

If the underlined word or words are used incorrectly, write the correction in the space.

1. More people are involved in silk production than in any <u>another</u> activity in the village. _____

2. One of Mars's two moons is called Phobos and <u>other</u> is called Deimos. _____

3. Like most of <u>the other</u> language skills, reading requires practice. _____

4. Preserved in the shadows were bones, a skull, and <u>other</u> relics found when the building was erected. _____

5. Breathing into a paper bag is yet <u>others</u> cure for the hiccups. _____

6. Wool, as well as certain <u>other</u> fabrics, can cause skin irritation. _____

7. Some artists use traditional designs while <u>another</u> use more modern themes. _____

8. Western historians believe that the charges against Nikolay Bukharin and <u>another</u> old Bolsheviks were fraudulent. _____

Answers to Exercise S50 are on page 457.

Exercise S51   ***Checking frequently confused words***

Circle the underlined word which correctly completes the sentence.

Example   Alfred cut the photograph separate/apart.

1. Undersea cables <u>able/enable</u> people to telephone friends in other parts of the world.

2. Disney World has many robots that look <u>alive/life</u>.

3. Although fascinating, the book is <u>some/somewhat</u> depressing.

4. Satellites have made communication with other <u>person/people</u> fast and efficient.

5. A great <u>number/amount</u> of buffalo were shot from train windows in nineteenth-century America.

6. Humans <u>have done/have made</u> great advances in technology at the expense of the environment.

7. The American national symbol, the bald eagle, is <u>live /alive</u> and thriving in Alaska.

8. Ann set <u>aside/beside</u> 10 percent of her paycheck to buy a new car.

9. The Mayans' <u>observance/observation</u> of the heavenly bodies helped them make an accurate calendar.

10. The Rocky Mountains boast a large <u>number/quantity</u> of peaks over 10,000 feet high.

Answers to Exercise S51 are on page 458.

CHECK YOUR PROGRESS

Check your progress in using the skills you have been practicing in Exercises S38– S51 by completing the following mini-test. This exercise uses the same format as questions 16–40 of the Structure and Written Expression section on the TOEFL.

Exercise S52   **Mini-test**   *(Time – 15 minutes)*

Directions: In questions 1–25 each sentence has four underlined words or phrases. The four underlined parts of the sentence are marked (A), (B), (C), and (D). Identify the <u>one</u> underlined word or phrase that must be changed in order for the sentence to be correct. Then circle the letter that corresponds to the answer you have chosen.

Example   In medieval times <u>helmets</u> were <u>most</u> of metal and <u>varied</u> in shape from
                       A   B   C

    reign <u>to</u> reign.
        D

The underlined word "most" (B) should be in the adverb form "mostly."

1. The <u>earliest</u> references to Jericho <u>so</u> a city <u>date</u> back <u>several</u> thousand years.
       A   B   C   D

2. <u>Much</u> unknown plants and animals are disappearing <u>as</u> the <u>tropical</u> forests are
    A   B   C
    <u>destroyed</u>.
      D

3. <u>Wooden</u> in summer <u>grows</u> more <u>slowly</u> and is <u>darker</u>.
     A   B   C   D

4. Blowing out birthday candles is an <u>ancient</u> test to see if a <u>growing</u> child is
                                   A   B
    <u>enough strong</u> to blow out a greater <u>number</u> each year.
        C   D

5. <u>Cloudy</u> recorded in time lapses <u>moved</u> <u>counterclockwise</u> faster than <u>the</u> planet
     A   B   C   D
    rotated.

6. It is <u>the</u> dream of every <u>mountaineers</u> to climb the world's <u>highest</u> peak.
    A B   C   D

7. The caverns were <u>more exciting</u> before the <u>guides</u> came and took away the
    A   B   C
    <u>adventurously</u> aspect.
       D

8. The council set off <u>controversial</u> by its <u>strong</u> position on <u>wildlife</u> management.
    A   B   C   D

9. While <u>searching</u> for gold, the Spanish <u>found</u> the Grand Canyon <u>to be</u> an <u>impassably</u>
         A   B   C   D
    barrier.

10. The assassins hastily to hide the evidence against them.
         A   B   C   D

11. The figure was carved on a hillside enough that it could be seen from a distance of
                  A   B   C   D
    several miles.

12. In ancient Greek traditional, weapons and stable gear were placed upon the grave.
       A   B   C   D

13. During the bleak winter, food became too scarce that starvation and famine were
            A   B   C
    widespread.
      D

14. Transplanting organs such hearts and kidneys has proved easier than transplanting
          A   B   C
    muscles.
      D

15. The grenade is a small bomb done to be thrown by hand or shot from a modified
                   A   B C   D
    rifle.

16. There is not enough room in zoos to house all the others subspecies that need
            A   B   C
    preserving.
      D

17. The high cost of testing new pesticides inadvertently discourages the develop of
      A   B   C
    viruses, protozoa, bacteria, and molds for pest control.
                    D

18. The glider uses gravity to keeping flying and updrafts of air to gain altitude.
      A   B   C   D

19. A pure gold Islamic coin is expected to bring some between $8 million and
        A   B
    $10 million at the auction next week.
            C   D

20. Unlike a tractor is, a mule won't turn over on a steep hillside and crush the driver.
      A   B   C   D

21. The rattlesnake coils to able it to spring forward and strike its victim.
            A   B   C   D

22. Faint is not uncommon in elderly people who stand up suddenly.
      A   B   C   D

23. Bicyclists joy riding across country and through small towns.
      A B   C   D

24. He didn't <u>attend</u> to bring the <u>stack</u> of <u>papers</u> <u>home</u>.
             A   B   C   D

25. A <u>baby</u> elephant <u>sucks</u> its trunk <u>alike</u> a human baby sucks its <u>thumb</u>.
    A   B   C   D

Answers to Exercise S52 are on page 458.

PRACTICE WITH CLAUSES

A clause is a group of words that contains a subject and a verb. Ask yourself these questions when checking clauses.

1. Is the clause independent?

Independent clauses are complete sentences. They contain a subject and verb. Three different types of sentences contain independent clauses.

(A) Simple sentences.

Simple sentences are made up of one independent clause.

    S V
The cat ran.

                  S   **V**
Late last night the fat, black cat swiftly ran under the speeding blue sports car.

(B) Compound sentences.

Compound sentences are made up of two (or sometimes more) independent clauses that are joined by a conjunction (such as "and," "but," "or," "nor," and "yet").

    S V   **S V**
The cat ran **and** the dog chased it.

    S   **V**   **S**   **V**
Kelly wanted to take the geometry course, **but** it was offered at the same time as her biochemistry lab.

    S   **V**   **S**   **V**
We could trade in our old car, **or** we could keep it as a second car.

(C) Complex sentences.

Complex sentences are made up of one or more independent clauses and one or more dependent clauses. (A dependent clause is an incomplete sentence. It needs to be connected to an independent clause. See 2 on page 177.)

          DEPENDENT
    S ┌**CLAUSE**┐ **V**
The cat that I saw ran.

                    S ┌**DEPENDENT CLAUSE**┐   **V**
Last night the fat, black cat that I saw in the street swiftly ran under the speeding

                   ┌_____**DEPENDENT CLAUSE**_____┐
blue sports car as the big shaggy dog chased after it.

2. Is the clause dependent?

Dependent clauses have a subject and a verb, but they do not form complete sentences. They must be connected to an independent clause. Look at the following dependent clauses.

> that I saw
> as the dog played with it

Both of the clauses have a subject and a verb. However, they are not complete sentences.

> The TV program **that I saw** was interesting.

The sentence above is complete. The dependent clause "that I saw" has been connected to the independent clause "The TV program was interesting." The dependent clause gives further information; for example, it says who saw the TV program.

> The toy was torn to pieces **as the dog played with it.**

The sentence above is complete. The dependent clause "as the dog played with it" has been connected to the independent clause "The toy was torn to pieces." The dependent clause gives additional information; for example, it says *who* tore apart the toy (the dog) and *how* the toy was torn apart (the dog played with it).

There are three kinds of dependent clauses: noun clauses, adjective clauses, and adverb clauses. (For more information see Practice with Noun Clauses, page 179, Practice with Adjective Clauses, page 186, and Practice with Adverb Clauses, page 199.)

(A) Noun clauses, like nouns, can be used in any noun position (see Practice with Nouns, page 114).

> *Subject* **Who does the work** is not important.
> *Object* I didn't see **what they did**.
> *Object of the preposition* I don't understand the implications of **what he said**.

(B) Adjective Clauses, like adjectives, are used to describe a noun (see Practice with Word Forms, 2C, page 161).

> The car **that is blue** is mine.
> Sam wrote the paper **that caused the controversy**.

(C) Adverb clauses are used in the same way as an adverb (see Practice with Word Forms, 2D, page 161). Generally, adverb clauses can appear at either end of the sentence without changing the meaning of the sentence. When it begins the sentence, it is usually set off by a comma.

> **When I leave**, I'll take the papers.
> I'll take the papers **when I leave**.

Use Exercises S53–S54 to develop your skills in clause recognition.

Exercise S53   *Recognizing complete simple sentences*

Write an "I" if the clause is independent (a complete sentence). Write a "D" if the clause is dependent (an incomplete sentence).

Examples   _D_   The eagle spreading its wings.
            _I_   The rain came suddenly.

1. _____   Swimming is an invigorating sport.

2. _____   Acupuncture's start in China.

3. _____ Lightning striking a hut can kill the people inside.

4. _____ A hormone in the body called androvine.

5. _____ It has been discovered.

6. _____ To be happy is a common personal goal.

7. _____ At the foot of the peak workers using bulldozers.

8. _____ What a good idea the committee presented.

Extended practice: Correct the incomplete sentences in this exercise.

Answers to Exercise S53 are on page 458.

Exercise S54   **Recognizing complete complex sentences**

Write "C" in the space if the sentence is complete. Write "I" if the sentence is incorrect because there is missing information.

Examples   _C_   The people who lived in the wilderness of the Yukon had to be self-sufficient.

      _I_   The lighthouse that had burned down no longer warning sailors of the rocks.

The second sentence cannot be understood because the verb for the independent clause is missing.

1. _____ The report, which covers many regions, states that the situation is nothing short of catastrophic.

2. _____ More than thirty fatalities had been reported before the year's rainy season started in earnest.

3. _____ Lightning produced in cumulonimbus clouds which occur in thunderstorms.

4. _____ The hard part is to locate the answer on the map with a gadget called a reticle.

5. _____ Any offer that doesn't have the necessary documents attached not to be considered.

6. _____ While large numbers of eagles have long converged in national parks, only recently the birds generating outside curiosity.

7. _____ They are worried about what they consider to be a failure of leadership and funding.

8. _____ The most convincing evidence that several tribes in the area use Aspilia for medicinal purposes.

Extended practice: Correct the incomplete sentences in this exercise.

Answers to Exercise S54 are on page 459.

PRACTICE WITH NOUN CLAUSES

Ask yourself the following questions about noun clauses.

1. Is the clause a noun clause?

A noun clause has a subject and a verb. It is introduced by a clause marker (see 2 below) and can be used in exactly the same way as a noun. Compare the following uses of nouns and noun clauses.

As subjects	Sam's **jokes** are very funny. (noun)
	What Sam says is very funny. (noun clause)
As objects	The man told us the **address**. (noun)
	The man told us **where he lived**. (noun clause)
As objects of the preposition	I wasn't asked about the **party**. (noun)
	I wasn't asked about **who was invited**. (noun clause)

2. Is the correct clause marker used?

A clause marker *introduces* a clause.

Noun clause markers	Examples
"That" indicates a fact.	I knew **that** he had to go.
"What" focuses on a fact.	Everyone was surprised at **what** he brought for the picnic.
"When" indicates a time.	He told us **when** the plane would arrive.
"Where" indicates a place.	**Where** they are going on their honeymoon is a secret.
"Why" indicates a reason.	She wouldn't say **why** he left so early.
"Who" indicates a person.	**Who** sent the letter is a mystery to me.
"How many" indicates a quantity.	I've lost count of **how many** times I've broken my glasses.
"How much" indicates an amount.	He wasn't paying attention to **how much** he ate.
"How" indicates a manner.	He showed us **how** he was going to win the race.
"Which" indicates a choice.	I didn't know **which** book I was supposed to read.
"Whether" indicates two or more alternatives.	I didn't know **whether** I should bring my bike or leave it at home.
"Whose" indicates possession.	I never found out **whose** car was parked outside our house.
"Whom" indicates a person.	Sue didn't know to **whom** he was engaged.
"If" indicates alternatives.	I didn't know **if** I should bring my bike.

When used as clause markers, "if" and "whether" are interchangeable.

3. Is the clause marker missing?

Wh- words used as clause markers cannot be left out of the sentence. "That" can sometimes be left out.

(A) "That" cannot be left out if the noun clause is the subject of the sentence.

   Subject position   **That he passed** is a miracle.

(B) "That" can be left out if the noun clause is the object of the sentence.

   Object position   Janet noticed **that the window was broken.**

This sentence is also correct without the word "that":

   Janet noticed **the window was broken.**

4. Is there a subject and a verb in the noun clause?

The noun clause must have a subject and a verb to be complete.

                                       S   V
   One additional feature of the car is **that it has push button windows.**

   S   V
   What was in the box surprised everyone.

5. Does the noun clause complete the independent clause?

If the noun clause is used in the subject position, there must be a verb in the independent clause.

              S   V
   That he might fall worries me.

If the noun clause is used in the object position, there must be a subject and a verb in the independent clause.

   S   V   OBJECT
   Sam knew **what he had to do.**

6. Does the verb tense in the noun clause agree with the verb tense in the independent clause?

   Correct   Last week Alfred asked where we were going.

"Last week" indicates that the action of asking took place in the past. The verb tense "were going" indicates that the action of going could have occurred at any point in time after Alfred asked the question.

   Correct   Last week Alfred asked where we had gone.

"Last week" indicates that the action of asking took place in the past. The verb tense "had gone" indicates that the action of going occurred before Alfred asked the question.

   Incorrect   Last week Alfred asked where we will go.

The verb tense "will go" (future) in the noun clause does not agree with the verb tense "asked" (past) in the independent clause.

Use Exercises S55–S60 to develop your skills in identifying noun clauses.

Exercise S55　　***Identifying noun clauses***

Circle the words that identify the following phrases.

Examples　　that book was very interesting
　　　　　　　　(noun clause/independent clause)

　　　　　　　　that the book was on the table
　　　　　　　　(noun clause)/independent clause

　　　　　　　　where is the book
　　　　　　　　noun clause/(independent clause)

You should circle both "noun clause/independent clause" in the first example because the phrase could be either a noun clause or an independent clause. You should circle "noun clause" in the second example because the phrase is a noun clause and needs to be in the noun position of an independent clause. You should circle "independent clause" in the third example because the phrase is an independent clause in the question form.

1. that he is a good actor
　　noun clause/independent clause

2. whichever program you prefer
　　noun clause/independent clause

3. that crisis happened only a few years ago
　　noun clause/independent clause

4. who is he
　　noun clause/independent clause

5. whose house is across the street
　　noun clause/independent clause

6. where she lives
　　noun clause/independent clause

7. when are you going
　　noun clause/independent clause

8. that picture was in the library
　　noun clause/independent clause

Answers to Exercise S55 are on page 459.

Exercise S56　　***Identifying noun clause functions***

Underline the noun clause. Write "S" in the space if the noun clause is the subject and "O" if the clause is an object.

Examples　　_S_　That most fast-food meals are high in fat has become an increasing concern.
　　　　　　　_O_　It is easy to understand why fast-food restaurants are so popular.

1. _____ How the buildings are constructed to keep their inhabitants cool is one of the most striking aspects of the Bahraini architecture.

2. _____ What the doctor advised was a vacation away from the hustle and bustle of the city.

3. _____ When the city of Rome was actually founded is a matter of dispute among historians.

4. _____ Marie Curie showed that a woman can be as good a scientist as a man can be.

5. _____ The general decided which troops were to be moved.

6. _____ By the latest accounts, what really occurred during the fight was censored by the government.

7. _____ The president told the youths that their journey was a noteworthy achievement.

8. _____ That the city has lost its charm in its zeal to modernize is a common perception.

Answers to Exercise S56 are on page 459.

Exercise S57   ***Locating subject and verb in independent clauses***

Locate the subject and verb of the independent clause. Underline the verb and circle the complete subject.

Example   (That lightning is electrical in nature) was suggested by Benjamin Franklin.

1. That rent control laws inhibit landlords from repairing properties is unfortunate, but true.

2. Sophia realized that the experience caused her to see her world differently.

3. How glass is blown in a cylinder was demonstrated at the Stuart Crystal factory.

4. A top architect lamented that cultural uniqueness has been replaced by international sameness.

5. Why consumers hesitated to buy the controversial digital audiotape players is a subject the article ignored.

6. Whom the late Dr. Bishopstone left his fortune to will be revealed this afternoon.

7. Richards claimed that the documents were taken from archives in Portugal.

8. What the manufacturer does to syrup results in one of three basic kinds of candy.

Answers to Exercise S57 are on page 459.

Exercise S58   ***Locating subject and verb in noun clauses***

Locate the subject and verb of the noun clause. Underline the verb and circle the subject.

Example   One of the characteristics of leather is that (it) has a fibrous structure.

1. Whose property that is still remains a mystery.

2. Herbal medicine companies stress that no alcohol or chemicals are included in their formulas.

3. In 590 B.C. the Greek traveler Solon learned from Egyptian historians how a disaster had struck the island of Thera.

4. That many nonsmokers find the odor of cigarettes objectionable surprises many smokers.

5. That radioactive antibodies can help locate tumors is a recent medical discovery.

6. A leading professor of tropical medicine said that far too little is being done to fight malaria.

7. That the poverty action group was set up in the 1970s was a sign of public awareness during that decade.

8. How witch doctors cure illnesses still mystifies physicians today.

Extended practice: Locate the subject and verb in the noun clauses in Exercise S57 and the subjects and verbs in independent clauses in Exercise S58.

Answers to Exercise S58 are on page 459.

Exercise S59   ***Checking verbs in the noun clause***

If the verb in the noun clause is used incorrectly, cross it out and write the correct form.

Example   Mary wondered what the extent of the destruction ~~will~~ be. [would]

1. In 1776, the U.S. Congress resolved that the authority of the British crown will be suppressed.

2. The orders to General J. Pershing were that he was to capture Mexico's revolutionary leader, Pancho Villa.

3. Peter fears that he might not have been able to master the intricacies of the craft.

4. What will prove to be a mistaken identity caused him many problems.

5. What you will already make is sufficient to buy the house.

6. East Coker is where the Anglo-American poet T. S. Eliot was buried in 1965.

7. That Thomas Hardy used real locations in his novels is disguised by his having altered place names.

8. Many people believed that space exploration is impossible.

> Answers to Exercise S59 are on page 459.

Exercise S60   ***Choosing the correct clause marker***

Circle the letter of the clause marker that correctly completes the sentence.

Example   ----- raiding for camels was a significant part of Bedouin life is no wonder.
  (A) That
  (B) Which
  (C) What
  (D) Where

You should circle (A) because "that" is the clause marker indicating a fact.

1. Bracewell told the people ----- effect a drought would have on the Great Plains.
   (A) that
   (B) how
   (C) what
   (D) then

2. The thieves knew precisely ----- the collection of priceless jewels was hidden.
   (A) where
   (B) then
   (C) who
   (D) what

3. ----- adults come to night classes eager to learn has been the experience of most adult education teachers.
   (A) That
   (B) When
   (C) Where
   (D) Which

4. Just ----- created the fantastic jade masterpiece is unknown.
   (A) whether
   (B) why
   (C) who
   (D) by whom

5. The report recommended ----- colleges should prize good teaching as well as good research.
   (A) not only
   (B) both
   (C) that
   (D) where

6. The secretary identified ----- reports treated new issues as well as old ones.
   (A) those
   (B) which
   (C) that
   (D) both

7. The coaches taught the contestants ----- they should walk, sit, and even apply makeup.
   (A) what
   (B) which
   (C) then
   (D) how

8. Political researchers explained ----- female candidates have a difficult time raising campaign money.
   (A) which reasons
   (B) because
   (C) the result
   (D) why

Answers to Exercise S60 are on page 459.

CHECK YOUR PROGRESS

Check your progress in using the skills you have been practicing in Exercises S53–S60 by completing the following mini-test. This exercise uses the same format as questions 1–15 of the Structure and Written Expression section on the TOEFL.

Exercise S61   ***Mini-test***   *(Time – 10 minutes)*

Directions: Questions 1–15 are incomplete sentences. Beneath each sentence you will see four words or phrases marked (A), (B), (C), and (D). Choose the one word or phrase that best completes the sentence. Then circle the letter that corresponds to the answer you have chosen.

Example   ----- the Anasazi deserted their cliff dwellings is not clearly understood.
   (A) What
   (B) Who
   (C) Where
   (D) Why

You should circle (D) because it is why this took place that people do not clearly understand.

1. ----- Freud and Marx were motivated primarily by compassionate concern for suffering humanity is elaborated upon in Fromm's biography.
   (A) Both are
   (B) What both
   (C) Both
   (D) That both

2. Scientists have speculated that the destruction of Earth's ozone layer would ----- us to damaging ultraviolet rays.
   (A) exposed
   (B) have exposed
   (C) expose
   (D) have been exposing

3. ----- Latin speakers originally borrowed the word "caupo" meaning "merchant" from Germanic speakers or vice versa is not clear.
   (A) Then
   (B) Whether
   (C) Because
   (D) Which

4. The world still admires ----- great Doric temples in Greece.
   (A) that
   (B) those
   (C) when
   (D) how

5. The problem facing most tourists is ----- among so many possibilities.
   (A) what they should see
   (B) what should they see
   (C) should they see what
   (D) they should see what

6. That acne ----- by daily consumption of zinc sulfate tablets gives patients much encouragement.
   (A) has been controlled
   (B) controlled
   (C) will have been controlled
   (D) had controlled

7. One of the lesser well-known treasures of Paris is ----- Parisians call "La Mosquée d'Islam."
   (A) that
   (B) why
   (C) what
   (D) where

8. ----- patients should try to reduce needless office visits for colds and minor respiratory illnesses.
   (A) Doctors that agree
   (B) That doctors agree
   (C) Doctors agreeing that
   (D) Doctors agree that

9. Differences among environmental groups illustrate ----- a broad range of philosophies and tactics.
   (A) that is
   (B) that is there
   (C) that there
   (D) that there is

10. ----- half the world's tropical forests have vanished since the 1940s.
    (A) World Wildlife Fund statistics show that
    (B) World Wildlife Fund statistics showing that
    (C) That showing World Wildlife Fund statistics
    (D) That World Wildlife Fund statistics show

11. Stallholders in the old market wondered how much ----- be able to stay there.
    (A) would they longer
    (B) they would longer
    (C) longer they would
    (D) they longer would

12. ----- disabled children cannot enjoy toys designed for nondisabled youngsters is the subject of the report.
    (A) What
    (B) Those
    (C) That
    (D) Because

13. ----- capable of machine automation and parts handling has been developed.
    (A) A robot
    (B) That a robot
    (C) These robots
    (D) Robots

14. NASA reported ----- a hypersonic aircraft is being designed for military missions and as a space launch vehicle to carry supplies.
    (A) there is
    (B) both
    (C) not only
    (D) that

15. Science has not yet made a machine that can learn ----- a young child can learn in a few days – how to tie a pair of shoes.
    (A) where
    (B) what
    (C) which
    (D) when

Answers to Exercise S61 are on page 459.

PRACTICE WITH ADJECTIVE CLAUSES

Ask yourself the following questions about adjective clauses.

1. Is the clause an adjective clause?

An adjective clause has a subject and a verb. It is a dependent clause because it does not form a complete sentence. It is used like an adjective to describe, identify, or give more information about nouns and indefinite pronouns such as "someone," "anyone," and "everything."

       NOUN _____ **ADJ CLAUSE**_____
The **house** that has the green shutters is for sale.

       NOUN _____ **ADJ CLAUSE**_____
The **woman** whose son won the award was out of town.

   PRONOUN _____**ADJ CLAUSE**_____
Anybody who finishes the test early can leave.

       NOUN ___**ADJ CLAUSE**___
Sam's **uncle**, who is very rich, came for a visit.

2. Is the correct clause marker used?

The adjective clause is introduced by the clause markers "that" or a *Wh-* word. The clause marker refers to the noun or pronoun it follows.

(A) The most common clause markers are the relative pronouns: "who," "whom," "which," "whose," and "that."

"Who" and "whom"* are used to refer to people.

> The man **who** saw the child works nearby. ("Who" refers to the man.)
> The man **whom** we saw works nearby. ("Whom" refers to the man.)

*"Who" is used in the subject position of a clause and "whom" is used in the object position. However, you will not be tested on the difference between "who" and "whom" on the TOEFL.

"Which" is used to refer to things.

> The watch **which** I lost was not valuable. ("Which" refers to the watch.)

"That" can be used to refer to either people or things.

> The man **that** was hired lives in the blue house. ("That" refers to the man.)
> The vase **that** I bought was handmade. ("That" refers to the vase.)

"Whose" is used to refer to the person or thing that possesses something.

> The woman **whose** car broke down needs a ride. ("Whose" refers to the woman. She owns the car.)

(B) Clause markers "where," "when," and "whereby" can also be used to introduce an adjective clause.

"Where" is used to refer to a location or the name of a location.

> The school **where** I met my husband is now closed. ("Where" refers to the location, school.)

"When" is used to refer to a time.

> That was the year **when** we moved to Alaska. ("When" refers to the year.)

"Whereby" is used to refer to words indicating an agreement.

> They made a deal **whereby** she would pay for the expenses and he would complete the work by Saturday. ("Whereby" refers to the deal.)

(C) Sometimes the adjective clause is used with a preposition. In conversational English the preposition usually goes at the end of the clause, but in formal and written English it goes at the beginning.

Informal	He asked questions that there were no answers **for.**
Formal	He asked questions **for** which there were no answers.
Informal	Mac was the man whom Linda was referring **to.**
Formal	Mac was the man **to** whom Linda was referring.

3. Is the clause marker in the correct position?

(A) Within the adjective clause, relative pronouns are used in the same positions as a noun.

> **S   V   ___OBJ___**
> *As subject*   The woman **who** wrote the book has just left.

> **OBJ   S   V**
> *As object*   The woman **whom** I saw was in a hurry.

> **OBJ OF**
> **PREP S   V**
> *As object of the preposition*   The woman to **whom** I owe my good fortune lives nearby.

(B) The clause markers "where," "when," and "whereby" take an adverb position.

ADV S   V   ___OBJ___

The store **where** I bought my camera is having a sale.

4. Is the clause marker missing?

(A) If the relative pronoun is the subject of the adjective clause, it cannot be omitted.

S   V

The man **who** quit forgot his papers.

(B) If the relative pronoun is the object of the adjective clause, it can be omitted.

OBJ S   V

The picture **that** I wanted had been sold.
The picture I wanted had been sold.

(C) If the relative pronoun is the object of the preposition in the adjective clause, it can be omitted, and the preposition goes to the end of the clause.

OBJ OF
PREP S   V

The man for **whom** I work gave me a bonus.

S   V   PREP

The man I work for has given me a raise.

(D) The relative pronoun "whose" cannot be omitted.

The man **whose** opinion we respect teaches at the local community college.

(E) The clause marker "when" can be omitted.

That was the year **when** the miners were on strike.
That was the year the miners were on strike.

(F) "Where" and "whereby" cannot be omitted.

That's the room **where** I was born.
The factory devised a system **whereby** we could get more overtime work.

5. Does the adjective clause have a subject and a verb?

The adjective clause must have a subject and a verb to be complete.

S   V

The music **that we heard** was composed by Bach.

S   ____V____

The music **that was played** made me sad.

6. Is the independent clause that contains the adjective clause complete?

The independent clause must have a subject and a verb.

S   V

Last night on TV we watched a clown **who could juggle bowling balls**.

S   V

The clown **who juggled bowling balls** was very funny.

7. Does the verb of the adjective clause agree with the verb in the independent clause?

Although the tenses of the adjective clause may vary, they must be logical. In both of the following sentences the verb in the adjective clause is in the past tense and the verb in the independent clause is in the present progressive tense. However, the first sentence is correct and the second one is incorrect.

Correct   The man who sang at the concert last night is sitting over there.
Incorrect   The dog that was killed is wagging its tail.

In the second sentence, it is illogical for a dog to have been killed in the past and be wagging its tail now.

Use Exercises S62–S67 to develop your skills with adjective clauses.

Exercise S62   **Locating clause markers**

Circle the clause markers in the following sentences.

Example   The new book (which) I read in two days will leave a lasting impression.

1. One of the German officers who attended the meeting was Field Marshal Erwin Rommel.

2. Agriculture relies on water, which may be scarce at times.

3. A museum curator who was determined to read the label at every exhibit spent five full days at the museum.

4. The flight of stairs led to dungeons where men were penned with beasts until their execution.

5. The village had a church which was probably built in the fifth century.

6. The storks that stop at the lagoon on their way north are protected.

7. The tourists whom the guide had shown through the museum were impressed with the collection.

8. The largest mosaic in the world is in Mexico City where Juan O'Gorman's work covers 1,000 square meters of the university library walls.

Answers to Exercise S62 are on page 460.

Exercise S63   **Locating adjective clauses**

Underline the adjective clause and circle the word in the independent clause which it refers to.

Example   I finally met (someone) who knew the answer.

1. The date on which Romulus founded Rome is generally considered to be 753 B.C.

2. Chekhov's calling *The Seagull* a comedy is a description that has puzzled playgoers, directors, and even critics.

3. Those who flip through this brochure will find it very entertaining.

4. The common hedgehog, which has outlived the mammoth and the sabre-toothed tiger, is now threatened by traffic.

5. Shakespeare wrote plays people have enjoyed for four centuries.

6. The impression he gave was that he wouldn't arrive before Monday.

7. An added attraction to the park is an enclosure where children can play with baby goats.

8. A balance between nature and human beings which will safeguard succeeding generations is what humanity should strive for.

Answers to Exercise S63 are on page 460.

Exercise S64   ***Checking clause markers***

Write "C" if the correct clause marker has been used. Write "IC" if an incorrect clause marker has been used.

Example _IC_   The car <u>who</u> I brought is my father's.

You should write "IC" in the space because the relative pronoun "who" refers to people, but the word "car" is a thing and therefore takes the pronoun "that" or "which."

1. _____ California's San Joaquin Valley, <u>where</u> has lured settlers throughout the years, is rimmed by beautiful mountains.

2. _____ Edward Kazarian, <u>which</u> is a master of making miniatures, uses microscopes and diamond-tipped tools to create figures the size of the head of a pin.

3. _____ People <u>who</u> love car racing always enjoy the Indianapolis 500.

4. _____ The vast oil spill <u>that</u> smeared the coast cost millions to clean up.

5. _____ The person <u>whose</u> is in charge of reservations warns people to call in early.

6. _____ Using low doses of antibiotics <u>which</u> don't kill the bacteria only helps it develop its resistance.

7. _____ The last city of the Pyu civilization, <u>who</u> flourished from the first to ninth centuries B.C., lies about 160 miles from Rangoon, Burma.

8. _____ Anna Freud, <u>when</u> was the daughter of Sigmund Freud, was an eminent psychoanalyst as well.

Extended practice: Write the correct clause marker for the items that were incorrect.

Answers to Exercise S64 are on page 460.

Exercise S65   ***Choosing the correct clause marker***

Circle the letter of the word that correctly introduces the adjective clause.

Example   A new species of tomato ----- is adapted to harsh climatic conditions has been developed.
(A) what
(B) where
(C) that
(D) who

The word being referred to is "tomato." "What" in (A) is not a clause marker for an adjective clause. "Where" in (B) refers to a location. "Who" in (D) refers to a person.

You should circle (C) because "that" is the clause marker that can refer to either a person or a thing.

1. New Orleans is a city ----- older traditions can still be seen.
   (A) those
   (B) that
   (C) which
   (D) where

2. The preservation of ancient sites and historical buildings is a job ----- requires a person ready to fight a long battle.
   (A) whose
   (B) which
   (C) whom
   (D) where

3. Monteverdi, ----- works were mainly written on commission for private theaters of wealthy Italian nobility, wrote his final opera in 1642.
   (A) which
   (B) who
   (C) whom
   (D) whose

4. Crossing Death Valley, ----- temperatures reach well above 110° Fahrenheit, was a near insurmountable task for the early pioneers.
   (A) when
   (B) where
   (C) that
   (D) those

5. Marine excavation is a race against time, the sea, and the looters ----- want history's treasures for themselves.
   (A) which
   (B) who
   (C) whose
   (D) those

6. Those for ----- skiing is an obsession would find life in the Snowy Mountains to their liking.
   (A) which
   (B) where
   (C) whom
   (D) whose

7. T. A. Watson's business involved building models for inventors ----- had ideas but lacked the means or skills to execute them.
   (A) who
   (B) when
   (C) whose
   (D) to whom

8. Glaucoma, ----- is often called tunnel vision, happens when a buildup of pressure in the eye gradually shrinks the field of vision.
   (A) where
   (B) why
   (C) which
   (D) when

Answers to Exercise S65 are on page 460.

Exercise S66   *Locating the subject and verb in the adjective clause*

Circle the complete subject and underline the verb of the adjective clause.

Example   The painting which (William Gear) exhibited in the New York gallery was from the Cobra period.

The adjective clause is "which William Gear exhibited in the New York gallery."

1. Anne Boleyn, who was the second wife of King Henry VIII, was beheaded at the age of 29.

2. Many words that people use daily have origins in other countries and cultures.

3. The report counters the belief that population growth is environmentally neutral.

4. Botulism spores, which bees carry from certain kinds of plants, have been found in jars of honey.

5. Locusts breed in remote desert areas where they go unnoticed.

6. Collapsed stars can form a black hole, which is matter so dense that its gravity sucks in even light.

7. Those patients whom the doctors found to have tumors were treated with a radioactive antibody.

8. Sharks, whose appetites are notorious, have acquired a taste for the cables that carry international telephone calls.

Extended practice: Write "S" above the subject and "V" above the verb of the independent clause in the above sentences.

Answers to Exercise S66 are on page 461.

Exercise S67   *Checking verbs in adjective clauses*

If the verb in the adjective clause is used incorrectly, cross it out and write the correct form.

Example   Sam will never forget what happened the day he ~~will meet~~ *met* Sue.

The verb "happened" indicates that the event of meeting Sue took place in the past. Therefore, the verb in the adjective clause should also be in the past.

1. Bicyclists pedal through the countryside during a week-long ride which is holding every summer in Iowa.

2. In 1918, Charles Strite invented the timer that turns off the toaster when the bread is toasted.

3. It is Earth's magnetic field that made a compass work.

4. A vending machine is a kind of robot salesperson which automatically gave out candy or other items when money is inserted.

5. Hans Christian Oersted, the man who made the electric motor possible, was a Danish scientist.

6. A laser cane, which the blind find useful, sends out beams that detecting obstacles.

7. For the foreign buyers to whom Canada supplying furs, the industry has never been healthier.

8. Lucid dreamers are those people who recognize when they are dreaming and thus controlling the plot of their dreams.

Answers to Exercise S67 are on page 461.

PRACTICE WITH REDUCED ADJECTIVE CLAUSES

Adjective clauses can be reduced to phrases. Unlike a clause, a *phrase* is a group of words that does *not* contain a subject and a verb. Ask yourself the following questions concerning adjective phrases.

1. Is the phrase a reduced adjective clause?

An adjective clause can often be reduced to an adjective phrase when the relative pronoun of the adjective clause is the *subject* of the clause. You can reduce the clause by either: (1) omitting the "be" verb or (2) changing the form of the verb to *-ing*. Study the following examples.

(A) Active voice:

The man **who is driving** has a new car.   (clause)
The man **driving** has a new car.   (phrase)

Christopher de Hamel has published a book which **contains descriptions of
    illuminated manuscripts**.   (clause)
Christopher de Hamel has published a book **containing descriptions of illuminated
    manuscripts**.   (phrase)

(B) Passive voice:

The magazine ad **which was printed in *Shoppers' Weekly*** showed the city
    skyline.   (clause)
The magazine ad **printed in *Shoppers' Weekly*** showed the city skyline.   (phrase)

The ideas **which had been presented in the previous meeting** were discussed.
    (clause)
The ideas **presented in the previous meeting** were discussed.   (phrase)

(C) Subject + *to be* + adjective:

The man **who is responsible** said the underground water had a high salt content.
    (clause)
The man **responsible** said the underground water had a high salt content.   (phrase)

(D) Subject + *to be* + noun:

Her name, **which is Lou Ann**, contains easy sounds for the deaf to pronounce.
    (clause)
Her name, **Lou Ann**, contains easy sounds for the deaf to pronounce.   (phrase)

(E) Subject + *to be* + prepositional phrase:

The books **that are on the table** belong to Emma.   (clause)
The books **on the table** belong to Emma.   (phrase)

2. Is the verb form in the phrase correct?

The *-ing* form is used for the active voice, and the *-ed* form is used for the passive voice.

(A) A verb that is used to indicate a permanent characteristic uses the *-ing* form.

Present
The window which **overlooks** the garden is broken.
The window **overlooking** the garden is broken.

Past
The window which **overlooked** the garden was broken.
The window **overlooking** the garden was broken.

(B) A verb that is used to indicate an ongoing activity uses the *-ing* form.

Present progressive
The detective who is **investigating** the case has found an important clue.
The detective **investigating** the case has found an important clue.

Past progressive
The detective who **was investigating** the case has found an important clue.
The detective **investigating** the case has found an important clue.

(C) A verb that is used in the passive uses the *-ed* form (the past participle).

The woman that **was invited** to join the club declined.
The woman **invited** to join the club declined.

Remember that the past participle forms of many verbs are irregular.

I like yogurt that **is made** in France.
I like yogurt **made** in France.

The house that **has been built** in the forest doesn't have electricity.
The house **built** in the forest doesn't have electricity.

3. Is the phrase correct?

(A) When the clause marker is in the object position it cannot be reduced to an adjective phrase.

The books **that I checked out of the library** are due today.

The adjective clause cannot be shortened to "checking out of the library" because the subject "books" is not the subject for the verb "check." Books cannot "check" themselves out.

(B) The adjective clause beginning with "whose" cannot be reduced without a change in meaning.

The woman **whose son is blocking the entrance** works upstairs.
The woman **blocking the entrance** works upstairs.

Although the second sentence is grammatically correct, it does not mean the same as the first sentence. In the first sentence, the son is blocking the entrance. In the second sentence, the woman is blocking the entrance.

(C) The adjective clause beginning with a clause marker that takes the adverb position cannot be reduced to an adjective phrase.

The time **when Andrew arrived** was inconvenient.

" The time arriving was inconvenient" is incorrect because the time did not arrive, Andrew did.

The house **where we grew up** was torn down.

" The house growing up was torn down" is incorrect because the house did not grow up, we did.

Use Exercises S68–S71 to develop your skills with reduced adjective clauses.

Exercise S68   **Locating adjective phrases**

Underline the adjective phrase in each of the following sentences.

Example   People living in a foreign country face many problems.

"Living in a foreign country" is shortened from the adjective clause "who are living in a foreign country."

1. Passengers suffering from the heat on warm summer days should close the windows if the air-conditioning is to work effectively.

2. Bookworms can browse through or buy from a large selection of the literature on display at the book festival.

3. The fifteenth-century mystery plays first revived in 1951 in York are performed every four years at St. Mary's Abbey.

4. Leaflets giving full details of the program are available at the information desk.

5. The tough palm fiber used in the street-sweeping machines is piassava.

6. Local people consenting to help erect the building were promised a lifetime membership to the museum.

7. For towns in remote areas, the airplane is the only means of external communication.

8. In ancient Greece, a person lucky enough to be wealthy and male could join a birthday club composed exclusively of men born the same day.

Extended practice: Change the phrases into adjective clauses.

Answers to Exercise S68 are on page 461.

Exercise S69   **Identifying adjective phrases and clauses**

Underline the adjective phrase and/or clause in each of the following sentences. Then write "C" if the sentence contains an adjective clause or "P" if it contains an adjective phrase. If it contains both, write "P/C."

Examples   _C_   The bone that he broke was the clavicle.

   _P_   The hills seemed like mountains rising from the gentle expanse.

   _P/C_   The world's first jigsaw puzzles, which appeared in the 1760s, were cut up maps intended to help children learn geography.

In the first sentence, "that he broke" is a clause because it has a subject and a verb.

In the second sentence, "rising form the gentle expanse" is a phrase (reduced from the clause "which were rising from the gentle expanse").

In the last sentence, "which appeared in the 1760s" is a clause, and "intended to help children learn geography" is a phrase.

1. _____ The cultural revolution which historians call the Renaissance has left a remarkable legacy in Italy.

2. _____ The road leading into the city is lined with overlapping trees which create a green tunnel.

3. _____ About 55 percent of those exiled to Siberia in czarist Russia were not sentenced by judicial process.

4. _____ The Romans recognized the need for a canal linking the southwestern corner of France to the Mediterranean.

5. _____ The "Four Corners" world bike riders, the first of whom pedaled off in September, are now scattered across the globe.

6. _____ The highest ruins found in the Andes have yet to be properly examined because of their inaccessibility.

7. _____ Strong winds flowing over weaker ones can cause tornadoes.

8. _____ Gray whales migrate 5,000 miles from Arctic waters to bays in Baja California where they give birth to their calves.

Answers to Exercise S69 are on page 461.

Exercise S70   ***Recognizing whether or not clauses can be reduced***

If the adjective clause can be reduced without a change in meaning, write the changes that are necessary.

Examples   George Washington, ~~who was~~ the first president of the United States, lived at Mount Vernon.

Mount Vernon, where George Washington lived, is in the state of Virginia.

The clause in the first sentence can be reduced because the relative pronoun is the subject of the clause. The clause in the second sentence cannot be reduced because "George Washington," the subject of the clause, is not a relative pronoun and does not refer to "Mount Vernon."

1. The letter "M" may have originated as a hieroglyphic symbol which represented the crests of waves and meant "water."

2. There are still people who are dying from diseases that are preventable and controllable.

3. Before the age of steam, hemp, which was used for ropes on ships, was an important commodity.

4. Brabant Island, where the research team spent the winter, is an inhospitable and violent terrain near Antarctica.

5. The film *The Jazz Singer* was produced many years ago, when the talking movie industry was still in its infancy.

6. Rings, which were probably invented by the Egyptians, were an easy way to display authority.

7. Wind that is deflected down the face of tall buildings causes gusty swirling winds in the streets.

8. Pain is the body's warning signal that calls attention to a potentially harmful condition.

Answers to Exercise S70 are on page 461.

Exercise S71   ***Checking verb forms***

If any verb form in an adjective phrase is incorrect, cross it out and write the correct form above the verb.

meaning
Example   The word "Minnesota," ~~means~~ many lakes, is another example of an
found
Indian word ~~finding~~ in American English.

1. Ambroise Paré, knowing as the father of modern surgery, brought medicine out of the Dark Ages.

2. Each child enter the school is individually screened.

3. Natural oils taken from the rose and the jasmine flower are valuable ingredients of perfume.

4. Scissors, a Bronze Age invention remained basically unchanged to this day, consist of two blades linked by a C-shaped spring.

5. The protesters chained themselves to the trees marked to be cut down.

6. Butterfly wings have iridescent scales consist of thin, interlaced layers.

7. Glacier National Park is impressive with its mountain peaks are towering over splendid lakes.

8. The medicine finding in the cabinet had expired.

Answers to Exercise S71 are on page 461.

CHECK YOUR PROGRESS

Check your progress in using the skills you have been practicing in Exercises S62– S71 by taking the following mini-test. This exercise uses the same format as questions 1–15 of the Structure and Written Expression section on the TOEFL.

Exercise S72   ***Mini-test***   *(Time – 10 minutes)*

Directions: Questions 1–15 are incomplete sentences. Beneath each sentence you will see four words or phrases marked (A), (B), (C), and (D). Choose the <u>one</u> word or phrase that best completes the sentence. Then circle the letter that corresponds to the answer you have chosen.

Example   A loudspeaker is an instrument ----- electrical energy into sound energy.
    (A) that
    (B) who is transforming
    (C) transformed
    (D) which transforms

The adjective clause is missing a subject and a verb. Answer (D) "which transforms" has both a subject and a verb and completes the sentence.

1. Researchers may be able to find and monitor San Andreas earthquake fault lines ----- since 1857 or earlier.
   (A) where have not slipped
   (B) have not slipped
   (C) that have not slipped
   (D) have not been slipping

2. The trail led over sandhills ----- thin grasses and thorny bushes grew.
   (A) where there were
   (B) where
   (C) that were
   (D) that

3. ----- whose fauna and flora create an enchanted world.
   (A) A biological park
   (B) Where a biological park
   (C) It is a biological park
   (D) Being a biological park

4. ----- found in New Zealand were brought there by homesick immigrants.
   (A) The hedgehogs which
   (B) The hedgehogs
   (C) Where the hedgehogs
   (D) The hedgehogs are

5. Communication companies have been experimenting with a fiber-optic cable ----- international telephone transmissions.
   (A) can carry
   (B) can carry it
   (C) that can carry
   (D) that it can carry

6. The stolen items came into the hands of an art dealer ----- to the museum.
   (A) who returned them
   (B) returned
   (C) he returned them
   (D) returning them

7. Nantucket ----- a little island 20 miles off Cape Cod, Massachusetts.
   (A) which is
   (B) where
   (C) is
   (D) it is

8. The woolly musk ox, -----, survives on Ellesmere Island.
   (A) once hunted almost to extinction
   (B) hunted almost once to extinction
   (C) almost hunted once to extinction
   (D) hunted almost to once extinction

9. For villagers ----- to read, instructions have been developed using special symbols.
   (A) who unable
   (B) they are unable
   (C) unable
   (D) where they are unable

10. North Carolina ----- because of its production of tar, turpentine, and pitch.
    (A) called the Tar Heel State
    (B) it is called the Tar Heel State
    (C) which the Tar Heel State is called
    (D) is called the Tar Heel State

11. The Cherokee Indians, ----- west on the Trail of Tears in the late 1830s, were originally from the Appalachian Mountains.
    (A) forcing
    (B) forced
    (C) had forced
    (D) are forced

12. The many people ----- must be willing to commute a long distance to work.
    (A) wished to live in rural areas
    (B) wished they lived in rural areas
    (C) those wishing to live in rural areas
    (D) who wish to live in rural areas

13. After 116 million dollars had been spent, the Supreme Court stopped construction of the dam because of a little fish, ----- .
    (A) the famous endangered snail darter
    (B) it was the famous endangered snail darter
    (C) being the famous endangered snail darter
    (D) which the famous endangered snail darter

14. The black moths ----- have genetically become more tolerant of pollution.
    (A) survive in industrial areas
    (B) survived in industrial areas
    (C) survival in industrial areas
    (D) surviving in industrial areas

15. The king's burial shoes, ----- except for some decorative strips of gold, were displayed on a clay model.
    (A) who were disintegrating
    (B) when disintegrating
    (C) which had disintegrated
    (D) whose had disintegrated

Answers to Exercise S72 are on page 462.

PRACTICE WITH ADVERB CLAUSES

Ask yourself the following questions about adverb clauses.

1. Is the clause an adverb clause?

An adverb clause is a dependent clause (incomplete sentence) with a subject and a verb. It may occur at the beginning of a sentence before the independent clause or at the end of the sentence after the independent clause. When it occurs at the beginning, it is frequently separated from the independent clause by a comma.

> **Even though Ted knew the material**, he failed the exam.
> Ted failed the exam **even though he knew the material**.

2. Is the correct clause marker used?

The following clause markers are some of the more common ones used to introduce an adverb clause.

(A) Clause makers indicating time.

after	by the time	until
as	now that	when
as long as	once	whenever
as soon as	since	while
before		

Examples

The people danced **as** the music played.
We worked **as long as** we could.

(B) Clause markers indicating concessions.

although	except that	though
despite the fact that	in spite of the fact that	whereas
even if	much as	while
even though	not that	

Examples

Jim goes hiking **despite the fact that** he has asthma.
Jenny's smile is an important aspect of her personality, **even if** she doesn't realize
   it.

(C) Clause markers indicating cause and effect (reason).

as	in case	so
because	since	

Examples

We should take a safety kit **in case** there is an accident.
Since Max seldom talks about himself, I didn't know he liked classical ballet.

(D) Clause markers indicating results.

so that	such . . . that

Examples

The lock on my suitcase broke **so that** all my belongings fell onto the conveyor
   belt.
She got **such** a shock **that** she dropped the tray.

(E) Clause markers indicating purpose.

in order that	so	so that

Examples

He wrote that memo **in order that** there would be no misunderstandings.
I bought the book **so that** I could read on the flight.

(F) Clause markers indicating manner.

as	as if	as though	just as	like

Examples

Betty looks **as if** something is wrong.
The wind was cold yesterday **just as** it had been all week long.

(G) Clause markers indicating place.

where	wherever	everywhere

Examples

Wherever I looked, I found fingerprints.
Everywhere he went, people admired him.

(H) Clause markers indicating conditions.

even if	if	only if	provided	unless

Examples

We can go camping with Bill **provided** we bring our own equipment.
Lucy can't attend the meeting **unless** she finds a baby-sitter.

3. Is the clause marker missing?

(A) An adverb clause must begin with a clause marker.

When Sam arrives, we'll open the gifts.
I want to leave now **so** I will get home early.

(B) If the aux-word or verb in a conditional clause is "should," "were," or "had," it is sometimes put at the beginning of the clause and the clause marker "if" is omitted.

If he had planned on going, he would have let us know.
Had he planned on going, he would have let us know.

4. Is there a subject and a verb in the adverb clause?

                                      S   **V**
Mike wears glasses, **whereas his brother wears contact lenses**.

              S   **V**
Whenever Ralph drinks cold water, he gets a toothache.

5. Is the adverb clause used with an independent clause?

INDEPENDENT
_____**CLAUSE**_____ _____**ADV CLAUSE**_____
Lenny can't work until the cast is off his foot.

__**ADV CLAUSE**__ _____**INDEPENDENT CLAUSE**_____
After he leaves, we'll bring in the lawn chairs.

6. Is the verb of the adverb clause used correctly?

In most adverb clauses, the verb has the same tense as the verb in the independent clause. The following cases are exceptions.

(A) Clauses of time.

If the time refers to something that will happen, you use a present tense.

As soon as I **find** my car keys, we'll leave.

(B) Clauses of reason.

If the clause of reason introduced by the markers "in case" or "just in case" refers to a possible future situation, the reason clause is in the simple present tense.

I'm bringing my umbrella in case **it rains**.

(C) Clauses of purpose.

If the verb in the independent clause is in the present tense or in the present perfect tense, one of the modals "can," "may," "will," or "shall" is usually used.

I want to learn typing so that I **can type** my own essays.

If the verb in the independent clause is in the past tense, one of the modals "could," "might," "would," or "should" is usually used.

Margo wrote the items on a list so that we **would remember** everything.

(D) Clauses of condition.

If the sentence concerns a common occurrence, the simple present tense or the present continuous tense is used in both the adverb clause and the independent clause.

If someone **speaks** to Lily, she **turns** red.

If the sentence concerns a common occurrence in the past, the simple past tense or the past continuous tense is used in the adverb clause, and the simple past and a modal are used in the independent clause.

He **couldn't sleep** unless he **got** a lot of exercise.

If the sentence concerns a possible situation in the present, the simple present tense or the present perfect tense is used in the adverb clause and a modal is used in the independent clause.

If you **don't believe me**, you **can ask** Mike.
If you **haven't tried** this kind of cookie, we **should buy** a package.

If the sentence concerns a possible future occurrence, the simple present tense is used in the adverb clause and the simple future tense is used in the independent clause.

If he **goes**, I **will go** too.

(Notice these more formal ways of expressing a possible future occurrence.

If he **should go**, I **would go** too.
If he **were to go**, I **would go** too.)

If the sentence concerns an unlikely situation, the simple past tense is used in the adverb clause and "would," "should," or "might" is used in the independent clause.

If I **asked** for another raise, my boss **would fire** me.

If the sentence concerns something that might have happened in the past but did not happen, the past perfect tense is used in the adverb clause, and "would have," "could have," "should have," or "might have" is used in the independent clause.

If I **had realized** the danger at that time, I **would have taken** more precautions.

Use Exercises S73–S77 to develop your skills in identifying adverb clauses.

Exercise S73 **Locating adverb clauses**

Underline the adverb clauses in the following sentences.

Example   By the time the Privacy Act became law, the Freedom of Information Act had been in use for eight years.

"By the time the Privacy Act became law" relates to when the Freedom of Information Act had been in use.

1. The Romans built raised sidewalks of stone in Pompeii so that pedestrians would not get their feet muddy.

2. Although the existence of germs was verified in about 1600, scientists did not prove the connection between germs and diseases until the mid-nineteenth century.

3. If you should step on a stingray, it will whip its spine into your foot or calf.

4. While the men were arguing, a stranger leading two horses appeared on the riverbank.

5. The noisy chattering of a troop of monkeys ended as soon as the hunter entered the jungle.

6. Sun-dried clay returns to its malleable state when wet, whereas fired clay does not.

7. When an Easterner in 1886 described St. Paul, Minnesota, as another Siberia, the people responded by holding a winter carnival.

8. Since the search to find and document sites of Indian cave paintings was first begun, more than 200 have come to light.

Answers to Exercise S73 are on page 462.

Exercise S74 **Identifying adverb clauses**

If the sentence contains an adverb clause, underline the clause.

Examples After the work is completed, we can leave for the rest of the week.

The picture was exhibited in the gallery for over a month.

In the first sentence, "after the work is completed" is an adverb clause indicating when we can leave. There is no adverb clause in the second sentence.

1. The word "moon" is an ancient word related to "month."

2. Even though it contains no fish, Mono Lake teems with brine shrimp.

3. As traders mill about in the New York Stock Exchange, information is flashed instantly on exchange tickers and display boards around the world.

4. An incredible 800,000 feeding birds were counted on Negit Island in one day.

5. Using computers in schools not only speeds the rate of learning but also frees the teacher to explain new concepts.

6. Aphrodisias continued as a Byzantine center until violent earthquakes and invasions brought its prosperity to an end.

7. Smoke from the blazing fire forced the fire fighters to retreat.

8. To combat damaging impurities that have penetrated the marble, sculptures are placed into tubs of water and soaked for up to a month.

Answers to Exercise S74 are on page 462.

Exercise S75 **Locating subjects and verbs of adverb clauses**

Locate the subject and verb of the adverb clause. Underline the verb and circle the complete subject.

Example   Antiochus was overthrown by Rome around 34 B.C. after (he) apparently <u>used</u> some of his funds to support a local rebellion backed by the Persians.

You should circle "he" and underline "used" because they are the subject and verb of the adverb clause "after he apparently used some of his funds to support a local rebellion backed by the Persians."

1. Although monitoring earthquakes is a complex problem, seismologists are making considerable advances.

2. More than 100 pandas starved to death when one of the species of bamboo on which they feed died out.

3. Since oceans cover so much of Earth's surface, it is natural to explore them for future resources.

4. Even though the Chinese sage Confucius lived in the sixth century B.C., his teachings still profoundly influence daily life.

5. The people rely on their fishing industry because less than four percent of the land is tillable.

6. While the world population continues to grow, natural resources remain finite.

7. Although some Eskimos still migrate using dogsleds, many now make the trek with snowmobiles.

8. As the father repaired the tractor, the children played in the field.

Extended practice: Locate the subject and verb of the independent clause in these sentences.

Answers to Exercise S75 are on page 463.

Exercise S76 **Checking verb tense and form**

Check the verb tense and form of the adverb clause. If it is incorrect, cross it out and write the correct form above.

encountered
Example   Even though the team of scientists ~~encounter~~ snow and strong winds, they continued their excavation.

The verb in the adverb clause must be in the past tense for the action to agree in time with the verb "continued."

1. As dusk settling, fireflies begin to signal.

2. If the Italian authorities hadn't took measures to control the smuggling of national treasures, many Roman artifacts would have been lost.

3. Sixteenth-century mariners called Bermuda the "Isle of Devils" partly because breeding seabirds are making horrid sounds in the night.

4. As the numbers of shellfish diminished in the shallow waters, the divers were forced to dive deeper.

5. NASA does not quarantine space crews, since returning astronauts have carried no harmful agents or living organisms.

6. Whenever privateering falls off, the natives rearranged beacons to lure ships onto the reefs.

7. While students practice doctoring a plastic automated mannequin, the instructor uses a computer to vary the mannequin's reactions.

8. When a key pressed, a series of levers opens the hole in the pipe and air is pumped through.

> *Answers to Exercise S76 are on page 463.*

Exercise S77 **Choosing the correct clause marker**

Circle the letter of the correct clause marker needed to complete the sentence.

Example The dog spent three days in the central plaza howling and barking, ----- it were pleading for help.
(A) as though
(B) even though
(C) although
(D) though

"As though" indicates a manner and correctly completes the sentence. (B), (C), and (D) all indicate concession.

1. ----- the wasp deposits an egg, the flower grows a protective covering.
(A) Then
(B) As if
(C) In fact
(D) After

2. The region is referred to as the "Land of Fruit" ----- it yields a bountiful harvest of oranges and apples.
(A) although
(B) because
(C) so that
(D) such as

3. Seat belt laws were introduced ----- traffic fatalities would be reduced.
(A) so that
(B) then
(C) when
(D) as if

4. ----- the fires were blazing, the skewers impaling the fish were tilted toward the flames.
(A) As soon as
(B) So that
(C) As if
(D) Such as

5. The great stone city Angkon flourished for six centuries ----- it fell in 1431 and lay prey to the jungle for four long centuries.
   (A) as soon as
   (B) because
   (C) until
   (D) so that

6. The most modern ladders cannot reach above seven stories, ----- fire fighters must enter skyscrapers dressed in suits designed to supply oxygen and reflect heat.
   (A) before
   (B) so
   (C) as
   (D) until

7. ----- Kublai Khan's archers destroyed the Burmese war elephants, he shattered the elephant cavalry's myth of invincibility.
   (A) Although
   (B) Until
   (C) When
   (D) So that

8. ----- the government disapproves, cultivation of the opium poppy thrives.
   (A) As if
   (B) Until
   (C) So that
   (D) Even though

Answers to Exercise S77 are on page 463.

PRACTICE WITH REDUCED ADVERB CLAUSES

Some adverb clauses can be reduced to phrases without changing the meaning. Ask yourself the following questions concerning adverb phrases. Remember: A clause contains a subject and a verb, but a phrase does not contain both a subject and a verb.

1. Is the phrase a reduced adverb clause?

An adverb clause can be reduced to an adverb phrase only when the subject of the independent clause is the same as the subject of the adverb clause. Notice how the following adverb clauses change to phrases.

(A) Time sequences: "after," "before," "once," "since," "until," "when," and "while."

┌─── **SAME SUBJECT** ───┐

Clause	**After they sang two songs**, they did a dance.
Phrase	**After singing two songs**, they did a dance.
Clause	**Before he answered the phone**, he grabbed a pencil and notepad.
Phrase	**Before answering the phone**, he grabbed a pencil and notepad.
Clause	**Once he had been challenged to play tennis**, Tim wouldn't stop practicing.
Phrase	**Once challenged to play tennis**, Tim wouldn't stop practicing.
Clause	**Since she finished studying at the university**, Ellen has gone on to become a successful designer.
Phrase	**Since studying at the university**, Ellen has gone on to become a successful designer.
Clause	We worked on the project **until we finished it**.
Phrase	We worked on the project **until finishing it**.
Clause	**When he is working on a car**, Jan always works overtime.
Phrase	**When working on a car**, Jan always works overtime.

Clause	**While George was in London**, he wrote daily.	
Phrase	**While in London**, George wrote daily.	

(B) Reason: "because." When a clause introduced by "because" is reduced, "because" is omitted and the verb changes form.

Clause	**Because she had always been interested in sports**, Linda became an avid supporter of the team.
Phrase	**Having always been interested in sports**, Linda became an avid supporter of the team.

(C) Clauses of concession: "although," "despite, "in spite of," "though," and "while."

Clause	**Although he was hurt**, Jack managed to smile.
Phrase	**Although hurt**, Jack managed to smile.

Clause	**Despite the fact that she was ill**, Lisa went on stage.
Phrase	**Despite being ill**, Lisa went on stage.

Clause	**In spite of the fact that she works long hours**, Joan spends a lot of time with her family.
Phrase	**In spite of working long hours**, Joan spends a lot of time with her family.

Clause	**Though I am capable of making cakes**, I prefer to bake cookies.
Phrase	**Though capable of making cakes**, I prefer to bake cookies.

Clause	**While I am fond of Jeff**, I do not want to marry him.
Phrase	**While fond of Jeff**, I do not want to marry him.

2. Is the verb form in the clause correct?

(A) Active voice:

Present tense	**When I work**, I forget to eat. **When working**, I forget to eat.
Past tense	**While he was studying**, he heard the explosion. **While studying**, he heard the explosion.
Perfect tenses	**After he had finished the book**, he put it on the table. **After finishing the book**, he put it on the table. *or* **After having finished** the book, he put it on the table.

(B) Passive voice:

Present tense	The building will be used as a convention center **when it is completed**. **When completed**, the building will be used as a convention center.
Past tense	**When the boy was told to go to bed**, he began to cry. **When told to go to bed**, the boy began to cry.
Perfect tenses	**Because the car has been built by hand**, it is in superb condition. **Having been built by hand**, the car is in superb condition.

3. Is the phrase correct?

(A) When the subject of the adverb clause and the subject of the independent clause are not the same, the clause cannot be reduced.

Same subject:

Clause	Since **she** graduated, **she** has become an engineer.
Phrase	Since graduating, she has become an engineer.

Different subjects:

Clause	After **she** graduated, **her parents** retired. (= The daughter graduated, then her parents retired.)
Phrase	After graduating, her parents retired. (= Her parents graduated, then her parents retired.)

(Reducing the adverb clause changes the meaning.)

(B) Some adverb clauses, such as those beginning with "as" or "as soon as," cannot be reduced.

Correct	As he was walking, he kept stopping to look at the flowers.
Incorrect	As walking, he kept stopping to look at the flowers.

Use Exercises S78–S81 to develop your skills with reduced adverb clauses.

Exercise S78   *Identifying phrases and clauses*

Write "C" if the sentence contains an adverb clause. Write "P" if the sentence contains an adverb phrase.

Examples ___P___ After finishing supper, Max went to the club to play basketball.

___C___ Because the spare parts are difficult to buy here, I recommend that you don't get that car.

1. _____ These steps are repeated for successive colors until a multihued design is complete.

2. _____ While staying at the Greyfield Inn, the tourist visited the ruins of Dungeness, the most famous Carnegie mansion.

3. _____ Before migrating whales head for Baja, California's lagoons, they feed on krill in the Arctic waters.

4. _____ When photographing the set, the camera operators corrected the change in positions.

5. _____ Cowboys train their horses to neck-rein because holding the reins in one hand frees the other hand for roping.

6. _____ After harpooning the walruses, the hunters drag the carcasses to camp for cutting.

7. _____ Before Disneyland's opening in 1955, Anaheim was a pastoral community of citrus groves.

8. _____ After having convinced himself that the Hudson was only a river and not the Northwest Passage, Henry Hudson sailed back south.

Answers to Exercise S78 are on page 463.

Exercise S79   ***Recognizing clauses that can be reduced***

If the sentence contains an adverb clause that can be reduced, write the changes necessary to reduce it.

a cowboy

Examples   When ~~a cowboy is~~ working on the range, ~~he~~ goes for a long period of time without seeing his family.

The most recent glaciation on Mount Kilimanjaro occurred between 1400 and 1700, when the Northern Hemisphere was in the grip of the Little Ice Age.

1. No two of them are alike, so you have to learn by experience.

2. In winter, the Magdalen Islands are almost as isolated as when Cartier first discovered them.

3. While the crew was waiting for the tide to come in, they checked all their equipment.

4. After they end their larval period, the worms suddenly grow sluggish and enter the stage of metamorphosing into adults.

5. By the time the permit was ready, it was too late to leave for the trip.

6. While knowledge about the brain is growing, many riddles of the thought process remain unsolved.

7. When they built the wall, the Romans also erected forts every mile.

8. The Hutterites had fled persecution in central Europe and Russia before they came to settle in the United States.

Answers to Exercise S79 are on page 463.

Exercise S80   ***Checking verb form***

If the verb form of the adverb phrase is incorrect, cross it out and write the correction.

coming

Example   Before ~~came~~ to the country, Mary had never seen a camel.

1. While chipped away with a long-handled ax, the woodsman tore his coat.

2. Before going on a long-distance hike, you should soak your feet in cold salty water to toughen the skin.

3. Having bitten by the snake, the farmer quickly tied a tourniquet above the wound.

4. After reconstructed the newly found skull, the anthropologist found it to be similar to human skulls.

5. Since came to the area, the company has brought many new jobs to the community.

6. Having been exiled from her country, the woman made France her new home.

7. After bump our way over dirt tracks, we were relieved to reach a paved road.

8. While entering the canal, the boat enthusiasts made ready to go through the locks.

Answers to Exercise S80 are on page 464.

Exercise S81   *Choosing the correct clause marker*

Circle the letter of the correct clause marker needed to complete the sentence.

Example   Mary was reading a book ----- waiting for the bus.
     (A) as though
     (B) as soon as
     (C) while
     (D) so that

"While" indicates that two actions are occurring at the same time: reading a book and waiting for the bus.

1. ----- capable of walking upright, apelike Australopithecus did so only for short periods of time.
     (A) As if
     (B) Though
     (C) Until
     (D) Because

2. ----- erupting in May 1980, Mount Saint Helens continued erupting intermittently throughout the following year.
     (A) After
     (B) Such as
     (C) Since
     (D) As if

3. The boys were challenged to enter the house ----- having been told the ghost story.
     (A) until
     (B) because
     (C) since
     (D) after

4. ----- entering the starting gate, the horse reared up and knocked down the trainer.
     (A) So that
     (B) When
     (C) Though
     (D) So

5. ----- watching the bullfight, the crowds cheered the bullfighter on.
     (A) As soon as
     (B) Since
     (C) While
     (D) So that

6. ----- declaring the area useless, Daniel Webster could not have foretold how irrigation would make California's Imperial Valley bloom.
     (A) Because
     (B) When
     (C) Though
     (D) So that

7. ----- plowing the field, the farmer uncovered a dinosaur jawbone.
     (A) As though
     (B) While
     (C) Since
     (D) Until

8. ----- struck by lightning, the tree continued to thrive.
     (A) As if
     (B) After
     (C) When
     (D) Although

Answers to Exercise S81 are on page 464.

CHECK YOUR PROGRESS

Check your progress in using the skills you have been practicing in Exercises S73–S81 by completing the following mini-test. This exercise uses the same format as questions 1–15 of the Structure and Written Expression section on the TOEFL.

Exercise S82   *Mini-test*   *(Time – 10 minutes)*

Directions: Questions 1–15 are incomplete sentences. Beneath each sentence you will see four words or phrases marked (A), (B), (C), and (D). Choose the <u>one</u> word or phrase that best completes the sentence. Then circle the letter that corresponds to the answer you have chosen.

Example ---- waiting for the bus, many people read newspapers.
   (A) During
   (B) If
   (C) As
   (D) While

You should circle (D) because "while" can introduce an adverb clause that has been reduced.

1. -----, their small size and the thin soil make them easy prey to a hiker's heel.
 (A) Alpine flowers which can resist wind, cold, and snow
 (B) When alpine flowers can resist wind, cold, and snow
 (C) While alpine flowers can resist wind, cold, and snow
 (D) Alpine flowers resisting wind, cold, and snow

2. ----- pandas eat bamboo almost exclusively, they are also carnivorous.
 (A) Not only
 (B) Until
 (C) As soon as
 (D) Although

3. Although ----- a country illegally is risky, the alien who finds work may believe the risk worthwhile.
 (A) when entering
 (B) he enters
 (C) entering
 (D) having entered

4. The Andean condor glides on air currents and doesn't flap its wings ----- it must do so to reach updrafts.
 (A) because
 (B) until
 (C) that
 (D) as if

5. ----- sighting an approaching car, some drivers tend to speed up.
 (A) When slowing down instead of
 (B) Instead when slowing down at
 (C) When instead of slowing down
 (D) Instead of slowing down when

6. ----- to England remain strong, the Channel Islanders are exempt from most British taxes.
 (A) Although their ties
 (B) Although tied
 (C) Before their ties
 (D) Tied

7. -----, the travelers found that their flight had been canceled because of the severe snowstorm.
 (A) That they arrived at the airport
 (B) As soon as arriving at the airport
 (C) At the airport
 (D) They arrived at the airport

8. When competing in a demolition derby, ----- until their cars are demolished.
 (A) that drivers continue
 (B) drivers must continue
 (C) drivers continuing
 (D) although drivers must continue

9. ----- governments point with pride to increasing mechanization in agriculture, human and animal power still produce a significant portion of the world's food.
   (A) Since
   (B) Because
   (C) So that
   (D) While

10. -----, tobacco farmers had not yet felt its effect.
    (A) Though a campaign against smoking
    (B) That there was a campaign against smoking
    (C) Even though there was a campaign against smoking
    (D) There was a campaign against smoking

11. There were few settlements along the North Carolina coast ----- many problems for seafarers.
    (A) because the offshore barrier posed
    (B) before posing the offshore barrier
    (C) while posing the offshore barrier
    (D) that the offshore barrier had posed

12. ----- since the death of her father.
    (A) The ancestral home of my mother abandoned
    (B) My mother's ancestral home standing abandoned
    (C) My mother's ancestral home has stood abandoned
    (D) My mother's ancestral home which has stood abandoned

13. ----- the owner and buyer finally agreed on a price for the house.
    (A) They had been bargaining for several weeks,
    (B) After bargaining for several weeks,
    (C) After several weeks they began bargaining,
    (D) As if bargaining for several weeks,

14. ----- of the tranquilizer, the scientist put a tag on its ear and recorded details about the animal.
    (A) While under the effect the deer
    (B) While being under the effect the deer
    (C) While the deer was under the effect
    (D) While the deer under the effect

15. ----- the finish line first, the runner gave up.
    (A) Having failed to reach
    (B) Having failed reaching
    (C) He failed to reach
    (D) That he failed reaching

Answers to Exercise S82 are on page 464.

PRACTICE WITH COMPARING

Ask yourself the following questions about comparatives and superlatives.

1. Is the comparative or superlative form correct?

(A) One-syllable adjectives and adverbs form their comparative and superlative forms by adding *-er* and *-est* to the base.

Base	Comparative	Superlative
small	smaller	smallest
fast	faster	fastest

This ring is **smaller** than that ring.
It is the **smallest** one in the box.

Note: The superlative structure includes "the." The comparative structure includes "the" only when the comparative takes a noun position (for example, "I like **the smaller** of the two").

(B) Two-syllable adjectives and adverbs ending in *-er, -y,* or *-ly* add *-er* or *-est* to the base form.

Base	Comparative	Superlative
clever	cleverer	cleverest
happy	happier	happiest
early	earlier	earliest

(C) Some two-syllable adjectives and adverbs and all those with three or more syllables use "more" and "most" with the base form.

Base	Comparative	Superlative
joyful	more joyful	most joyful
intelligent	more intelligent	most intelligent
happily	more happily	most happily

(D) Irregular comparatives and superlatives are as follows:

Base	Comparative	Superlative
good (ADJ)	better	best
well (ADV)	better	best
bad (ADJ)	worse	worst
badly (ADV)	worse	worst
little (ADJ & ADV)	less	least
many (ADJ)	more	most
much (ADJ & ADV)	more	most
far (ADJ & ADV)	farther	farthest
	further	furthest
late (ADV)	later	last
old (ADJ)	older	oldest
	elder	eldest

(E) The comparative form "less" and the superlative form "least" are used with adjectives and adverbs to indicate that something does not have as much of a quality as what it is being compared to.

> I have become **less** anxious about the project.
> This is the **least** popular of the perfumes.

2. Is the comparative or superlative used correctly?

(A) Comparatives and superlatives can be used to modify a noun.

> A **harder** exam would discourage the students.
> The **taller** boy won the wrestling match.
> The **earliest** time I can come is 10:00.

(B) Comparatives and superlatives can be used after a verb.

> We need to be **more** understanding.
> The black horse is the **fastest**.

(C) Some structures using comparatives take the word "than." (*Note:* The words "the" and "than" are not used together in a comparative structure.)

Before noun	Jackie is **more active than** her brother.
Before phrases	Last year the test results were **better than** in previous years.
Before clauses	He is **taller than** I thought he was.

(D) The superlative is used in the following structures.

With prepositions	The first step is **the most** important of all.
	He has **the worst** temper in the world.
With clauses	That book is **the best** I'm likely to find.
	That is **the most convincing** movie I've ever seen.

3. Is the expression of equality or inequality used correctly?

Expressions of equality or inequality can be made using the base form of the adjective or adverb with "as . . . as," "not as . . . as," or "not so . . . as."

> Jim is **as clever as** Nancy, but he doesn't work **as hard as** she does.
>
> I am just **as good** a typist **as** Bobby is.

4. Is the parallel comparison used correctly?

When a two-clause sentence begins with a comparative, the second clause also begins with a comparative.

> **The more encouragement** Edna got, **the harder** she tried to succeed.

Use Exercises S83–S88 to develop your skills in identifying comparisons.

Exercise S83   Locating phrases

Underline the comparatives, superlatives, and expressions of equality and inequality in the following sentences.

Example   Mount Everest is the highest mountain in the world.

You should underline "the highest" because this phrase is a superlative comparing Mount Everest with all the mountains in the world.

1. The largest known gathering of bald eagles anywhere is on the Chilkat River.

2. Settlers from Europe brought with them smallpox, which aided the conquest of the Americas by killing as much as half the native population.

3. As recently as the 1930s Yemen was inaccessible to travelers.

4. The increasing popularity of tennis and bigger crowds meant that a grandstand had to be built at Wimbledon in 1880.

5. Most delectable, king salmon are also the rarest.

6. Once the world's largest church, Hagia Sophia is now a museum.

7. The more isolated the area, the happier the campers were.

8. Rough woven washcloths rub off dirt as well as sponges do.

Answers to Exercise S83 are on page 465.

Exercise S84   *Identifying the kind of phrase*

Write "C" if the underlined phrase is a comparative, "S" if the phrase is a superlative, and "E" if the phrase is an expression of equality or inequality.

Example   _E_   He ate as much as his older brother.

1. _____ Lower prices have forced people in the fishing industry to seek fish other than salmon.

2. _____ The port of Mocca gave its name to what is possibly the most distinctive coffee in the world.

3. _____ Attempts to abolish the court cards from playing cards have proved as unsuccessful as trying to abolish royal figures from the game of chess.

4. _____ The oldest known dam, an engineering wonder of the ancient world, lies near Marib, once the home of the Queen of Sheba.

5. _____ Perhaps the most coveted prize of them all is the Nobel Peace Prize.

6. _____ More pioneers walked across the continent than rode in wagons or on horses.

7. _____ The Mexico earthquake of 1985 was far worse than that of 1979.

8. _____ Mice aren't really as attracted to cheese as they are to grains.

Answers to Exercise S84 are on page 465.

Exercise S85   *Checking comparatives*

Circle any comparative that is used incorrectly.

Example   Northern Mexico generally receives (the less rain than) does Central Mexico.

You should circle "the less rain than" because the words "the" and "than" are not used together in a comparative structure.

1. More often than not a honking goose frightens off strangers best than a barking dog.

2. Australia is the flatter and drier of all the continents.

3. Iowa produces the more feed corn than any other state.

4. The calmer of the two horses was more suitable for amateur riders.

5. The northern side of the mountain has a better scenic view.

6. Waiting to be developed is smaller of the two islands.

7. The history of the United States as a nation spans less time than most major Chinese dynasties.

8. The hunter fired his gun when the heavy of the two bears charged at him.

Extended practice: Rewrite the incorrect sentences using the correct form of the comparative.

Answers to Exercise S85 are on page 465.

Exercise S86   Checking parallel comparatives

Circle any parallel comparative that is used incorrectly.

Example   The more advances and improvements are made in technology, (the more convenient than) the banking transactions become.

1. The more populated the area becomes, the more noise one has to contend with.

2. The finer the particles, the better they bond together when compacted.

3. The more the grasslands are overgrazed, the fast they become deserts.

4. Harder the government tried to settle the nomads, the stronger their resistance to change became.

5. The lower the temperature and longer the cooking time used for a baked potato, the crunchier and tough the skin will be.

6. The further west the Indians were driven, the harder they fought to secure their lands.

7. The faster he tried to work, the less he was able to accomplish.

8. The more development that takes place on the island, the less likelier the native wildlife will survive.

Extended practice: Rewrite the incorrect sentences using the correct form of the parallel comparative.

Answers to Exercise S86 are on page 465.

Exercise S87   Checking superlatives

Circle any superlative that is used incorrectly.

Example   He is (the intelligentest) of all the people at the university.

You should circle "the intelligentest" because the correct superlative is "the most intelligent."

1. Turkey's the largest city, Istanbul, played a central role in history as Constantinople, the capital of the Byzantine Empire.

2. Only the 100 wealthiest were allowed to become members of the club.

3. The water in Half-Moon Bay is the bluest of blues.

4. Blown in from deserts to the north and west, China's loess deposits are the world's greater.

5. The most early set of cards found in Italy is the Tarot deck.

6. Once one of the southernmost towns of biblical Palestine, Beersheba contains a well believed to have been dug by Abraham.

7. The *George W. Wells*, a six-masted schooner, was a largest sailing ship lost on the East Coast.

8. The world's longest running sports competition began at Olympia in 776 B.C.

Extended practice: Rewrite the incorrect sentences using the correct form of the superlative.

Answers to Exercise S87 are on page 465.

Exercise S88   *Checking expressions of equality and inequality*

Circle any expression of equality and inequality that is used incorrectly.

Example   He likes cake (too much as) cookies.

You should circle "too much as" because the correct expression of equality is "as much as."

1. Every year many pounds of peanuts are grown as sweet potatoes in the fertile soil of the Tidewater region.

2. As idyllic as the setting is, it has its drawbacks.

3. Not as many ice skaters take part in the games they used to.

4. Although the drought was as not severe as the previous one, its effect was more damaging.

5. Henry David Thoreau wanted to be as far from the noise of the crowded city as possible.

6. Though St. Paul is not as larger as Minneapolis, it shares the fame of being one of the "Twin Cities."

7. Elephants can siphon up their trunks as much as a gallon and a half of water before spraying it into their mouths.

8. Not as popular a sport as downhill skiing, cross-country skiing has its advantages.

Extended practice: Rewrite the incorrect sentences using the correct form of the expression of equality.

Answers to Exercise S88 are on page 466.

PRACTICE WITH PARALLEL STRUCTURES

Many sentences present information in a list or series. The list or series may consist of two or more parts that have the same grammatical function. This listing is known as parallel structure.

1. Do the parts in the list have the same grammatical function?

Notice how the words in the following sentences are parallel.

Noun	The children played on the **swings, slides,** and **seesaw.**
Gerunds	**Reading, writing,** and **calculating** are important skills to learn.
Infinitives	After her accident, Emma had to learn how **to speak, to walk,** and **to write** again.
Verbs	We will **run, swim,** and **play** at the beach.
Adjectives	Betty is **short, chubby,** and **vivacious.**
Adverbs	This car runs **efficiently, quietly,** and **dependably.**
Subjects	**Vendors selling postcards, artists drawing on the pavement,** and **folk singers strumming guitars** can all be seen at the summer festival in the park.
Phrases	For all her years **of triumph and tragedy, of glory and ruin, of hope and despair,** the actress was still able to draw a crowd.
Clauses	The creation of a map is a compromise of **what needs to be shown, what can be shown in terms of map design,** and **what we would like to include.**

2. Are the parallel parts joined correctly?

Parallel structures may be joined by the following words or phrases:

and	both . . . and
but	not only . . . but also
or	either . . . or
nor	neither . . . nor

3. Are any necessary words missing from the parallel parts?

Study the following sentences.

Incorrect	The eagle swooped down, caught the rabbit, and brought back to its nest.
Correct	The eagle swooped down, caught the rabbit, and brought it back to its nest.

The verb "swoop" does not take an object. The verb "caught" has the object "rabbit." The verb "brought" must have an object. The pronoun "it" in the corrected sentence refers to "the rabbit."

Use Exercises S89–S91 to develop your skills in identifying parallel structures.

Exercise S89   Locating parallels

Underline the parallels in the following sentences.

Example   The dog wagged its tail, sat up, and barked.

1. In the Welsh hills one can easily imagine gnomes, sprites, and elves.

2. Warm ocean conditions, regulation of foreign catches within the U.S. 200-mile limit, and international agreements reducing fishing fleets have played a part in saving the pink salmon from extinction.

3. Silk has been woven into luxurious tapestries, rugs, clothes, and accessories for some 4,000 years.

4. A remarkable system of aqueducts, cisterns, and drains provided water and sanitation for the old city.

5. Pesticides protect us from insects, weeds, disease, and hunger, but some pose a risk of cancer, birth defects, genetic mutations, and sterility.

6. Lashed by storms, violated by opportunists plundering its resources, and struggling against today's economic pressures, Pennsylvania has endured.

7. The crops haven't been developed because of the instability of the economy, the high inflation, and the exchange-rate fluctuations.

8. The grottos have been a den for thieves, a hideout for guerrillas, and a tomb for unwary explorers.

Answers to Exercise S89 are on page 466.

Exercise S90   *Checking for parallels*

Write "Y" (for "yes") if the sentence contains a parallel structure. Write "N" (for "no") if the sentence contains no parallel structure.

Example   _N_   Learning how to row a boat can be tricky at first.

1. _____ Undisturbed by the pesticide, resistant insects can breed, multiply, and injure crops.

2. _____ The eisteddfods are an ancient tradition full of pageantry, ritual, and fanfare.

3. _____ Exploring Chesapeake Bay in 1608 for gold, Captain John Smith discovered ` instead a pathway for settlers.

4. _____ Hungry for freedom and land, the Swedes, Dutch, and English settled the Delaware Valley.

5. _____ The Philadelphia Museum of Art has a community program of public murals, free art instruction, and special exhibitions.

6. _____ You can see the Amish on the country roads, driving their handsome little black horse-drawn carriages.

7. _____ The paint used is a mixture of pollen, cornmeal, and ground-up stones.

8. _____ During the four ceremonial days, the dancer could not bathe, touch her skin, or drink from a glass.

Answers to Exercise S90 are on page 466.

Exercise S91   *Checking parallels*

Circle any incorrect parallels in the following sentences.

Example   At the party the children joined hands, sang songs, and (were playing) circle games.

You should circle "were playing" because the past progressive tense of the verb is not parallel to the simple past tense of the other verbs in the sentence.

1. On the stones of the Sacra Via, patricians and plebeians bargained, elected officials, heard speeches, and were paying homage to pagan gods.

2. Following Charles V's death, the Louvre reverted to its former uses as a fortress, a prison, an arsenal, and a treasure house.

3. The towering pinnacles of Bryce Canyon, the eroded valleys of the Grand Canyon, and across Death Valley are sights the tourist will always remember.

4. The money raised goes directly to schooling for the children, teaching survival skills to women, and most importantly medical supplies.

5. The farmer explained which kind of apples are used for cider, how they are processed, and the small bitter apples make the best cider.

6. The chicks have been raised on a diet of liquidized mice, dogfood, fish, proteins, and vitamins.

7. The Dartmoor sheep produces quality fleece, is comparatively prolific, and has lambs that fatten readily.

8. Filming a wild animal in its habitat requires meticulous preparation, unending patience, and at times, one must be courageous.

Extended practice: Rewrite the incorrect sentences using the correct parallel structure.

Answers to Exercise S91 are on page 466.

PRACTICE WITH PREPOSITIONAL PHRASES

Ask yourself the following questions about prepositional phrases.

1. Is the phrase correct?

The prepositional phrase consists of a preposition and an object. The object is a noun or pronoun.

> **PREP   OBJ**
> into the house

> **PREP OBJ**
> above it

The noun can have modifiers.

> **PREP   OBJ**
> into the old broken-down house

2. Is the phrase in the correct position?

(A) Prepositional phrases that are used as adverbs can take various positions.

> The city park is just **around the corner**.
> Just **around the corner** is the city park.

"Around the corner" answers the question "Where is the city park?" and therefore is used like an adverb. (See Practice with Adverb Clauses, page 199.)

(B) Prepositional phrases that are used as adjectives *follow* the noun they describe.

NOUN _____**PREP PHRASE**_____
I walked into the house **with the sagging porch.**

"With the sagging porch" describes the house and therefore is used like an adjective.

3. Is the correct preposition used to introduce the phrase?

(A) Some of the words and phrases that are commonly used as prepositions are:

about	behind	in	through
above	below	in spite of	throughout
across	beneath	into	till
after	beside	like/unlike	to
against	between	near	toward
along	beyond	of	under
among	by	off	until
around	despite	on	up
as	down	out	upon
at	during	out of	with
because of	for	over	within
before	from	since	without

(B) Some of the words that are used as prepositions can be used in other ways. To check whether a prepositional phrase is being used, look for a preposition and an object.

___**PREP**___ ___**OBJ**___
Because of the time, we had to leave.

CLAUSE
MARKER ___**CLAUSE**___
Because it was late, we had to leave.

PREP ___**OBJ**___
We wrote the correction **above the error**.

ADV
Study the sentences **above**.

PREP_____**OBJ**_____
We climbed **up the spiral staircase**.

PHRASAL
VERB*
We had to **get up** early.

*A phrasal verb is a verb + one or two other words which gives the verb a different meaning. "Get" means "obtain," whereas "get up" means "arise."

(C) Some prepositions have several meanings.

I hung the picture **on** the wall.	(upon)
I bought a book **on** philosophy.	(about)
I called her **on** the phone.	(using)
I worked **on** the research committee.	(with)

Use Exercises S92–S95 to develop your skills in identifying prepositions.

Exercise S92   *Identifying prepositional phrases*

Write "Y" (for "yes") if the phrase is a prepositional phrase. Write "N" (for "no") if the phrase is not a prepositional phrase.

Example   <u> N </u>   to go home

               <u> Y </u>   to the store

You should write "N" in the first space because "go" indicates that the phrase is an infinitive phrase. You should write "Y" in the second space because this prepositional phrase has the preposition "to" + the article "the" and the object "store."

1. _____ because of the promise

2. _____ by walking

3. _____ to bring the paper

4. _____ in the summertime

5. _____ because they left

6. _____ between the houses

7. _____ for drawing the plans

8. _____ during the evening

Answers to Exercise S92 are on page 466.

Exercise S93   *Locating prepositional phrases*

Underline the prepositional phrases in the following sentences.

Example   <u>In a palm-shaded beach house</u> south <u>of Bombay,</u> Professor Salim Ali is battling <u>against time and illness</u> to complete his 10-volume handbook <u>of the birds</u> <u>of India and Pakistan.</u>

1. In the aftermath of the explosion, people worked night and day to clear the area.

2. Having been to the park on several occasions, Dr. Jenkens was pleased to find that the new gates were enabling wild animals to move freely through the range.

3. For several weeks the tiny asteroid orbited close to Earth.

4. Even though her watch got mixed in with the laundry and was put into the washing machine, it still kept relatively good time.

5. John Wesley Hyatt discovered plastics by accident while cooking up a recipe for the billiard ball.

6. When buying property, it is a wise idea to consult a lawyer about the various legal aspects.

7. It was well after midnight when she left her friend's house in the French quarter of New Orleans and set out to search for a taxi.

8. The picnic evolved in Europe as a pastime of the upper classes, whose outings would be attended by the bustle of servants.

Answers to Exercise S93 are on page 466.

Exercise S94   *Identifying the correct preposition*

Circle the letter of the preposition that correctly completes the sentence.

Example   Information ----- bird-banding fills huge gaps in our knowledge of bird behavior and migration.
(A) by
(B) from
(C) with
(D) during

You should circle (B) because "from" indicates "the source of the information."

1. Meriwether Lewis and William Clark made their epic journey across North America in the years 1804 ----- 1806.
   (A) to
   (B) between
   (C) over
   (D) for

2. Clay incense burners ----- effigy lids were excavated near Becan.
   (A) out
   (B) from
   (C) with
   (D) before

3. The black bear suddenly appeared from ----- the tent.
   (A) behind
   (B) out
   (C) with
   (D) after

4. Wilbur Wright flew his airplane ----- France in 1909.
   (A) on
   (B) upon
   (C) until
   (D) over

5. Mount Rainier towers nearly three miles ----- sea level.
   (A) up
   (B) at
   (C) along
   (D) above

6. The winter snow was ----- 16 feet deep in places.
   (A) across from
   (B) up to
   (C) out from
   (D) out of

7. While ----- a visit to Georgia, Eli Whitney learned of the need for a machine that could clean cotton.
   (A) of
   (B) on
   (C) above
   (D) for

8. As densely populated as the city is, there are surprisingly few people seen ----- the streets.
   (A) to
   (B) at
   (C) of
   (D) on

Answers to Exercise S94 are on page 466.

Exercise S95   *Identifying the correct phrase*

Circle the letter of the phrase that correctly completes the sentence.

Example   The man moved awkwardly ----- of a cane.
(A) with the aid
(B) while the aiding

1. ----- his adventurous feelings often returned.
   (A) As the years
   (B) Through the years

2. The Mississippi region is ----- astonishingly diverse people.
   (A) full of
   (B) entirely filled

3. The members expected ----- would cause controversy.
   (A) that the report
   (B) from the report

4. ----- the encouraging response, the manager decided to continue the project.
   (A) Because
   (B) Because of

5. The original story has not been changed ----- the names of the characters.
   (A) except that
   (B) except for

6. The dates, places, and times ----- were listed in the brochure.
   (A) the carnival was
   (B) of the carnival

7. The documentary stressed the need ----- toward our planet.
   (A) for a new attitude
   (B) being a new attitude

8. A graceful carved statue ----- in Asyut is the centerpiece of the exhibition.
   (A) from a tomb
   (B) that a tomb

Answers to Exercise S95 are on page 467.

PRACTICE WITH REDUNDANCIES

Ask yourself the following question about repeated information.

Have words that repeat unnecessary information been used?

(A) When two words have essentially the same meaning, use one or the other, but not both.

Correct	It was **very** important.
	It was **extremely** important.
Incorrect	It was very, extremely important.

Because "very" and "extremely" have essentially the same meaning, they should not be used together.

Correct	Money is required for research to **advance**.
	Money is required for research to move **forward**.
Incorrect	Money is required for research to advance forward.

The word "advance" indicates "going forward." Therefore, the word "forward" is unnecessary.

(B) In general, avoid these combinations:

advance forward	repeat again
join together	reread again
new innovations	return back
only unique	revert back
proceed forward	same identical
progress forward	sufficient enough

Use Exercises S96–S97 to develop your skills in identifying redundancies.

Exercise S96   **Checking phrases**

If the following phrases are redundant, cross out "and" and the second word.

Examples   established ~~and founded~~
salt and pepper

In the first example, you should cross out "and founded" because "established" means "founded." In the second example, you should leave "salt and pepper" as it is because "salt" is different from "pepper."

1. enlarged and grew

2. wounded and injured

3. small and single

4. sneeze and cough

5. long and slender

6. protect and guard

7. divide and conquer

8. original and first

Answers to Exercise S96 are on page 467.

Exercise S97   **Identifying redundancies**

If there are any redundancies in the following sentences, cross them out.

Example   The house was enlarged ~~and made bigger~~ as the family grew.

1. Conservationists have been collecting data to save these shy and timid creatures.

2. Drastic measures are necessary and needed to stop the famine.

3. Labels should include the information that allows shoppers to compare the ingredients and contents of the food they are buying.

4. Illnesses caused by viruses and bacteria may lower the level of vitamins in the blood stream.

5. Heavy consumption of alcohol and drinking a lot of wine may interfere with the body's utilization of folic acid.

6. Both overeating and skipping meals can cause adverse effects.

7. Montreal is the charming and enchanting old capital city of Quebec.

8. A 1,300-year-old Byzantine ship and another old, ancient vessel have been retrieved from watery graves.

Answers to Exercise S97 are on page 467.

CHECK YOUR PROGRESS

Check your progress in using the skills that you have been practicing in Exercises S83–S97 by completing the following mini-test. This exercise uses the same format as questions 1–15 of the Structure and Written Expression section on the TOEFL.

Exercise S98   **Mini-test**   *(Time – 10 minutes)*

Directions: Questions 1–15 are incomplete sentences. Beneath each sentence you will see four words or phrases marked (A), (B), (C), and (D). Choose the <u>one</u> word or phrase that best completes the sentence. Then circle the letter that corresponds to the answer you have chosen.

Example   More advancements have been made in technology in the last 100 years -----
in all the rest of human history.
(A) than
(B) as
(C) and
(D) as well as

"Than" is the word used in comparatives, and the advancements in the last 100 years are
being compared to the advancements in all the rest of history.

1. The treasures came from a second, ----- room.
    (A) the smallest
    (B) as small as
    (C) much smaller
    (D) more small

2. Bryce Canyon is 56 square miles of badlands, towering pinnacles, and -----.
    (A) it has eroded forms that are grotesque
    (B) forming grotesque erosion
    (C) there are grotesque forms of erosion
    (D) grotesque eroded forms

3. The shrinking range poses ----- to Africa's elephants.
    (A) a graver threat that is long term
    (B) the gravest long-term threat
    (C) long term the gravest threat
    (D) a long-term threat graver

4. ----- in astronomy, the discovery of Uranus was by accident.
    (A) It was like many finds
    (B) Like many finds
    (C) Alike many finds
    (D) Many alike finds

5. -----, the condor in Peru is threatened by the rapid encroachment of humans.
    (A) As isolated as its few remaining habitats may be
    (B) As its few remaining isolated habitats may be
    (C) May its few remaining habitats be as isolated
    (D) Its few remaining habitats may be as isolated as

6. The stories show how ----- humans have been trying to live in harmony with nature.
    (A) during the earliest times
    (B) that the earliest times
    (C) from the earliest times
    (D) because earliest times

7. -----, Mozart had already written his first composition.
    (A) His age was six
    (B) By the age of six
    (C) He was six
    (D) Six years old

8. Julius Caesar did not conquer Britain but instead stayed a few weeks, took some
    hostages, and -----.
    (A) before returning to Boulogne
    (B) he returned to Boulogne
    (C) then to Boulogne
    (D) returned to Boulogne

9. Today shire horses are seen more and more in their traditional role ----- work horses.
   - (A) alike
   - (B) as
   - (C) like
   - (D) as if

10. ----- was debated, the more people became involved.
    - (A) The longer the issue
    - (B) The longer issue
    - (C) The long issue
    - (D) The longest issue

11. The Viking Ship Museum houses ----- ever recovered.
    - (A) three finest funeral ships
    - (B) the finest three funeral ships
    - (C) the three finest funeral ships
    - (D) the three funeral finest ships

12. -----, black bears climb trees.
    - (A) Unlike grizzly bears are
    - (B) Grizzly bears are unlike
    - (C) Grizzly unlike bears
    - (D) Unlike grizzly bears

13. The exquisite antique bottle was carved ----- marble.
    - (A) from
    - (B) by
    - (C) about
    - (D) at

14. The Searight collection ----- of the Middle East by European artists covers the past two centuries.
    - (A) of some 6,000 drawings and paintings
    - (B) about 6,000 drawings and paintings
    - (C) some 6,000 drawings and paintings big
    - (D) about 6,000 drawings and paintings in all

15. A fist-sized tarantula was crawling ----- of his hand.
    - (A) by the yard
    - (B) between a yard
    - (C) in yards
    - (D) within a yard

Answers to Exercise S98 are on page 467.

Exercise S99   *Structure and Written Expression Practice Test*

When you have completed the exercises as recommended by the Diagnostic Test, test your skills by taking this final TOEFL Structure and Written Expression Practice Test. Maintain the same test conditions that would be experienced during the actual TOEFL test. Time the test and tear out and use the answer sheet on page 545.

Answers to Exercise S99 are on page 468.

SECTION 2
STRUCTURE AND WRITTEN EXPRESSION

Time – 25 minutes

This section is designed to measure your ability to recognize language that is appropriate for standard written English. There are two types of questions in this section, with special directions for each type.

Directions: Questions 1–15 are incomplete sentences. Beneath each sentence you will see four words or phrases marked (A), (B), (C), and (D). Choose the one word or phrase that best completes the sentence. Then, on your answer sheet, find the number of the question and fill in the space that corresponds to the letter of the answer you have chosen. Fill in the space so that the letter inside the oval cannot be seen.

Example   Baby teeth require just ----- later permanent teeth.

    (A) as careful as
    (B) more care than
    (C) as much care as
    (D) the most care

Sample Answer
Ⓐ Ⓑ ● Ⓓ

The sentence should read, "Baby teeth require just as much care as later permanent teeth." Therefore, you should choose answer (C).

After you read the directions, begin work on the questions.

1. Deep in the Rio Bec area of Mexico's Yucatan Peninsula -----.
    (A) does a 1,250-year-old pyramid lie
    (B) a 1,250-year-old pyramid lie
    (C) lies a 1,250-year-old pyramid
    (D) is a 1,250-year-old pyramid lying

2. The architecture and pottery uncovered in ----- revealed Middle Eastern cultural relationships.
    (A) this area has
    (B) the areas has
    (C) area have
    (D) this area have

3. The Pacific Crest Trail is America's -----.
    (A) longest footpath
    (B) the long footpath
    (C) footpath the longest one
    (D) the longest footpath

4. Air pollution ----- almost every major city in the world.
    (A) that now afflicts
    (B) it now afflicts
    (C) now afflicts
    (D) what now afflicts

5. Today, "carpet" refers to floor coverings that reach from wall to wall ----- "rug" refers to a piece of material that covers only one section of the floor.
    (A) therefore
    (B) whereas
    (C) in as much as
    (D) among

6. The triple function of Bodiam Castle's moat was to be defensive, decorative, and -----.
    (A) to double the impression of impregnability
    (B) to be double the impression of impregnability
    (C) double the impression of impregnability
    (D) for doubling the impression of impregnability

7. ----- is that a chicken stands up to lay its eggs.
    (A) Many people don't realize
    (B) What many people don't realize
    (C) It is that many people don't realize
    (D) Because many people don't realize

8. The tiger heard the splashing, rolled into ambush position, and crouched down in the grass -----.
    (A) readied itself to attack
    (B) made itself ready for the attack
    (C) to ready itself and attacked
    (D) to ready itself for the attack

9. ----- before the stork chick moves even six inches in the nest.
    (A) Just over five months is
    (B) It takes just over five months
    (C) When just five months are over
    (D) That it takes just over five months

GO ON TO THE NEXT PAGE

10. Thor Heyerdahl ----- from Peru in a frail balsa craft to prove his theory of South American migration to Polynesia.
(A) set sail
(B) who set sail
(C) he set sail
(D) whom set sail

11. Napoleon III eventually landed in England -----.
(A) not only as a dethroned exile
(B) but only as a dethroned exile
(C) but a dethroned exile
(D) but being only a dethroned exile

12. Jacob Lawrence is considered by many critics -----.
(A) to be the foremost African-American artist
(B) the foremost African-American artist is
(C) foremost African-American artist
(D) is the foremost African-American artist

13. Within the first ten minutes the chairperson knew the meeting -----.
(A) would nothing come to
(B) would come nothing
(C) would come to nothing
(D) nothing would come to

14. ----- of true seals, the monk seals are considered to be the most primitive.
(A) The 18 species
(B) 18 species are
(C) There are 18 species
(D) Of the 18 species

15. Traditional sailors ----- many of the same dangers as their predecessors.
(A) face is
(B) is facing
(C) face
(D) are faced

Directions: In questions 16–40 each sentence has four underlined words or phrases. The four underlined parts of the sentence are marked (A), (B), (C), and (D). Identify the one underlined word or phrase that must be changed in order for the sentence to be correct. Then, on your answer sheet, find the number of the question and fill in the space that corresponds to the letter of the answer you have chosen.

Example   When moist air rises into <u>lowest</u> temperatures and becomes <u>saturated</u>, condensation
                     A   B   C
<u>takes</u> place.
   D

Sample Answer
Ⓐ ● Ⓒ Ⓓ

The sentence should read, "When moist air rises into lower temperatures and becomes saturated, condensation takes place." Therefore, you should choose answer (B).

After you read the directions, begin work on the questions.

16. Small animals can <u>to</u> survive the desert heat <u>by finding</u> shade <u>during</u> the <u>daytime</u>.
                                    A   B   C   D

17. Motoring authorities <u>credit</u> mandatory seat belt laws <u>by</u> the <u>reduction</u> in traffic <u>fatalities</u>.
                                          A   B   C   D

18. Vancouver, British Columbia, <u>was named</u> <u>after</u> the man <u>which</u> explored the <u>area</u> in 1792.
                                                         A   B   C   D

19. Belgian chocolate is <u>considered</u> <u>by</u> many <u>to</u> be the <u>fine</u> in the world.
                                          A   B   C   D

20. The dream of building a <u>permanently</u> staffed space station may soon <u>to become</u> a <u>reality</u>.
                                             A   B   C   D

GO ON TO THE NEXT PAGE

21. It is a <u>well-know</u> fact <u>that</u> camels can <u>go</u> for extended periods <u>without</u> water.
      A   B   C   D

22. Several <u>expeditions</u> have attempted <u>finding</u> the <u>remains of</u> Noah's ark <u>on</u> the slopes of
        A   B   C   D
Mount Ararat.

23. Scientists <u>worry</u> that the <u>continued</u> use of <u>certain</u> pollutants may damage <u>an</u> Earth's
         A   B   C   D
ozone layer.

24. The artists John Constable and Thomas Gainsborough <u>were born</u> at a <u>few</u> miles of each
                                             A   B   C
<u>other</u>.
 D

25. Starches <u>provide</u> important nutrients and <u>satisfy</u> hunger <u>without</u> <u>add</u> excess weight.
        A   B   C   D

26. Prices are <u>increasingly</u> going up <u>as</u> the economy <u>falters</u>.
    A   B   C   D

27. Norma Jean Baker <u>was</u> the <u>real</u> name of the <u>famous</u> Hollywood actress known <u>such as</u>
                 A   B   C   D
Marilyn Monroe.

28. The <u>capital</u> of North Yemen <u>is situating</u> 2,190 meters <u>above</u> sea level.
     A   B C   D

29. *Bleak House* is in <u>many</u> ways <u>the most</u> controversial of the <u>novel</u> that Charles Dickens
                 A   B   C   D
wrote.

30. The Aswan High Dam <u>has protected</u> Egypt <u>of</u> the <u>famines</u> of <u>neighboring</u> countries.
                      A   B   C   D

31. <u>Some</u> 2,300 years <u>ago</u>, Greek philosophers <u>gave</u> the name "atom" to the <u>smaller</u> particle
     A   B   C   D
of matter in nature.

32. <u>As</u> the first recreation chief of the U.S. Forest Service, Bob Marshall <u>helped</u> <u>preserving</u>
 A   B   C
millions of acres <u>of</u> wilderness.
            D

33. When John Speke <u>discovered</u> Lake Victoria in 1858, <u>he</u> believed was the <u>source</u> of
   A   B   C   D
the Nile.

GO ON TO THE NEXT PAGE ➡

34. <u>With</u> the discovery of Pluto's moon, Charon, astronomers now <u>think</u> Pluto is <u>the</u>
      A   B   C

    smallest planet in <u>ours</u> solar system.
                  D

35. The psychological school of <u>behaviorism</u> was <u>found</u> by J. B. Watson.
     A   B   C D

36. The <u>first</u> wagon train on <u>the</u> Oregon Trail <u>setting</u> out <u>from</u> Independence, Missouri,
       A   B   C   D

    in 1841.

37. The <u>discovery</u> of gold in 1849 <u>brought</u> California nationwide <u>attentive</u>.
        A   B   C   D

38. The Kerma <u>civilization</u> was <u>some</u> of the <u>earliest</u> indigenous African <u>tribal</u> groups.
             A   B   C   D

39. Human beings <u>which</u> live <u>longer</u> than one hundred years <u>are</u> a <u>rarity</u>.
            A   B   C   D

40. Scientists <u>have</u> identified several hundred subatomic <u>particle</u> <u>held</u> together by a
         A   B   C   D

    nuclear force.

THIS IS THE END OF THE STRUCTURE AND WRITTEN EXPRESSION PRACTICE TEST.

SECTION ·3·

VOCABULARY AND READING COMPREHENSION

VOCABULARY

Section 3 of the TOEFL, Vocabulary and Reading Comprehension, consists of 60 questions. Thirty of these are vocabulary items. Each item consists of a sentence with one word or phrase underlined. Following each sentence are four words or phrases. You must choose the one word or phrase that could be used in place of the underlined word without changing the meaning of the sentence.

STRATEGIES TO USE FOR BUILDING VOCABULARY

1. Read extensively.

The kind of vocabulary that you will encounter on the TOEFL is formal and academic. Read as much as you can – particularly newspapers, magazine articles, and encyclopedia entries that are academic in nature. By reading this type of material, you will encounter the kind of words that will be useful for you to learn.

When you are reading, try to guess the meaning of unknown words from the context. To do this, use other words in the sentence or passage as clues that show you the meaning of unfamiliar words. If you still are not certain, look the word up in your dictionary and check if your guess was correct.

2. Use notecards.

When you come across a word you don't know, first write it on a notecard and then look it up in a dictionary. On the back of the notecard write down the meaning and any other information that will help you to learn the word.

Increase your vocabulary by studying your notecards. Write sentences using the new words. Try to add at least three new words with their synonyms (words that mean the same) and antonyms (words that mean the opposite) to your vocabulary every day.

3. Use a dictionary.

Invest in a good English dictionary (not a learner's dictionary). Dictionaries vary greatly. A good dictionary will have more information than just meanings. Look for a dictionary that includes the following information:

(A) The pronunciation of the word.
(B) Information on how the word is used grammatically. For example, is it a noun (n.), verb (v.), etc.?
(C) Clear meanings.

(D) An example of the word used in a sentence or phrase.

(E) Optional: The origins of words. This information may help you learn new words by giving you the meanings of the parts of the word (prefixes, roots, and suffixes).

Study the following entry:

succeed \sək si:d\, v.t. & i.   1.   take the place previously filled by, follow (t. & i.) in order, come next (to), ensue, be subsequent (to), come by inheritance or in due order to or to office or title or property, (day ____s day; agitation ____ed calm; ____ing ages will reverence his memory; Elizabeth ____ed Mary to the throne).   2.   Have success (in doing, etc.), be successful, prosper, accomplish one's purpose (of plan, etc.), be brought to successful issue. [ME, f. OF succeder or L SUC (cedere cess – go)]

The word "success" is followed by letters between slash marks. This is the pronunciation of the word. Next is the grammatical usage of "success." It can be used as either a transitive verb, v.t. (a verb that takes an object), or an intransitive verb, v.i. (a verb that does not take an object). The first meaning of the word is given with examples in parentheses. The space ____ is where the word "success" would be used. Following the second meaning of the word is the history or origins of the word "success." "Success" came into Modern English from Middle English (ME) via the Old French (OF) word "succeder" or the Latin (L) word "succedere." The capital letters for the Latin prefix "suc" indicate that this prefix is defined under the dictionary entry "suc-." "Suc-" is a variation of the prefix "sub-" meaning "under." The Latin word "cedere" means "go." The word "success" comes from the word "undergo."

4. Learn prefixes, suffixes, and roots.

Prefixes and suffixes are additions placed at the beginning and end of a root word to modify its meaning. A knowledge of these additions will help you expand your vocabulary. (See Practice with Prefixes, Roots, and Suffixes for more information.)

5. Use a thesaurus.

It is easier to remember a word if you know related words. A thesaurus is a good source for finding words that are related. It may also list expressions that the words are used in.

To use a thesaurus, you look up the word you want in the index at the back. The index entry is followed by one or more references, all of which are in some way related to the word you are looking up (although they are not necessarily synonyms). A number following each reference will direct you to a section that contains lists of further related words. Use your dictionary to find the precise meaning for any word you are unsure of.

6. Use a dictionary of synonyms and antonyms.

A dictionary of synonyms and antonyms is useful because it lists both words that mean the same and words that mean the opposite. Expand your vocabulary by adding words that mean the opposite to your list of vocabulary.

7. Make word diagrams.

It is easier for some people to remember related words if they use symbols, diagrams, or "word maps." Here are a few examples.

This is a word map for adjectives that mean the same as "strange."

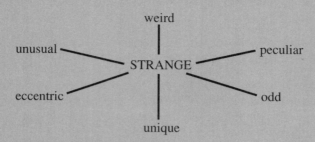

Here is a word chart for professions:

Concerning money	Helping people	Working with machinery
economist	social worker	engineer
banker	therapist	mechanic
stock broker	counselor	

Here is a way to write words and their opposites: poor ≠ rich

destitute ≠ affluent

indigent ≠ wealthy

By showing relationships between words, it is often easier to remember new vocabulary.

8. Make good use of your free time.

People spend a lot of time waiting. Keep your notecards with you. The next time you are waiting for a bus, sitting in a doctor's office, or standing in a line, get out your cards and review your words.

STRATEGIES TO USE FOR THE VOCABULARY SECTION

1. Read the complete sentence and all *possible answers.*

Example This assignment is turning into a <u>regular</u> disaster.
    (A) veritable
    (B) permanent
    (C) standard
    (D) habitual

All of the possible answers are synonyms of the word "regular."

(A) "Regular" means "veritable" in the following sentence: "He is a regular genius when it comes to fixing cars."

(B) "Regular" means "permanent" in the following sentence: "The regular night nurse was on duty when the accident occurred."

(C) "Regular" means "standard" in the following sentence: "Regular-sized note book paper is required for the project."

(D) "Regular" means "habitual" in the following sentence: "His regular customers helped him through the recession."

If you read only the underlined word and the possible answers, you might choose the synonym for "regular" which you are most familiar with. Only by reading the complete sentence do you know which of the answers is the synonym of "regular" in this case.

2. Answer the vocabulary items carefully, but quickly.

The combined time for the Vocabulary and Reading Comprehension section is only 45 minutes. Don't waste time on vocabulary that you don't know. If there is time, you can return to the vocabulary section after you have finished the readings.

3. Use your time wisely.

Do not waste time attempting to answer vocabulary items in the following ways.

(A)　Searching for context clues.

There are virtually no clues in the sentence to help you understand a word you don't know.

> **Example**　This assignment is turning into a regular disaster.
> (A) veritable
> (B) permanent
> (C) standard
> (D) habitual

If you do not know what the word "regular" means in the example, you cannot figure out its meaning from clues in the sentence. Only if you know the various meanings for "regular" will the context of the sentence help you.

(B)　Searching for grammatical clues.

　All the possible answers can fit into the sentence grammatically.

(C)　Analyzing a word.

While the knowledge of word parts will help you increase your vocabulary greatly, it may not always help you identify a correct answer.

> **Example**　Rachel is rearranging the furniture.
> (A) removing
> (B) fixing
> (C) shifting
> (D) renovating

The word "rearrange" is composed of "re-" meaning "again" and "arrange" meaning "organize." Rachel is organizing the position of her furniture again. Because the word "removing" is composed of "re-" meaning "again" and "move" meaning "change positions," you might suspect that "removing" means "rearranging." However, the correct answer is (C), "shifting."

4. Know what works for you.

If you are uncertain which answer is correct, you can do one of two things:

(A) Use your intuition (instincts).
(B) Guess.

Sometimes you do not know the answer but have an unexplained feeling that one of the answers is correct. You have no other reason to believe it is correct. This is your intuition. Test your *intuition* while working through the mini-tests in this book by marking items that you answered intuitively. If your intuition is usually correct, trust it when you take the TOEFL.

Sometimes students answer intuitively and then change their answers. Check yourself while working through the mini-tests in this book. Do you frequently change right answers to wrong ones, or are your changes usually correct? If your first answer is usually the correct one, don't change your answers on the TOEFL.

Remember that wrong answers will not count against you. If you don't know an answer and have no feeling about which of the four choices may be correct, use a *guess letter.* A guess letter is one letter (A, B, C, or D) that you can use to answer all items you don't know. You are more likely to get some correct answers if you use one letter consistently than if you use all letters randomly.

5. Answer every item.

If you do not know the answer, do not leave a blank space. Answer it using your intuition or a guess letter. Mark the item you are unsure of in the test booklet. If you have time, you can go back and think about the marked items. If you change any answer, be sure you thoroughly erase your first answer.

PRACTICE WITH SYNONYMS, ANTONYMS, SHADES OF MEANINGS, AND MULTIPLE MEANINGS

In the following vocabulary exercises, concentrate on building your knowledge of synonyms, antonyms, shades of meanings, and multiple meanings. As you continue to study the other sections of the TOEFL, add any unknown vocabulary words to your list and add their synonyms, antonyms, shades of meanings, and multiple meanings. Also, write their noun, adjective, adverb, and verb forms both for learning the vocabulary and for helping you in the grammar section.

Exercise V1   ***Identifying synonyms***

Write an "S" in the space next to each word that means the same or almost the same as the given word. There may be more than one possible right answer.

Example   seashore

    _____ gulf

    _*S*__ coast

    _____ canal

    _____ sea

    _*S*__ beach

While all the words concern water areas, the word "seashore" concerns the area where the water and land meet. The words in the list that also relate to where water and land meet are "coast" and "beach."

1. gem

_____ jewel

_____ boulder

_____ sand

_____ stone

_____ pebble

2. eradicate

_____ consume

_____ exterminate

_____ devour

_____ destroy

_____ devastate

3. liberate

_____ redeem

_____ release

_____ free

_____ salvage

_____ rescue

4. provoke

_____ arouse

_____ explode

_____ offend

_____ incense

_____ irritate

5. guilty

_____ bad

_____ shameful

_____ offensive

_____ at fault

_____ to blame

6. motive

_____ reason

_____ urge

_____ push

_____ cause

_____ induce

7. scent

_____ stink

_____ perfume

_____ odor

_____ fragrance

_____ smell

8. stare

_____ glance

_____ blink

_____ glimpse

_____ gaze

_____ gape

9. wander

_____ rove

_____ ramble

_____ meander

_____ travel

_____ tour

10. inn

_____ dwelling

_____ hotel

_____ lodge

_____ tent

_____ hovel

Answers to Exercise V1 are on page 469.

Exercise V2   ***Replacing words in sentences***

The following sentences each contain an underlined word. Write "S" in the space next to each word that has a similar meaning and could replace the underlined word in the sentence.

Example   Whether on stage or in the movies, that actor does a superb job.

_____ villain

_____ hero

_S_ entertainer

_S_ performer

_____ idol

"Villain" and "hero" are specific roles on stage or in the movies. An "actor" is the person whose profession is to play any of these roles. "Entertainers" and "performers" can be actors (or singers, dancers, comedians, etc.) who work on the stage or in the movies, so you should write "S" beside these words. An "idol" is someone that somebody else adores, and it has nothing to do with the acting profession.

1. The ship steamed into the harbor last week.

_____ train

_____ plane

_____ bus

_____ vessel

_____ boat

2. His preposterous remark embarrassed his friends.

_____ indiscreet

_____ ambiguous

_____ absurd

_____ ridiculous

_____ rude

3. The caves had been inhabited by ancient peoples.

_____ caverns

_____ mines

_____ shafts

_____ grottos

_____ tunnels

4. A ferocious dog chased away the mail carrier.

_____ angry

_____ irritating

_____ fierce

_____ annoying

_____ savage

5. The audience stood and vigorously clapped after the performance.

_____ viciously

_____ naturally

_____ heartily

_____ energetically

_____ haughtily

6. The government tried to ban all public meetings.

_____ prohibit

_____ discontinue

_____ complete

_____ forbid

_____ antagonize

7. Did you <u>witness</u> the crime?

_____ observe

_____ predict

_____ spy

_____ foresee

_____ see

8. The campsite was chosen because of <u>an abundant</u> supply of fresh water.

_____ a plentiful

_____ an exuberant

_____ an ample

_____ an extreme

_____ a varied

9. Professor Shepard's <u>lecture</u> was well attended.

_____ proposal

_____ speech

_____ talk

_____ chatter

_____ utterance

10. An ancient Mayan city was <u>concealed</u> by the jungle.

_____ hidden

_____ covered

_____ prevented

_____ deposited

_____ ruined

11. The <u>tired</u> traveler searched for accommodations.

_____ weary

_____ misled

_____ exhausted

_____ collapsed

_____ wasted

12. The father wanted to give his <u>offspring</u> a large amount of money.

_____ children

_____ progenitors

_____ forefathers

_____ predecessors

_____ descendants

Answers to Exercise V2 are on page 469.

Exercise V3   ***Recognizing multiple meanings***

The given word may have several different possible meanings. Some of those meanings may apply to different forms of the given word (e.g., noun, verb, adjective, or adverb). Write a check (√) in the blank before each word that could be a meaning of the given word.

Example   note

√ message

√ jot down

_____ dim

√ take notice of

_____ remain

The noun "note" can mean a "message." The verb "to note" can mean "to jot something down." The verb "to note" can also mean "to take notice of something."

1. pilot

_____ test

_____ landing

_____ fault

_____ restrain

_____ navigate

2. gain

_____ profit

_____ gallows

_____ win

_____ acquire

_____ distort

3. annual

_____ crowd

_____ endure

_____ yearbook

_____ holiday

_____ yearly

4. foundation

_____ endowment

_____ hinder

_____ installation

_____ justification

_____ base

5. list

_____ lean

_____ garb

_____ brag

_____ enumerate

_____ mediocrity

6. range

_____ vary

_____ extent

_____ attic

_____ breathe

_____ grazing lands

7. loose

_____ decorate

_____ limp

_____ unfastened

_____ vacant

_____ free

8. border

_____ barrier

_____ frontier

_____ boundary

_____ edge

_____ projection

9. absorb

_____ jeer

_____ take in

_____ effect

_____ consume

_____ monopolize

10. shed

_____ hut

_____ shelf

_____ emit

_____ filter

_____ cast off

Answers to Exercise V3 are on page 470.

Exercise V4   ***Using words with multiple meanings in sentences***

Write a check ($\sqrt{}$) in the space before the sentence if the given word could replace the underlined word without changing the meaning of the sentence.

Example   poor

$\underline{\quad\sqrt{}\quad}$ The <u>inferior</u> quality of the metal makes it unsuitable for use in building construction.

$\underline{\qquad\qquad}$ The <u>denial</u> added insult to injury.

$\underline{\quad\sqrt{}\quad}$ The family sat down to a <u>meager</u> meal.

$\underline{\quad\sqrt{}\quad}$ The agriculture specialists analyzed the contents of the <u>impoverished</u> soil.

1. lot

$\underline{\qquad\qquad}$ The <u>exact</u> number of stars in the galaxy is not known.

$\underline{\qquad\qquad}$ The <u>fate</u> of many Indian tribes was tragic.

$\underline{\qquad\qquad}$ The family bought the <u>portion of land</u> beside their farm.

$\underline{\qquad\qquad}$ Homing pigeons lose their sense of <u>direction</u> in fog.

2. stock

$\underline{\qquad\qquad}$ Some stores keep a large <u>inventory</u> of goods on reserve.

$\underline{\qquad\qquad}$ Many scientists believe that human beings and apes are descended from a common <u>ancestor</u>.

$\underline{\qquad\qquad}$ Sigmund Freud claimed that an individual's <u>character</u> results from primitive biological drives.

$\underline{\qquad\qquad}$ Al Capone, the gangster, was finally brought to <u>trial</u> for income tax evasion.

3. pelt

$\underline{\qquad\qquad}$ A quartet is a musical <u>composition</u> for four voices or instruments.

$\underline{\qquad\qquad}$ The robin nests in a great <u>variety</u> of locations.

$\underline{\qquad\qquad}$ The <u>skin</u> of the common raccoon is considered valuable.

$\underline{\qquad\qquad}$ To <u>bombard</u> a prisoner with garbage was once a common form of punishment.

4. stage

$\underline{\qquad\qquad}$ The <u>grain</u> in a rice husk is known as "paddy."

$\underline{\qquad\qquad}$ The <u>part</u> of a journey spent waiting in an airport is often the most tiresome.

$\underline{\qquad\qquad}$ The theatrical company wanted to <u>perform</u> a one-act play at the centennial festivities.

$\underline{\qquad\qquad}$ The child was in Piaget's second <u>period</u> of development.

5. mean

$\underline{\qquad\qquad}$ Most governments <u>intend</u> to improve the living standards of their citizens.

$\underline{\qquad\qquad}$ The <u>average</u> age of the North American population is increasing.

$\underline{\qquad\qquad}$ Dogs of certain species can become <u>vicious</u> if ill-treated.

$\underline{\qquad\qquad}$ Plantar warts, which occur on the soles of feet, cause a good <u>deal</u> of discomfort.

6. word

_____ The <u>term</u> "mortgage" originally comes from Norman-French.

_____ It is considered unethical to break one's <u>promise</u>.

_____ The <u>oath</u> of a witness is a legal requirement.

_____ Archaeological discoveries show that the ancient <u>legend</u> has a factual basis.

7. yield

_____ Many factors contribute to the <u>output</u> of cultivated crops.

_____ Vehicles must <u>give way</u> when approaching a road intersection.

_____ Archaeologists <u>deduce</u> the activities of prehistoric peoples from various sources.

_____ Careful planning should <u>produce</u> accurate results.

8. bore

_____ The <u>diameter</u> of an engine cylinder can be carefully calculated.

_____ Geologists <u>drill</u> deep holes in the ground in their search for oil.

_____ Too many commercials <u>tire</u> the television watcher.

_____ To help people was Mother Teresa's <u>desire</u>.

9. pen

_____ A well-built <u>enclosure</u> is necessary to prevent farm animals from wandering.

_____ The author was asked to <u>write</u> an article for the magazine.

_____ In seventeenth-century Europe, people thought it necessary to <u>confine</u> the insane in prisons.

_____ Unlike most farm animals, poultry <u>swallow</u> their food whole.

10. peer

_____ Some scholars argue that Hawthorne's *The Scarlet Letter* has no <u>equal</u> among nineteenth-century American novels.

_____ The gang leader John Dillinger managed to <u>escape</u> from prison using a false gun made from soap.

_____ The scabies mite was the cause of the <u>itch</u> the child complained of.

_____ People who <u>look</u> at computer screens for extended periods may develop eye problems.

Answers to Exercise V4 are on page 470.

Exercise V5   ***Recognizing synonyms and antonyms***

Write an "S" in the space if the words are synonyms (their meanings are the same), or an "A" if they are antonyms (their meanings are the opposite). Leave the space blank if the words are neither synonyms nor antonyms.

Example   _S_ jump   leap

_A_ outgoing   introverted

1. _____	polish	shine	9. _____	feeble	strong
2. _____	especially	notably	10. _____	roughly	sturdily
3. _____	state	declare	11. _____	hatch	die
4. _____	wound	heal	12. _____	sensation	sensitive
5. _____	folded	outstretched	13. _____	coverage	reportage
6. _____	liquids	fluids	14. _____	rival	ally
7. _____	obliquely	directly	15. _____	heyday	tradition
8. _____	compulsory	mandatory			

Answers to Exercise V5 are on page 470.

Exercise V6   **Finding synonyms and antonyms**

Read the following sentences. Use your dictionary, synonym dictionary, or thesaurus to find a word that could replace the word that is underlined. Then find a word that is opposite in meaning.

Example   The fruit shriveled in the hot sun.

synonym: *withered*

antonym: *flourished*

1. The foundation of the old hotel was damaged in the earthquake.

synonym: _____

antonym: _____

2. The discovery of DNA has led to many breakthroughs in finding cures for hereditary diseases.

synonym: _____

antonym: _____

3. The man who was leading the group through the jungle had been raised there.

synonym: _____

antonym: _____

4. A former Olympic ice skater has accepted the position of instructor at the skating rink.

synonym: _____

antonym: _____

5. The towering decorated tree in the city square was a marvelous sight to see.

synonym: _____

antonym: _____

6. The prairie grass vanished in a summer storm of locusts.

synonym: _____

antonym: _____

7. The two countries decided that a mutual trade agreement was the solution to the problem.

synonym: _____

antonym: _____

8. The beaming child had a look of total innocence about her.

synonym: _____

antonym: _____

9. Consumers are reluctant to change their spending habits.

synonym: _____

antonym: _____

10. A musty atmosphere permeated the room.

synonym: _____

antonym: _____

Answers to Exercise V6 are on page 471.

Exercise V7   **Finding synonyms for words with multiple meanings**

The underlined words in the following sentences have several different meanings. Use your dictionary, synonym dictionary, or thesaurus to find synonyms for these words. Write your synonyms in the space.

Example   They are planning to build a patio in their backyard.

   construct _____

   One of the committee's goals is to build a more trusting relationship between the staff and the management.

   develop _____

   The bank robber had the build of a heavyweight wrestler.

   physique _____

(The answers in the spaces above are possible answers. Yours may differ.)

1. (A) The vegetables in the pantry were left too long and became spoiled.

   _____

   (B) Nobody has spoiled a child as much as they have.

   _____

   (C) The marauding tribe took all the spoils.

   _____

2. (A) Many early settlements crowded around the banks of the Hudson River.

   _____

   (B) The airplane banked sharply before coming in to land.

   _____

   (C) The cloud bank indicated the advance of the storm.

   _____

3. (A) The violent waves rocked the small boat.

   _____

   (B) The boys were practicing their aim by throwing rocks at the post.

   _____

   (C) He is the rock of that organization.

   _____

4. (A) She found the article while paging through the magazine.

   _____

   (B) They were paging a doctor in the theater last night.

   _____

   (C) In the movie John plays the part of a page for one of King Arthur's knights.

   _____

5. (A) The children waved to the passengers as the train entered the tunnel.

   _____

   (B) The performer had trained his dogs to jump through a flaming hoop.

   _____

   (C) The commotion caused me to lose my train of thought.

   _____

6. (A) They set out on the trail through the forest at dawn.

   _____

   (B) The dogs lost the escaped convict's trail at the river.

   _____

   (C) The child was trailing her blanket behind her.

   _____

7. (A) The <u>press</u> had news of the revolt almost immediately.

    _____

   (B) The suit had to be <u>pressed</u> before it could be worn.

    _____

   (C) The explorers <u>pressed</u> on toward the South Pole.

    _____

8. (A) We heard the rifle <u>shot</u> in the early hours of the morning.

    _____

   (B) Tomorrow a nurse will come to the school to give the children a flu <u>shot</u>.

    _____

   (C) It would have been a good <u>shot</u>, but the camera had just run out of film.

    _____

9. (A) We lost our last tennis <u>game</u> of the season.

    _____

   (B) Mr. Richard's likes to hunt big <u>game</u>.

    _____

   (C) We didn't want to trust them until we knew what their <u>game</u> was.

    _____

10. (A) The man <u>slipped</u> on the ice and broke his hip.

    _____

   (B) The spy <u>slipped</u> through the gate unseen by the guards.

    _____

   (C) The girl was embarrassed because her <u>slip</u> was showing.

    _____

Answers to Exercise V7 are on page 471.

Exercise V8   **_Building word charts_**

Study the chart. You will notice that the heading word is followed by a list of synonyms.
Fill in the spaces with more words that mean the same as those synonyms.

Example   master

Nouns:	teacher	*instructor*
		educator
	artist	*painter*
		sculptor
	conqueror	*victor*
	expert	*mastermind*
		genius
		prodigy
	chief	*head*
		leader
		superior
		senior

Verbs: know well   *have a thorough knowledge*

                       be well informed

         learn   *gain command of*

                       become adept in

                       gain thorough knowledge

         conquer   *vanquish*

                       subdue

                       subjugate

                       dominate

Adjectives:

         main   *chief*

                       principal

                       foremost

                       leading

                       dominant

1. grant

    Nouns: sanction   _____

                       _____

           gift   _____

                       _____

           subsidy   _____

                       _____

                       _____

    Verbs: allow for   _____

           acknowledge _____

           permit   _____

                       _____

                       _____

           give   _____

                       _____

                       _____

    Expressions:

           grant amnesty to   _____

           take for granted   _____

2. spread

    Nouns: expanse   _____

                       _____

           covering   _____

                       _____

feast _____
       _____

Verbs: expand _____
                 _____

extend _____

apply _____
       _____
       _____

make known _____
            _____

disperse _____
          _____

separate _____

Expressions:
spread one's wings _____
spread oneself thin _____

3. bump

Nouns: swelling _____
                   _____
                   _____

push _____
      _____

collision _____
           _____

thud _____
      _____

Verbs: push _____
               _____
               _____

collide _____
         _____
         _____

discharge _____
           _____
           _____
           _____

shake _____
       _____
       _____

demote   _____

_____

_____

Expressions:

bump into   _____

bump off   _____

4. match

Nouns: counterpart   _____

_____

_____

equal   _____

_____

_____

two   _____

_____

_____

contest   _____

_____

_____

game   _____

_____

_____

marriage   _____

_____

_____

Verbs: coincide   _____

_____

be alike   _____

_____

correspond   _____

_____

_____

equal   _____

_____

_____

pair   _____

_____

size _____
_____
_____

oppose _____
_____
_____

compare _____
_____
_____

marry _____
_____
_____

5. act
   Nouns: process _____
   _____
   _____

   action _____
   _____
   _____

   law _____
   _____
   _____

   Verbs: function _____
   _____
   _____

   impersonate _____
   _____
   _____

   portray _____
   _____
   _____

   pretend _____
   _____
   _____

   officiate _____
   _____
   _____

   behave _____
   _____
   _____

Expressions:

catch in the act or catch red-handed _____

in the act of _____

put on an act _____

act a part _____

act for _____

act of grace _____

act on _____

act one's part _____

act out _____

act the part of _____

act up _____

act one's age _____

6. leave

Nouns: departure _____

_____

_____

vacation _____

_____

_____

permission _____

_____

_____

Verbs: depart _____

cease _____

_____

abandon _____

_____

_____

_____

resign _____

_____

_____

bequeath _____

_____

_____

Expressions:

by one's leave _____

give leave _____

on leave _____

leave in the cold _____

leave in the lurch _____

leave no stone unturned _____

leave no trace _____

leave off _____

leave one cold _____

leave out _____

leave the beaten path _____

leave the door open _____

leave well enough alone _____

leave word _____

7. change

Nouns: alteration _____

_____

_____

substitution _____

_____

_____

money _____

_____

_____

Verbs: alter _____

_____

_____

_____

substitute _____

_____

_____

_____

move _____

_____

trade _____

_____

Expressions:

change back _____

change hands _____

change one's mind _____

change one's ways _____

8. end

Nouns: cessation _____

_____

completion _____
_____
_____
_____

tip _____
_____
_____

death _____
_____
_____

limit _____
_____
_____

remainder _____
_____

fate _____
_____

ruin _____
_____

Verbs: terminate _____
_____

stop _____
_____
_____

kill _____
_____

perish _____
_____
_____
_____

Expressions:

at loose ends _____
at the end of one's rope_____
dead end _____
end of the line _____
end on that note_____
end to end _____
make both ends meet _____
no end _____
on end _____

put an end to _____

to that end _____

end up in smoke _____

end-all _____

odds and ends _____

the end _____

9. top

   Nouns: summit   _____

   _____

   _____

   _____

   lid   _____

   shirt   _____

   Verbs: dominate   _____

   _____

   _____

   _____

   crown   _____

   _____

   Adjectives:

   supreme   _____

   _____

   _____

   _____

   _____

   Expressions:

   at the top of the ladder _____

   on top _____

   on top of _____

   on top of the heap _____

   top off _____

   go to the top _____

   on top of the world _____

   off the top of one's head _____

10. part

   Nouns: share   _____

   _____

   _____

   _____

   _____

region
_____
_____
_____
_____

piece
_____
_____
_____
_____

role
_____
_____

component _____
_____

function _____
_____

Verbs: separate
_____
_____
_____
_____
_____

die
_____
_____
_____
_____
_____

disband
_____
_____

open _____
_____

share
_____
_____

Expressions:

do one's part _____

in part _____

on the part of _____

take the part of _____

part company with _____

part with _____

part ways _____

for the most part _____

Extended practice 1: Make your own charts using the following words: last, run, dark, cold, check, get, stand, lock, course, bear, chance, mark, make, shade, cool, break, beat, band, shoot.

Extended practice 2: Make your own charts using your own words.

Extended practice 3: Make sentences using the words from your charts in Extended Practice 2.

Answers to Exercise V8 are on page 471.

Exercise V9   **Finding unrelated words**

Circle the word that doesn't belong in the list. Then use your dictionary to find at least three words that mean the same as the circled word. Write the words you found.

Example   glad   happy   (miserly)   joyful

cheap   _stingy_   _tightwad_

(The answers in the space above are possible answers. Others may also be correct.)

1. considerable   great   tremendous   exclusive

2. withheld   stole   retained   kept

3. trap   summit   peak   crest

4. excite   arouse   stimulate   endear

5. store   career   profession   trade

6. abound   reserve   teem   overflow

7. vast   huge   minute   colossal

8. shy   brash   timid   bashful

9. exodus   departure   exit   expire

10. incessantly   nonstop   constantly   intermittently

11. slender   thin   flabby   slim

12. basically   fundamentally   definitely   essentially

_____

13. fickleness   steadfastness   loyalty   fidelity

_____

14. dampen   dwindle   decrease   diminish

_____

15. distant   territory   remote   faraway

_____

16. competent   proficient   capable   enable

_____

17. prompting   dazzling   sparkling   twinkling

_____

18. sequence   order   contingent   progression

_____

19. fasten   sieve   attach   affix

_____

20. congested   clogged   spacious   crowded

_____

Answers to Exercise V9 are on page 475.

Exercise V10   *Correcting synonyms*

Each sentence contains an underlined word. If the word following the sentence does not mean the same as the underlined word, cross it out and supply your own synonym.

Example   The boy's job was to polish shoes.

~~spike~~   *shine* _____

1. The man was too meek for the position he held.

   erudite _____

2. Total anarchy reigned for several months after the revolution broke out.

   chaos _____

3. A strong gust of wind disseminated the remaining seeds from the pod.

   apportioned _____

4. The preliminary investigation was too superficial to yield useful results.

   ample _____

5. The <u>immensity</u> of such a project as colonizing the moon is hard to appreciate.

   sublimity _____

6. The releasing of rabbits not native to Australia has had <u>dire</u> consequences.

   thriving _____

7. Overzealous people have been killing even the <u>innocuous</u> snakes in the area.

   benign _____

8. The starfish clung <u>tenaciously</u> to the rocks.

   courageously _____

9. A festive clatter was coming from the <u>adjacent</u> house.

   hospitable _____

10. The fire caused <u>extensive</u> damage to the forest and surrounding communities.

    widespread _____

Answers to Exercise V10 are on page 475.

Exercise V11   **Shades of meaning**

The following pairs of words are close in meaning. Write how they are the same and how they are different. Use your dictionary if necessary.

Example   song/chant

> *Both a song and a chant are pieces of music with words. However,*
>
> *a chant is different from a song in that it is repetitive and uses only*
>
> *a few notes.*

1. carve/cut

   _____

   _____

   _____

2. smolder/blaze

   _____

   _____

   _____

3. emblem/symbol

   _____

   _____

   _____

4. glance/stare

_____

_____

_____

5. evade/escape

_____

_____

_____

6. letter/card

_____

_____

_____

7. band/quartet

_____

_____

_____

8. chuckle/snicker

_____

_____

_____

9. bizarre/strange

_____

_____

_____

10. exiled/expelled

_____

_____

_____

11. tease/mock

_____

_____

_____

12. gaudy/colorful

_____

_____

_____

13. gossip/talk

_____

_____

_____

14. vow/promise

_____

_____

_____

15. skeptical/cynical

_____

_____

_____

Answers to Exercise V11 are on page 475.

Exercise V12   **Completing sentences**

Circle the word that best completes the sentence.

Example   The grass was ----- after the storm.

moist/soaked

You should circle "soaked" because a storm (heavy rain) would have left the grass very wet and not just "moist" (damp).

1. After the long flight across the Atlantic, Judy ----- for 10 hours.

   slept/napped

2. That vacant lot on East 3rd Street is the building ----- for the new National Bank.

   site/spot

3. The old woman attributed her accurate weather ----- to her rheumatism, which flared up before rainstorms.

   prophesy/prediction

4. The president gave an interesting ----- at the inauguration.

   lecture/speech

5. In the race, the children had to ----- along holding one foot behind them.

   leap/hop

6. All the ----- in the kingdom were invited to the festivities.

   kings/aristocrats

7. There was only just ----- amount of food to go around.

   an abundant/a sufficient

8. Elizabeth had a right to be ----- about her achievement.

proud/vain

9. Although Diane and Barbara met as students at the business college, they never were more than mere -----.

acquaintances/friends

10. It was very ----- of the boy to figure out the mathematical problem so quickly.

wise/clever

Answers to Exercise V12 are on page 476.

Use the following exercises in different sections of this book to build your vocabulary:

Listening Comprehension Exercises L4–L6, L9–L11, L22–L24, L28–L30, L47–L50, and L67–L70
Structure and Written Expression Exercises S38–S43, S51, and Practice with Word Choices (8), page 169
Reading Comprehension Exercise R1

CHECK YOUR PROGRESS

Check your progress with vocabulary building skills (Exercises V1–V12) by completing the following mini-test. This exercise contains more vocabulary words that you can add to your list if you are uncertain of their meanings, and it uses a format similar to that used in the Vocabulary section of the TOEFL.

Exercise V13   **Mini-test**   *(Time – 10 minutes)*

Directions: Each of the following sentences has an underlined word or phrase. Below each sentence are four other words or phrases, marked (A), (B), (C), and (D). You are to choose the one word or phrase that best keeps the meaning of the original sentence if it is substituted for the underlined word or phrase. Then circle the letter of that answer in your book.

Example   Helmeted diving suits were first devised in the seventeenth century and improved versions are still used.
(A) regarded
(B) invented
(C) envisioned
(D) verified

You should circle (B) because "Helmeted diving suits were first invented in the seventeenth century and improved versions are still used" is closest in meaning to the original sentence.

1. The park offered a myriad of activities during the summer holidays.
(A) dearth
(B) variety
(C) series
(D) tribe

2. Fur traders carried trinkets to exchange for pelts with the Indians.
(A) tools
(B) guns
(C) knives
(D) baubles

3. The bighorn sheep tends to remain <u>aloof</u>.
   (A) distant
   (B) lofty
   (C) skittish
   (D) playful

4. A pungent smell <u>permeated</u> the hallways of the hotel.
   (A) penetrated
   (B) insinuated
   (C) stormed
   (D) rampaged

5. Although the <u>prank</u> was meant in fun, the man became very angry.
   (A) remark
   (B) praise
   (C) trick
   (D) game

6. It was impossible to known how <u>precarious</u> the situation was.
   (A) hazardous
   (B) ludicrous
   (C) facetious
   (D) marvelous

7. Crime frequently increases during periods of social <u>upheaval</u>.
   (A) ruin
   (B) unrest
   (C) havoc
   (D) trends

8. The fact that this metal is <u>pliant</u> is an advantage for many industrial purposes.
   (A) caustic
   (B) durable
   (C) yielding
   (D) polished

9. The early colonists <u>bore</u> many hardships.
   (A) reached
   (B) endured
   (C) exposed
   (D) allowed

10. Sara's peers found her <u>haughtiness</u> overbearing.
    (A) insincerity
    (B) pertinence
    (C) vexation
    (D) arrogance

11. The post office purchased a new machine to <u>sort</u> the mail.
    (A) sift through
    (B) stamp
    (C) weigh
    (D) carry out

12. The inventor had to <u>mull over</u> his idea for several days.
    (A) scrutinize
    (B) ponder
    (C) remember
    (D) organize

13. The students came up with some <u>novel</u> ideas for fund-raising.
    (A) unique
    (B) bookish
    (C) educational
    (D) radical

14. When attacking their prey, eagles reach out with their <u>talons</u>.
    (A) wings
    (B) claws
    (C) beaks
    (D) legs

15. A small group of rebels <u>usurped</u> the president.
    (A) advised
    (B) assassinated
    (C) supplanted
    (D) rewarded

16. The origin of this <u>shard</u> of pottery cannot be identified.
    (A) pattern
    (B) sliver
    (C) example
    (D) amount

17. The lion searched the jungle for its <u>quarry</u>.
    (A) prey
    (B) lair
    (C) mate
    (D) cubs

18. The millstone used for <u>grinding</u> wheat was damaged in the flood.
    (A) dusting
    (B) ransacking
    (C) smothering
    (D) pulverizing

19. Mark Twain is well known for his wit.
    (A) insight
    (B) stories
    (C) vision
    (D) humor

20. The player was ostracized by his teammates.
    (A) beleaguered
    (B) counteracted
    (C) endorsed
    (D) excluded

21. The child was scarred in the car accident.
    (A) orphaned
    (B) disfigured
    (C) killed
    (D) bruised

22. The people complained about the gas canister that was left in front of the building.
    (A) device
    (B) container
    (C) propellant
    (D) equipment

23. The car skidded around the corner with the police close behind it.
    (A) slid
    (B) screeched
    (C) rolled
    (D) zoomed

24. Jack thought that his teacher was being rather finicky about the final draft of the paper.
    (A) detrimental
    (B) aggravating
    (C) meddlesome
    (D) fastidious

25. The police academy trains its dogs to fetch things on command.
    (A) sniff out
    (B) retrieve
    (C) attack
    (D) search for

26. The clear mountain air added to the serenity of the Alpine village.
    (A) lucidity
    (B) wholesomeness
    (C) tranquility
    (D) brilliance

27. Each time the storyteller told about the encounter, she embellished the plot.
    (A) exaggerated
    (B) enhanced
    (C) altered
    (D) rectified

28. The evening would have been more enjoyable if all the extraneous activities had been dropped from the program.
    (A) irrelevant
    (B) excessive
    (C) overextended
    (D) exceptional

29. The farmer studied the ominous clouds thoughtfully.
    (A) billowing
    (B) gloomy
    (C) menacing
    (D) feathery

30. Janice could not put her ephemeral thoughts into words.
    (A) fleeting
    (B) profound
    (C) vacuous
    (D) ethereal

Answers to Exercise V13 are on page 476.

PRACTICE WITH PREFIXES, ROOTS, AND SUFFIXES

By learning to recognize prefixes, roots, and suffixes, you can learn how to guess the meanings of words you have never seen before.

1. A root is the base element of a word. For example:

"Pose" is a root meaning "put."

2. A prefix *is a word element that is placed before a root. Adding a prefix to a root changes the meaning. For example:*

(A) *ex-* is a prefix meaning "out" or "from."

"Expose" (prefix + root) means to uncover, disclose, or reveal (to "put out").

   When the tide went out, the ship wreck was **exposed**.

(B) *im-* is a prefix meaning "in," "on," "into," "toward," or "against."

"Impose" (prefix + root) means to place upon.

   The government is debating the possibility of **imposing** yet another tax.

3. A suffix *is a word element that is placed after a root. It, too, changes the meaning of a root. For example:*

(A) *-ion* is a suffix that indicates a noun form.

An "imposition" (prefix + root + suffix) is a state of affairs in which someone or something inflicts (imposes) on someone a set of conditions that need to be met.

   It was an **imposition** to ask him to go miles out of his way to pick up your package.

(B) *-ure* is a suffix that indicates a noun form.

"Exposure" (prefix + root + suffix) is the state of being in a position where something is revealed to you or you reveal something.

   The **exposure** to a constant high level of noise in the factory affected his hearing.

Review suffixes by completing Exercise S38, page 164. Then use Vocabulary Exercises V14–V27 to enlarge your vocabulary and strengthen your ability to recognize words in context.

Exercise V14   ***Adding vocabulary with prefixes and roots***

Study the following prefixes and roots.

Prefixes	
ad-, as-	= to, toward
dis-	= not, away, apart, remove
e-, ex-	= out, from
in-, im-	= in, into
re-	= back, again

Roots	
pel, pulse	= push, drive
quire	= ask, seek
solve, solut	= loosen
spect, spic	= look at, see
vene, vent	= come
pose	= put

Use the preceding lists of prefixes and roots to help find the meanings of the words. Circle the letter of the word that could replace the underlined word without a change of meaning. Try not to use your dictionary.

Example   The snow receded with the <u>advent</u> of spring.
   (A) coming
   (B) returning
   (C) look
   (D) sight

Although (A), (B), (C), and (D) could all grammatically replace the underlined word, only (A) does not change the meaning of the sentence. *Ad-* means "toward" and *-vent* means "come." Therefore, you should circle (A).

1. The expelled students petitioned the dean.
   (A) required
   (B) disposed
   (C) dismissed
   (D) rejected

2. The problem was resolved at the meeting.
   (A) taken care of
   (B) brought up
   (C) debated
   (D) verified

3. The secretary disposed of the clutter on the desk.
   (A) filed
   (B) got rid of
   (C) returned
   (D) mailed

4. Mary bought her new coat on an impulse.
   (A) a shopping trip
   (B) sale
   (C) credit
   (D) a whim

5. William studied the various aspects of the situation.
   (A) facets
   (B) airs
   (C) visages
   (D) poses

6. This material repels water.
   (A) filters
   (B) alters
   (C) extracts
   (D) sheds

7. Last night's event was remarkable.
   (A) happening
   (B) blizzard
   (C) escapade
   (D) rampage

8. Sam hasn't made any money on his invention.
   (A) fabrication
   (B) anecdote
   (C) creation
   (D) composition

9. The club was dissolved after a few years.
   (A) disbanded
   (B) reestablished
   (C) perpetuated
   (D) assisted

10. The inquiry took more than two hours.
    (A) deliberation
    (B) appraisal
    (C) commentary
    (D) investigation

Answers to Exercise V14 are on page 477.

Exercise V15   Adding more prefixes and roots

Study the following prefixes and roots.

Prefixes	
con-*, com-, co-	= together or with
pre-, pro-	= [GK] before, in front of, on behalf of;
	= [L] before, for, instead of
de-	= from, off, down
intro-	= into
inter-	= between, among
intra-	= within, on the inside
sub-	= under, lower

Roots	
sume	= use up, take
vert	= turn
sign	= mark, sign
ject	= throw
duce, duct	= lead
hes, here	= stick
tract	= draw away, pull

*con- is frequently used to intensify a meaning (make it stronger).

Note: "[GK]" indicates that the meanings that follow are the meanings for the Greek prefix. "[L]" indicates the meanings for the Latin prefix.

Use the prefixes and roots on page 264 to help find the meanings of the words. Circle the letter of the word that could replace the underlined word without a change of meaning.

Example   The metal contracted when the weather changed.
    (A) shrunk
    (B) stuck
    (C) twisted
    (D) broke

Although (A), (B), (C), and (D) can all replace "contracted" grammatically, only (A) means contracted. *Con-* means "together" and *-tract* means "draw." To "draw together" can mean to "get smaller" or "shrink."

1. We have been conducting a survey on the dietary habits of university graduates.
    (A) running
    (B) examining
    (C) condemning
    (D) discussing

2. The Concorde aircraft consumes a great amount of fuel.
    (A) needs
    (B) wastes
    (C) leaks
    (D) uses

3. Lisa felt dejected after the interview.
    (A) elated
    (B) determined
    (C) discouraged
    (D) convinced

4. The speaker interjected anecdotes about the football team.
    (A) inserted
    (B) transformed
    (C) interrupted
    (D) delivered

5. The group was involved in several subversive activities.
    (A) charitable
    (B) rebellious
    (C) preposterous
    (D) questionable

6. The professor wants Jan to improve the coherence of his term paper.
    (A) rationality
    (B) consistency
    (C) penmanship
    (D) distinctiveness

7. The explosion projected pieces of masonry and debris for several miles.
    (A) destroyed
    (B) melted
    (C) wrecked
    (D) hurled

8. Lucy deduced what had happened in the playground.
    (A) surmised
    (B) provoked
    (C) appealed
    (D) condoned

9. Bill has a tendency to be introverted.
    (A) biased
    (B) haughty
    (C) reserved
    (D) devious

10. Susan was subjected to Tony's cooking last night.
    (A) converted
    (B) diverted
    (C) exposed
    (D) opposed

Answers to Exercise V15 are on page 477.

Exercise V16   ***Adding more prefixes and roots***

Study the prefixes and roots in the charts on the top of page 266 before doing the exercise.

Prefixes	
retro-	= backward, behind
trans-	= across, beyond, through, on or to the other side
ante-	= before
se-	= away, apart, without
ob-, of-	= against, toward
circum-	= around, about
super-	= over, beyond

Roots	
act	= do, make
ced, cede, ceed, cess	= go, come
flex	= bend
gress	= step, move
fer	= carry, bring
scend	= climb

Use the preceding prefixes and roots to help find the meanings of the words. Circle the letter of the word that could replace the underlined word without a change of meaning.

Example   Those who transgress the laws of society can be punished.
(A) disagree with
(B) disperse
(C) violate
(D) interfere with

(A)–(D) can all replace "transgress" grammatically, but only (C) means "transgress." "To violate" means "to offend against." *Trans-* means "across" and *gress* means "move" or "step." "To transgress the law" means to step or move across what is permitted.

1. The law was retroactive to 1980.
   (A) abolished in
   (B) enacted in
   (C) backdated to
   (D) overturned in

2. The Southern states seceded from the union in 1860.
   (A) benefitted from
   (B) withdrew from
   (C) terminated
   (D) discriminated against

3. The operator was transferred after twenty years at her job.
   (A) relocated
   (B) dismissed
   (C) retired
   (D) honored

4. Jet propulsion aircraft superseded airplanes driven by propellers.
   (A) supplanted
   (B) maintained
   (C) enhanced
   (D) transgressed

5. A retroflexed tongue position is used to make that sound.
   (A) curled
   (B) curious
   (C) backward
   (D) flexible

6. I had to complete several transactions before the house could be sold.
   (A) deals
   (B) renovations
   (C) alterations
   (D) removals

7. The circumference of the property has only been estimated.
   (A) caliber
   (B) expenses
   (C) perimeter
   (D) territory

8. The antecedent of the horse was a small four-toed animal.
   (A) breeder
   (B) predecessor
   (C) competitor
   (D) rival

9. Medical services retrogressed after funding had been cut.
   (A) progressed
   (B) modernized
   (C) transformed
   (D) regressed

10. The man offered to fix the television.
    (A) refused
    (B) attempted
    (C) charged
    (D) volunteered

Answers to Exercise V16 are on page 477.

Exercise V17   **Adding words using the prefix ad-**

Study how the prefix *ad-*, meaning "toward, to, forward," is joined to some roots.

1.	ad + apt (fit, fasten)	= adapt
2.	ad + cede (go or come)	= accede
3.	ad + fluent (flow)	= affluent
4.	ad + gression (step or move)	= aggression
5.	ad + here (stick)	= adhere
6.	ad + locate (place)	= allocate
7.	ad + nounce (proclaim)	= announce
8.	ad + petite (seek, desire)	= appetite
9.	ad + scend (climb)	= ascend
10.	ad + sign (mark or sign)	= assign
11.	ad + sume (use up or take)	= assume
12.	ad + tract (draw away or pull)	= attract

Write what you think the preceding words mean. Check the meanings in your dictionary.

1. _____
2. _____
3. _____
4. _____
5. _____
6. _____
7. _____
8. _____
9. _____
10. _____
11. _____
12. _____

Extended practice: Write sentences using these words.

Answers to Exercise V17 are on page 478.

Exercise V18   **Defining the root fer**

The root *fer* means "to carry or bring." Write what you think these words mean. Check the meanings in your dictionary.

1. confer _____
2. defer _____
3. infer _____
4. prefer _____
5. refer _____
6. transfer _____

Extended practice: Write sentences using these words.

Answers to Exercise V18 are on page 478.

Exercise V19   Adding the suffix -ion

The suffix *-ion* turns a word into a noun. It means "in the condition or action of." Write what you think these words mean. Check the meanings in your dictionary.

1. aggression _____

2. ascension _____

3. convention _____

4. distraction _____

5. expulsion _____

6. induction _____

7. introspection _____

8. reflection _____

9. resolution _____

10. subtraction _____

Extended practice: Write sentences using the words that you found.

Answers to Exercise V19 are on page 478.

Exercise V20   Adding the suffix -ive

The suffix *-ive* turns a word into an adjective. It means "having the nature of." Write what you think these words mean. Check the meanings in your dictionary.

1. aggressive _____

2. attractive _____

3. deductive _____

4. distractive _____

5. excessive _____

6. impulsive _____

7. inventive _____

8. objective _____

9. respective _____

10. subjective _____

Extended practice: Write sentences using these words.

Answers to Exercise V20 are on page 479.

Exercise V21   Adding more prefixes

Write at least one word that uses each prefix and its meaning. Check its meaning in your dictionary.

1. ambi- (both) _____

2. contra- (against, opposing) _____

3. en-, em- (put into) _____

4. extra(o)- (outside, beyond) _____

5. infra- (below) _____

6. mal- (bad, wrong) _____

7. multi- (many) _____

8. per- (through) _____

9. post- (after) _____

10. preter- (more than) _____

11. syn- (together) _____

12. ultra- (beyond) _____

Extended practice: Write sentences using the words you wrote.

Answers to Exercise V21 are on page 479.

Exercise V22   ***Adding prefixes meaning "not"***

Write at least one word that uses each prefix and its meaning. Check its meaning in your dictionary.

1. a- _____

2. dis- _____

3. mis- _____

4. in- _____

5. im- _____

6. il- _____

7. ir- _____

8. non- _____

9. un- _____

Extended practice: Write sentences using the words you wrote.

Answers to Exercise V22 are on page 479.

Exercise V23   ***Adding more roots***

Look up the following words in your dictionary. Write what you think the underlined root means in the space.

1. <u>ambul</u>ate, per<u>ambul</u>ator _____

2. <u>ami</u>able, en<u>amor</u>ed _____

3. <u>aque</u>duct, <u>aqu</u>atic _____

4. <u>anthrop</u>ology, mis<u>anthrop</u>ist _____

5. <u>carn</u>ivorous, rein<u>carn</u>ation _____

6. <u>infant</u>icide, <u>suic</u>idal _____

7. <u>frag</u>ment, <u>fract</u>ure _____

8. refugee, fugitive _____

9. herbicide, herbivore _____

10. illuminate, luminous _____

11. magnificent, magnanimous _____

12. omnipotent, omnivore _____

13. paternity, patriarch _____

14. infidelity, confidence _____

15. pendulum, dependent _____

Answers to Exercise V23 are on page 479.

Exercise V24   **Adding number prefixes**

Cardinal numbers		Ordinal numbers	
uni	1	primo	1st
du, bi	2	second	2nd
tri	3	terti	3rd
quadru, quadri	4	quart	4th
quinque/quinqu	5	quint	5th
sex	6	sext	6th
sept/septem	7	sept	7th
octo(i)	8	octav	8th
nov/novem	9	non	9th
dec/deci/decem	10	decim	10th
cent/centi	100	centi	100th
mill/milli	1,000	milli	1,000th

Answer the following questions which contain words with number prefixes. Try to work out the definitions without a dictionary. Check your answers with a dictionary after you complete the exercise.

1. What is primacy? _____

2. What is an octave? _____

3. What is a unicycle? _____

4. What is a triangle? _____

5. What is a duet? _____

6. What is a centipede? _____

7. What is a centennial? _____

8. What are quintuplets? _____

9. What is the decimal system? _____

10. What is secondary school? _____

Extended practice: Write sentences using the words in the exercise.

Answers to Exercise V24 are on page 480.

Exercise V25   Reviewing prefixes

Cover columns 2 and 3 with a sheet of paper. Put a check beside the prefixes you know. Study the prefixes you are unsure of.

1 Prefix	2 Meaning	3 Example
a-	to, toward	ashore, aside
a-, an-	not, without	amoral
ab-, abs-	away from	abstraction
ad-, ac-, ag-, al-, an-, as-, at-	to	adhere
ambi-	both	ambidextrous
ante-	before	anterior
anti-	against	antisocial
auto-	self	automation
bene-	well	benefactor
bi-	two	biceps
cata-	down	catastrophe
circum-	around	circumvent
con-, com-, co-, cog-, col-, cor-	together, with	cognate
contra-	against	contraception
de-	from	deferral
di-, dif-, dis-	part, separate	divide
dis-	not	disillusioned
en-, em-	put into	enthralled
e-, ex-	out, from	extract
extra(o)-	beyond	extraterrestrial
il-, in-, im-, ir-	not	impartial
in-, im-	in, into	involved
infra-	below	infrared
inter-	between, among	interfere
intro-	into	introduce
intra-	within	intramural
mal-	bad	maladjusted
meta-	beyond	metaphysics
micro-	small	microscope
mis-	wrong	misdeed
mono-	one	monogamy
multi-	many	multitude
non-	not	nonentity
ob-, oc-, of-, ops-	against	obstruct
out-	surpass	outmaneuver
over-	excessive	overconfident
para-	beside	paramedic
per-	through	permeate
poly-	many	polyglot
post-	after	posthumous
pre-	before	premeditated
preter-	more than	preternatural
pro-	for	proceed
re-	back, again	regain
retro-	backward	retroactive
se-	apart	sequential
semi-	half	semicolon
sub-, suc-, suf-, sug-, sup-, sur-	under	submarine
super-	over	superfluous

Box continued

1 Prefix	2 Meaning	3 Example
syn-, sym-, syl-, sys-	together	symbol
trans-	across	transmute
ultra-	beyond	ultrasound
un-	not	uncertain

Exercise V26   Reviewing roots

Cover columns 2 and 3 with a sheet of paper. Put a check beside the roots you know. Study the roots you are unsure of.

1 Root	2 Meaning	3 Example
act	do	activate
ambula	walk	ambulate
ami, amo	love	enamored
annus	year	annual
aqua	water	aquarium
anthrop	humankind	anthropomorphic
astr	star	astronaut
audi	hear	audition
biblio	book	bibliography
bio	life	biography
carni	meat	carnivorous
ced, cede, ceed, cess	go, come	precede
chronos	time	chronometer
cide	kill	homicide
claudo	close	claustrophobia
dict	say	dictation
dorm	sleep	dormitory
duct	lead	conduct
ego	self	egocentric
fact	make	factory
fer	carry	transfer
fem	woman	effeminate
fidel	trust	fidelity
flex	bend	flexible
fluent, flou	flow	superfluous
frac, frag	break	fracture
frat	brother	fraternal
fuge	flee	fugitive
gam	marriage	bigamist
gen	birth, race	genocide
geo	earth	geology
gnostos	know	prognosis
gram	letters	grammar
graph	writing	telegraph
gress	step, move	ingress
gyn	woman	gynecologist
herbi	grass	herbivore
host	enemy	hostile
here	stick	coherence
hetero	different	heterogeneous
homo	alike	homogeneous
hydro	water	hydraulic

Box continued

1 Root	2 Meaning	3 Example
ject	throw	interjection
later	side	lateral
lingua	tongue	linguistics
lithos	stone	paleolithic
logy	study	biology
lumin	light	illuminate
manu	hand	manipulate
magni	big	magnify
mania	madness	megalomaniac
masc	male	masculine
matri	mother	matriarch
metron	measure	metrical
mit, miss	send	transmit
morph	form	metamorphic
mort	death	immortal
nym	name	synonym
omni	all	omnipotent
ops	eye	optical
pater, patri	father	paternal
pathy	feelings	sympathy
ped	foot	pedestrian
pel, pulse	push, drive	repulsive
pend	hang	appendage
phil	love	philosophy
phobia	fear	acrophobia
phon	sound	microphone
port	carry	transport
pose	put	composition
pseudo	false	pseudonym
psych	mind	psychopathic
quire	seek	acquire
scend	climb	transcendental
scope	see	telescope
script	write	inscribe
sec	cut	dissect
sed	sit	sedentary
sentio	feel	resentful
sequ	follow	consecutive
sign	mark	consignment
spect	view	inspector
soro	sister	sorority
solve	loosen	resolution
soph	wise	philosopher
sui	self	suicidal
sume	use up, take	consumption
tact	touch	contact
tele	distance	telepathy
terre	earth	terrestrial
thermo	heat	thermostat
theo	god	monotheist
tract	draw away	traction
vene	come	intervene
vert	turn	diversion
vis	see	invisible
vore	eat	carnivore
zoo	animal	zoologist

Exercise V27   *Reviewing suffixes*

Cover columns 2 and 3 with a sheet of paper. Put a check beside the suffixes you know. Study the suffixes you are unsure of.

1 Suffix that forms a noun	2 Meaning	3 Example
-acy, -cy	state or quality	accuracy, infancy
-age	activity	courage
	result of activity	drainage
-al	action	refusal, rival
-ance, -ence	action or process	assistance, dependence
-ant, -ent	agent	disinfectant, dependent
-ate	state	magistrate
-ation	resulting state	starvation
	action	exploration
	institution	organization
-dom	rank, condition, domain	kingdom
-ee	affected person	employee
-eer	person concerned with	volunteer
-en	diminutive	maiden
	plural form	oxen
-er, -or	person who does something	astronomer, translator
-ese	inhabitants, language	Chinese
-ess, -tress	female form	authoress, enchantress
-ful	an amount	handful
-hood	status	childhood
-ian, -an	pertaining to	Polynesian, republican
-ia	names	dahlia, Australia
	illnesses	phobia, hysteria
	classes	reptilia
-ic, -ics	arts and sciences	logic, music, arithmetic, physics
-id	name	orchid, pyramid
-ide	names of elements	chloride, dioxide
-in, -ine	names of substances	gelatin, margarine
-ing	material made of	roofing
	activity	driving
	result of activity	building
-ion	condition or action	communication
-ism	attitude	idealism
	action	baptism
	conduct	heroism
	condition	alcoholism
-ist	member of a party	socialist
	occupation	cellist
-ite	a member of a community	socialite
-ity	state or condition	purity
-ive	condition	captive
-let, -ette	diminutive	booklet, kitchenette
-ling	diminutive	fledgling
-ment	result	fragment
-ness	state or condition	happiness
-ocracy	system	democracy

Box continued

1 **Suffix that forms a noun**	2 **Meaning**	3 **Example**
-ry, -ary	place of activity	refinery, military
-ery	collectively	machinery
-ship	status, condition	friendship
-ster	occupation	gangster
-tive	condition	captive
-y	state or condition	fury
	the results of an activity	victory
	location	library, company
-y, -ie	endearment	daddy, auntie

1 **Suffix that forms a verb**	2 **Meaning**	3 **Example**
-ate	put in a state	isolate
-ed	past tense	walked
-en	become	moisten
	cause	deafen
-er	action	wander, waver
	imitating sounds	chatter
-ify	cause	simplify
-ing	present participle	working
-ize (-ise in British English)	cause	epitomize

1 **Suffix that forms an adjective**	2 **Meaning**	3 **Example**
-able, -ible	worthy	valuable, sensible
-al, -ial, -ical	quality	criminal, social, musical
-ant, -ent	kind of agent	malignant, apparent
-ate	kind of state	desolate
-ed	having	wooded
-en	material	woolen, golden
-er	comparative	grander
-ese	origin	Japanese
-ful	having, giving	useful
-ian	in the tradition	Georgian
-ic	quality	heroic
-ing	activity	working
-ile	having the qualities	infantile
-ish	belonging to	Swedish
	having the character of	foolish
	somewhat	youngish
-ive, -ative, -itive	having the quality of	passive, attractive, sensitive
-less	without	helpless
-like	having the qualities of	childlike
-ly	having the qualities of	friendly
-ous, -eous, -ious	having the quality of	virtuous, courteous, vivacious
-y	full of	creamy, bony

1 **Suffix that forms an adverb**	2 **Meaning**	3 **Example**
-ly	in a manner of	happily
-ward(s)	in a manner or direction	backward(s)
-wise	in a manner or direction	clockwise

CHECK YOUR PROGRESS

Check your progress with vocabulary building skills through recognition of prefixes, roots, and suffixes (Exercises V14–V27) by completing the following mini-test. This exercise contains more vocabulary words that you can add to your list if you are uncertain of their meanings, and it uses a format similar to that used in the Vocabulary section of the TOEFL.

Exercise V28   *Mini-test*   *(Time – 10 minutes)*

Directions: Each of the following sentences has an underlined word or phrase. Below each sentence are four other words or phrases, marked (A), (B), (C), and (D). You are to choose the <u>one</u> word or phrase that <u>best keeps the meaning</u> of the original sentence if it is substituted for the underlined word or phrase. Then circle the letter of that answer in your book.

Example   Believing the Spanish conquerors to be <u>descendants</u> of the god Quetzalcoatl, Montezuma gave them gifts to persuade them to leave.
(A) messengers
(B) representatives
(C) angels
(D) progeny

You should circle (D) because "Believing the Spanish conquerors to be progeny of the god Quetzalcoatl, Montezuma gave them gifts to persuade them to leave" is closest in meaning to the original sentence.

1. The way the nervous system develops in fruit flies and mice <u>corresponds</u> closely, even though their bodies are radically different.
   (A) corroborates
   (B) coincides
   (C) reciprocates
   (D) combines

2. Physicians from all parts of the world meet yearly in Hiroshima to attend <u>a conference</u> on atomic war threats.
   (A) a symposium
   (B) a rehearsal
   (C) a briefing
   (D) an assignment

3. The famous racehorse Secretariat had to be destroyed because of a painful, <u>incurable</u> hoof disease.
   (A) disabling
   (B) vexatious
   (C) dangerous
   (D) irreparable

4. In most countries, <u>compulsory</u> military service does not apply to women.
   (A) superior
   (B) mandatory
   (C) beneficial
   (D) constructive

5. When normal tissue of the liver is destroyed, the circulation of the blood through the liver is <u>impeded</u> and its detoxifying powers are reduced.
   (A) hampered
   (B) barricaded
   (C) dissolved
   (D) unadulterated

6. UNICEF has <u>assumed</u> the responsibility of aiding children in need.
   (A) taken on
   (B) effected
   (C) evaded
   (D) violated

7. Minimum wages are aimed at <u>assuring</u> workers a reasonable standard of living.
   (A) depriving
   (B) extending
   (C) promising
   (D) awarding

8. Scientists warn of the <u>impending</u> extinction of many species of plants and animals.
   (A) irrefutable
   (B) imminent
   (C) formidable
   (D) absolute

9. The <u>predominant</u> art forms created by Africans inhabiting areas south of the Sahara are masks and figures.
   (A) phenomenal
   (B) sporadic
   (C) principal
   (D) exquisite

10. Needlepoint lace, done with a needle in <u>variations</u> of the buttonhole stitch, arose in Italy during the Renaissance.
    (A) modifications
    (B) inventions
    (C) implications
    (D) insinuations

11. The aircraft carrier is <u>indispensable</u> in naval operations against sea- or shore-based enemies.
    (A) unique
    (B) novel
    (C) exotic
    (D) vital

12. Agricultural <u>diversification</u> in America's Deep South began after an insect infestation of the cotton fields.
    (A) pesticides
    (B) evacuation
    (C) sterilization
    (D) variegation

13. Josef Albers is best known for a <u>sequence</u> of paintings that portrays colors in concentric squares.
    (A) landscape
    (B) succession
    (C) studio
    (D) summation

14. In 1952 Akihito was officially <u>proclaimed</u> heir to the Japanese throne.
    (A) declared
    (B) denounced
    (C) inculcated
    (D) installed

15. The Italian dramatist and poet Ugo Betti was a judge who gained literary <u>recognition</u> late in life.
    (A) knowledge
    (B) prestige
    (C) perception
    (D) ambition

16. The eating disorder bulimia is found almost <u>exclusively</u> among young women.
    (A) luxuriously
    (B) perpetually
    (C) uniquely
    (D) eminently

17. Several members of the British Parliament called for <u>conciliation</u> with the American colonists.
    (A) reservation
    (B) transaction
    (C) appeasement
    (D) disengagement

18. The CAT scan allows a safe, painless, and rapid diagnosis of previously <u>inaccessible</u> areas of the body.
    (A) immaculate
    (B) unrestricted
    (C) imprecise
    (D) unreachable

19. Medieval French dialects <u>persist</u> in some rural areas.
    (A) survive
    (B) succeed
    (C) improve
    (D) prevail

20. Marco Polo's account of his travels has been <u>invaluable</u> to historians.
    (A) immaterial
    (B) unpalatable
    (C) irreplaceable
    (D) deplorable

21. Petty larceny is a <u>misdemeanor</u> distinguished from grand larceny by the value of the property involved.
    (A) crime
    (B) hobby
    (C) career
    (D) chore

22. The <u>symmetrical</u> branches of the monkey-puzzle tree are covered by stiff overlapping leaves.
    (A) matured
    (B) extended
    (C) pointed
    (D) balanced

23. An artificial pacemaker can be <u>implanted</u> in a body when the heart does not function properly.
    (A) assembled
    (B) anchored
    (C) enclosed
    (D) inserted

24. Called the great <u>benefactor</u> of humanity, Osiris brought to the people knowledge of agriculture and civilization.
    (A) patron
    (B) conjurer
    (C) deceiver
    (D) client

25. Eyeglasses with concave lenses can <u>compensate</u> for the refractive error in nearsightedness.
    (A) avenge
    (B) charge
    (C) account
    (D) adjust

26. Ralph Nader was the most <u>prominent</u> leader of the U.S. consumer protection movement.
    (A) significant
    (B) aggressive
    (C) promiscuous
    (D) discriminating

27. Electronic games challenge eye-hand <u>coordination</u> in a setting designed to provide entertainment.
    (A) exploitation
    (B) determination
    (C) synchronization
    (D) alleviation

28. Albert Einstein is <u>lauded</u> as one of the greatest theoretical physicists of all time.
    (A) acclaimed
    (B) described
    (C) dictated
    (D) ordained

29. Selective herbicides attack weeds without <u>permanently</u> harming crops.
    (A) negligibly
    (B) irrevocably
    (C) remotely
    (D) formally

30. Rubies that exhibit an <u>internal</u> star when cut with a rounded top are relatively rare.
    (A) inferior
    (B) interior
    (C) indifferent
    (D) intimate

Answers to Exercise V28 are on page 480.

READING COMPREHENSION

The Reading Comprehension section of the TOEFL contains reading passages which are followed by a number of questions about each passage. There are 30 questions in each TOEFL test. All the information needed to answer the questions is in the passages. If you have worked quickly through the Vocabulary section, you should have more than 30 minutes to complete this section.

STRATEGIES TO USE FOR BUILDING READING FLUENCY

1. Read extensively.

The more you read, the better you become at reading. Read on a variety of topics in order to build your vocabulary. The larger the vocabulary you have, the less time you will have to spend trying to understand words in context and the more time you will have for accurate reading.

2. Read challenging material.

If you always read things that are easy for you, you will not develop your ability to read more difficult material.

3. Read the material critically.

Think about what you are reading. Ask yourself what the reading is really about. Ask yourself how the writer defends the ideas presented.

STRATEGIES TO USE FOR READING COMPREHENSION

1. Read the questions.

Before you read the passage, you should read the questions in order to have an idea of the information you are looking for.

2. Skim the passage.

Read the passage quickly to determine its organization, the main idea, and the location of the information asked about in the questions.

3. Answer the easy questions first.

Answer all the questions about the passage that you can after you have skimmed it.

4. Read the passage.

Read the passage carefully to find the answers to the more difficult questions. All the answers are either stated or implied in the reading.

5. Use context clues to understand the passage.

Even native speakers do not always understand all the vocabulary used in the passages. Instead, they use clues from other words in the sentence or passage to determine the meaning of unfamiliar words.

6. Read the passage even if you are familiar with the topic.

Sometimes you will find a passage about a topic you are familiar with. However, you should read the passage anyway. It might contain new information concerning the topic or concepts that conflict with your ideas about the topic.

7. Know what works for you.

If you are uncertain which answer is correct, you can do one of two things:

(A) Use your intuition (instincts).
(B) Guess.

Sometimes you do not know the answer but have an unexplained feeling that one of the answers is correct. You have no other reason to believe it is correct. This is your *intuition*. Test your intuition while working through the mini-tests in this book by marking items that you answered intuitively. If your intuition is usually correct, trust it when you take the TOEFL.

Sometimes students answer intuitively and then change their answers. Check yourself while working through the mini-tests in this book. Do you frequently change right answers to wrong ones, or are your changes usually correct? If your first answer is usually the correct one, don't change your answers on the TOEFL.

Remember that wrong answers will not count against you. If you don't know an answer and have no feeling about which of the four choices may be correct, use a *guess letter*. A guess letter is one letter (A, B, C, or D) that you can use to answer all items you don't know. You are more likely to get some correct answers if you use one letter consistently than if you use all letters randomly.

8. Answer all the questions.

Answer all the items of one passage before you go on to the next passage. If you do not know the answer to a question, do not leave a blank space. Answer it using your intuition or a guess letter. Mark the item you are unsure of in the test booklet. If you have time, you can go back and think about the marked items. If you change any answer, be sure you thoroughly erase your first answer.

PRACTICE WITH UNDERSTANDING WORDS IN CONTEXT

It may be possible to guess the meaning of a word from the context. For example, consider this sentence:

Timothy **scowled** when he saw the dent in his new car.

We can guess that Timothy is upset when he notices a dent in his new car. Although we can't know the *exact* meaning of "scowl" from the context, we can guess that it is a way of showing displeasure. We might further guess that most people show they are upset by their facial expression. Thus, we have arrived at a definition of "scowl": a facial expression that shows displeasure.

It's not always possible to get a clue to the meaning of a word from the context. For example, consider this sentence:

Timothy **scowled** when he saw Aunt Agatha.

Unless we know what Timothy's opinion of Aunt Agatha is, we cannot guess the meaning of "scowled" here. However, other sentences in the passage might indicate what his opinion is, and these could give a clue to the meaning.

While the Vocabulary section does not give context clues, you will find that your skills in understanding words through context will be helpful in the Reading Comprehension section. Vocabulary meanings are given in English in various ways. The following exercises reflect some of these ways.

Exercise R1   ***Understanding words in context***

Look at the underlined word and write its meaning on the line.

Example   A cutlass is a short curved sword.

sword
_____

You should write "sword" as the meaning of "cutlass" because the definition of "cutlass" is included in the sentence.

USING THE VERB "TO BE"

The object following the verb "to be" is frequently used to identify the subject.

Example   A salmon is a fish.

The meaning of "salmon" is identified by the word "fish."

1. Hypoxia is an illness caused by a deficiency of oxygen in the tissues of the body.

   _____

2. A porcupine is a large climbing rodent that is covered with sharp spines for defense.

   _____

3. The atom is the smallest part of a chemical element that can exist and still have the properties of the element.

   _____

4. A meteorite is a falling star that reaches the earth without burning up.

   _____

5. A drone is a male bee.

   _____

USING APPOSITIVES

A noun or noun group which follows a noun and is set off by commas is an appositive. It identifies the noun it follows.

Example   Mercury, **the silver-colored metal used in thermometers**, is usually in a liquid form.

The meaning of "mercury" is identified by its appositive, "the silver-colored metal used in thermometers."

By adding the words "which is/are" or "who is/are," you can test if the noun is an appositive.

Example *Mercury*, **which is** the silver-colored metal used in thermometers, is usually in a liquid form.

6. The coelacanth, a large-bodied hollow-spined fish, was thought to be extinct until recently.

_____

7. Pacemakers, small electrical devices that stimulate the heart muscle, have saved many lives.

_____

8. Many residents of Hawaii used to believe that the volcano's flarings were tirades of their goddess, Pele.

_____

9. Morse code, a system of telegraphic signals composed of dots and dashes, was invented by Samuel F. B. Morse.

_____

10. Studying supernovas, the catastrophic explosions of dying stars, may give answers to questions of modern cosmology.

_____

USING PUNCTUATION

Punctuation marks are sometimes used to set off a word which is being used to identify another word. Some of the punctuation marks you may see used in this way are:

commas	,	brackets	[ ]
dashes	–	single quotation marks	' '
parentheses	( )	double quotation marks	" "

Example In laser printing, the greater the number of dpi (**dots per inch**), the higher the quality of the image produced.

The meaning of "dpi" is identified by the words in parentheses, "dots per inch."

11. Intensity – loudness or softness – depends on the extent or amplitude of vibrations.

_____

12. The use of carved birds, "decoys," is not a new idea in hunting.

_____

13. If you are ectomorphic (the slender type), you are likely to be good in such sports as track, tennis, and basketball.

_____

14. A path to the chieftain's headquarters winds through ancient petroglyphs – inscriptions in stone.

_____

15. Oral history – the use of the tape recorder to capture memories of the past in private interviews – has become increasingly popular among professional historians.

_____

USING "OR"

A word is sometimes identified by a synonym following the word "or."

Example   The husky, or sled dog, of the North is a hardy breed.

The meaning of the word "husky" is identified by the words "sled dog" following the word "or."

16. Altitude, or the height above sea level, is a factor that determines climate.

_____

17. Vespers, or evening worship, can be heard at St. Matthew's Cathedral.

_____

18. In some American Indian tribes, the squaw, or woman, was the owner of all property.

_____

19. The central nervous system of grasshoppers, fruit flies, and other insects includes both the brain and a chain of simpler segmental ganglia, or groups of nerve cells.

_____

20. Claustrophobia, or the fear of being enclosed, is more common than many people realize.

_____

USING EXAMPLES

A word is sometimes identified by examples. These terms often introduce examples:

as	for example	such as
like	for instance	

Example   Percussion instruments, **such as** drums, cymbals, and tambourines, were the preferred instruments in the study.

The meaning of "percussion instruments" is identified by the three examples: "drums," "cymbals," and "tambourines."

21. Such large fish as groupers and moray eels recognize the wrasse as a friend that will help them.

_____

22. Creatures such as the camel and the penguin are so highly specialized that they can only live in certain areas of the world.

_____

23. The sand absorbs enough moisture to support drought-resistant plants such as mesquite, as well as several species of grasses.

_____

24. Camping paraphernalia such as tents, sleeping bags, and cooking equipment can range from very simple to quite complex.

_____

25. Much can be done to halt the process of desertification. For example, an asphaltlike petroleum can be sprayed onto sand dunes, and seeds of trees and shrubs can then be planted. The oil stabilizes the sand and retains moistuire, allowing vegetation to become established.

_____

USING CLAUSES

Adjective clauses sometimes identify words, They are introduced by the words;

that	where	who
when	which	whom

Example   Airships, **which** are cigar-shaped, steerable balloons, have many uses, such as filming, advertising, and entertainment.

The meaning of "airships" is identified by the adjective clause "which are cigar-shaped, steerable balloons."

26. Recent tests show that silver sulfadiazine, which is a compound used in the treatment of burns, can cure the most serious types of African sleeping sickness.

_____

27. The kiva, where Pueblo Indians hold their secret ceremonies, is entered by an opening in the roof.

_____

28. Melody, which is the succession of sounds, takes on new interest when fit into a rhythmic pattern.

_____

29. Nonlethal techniques, those that do not kill coyotes, are being developed to protect sheep and other livestock.

_____

30. The "O" in many Irish names comes from the Gaelic word ua, which means "descended from. "

_____

USING REFERENTS

Referents are words that refer back or forward to other words in the sentence or paragraph.

Example   The solar-powered batteries in the ERS-1 are expected to function for at least two years, during which time the **satellite** will be able to gather more information than any previous satellite.

The meaning of "ERS-l" is identified by its referent "satellite."

31. The farmers were concerned about the growing number of boll weevils. An infestation of these insects could destroy the cotton crop overnight.

_____

32. At least 50 weed species fight off competitors by emitting <u>toxins</u> from their roots, leaves, or seeds. These poisons do their work in a dozen ways, such as inhibiting germination of seeds and destroying photosynthesis abilities.

33. Important officials visiting president Roosevelt were surprised by his <u>menagerie</u> of pets. No previous president had filled the White House with such a variety of animals.

34. The groom struggled with his <u>tuxedo</u>. He wondered why he had to wear these kinds of clothes to get married.

35. Emma was told to put the sheets in the <u>hamper</u>, but she found the basket too full of soiled clothes to fit the sheets in.

USING CONTRASTS

Sometimes the meanings of words can be understood because they are in contrast to another word in the sentence. Words that indicate a contrast are.

but	in contrast	or
despite	in spite of	unlike
however	instead	whereas

Example The <u>brief</u> scenes in the movie focus on the boy's point of view, **whereas** the longer scenes depict the father's side.

"Brief" scenes are understood to be "short" scenes because they are in contrast to the "longer" scenes.

36. The bite of a garter snake, unlike that of the deadly cobra, is <u>benign</u>.

37. The bluebonnet, the Texas state flower, <u>thrives</u> in dry, poor soil but dies in overly wet conditions.

38. Despite proposed <u>cutbacks</u> in financial support for domestic students, assistance for foreign students studying and training in the United States is to be sharply increased.

39. Unlike her <u>gregarious</u> sister, Jane is a shy, unsociable person who does not like to go to parties.

40. At the Indian Reservation Trading Post, tourists can buy <u>trinkets</u> or they can buy expensive handmade items.

USING OTHER WORDS IN THE SENTENCE

Other words in a sentence can sometimes help identify a word.

Example   In order to sip the <u>nectar</u> with its long tongue, the bee must dive into the flower and in so doing becomes dusted with the fine pollen grains from the anthers.

We can guess that "nectar" is the substance that bees collect from a flower because the bee must "sip . . . with its long tongue" and "dive into the flower." We can guess that "anther" is a part of the flower because the bee gets "dusted with the fine pollen grains from the anthers" when it dives into the flower.

41. The bright purple <u>gentian</u> grows wild in Colorado and blooms in late summer.

   _____

42. While blowing air into the leather bag, the bagpipe player produces melodies by fingering the <u>chanter</u>.

   _____

43. Unfortunately, the plant's hairs kill useful insects, but this problem can be <u>alleviated</u> by controlling the amount of hair.

   _____

44. The much larger <u>hull</u> of the multidecked round ship allowed it to carry more supplies, more men, more guns, and more sails, all of which were necessary for long voyages of commerce and discovery.

   _____

45. In the third century B.C., Ctesibuis, the Greek engineer and theorist, first exercised his <u>inventive</u> talents by making an adjustable mirror and then creating ingenious toys which could move under their own power.

   _____

Answers to Exercise R1 are on page 481.

PRACTICE WITH REFERENTS, TRANSITIONS, AND CONNECTORS

In order to understand a reading passage, you need to be able to:

1. Identify what the referents are referring to.
2. Follow the flow of ideas by paying attention to transitions and connectors.
3. Break complex sentences into simple sentences in order to understand the ideas.

Use Exercises R2–R4 to build your skills in understanding passages.

Exercise R2   *Locating referents*

Read the following statements. Find the referent for the underlined word or words and write it in the space. (For additional practice, see Exercises L58 and L59.)

Example   Because of their vitality and pervasiveness, some familiarity with Greek myth and legend is almost indispensable to a full appreciation of European culture.

their   _____*Greek myth and legend*_____

"Vitality and pervasiveness" belong to "Greek myth and legend.

1. The first complete American dictionary of the English language was compiled in 1828 by the lawyer and lexicographer Noah Webster, who was particularly keen to show that American English was distinct from that spoken in Britain.

   who _____

   that _____

2. Under the ice, bubbles gather against the ice roof until they overflow and escape through the tide cracks.

   they _____

3. Amnesty International consists of over 900 groups of individuals who work for the release of political prisoners incarcerated for their beliefs.

   who _____

   their _____

4. Seward's Folly is what people called Alaska when U.S. Secretary of State William Seward arranged to purchase it from Russia in 1867.

   it _____

5. The Royal Canadian Mounted Police use horses and wear their famous red uniforms on ceremonial occasions.

   their _____

6. Some psychiatrists believe that every person is surrounded by a force field that broadcasts his or her emotions to other people.

   his _____

   her _____

7. In 1863, when a Hungarian count recognized the potential of Californian soil and sun for growing wine grapes, he planted the first European variety there near the town of Sonoma.

   when _____

   he _____

   the first European variety _____

   there _____

8. Research in sensory deprivation has revealed that the human mind cannot operate normally unless it receives a constant succession of stimuli.

   it _____

9. Novelist Willa Cather used the frontier life of the Nebraska prairie of <u>her</u> youth for her <u>subject matter</u>.

her _____

subject matter _____

10. Arctic people must not only defend <u>themselves</u> from the environment and wild animals, but <u>they</u> must also protect <u>these natural resources</u>.

themselves _____

they _____

these natural resources _____

Answers to Exercise R2 are on page 482.

Exercise R3   *Understanding transitions and connectors*

Study the following list of transition words and connecting words.

Words that:

qualify	but, however, although, yet, except for
emphasize	surely, certainly, indeed, above all, most importantly
illustrate	for example, next, for instance, thus, such, such as
contrast	unlike, in contrast, whereas, on the other hand, instead
concede	although, yet, nevertheless, of course, after all
conclude	finally, in conclusion, at last, in summary, to sum up
add	in addition, also, moreover, then, first, second (etc.)
compare	similarly, like, in the same way, both, equally important
explain	now, in addition, furthermore, in fact, in this case, at this point
state a consequence	therefore, as a result, consequently, accordingly, otherwise

Complete the following sentences by choosing the phrase that would follow the underlined transition words or connectors. Circle the letter of the phrase.

Example   Although potatoes are richer in food value than any other vegetable, they are not always a wise choice for a garden crop because they need a considerable amount of room. <u>Consequently,</u>
(A) they are the most common vegetable in a garden.
(B) people don't eat potatoes very much.
(C) they can be more economically grown on farms.
(D) farmers overcharge for their potatoes.

You should circle (C) because if potatoes are not a wise choice for a garden because of the amount of room they need, they could be grown on a farm more economically, since a farm does have adequate space.

1. Glass was precious to Egyptians, who used it interchangeably with gemstones, <u>but</u>
(A) it is over 4,000 years old.
(B) its novelty as an artist's material prevents its being taken seriously.
(C) today it has come out of factories and into the workshops.
(D) today it is so commonplace in everyday objects that it is seldom given a second thought.

2. Glimpses into the prenatal world via ultrasound imaging occasionally show behavior such as
   (A) the development of the central nervous system.
   (B) the sex of the baby-to-be.
   (C) a fetus sucking its thumb.
   (D) structures as small as the pupil of an eye of a second-trimester fetus.

3. Although the animals and plants that live in the world's various deserts come from different ancestral stocks,
   (A) they have solved their problems of survival differently.
   (B) none of them have adapted to the jungles.
   (C) they are from different deserts.
   (D) they resemble one another to a surprising degree.

4. Children dress up in witches' hats or goblin suits to play pranks when celebrating the ancient pagan holiday of Halloween. In contrast,
   (A) Thanksgiving is a traditional holiday.
   (B) Thanksgiving is always celebrated on the fourth Thursday of November.
   (C) families dress more formally and set elegant tables for the more serious occasion of Thanksgiving.
   (D) children enjoy Thanksgiving.

5. Everything from chairs and fishing poles to rope and paper can be made from bamboo. Equally important,
   (A) this giant grass grows in warm climates.
   (B) fresh spring bamboo shoots take longer to cook than winter ones.
   (C) a variety of food can be made from this giant grass.
   (D) preserved bamboo shoots can be used in soups instead of fresh ones.

6. Earth satellites transmit telephone and television signals, relay information about weather patterns, and enable scientists to study the atmosphere. This information has helped people communicate ideas and expand their knowledge. In conclusion,
   (A) satellites have enriched the lives of humankind.
   (D) satellites are expensive to send into space and sometimes are difficult to maintain.
   (C) a dish antenna can pick up 300 TV channels from satellites.
   (D) satellites are placed in an orbital region around Earth called the geostationary belt.

7. In the 1940s, when many of today's astronauts hadn't even been born, comic strip detective Dick Tracy fought crime in an atomic-powered space vehicle. In addition to that,
   (A) many of today's astronauts have used a kind of atomic-powered space vehicle.
   (B) he used lasers to process gold and a two-way wrist TV for communication.
   (C) Dick Tracy was a very popular comic strip in the U.S.
   (D) astronauts used lasers to process gold and communicated on long-distance flights using two-way wrist TVs.

8. Until recently, chlamydial infections could be detected only by a complicated test that took up to seven days to complete and which was offered only at a few medical centers. As a result,
   (A) up to 10 percent of all college students are afflicted with it.
   (B) chlamydial infections were rarely diagnosed.
   (C) chlamydial infections are treated promptly.
   (D) doctors prescribe large doses of antibiotics to treat the infections.

9. Medical researchers have recently developed a nonsurgical method of treating heart disease that, <u>in some cases,</u>
   - (A) is just as effective as coronary bypass surgery but is much less expensive and disabling.
   - (B) can replace a clogged artery by the transplanting of a vein or artery from another part of the body.
   - (C) continues to be underused because coronary bypass operations are lucrative for hospitals and surgeons.
   - (D) requires opening up the chest and operating under local anesthesia.

10. Neurons, which cannot divide, are the basic cells of the brain. Glial cells, which can increase in number, provide support and nourishment to the neurons. It was hypothesized that if Einstein's brain was more active in some areas, more glial cells would be found there. <u>Indeed,</u>
   - (A) scientists found that the physicist's brain contained more glial cells per neuron in all four areas, compared with the brains of eleven normal males.
   - (B) scientists' previous work had shown that animals put in environments that stimulate mental activity develop more glial cells per neuron.
   - (C) scientists examined sections of the upper front and lower rear of both hemispheres because these areas are involved in "higher" thinking.
   - (D) scientists found that even though there was evidence he had greater intellectual processing, it cannot be determined if Einstein was born with this or developed it later.

Answers to Exercise R3 are on page 482.

Exercise R4   ***Understanding complex structures***

Break the following complex sentences into short, simple sentences in order to understand all the ideas.

Example   The advantages of such a bridge being built across the point where the two rivers join far outweigh the disadvantages of the cost and labor it will entail.

A bridge may be built across two rivers. The bridge will cross where the two rivers join. The advantages of the bridge being built here are greater than the disadvantages. The disadvantages are the cost and the labor.

1. Although critics separate Charles Dickens' earlier novels from his mature work by degree of structural complexity, the earlier works are also masterpieces of narrative.

   _____

   _____

   _____

   _____

2. Recycled rubber from discarded automobile tires can be used to react with hot asphalt in a process which gives the asphalt elasticity and prevents it from cracking when it is used for surfaces, such as airport runways, that are subjected to great stresses.

   _____

   _____

   _____

   _____

3. In 1785, when the Frenchmen Pilatre de Rozier and Pierre Romain tried to cross the English Channel in a balloon, their balloon, which was filled with a mixture of hot air and hydrogen, caught fire and fell to the ground.

_____

_____

_____

_____

4. Although originally formed to prevent illegal trade in whiskey, the Royal Canadian Mounted Police, or Mounties as they are informally called, now enforce all federal laws throughout Canada.

_____

_____

_____

_____

5. The historic centers of the sister cities of Savannah and Charleston have fortunately been saved from demolition or neglect and now attract tourists eager to view the gracious old houses.

_____

_____

_____

_____

Answers to Exercise R4 are on page 483.

PRACTICE WITH MAIN IDEAS

All well-written paragraphs have a main idea. The main idea is what the paragraph is about. TOEFL questions concerning the main idea may be phrased in different ways. Here are some examples:

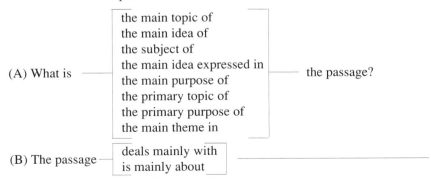

(A) What is
- the main topic of
- the main idea of
- the subject of
- the main idea expressed in
- the main purpose of
- the primary topic of
- the primary purpose of
- the main theme in

the passage?

(B) The passage
- deals mainly with
- is mainly about

(C) With what topic is the passage primarily concerned?

The topic of the passage is usually stated in the first sentence, although other positions are also possible. Read the following paragraph:

> The family heard the siren warning them that the tornado was coming. They hurried to the cellar. The roar of the tornado was deafening, and the children started crying. Suddenly it was silent. They waited a while before they went outside to survey the damage.

In the preceding paragraph, the topic – the tornado – is stated in the first sentence. In the following paragraph, the main topic is stated in the last sentence.

> The family hurried to the cellar and waited. First, they heard the pounding of the hailstones. The wind became deafening, and the children started crying. Suddenly it was silent. They waited a while before they ventured outside to see the damage the tornado had done.

Sometimes the topic is not stated in the passage at all but is implied, as in the following passage.

> The sky became dark and threatening. A funnel of dust began forming in the air and soon reached down to touch the ground. Debris was seen swirling around as everything was swallowed up, twisted, and then dropped.

Although "tornado" is not mentioned in the passage, it has been implied by the description ("a funnel of dust in the air," "debris . . . swirling," "twisted").

Use Reading Exercises R5–R8 to develop your skills in identifying the main ideas in the reading passages.

Exercise R5   *Locating topics*

Read the following passages. Underline the word or words that give the "topic" of each passage. If the topic is implied, then write the topic in the space.

Example   Gilbert and Sullivan are best known for a series of operas which they collaborated on. Gilbert's humorous plots and paradoxes combined with Sullivan's music have made their operas unforgettable. Written in the nineteenth century, these operas maintain their popularity today.

_____

You should underline "Gilbert and Sullivan" and "operas" because the passage is mainly about the operas that Gilbert and Sullivan wrote. You would leave the space empty because the topic is stated rather than implied.

1. The Japanese macaque is an endangered monkey. It inhabits an area farther north than any other primate except for humans. The Japanese call this animal the snow monkey because it can be found in the snowy regions of Japan. Ironically, some troops of macaques have been relocated in Texas to ensure their survival.

_____

2. Originally, robots were found only in science fiction movies and books. Today, they have become science fact as technology has turned them into a feasible means of increasing productivity. The robot industries may still be in their infancy, but their products are no longer being ridiculed as an impossibility.

_____

3. By nine o'clock in the morning, the streets are lined with people. Somewhere in the distance, a band is heard playing a marching song. Shopkeepers are locking their doors and joining the crowds. Everyone is craning their necks to see how long it will be before the first float reaches them.

4. Parsley, a good source of iron and vitamins A, C, and E, is a common herb of the Mediterranean area. The ancient Greeks considered it sacred and therefore did not eat it. The Romans served it as a garnish and to improve the taste of food.

5. For thousands of years, desert dwellers have sheltered themselves in extremely functional buildings constructed of one of the most readily available, dependable, and inexpensive materials we know of. This ideal insulator, which absorbs heat during the day and slowly releases it at night, is mud.

6. Before World War II, Hay-on-Wye was a bustling little market town on the border of Wales and England. However, it became a dying town when Welsh agriculture declined, forcing many farmers off their land and to factory jobs in England. Today, Hay is flourishing again because of a flamboyant gentleman who has turned the town into the world's largest secondhand bookstore.

7. The Queens' Children's Psychiatric Center on the eastern outskirts of New York is recruiting elderly men and women to work as foster grandparents for the children in the hospital. Even though these grandparents have no experience or training in dealing with emotionally disturbed children, they have lots of experience in being parents. It has been found that both foster grandparents and foster grandchildren benefit immensely from this relationship.

8. The koto is a traditional Japanese instrument originating in China. It is made by stretching 13 strings of tightly coiled silk over an arched body of paulownia wood. The player plucks the strings to make the gentle zitherlike tones.

9. Parents are allowed at the starting gate only for the 6-and-under and the 5-and-under classes. Most of the bicycle racers in the 17-and-over expert classes have sponsors. Some of the racers even have an income.

10. Human beings are capable of thinking in two basic ways. Convergent thinking neatly and systematically tends toward an answer. Divergent thinking tends away from a center, perhaps in several directions at once, seeking avenues of inquiry rather than a particular destination. Scientists, on the whole, engage in convergent thinking, but it is divergent thinking that breaks with the past and leads to unpredictable conclusions.

Answers to Exercise R5 are on page 483.

Exercise R6   ***Selecting a topic sentence***

In the following passages only the supporting ideas are given. The passages are followed by three possible topic sentences. Circle the letter of the sentence which would best introduce the passage.

Example   In Greek and Roman times, the cavalry was comprised of members of noble families. This distinction continued up to the Middle Ages. After the invention of gunpowder, this branch of the military service underwent great changes. With the development of heavy artillery and air forces, this service has almost disappeared.

(A) The cavalry has been displaced by armored regiments.
(B) Cavalry regiments still retain a mounted squadron for ceremonial duties.
(C) The cavalry is the part of an army consisting of troops that serve on horseback.

Both (A) and (B) discuss the cavalry situation of today. However, the passage discusses the cavalry from Greek and Roman times until today. Therefore, you should circle (C) because it introduces the topic of a cavalry by giving an explanation of what a cavalry is.

1. There appear to be tracks of young dinosaurs near tracks of older ones in the area. These dinosaur tracks are in sequences of eight to ten paces. They enable scientists to calculate the animals' weight, stride, and speed.
   (A) Important dinosaur tracks have been found in areas that were near ancient seas.
   (B) Some recently discovered tracks are giving important information about dinosaurs.
   (C) Dinosaurs may weigh as much as 10,000 pounds and be 23 feet tall.

2. This spider, named *Micromygale debliemma*, has only two eyes where most spiders have six or eight. Unlike most spiders, it does not have lungs but instead absorbs oxygen through its skin. Just three one-hundredths of an inch long, Micromygale is one of the world's smallest spiders.
   (A) Scientists have discovered a spider which is remarkably different from any other known spider.
   (B) Scientists have discovered a spider which is the size of the head of a pin.
   (C) Scientists have discovered a spider which inhabits the coastal forested regions of Panama.

3. Trees can defend themselves against devouring insects by undergoing changes in the nutritional quality of their leaves. The leaves of nearby trees undergo the same changes in nutritional quality as do those attacked. It is hypothesized that trees emit chemical substances that transmit information to other trees concerning the attack.
   (A) Scientists believe that the nutritional quality of leaves causes chemical substances to transmit information.
   (B) Scientists believe that studies in tree communication could affect pest control programs.
   (C) Scientists believe that trees attacked by insects may communicate information to neighboring trees, which act accordingly.

4. Satellites routinely relay pictures of desert areas on Earth, from which it can be determined where locusts are likely to breed. A single swarm of locusts can devour 80,000 tons of corn a day – sustenance for half a million people for one year. With information on the locusts' breeding areas, agriculture officials can use pesticides to kill the locusts before they become a menace.
   (A) Aerial pictures transmitted from satellites will be used to dramatically curtail infestations by locusts.
   (B) Scientists have found that images from satellites reveal regions about to be infested by locusts.
   (C) Locusts must be eradicated before they strike and cause thousands of people to starve.

5. Scientists used to believe that animal screams startled predators into loosening their grip. However, now some researchers have concluded that the piercing, far-reaching screams of animals caught by predators are not warnings to kin or cries for help. Recent studies indicate that these screams may be to attract other predators, which will give the prey a chance to escape during the ensuing struggle between predators.
   (A) Animal screams attract buzzards, hawks, foxes, feral cats, and other predators.
   (B) Researchers broadcasted the fear screams of the European starling from a concealed loudspeaker.
   (C) New research in animal behavior has come to surprising conclusions about animal screams.

6. It has an enameled surface decorated with elaborate designs, the outlines of which are formed by small bands of metal. The Byzantines excelled in making this kind of pottery. However, in the twentieth century, Japan and China have led in the production of cloisonné.
   (A) Cloisonné is a kind of fine pottery.
   (B) Pottery is fired in a kiln.
   (C) Fine pottery is made with a particular kind of clay.

7. Immunization can significantly reduce the microorganisms thought to cause cavities. The Federal Drug Administration needs to approve the vaccine before it can be sold to the public. Consequently, the vaccine will have to undergo a three-year trial period.
   (A) A new cavity-preventing vaccine may soon be on the market.
   (B) Vaccines given to animals can reduce tooth decay by 50 to 60 percent.
   (C) The National Caries Program of the National Institute of Dental Research does research on immunizations.

8. Cirrus clouds are thin and delicate, whereas cumulus clouds look like cotton balls. Nimbus clouds are dark and ragged, and stratus clouds appear dull in color and cover the entire sky.
   (A) A stratus cloud on the ground is called fog.
   (B) There are four basic cloud types – cirrus, cumulus, nimbus, and stratus.
   (C) It is possible to predict the weather by studying clouds.

9. For example, King William the First, better known as William the Conqueror, was the first Norman king of England. Perhaps the most famous English writer of all times was William Shakespeare. And who can forget the American hero of the West, Buffalo Bill (William) Cody?
   (A) One of the most common boys' names in English is "William."
   (B) "William" is not only a popular name today but was also the name of many famous people in the past.
   (C) If your name is William, you have the same name as many other people.

10. Straw, which can absorb up to four times its weight in oil, can be thrown on the spill and then be burned. Oil can be broken up and sunk by either sand, talcum powder, or chalk. Under experimentation, some chemicals have been shown to disperse the spill into droplets, which microbes can then destroy.
    (A) There are many ways in which oil spills in the sea can be dealt with.
    (B) Contamination of the sea by oil spills is a critical problem.
    (C) Wind and wave action can carry oil spills a great distance across the sea.

Answers to Exercise R6 are on page 483.

Exercise R7   *Identifying supporting ideas*

You are given a sentence containing a main idea followed by a list of sentences. Circle the letter of each sentence that supports the main idea.

Example   The Henry Ford Museum has redesigned its display of old cars to show the changes brought about by the automobile.
   (A) The Henry Ford Museum was founded in 1929 in Dearborn, Michigan, about 12 miles west of downtown Detroit.
   (B) One exhibit which shows the evolution of roadside services contrasts a 1940s diner with a 1960s fast-food restaurant.
   (C) The museum is open daily from 9 to 5 except on national holidays.
   (D) The "Getting Away From It All" exhibit presents an assortment of recreational vehicles dating from Packard's 1916 camp truck to today's mobile home.
   (E) Changes in roadside objects such as billboards can be seen along the museum's roadway, where 108 cars are lined up as if traveling.

(B), (D), and (E) are good choices because they tell of specific "changes" caused by the automobile. The other choices are not related to the idea of change.

1. Vitamin D is called the sunshine vitamin.
   (A) Bare skin absorbs vitamin D from the sun.
   (B) Vitamin D is used by the body to form strong bones.
   (C) The lack of vitamin D can cause the disease rickets.
   (D) Growing children need vitamin D.
   (E) People who are not exposed to the sun become deficient in vitamin D.

2. Waste that has been made useful is said to have been recycled.
   (A) Nobody likes to see garbage strewn along the highways.
   (B) Empty bottles could be returned and used again.
   (C) Other things that can be recycled are paper, glass, and coffee.
   (D) Recycling waste is an environmentally sound idea.
   (E) New uses for many common waste materials have been found.

3. Although edelweiss is the Swiss national flower, it is also found in the Rocky Mountains of North America.
   (A) The Rocky Mountains have many high peaks to challenge mountain climbers.
   (B) Frequently edelweiss can be found in steep rocky crevices.
   (C) People like to ski both the Swiss Alps and the Rocky Mountains.
   (D) Edelweiss has small, white, star-shaped blossoms.
   (E) Edelweiss grows wild near areas with year-round snow.

4. It was only with the invention of lightweight steel frames that the building of skyscapers became possible.
   (A) Steel frames are strong but not bulky.
   (B) Although a high wind can move steel-framed buildings, it cannot damage them.
   (C) The twin towers of the World Trade Center are the tallest skyscrapers in New York City.
   (D) Steel was perfected in the early 1900s.
   (E) Many modern cities have spectacular skylines.

5. Perhaps the most fascinating thing about a snake is its jaws.
   (A) Some snakes have rattles on their tails to warn off predators.
   (B) A snake smells with its tongue.
   (C) Unlike other reptiles, a snake's jaws are not hinged.
   (D) The teeth, which are not good for chewing, point to the back of the jaw while the snake is eating so they don't get in the way.
   (E) The jaw can be opened wide enough for a snake to swallow a larger animal whole.

6. Pennsylvania Avenue is the main street of Washington, D.C.
   (A) Pierre Charles L'Enfant was the city planner at this time.
   (B) Pennsylvania Avenue connects the Capitol to the White House.
   (C) The Old Post Office is one of the interesting buildings which lines Pennsylvania Avenue.
   (D) Pennsylvania Avenue is lined by a collection of old and new architectural styles.
   (E) The Treasury Department blocks the view of the Capitol from the White House.

7. The English longbowmen did not draw their bows but bent them.
   (A) Archers bent their bows by leaning on them with one arm and the upper part of their body.
   (B) Bending a bow utilized the strength of the body instead of just the arm.
   (C) Bending a bow gave the archers endurance to use them longer.
   (D) Robin Hood may have been a longbowman.
   (E) A hit using a longbow was more by chance than by accuracy.

8. The Aleutian Islands are North America's farthest west extension, as well as its farthest east extension.
   (A) In 1913, the Aleutian Islands were declared a wildlife refuge.
   (B) The Aleutian Islands sweep west and cross the 180 degree longitude into the Eastern Hemisphere.
   (C) The Aleutian Islands are a long range of active volcanos.
   (D) The outermost island is within 600 miles of the Asian mainland.
   (E) During World War II, the Battle of Attu took place on Attu Island of the Aleutian Islands.

Answers to Exercise R7 are on page 484.

Exercise R8   ***Identifying irrelevant ideas***

Each of the following passages contains an irrelevant idea – one that does not support the main idea of the passage. Read the following passages. Identify the main idea. Then, cross out the sentence that does not support the main idea of the passage.

Example   (1) The Pre-Raphaelite brotherhood was a school of artists formed about 1848.   (2) Their ideal was absolute fidelity to Nature.   (3) Ruskin was an art critic.   (4) For a time, the school greatly influenced art developments.   (5) However, by the end of the century, the movement had been abandoned.

You should cross out sentence (3). The topic is the Pre-Raphaelite school of artists. Ruskin was an art critic, not an artist. There is no clear relationship in the passage between Ruskin and the Pre-Raphaelite school of artists.

1. (1) The earliest known domestic turkeys were found in Mexico among the Aztecs. (2) Hernando Cortés, the Spanish conquistador, took specimens back to Spain. (3) The turkey spread throughout Europe.   (4) The wild turkey is a close relation to the domestic turkey.   (5) The Pilgrims then brought the domestic turkey back to the Western Hemisphere from England.

2. (1) Among the major grain crops, the only one that is grown almost exclusively as human food is rice.   (2) Rice constitutes half the diet of 1.6 billion people, and another 400 million people rely on it for between one-fourth and one-half of their diet.   (3) Rice originated in the hot, humid tropics, where monsoon rains and flood waters create an aquatic environment for at least part of the year.   (4) Millions of people would have been severely underfed had it not been for a series of remarkable genetic advances that have made possible the cultivation of high-yield varieties that are resistant to disease and insect pests.

3. (1) Addiction to cigarette smoking is basically an addiction to nicotine. (2) Cigar or pipe smokers are more likely to get lip cancer than lung cancer. (3) Switching to low-nicotine cigarettes simply causes problem smokers to smoke more. (4) Zero-nicotine cigarettes are usually rejected. (5) For these reasons, a chewing gum containing nicotine may be an effective aid for those who want to stop smoking.

4. (1) A meteorite is a meteor that reaches Earth without burning up. (2) Approximately 500 meteorites reach Earth every year, but only about five or six of these are actually seen as they fall through the air. (3) Meteorites can bury themselves 10 feet deep or more with the force of their impact. (4) If a meteorite were found with a fossil inside, it would mean there was life somewhere else in the universe.

5. (1) Underground homes are more expensive to build than conventional houses. (2) Earth shelters are nothing like a dank, dark basement. (3) Well-placed windows and skylights ensure brightness and fresh air. (4) Sophisticated waterproofing techniques keep moisture out. (5) Heating and air-conditioning require less energy because the soil temperature is relatively stable and the concrete walls can store the sun's heat and radiate it into the rooms at night.

6. (1) Every spring, windstorms collect dust from the great deserts of China. (2) The dust forms a dense cloud that is hundreds of miles wide. (3) It is blown thousands of miles across the Pacific Ocean. (4) As much as 10 percent of the soil in Hawaii is composed of dust particles from China. (5) The dust travels from the North Pacific to the Gulf of Alaska and from there moves south and then east.

7. (1) At least 18 species of birds – a total of 17 million birds – have either left or perished on Christmas Island. (2) Christmas Island was discovered by Captain James Cook on Christmas Eve in 1777. (3) It is suspected that the cause of the disappearance may be related to a cyclical weather phenomenon in the Pacific that alters wind patterns, salinity, and ocean currents. (4) These conditions have resulted in higher water temperatures, which may have killed the fish and squid that the birds live on.

8. (1) Plant researchers have successfully crossed the common potato with a hairy wild variety from Bolivia that emits a strong glue from the end of its hairs to trap and kill insects. (2) The new hairy potato not only reduces aphid populations by 40 percent to 60 percent, but it also emits a substance that checks the population of the Colorado potato beetle, one of the most destructive potato pests. (3) Unfortunately, the hairs also trap beneficial insects, but this problem can be alleviated by limiting the density of hairs. (4) Potatoes, which are nutritious and tasty, are tubers that grow underground.

9. (1) In 1772, Caroline Herschel leaped at the chance to live in England with her astronomer brother, William. (2) He taught her mathematics, and she began to help him keep a record of his discoveries. (3) In Germany, her mother only allowed her to learn how to knit. (4) The two of them would often stay up until dawn and in all temperatures, gazing upward. (5) They built their own telescopes, which were even bigger and better than those at the Royal Observatory in Greenwich.

10. (1) Winning or losing a race in skiing can be a matter of a hundredth of a second. (2) To increase speed, skiers wear one-piece suits that cling to their bodies in order to reduce wind resistance. (3) Nothing is worn under these tight-fitting suits. (4) Skiing equipment has changed over the years.

Answers to Exercise R8 are on page 484.

CHECK YOUR PROGRESS

Check your progress in identifying the topic sentences (Exercises R5–R8) by completing the following mini-test. This exercise uses a format similar to that used in the Reading Comprehension section of the TOEFL.

Exercise R9   ***Mini-test***   *(Time – 15 minutes)*

Directions: You will read several passages. Each reading passage is followed by a question. Choose the best answer, (A), (B), (C) or (D), to each question. Then circle the letter of your answer in your book.

Example   Between the late 1920s and 1950s, the Osborne Calendar Company produced a series of calendars featuring trains of the Pennsylvania Railroad. Up to 300,000 of these, featuring large colorful scenes of trains at work, were published each year to hang in depots and shippers' offices along the lines of the famous railroad company. The scenes, mostly painted by one artist, Grif Teller, are now valuable collectibles.

What is the subject of this passage?
(A) trains at work
(B) calendars of the Pennsylvania Railroad trains
(C) valuable calendars
(D) Grif Teller's paintings of trains

The passage mainly discusses the calendars of the trains of the Pennsylvania Railroad produced by the Osborne Calendar Company. Therefore, you should circle (B).

1. Yuzen dyeing is a Japanese art that produces a lavish, multicolored type of kimono design that dates from the seventeenth century. First, a pattern is sketched on a kimono of plain, undyed silk. The garment is then taken apart and the design carefully painted onto the fabric with a paste that prevents the fabric from absorbing dye. Next, dyes are brushed over the silk, their colors penetrating only the untreated areas. After the paste is rinsed out, the strips of silk are again sewed into the kimono. Elaborate embroidery often completes the decoration.

What is the main subject of this passage?
(A) kimono design dating from the seventeenth century
(B) a description of Yuzen dyeing
(C) how kimonos are made
(D) the elaborate embroidery done on kimonos

2. The bioluminescent flashlight fish does not actually light up but has a saclike organ under each eye that contains luminous bacteria. Although the bacteria glow constantly, the fish can control the light by eye movements. The flashlight fish uses its lights to search for food in the dark depths. Upon finding the food, the fish blinks rapidly to signal its mates. If an intruder threatens, the fish can startle it by shining its light. Predators can be confused by the flashlight fish's flashing its light and abruptly changing directions.

What is the main idea of this passage?
(A) the flashlight fish uses its bioluminescence for different purposes
(B) bioluminescence can save the life of the flashlight fish
(C) bioluminescence in the flashlight fish is due to the luminous bacteria in the eye organs
(D) different fish use bioluminescence in different ways

3. Cole Porter was never regarded in his lifetime as socially conscious. Society-conscious, yes; he was born rich, and married richer, to Linda Lee Thomas, a wealthy divorcee. Songwriting made him a third fortune. He was not just rich and famous, he was famous for being rich. Though not a native New Yorker – he was a backcountry boy from Peru, Indiana – he and his work came to typify smart Manhattan society. His music was a highly personal mixture and had huge appeal. Porter, as an admiring contemporary remarked, made sophistication popular.

What is the subject of this passage?
(A) a socially conscious musician
(B) becoming rich and famous
(C) the life of a songwriter
(D) popularizing sophistication

4. The beaver's comical-looking flat tail, which is three quarters of an inch thick, six or seven inches wide, and perhaps a foot long, is unique in the animal world. In the water, it serves as a rudder for swimming, and on land it props the beaver upright while the animal is cutting trees. It also serves as a radiator through which the heavily insulated beaver passes off excess body heat. The beaver uses its broad tail for an early warning system by slapping it against the water's surface, making a resounding whack that can be heard half a mile away.

What is the purpose of this passage?
(A) to describe what the beaver's tail looks like to the reader
(B) to inform the reader about the many uses of a beaver's tail
(C) to give the reader a lesson in nature studies
(D) to teach the reader how to use a beaver's tail

5. Tree rings have long been used to determine the ages of trees and to gauge past climatic conditions. New evidence adds considerable weight to the theory that tree rings also record earthquakes. The rings reflect the effects of earthquakes, such as tilting, the disruption of root systems, and breakage, as well as shifts in environments. Older trees and petrified trees may give information about earthquakes that took place hundreds and even thousands of years ago.

What is the main theme of this passage?
(A) how earthquakes affect tree rings
(B) how tree rings can be used to warn people of impending earthquakes
(C) what information might be gained from studying tree rings
(D) why tree rings are used to determine tree ages, climatic conditions, and earthquakes

Answers to Exercise R9 are on page 484.

PRACTICE WITH RESTATEMENT

Restatement questions require you to recognize information from the passage that is stated in a different way. On the TOEFL, these questions are frequently asked in the following manner:

According to the passage . . .
It is stated in the passage that . . .

Use Exercises R10–R13 to develop your skills in recognizing details from the passage that are stated in a different way in the questions and answers.

Exercise R10   *Identifying if statements are the same or different*

Write an "S" in the space if the two sentences mean the same. Write a "D" in the space if they have different meanings.

Example   _D_   (A) A collection of fascinating tales called *The Arabian Nights* was introduced into Europe by the French scholar Antoine Galland.

(B) The French scholar Antoine Galland introduced into Europe a collection of fascinating tales which he called *The Arabian Nights*.

You should write "D" in the space because the sentences do not mean the same thing. In the first sentence, the scholar introduced the tales, whereas in the second sentence, the scholar introduced and named the collection of tales.

1. _____ (A) Scree, which abounds in the Rocky Mountains, has its origins in the ice ages.

(B) The Rocky Mountains have a lot of scree, whose formation dates back to the ice ages.

2. _____ (A) The drum and flute music once heard in the streets has been replaced by noisy radios and cassette players.

(B) Radios and cassette players are now heard in the streets, which once were filled by the sounds of drum and flute music.

3. _____ (A) Many reef organisms avoid dead-end caves, which lack the steady currents necessary for bringing a continuous food supply.

(B) Dead-end caves don't have currents which bring in food supplies, so many reef organisms don't go there.

4. _____ (A) Instead of being overwhelmed by the hard life in Montana, Evelyn Cameron reveled in it.

(B) Evelyn Cameron revealed how difficult life was in Montana.

5. _____ (A) Two theaters in Stratford-upon-Avon and two in London are regularly used by the Royal Shakespeare Company.

(B) The Royal Shakespeare Company regularly uses four theaters – two in Stratford-upon-Avon and two in London.

6. _____ (A) Police reconstruct scenes because people seem to recall things best when they are in the same physical situation.

(B) When people are in the same physical situation, they seem to remember better scenes than the ones police have reconstructed.

7. _____ (A) Despite the cold Alaskan temperatures, which freeze perspiration and breath in a man's beard, cabin fever forces inhabitants to challenge the elements.

(B) The Alaskan inhabitants suffer from cabin fever, which causes perspiration and breath to freeze in the men's beards.

8. _____ (A) Leather, when improperly handled and exposed to changeable temperatures, cracks easily.

(B) Leather cracks easily when it is handled incorrectly and is exposed to variable temperatures.

9. _____ (A) Despite the increasing pollution of their shorelines, oceans have become cleaner in the vast open-sea areas over the past decade.

(B) During the last 10 years, pollution has been increasing along the coasts of the oceans and spreading to the once clean open-sea areas.

10. _____ (A) The Hitler diaries, the greatest known publishing fraud in history, were written by a man who copied material from Hitler's speeches and medical reports.

(B) By copying material from Hitler's speeches and medical reports, a man wrote the Hitler diaries, which became known as the greatest publishing fraud in history.

Answers to Exercise R10 are on page 485.

Exercise R11   *Identifying restatements*

Read the following statements. Circle the letter of the statement that has the same meaning as the given statement.

Example   The bulk of Kafka's writings was not published until after his early death from tuberculosis.

(A) It was not until after Kafka's early death from tuberculosis that the bulk of his writings was published.

(B) After the bulk of his writings was published, Kafka died an early death from tuberculosis.

(C) After Kafka had written the bulk of his published writings, he met with an early death from tuberculosis.

(D) An early death from tuberculosis kept Kafka from publishing the bulk of his writings.

You should circle (A) because this is the only sentence which contains the same information as the first sentence. First Kafka died, and then most of his writings were published.

1. Fainting is caused by a sudden drop in the normal blood supply to the brain.
   (A) The brain reacts to a drop in the normal blood supply by fainting.
   (B) Fainting occurs when the brain suddenly loses its normal blood supply.
   (C) Fainting happens when the brain drops its normal blood supply.
   (D) The brain faints when the normal blood supply drops.

2. Gorillas, which are vegetarians, have been observed to demonstrate gentle behavior toward small creatures in the wild.
   (A) Vegetarians have been observed to demonstrate gentle behavior toward gorillas and small creatures in the wild.
   (B) Only vegetarian gorillas have been observed as demonstrating gentle behavior toward small creatures in the wild.
   (C) Small creatures in the wild have been observed as behaving gently and demonstratively when near gorillas.
   (D) It has been observed in the wild that gorillas, by nature vegetarians, treat small animals gently.

3. In fighting forest fires, the initial attack crews dig a fire line, which varies in width depending on the strength and nature of the fire.
   (A) Initial attack crews dig a forest fire to vary the fire line's width.
   (B) Initial attack crews depend on the strength and nature of the fire to vary the fire line.
   (C) The width of the fire line, which the initial attack crews dig, varies according to the strength and nature of the fire.
   (D) In digging a fire line, the initial attack crews depend on fighting forest fires.

4. Medical quackery, which promises cures for all existing and even nonexisting diseases, has a powerful appeal even to the well educated.
   (A) Well-educated people in medicine promise to find powerful cures for diseases.
   (B) Even well-educated people are attracted to fake cures for diseases that may or may not exist.
   (C) Medical quackery promises the well educated a cure for diseases.
   (D) The medical profession has appealed to the well educated for funding to find cures for diseases.

5. A silver compound has been found to kill the parasitic protozoa which are carried by the dreaded tsetse fly and cause sleeping sickness.
   (A) The dreaded tsetse fly causes sleeping sickness and kills the parasitic protozoa used for finding silver compounds.
   (B) It has been found that the silver compound which is carried by the dreaded tsetse fly and causes sleeping sickness kills the parasitic protozoa.
   (C) Sleeping sickness, which is caused by the dreaded tsetse fly, has been found to kill the parasitic protozoa in silver compounds.
   (D) Parasitic protozoa which cause sleeping sickness and are carried by the dreaded tsetse fly can be killed with a silver compound.

6. While working as a fire fighter at the University of Mississippi, William Faulkner submitted 37 stories to magazines, six of which were accepted.
   (A) Of the 37 stories that Faulkner wrote while working at the University of Mississippi as a fire fighter, six became published in magazines.
   (B) Faulkner wrote six out of 37 stories after accepting a job as fire fighter at the University of Mississippi.
   (C) Faulkner published 37 stories in magazines, six of which were accepted by the University of Mississippi.
   (D) The six accepted stories by Faulkner were about his job as a fire fighter at the University of Mississippi.

7. The continental drift theory proposes that the earth's crustal plates are driven by a global system of convection currents in the hot magma below that behave like giant conveyor belts.
   (A) Theoretically, the earth's crustal plates behave like giant conveyor belts, driving the convection currents across the hot magma which causes the continents to drift.
   (B) A global system of convection currents in the underlying hot magma acts as giant conveyor belts to drive the earth's crustal plates.
   (C) The continental drift theory suggests that global plates cover hot magma, which acts as a giant conveyor belt below the convection currents.
   (D) The continental drift theory is proposed by the earth's crustal plates, which drive a global system of convection currents in the hot magma below, behaving like giant conveyor belts.

8. Medical authorities have been reluctant to support the findings of some nutritionists that vitamin C given in large doses can prevent the common cold.
   (A) Medical authorities support the nutritionists' views about the value of vitamin C in preventing the common cold.
   (B) Nutritionists have found that medical authorities are not in favor of using vitamin C to prevent the common cold.
   (C) Some nutritionists have found that large doses of vitamin C can prevent the common cold, but this has not been completely accepted by medical authorities.
   (D) According to nutritionists and some medical authorities, the common cold can be prevented by giving large doses of vitamin C.

9. Female cowbirds, which cannot sing, are nonetheless able to teach songs to their young by responding to specific chirps and ignoring others.
   (A) Even though female cowbirds cannot sing, they teach their chicks to do so by responding to specific chirps and ignoring others.
   (B) Female cowbirds can neither sing nor teach songs to their babies by responding to certain chirps more than to others.
   (C) Female cowbirds, which cannot sing, have certain other birds teach their young to sing.
   (D) Female cowbirds, which cannot sing, unsuccessfully attempt to teach their young to sing by responding to other bird songs.

10. The conflict between those who wish to conserve a large area of unaltered and unimproved spaces and those who want the abolition of the last remnants of wilderness in the interest of industrial profit will not be resolved in the near future.
   (A) The people who desire to conserve a large area of untouched natural land and those who want to use all land for industrialization are in a conflict which will not have an immediate resolution.
   (B) The conflict over whether a large area of unaltered and unimproved space should be given over for industrial development and profit is of interest to those resolved to abolish the last remnants of wilderness.
   (C) Lawyers are profiting from the unresolved conflict between the people who wish to save the last remnants of wilderness and those who want to alter and improve the space for industry.
   (D) There is an unresolved conflict caused by people who wish to abolish industry and turn the spaces back into a natural wilderness state.

Answers to Exercise R11 are on page 485.

Exercise R12   *Locating restated information*

Underline the words or phrases in the passage that give the information that is restated in the sentence following the passage.

Example   The damp British climate may be infuriating to humans, but it's ideal for plants. The Gulf Stream flows across the Atlantic to warm the west coast of these Isles, which occupy the same latitudes as Newfoundland. Moisture-laden Atlantic winds bring almost constant rain and mist, so plants don't dry out.

The perfect weather conditions for plants to flourish are found in the wet British Isles.

You should underline "British climate" (weather conditions in the British Isles), "ideal for plants" (perfect for plants), and "constant rain and mist" (wet) because these are the words from the passage that are restated.

1. Europa, one of Jupiter's moons, is the only place in the solar system – outside of Earth – where enormous quantities of water are known to exist. Although this water is in ice form, there is a possibility that there is only a crust of ice with a liquid ocean underneath. Because of powerful thermal pulses caused by the tidal forces of Jupiter and the other moons, Europa may be the best place in the solar system for finding life forms.

   Europa's vast oceans are unequaled in the solar system, with one exception.

2. Using sophisticated instrumentation, lightning experts have learned that lightning travels at one-third the speed of light. A lightning bolt is five times hotter than the surface of the sun and can have 10 times more power than the output of a large power company. A single discharge can actually contain 20 or more successive strokes, occurring too fast for the eye to separate. Some seem to stretch for 500 miles when observed from outer space.

   It is possible that a lightning bolt, which seems very large, is really a series of bolts.

3. Once porpoises reach speeds of 12 miles per hour, they leap out of the water to escape the pull of surface drag. At that point, leaping out of the water actually requires less energy than swimming. These leaps are most efficient at speeds of 40 miles per hour and greater.

   Porpoises conserve energy by traveling through the air, which creates less drag than water.

4. In the earliest stages of a star's formation – a process that takes some 10,000 years – the star is surrounded by an extremely dense layer of gas and dust. This matter eventually condenses and heats up to 1 million degrees and hotter, triggering a thermonuclear explosion. During the flare-up, strong winds blowing off the surface of the star disperse the surrounding dust and expose the newborn star to observers on Earth.

   People can see the birth of a star because of the strong winds that scatter the dust particles.

5. Perhaps the greatest navigators in history were the Vikings. Without compasses or other modern instruments, they explored Iceland, Greenland, and even crossed the Atlantic Ocean to the shores of North America. To find their way, they stayed close to shorelines or used the position of the sun to plot the latitude.

   The Vikings were expert sailors.

6. Since the first dolphin was trained by the United States Navy in 1965 to help divers in their underwater home, Sealab II, many other dolphins have been drafted into the Navy. Originally, dolphins were used as messengers or to answer calls for help. Today, dolphins do such dangerous and necessary work as locating explosives hidden in the sea and helping ships navigate safely in war zones.

   An important task for a dolphin is to find mines.

7. There are many specifications that a good city tree must meet. First, it must be able to withstand air pollution from car exhaust and factories. Second, it must have both shallow roots that won't damage underground pipes and short branches that won't get entangled with electrical lines. Last, it shouldn't grow fruit that falls and rots on the sidewalks.

   A city tree has to be tough to survive.

8. Saint Bernard dogs are large and shaggy animals. They were bred by Augustinian monks, who trained them to search for travelers lost in snowstorms or avalanches in the Alps. For hundreds of years, Saint Bernards served this purpose. But nowadays the journey across the Alps is on well-maintained road and tunnel systems, and the dogs are no longer needed.

Saint Bernards aided travelers for centuries.

9. Every year in Japan, the competitions for the longest unpowered flights are held. Out on Lake Biwa, participants attempt to break records by flying their own inventions over the water without propeller or jet assistance. The would-be human birds glide until their craft meets its inevitable crash landing. A flotilla of small boats line the flight path waiting to rescue the pilot. In the first Japanese event, a world record of 88.53 meters was established. Since then, new records have been made every year.

Participants fly in crafts they have designed themselves.

10. Protecting pearls properly can make them last for centuries. One of the reasons a pearl loses its luster or cracks is due to the mineral constituent of the pearl being dissolved by weak acids. There are several kinds of acids that pearls may come in contact with. The acidic nature of perspiration is one such acid. Much of the cotton that pearls are wrapped in when not in use is treated with an acid. Another kind of acid that damages pearls is found in many modern cosmetics. Cosmetics seep into the string canal and may penetrate into the layers of the pearl and cause deterioration. The best protection to give a pearl to ensure its long life is having it cleaned and restrung at prescribed intervals.

Sweating can cause damage to a pearl.

Answers to Exercise R12 are on page 485.

Exercise R13   Finding facts

Read each passage and the statements that follow. Write "T" in the space if the statement is true according to the information in the passage. Write "F" in the space if the statement is false or if the information is not given in the passage.

Example   The earliest form of dueling was the clash of mounted knights armed with lances in medieval tournaments. These duels were often purely sporting affairs in which special nonlethal lances were used. They provided entertainment for the spectators and kept the knights in good condition for battle. In Elizabethan days, duels no longer took place on horseback, and the lance was exchanged for a sword and dagger. The sword was held in the right hand and used for attacking, while the dagger was held in the left hand and used for defense. Dueling with swords as a means to decide a point of honor became obsolete with the invention of pistols. Pistols brought about a whole new set of rules and etiquette unique to that form of dueling.

(A) _F_   A duel is a battle between armies of knights on horseback.

(B) _T_   The knights used lances to fight their duels.

(C) _F_   Spectators enjoyed watching knights kill other knights in tournaments.

(D) _T_   Fighting duels was a good way for knights to maintain their physical fitness.

(E) _F_   It became very dishonorable to duel with swords after the invention of pistols.

Statement (A) is false because there is no mention of armies battling in the passage. Statement (B) is true because according to the passage the mounted knights were armed with nonlethal lances. Statement (C) is false because according to the passage the knights fought with nonlethal lances in purely sporting affairs. Statement (D) is true because according to the passage duels kept the knights in good condition for battle. Statement (E) is false because there is no information concerning the honor of dueling with swords after the invention of pistols.

1. The plan to join the British Isles to the European continent by boring a tunnel under the sea between Dover, England, and Calais, France, was originally proposed in the second half of the nineteenth century. The bill authorizing the work was rejected in 1883. The plan was again proposed in 1930 by many enthusiastic supporters. The tunnel was to be the longest ever made and an engineering wonder. However, the estimated cost, the military risks, and the doubt as to the feasibility of construction led to the rejection of the proposal in June 1930. Finally, in the 1980s, the proposal was accepted and tunneling began.

   (A) _____ The plan to unite the British Isles with the European continent has been proposed three times.

   (B) _____ The plan to unite the British Isles with the continent has been rejected three times.

   (C) _____ It was believed by some that the tunnel posed a threat to national security.

   (D) _____ Some people did not believe that the tunnel was a viable idea in the 1930s.

   (E) _____ Tunneling originally began in Calais, France.

   (F) _____ The plan was rejected in 1883 because the people were bored.

   (G) _____ The construction of the tunnel led to the rejection of the proposal in 1930.

   (H) _____ The tunnel made in 1930 was the longest ever made.

   (I) _____ The supporters of the tunnel wanted to hire a wonderful engineer.

   (J) _____ The estimated cost of the tunnel was prohibitive in 1930.

2. Cheese is made from the curd of milk. While there are literally thousands of varieties, which differ according to the method of preparation and quality of milk, they can be divided into three main classes. Soft cheeses are those with rinds and very soft creamy centers. Of these, Brie and Camembert are perhaps the most famous. Blue-veined cheeses have been injected with a penicillin mold, which creates the characteristic blue veins. Roquefort is perhaps the best known of the blue-veined cheeses. Pressed cheeses are those placed in a mold and firmly pressed. There are uncooked pressed cheeses, such as Cheddar, and cooked pressed cheeses, such as Gruyère.

   (A) _____ There are three varieties of cheese.

   (B) _____ One method of preparing cheese is using the curd.

   (C) _____ The quality of milk will determine the kind of cheese it will be made into.

   (D) _____ Brie is an example of a soft cheese.

   (E) _____ Blue-veined cheeses are put into a mold.

   (F) _____ Penicillin mold is used in the production of some cheeses.

   (G) _____ Roquefort is used for injections.

   (H) _____ Cheddar and Gruyère are both pressed cheeses.

   (I) _____ Penicillin is injected into the mold of pressed cheeses.

   (J) _____ Cheddar cheese is unlike Gruyère in that it is cooked.

3. The homing instinct of pigeons has made them popular for the sport of pigeon racing. A young bird's training begins when it is about seven weeks old. This training consists of giving it short exercise flights, teaching it to recognize its owner's call, and teaching it to enter inside of its cote, or home. The next phase of training is started when the bird is about four months old. The pigeon is taken short distances from its home and is released. These flights are gradually extended from three miles to 100 miles as the bird's stamina increases. When the bird is ready, the owner may enter it in a race against other trained pigeons. The owners take their birds to a central meeting place where all the birds are tagged and released simultaneously. A bird is not considered to be home until it has entered its cote and its owner has removed the tag and inserted it into a clock that records the bird's arrival time. Because owners live at varying distances from the release point, the first bird home may not be the fastest flyer. The bird that makes the best time in flying the distance home is the winner.

(A) _____   The popularity of homing pigeons is due to their instinct for racing.

(B) _____   A pigeon's instincts make it difficult to train them.

(C) _____   Pigeons can recognize their owner's call.

(D) _____   A cote is where a pigeon lives.

(E) _____   A pigeon's training begins when it is four months of age.

(F) _____   When a pigeon is first raced, it can only fly for a short distance.

(G) _____   A bird's stamina is increased gradually.

(H) _____   A bird must be able to fly 100 miles because the race is 100 miles long.

(I) _____   A bird wins when it enters its cote.

(J) _____   The bird that gets home first is the winner.

4. Playing marbles was supposedly popular in ancient Egypt, and it has yet to lose its popularity. There are several different games played with marbles, but the main object of all marble games is hitting a target by flicking a marble held between the forefinger and thumb at the target. The best-known marble game is called ringtaw. In this game, the players draw a circle on the ground. From a prearranged distance, the players take turns at shooting one of their marbles at the marbles in the circle. The object is to knock as many marbles out of the circle as possible. In another game, fortification, the marbles are placed in the center of a series of concentric circles marked on the ground. The players must knock marbles out of the center circle and into the adjacent circle. A marble is considered out when the player has knocked it through all the circles. A third popular game is one that uses holes instead of circles. In fact, this game is called holes. Here, the players shoot their marbles into shallow holes dug in the ground.

(A) _____   To be popular in ancient Egypt, one had to play marbles.

(B) _____   To play marbles, one has to flick the target.

(C) _____   In all marbles games, a marble is used to hit another marble.

(D) _____   Ringtaw is the most famous of marbles games.

(E) _____   In ringtaw, the players try to shoot as many of their marbles as possible into the circle.

(F) _____   There are several circles used in the game of fortification.

(G) _____   The object of both ringtaw and fortification is to knock the marbles out of a circle.

(H) _____   In the game of holes, players shoot their marbles at other marbles placed in holes.

(I) _____   The game of holes does not use circles.

(J) _____   Ringtaw, fortification, and holes are the only games that are played with marbles.

5. We all know that people can and do influence each other. But the disturbing question is how far people's minds can be influenced against their own wills. There are three techniques that have been used in attempts to control other people's behavior.

One technique, subliminal perception, is frequently referred to as *subception*. This technique is based on the observation that people notice a great deal more than they consciously realize. This is not a new observation, but it has been given special attention since the results of an experiment in a New York movie theater were reported. In the experiment, an advertisement for ice cream was flashed onto the screen during the feature film. The ad was shown for such a brief period that no one consciously saw the intrusion, yet ice cream sales soared for the period of time the experiment continued.

Hypnosis is another technique that can be used for controlling people's minds. While in a deep trance, people can be told to do something at a specific time or at a certain signal. They can be told that they won't remember what has been said once out of the trance. This is called a post-hypnotic suggestion. It is still uncertain whether a subject can be made to carry out an action that otherwise would be unacceptable in that person's mind.

Yet another technique is called brainwashing. Brainwashing entails forcing people to believe something, usually something false, by continually telling them or showing them evidence that is supposedly true and preventing them from thinking about it properly or considering other evidence. Brainwashing can take extreme forms. For example, brainwashing can be done by first causing a complete breakdown of individuals through acts such as starving them, preventing them from sleeping, intimidating them, and keeping them in a state of constant fear. When the individuals lose their sense of reality, new ideas can be planted in their minds.

(A) _____   There are three methods that are used to disturb people's minds.

(B) _____   The term "subception" refers to a person's unconscious perceptions.

(C) _____   Subception is not only a new observation, but it has also been given special attention.

(D) _____   People in New York were very upset by the intrusion of advertisements for ice cream.

(E) _____   More ice cream was sold during the period the experiment was conducted than before or after the experiment took place.

(F) _____   A post-hypnotic suggestion is a suggestion made after a person is no longer under hypnosis.

(G) _____   When under the effects of hypnosis, a person can be made to carry out an act he or she would normally consider unethical.

(H) _____   Brainwashing is a technique used for controlling people.

(I) _____   When brainwashed, people force others to look at evidence that is true.

(J) _____   New ideas can be put into the minds of individuals who have been denied sleep.

6. In the eleventh century, people noticed that if there was a small hole in one wall of a darkened room then the light coming through the hole would make a faint picture on the opposite wall of the scene outside the room. A room like this was called a camera obscura. Artists later used a box "camera obscura" with a lens in the hole to make the picture clearer. But it was not possible to preserve the image that was produced in the box.

In 1727, Johann Heinrich Schulze mixed chalk, silver, and nitric acid in a bottle. He found that when the mixture was exposed to the light it became darker. In 1826, Joseph Nicéphore Niepce put some paper dipped in a light-sensitive chemical into his camera obscura which he left on a window. The result was probably the first permanent photographic image.

The image Niepce made was a "negative," a picture where all the white parts are black and all the black parts are white. Later, Louis Daguerre found a way to reverse the black and white parts to make "positive" prints. But when he looked at the pictures in the light, the chemicals continued to react and the pictures went dark. In 1837, he found a way to "fix" the image. These images are known as *daguerreotypes*.

Many developments were made in the nineteenth century. Glass plates coated with light-sensitive chemicals were used to produce clear, sharp, positive prints on paper. In the 1870s, George Eastman proposed using rolls of paper film, coated with chemicals, to replace glass plates. Then, in 1888, Eastman began manufacturing the Kodak camera, the first "modern" lightweight camera which people could carry and use.

During this century, many great technological improvements have been made. One of the most important is color film. This is made from layers of chemicals that are sensitive to red, green, and blue light, from which all other colors can be made. Although now, for example, we make and see photos of the earth from space, the basic principles of photography have not changed since Niepce took his first photograph.

(A) _____   Originally, the camera obscura was nothing more than a dark room in which an image was projected onto a wall through a hole.

(B) _____   In the original camera obscura, people could observe on their wall a scene taking place on the outside of the building.

(C) _____   In an attempt to preserve the image, artists added a lens to the camera obscura.

(D) _____   Niepce used Schulze's mixture in his camera obscura to produce an image on paper.

(E) _____   Niepce and Schulze worked together to make the first permanent picture.

(F) _____   In Daguerre's pictures, the white objects were seen as white and the black objects were seen as black.

(G) _____   George Eastman replaced glass plates with light-sensitive film in the nineteenth century.

(H) _____   The Kodak camera was the first portable camera to be developed.

(I) _____   Eastman was responsible for the development of color film.

(J) _____   Photographs of the earth from space are taken using a camera obscura.

Answers to Exercise R13 are on page 486.

CHECK YOUR PROGRESS

Check your progress in recognizing restatement (Exercises R10–R13) by completing the following mini-test. This exercise uses a format similar to that used in the Reading Comprehension section of the TOEFL.

Exercise R14   **Mini-test**   *(Time – 20 minutes)*

<u>Directions</u>: You will read several passages. Each reading passage is followed by several questions about it. Choose the best answer, (A), (B), (C), or (D), to each question. Then circle the letter of your answer in your book.

Example   Pragmatism is essentially an American school of thought that has had few supporters elsewhere. Pragmatists believe that the test of any belief should be its practical consequences. One of the first pragmatists, William James, wrote that it was impossible to discover the "real" world outside our senses and therefore we must concern ourselves primarily with human experience. Because the world would be a worse place without a belief in human responsibility, morals, and the freedom of will, it was necessary, he considered, to believe in these concepts.

According to the passage, pragmatism is
(A) popular worldwide
(B) impossible to discover
(C) an American philosophy
(D) primarily a human experience

The passage says that "Pragmatism is essentially an American school of thought that has had few supporters elsewhere." Therefore, you should circle (C).

Questions 1–3

The 50-million-year-old fossils of an ancient whale found in the Himalayan foothills of Pakistan give strong evidence that modern whales are descended from a four-legged, land-dwelling animal. The fossils consist of part of the skull, some teeth, and the well-preserved middle ear of an animal that was 6 to 8 feet long, weighed 350 pounds, had a wolflike snout, and had two foot-long jaws with sharp, triangular teeth. It is the middle ear which suggests that the ancient whale lived on land. Analysis indicated that the animal had eardrums, which do not work in water and which modern whales have only in vestigial form. Furthermore, the right and left ear bones were not isolated from each other. The separation of these bones in marine whales enables them to detect the direction of underwater sounds.

1. The 50-million-year-old fossils found in Pakistan
   (A) are 6 to 8 feet long and 350 pounds in weight
   (B) are descended from a four-legged, land-dwelling animal
   (C) proves the Himalayan foothills were once under water
   (D) includes the middle ear of an ancient whale

2. Whales with eardrums
   (A) would not be able to hear well in water
   (B) were marine creatures
   (C) could distinguish where underwater sounds originated
   (D) could not live on land

3. A marine whale can recognize the source of a sound because
   (A) the right and left ear bones are isolated from each other
   (B) the middle ear is in a vestigial form
   (C) it lives under water instead of on land
   (D) it has a well-preserved middle ear

Questions 4–6

The most traditional American food may well be cornmeal. Cornmeal, as we know it today, began as an Indian staple. The Indians grew corn of six diferent colors – black, red, white, yellow, blue, and multicolored. They ground the corn kernels into cornmeal and mixed it with salt and water, then baked it. This recipe was introduced to the early colonists, who experimented with it and developed their own uses for cornmeal. Succotash, a meat stew with cornmeal added, and mush, leftover cornmeal porridge cut and fried, are two meals invented by early colonists.

Visitors can travel south and enjoy spoonbread, a smooth puddinglike dish, or to New England for johnnycakes, a kind of flat pancake. But probably the most common forms of cornmeal nationwide are cornbread, cornmeal muffins, and the "hushpuppy," a round ball of cornmeal batter that is fried in oil.

4. According to the passage, cornmeal was originally used by
   (A) the early colonists
   (B) the New Englanders
   (C) the American Indians
   (D) the people in the south

5. According to the passage, mush is
   (A) a batter that is fried in oil
   (B) fried leftovers from a cornmeal dish
   (C) added to meat stew to make succotash
   (D) one of two meals developed by the Indians

6. According to the passage, common forms of cornmeal are
   (A) no longer popular
   (B) restricted to certain regions
   (C) found nationwide
   (D) multicolored

Questions 7– 9

A Stradivarius violin is unmatched in tonal quality and responds more quickly and easily to the touch than any other violin. Unfortunately, the secrets for making such a superb instrument were lost in 1737 with the death of Antonio Stradivari, the master craftsman who built them. Many attempts have been made to reproduce an instrument of such quality, but all have failed. It is believed that the secret lies in the wood that was used and the distinctive varnish, which ranges from orange to a deep reddish-brown color. Only around 650 Stradivarius violins are believed to be in existence today, and the price for such a rare instrument is well in the hundreds of thousands of dollars. Even a cheap Stradivarius costs around a quarter million dollars. It is not surprising that a Stradivarius is sought after by great violinists and musical instrument collectors alike.

7. The main qualities of the Stradivarius are its
   (A) age and number
   (B) violinists and musical instrument collectors
   (C) tone and response
   (D) orange to reddish-brown color

8. According to the passage, how many Stradivarius violins are there?
   (A) 1737
   (B) 650
   (C) 250,000
   (D) 100,000

9. According to the passage, a Stradivarius that costs a quarter million dollars is
   (A) the rarest kind
   (B) the most expensive one
   (C) a cheap reproduction
   (D) an inexpensive one

Questions 10–12

In the twentieth century, architects in large cities designed structures in a way that reduced noise and yet made living as comfortable as possible. They used such techniques as making walls hollow and filling this wall space with materials that absorb noise. Thick carpets and heavy curtains were used to cover floors and windows. Air conditioners and furnaces were designed to filter air through soundproofing materials. However, after much time and effort had been spent in making buildings less noisy, it was discovered that people also reacted adversely to the lack of sound. Now architects are designing structures which reduce undesirable noise but retain the kind of noise that people seem to need.

10. Which of the following is not mentioned as absorbing sound?
    (A) filled hollow walls
    (B) thick carpets and heavy curtains
    (C) air conditioners and furnaces
    (D) air filters

11. Architects are now designing
    (A) new techniques of soundproofing
    (B) the ideal noise
    (C) structures with some noise
    (D) adverse buildings

12. According to the passage, people live most comfortably with
    (A) noisy furnaces
    (B) silence
    (C) reduced noise
    (D) certain noises

Questions 13–15

The quality of the graphics output on a computer printer is measured in dpi (dots per inch). Simply by changing the density of dots that make up each part of an image, the printer can produce graphics that look almost photographic. To understand how this works, consider how a black-and-white photograph shows the shades which, in real life, are colors. Each color is a different shade of gray. For graphics to be produced on the computer printer, a piece of software called a printer driver decides upon a dot pattern which will represent each color shade. These different patterns or textures each create an individual effect which your eye translates into gray shades. The closer you look at the image, however, the less lifelike it looks.

13. According to the passage, a computer printer can
    (A) measure dots per inch
    (B) change photographs
    (C) look photographic
    (D) produce pictures

14. Graphics are like black-and-white photographs in that
    (A) they are produced by computers
    (B) a dot pattern is decided by a printer driver
    (C) each color is seen as a different shade of gray
    (D) they each create an individual effect

15. According to the passage, the graphics image
    (A) is an exact reproduction of the photograph
    (B) has the same quality as a photograph
    (C) loses its natural look when viewed close up
    (D) changes the density of dots

Answers to Exercise R14 are on page 487.

PRACTICE WITH INFERENCES

When you read a passage, some details are not stated explicitly, but they can be understood from the other details that are stated. Read the following statement:

> Dr. Smitten and two other psychologists chose 25 children for their study: 5 from Campbell, 10 from other multiracial schools in Miami, and the rest from multiracial schools in other cities in Florida.

The details stated are:

1. Dr. Smitten and two other psychologists chose 25 children for a study.
2. 5 children were from Campbell.
3. 10 children were from other schools in Miami.
4. The rest were from schools in other Florida cities.

What is not stated but must be understood:

1. What kind of doctor is Dr. Smitten?
   You understand that Dr. Smitten is a psychologist because it can be inferred from the phrase "and two other psychologists."
2. How many psychologists were doing the study?
   You understand that three psychologists were doing the study because it can be inferred from the phrase "Dr. Smitten and two other psychologists."
3. What and where is Campbell?
   You understand that Campbell is a multiracial school in Miami because it can be inferred from the phrase "other multiracial schools in Miami."
4. What and where is Miami?
   You understand that Miami is a city in Florida because it can be inferred from the phrase "other cities in Florida."
5. How many children from other cities in Florida were chosen for the study?
   You understand that 10 children came from other cities because it can be inferred from the phrase "chose 25 children, 5 from . . ., 10 from. . ., and the rest from other cities."
6. What was the study probably about?
   You understand that the study was probably about some aspect of children in multiracial school environments because it can be inferred from the phrases "multiracial schools in Miami" and "multiracial schools in other cities" that "multiracial" was an important factor in choosing the children from those schools.

Some details are neither stated nor inferred. Therefore, you cannot answer the following questions.

1. When did the study take place?
2. Why was the study done?
3. What were the results of the study?

On the TOEFL, you will have to make inferences from the passages that you read. Sometimes you must use the information given to you in the passage to draw some conclusion about the topic. Practice making inferences and drawing conclusions in Exercises R15–R19.

Exercise R15   *Identifying inferences in statements*

Circle the letter of those inferences which can be made from the information given in the statement. There may be more than one possible inference.

Example   The lesser North American poets are more popular with children than major poets because they are direct and clear.

    (A) Children have difficulty understanding major poets.
    (B) Minor poets write poetry for children.
    (C) There are fewer poets writing for children than writing for adults.
    (D) Indirect and hidden meanings are used in the poetry of major poets.

You should circle (A) because it can be inferred that the poetry of major poets is difficult for children because, unlike that of minor poets, it is not direct and clear. You should not circle (B) because it cannot be inferred whether either minor or major poets write for children, or (C) because "lesser" means "minor poets," not "fewer poets." You should circle (D) because it can be inferred that if children like the lesser poets because they write more directly and clearly, the major poets use indirect ways of expressing ideas and hide meanings by use of symbols.

1. Three of the published reports came from official investigations, but the other two came from private individuals.
    (A) Private individuals cannot submit reports for publication.
    (B) Only the three official reports were considered for the publication.
    (C) Five reports were published.
    (D) Official investigations were made on private individuals.

2. The Institute of Anthropology plans to computerize archaeological data to help restore the North American Indian villages in Chaco Canyon.
    (A) The Chaco Canyon Indian villages were destroyed by European people.
    (B) The Institute of Anthropology collects information about Indian villages that are in ruins.
    (C) The North American Indians in Chaco Canyon have computers to help them store data.
    (D) Computers can be helpful to restore archaeological plans.

3. Some scientists believe that the African bees which have devastated the Latin American beekeeping industry will become gentler as they interbreed with the previously introduced European varieties.
    (A) European bees will not be advantageous to the Latin American beekeeping industry.
    (B) African bees are ferocious and destructive.
    (C) The Latin American beekeeping industry will become gentler as African bees and European bees interbreed.
    (D) African bees as well as European bees live in Latin America.

4. The need for a person to love and be loved is so pressing that when it is frustrated, the person will find a substitute, which can range from having a pet to collecting antiques.
    (A) Animal owners are people who think that nobody likes them.
    (B) A person who feels rejected may lavish an abnormal amount of affection upon a stray cat.
    (C) To show your love for someone, you should give that person a pet.
    (D) Collecting stamps can be a substitute for needed attention.

5. From the start of training to the finish of a race, the attention that endurance race contestants give their horses to ensure their being in top condition for competing is more than these riders give to themselves.
    (A) To a contestant, the good condition of the horse is more important in winning an endurance race than the condition of the rider.
    (B) The riders in an endurance race like their horses better than they like themselves.
    (C) In order to win, the horses don't give themselves as much attention as the riders give to themselves.
    (D) After a race, endurance race contestants give themselves more attention than they give their horses.

6. No partner helps the male pheasant-tailed jacana protect and nurture his chicks in their floating nest.
   (A) The female pheasant-tailed jacana does not take care of her babies.
   (B) The jacana is an aquatic bird.
   (C) The male pheasant-tailed jacana doesn't help to protect and nurture its partner.
   (D) The male pheasant-tailed jacana does not mate.

7. Elephants are slowly becoming trapped in isolated forest enclaves completely surrounded by land cleared for agriculture.
   (A) Hunters are trapping elephants in isolated forest enclaves to get their ivory tusks.
   (B) People are destroying the elephants' habitat to make farms.
   (C) Elephants would have to cross though farmland to migrate to different forests.
   (D) People are trapping elephants to use them for clearing land for agriculture.

8. To safeguard sunken ships from adventurers or thieves, ship salvagers keep the wrecks under constant surveillance by electronic and other means.
   (A) Thieves sunk the ships to steal the cargo.
   (B) Sunken ships contain things that are valuable.
   (C) Ship salvagers are usually caught before they steal anything because of safeguards.
   (D) There are various ways to guard sunken ships from pilferers.

9. A species of weed known as the gopher plant has earned a new name – the gasoline plant – because it yields a milky latex containing hydrocarbons that can be refined into substitutes for crude oil and gasoline.
   (A) Some weeds have been renamed "gasoline plants" because their latex can be made into gasoline.
   (B) Substitutes for crude oil and gasoline can come from hydrocarbons.
   (C) Gasoline refined from the gasoline plant will soon replace the need for gasoline from other sources.
   (D) Milk contains hydrocarbons necessary for crude oil and gasoline substitutes.

10. Not yet profitably synthesized, morphine, a drug unsurpassed for controlling pain, is still being scraped from opium poppy heads as it was at least 5,000 years ago.
    (A) Morphine, a drug from the poppy plant, is no longer profitable to cultivate.
    (B) Cocaine is not as effective as morphine for stopping pain.
    (C) Morphine has been used for pain control for at least 5,000 years.
    (D) It is possible to make artificial morphine economically.

Answers to Exercise R15 are on page 488.

Exercise R16   *Locating inferred information*

Read the passages and the inferred statements that follow. Underline the part or parts of the passage from which the inference can be made.

Example   Is it true that <u>crime</u> doesn't pay? Although it is impossible to report every <u>dollar that was generated into the American economy by Watergate</u>, figures pointed at what could be termed a first-class growth industry. Fees, royalties, fines, bills, and other miscellaneous payments added up into the millions of dollars moving around in the U.S. economy.

It can be inferred that Watergate is the name for a crime that took place in America.

You should underline "crime" and "dollar that was generated into the American economy by Watergate" because it can be inferred that Watergate was a crime or else it wouldn't have been cited in the discussion of how crime pays. The passage goes on to discuss how crime has paid by generating money into the American economy.

1. Unlike other toads, the male golden toad is nearly voiceless. It attracts its mate by its unmistakable orange color. When the clouds are thick in the rain forest, usually in April and May, the male toads appear like flashing neon signals, which is as effective as croaking in luring females during the mating season.

   It can be inferred from this passage that most toads attract their mate by making sounds.

2. The great temple of Borobudur is a stepped pyramid of unmortared andesite and basalt volcanic stone, standing 403 feet square and 105 feet high. This holy place lay abandoned and forgotten for more than 800 years after a devastating earthquake and an eruption of one of the four surrounding volcanos caused its population to flee in 1006. Besides earthquakes and volcanos, torrential rains, encroaching tropical vegetation, and time have all taken their toll.

   It can be inferred from this passage that the temple of Borobudur is in ruins.

3. Some multiple sclerosis victims are experimenting with deadly snake venom to ease the pain and tiredness caused by their disease. First, the poison is milked from cobra, krait, and viper snakes. One part of it is then mixed to 4,000 parts of a saline solution. Although medical authorities are skeptical of the treatment, those using it claim that the venom has startling healing qualities.

   It can be inferred that snake venom for the treatment of multiple sclerosis has not yet been approved by doctors.

4. The cassowary, one of the world's largest and least known birds, grows to a height of 6 feet and a weight of 120 pounds. Its powerful legs, which it uses for defense, are fearful weapons, because the inner toe of each foot is equipped with a sharp claw, 4 inches long. The cassowary has glossy black plumage which hangs coarse and brushlike because it lacks the barbules that are needed to lock feathers into a flat vane. The naked neck is of iridescent blue on the sides and pink on the back. Its head is crowned by a leathery helmet that protects it when it is charging through the jungle.

   It can be inferred that the cassowary probably doesn't fly.

5. Prior to 1870, little stone decoration was done on New York buildings, except for churches and public buildings. With the arrival of artisans among the groups of European immigrants, architectural carving began to flourish. Architects would buy sculptures already done or show sketches of what they wanted carved. Away from the master carver who dictated what was to be carved, the artisans created eclectic and uninhibited sculptures, which became integrated into a purely American style.

   It can be inferred from the passage that in Europe artisans did not carve what they wanted to carve.

6. The Society for Creative Anachronism Inc., is a nonprofit club which joins together those people who enjoy reenacting life as it was lived before the 1700s. Members of both sexes not only learn the art of sword fighting in mock combat but learn a wide range of authentic medieval skills as well. These include such skills as armor making, equestrian arts, games, jewelry making, astrology, and magic. Since the first tournament held in 1966, in which a dozen fighters took part, the society has grown to some 5,000 members.

   It can be inferred from the passage that women members of the Society for Creative Anachronism fight in battles.

7. Computer-driven cameras, lights, and servomotors as well as lasers and tiny lens assemblies are just a few of the complex instruments that have brought to today's television viewers effective scientific informational films. Two crucial problems in such films are finding arresting visuals and creating special effects to illustrate complex scientific concepts. Computer-generated motion pictures allow the viewer to see the meaning of data and complex relationships instantly and are a new aid to human understanding of almost limitless power.

It can be inferred from this passage that computers used in the film industry have enabled people to understand science better.

8. Fish rubbings and nature printing have been developing as art forms in North America over the past 40 years, although the techniques may date as far back as the time of early cave dwellers. To make a fish print, one should choose a very fresh fish with large rough scales and a flat body. Other needed materials are several brushes, including a fine brush for painting the eyes on the print, a thick waterbased ink, newspaper, modeling clay for supporting the fins, straight pins, and cloth or absorbent paper such as newsprint. Handmade paper is best, but it is more expensive and not recommended for beginners. The fish should be washed, dried, and laid out on the newspaper. A thin layer of ink should be brushed on in both directions. The paper is then placed over the fish and pressed carefully with the fingers, avoiding wrinkles or movement of the paper.

It can be inferred from the passage that it takes practice to become proficient in using in this technique.

9. Characteristics of tropical rain forests are high and steady levels of heat and moisture, as well as a wide variety of organisms. It is believed that two-thirds of all species live in the tropics, and half of those live in the tropical rain forests. Nowhere else, except perhaps in tropical coral reefs, is nature so great in its diversity of organisms and complex in its biological interaction.

It can be inferred from this passage that tropical coral reefs contain a wide variety of organisms.

10. Even though historians think that ice-skating has been a sport for the last 2,000 years, it is within the last five decades that skating has gained recognition as a form of art. Champion athletes combine new heights of athleticism with the elegance of dance in what is now called figure skating. Ice skaters performing daring jumps in flamboyant costumes have brought ballet to the ice rink. Ice-skating is now seen as an exciting and innovative sport that has won millions of new admirers.

It can be inferred that ice skaters are both athletes and artists.

Answers to Exercise R16 are on page 489.

Exercise R17   ***Checking if a statement can be inferred***

Answer "yes" or "no" to the question that follows each statement.

Example   Volunteers for organizations such as Save the Children make an extremely important personal contribution toward improving the daily lives of millions of children throughout the world.

Can it be inferred that Save the Children volunteers contribute a lot of money to aid children?   *no*

You should write "no" in the space because a "personal contribution" does not necessarily mean a monetary contribution. Volunteers may contribute time or a special personal skill that they have in order to aid children.

1. Each day, more and more communities discover that they have been living near dumps or on top of ground that has been contaminated by toxic chemicals.

   Can it be inferred that communities aren't always told when and where toxic wastes are being disposed? _____

2. E. B. White's death, at 86, was cause for sadness in millions of homes.

   Can it be inferred that E. B. White was famous? _____

3. Charles F. Richter helped devise a scale that is universally used to measure the magnitude of earthquakes.

   Can it be inferred that the Richter scale was named for a devastating earthquake? _____

4. There is evidence that a global firestorm raged about the time the dinosaurs disappeared.

   Can it be inferred that dinosaurs became extinct because of a global firestorm? _____

5. Of the twelve sulfite-associated deaths, one was caused by wine, one by beer, and one by hashed brown potatoes; the rest were linked to fresh fruits or vegetables.

   Can it be inferred that nine people died from sulfite-contaminated fresh foods? _____

6. Tattooing a thin dark line along the upper and lower eyelids to replace eyeliner is an operation which appeals to athletic women who don't want to wear eyeliner that smears.

   Can it be inferred that athletic women are lazy about putting on cosmetics? _____

7. Early evaluation of data from *Vega I* showed that it encountered less dust than expected as it approached Halley's comet.

   Can it be inferred that *Vega I* is an unidentified flying object, or "UFO"? _____

8. Quinolone, a recently discovered antibiotic, inhibits an enzyme that controls the way bacterial DNA unravels and rewinds when microbes reproduce.

   Can it be inferred that quinolone will eventually replace all other antibiotics? _____

9. Bifocal lens wearers may soon be able to use contact lenses that take advantage of the way the eye reacts to light.

   Can it be inferred that people who need bifocals cannot presently use contact lenses? _____

10. For people whose nerves have been damaged by illness or injuries, actions such as walking or grasping an object may be impossible.

    Can it be inferred that the nervous system is important for muscle control? _____

Answers to Exercise R17 are on page 489.

Exercise R18   *Identifying inferences in paragraphs*

Read the passages and the statements that follow. Write "I" in the space if the statement is an inference. Write "R" if the statement is a restatement. Leave the space blank if the statement is neither an inference nor a restatement.

Example   Francis Gary Powers survived when his high-flying reconnaissance aircraft was shot down over the Soviet Union in 1960. He was convicted of espionage after a trial in Moscow. Later, Powers was returned to the United States in exchange for Soviet spy Rudolf Abel. Powers was killed in a helicopter crash in California in 1977.

   (A) _____   Powers was not injured when his aircraft was shot down over the Soviet Union.

   (B) _R_   Powers was found guilty of spying in the Soviet Union.

   (C) _I_   Rudolf Abel was being held by the Americans for spying.

   (D) _____   Powers was killed during a reconnaissance mission.

You should leave (A) blank because we do not know from the given information whether or not Powers was injured. You should write an "R" for (B) because to be "convicted of espionage" means the same as to be "found guilty of spying." You should write "I" for (C) because Rudolf Abel must have been held by the Americans if they exchanged him for Powers. You should leave (D) blank because no information is given on why Powers was flying the helicopter (for example, for work or for recreation).

1. The MacArthur prizes, or "genius awards," are grants of money ranging from $128,000 to $300,000 given to individuals who show outstanding talents in their fields. According to a foundation spokesperson, this money frees geniuses from financial worries and allows them the time to devote themselves to creative thinking. The recipients of the MacArthur prizes are people who have already achieved considerable success. It may be asked whether they attained success despite the fact that they had to worry about money or because of it.

   (A) _____   People who are not already known in their field will probably not be a recipient of the MacArthur prize.

   (B) _____   Some people may become successful because they are worried about money.

   (C) _____   Money can buy time.

   (D) _____   Some individuals receive as much as $300,000 to think.

2. The CDC (Centers for Disease Control) is responsible for the research done in solving or attempting to solve medical mysteries. Teams of epidemiologists crisscross the country investigating outbreaks of disease. They ask questions, look for clues, and track down pieces of puzzles in a relentless pursuit to find answers that will bring about breakthroughs in the prevention or cure of serious diseases. The CDC rushes in to study epidemics because it is possible to quickly determine patterns and common links among the victims.

   (A) _____   The Centers for Disease Control is not always successful in its research of diseases.

   (B) _____   Epidemiologists travel across the nation to do their research.

   (C) _____   Because there are more victims when an epidemic strikes, more data can be collected to find answers to medical questions.

   (D) _____   To make a breakthrough in science, a lot of research usually needs to be done.

3. Astronomers have long believed that frozen gases and water account for up to 80 percent of a comet's mass. While observing Comet Bowell, astronomers were able to measure the amount of light this comet absorbed and reflected. On the basis of these observations, they determined that comets do indeed contain frozen water.

(A) _____ Astronomers have proved the theory that comets contain frozen water.

(B) _____ The ice content of other comets can be ascertained by measuring how much light they absorb and reflect.

(C) _____ Astronomers are scientists that study heavenly bodies such as the sun, moon, stars, and planets.

(D) _____ The name of the observed comet is Bowell.

4. Although most honeybees die in the field while gathering pollen, some bees die in the hives and must be removed in order to prevent the spread of disease and to keep the nest from filling up with corpses. These corpses emit a chemical that signals death. Most of the bees either ignore the corpses, poke at them, lick them, or inspect them. Usually within an hour, the bees that are in charge of removing dead bees grasp them in their mandibles, pull them through the hive toward the entrance, then fly away and drop them as far as 400 feet from the hive.

(A) _____ When a bee is dying, it signals the other bees by emitting a chemical.

(B) _____ Dead bees cannot be left in the hive because they may make the other bees sick.

(C) _____ The honeybees know there is a dead bee in the hive because of the death chemical that is emitted.

(D) _____ In less than one hour, the dead bees have usually been removed from the hive.

5. The northern elephant seal, a 2,000-pound mammal, is making a dramatic comeback after being hunted to near extinction in the late nineteenth century. The seals that once thrived off the coast of California now receive protection from both the Mexican and American governments. A contributing factor to their survival is the reduced demand for seal oil due to the availability of petroleum products.

(A) _____ There used to be a large number of northern elephant seals living near California.

(B) _____ Products that were once made from seal oil are now made from petroleum.

(C) _____ Petroleum is easier to obtain now than seal oil is.

(D) _____ Northern elephant seals are now numerous.

6. Diverse in culture and language, the tenacious men and women who inhabit the world's harshest environment, the land above the Arctic Circle, probably descended from hunting societies pushed north from Central Asia by population pressure about 10,000 years ago. "Scarcity" is the word that best describes the Arctic ecosystem, where life-giving solar energy is in short supply. In the winter, the sun disappears for weeks or months depending on the latitude. Even during the months of prolonged sunlight, the slanted rays cannot thaw the frozen subsurface soil. But more than the severe cold, the lack of resources for food, clothing, and shelter define the lifestyles that the Arctic peoples lead.

(A) _____ During the summer months, the sun shines day and night.

(B) _____ Scarcity of food, clothing, and shelter influences Arctic living conditions more than the harsh climate does.

(C) _____ Anthropologists are not completely certain about the ancestry of the Arctic peoples.

(D) _____ The further north one is, the less sunshine there is.

7. Half of all the astronauts on space flights are afflicted with debilitating space sickness, an ailment akin to car sickness and marked by nausea and vomiting. It is believed that zero gravity and its effect on the inner ear and the flow of body fluids is the cause. Scientists are attempting to find a way to predict who is susceptible to the illness, because it interferes with the important work that must be done efficiently during space missions.

(A) _____ Scientists cannot tell whether an astronaut who suffers from car sickness will suffer from space sickness.

(B) _____ Space sickness makes it difficult for afflicted astronauts to do their work.

(C) _____ Space sickness and car sickness are related illnesses.

(D) _____ The effect of gravity on the inner ear of car passengers causes car sickness.

8. The white shark, which has acquired a reputation for mindless ferocity unequaled among terrestrial or aquatic predators, belongs to the family known as the mackerel sharks. Nothing about this terrifying fish is predictable: not its behavior, range, or diet. Evidence from the remains of victims of shark attacks suggest that the white shark does not eat people.

(A) _____ White sharks sometimes kill people but not to eat them.

(B) _____ The white shark has gained a terrifying reputation because it attacks people.

(C) _____ The white shark attacks its victims for reasons other than hunger.

(D) _____ At least one kind of mackerel shark does not eat people.

9. Because they seem to be taking a measure with each looping stride, some caterpillars are called geometrids, or earth measurers. From this comes their common name, inchworms. This caterpillar grasps a twig with its back legs, extends itself forward, then draws its back end up to its front legs and repeats the sequence. Because its rudimentary eyes primarily discern only light and dark, when searching for a different perch, it gropes along slowly, reminiscent of a blind person without a cane.

(A) _____ The geometrid moves by stretching forward then moving its back to its front, then repeating this process.

(B) _____ Not all caterpillars are inchworms.

(C) _____ A loop is formed when the geometrid draws its back legs forward to meet the front legs.

(D) _____ All inchworms are earth measurers.

10. The Merlin is propelled by six compact engines, each encased in a separate duct. With no exposed blades, the craft is much safer to maneuver on the ground than either a helicopter or small plane. The Merlin takes off and hovers by blasting a column of air straight down and moves forward by directing some of that air backward with movable vanes behind each engine.

(A) _____ The Merlin is a kind of aircraft.

(B) _____ Exposed blades make some aircraft unsafe.

(C) _____ Production of the Merlin has not yet begun.

(D) _____ A pilot controls the Merlin.

Answers to Exercise R18 are on page 489.

Exercise R19   *Drawing conclusions*

Read the following statements and circle the letter of the best answer based on the information given.

Example   Few school curriculums include a unit on how to deal with bereavement and grief, and yet all students at some point in their lives suffer from losses through death and parting.

What topic would not be included in a unit on bereavement?
(A) how to write a letter of condolence
(B) what emotional stages are passed through in the healing process
(C) how to give support to a grieving friend
(D) what the leading causes of death are

Bereavement is the state of experiencing the death of a relative or friend. Since the leading causes of death are not relevant to the particular death that a person may have to deal with, you should circle (D).

1. Studies show that bike races in Mexico City, where air is 20 percent less dense than at sea level, tend to be 3 to 5 percent faster than at lower altitudes.

   In which area would a bike race probably be the slowest?
   (A) along the coast
   (B) on an indoor track
   (C) on a high plateau
   (D) at the snowline of a volcano

2. Owners of famous and valuable paintings have recently been commissioning talented artists to paint copies of these art treasures to exhibit in their homes.

   What is the most likely reason an owner of a valuable painting might want to exhibit a copy instead of the original?
   (A) because they need to trick the experts
   (B) because they hope to foil would-be thieves
   (C) because they want to encourage talented artists
   (D) because they enjoy buying fake paintings

3. The Academy of Dog Training supplies law enforcement agencies with German shepherds which are trained to recognize the smell of marijuana and other drugs.

   In which of the following places would these German shepherds most likely be used?
   (A) at scenes of violent crimes
   (B) where burglaries have taken place
   (C) at sports arenas
   (D) at customs checks between borders

4. Schools based upon the philosophy of Rudolph Steiner are all coeducational, practice mixed-ability teaching, and discourage competition between children.

   Which of the following activities would probably not be seen in a Steiner school?
   (A) a class period devoted to the teaching of mathematics
   (B) a game involving both boys and girls
   (C) a poetry writing contest
   (D) a classroom of children reading at different levels

5. The microbiologist exposed bacteria to increasingly higher levels of cyanide until he had a type of bacteria that could destroy the cyanide that had been dumped into rivers by chemical plants.

 In what way could this bacteria be useful?
(A) for saving the water life from toxic wastes
(B) for poisoning undesirable fish
(C) for cleaning swimming pools
(D) for increasing the cyanide in the chemical plants

Answers to Exercise R19 are on page 491.

CHECK YOUR PROGRESS

Check your progress with inference skills (Exercises R15–R19) by completing the following mini-test. This exercise uses a format similar to that used in the Reading Comprehension section of the TOEFL.

Exercise R20 **Mini-test** *(Time – 20 minutes)*

Directions: You will read several passages. Each one is followed by several questions about it. Choose the best answer, (A), (B), (C), or (D), to each question. Then circle the letter of your answer in your book.

Example As modern medicine becomes more sophisticated, more cases of the phenomenon of near-death encounters (NDEs) are being reported. NDEs are out-of-body experiences which many people reportedly have undergone during moments when they have been near death or have actually experienced clinical death before being revived. Many doctors have confirmed that their patients have described death as a perception of leaving their bodies, traveling down a tunnel to a heavenly paradise, and meeting deceased relatives before being called back to their bodies.

It can be concluded that
(A) heaven has been proven to exist
(B) modern medicine makes some people hallucinate about an afterlife
(C) some people pronounced dead are actually alive
(D) near-death encounters had been experienced before modern medicine became so sophisticated

If more cases of NDEs are being reported with the advent of modern medicine, then there must have been some cases previously reported. Therefore, you should circle (D).

Questions 1–3

Time can be regarded as neither a biological nor a physical absolute but a cultural invention. Different cultures have differing perceptions about the passage of time. At the opposing ends of the spectrum are the "monochronic," or linear, cultures and the "polychronic," or simultaneous, cultures. In monochronic societies, schedules and routines are primary. Monochronic societies tend to be more efficient and impartial. However, they are blind to the humanity of their members. In polychronic societies, people take precedence over schedules. People are rarely alone, not even at home, and are usually dealing with several people at once. Time and schedules are not priorities.

1. It can be inferred from the passage that
   (A) people who are blind live in monochronic societies
   (B) it may be frustrating for monochronic and polychronic societies to deal with each other
   (C) monochronic cultures are concerned with schedules and linear cultures are concerned with people.
   (D) in monochronic cultures, one person takes precedence over schedules, and in polychronic cultures, many people take precedence over schedules

2. It can be inferred from the passage that
   (A) in a polychronic society, a person will skip an appointment if a family member needs some advice
   (B) in a monochronic society, a person will skip an appointment for a blind friend
   (C) in a polychronic society, a person will be on time for an appointment if the other person is from a monochronic society
   (D) in a monochronic society, people will look for any excuse in order to skip an appointment

3. It can be inferred from the passage that
   (A) there are other cultures that regard time differently than polychronic and monochronic cultures do
   (B) there are four different ways cultures regard time: monochronic, linear, polychronic, and simultaneous
   (C) a spectrum of time is not a culture's invention nor a physical absolute
   (D) cultures invent biological and physical absolutes

Questions 4–6

Erosion of America's farmland by wind and water has been a problem since settlers first put the prairies and grasslands under the plow in the nineteenth century. By the 1930s, more than 282 million acres of farmland were damaged by erosion. After 40 years of conservation efforts, soil erosion has accelerated due to new demands placed on the land by heavy crop production. In the years ahead, soil erosion and the pollution problems it causes are likely to replace petroleum scarcity as the nation's most critical natural resource problem.

4. Land erosion is probably worse in which of the following areas?
   (A) areas which were once prairies
   (B) areas which were once grasslands
   (C) areas which produce many crops
   (D) areas which have a lot of petroleum production

5. It can be inferred from the passage that
   (A) soil erosion today is worse than it was in the nineteenth century
   (B) after 40 years of conservation efforts, up to 282 million acres were damaged by erosion
   (C) the settlers of the nineteenth century followed better environmental practices than those of the 1930s
   (D) heavy crop production is necessary to meet the demands of the nation and prevent a critical disaster

6. It can be inferred from the passage that
   (A) petroleum will be the most critical natural resource problem
   (B) petroleum is causing heavy soil erosion and pollution problems
   (C) soil erosion has caused humans to place new demands on heavy crop production
   (D) soil erosion, pollution, and petroleum scarcity are critical problems that the nation faces

Questions 7–9

An ultralight airplane is very different from a conventional airplane. It looks like a lawn chair with wings, weighs no more than 254 pounds, flies up to 60 miles an hour, and carries about 5 gallons of fuel. Most ultralights are sold as kits and take about 40 hours to assemble. Flying an ultralight is so easy that a pilot with no experience can fly one. Accidents are rarely fatal or even serious because the ultralight lands so slowly and gently and carries so little fuel. Some models now have parachutes attached, while others have parachute packs which pilots can wear.

7. It can be inferred from the passage that
   (A) ultralights are powered by an engine
   (B) ultralights are powered by human energy
   (C) ultralights are powered by remote control
   (D) ultralights are powered by solar energy

8. It can be inferred from the passage that
   (A) people can put their own ultralights together
   (B) an ultralight can be purchased at the airport
   (C) people who fly ultralights have no experience
   (D) ultralight builders need to have training in aviation

9. It can be inferred from the passage that
   (A) accident statistics are inaccurate because ultralights are not registered at airports
   (B) fatal accidents are frequent because of the lack of experienced pilots
   (C) ultralight pilots can walk away from most of the accidents they are in
   (D) because of the frequency of fatal accidents, laws requiring parachutes have been enacted

Questions 10–12

The Mississippi River and its tributaries form the world's fourth longest river system. Two Canadian provinces and all or parts of 31 states in the United States have rivers that drain into the Mississippi. As the Mississippi River flows down to join the sea, it deposits sand, silt, and clay, building the delta seaward across Louisiana's shallow continental shelf. The delta marsh and its bays, lakes, and sounds provide shelter and nutrients for North America's most fertile marine nursery.

10. It can be inferred from the passage that
    (A) Canada has only two drainage areas in its provinces
    (B) there are 31 states in the United States
    (C) the 31 states mentioned have no other river systems to carry silt, sand, and clay
    (D) some of the silt deposited in the Louisiana delta is from Canada

11. It can be inferred from the passage that
    (A) the delta system formed by the Mississippi River is very important for marine life
    (B) nurseries have been set up in the delta so that children can take part in aquatic sports in the bays, lakes, and sounds
    (C) the delta marshlands is an excellent area for medical people to study diseases caused by mosquitoes and other insects
    (D) the United States has established nurseries to provide shelter and food for migrating birds

12. It can be inferred from the passage that
   (A) the delta is being destroyed by the Mississippi River's depositing sand, silt, and clay
   (B) the geographic features of the delta are always changing
   (C) the sea movement is building a delta on the continental shelf at the mouth of the Mississippi
   (D) the river, delta, and sea all play an important role in building Louisiana's continental shelf

Questions 13–16

The Malabar pied hornbill usually nests in the fruit trees that bear its food. The female enters a hole in the tree and molts. She and her mate seal the hollow with mud and dung, leaving a crack through which he feeds her. When the chicks hatch and her plumage returns, she breaks out, resealing the nest to guard the young, which emerge later.

13. The Malabar pied hornbill is probably
   (A) a chicken
   (B) a seal
   (C) a bird
   (D) a bear

14. It can be inferred from the passage that
   (A) the Malabar pied hornbill's nest is lined with feathers
   (B) the hole in the tree is so warm it causes the Malabar pied hornbill female to lose its plumage
   (C) the female Malabar pied hornbill breaks up the nest after it molts
   (D) the Malabar pied hornbill female plucks off its feathers in order to cover the crack in the nest

15. Which of the following statements can be inferred?
   (A) The female purposely imprisons herself to lay her eggs.
   (B) The male is afraid of other males and, therefore, forces his mate into the nest and seals it.
   (C) The female is so involved in building her nest that she doesn't realize she's locked herself inside it.
   (D) The female has to keep the male from hurting the babies, so she encloses herself in the nest.

16. It can be inferred from the passage that
   (A) the male feeds the eggs through a crack in the nest
   (B) the male doesn't help the female until she has enclosed herself in the nest
   (C) the male uses his plumage to guard the recently hatched chicks
   (D) the male doesn't hatch the eggs by keeping them warm with its own body

Answers to Exercise R20 are on page 491.

PRACTICE WITH READING AND CONTEXT

Occasionally the TOEFL includes a section with passages that test your reading skills and understanding of context. The passages are in a cloze format (fill in the blank) with multiple choice answers. Use Exercises R21 and R22 to develop your skills in reading and understanding context.

Exercise R21   *Completing short sentences*

The following sentences are incomplete. Circle the letter of the one word or phrase that best completes the sentence.

Example   Ice used to be shipped to ----- as far away from New England as Asia and Australia.
(A) extremes
(B) departures
(C) exports
(D) regions

You should circle (D) because "regions" best completes the sentence.

1. An irrational fear or phobia can ----- almost over any object or situation.
(A) harbor
(B) appear
(C) develop
(D) recover

2. Truffles, the rare and costly relative ----- the mushroom, are a gourmet's delight.
(A) at
(B) in
(C) of
(D) by

3. Radio amateurs can communicate with each ----- by voice or by special signals.
(A) other
(B) ones
(C) every
(D) either

4. The possessor of perfect pitch is ----- to identify any musical note that is heard.
(A) can
(B) able
(C) ability
(D) enable

5. Some people believe dogs see the ----- departing from the body of a dying master.
(A) plane
(B) howl
(C) death
(D) soul

6. A termitarium, the home of at ----- two million termites, is built of wood particles cemented together.
(A) last
(B) latter
(C) least
(D) later

7. A common desert phenomenon is a ----- that looks like a shimmering pool of water.
(A) mirage
(B) sandy
(C) camel
(D) dune

8. Complete silence can be found only ----- laboratories called anechoic rooms.
(A) in
(B) about
(C) for
(D) by

9. Transitory pains are those that come ----- go quickly, rarely return, and signify nothing.
(A) however
(B) instead
(C) not
(D) and

10. There is scarcely a country in ----- world where the beginning of a new year is not celebrated.
(A) an
(B) a
(C) the
(D) that

Answers to Exercise R21 are on page 493.

Exercise R22 ***Completing short passages***

The following passages are incomplete. Circle the letters of the words or phrases that best complete the passage. Before choosing your answers, read the passage quickly for comprehension.

Questions 1–5

While a dark suntan may look ___(1)___, it may, in fact, be hazardous. ___(2)___

(A) awful	(A) For
(B) happy	(B) To
(C) healthy	(C) With
(D) sunny	(D) At

achieve a dark suntan, the skin ___(3)___ be exposed to ultraviolet light ___(4)___ sun

(A) could	(A) for
(B) must	(B) since
(C) had to	(C) by
(D) would	(D) from

rays. Unfortunately, skin cancer has ___(5)___ linked to this kind of exposure.

(A) been
(B) was
(C) had
(D) became

Questions 6–11

One of the ways cultural anthropologists ___(6)___ really study a culture is

(A) can
(B) want
(C) have
(D) need

by ___(7)___ through its garbage dumps. Garbage is ___(8)___ remains of what that

(A) eating	(A) that
(B) driving	(B) there
(C) sifting	(C) maybe
(D) mixing	(D) the

society actually___(9)___ or threw away. An analysis of ___(10)___ is discarded gives

(A) has	(A) which
(B) was	(B) what
(C) used	(C) that
(D) buys	(D) any

interesting insights into ___(11)___ behavior.

(A) automobile
(B) road
(C) city
(D) human

Questions 12–16

"Moonshiner" was the name given to a ___(12)___ who made illegal alcohol.

(A) customer
(B) person
(C) client
(D) thief

Many people ___(13)___ the taste of whiskey made in ___(14)___ old-fashioned way,

(A) selected	(A) a
(B) preferred	(B) each
(C) compared	(C) them
(D) sought	(D) the

from recipes and ___(15)___ dating back to America's earliest Scotch-Irish ___(16)___.

(A) techniques	(A) potatoes
(B) remedies	(B) pioneers
(C) ancients	(C) growth
(D) times	(D) countries

Questions 17–22

Polio is a crippling disease that ___(17)___ epidemic proportions during the 1950s.

(A) became
(B) stretched
(C) formed
(D) reached

Unfortunately ___(18)___ sufferers from that decade started experiencing

(A) more
(B) many
(C) other
(D) extra

___(19)___ return of the symptoms 30 years ___(20)___. The reason behind this

(A) all	(A) later
(B) a	(B) ago
(C) their	(C) then
(D) this	(D) before

recurrence is ___(21)___ yet understood, but it has given ___(22)___ new knowledge

(A) not	(A) medicine
(B) never	(B) pharmacies
(C) nor	(C) scientists
(D) neither	(D) patients

about polio.

Questions 23–30

A model of a sailing ship ___(23)___ a small-necked bottle is fascinating to

(A) inside
(B) inside out
(C) upside down
(D) sideways

___(24)___ people. The secret of getting the ___(25)___ into the bottle lies in making

(A) most	(A) neck
(B) more	(B) bottle
(C) other	(C) ship
(D) each	(D) sail

___(26)___ parts hinged so that they can ___(27)___ collapsed, pushed through the

(A) them	(A) have
(B) the	(B) be
(C) every	(C) had
(D) very	(D) been

neck, and ___(28)___ drawn upright by threads which extend ___ (29)___ holes in the

(A) because
(B) than
(C) by
(D) then

(A) forward
(B) encircled
(C) through
(D) backward

ship's bow. The threads are then ___(30)___ and the holes are covered.

(A) cut
(B) shredded
(C) plucked
(D) run

Questions 31–38

A fossil that has been identified ___(31)___ history's largest flying seabird has recently

(A) as
(B) since
(C) like
(D) thus

___(32)___ excavated in the United States. Extinct ___(33)___ previously unknown, this

(A) be
(B) been
(C) being
(D) is

(A) and
(B) nor
(C) but
(D) or

species had a ___(34)___ of more than 18 feet and ___(35)___ have weighed close to

(A) seabird
(B) history
(C) fossil
(D) wingspan

(A) had
(B) probably
(C) may
(D) even

90 pounds. ___(36)___ albatross, which weighs up to 20 ___(37)___ and has a

(A) A
(B) That
(C) The
(D) Another

(A) weight
(B) pounds
(C) meters
(D) large

wingspan of 11 ___(38)___, is the largest living seabird today.

(A) long
(B) length
(C) times
(D) feet

Questions 39–45

The advantages of herding animals over ___(39)___ them are numerous. Besides the

(A) watching
(B) classifying
(C) hunting
(D) identifying

obvious ___(40)___ of not having to search for ___(41)___, there is the opportunity of

(A) adventure
(B) advantage
(C) advertisement
(D) additives

(A) food
(B) commerce
(C) grasslands
(D) shelter

keeping ___(42)___ animal alive until needed. Consequently, the ___(43)___ is fresh.

(A) it
(B) those
(C) a
(D) the

(A) meat
(B) bone
(C) skin
(D) milk

Also, the animals can ___(44)___ bred selectively for better tasting ___(45)___.

(A) have	(A) grain
(B) be	(B) beef
(C) may	(C) health
(D) might	(D) meat

Questions 46–52

Scientists have reported that positive thinkers ___(46)___ to live healthier lives. Even

(A) seem
(B) have
(C) capable
(D) enabled

though ___(47)___ theory has not yet been proved, ___(48)___ is no doubt that

(A) those	(A) they
(B) these	(B) there
(C) this	(C) their
(D) them	(D) they're

positive thinkers live ___(49)___ lives. They look at life with ___(50)___ attitude of

(A) stronger	(A) an
(B) wealthier	(B) a
(C) stingier	(C) any
(D) happier	(D) all

hope that influences their ___(51)___ in a way that creates positive ___(52)___.

(A) environmental	(A) reasons
(B) social	(B) areas
(C) surroundings	(C) results
(D) encompass	(D) causes

Questions 53–58

Mother whales have been observed to ___(53)___ their babies up to show them

(A) handle
(B) hold
(C) hatch
(D) harass

___(54)___ to humans in boats. They even ___(55)___ them close enough to the

(A) of	(A) persuade
(B) in	(B) bring
(C) by	(C) smother
(D) off	(D) catch

boats ___(56)___ people to reach out and pet ___(57)___. This kind of trust is

(A) for	(A) them
(B) forward	(B) they
(C) towards	(C) their
(D) from	(D) theirs

unparalleled ___(58)___ the animal world.

(A) on
(B) under
(C) in
(D) through

Questions 59–64

In a recent survey on smell, men ___(59)___ women were asked to smell samples

(A) or
(B) both
(C) and
(D) also

___(60)___ scents and identify them. It was ___(61)___ that women in general smell

(A) at   (A) established
(B) for   (B) inferred
(C) of   (C) implied
(D) by   (D) disputed

more ___(62)___ than men unless pregnant, when, contrary ___(63)___ popular belief,

(A) seldom   (A) by
(B) imaginatively   (B) for
(C) stressfully   (C) to
(D) acutely   (D) after

a temporary loss of ___(64)___ occurs.

(A) hearing
(B) smell
(C) vision
(D) taste

Answers to Exercise R22 are on page 493.

CHECK YOUR PROGRESS

Check your progress with reading skills and guessing words from context (Exercises R21–R22) by completing the following mini-test. This exercise uses a format similar to that used in the Reading Comprehension section of the TOEFL.

Exercise R23   **Mini-test**   *(Time – 45 minutes)*

<u>Directions</u>: Read the following passages. Choose the one answer that is most appropriate to fill in the blank. Circle the letters of the words that best complete the passage. Before choosing your answers, read the passage quickly for comprehension.

Examples   The extraordinary efficiency of snow ___(1)___ an insulator

(A) like
(B) same
(C) over
(D) as

makes it difficult to find a person ___(2)___ in an avalanche.

(A) buried
(B) confined
(C) outstretched
(D) consumed

Questions 1–13

The world's heaviest gold coin is worth about $10 million. Minted in the year 1613 in India, the ___(1)___ of its issuer, Mughal Emperor Jehangir, is ___(2)___ on the coin.

(A) gold	(A) planted
(B) word	(B) signed
(C) value	(C) stamped
(D) name	(D) viewed

Prior to this Muslim emperor, ___(3)___ in India obtained permission to ___(4)___ coins

(A) rulers	(A) invent
(B) people	(B) describe
(C) warriors	(C) put
(D) knights	(D) mint

from the caliph in Baghdad. ___(5)___, Emperor Jehangir changed this tradition and

(A) However
(B) Moreover
(C) Surely
(D) Despite

___(6)___ his own policy of issuing coins ___(7)___ his own name. It was ___(8)___

(A) proved	(A) for	(A) during
(B) started	(B) at	(B) against
(C) told	(C) of	(C) among
(D) qualified	(D) in	(D) between

the time of the Mughal dynasty that many art ___(9)___ were encouraged to flourish.

(A) pieces
(B) sales
(C) forms
(D) performances

___(10)___, it is not surprising that the art of minting ___(11)___ began and reached its

(A) Anyway	(A) coins
(B) Such	(B) forms
(C) Therefore	(C) names
(D) Nevertheless	(D) gold

___(12)___ of perfection during Emperor Jehangir's ___ (13)___.

(A) peak	(A) vision
(B) top	(B) reign
(C) high	(C) enterprise
(D) chief	(D) position

Questions 14–26

The joints in the body are dependent upon the synovial membranes. These membranes consist of cells which ___(14)___ fluids to lubricate the areas between ___(15)___

(A) show	(A) these
(B) produce	(B) the
(C) protect	(C) their
(D) join	(D) such

bones. They are also important in ___(16)___ nutrients and removing the waste

(A) pushing
(B) loading
(C) picking
(D) carrying

___(17)___ that are involved in the metabolism ___ (18)___ the cartilage tissues. These

(A) bodies
(B) substances
(C) parts
(D) particulars

(A) of
(B) after
(C) with
(D) to

tissues protect the ___(19)___ of the bones by acting much ___(20)___ elastic shock

(A) ends
(B) outside
(C) tops
(D) backs

(A) for
(B) towards
(C) same
(D) like

absorbers. If the tissues ___(21)___ damaged, regeneration is impeded. However,

(A) be
(B) is
(C) been
(D) are

experiments are ___(22)___ conducted to renew damaged cartilage ___(23)___

(A) having
(B) doing
(C) being
(D) seeming

(A) at
(B) from
(C) with
(D) by

transplanting the synovial membrane cells. So ___(24)___, the results have been very

(A) far
(B) now
(C) till
(D) soon

encouraging, ___(25)___ further experiments need to be conducted before a ___(26)___

(A) and
(B) or
(C) but
(D) so

(A) guess
(B) decision
(C) selection
(D) position

can be made concerning their use on humans.

Questions 27–38

Many laws which have been passed in the various states of the United States are out of

date or just plain ludicrous. These laws remain unchanged because of the ___(27)___

(A) time
(B) occasion
(C) ages
(D) hours

and cost to the ___(28)___ for the state legislature to ___(29)___ and make changes in

(A) taxpayer
(B) president
(C) money
(D) change

(A) talk
(B) debate
(C) chatter
(D) speak

existing laws. The laws in one state make it ___(30)___ for women to expose their

(A) bad
(B) difficult
(C) detestable
(D) illegal

ankles and men to go without their guns. ___ (31)___, virtually everyone has broken the

(A) Thus
(B) In spite of
(C) Because
(D) Such

law. Another law makes it illegal to tether one's ___(32)___ to the fence surrounding

(A) gun
(B) boots
(C) hat
(D) horse

that state's capitol building. Perhaps one of the ___(33)___ ludicrous laws is one passed

(A) most
(B) much
(C) many
(D) so

___(34)___ the city of Pocatello, Idaho, which ___(35)___ that it is illegal to frown.

(A) on
(B) among
(C) in
(D) towards

(A) gives
(B) describes
(C) states
(D) argues

According to the ___(36)___, some council members went to the bank for personal loans

(A) joke
(B) story
(C) law
(D) memory

and the ___(37)___ were unfriendly, so the council members passed a ___(38)___

(A) keepers
(B) salespersons
(C) bankers
(D) officers

(A) law
(B) loan
(C) order
(D) ticket

making it illegal to frown.

Questions 39–53

Sound-activated toys are an example of how high technology has affected childhood experiences. When a child talks to a sound-activated toy, the ___(39)___ talks back.

(A) child
(B) toy
(C) sound
(D) technology

There is a doll ___(40)___ the market that has a more ___(41)___ memory than a

(A) with
(B) under
(C) over
(D) on

(A) instinctive
(B) cumbersome
(C) extensive
(D) disposable

personal computer. It has ___(42)___ soft face that looks alive because it ___(43)___

(A) a
(B) some
(C) the
(D) that

(A) moves
(B) speaks
(C) listens
(D) looks

when the doll talks. Its eyes ___(44)___ sensitive to light, its hands are ___(45)___ heat,

(A) is
(B) be
(C) have
(D) are

(A) opposed to
(B) sensitive to
(C) interested in
(D) converted to

and it has a voice ___(46)___ facility which gives it the ability to ___(47)___ to the child

(A) possession
(B) exception
(C) recognition
(D) discussion

(A) question
(B) express
(C) respond
(D) laugh

playing with it. ___(48)___, with all the high technology going into making ___(49)___

(A) In addition
(B) Also
(C) Despite
(D) However

(A) expensive
(B) technique
(C) living
(D) facility

toys, it may be surprising to find ___(50)___ the toys children ___(51)___ return to

(A) which
(B) that
(C) who
(D) what

(A) rarely
(B) always
(C) occasionally
(D) now and then

after the ___(52)___ of a new toy has worn off are the ball, the ___(53)___ stick, and the

(A) gift
(B) talking
(C) novelty
(D) technology

(A) invigorating
(B) ordinary
(C) malevolent
(D) allusive

common cardboard box.

Questions 54–70

People have made a living from the sea in many ways. Perhaps one of the most

dangerous was that of ___(54)___ for pearls. Only the most ___(55)___ would go out

(A) sailing
(B) boating
(C) running
(D) diving

(A) daring
(B) boring
(C) clinging
(D) scattering

to sea to dive. The technique was ___(56)___. Divers were attached to

(A) simple
(B) ridiculous
(C) intricate
(D) sane

___(57)___ which were used to keep them in ___(58)___ with an assistant on

(A) blades
(B) pillars
(C) helpers
(D) ropes

(A) agreement
(B) contact
(C) contempt
(D) harmony

board the ship. The assistant used the rope to ___(59)___ the divers up when they

(A) load
(B) ascend
(C) haul
(D) lighten

signaled their intention to ___(60)___. To speed their descent and ___(61)___ their

(A) drown
(B) search
(C) drift
(D) surface

(A) replenish
(B) exhale
(C) monitor
(D) conserve

breath for searching the sea bed, divers ___(62)___ large weights which they ___(63)___

(A) used
(B) lifted
(C) threw
(D) attracted

(A) entangled
(B) devoted
(C) attached
(D) assailed

to a different rope. Divers used noseclips, ___(64)___ gloves to protect their hands from

(A) real
(B) heavy
(C) wide
(D) slim

___(65)___ sharp edges of the oyster ___(66)___, and a net slung around their necks in

(A) some	(A) points
(B) the	(B) shells
(C) these	(C) fish
(D) a	(D) crab

which they ___(67)___ the oysters. Later, the pearls taken from the oysters were sifted

(A) collected
(B) salvaged
(C) pursued
(D) searched for

through sieves and ___(68)___ according to size and quality. The profession of pearl

(A) broken
(B) spoiled
(C) cut
(D) graded

diving has largely ___(69)___ with the development of the cultured ___(70)___.

(A) outlived	(A) rock
(B) suspended	(B) diver
(C) disappeared	(C) pearl
(D) postponed	(D) sea

Answers to Exercise R23 are on page 493.

Exercise R24   *Vocabulary and Reading Comprehension Practice Test*

When you have completed the exercises as recommended by the Diagnostic Test, test your skills by taking this final TOEFL Vocabulary and Reading Comprehension Practice Test. Maintain the same test conditions that would be experienced during the actual TOEFL test. Time the test and tear out and use the answer sheet on page 545.

Answers to Exercise R24 are on page 493.

SECTION 3
VOCABULARY AND READING COMPREHENSION

Time – 45 minutes

This section is designed to measure your comprehension of standard written English. There are two types of questions in this section, with special directions for each type.

Directions: In questions 1–30 each sentence has an underlined word or phrase. Below each sentence are four other words or phrases, marked (A), (B), (C), and (D). You are to choose the one word or phrase that best keeps the meaning of the original sentence if it is substituted for the underlined word or phrase. Then, on your answer sheet, find the number of the question and fill in the space that corresponds to the letter you have chosen. Fill in the space so that the letter inside the oval cannot be seen.

Example   Mackinac Island, Michigan, has retained its Victorian aura.
      (A) regained
      (B) preserved
      (C) reformed
      (D) subdued

Sample Answer
Ⓐ ● Ⓒ Ⓓ

The best answer is (B) because "Mackinac Island, Michigan, has preserved its Victorian aura" is closest in meaning to the original sentence. Therefore, you should choose answer B.

1. More than 15,000 species of ants have been underlined{identified} by scientists.
   (A) chosen
   (B) grouped
   (C) named
   (D) seen

2. Pioneers crossing the continent on the Oregon Trail carved their names on Independence Rock.
   (A) penned
   (B) scratched
   (C) buried
   (D) described

3. When running, grizzly bears are capable of attaining speeds of 35 miles an hour.
   (A) traveling
   (B) aiming
   (C) sprinting
   (D) achieving

4. Strong waves can put forth a pressure of 6,000 pounds per square foot.
   (A) exert
   (B) manage
   (C) create
   (D) display

5. Each grain of wheat contains three basic components: the germ, the endosperm, and the bran.
   (A) admits
   (B) involves
   (C) includes
   (D) implies

6. Although some people prefer white eggs to brown, the contents are identical.
   (A) substances
   (B) stuffings
   (C) ingredients
   (D) insides

7. Peter Roget is widely acclaimed for his work in classifying and arranging words and phrases.
   (A) recommended
   (B) approved
   (C) cheered
   (D) hailed

8. Middle English was spoken from roughly the twelfth century through the fifteenth.
   (A) nearly
   (B) approximately
   (C) crudely
   (D) abruptly

GO ON TO THE NEXT PAGE ➤

9. "Inky cap" is the name given to mushrooms which give off an inklike liquid after discharging their spores.
   (A) loosening
   (B) releasing
   (C) clearing
   (D) delivering

10. William Faulkner is regarded by many as the greatest North American novelist of the twentieth century.
    (A) considered
    (B) concluded
    (C) determined
    (D) distinguished

11. Asthma is a chronic disease whose chief symptom is difficulty in breathing.
    (A) supreme
    (B) large
    (C) principal
    (D) prestigious

12. Many nations are still trying to eliminate rabies from their territories.
    (A) leave out
    (B) cancel
    (C) separate
    (D) eradicate

13. Map reading is a skill which is acquired through practice.
    (A) produced
    (B) found
    (C) gained
    (D) maintained

14. An etymologist traces the history of linguistic form.
    (A) certifies
    (B) marks
    (C) tracks
    (D) draws

15. Between the ice ages there were periods when the climate became temperate.
    (A) regulated
    (B) moderate
    (C) tropical
    (D) chaotic

16. The length of an X-ray wave is incredibly small: less than one ten-millionth of a millimeter.
    (A) considerably
    (B) unbelievably
    (C) notably
    (D) sufficiently

17. Deerlike figures made from willow shoots are the oldest evidence of human habitation in the Grand Canyon.
    (A) dispute
    (B) proof
    (C) exhibit
    (D) clue

18. In the 1600s, many religious sects built settlements in Pennsylvania.
    (A) neighborhoods
    (B) districts
    (C) colonies
    (D) nations

19. New research suggests a link between nearsightedness and high intelligence.
    (A) connection
    (B) joint
    (C) cause
    (D) effect

20. The use of lasers in surgery has become relatively commonplace in recent years.
    (A) absolutely
    (B) relevantly
    (C) almost
    (D) comparatively

21. Sickle cell anemia afflicts black people almost exclusively.
    (A) repels
    (B) molests
    (C) offends
    (D) troubles

22. Pablo Picasso's celebrated painting *Guernica* was moved from New York to Spain in 1981.
    (A) worthy
    (B) expensive
    (C) famous
    (D) valuable

23. Over 40,000 horses and burros still roam wild in the western United States.
    (A) untamed
    (B) savagely
    (C) unopposed
    (D) recklessly

GO ON TO THE NEXT PAGE

24. Many Chinese believe that powdered rhinoceros horn will <u>cure</u> various afflictions.
   (A) retard
   (B) heal
   (C) restore
   (D) subdue

25. The introduction of credit cards radically <u>modified</u> North Americans' spending habits.
   (A) resolved
   (B) devoted
   (C) reduced
   (D) altered

26. Manhattan has many <u>stylish</u> shops.
   (A) lavish
   (B) modern
   (C) fashionable
   (D) fine

27. Oregon has a range of seven mountain <u>peaks</u> called the Seven Sisters.
   (A) summits
   (B) stacks
   (C) valleys
   (D) inclines

28. A marine snail, the wentletrap, can <u>extend</u> its snout three times the length of its shell.
   (A) hold
   (B) stretch
   (C) increase
   (D) continue

29. A deficiency of vitamin D can lead to <u>permanent</u> bone deformities.
   (A) serious
   (B) irreparable
   (C) infinite
   (D) occasional

30. About 35,000 different commercial products are currently available to control crop <u>diseases</u>.
   (A) sprouts
   (B) harvests
   (C) plagues
   (D) insects

<u>Directions</u>: In the rest of this section you will read several passages. Each one is followed by several questions about it. For questions 31–60, you are to choose the best answer, (A), (B), (C) or (D), to each question. Then, on your answer sheet, find the number of the question and fill in the space that corresponds to the letter of the answer you have chosen.

Answer all questions following a passage on the basis of what is <u>stated</u> or <u>implied</u> in that passage.

Read the following passage.

F. Scott Fitzgerald was considered the literary spokesperson of the Jazz Age in America, during the 1920s. He wrote about people like himself who led celebrated lives in New York City and the French Riviera. In his later years, he was tormented by the insanity of his wife and his financial difficulties.

Example   It can be inferred from the passage that Fitzgerald was

Sample Answer
Ⓐ Ⓑ ● Ⓓ

   (A) a jazz singer
   (B) a speech writer
   (C) a celebrity
   (D) a Frenchman

The passage states that Fitzgerald "wrote about people like himself who led celebrated lives." Therefore, you should choose answer (C).

After you read the directions, begin work on the questions.

GO ON TO THE NEXT PAGE

Questions 31–37

1   Astronomers at Kitt Peak National Observatory near Tucson, Arizona, have discovered
2   what they claim are the largest structures yet observed in the universe. The structures are
3   glowing blue arcs of light nearly 2 million trillion miles in length. The discoverers of
4   these arcs think they are actually optical illusions created by light that has been bent due
5   to the immense gravitational pull of a massive galaxy. The arcs are probably formed
6   when the light from a distant galaxy is bent by the gravitational pull of another, less
7   distant, intervening galaxy. Even though such light-bending galaxies contain billions of
8   stars, they still do not contain enough visible stars which alone could exert the pull
9   needed to bend light in such a way. Therefore, it is theorized that there must be huge
10   amounts of invisible or "dark" matter within these galaxies. Furthermore, astronomers
11   say that there might be enough dark matter in the universe to supply enough gravity to
12   slow the expansion of the universe and then make it eventually collapse.

31. This passage mainly deals with
    (A) how the universe expands
    (B) what effects gravitational pull has on galaxies
    (C) what "dark" matter is
    (D) how arcs in space are created

32. According to the passage, galaxies can bend light through their
    (A) extreme distance
    (B) gravitational pull
    (C) stars
    (D) arcs

33. According to the passage, "dark" matter is
    (A) visible from other galaxies
    (B) visible only through telescopes
    (C) invisible
    (D) blue

34. The gravitational pull of some galaxies may be partly supplied by
    (A) the expanding universe
    (B) dark matter
    (C) blue arcs
    (D) light

35. According to some astronomers, the universe may eventually
    (A) expand
    (B) bend
    (C) collapse
    (D) intervene

36. According to astronomers, the blue arcs are
    (A) only illusions
    (B) only imaginary
    (C) invisible
    (D) galaxies

37. It can be inferred from the passage that
    (A) astronomers are not certain about the properties of dark matter
    (B) only astronomers at the Kitt Peak National Observatory have seen the arcs
    (C) astronomers don't know if there are enough visible stars to exert gravitational pull
    (D) astronomers are not certain whether or not arcs are visible

GO ON TO THE NEXT PAGE

Questions 38–45

1   Jacob Epstein's sculptures were the focus of much controversy during the sculptor's
2   lifetime. Epstein was born in the United States of Russian-Jewish immigrants in 1880.
3   He moved to Paris in his youth and later to England, where he eventually settled and took
4   out British citizenship in 1907. His first major public commission, on a building in
5   London, offended public taste because of the expressive distortion and nudity of the
6   figures. In 1937, the Rhodesian government, which at that time owned the building,
7   actually mutilated the sculptures to make them conform to public notions of decency.
8   Many other of Epstein's monumental carvings received equally adverse criticism. While
9   the general public denounced his work, many artists and critics praised it. They admired
10   in particular the diversity of his work and noted the influence on it of primitive and
11   ancient sculptural motifs from Africa and the Pacific. Today, Epstein's work has received
12   the recognition it deserves, and Epstein is considered one of the major sculptors of the
13   twentieth century.

38. Jacob Epstein's nationality was originally
    (A) Russian
    (B) Parisian
    (C) American
    (D) English

39. Epstein moved to Paris
    (A) in 1880
    (B) in 1907
    (C) when he was young
    (D) in the 1930s

40. Concerning Epstein's work, the tone of the article is
    (A) critical
    (B) derisive
    (C) amusing
    (D) admiring

41. Which of the following statements is NOT true?
    (A) Epstein's work is now almost forgotten.
    (B) Some critics admired Epstein's work.
    (C) Epstein lived in Paris.
    (D) Epstein's first major work was erected in London.

42. The word "denounced" in line 9 can best be replaced by
    (A) condemned
    (B) insulted
    (C) damaged
    (D) disclaimed

43. The passage states that some people didn't like some of Epstein sculptures because they found the sculptures
    (A) badly made
    (B) mutilated
    (C) offensive
    (D) ancient

44. Which of the following was most probably an important influence on Epstein's work?
    (A) Russian painting
    (B) public tastes
    (C) the Rhodesian government
    (D) African carvings

45. Today, a newly erected Epstein sculpture would probably
    (A) be mutilated
    (B) conform to public opinions
    (C) be well received
    (D) be expressive

GO ON TO THE NEXT PAGE

Questions 46–52

1   A Japanese construction company plans to create a huge independent city-state, akin
2   to the legendary Atlantis, in the middle of the Pacific Ocean. The city, dubbed
3   "Marinnation," would have about one million inhabitants, two airports, and possibly
4   even a space port. Marinnation, if built, would be a separate country but could serve as a
5   home for international organizations such as the United Nations and the World Bank.
6   Aside from the many political and social problems that would have to be solved, the
7   engineering task envisaged is monumental. The initial stage requires the building of a
8   circular dam 18 miles in diameter attached to the sea bed in a relatively shallow place in
9   international waters. Then, several hundred powerful pumps, operating for more than a
10 year, would suck out the sea water from within the dam. When empty and dry, the area
11 would have a city constructed on it. The actual land would be about 300 feet below sea
12 level. According to designers, the hardest task from an engineering point of view would
13 be to ensure that the dam is leak proof and earthquake proof.
14   If all goes well, it is hoped that Marinnation could be ready for habitation at the end of
15 the second decade of the twenty-first century. Whether anyone would want to live in
16 such an isolated and artificial community, however, will remain an open question until
17 that time.

46. The phrase "suck out" in line 10 could best be
    replaced by which of the following?
    (A) draw out
    (B) evaporate
    (C) dry up
    (D) haul

47. In line 2, to what does the phrase "the city" refer?
    (A) a Japanese contruction company
    (B) Atlantis
    (C) the United Nations
    (D) a future city

48. In the last sentence of the passage, the author
    implies that
    (A) Marinnation could never be built
    (B) people might not want to live in Marinnation
    (C) people don't believe Marinnation could ever be
        constructed
    (D) people ask many questions about how they can
        live in Marinnation

49. What kind of city will Marinnation be?
    (A) underground
    (B) underwater
    (C) marine
    (D) legendary

50. The tone of the passage is
    (A) sarcastic
    (B) humorous
    (C) judgmental
    (D) informative

51. The problems of Marinnation focused on here are
    mainly
    (A) human
    (B) engineering
    (C) political
    (D) social

52. By referring to Atlantis in the passage, the author is
    saying that
    (A) Marinnation will never be built
    (B) Marinnation is a city in the ocean
    (C) even if built, Marinnation will fail
    (D) Marinnation is only a dream

GO ON TO THE NEXT PAGE

Question 53–60

1   Until recently, the growth hormone could only be obtained from the pituitary glands of
2   dead people. This substance was used to treat children who did not produce enough of
3   their own growth hormone and who would, therefore, grow up as dwarfs. The natural
4   product was taken off the market after it was linked to a brain disease which attacked some
5   of the children undergoing treatment with it. But now, a new synthetic growth hormone
6   has been developed which, it is claimed, has no dangerous side effects. The new drug is
7   called "Somatrem" and can be produced in unlimited quantities.
8   For children who are deficient in their own growth hormone, Somatrem is an
9   important medical advance. The problem is that the drug may be abused by people who
10   are not medically in need of its benefits. For example, athletes may take the drug in the
11   belief that it will improve their physique and physical performance. Parents may want to
12   obtain the drug for their children who are only marginally under average height. For such
13   reasons, experts are recommending that registers be kept of Somatrem recipients. The
14   implications of the use of Somatrem must be thoroughly understood before widespread
15   distribution of the drug is undertaken.

53. According to the passage, natural growth hormone is not marketed now because
    (A) it may have caused a brain disease
    (B) people were killed by it
    (C) it failed to make people grow
    (D) not enough pituitary glands were available

54. The direct benefits of Somatrem will be gained by
    (A) professional athletes
    (B) undersized children
    (C) medical experts
    (D) concerned parents

55. What is the tone of the passage?
    (A) sarcastic
    (B) cautious
    (C) pessimistic
    (D) humorous

56. Why does the author claim that Somatrem is an improvement over the natural growth hormone?
    (A) It can be used by athletes.
    (B) It is not necessary to use pituitary glands from dead people.
    (C) It cannot be abused by people.
    (D) It does not have any adverse side effects.

57. What is this passage mainly about?
    (A) the side effects of growth drugs
    (B) a medical breakthrough in growth hormones
    (C) the abuse of growth hormones
    (D) the problems of growth hormone-deficient children

58. Doctors would probably want Somatrem administered only to
    (A) any very short person
    (B) children whose parents believe they are short
    (C) undersized athletes
    (D) specific children

59. One might expect that Somatrem will be
    (A) in short supply
    (B) forgotten soon
    (C) in demand
    (D) taken off the market

60. The people who could benefit from this drug are short because of
    (A) lack of a hormone
    (B) hereditary diseases
    (C) severe accidents
    (D) birth defects

THIS IS THE END OF THE VOCABULARY AND READING COMPREHENSION PRACTICE TEST.

STOP STOP STOP STOP STOP STOP STOP

THE TEST OF
·WRITTEN ENGLISH·

Five TOEFL tests a year include a writing section called the Test of Written English (TWE). When the TWE is included, it is the first section to be tested. In the writing test, you will have 30 minutes to write an essay of 250 to 300 words. The essay you write will be in response to a question in which you must do one of the following:

(A) Express and support an opinion.
(B) Choose and defend a point of view.
(C) Compare and contrast a topic.
(D) Present an argument.
(E) Persuade an audience.

Your essays will be scored holistically on a scale of 1 to 6, with 6 being the highest score. This means that your score will reflect how you organized and presented your ideas. There are no right or wrong answers to the questions. You are scored only on how well you have expressed yourself in addressing all parts of the question. Specific errors in grammar, punctuation, and spelling are not counted against you unless they affect the clarity of your essay.

STRATEGIES TO USE FOR THE ESSAY

1. Study the question carefully.

Be sure you understand what the question is asking. Consider some of the ways to address the question. Jot down a few of these ideas.

2. Organize your ideas with an outline.

Use the ideas that you have jotted down and organize them into a logical progression of ideas by using an outline.

3. Budget your time so that you will be able to complete and correct your essay.

You have only 30 minutes to write your essay. Organize your time into the following slots: reading and thinking about the question, organizing your ideas in an outline, writing the essay, and making minor corrections on the completed essay.

4. Use sentence structures and vocabulary you know to be correct.

You are more likely to make grammatical mistakes if you write long, complex sentences. Keep the sentences and vocabulary in your essay simple and precise.

5. Don't waste time worrying about spelling, punctuation, and grammar.

Incorrect spelling, punctuation, and grammar will only hurt your score if the errors make your essay difficult to understand. You should attempt to write your essay as correctly as possible, but don't waste time worrying whether or not each sentence is grammatical or each word is spelled correctly.

6. Don't waste time worrying about whether the evaluator agrees with your opinions and argument.

Your essay is evaluated on how you present your argument, not on whether the evaluator agrees with you. Be sure you have supported your argument well and have answered all parts of the question.

WRITING PARAGRAPHS

An essay is made up of several paragraphs. First study paragraph form and structure. Then study essay form and structure.

PRACTICE WITH TOPIC SENTENCES

The topic sentence states the topic and a controlling idea concerning that topic. Look at the following example.

> People give many reasons for owning a car.

The topic of the sentence is "owning a car." The controlling idea is "reasons." All the supporting ideas in the paragraph should be "reasons for owning a car."

The following phrases, or ones similar to these, can be used in your topic sentence to express the controlling idea:

the reasons for
the causes of (the effects of)
the steps for (the procedure for)
the advantages of (the disadvantages of)
the ways to (the methods of)
the different sections (parts, kinds, types) of
the characteristics (traits, qualities) of
the problems of
the precautions for
the changes to

Exercise W1   *Looking at topic sentences*

Write a topic sentence for each of the following topics. Use one of the phrases above or one of your own for your controlling idea.

Example   Catching colds

People can avoid catching a cold by taking certain precautions.

This topic sentence includes the topic "catching colds" and the controlling idea "taking precautions."

1. large cars

   _____

2. living in a remote area

   _____

3. studying abroad

   _____

4. accidents

   _____

5. airports

   _____

6. absenteeism

   _____

7. taking exams

   _____

8. computers

   _____

9. rice

   _____

10. camping

   _____

Answers to Exercise W1 are on page 494.

Exercise W2   ***Checking topic sentences***

Your topic sentence should tell the person who is reading your paragraph what the paragraph is about. Read the following paragraph and decide whether the topic sentence is strong or weak. (The topic sentence is underlined.)

> Baseball is a popular sport in the United States. There are two teams of nine players each. Players on one team take turns batting, and the other team tries to put the batters out. The batter hits the ball and then tries to run around the bases and get "home" safely. The other team tries to put the batter out by catching the ball before it hits the ground, throwing the ball to the base before the batter gets there, or by tagging the batter with the ball. The batter can stop at any one of the three bases if it is impossible to make it "home."

The topic sentence in the paragraph is weak because it tells us that "baseball is a popular sport," but the rest of the paragraph tells us how baseball is played. A stronger topic sentence would tell us, the readers, that the paragraph is going to describe how baseball is played. Here is a stronger topic sentence.

Baseball, a popular game in the United States, is played in the following way.

Now the reader knows that the paragraph will describe how baseball is played instead of where it is played, or who plays it, or why it is popular.

Read the following paragraphs. The topic sentences are underlined. If the topic sentence is weak, rewrite it in the space provided.

1. Even though the procedures followed to enroll in an American university vary according to each university, some steps are the same. First, you should contact the registration office of the university you want to attend to get the necessary forms and information concerning that particular university's entrance requirements. Then you must follow the steps outlined in their response. You will probably have to send copies of your high school diploma, get letters of recommendation, and write an essay on why you want to study there. You may have to achieve a certain score on the TOEFL test and have your scores forwarded to that university. Finally, you will have to contact the American Embassy to start the procedures to obtain a student visa.

   _____

   _____

2. I like to go to the beach whenever I have the opportunity. I start the day by enjoying a refreshing swim. Then I walk along the beach and collect shells. Later you'll find me relaxing in the warm sunshine and making sand castles. Then I sleep for a while before I open the basket of food and drinks that I always pack to take.

   _____

   _____

3. Many students cannot afford a car. The city bus service usually passes the university so those students can get to class on the bus. Many universities have a special shuttle bus that is provided for student transportation. Some students like to ride to class on bicycles. This is good exercise. Also it is easier to find a space to leave a bicycle than to find a parking space for a car on a crowded university campus. Those students who live close to campus or on campus can enjoy a leisurely walk to their classes.

   _____

   _____

Answers to Exercise W2 are on page 495.

Exercise W3   *Writing topic sentences*

The following paragraphs consist of the supporting ideas. Read each paragraph and ask yourself what is being discussed or described (the topic) and how the topic is approached (the controlling idea). Then write a topic sentence for each paragraph.

1. _____

   _____

   Pictures or posters on the wall make a dormitory room feel more like home. A rug on the floor beside the bed is a nice addition to an otherwise cold and hard floor. Besides textbooks, favorite books from home on the bookshelf and a photograph or two of the family on the desk also add a comforting touch to the impersonal dormitory room.

2. _____

_____

The white pages of an American telephone book give the phone numbers of residences. The blue pages contain the numbers of government offices, and the yellow pages have advertisements and business numbers. There are maps as well as indexes at the back of the book. The telephone books of larger cities may provide separate books for different sections of the city, while those of small towns may have room to include the numbers from several towns all in one book.

3. _____

_____

First, the fast-food restaurant is good for people who must have a quick bite because of a busy schedule. Second, the food is inexpensive yet tasty. A person can eat an enjoyable meal out and stay within a limited budget. Finally, the food is usually consistent. For example, a cheeseburger from a well-known fast-food restaurant looks and tastes about the same no matter where in the world it is purchased. Consequently, buyers know exactly what they are getting.

Answers to Exercise W3 are on page 495.

PRACTICE WITH SUPPORTING IDEAS

Your topic sentence tells the reader what the paragraph will be about. The ideas stated in the rest of the paragraph should all refer to the given topic and the controlling idea. Look at the following example.

> There are many ways to eat peanut butter. You can spread it on a slice of bread like butter, or you can make it into a sandwich with jam. Peanut butter can be a major ingredient of very tasty cookies as well as cakes and candies. It is delicious in ice cream. Peanut butter was invented by George Washington Carver. My favorite way to eat peanut butter is to lick it off a spoon.

Our topic sentence tells the reader that we are discussing peanut butter. The controlling idea is "ways of eating it." All of the sentences should be about ways of eating peanut butter. Are they? No. The sentence "Peanut butter was invented by George Washington Carver" does not refer to ways of eating peanut butter.

Exercise W4   *Checking supporting ideas*

Look at the following outlines. Circle the letter of the idea that does not support the topic.

1. I. Ways to get rid of hiccups
   A. breathe into a paper bag
   B. hold your breath to the count of 10
   C. have someone frighten you
   D. make an appointment with your doctor

2. I. Steps for planning a trip
   A. purchasing a map
   B. working late
   C. making an itinerary
   D. reserving a ticket

3. I. Reasons for car accidents
    A. fast driving
    B. drinking and driving
    C. not following traffic regulations
    D. giving signals

4. I. Advantages of small apartments
    A. good school facilities
    B. easy to clean
    C. cheaper to furnish
    D. relatively inexpensive

5. I. Characteristics of a good restaurant
    A. efficient waiters
    B. tasty food
    C. jacket and tie required
    D. pleasant atmosphere

Answers to Exercise W4 are on page 495.

Exercise W5   *Checking paragraphs for supporting ideas*

Read these paragraphs and cross out the one idea that doesn't support the topic sentence.

1. Working at a part-time job while studying at a university has many advantages. If students can get a job in their area of study, they are gaining valuable experience and putting their knowledge to use immediately. The extra money they can earn will be useful for meeting tuition fees and enjoying university activities. Also, they will have the personal satisfaction of having contributed to their own education. Students who need extra money can hold down a full-time temporary job during their summer vacation.

2. Hobbies are important for many reasons. First, a hobby can be educational. For example, if the hobby is stamp collecting, the person can learn about the countries of the world and even some of their history. Second, engaging in the hobby can lead to meeting other people with the same interests. A person can also meet other people by going to parties. Third, a person's free time is being used in a positive way. The person has no time to be bored or get into mischief while engaged in the hobby. Finally, some hobbies can lead to a future job. A person who enjoys a hobby-related job is more satisfied with life.

3. There are several features of spoken English that make it difficult for me to understand. First, many words are not pronounced as they are spelled, so when I learn new words through reading, I sometimes don't understand them when they are spoken. Second, native speakers contract words and phrases. "What are you doing?" becomes "Whacha doin'?" In my opinion, people should write clearly. Third, native speakers have a wide range of accents. A British accent is very different from a Texas one. Fourth, there are lots of idioms and slang expressions. These expressions also differ depending on the area a speaker is from. Finally, there are sounds that don't exist in my language that do exist in English and vice versa. These sounds are difficult for me to distinguish.

Answers to Exercise W5 are on page 495.

Exercise W6   *Writing supporting ideas*

Use the topic sentences that you wrote for Exercise W1. Outline four supporting ideas.

Example   Catching colds

    I. People can avoid catching a cold by taking certain precautions.
      A. avoid people with colds
      B. get plenty of sleep
      C. eat nutritious food
      D. take vitamin C

1. I. _____
    A. _____
    B. _____
    C. _____
    D. _____

2. I. _____
    A. _____
    B. _____
    C. _____
    D. _____

3. I. _____
    A. _____
    B. _____
    C. _____
    D. _____

4. I. _____
    A. _____
    B. _____
    C. _____
    D. _____

5. I. _____
    A. _____
    B. _____
    C. _____
    D. _____

6. I. _____
    A. _____
    B. _____
    C. _____
    D. _____

7. I. _____
    A. _____
    B. _____
    C. _____
    D. _____

8. I. _____
    A. _____
    B. _____
    C. _____
    D. _____

9. I. _____
    A. _____
    B. _____
    C. _____
    D. _____

10. I. _____
    A. _____
    B. _____
    C. _____
    D. _____

Answers to Exercise W6 are on page 495.

Exercise W7   ***Writing supporting ideas in a paragraph***

On your own paper write out the paragraphs you outlined in Exercise W6 by expanding your supporting ideas into complete sentences.

Example

Catching Colds

    People can avoid catching a cold by taking certain precautions. Perhaps the most important precaution is to avoid people who already have colds so that you are not exposed to cold germs. You should also get plenty of sleep so that your resistance is strong. Eating nutritious food will ensure that you have the vitamins that can help fight cold germs. Finally, you could try taking vitamin C supplements, which may help prevent your catching a cold.

Extended practice: Use the sample outlines in the Answer Key for Exercise W6 to practice writing more paragraphs.

Answers to Exercise W7 are on page 495.

PRACTICE WITH DETAILS

To make a more fully developed paragraph you need to add details to your supporting ideas. Your details can be *facts, examples, personal experiences*, or *descriptions*.
    Look at this topic sentence:

The Smithsonian Institution is worth visiting for a number of reasons.

The topic is "the Smithsonian Institution" and the controlling idea is "reasons for a visit."

Look at the following supporting ideas and details:

Supporting idea 1

The Smithsonian Institution is composed of various museums that offer something for everyone.

Details – facts:

These museums consist of the National Museum of History and Technology, the National Aeronautics and Space Museum, the National Collection of Fine Arts, the National Museum of Natural History, and several others.

Supporting idea 2

A person can do more than just look at the exhibits.

Details – example

For example, in the insect zoo at the National Museum of Natural History, anyone who so desires can handle some of the exhibits.

Supporting idea 3

The museums provide unforgettable experiences.

Details – personal experience

In climbing through Skylab at the National Aeronautics and Space Museum, I was able to imagine what it would be like to be an astronaut in space.

Supporting idea 4

Movies shown at regular intervals aid in building an appreciation of our world.

Details – description

In the National Aeronautics and Space Museum there is a theater which has a large screen. When the movie is shown, it gives the illusion that the viewer is in the movie itself, either floating above the earth in a hot-air balloon or hang gliding over cliffs.

Exercise W8   **Adding details**

Write one sentence that adds a detail to each of the following ideas. Use facts, examples, personal experiences, or descriptions.

1. The capital city of my country is _____(name)_____.

   _____

2. My favorite pastime is reading.

   _____

3. The videocassette player may make movie theaters obsolete.

   _____

4. It is very important for me to pass the TOEFL test.

   _____

5. A long vacation at the beach is a nice way to relax.

   _____

6. Habits such as smoking are hard to break.

_____

7. Many bad traffic accidents could be prevented.

_____

8. Modern architecture has its critics as well as its admirers.

_____

9. The city was built on an ancient site.

_____

10. The suburban mall has taken away a lot of business from city centers.

_____

Answers to Exercise W8 are on page 496.

Exercise W9   *Adding details to paragraphs*

Many paragraphs can be made better by adding details. Read the following paragraph.

> Although seat belts have been shown to save lives, people give a number of reasons for not using them. First, many people think they are a nuisance. Second, people are lazy. Third, some people don't believe they will have an accident. Finally, some people are afraid the seat belt will trap them in their car. All of these reasons seem inadequate, since statistics show that wearing seat belts saves lives and prevents serious injuries.

The paragraph can be improved. Read the following questions.

(A) Why don't people like seat belts?
(B) In what way are people lazy?
(C) Why do people think they won't have an accident?
(D) Under what circumstances might people get trapped?

Asking and answering these kinds of questions will help strengthen the paragraph. Now read the paragraph with details. Notice how adding the answers to these questions has improved it.

> Although seat belts have been shown to save lives, people give a number of reasons for not using them. First, many people think they are a nuisance. They say the belt is uncomfortable and inhibits freedom of movement. Second, many people are lazy. For them it is too much trouble to put on and adjust a seat belt, especially if they are only going a short distance. Third, some people don't believe they will have an accident because they are careful and experienced drivers. They think they will be able to respond quickly to avoid a crash. Finally, some people are afraid the seat belt will trap them in their car. If they have an accident, they might not be able to get out of a car that is burning, or they might be unconscious and another person won't be able to get them out. All of these reasons seem inadequate, since statistics show that wearing seat belts saves lives and prevents serious injuries.

Rewrite the following "weak" paragraphs by answering the questions and using those answers within the paragraph.

1. When you plant a tree, you are helping your environment in many ways. Your tree will provide a home and food for other creatures. It will hold the soil in place. It will provide shade in the summer. You can watch it grow and someday show your children or even grandchildren the tree you planted.

   (A) What kind of home would the tree provide?
   (B) What kind of food would the tree provide?
   (C) What kind of creatures might use the tree?
   (D) Why is holding the soil in place important?
   (E) Why is shade important?

2. Airplanes and helicopters can be used to save people's lives. Helicopters can be used for rescuing people in trouble. Planes can transport food and supplies when disasters strike. Both types of aircraft can transport people to hospitals in emergencies. Helicopters and airplanes can be used to provide medical services to people who live in remote areas.

   (A) In what situations do people need rescuing by helicopters?
   (B) What kinds of disasters might happen?
   (C) What kinds of emergencies may require transporting people to hospitals?
   (D) How can helicopters and airplanes be used to provide medical services to people in remote areas?

3. Studying in another country is advantageous in many ways. A student is exposed to a new culture. Sometimes he or she can learn a new language. Students can often have learning experiences not available in their own countries. A student may get the opportunity to study at a university where a leading expert in his or her field may be teaching.

   (A) How can exposure to a new culture be an advantage?
   (B) How can learning a new language be an advantage?
   (C) What kinds of experiences might a student have?
   (D) What are the benefits of studying under a leading expert?

Answers to Exercise W9 are on page 496.

Exercise W10   *Further practice in adding details to paragraphs*

The following paragraphs are weak. They could be improved by adding details. Write your own questions. Then make the paragraph stronger by inserting the answers to your questions.

1. Even though airplanes are fast and comfortable, I prefer to travel by car. When traveling by car, I can look at the scenery. Also, I can stop along the road. Sometimes I meet interesting people from the area I am traveling through. I can carry as much luggage as I want, and I don't worry about missing flights.

2. Wild animals should not be kept in captivity for many reasons. First, animals are often kept in poor and inhumane conditions. In addition, many suffer poor health from lack of exercise and indicate frustration and stress through their neurotic behavior. Also, some animals will not breed in captivity. Those animals that mate often do so with a related animal such as a sister or brother. In conclusion, money spent in the upkeep of zoos would be better spent in protecting natural habitats.

3. Good teachers should have the following qualities. First, they must know the material that they are teaching very well. Second, they should be able to explain their knowledge. Third, they must be patient and understanding. Last, they must be able to make the subject matter interesting to the students.

Extended practice: Add details to the paragraphs you wrote in Exercise W7.

Answers to Exercise W10 are on page 496.

PRACTICE WITH ORGANIZING AND WRITING PARAGRAPHS

Brainstorming means thinking of and writing down ideas concerning a topic. Ask yourself questions such as "who?" "what?" "where?" "when?" "why?" and "how?" to get ideas about your topic. Write down any idea that comes into your head. Later you can go through your list and pick the ideas you want to write about. You will have to do this quickly when you write the TOEFL essay. Practice first with simple topics, as in the following example:

Example

Topic: TV

Ideas

1. a TV set	11. makeup	21. private and public
2. programs	12. education	22. movies
3. sports	13. entertainment	23. actors and actresses
4. black-and-white	14. violence	24. camera operators
5. color	15. cable	25. soap operas
6. directors	16. public announcements	26. satellites
7. major studios	17. news	27. scriptwriters
8. cartoons	18. broadcaster	28. weather
9. schedules	19. technology	29. censorship
10. sound effects	20. commercials	30. documentaries

Exercise W11   *Brainstorming*

Take no more than 2 minutes to write as many ideas as you can about the topic "cars."

Topic: cars

1. _____	16. _____
2. _____	17. _____
3. _____	18. _____
4. _____	19. _____
5. _____	20. _____
6. _____	21. _____
7. _____	22. _____
8. _____	23. _____
9. _____	24. _____
10. _____	25. _____
11. _____	26. _____
12. _____	27. _____
13. _____	28. _____
14. _____	29. _____
15. _____	30. _____

Exercise W12   *Combining related ideas*

After you have listed your ideas in Exercise W11, group the related ideas together. In the following example about the topic "television,"

○ marks the ideas concerning programming,
□ marks the ideas concerning technology,
△ marks the ideas concerning people, and
◇ marks the ideas concerning informative programs

Notice that not all ideas have been used. Also, some ideas may fit into two categories.

Example

□ 1.	a TV set	◇ 16.	public announcements
○ 2.	programs	◇○ 17.	news
○ 3.	sports	△ 18.	broadcaster
□ 4.	black-and-white	□ 19.	technology
□ 5.	color	○ 20.	commercials
△ 6.	directors	21.	private and public
7.	major studios	○ 22.	movies
○ 8.	cartoons	△ 23.	actors and actresses
○ 9.	schedules	△ 24.	camera operators
□ 10.	sound effects	○ 25.	soap operas
□ 11.	makeup	□ 26.	satellites
◇○ 12.	education	△ 27.	scriptwriters
○ 13.	entertainment	◇○ 28.	weather
○ 14.	violence	○ 29.	censorship
□ 15.	cable	◇○ 30.	documentaries

Look for related ideas about the topic "cars" in Exercise W11. Use the symbols to mark your ideas into related groups, as in the preceding example. Write how the ideas are related in the spaces that follow. (*Note:* You don't have to label every idea. Also, you may have fewer or more groups of related ideas than four.)

○ _____
□ _____
△ _____
◇ _____
X _____
_____

Exercise W13   ***Writing topic sentences***

Each group of related ideas that you have marked in Exercise W12 can be made into a paragraph. A topic sentence is needed to introduce the paragraph.

Look at the following topic sentences which cover the related ideas concerning TV in Exercise W12.

Example   ○ A large variety of programs can be seen on TV today.

☐ Modern technology plays an important part in today's TV broadcasting.

△ Many highly trained and skilled people are involved in making and presenting the programs we watch.

◇ The main purpose of many programs on TV is to bring the viewer up to date on important world or regional events.

Write topic sentences for your related ideas concerning "cars."

○ _____

_____

☐ _____

_____

△ _____

_____

◇ _____

_____

X _____

_____

_____

_____

Exercise W14   ***Outlining***

Write an outline to put your ideas from Exercises W12 and W13 in order. You may want to leave some of the ideas out or add more.

Example

I. A large variety of programs can be seen on TV today.
   A. sports
   B. news
   C. children's programs
   D. educational programs
   E. movies
   F. soap operas

II. Modern technology plays an important part in today's TV broadcasting.
   A. satellites
   B. TV sets
   C. special effects

III. Many highly trained and skilled people are involved in making and presenting the programs we watch.
   A. directors
   B. actors and actresses
   C. camera operators
   D. costume designers
   E. hair stylists and makeup artists
   F. special effects experts

IV. The main purpose of many programs on TV is to bring the viewer up to date on important world or regional events.
   A. news
   B. public announcements
   C. weather

Write your outline about cars.

I. _____
   A. _____
   B. _____
   C. _____
   D. _____

II. _____
   A. _____
   B. _____
   C. _____
   D. _____

III. _____
   A. _____
   B. _____
   C. _____
   D. _____

IV. _____
   A. _____
   B. _____
   C. _____
   D. _____

V. _____
   A. _____
   B. _____
   C. _____
   D. _____

VI. _____
   A. _____
   B. _____
   C. _____
   D. _____

Exercise W15   ***Adding details to the outline***

Add details to your outline about cars in Exercise W14. As you do this, you may decide to revise your outline in some way.

Example

I. A large variety of programs can be seen on TV today.
   A. sports
      1. variety such as football, basketball
      2. day of week and time of day when shown
      3. Olympic games
   B. news
      1. local
      2. national
      3. international
   C. children's programs
      1. educational
      2. cartoons
   D. educational programs
      1. children
      2. university home study
      3. documentaries
   E. movies
      1. movies made for TV
      2. films shown on TV
      3. old movies
   F. soap operas
      1. variety
      2. time shown

Extended practice: Add details to all of your outlines from Exercise W6.

Exercise W16   ***More brainstorming***

For each of the following topics, write at least 12 ideas. Then combine related ideas and make an outline. Do not spend more than 5 minutes on any topic.

1. books
2. education
3. space exploration
4. travel
5. holidays

Exercise W17   ***Brainstorming for questions***

Read the following questions.

1. What things need to be considered before taking a long journey?
2. What are some of the advantages of large cars?
3. What factors should a student take into consideration when choosing a university?
4. What are some problems a person has to deal with when living with a roommate?
5. What are some of the disadvantages of having a job and being a student at the same time?

Use the steps in Exercises W11–W15 to write about the preceding five questions. First, brainstorm ideas about each question. Next, combine related ideas and write topic sentences. Then organize your ideas into an outline and add details. Your outlines do not have to be very elaborate. Don't spend more than 8 minutes on each question. Look at the following example first.

Example

What are some of the problems a working mother faces?

1. child care
2. sick children
3. exhaustion
4. raising children
5. worry and anxiety
6. housework after work
7. cost of transportation
8. child care expenses
9. getting time off
10. staying late at work

○ = children
□ = extra expenses
△ = physical problems
◇ = work-related problems

I. The major problems a working mother faces concern her children.
   A. child care
      1. finding a reliable person to be at home with the child
      2. finding a day-care center where the child can go
   B. sick children
      1. special arrangements
      2. mother must skip work
   C. raising children
      1. who's teaching mother's values
      2. how do smaller children attend activities after school

II. Even though a mother is frequently forced into working for economic reasons, she soon discovers that there are added expenses.
   A. child care expenses
   B. cost of transportation
      1. to work
      2. to day care
   C. clothes to work in

III. A working mother sometimes suffers physically.
   A. exhaustion
   B. worry and anxiety
      1. children's safety
      2. being a good parent
   C. extra work
      1. housework after job
      2. child care after job

IV. Women who have children sometimes face problems at work that don't affect other working women.
  A. can't stay late
    1. must pick up child
    2. must check up on child
  B. needs extra time off
    1. care for newborns
    2. has ill child
    3. must attend school meetings

Exercise W18 **Writing paragraphs**

Write paragraphs for the topics you outlined in Exercises W16 and W17.

Example

Paragraph for I

The major problems a working mother faces concern her children. She must either find a reliable person who will be loving toward the children or a good day-care center where the children can go. If a child gets sick, the mother must make special arrangements for the child to be cared for at home, or she must stay home from work. While at work, the mother may worry about her children. She may wonder if they are safe, if they are learning the values she wants them to have, and if her absence is hurting them emotionally. She may also regret not being able to take them to after-school activities or participate in family activities with them.

WRITING ESSAYS

For the Test of Written English, you will write an essay that answers a question.

The parts of an essay are much like the parts of a paragraph. The essay begins with an introductory paragraph which tells the reader what the essay is about, just as the topic sentence tells the reader what the paragraph is about. The body of the essay is made up of paragraphs that support the introduction, and the concluding paragraph completes the essay.

Study the following model essay.

Question

Some people believe that a mother should not work. Others argue against this. Consider the problems that a working mother faces. Do you believe a mother should work? Support your opinion.

Essay

Introductory paragraph

Nowadays it is very common for mothers to work outside the home. Whether a woman should stay at home or join the work force is debated by many people. Some argue that the family, especially small children, may be neglected. The fact is, however, that many women need to work because of economic reasons or want to work to maintain a career. I believe that every mother has the right to work, and the decision to work should be one that a woman makes on her own. But first she should carefully consider the many problems that affect mothers who work.

Supporting (developmental) paragraph I

The major problems a working mother faces concern her children. She must either find a reliable person who will be loving toward the children or a good day-care center where the children can go. If a child gets sick, the mother must make special arrangements for the child to be cared for at home, or she must stay home from work. While at work the mother may worry about her children. She may wonder if they are safe, if they are learning the values she wants them to have, and if her absence is hurting them emotionally. She may also regret not being able to take them to after-school activities or participate in family activities with them.

Supporting (developmental) paragraph II

Even though a mother is frequently forced into working for economic reasons, she soon discovers that there are added expenses. Her biggest expense is child care. Another expense is transportation. This may include purchasing and maintaining a car. Yet another expense is clothing, such as a uniform or stylish suits to maintain a professional appearance. Finally, if her company does not have a subsidized cafeteria, she will have to pay for food in restaurants.

Conclusion

After a mother takes into account all of the above problems and perhaps other problems unique to her situation, she must decide if a job is worth it. I believe that even though she faces major obstacles, these obstacles are not insurmountable. Many mothers do work and manage a family very successfully. In conclusion, it is a woman's right to make this choice, and only the woman herself should decide this matter.

Analysis

Introductory paragraph

Notice that the essay has an introductory paragraph which states the general topic "working mothers." It restates the information in the question about people being in disagreement. It states the opinion that every mother has the right to work and the decision to work should be a mother's choice. It then tells the reader that the essay will focus on a controlling idea – the problems that a woman must first consider before making this decision. The sentence containing the controlling idea of an essay is called the thesis statement. The *thesis statement* is usually the last sentence of the introductory paragraph.

Second paragraph

The second paragraph in this essay is the first paragraph of the body of the essay. It is called the first developmental paragraph. It supports the controlling idea of problems that was identified in the introduction. The topic sentence (the first sentence) of this paragraph states the idea of "problems concerning children." All the sentences in this paragraph describe either a problem concerning children or a detail explaining a problem concerning children.

Third paragraph

The third paragraph, or second developmental paragraph, in this essay also supports the controlling idea of problems that was identified in the introduction. The topic sentence of this paragraph states the idea "problems of added expenses." All the sentences in this paragraph describe either an added expense or a detail explaining the added expense.

Conclusion

The last paragraph in this essay is the conclusion. The conclusion restates the topic of working mothers. Again, the controlling idea of problems which face a working mother is repeated. Also, the opinion that it should be a woman's choice is restated. All of these restatements are in different words. The last statement is the concluding statement. It completes the essay.

PRACTICE WITH INTRODUCTIONS

To write an introduction for an essay that answers a question, follow these procedures. First, introduce the topic in general. Then narrow the topic down to focus more on the question. Restate the question in your own words and in statement form. The concluding statement of the introduction is the thesis statement and indicates the controlling idea of the essay. Study the following question and its introduction.

Question

Living in an apartment instead of a university dormitory has advantages and disadvantages. Discuss some of the advantages and disadvantages of apartment living and then defend your preference.

Introduction

When a person decides to enter a university away from home, he or she must also consider living accommodations. Although most universities offer student dormitories, students frequently opt to live in an apartment. While there are many advantages to apartment living, there are also many disadvantages. Before a student decides to live in an apartment, all the aspects of that kind of accommodation should be reviewed.

1. The first sentence introduces the general topic of university living accommodations.

   When a person decides to enter a university away from home, he or she must also consider **living accommodations**.

2. The second sentence narrows the topic down to apartment living.

   While most universities offer student dormitories, students frequently opt to live in **an apartment**.

3. The third sentence restates the specific question.

   While there are many **advantages** to apartment living, there are also many **disadvantages**.

4. The fourth sentence is the thesis statement. It gives the controlling idea of the essay.

   Before a student decides to live in an apartment, **all the aspects** of that kind of accommodation should be reviewed.

Exercise W19   *Rewriting introductions*

The following student-written introductory paragraphs are weak. Some of them don't state the problem. Some don't include a thesis statement. Others try to put into the introduction all the information that will be discussed in the body or developmental paragraphs of the essay.

Rewrite these essay introductions using the procedures stated above.

1. *Question:* In your opinion, what is the most dangerous threat the world faces today? Discuss some reasons for its existence. Give some possible ways of preventing its occurrence.

   Weak introduction: War is the most dangerous threat. Everyone in the world fears it. We must try to avoid it.

2. *Question:* Modern technology has brought about changes in the roles of men and women. Discuss some of these changes. Do you think these changes have been beneficial?

   Weak introduction: There are more changes in the roles of men and women due to technological development in recent times than in the past. This has changed our society.

3. *Question:* Advances in technology and science have solved many problems. However, they have also created new problems. Discuss some of the new problems caused by technological advancement and give your opinion on how they should be dealt with.

   Weak introduction: Nowadays, we have many great advantages in our society which came from technology and science. For that reason, we must protect our lives by taking care of the dangerous problems advanced technology has caused.

PRACTICE WITH DEVELOPMENTAL PARAGRAPHS

To write the body of an essay, follow the procedures used in Exercises W1–W18. The body of your essay should consist of at least two developmental paragraphs. Each developmental paragraph should have a topic sentence that supports the controlling idea mentioned in the thesis statement of your introduction. All the ideas in each paragraph should support their topic sentence.

Study the following developmental paragraphs of the essay about apartment living (see page 365 for the introductory paragraph).

> Living in an apartment has many advantages. First, students can choose to live in a quiet neighborhood. A quiet neighborhood is conducive to studying. Away from the distractions of campus life, students can be more serious about their studies. Second, apartment life allows students to be more independent. For example, they can cook whatever they want to eat and have their meals whenever they want them. Third, students can often find apartments that are cheaper than the fee for room and board in a dormitory.
>
> However, living in an apartment also has disadvantages. Being away from campus life can make students feel isolated. Another disadvantage is that apartments close to campus are usually expensive, and those farther away are not within walking distance. Therefore, transportation must be considered. Finally, students who live in apartments must cook their own meals, shop for food, perhaps carry their laundry to a laundromat, and clean their entire apartment – not just their room.

The first developmental paragraph in the body of the essay addresses the question of advantages. The second developmental paragraph addresses the question of disadvantages. Both paragraphs consider aspects of apartment living, which is the controlling idea or the thesis statement.

Exercise W20   *Writing developmental paragraphs*

Write the developmental paragraphs for the introductions that you rewrote in Exercise W19.

Exercise W21   *Comparing and contrasting*

When answering an essay question, you may need to compare and contrast some information. Look at the following question.

Question: Both living in an apartment and living in a university dormitory have advantages and disadvantages. Compare these two kinds of living accommodations and defend your preference.

To compare and contrast you may want to use some of the following words and phrases.

Words used for comparing

alike, like	identical	equivalent
similar, similarities	also	resembles
just as	likewise	corresponds to
the same	comparable to	by the same token

Words used for contrasting

unlike	more than, less than, fewer than
different, differences	is different from, differs from
in contrast	worse, better
whereas	conversely
but	on the other hand

To brainstorm for a developmental paragraph that compares and contrasts, list the ideas that are similar and those that are different.

Similarities	*Differences*
1. places to live	1. kitchen facilities
2. may need to share	2. space
3. housing rules	3. privacy
	4. rent

There are two ways you can approach writing this essay:

1. You can discuss both apartment and dormitory similarities in one developmental paragraph and both apartment and dormitory differences in the second developmental paragraph.

    or

2. You can discuss only apartments in one paragraph and only dormitories in the other paragraph.

Study the following developmental paragraph on the question concerning apartments and dormitories.

> Apartments and dormitories are similar in several ways. First, they are both living accommodations which provide a student with a place to sleep, wash, and keep belongings. They are also alike in that they require living with or near another person. An apartment is usually in a building that houses other people as well. Frequently the person renting the apartment has a roommate to share the expenses. Similarly, in a dormitory, there are many rooms, and students either share rooms or live next door to each other. Another similarity is that both apartments and dormitories have certain rules by which people must abide.

This paragraph uses the first type of development and discusses similarities. Write the second developmental paragraph and discuss the differences between apartments and dormitories. (You can use the list of differences on page 367 as a guide.)

Extended practice: Write two developmental paragraphs on this essay question using the second type of development. Discuss only apartments in one paragraph and only dormitories in the other paragraph.

PRACTICE WITH CONCLUSIONS

So far you have practiced writing the introduction (which restates the problem and states the controlling idea) and writing the body (which discusses the problem). To end the essay you need to write a concluding paragraph.

For the essay question your concluding paragraph will:

1. Restate the thesis statement.
2. Restate the topic sentences from the developmental paragraphs.
3. State your opinion or preference, make a prediction, or give a solution.
4. Conclude with a statement that sums up the essay.

Look at the essay question in Exercise W21 again and read the following conclusion.

Conclusion

Even though there are many advantages to apartment living, I would prefer to live in the university dormitory for the following reasons. First, I will be new at the university and meeting people will be easier in a dormitory setting. Second, I won't have to worry about purchasing and cooking food or cleaning up afterwards. Consequently, I will have more time for my studies. Finally, I will be within walking distance of my classes and the university library. In conclusion, living on campus is more advantageous for me than living in an apartment.

Notice that this conclusion restates the topic and gives a personal preference. The writer lists the reasons for the preference and concludes with a summary statement.

Exercise W22   *Rewriting conclusions*

The following student-written conclusions go with the essays you began writing in Exercise W19. These conclusions are weak. Some do not give a solution, prediction, reason, or opinion. Others have a topic sentence but do not support it.

Rewrite the following concluding paragraphs so that they are stronger. Do they apply to your introduction and developmental paragraphs from Exercises W19 and W20? If not, modify them. You will then have three complete essays.

1. In summary, there must be a solution to any threat in the world, but a possible solution for this problem is difficult to find. Indeed, there is one possible solution, and that is all people must become pacifists, but it is doubtful that will happen.

2. To summarize, technological development has given us a new and better life-style, and I hope that it will remain so.

3. For all these problems we must find a solution. They can destroy our lives by killing us and making our lives boring. Our lives depend on progress, so we cannot stop it. But at the same time, we cannot kill ourselves by avoiding finding a solution.

Answers to Exercises W19, W20, and W22 are on page 497.

PRACTICE WITH ANALYZING ESSAYS

Read the following checklist. You will not have time to rewrite your essay during the test. Therefore, keep this list in mind as you write your outline and essay.

1. Is there an introductory paragraph?
2. Does the introductory paragraph restate the question?
3. Does the introductory paragraph have a thesis statement (a controlling idea)?

4. Does each paragraph have a clear topic sentence?
5. Do the topic sentences of the developmental paragraphs support the thesis statement?
6. Do the ideas in each developmental paragraph support the topic sentence of the paragraph?
7. Are the details (examples, facts, descriptions, personal experiences) clear?

8. Is there a conclusion?
9. Does the concluding paragraph give (A) an opinion, preference, prediction, or solution and (B) reasons?
10. Does the essay end with a concluding statement?

11. Does the essay answer all parts of the question?
12. Has the grammar and spelling been corrected? (Incorrect grammar, spelling, punctuation, and word usage count against you if those errors lead to a lack of clarity. Your essay will be clearer if you correct as many of these errors as you can find in the limited time that you have.)

Exercise W23   *Analyzing essays*

Practice analyzing essays by reading the following student-written essays and answering yes or no to each of the 12 questions in the preceding checklist.

Question A

Both large cars and small cars have their advantages and disadvantages. Write about some of these advantages and disadvantages. State which car you prefer and why.

Essay

Both large and small cars have their advantages and disadvantages.

First, large cars have many advantages. For example, many people can be carried inside the car. Also, large cars are stronger in bad accidents, and they are very good for big families. About the disadvantages. Large cars cannot get through small streets, and they use a lot of gas to start and run.

Second, small cars also have advantages and disadvantages. About the advantages. You can drive the small car any place. Small car uses less gas and many people call them economical. The last advantage is that the small car is good for the small family like a father, mother, and one child. About the disadvantages of small cars. The small car is not strong if someone has a bad accident. Moreover, small cars cannot go very fast because of their size.

For all this I like small cars.

Question B

In your opinion, what is one of the major problems in the world today? Discuss some reasons for its existence. Give some possible solutions.

Essay

Every day on the radio, on TV, and in the newspapers, we hear, see, or read about many problems in the world. Because of this we must think about these problems. We must also try to find a solution for them. Our lives depend on this. For example, there are pollution problems.

Air pollution is the first kind. It mostly comes from fumes released from cars, airplanes, and trains. Also, factories dump waste anywhere, even in the city where many people are living. Public safety does not concern the factory owners, who must know that people don't want to live in pollution that is dangerous for their health. Nobody in this world wants to breath dirty air.

The second pollution problem is sea pollution. Many people earn their living from fishing in the sea, and the fish they catch feed many people. Their lives depend on the fish. But the sea has become so polluted from oil spills and factory wastes that the fish are dying. This pollution is not only killing the fish, but is also affecting those people who depend on the sea for food.

Seldom do you find a place nowadays that is not polluted. This problem is growing more difficult every day. We must find a good solution that makes the world a better place to live. A good way to keep these dangerous fumes away from the people must be found. Also, programs about pollution should be shown on TV. When people understand the bad effect of pollution on the human body maybe they will stop doing those things that make the air or the sea polluted. Also, we should plant trees, which are very useful for the land. In conclusion, I hope we can find a solution for every kind of pollution in the world.

Extended practice: Rewrite the preceding essays and improve them.

Answers to Exercise W23 are on page 498.

Exercise W24   *Scoring essays*

Give the following student essays a score: 6 is for essays that indicate strong writing abilities, 5 indicates average writing abilities, and 4 indicates minimal writing abilities. Scores of 3, 2, or 1 indicate a lack of writing abilities. Compare the score you gave the essay with the possible TWE score given in the Answer Key. Read the analysis of the essays to understand the given score.

Question: Some people claim that reading novels is a waste of time. They say that reading nonfictional works is more beneficial. Do you agree? Support your opinion.

1. Score _____

The main point is whether it is better to read fiction or nonfictional. The questions about this depends on the people who read. I am going to talk about both people.

The people who read the novels like to emphasize with the characters in the book. They can feel what to be another people. They can do things like traveling to the moon in their imagines during the read.

On the other hand, the people who read the nonfictional novels like to learn about facts. For these people, it solves problems and make them happy.

As you can see, I have discussed both novels and nonfictional works. Because of the above mentioned things both novels and nonfictional work is very important in our living.

2. Score _____

Some people claim that reading nonfictional works is beneficial whereas reading novels is a waste of time. Those who think this way do not realize the importance of the novel. The fictional world affects mankind in several ways.

When people read a novel, they are entering into a new world. Frequently, the story takes place in a real part of the world at a particular time in history. The reader then learns about this place and time. Also, the reader learns new words or about something unfamiliar. For example, someone who lives in the mountains might learn ship terms and how to sail a schooner.

Reading also stimulates the imagination. In our complex society, we need people who can find ways of solving problems. People who have been reading a lot of fiction have developed good imaginations. They can use their imaginations creatively to solve problems in ways that other people could never dream of.

Sometimes novels can change world events. For example, Harriet Beecher Stowe's antislavery novel may have helped end slavery in the United States. Sometimes novels can help us see things in a different way. *Animal Farm* may have influenced many reader about communism.

In conclusion, reading novels is not a waste of time. It provides readers with many satisfying hours that teaches them about life, stretches their imaginations, and focuses their minds on today's problems. Reading novels is and should always be an important activity for the people in the world.

3. Score _____

I think that reading novels is not a waste of time. In many years ago, people can't read. Therefore, grandfathers told their little boy about the stories. That is how knowledge about things that happen. For example, Helen of Troy. In these days, our grandfather don't tell stories. Most people in the life know how to read. We read the stories that in before times grandfathers say them. We can read about many adventures. It is very good to read. But people who don't want to read novels are not having a big adventure.

4. Score _____

I agree with the people who claim that reading novels is a waste of time. It is silly to spend the time reading about things that never can happen or that are not real such as science fiction is. But nonfictional works are beneficial.

There are many demands on our living these days. We must know about a lot of math and science. We must know more about computers and computer technology. Also, it is important to learn about other people and cultures. These are real things that we learn about them from nonfictional books.

People used to read novels for entertainment. We do not need to read fiction any more because of the television set. Now when people need to relax themselves, they can watch TV or go to the movies.

In conclusion, we need to read nonfictional works to improve our mental. Novels are no longer needed because things that are not real, we can see on TV. Therefore, reading nonfictional books is the more beneficial.

5. Score _____

Nowadays people read nonfictional works is better. Because it gave technology. Also, gave too much information the many things in the world. People need know too much nowadays can have a good life.

6. Score _____

   Nonfictional works refer to those books which are informative. Novels are books which tell a story. Sometimes the story is completely made up. Sometimes it has real facts inside it. Reading either kind of book is beneficial.

   Nonfictional works are not a waste of time. They are beneficial because they teach us things about our world. The things they teach us may be interesting information such as the history of our city. Sometimes the information is necessary for our lives such as a book on first-aid techniques.

   Novels are not a waste of time either. They are beneficial because they help us enjoy our lives. We can do things vicariously with the people in the book that we would never experience in real life. Sometimes true events in history are more interesting because of the viewpoint of the fictional character in the story.

   Since learning about life is necessary and since both kinds of books helps us understand our world better, we should read both kinds of books. Therefore, the people who claim that reading novels is a waste of time are wrong about that. But they are right that reading nonfictional books is beneficial.

Answers to Exercise W24 are on page 498.

PRACTICE WITH ANSWERING ESSAY QUESTIONS

Now that you have studied all the parts of an essay and have analyzed problems in other students' essays, review the steps used for writing essays that answer essay questions.

Step 1. Read the question carefully.

Ask yourself questions. (What is the question *about*? What is it asking me to *do*?) Underline and number the key parts of the question.

Question   Violent TV programs have been blamed for causing crime rates to rise in many cities. But many people do not agree that violence is related to TV viewing. Discuss the possible reasons for both opinions. Give your opinion as to whether or not violent programs should be taken off the air.

The question is about TV violence. It asks me to:

1. Discuss reasons for both opinions:
   A. opinion that TV violence is bad
   B. opinion that TV violence is acceptable
2. Give my own opinion.

Step 2. Brainstorm.

In 8 minutes or less, write down your ideas, group them into related ideas, and write a thesis statement and a *modified* outline. Compare the following complete outline and modified outline.

Example of a complete outline

   I. Introduction
      A. state general topic
      B. restate question
      C. give thesis statement – reasons for both sides

II. Body
  A. crime related to violent TV programs
     1. children imitate what they see
        a. learn unacceptable values
        b. copy behavior
     2. heroes are frequently violent
     3. gives ideas for crimes
  B. crime not related to violent TV programs
     1. crime related to social pressures
        a. unemployment
        b. homelessness
     2. aggressive feelings vicariously released
     3. parental guidance more influential
     4. frequently bad consequences of violence shown

III. Conclusion
  A. my opinion
     1. shouldn't be censored
        a. people enjoy it
        b. change station
        c. turn off
     2. censorship questions
        a. who decides?
        b. what else may they censor?
     3. concluding statement

Example of modified outline

T.S. (thesis statement) reasons support both
A. why crime related to TV
   imitate
   violent heroes
   gives ideas
B. why crime not related to TV
   social pressures – joblessness, homelessness
   rids aggression
   parental influence
   bad consequences
conclude with opinion
   no censor – enjoyment, change, or turn off
   censor – who decides what
C. S. (concluding statement) need evidence

Step 3. Check if the topic sentences will support the thesis statement.

According to the preceding outlines, the thesis statement will introduce the essay with reasons for both sides of the question.

Topic sentence A indicates that the paragraph will discuss one side of the question – "reasons crime is related to TV." This sentence supports the thesis statement.

Topic sentence B indicates that the paragraph will discuss the other side of the question – "reasons crime is not related to TV." This sentence supports the thesis statement.

Step 4. Check if all supporting ideas relate to the topic.

According to the preceding outlines, the first topic sentence will discuss "reasons crime is related to TV." The supporting ideas – imitate what is seen, heroes sometimes violent, and give ideas for crimes – support the argument that TV and crime are related.

The second topic sentence will discuss "reasons crime is not related to TV." The supporting ideas – social pressures, rids aggression, parental influence, and bad consequences – support the argument that TV and crime are not related.

Step 5. Add more details if necessary.

Step 6. Put ideas in a logical order if necessary.

Step 7. Write the introduction.

Keep in mind the checklist on page 369. You will not have time to rewrite your essay, so be certain your introduction is clear.

> The crime rate in many cities is rising alarmingly. Some people have the idea that violent TV programs are the cause of real crime. However, many others disagree that TV violence can be blamed for this rise. Both sides of the question of whether TV may or may not be to blame are supported by good reasons.

Step 8 Write the body.

Keep in mind the checklist on page 369. You will not have time to rewrite your essay, so be certain the paragraphs support the thesis statement.

> Those who believe that violent TV programs cause crime give many reasons. First, many viewers are children who have not formed a strong understanding of right and wrong. They imitate what they see. If a person on TV gets what he or she wants by stealing it, a child may copy this behavior. Thus the child has learned unacceptable values. Second, many heroes in today's programs achieve their goals by violent means. Unfortunately, viewers might use similar means to achieve their objectives. Finally, people get ideas about how to commit crimes from watching TV.
>
> Other people argue that violent programs have no relation to the rise in crime rates. First, they claim that social factors, such as unemployment and homelessness, are to blame. Second, some argue that watching violence on TV is an acceptable way to reduce aggressive feelings. In other words, people may become less aggressive through viewing criminal and violent scenes. Third, even though children learn by imitation, their parents are the most influential models. Finally, the villains are usually punished for their crimes.

Step 9. Write the conclusion.

Keep in mind the checklist on page 369. You will not have time to rewrite your essay, so be certain your conclusion completes the essay.

> Whether or not violent programs are a factor in the rising crime rate, I am against their removal for the following reasons. First, some people enjoy them, and those who don't can change channels or turn their TVs off. Second, I disagree with other people deciding what I should watch. If violent programs can be censored, perhaps other programs which may be important for our well-being will also be censored. In conclusion, even though I am not fond of violent programs, I am against their removal until conclusive evidence proves that viewing violence creates violence.

Step 10. Read over the essay.

Make any minor corrections in spelling and grammar that will make your essay clearer. Remember, you will not have time to make major changes.

Exercise W25   Writing essays

Now answer the following essay questions to practice your writing skills. Try to complete and check each essay within 30 minutes. This is how much time you will be given on the TOEFL test to write a 250- to 300-word essay.

1. Billions of dollars go into space exploration projects yearly. Some people feel that this money should be used to solve problems on Earth. Discuss reasons supporting both opinions. State and support your opinion.

2. Compare and contrast the advantages of city living and country living. Defend your preference.

3. "A universal language should replace all languages." Discuss the advantages and disadvantages of a universal language.

4. Compare and contrast the advantages of marrying at a young age to marrying at an older age. State and support your preference.

5. There are many people who wish to ban smoking in public places. Others don't agree. Give reasons for both opinions. Do you agree with a ban or not? Defend your answer.

6. The first Olympic games were held at Mount Olympus in Greece. Nowadays, each time they are held, they take place in a different area of the world. Many people would like the games to be held in one specific place each time. Some people believe Greece would be the best place. Many other people believe that the games should continue being held in different places. State what you think should be done and give reasons for your opinion.

7. Many people believe that parents are too permissive with their children nowadays. Do you agree that this is a problem? Defend your answer.

8. Some people believe that young people should work for their spending money. Other people believe that young people should be given an allowance (spending money given at a regular interval) without having to work for it. State your opinion concerning allowances and defend it.

9. Drug abuse has become a major social problem in many parts of the world. Discuss the consequences of drug abuse and ways to deal with the problem.

10. Compare and contrast the way of life that you have with that of your parents. What experiences from both your life and that of your parents would you like your children (or future children) to have?

PRACTICE
• TESTS •

Take these practice tests as if your were taking an actual TOEFL test. The format of these tests are the same as for the TOEFL. If you are unsure of TOEFL procedures, read the instructions on pages 1 and 2 in the Introduction to this book.

Before you take one of the practice tests, make the following preparations:

1. Arrange to have a quiet room where you will not be disturbed for the duration of the test. Each test will take approximately 2 1/2 hours.
2. Bring the following items: a cassette player, the cassette which contains the Practice Tests, two pencils with erasers, and a timing device such as an alarm clock or timer.
3. Tear one of the answer sheets for the Practice Tests out of this book. You will find them on pages 547 and 549.

When you have completed the test, check your answers against the Answer Key starting on page 499. If you marked a wrong answer, the Answer Key will tell you which exercises in the book will help you improve in that area. For example, you may see:

(See Exercises L4–L6.)

These are the exercises you should do for further practice.

If you use the book in this way, you will identify the areas where you may be weak and need practice. After you have completed the exercises that focus on these areas, you may want to review other material in the book.

PRACTICE TEST 1

TEST OF WRITTEN ENGLISH (TWE)
ESSAY QUESTION

Time – 30 minutes

DO NOT TURN THE PAGE UNTIL THE SUPERVISOR TELLS YOU TO DO SO.

The TWE essay question follows. You will have 30 minutes to plan, write, and correct your essay. Your essay will be graded on its overall quality.

1. When the Supervisor tells you to begin, turn the page and read the Essay Question carefully.
2. Think before you write. Making notes may help you to organize your essay. Below the Essay Question is a space for notes. Use only this area to outline your essay or make notes.
3. Write only on this topic. If you write an essay on a different topic, it will not be scored. Write clearly and precisely. Use examples to support your ideas. How well you write is much more important than how much you write, but to cover the topic adequately, you may want to write more than one paragraph.
4. Start writing your essay on the first line of Essay Page Side 3. Use Side 4 if you need more space. Extra paper will not be provided. Write neatly and legibly. Do <u>not</u> skip lines. Do not write in very large letters or leave large margins.
5. Check your work. Allow a few minutes <u>before</u> time is called to read over your essay and make small changes.
6. After 30 minutes, the Supervisor will tell you to stop. You <u>must</u> stop writing and put your pencil down. If you continue to write, it will be considered cheating.

STOP! WAIT FOR THE SUPERVISOR'S INSTRUCTIONS.

COMPOSITION

Time – 30 minutes

Directions: Write a composition on a separate sheet of paper.

It has been said that a good sense of humor is one of the most important human qualities. Argue for or against this statement.

THIS SPACE MAY BE USED FOR NOTES.

SECTION 1
LISTENING COMPREHENSION

In this section of the test, you will have an opportunity to demonstrate your ability to understand spoken English. There are three parts to this section, with special directions for each part. Do not read ahead or turn the pages while the directions are being read. Do not take notes or write in your workbook at any time.

Part A

Directions: For each question in Part A, you will hear a short sentence. Each sentence will be spoken just once. The sentences you hear will not be written out for you.

After you hear a sentence, read the four choices in your workbook, marked (A), (B), (C), and (D), and decide which one is closest in meaning to the sentence you heard. Then, on your answer sheet, find the number of the question and fill in the space that corresponds to the letter of the answer you have chosen. Fill in the space completely so that the letter inside the oval cannot be seen.

Listen to an example.

On the recording, you hear: *The new observatory is nothing less than outstanding.*

In your workbook, you read: (A) The new observatory is excellent.
(B) There is nothing outstanding to observe.
(C) You must stand outside to make the observance.
(D) His new observations are more outstanding than usual.

Sample Answer

The woman said, "The new observatory is nothing less than outstanding." Sentence (A), "The new observatory is excellent," is closest in meaning to what the woman said. Therefore, the correct choice is (A).

NOW WE WILL BEGIN PART A WITH QUESTION 1.

GO ON TO THE NEXT PAGE

1. (A) He has two plates.
   (B) He served himself too much food.
   (C) Two people ate the food.
   (D) The food on his plate was too mushy.

2. (A) The windows were dirty.
   (B) The windows are to be cleaned.
   (C) Edie was washing the windows.
   (D) Natalie watched from the windows.

3. (A) Mary is packing to go.
   (B) Mary is playing music.
   (C) Mary is practicing saying no.
   (D) Mary is studying Plato.

4. (A) Give me a loan.
   (B) Lend me the leaves.
   (C) Let it be.
   (D) Stop bothering me.

5. (A) John didn't forget to lock the door.
   (B) John remembered locking the door.
   (C) John recalls seeing the door lock.
   (D) John remembered that the door was locked.

6. (A) Is tomorrow the day you leave?
   (B) Do you have a coat for me to borrow?
   (C) Do you have a job for me to do?
   (D) Does Lee need you to work tomorrow?

7. (A) I'm accustomed to going to evening classes.
   (B) I don't go to evening classes now.
   (C) I usually go to evening classes.
   (D) I use the evening for studying.

8. (A) I was angry because he was driving fast.
   (B) I won't be angry if he arrives late.
   (C) He didn't arrive on time, so I was angry.
   (D) I will arrive on time so he won't be angry.

9. (A) Bob washed the dye off.
   (B) Bob is no longer watching what he eats.
   (C) Bob took his tie off.
   (D) Bob got down from his chair.

10. (A) She's never seen it rain so much.
    (B) Entertainment doesn't matter to her.
    (C) She has never been in a train.
    (D) She has never been more amused.

11. (A) Turn right when you stop.
    (B) Turn at the light on the right side.
    (C) Turn right at the traffic signal.
    (D) Stop at the traffic signal.

12. (A) My friends and I started out the door.
    (B) I went out when my friends returned.
    (C) Before I started out my friends came back.
    (D) I left before my friends came back.

13. (A) You cannot fish here.
    (B) A permit is required to fish.
    (C) We don't allow fish here.
    (D) The fish are banned.

14. (A) Her ideas for the party are agreeable.
    (B) Do you agree with her ideas for the party?
    (C) I like her ideas for the party.
    (D) I heard about her ideas for the party.

15. (A) Dawn likes to send letters from the post office.
    (B) The post office sent Dawn's letters on.
    (C) Dawn received four letters from the post office.
    (D) Dawn forgot her letters at the post office.

16. (A) Was your picnic spoiled by the rain?
    (B) We can't have a picnic now because it might rain.
    (C) If it rains, we can't have a picnic.
    (D) It may rain, so shall we have a picnic or not?

17. (A) Jean and Bill both took a long vacation.
    (B) Jean had a long vacation, but Bill didn't.
    (C) Jean should go on vacation, and so should Bill.
    (D) If Jean takes a long vacation, so should Bill.

18. (A) I can't believe he's already back from the store.
    (B) He won't be able to return to the store yet.
    (C) I don't believe he returned to the store.
    (D) He shouldn't have turned at the store.

19. (A) Peter got the car for Robert.
    (B) Peter allowed Robert to use the car.
    (C) Peter's car was lent by Robert.
    (D) Peter and Robert were permitted to use the car.

20. (A) The politician questioned the interviewer.
    (B) The interviewer asked questions about politics.
    (C) The politician asked the interviewer some questions.
    (D) The interviewer questioned the politician.

Part B

<u>Directions</u>: In Part B you will hear short conversations between two people. After each conversation, a third person will ask a question about what was said. You will hear each conversation and question about it only <u>one</u> time. After you hear a conversation and the question about it, read the four possible answers in your workbook and decide which <u>one</u> is the best answer to the question you heard. Then, on your answer sheet, find the number of the question and fill in the space that corresponds to the letter of the answer you have chosen.

Listen to an example.

On the recording, you hear: (First Man) *I think I'll have the curtains changed.*
(Woman) *They are a bit worn.*

(Second Man) *What does the woman mean?*

In your workbook, you read: (A) She thinks every bit of change is important.
(B) She wants to wear them.
(C) She thinks they've been worn enough.
(D) She thinks they are in bad condition.

Sample Answer

You learn from the conversation that the woman thinks the curtains are worn. The best answer to the question "What does the woman mean?" is (D), "She thinks they are in bad condition." Therefore, the correct choice is (D).

NOW WE WILL BEGIN PART B WITH THE FIRST CONVERSATION.

21. (A) At a restaurant.
    (B) At the hospital.
    (C) At the dentist's.
    (D) At a bakery.

22. (A) She's upset with Jill about not giving her notes back.
    (B) She wants to give Jill another piece of information.
    (C) She's thinking about binding her notes.
    (D) She wouldn't mind going to see Jill about the notes.

23. (A) Pick up something for a student.
    (B) Loan a student his truck.
    (C) Get a form for financial aid.
    (D) Borrow money in a hurry.

24. (A) A carpenter built it for them.
    (B) The members designed and made it.
    (C) The members made it from a carpenter's design.
    (D) A carpenter had it designed for them.

25. (A) He is indecisive.
    (B) He is moody.
    (C) He is not intelligent.
    (D) He puts things off.

26. (A) It was tailor-made.
    (B) It was made smaller.
    (C) It was given away.
    (D) It was exchanged.

27. (A) He's going to camp if it rains.
    (B) He's not changing his plans even if it rains.
    (C) He's going camping in May.
    (D) He's predicting it might rain.

28. (A) Nobody knows where Elm Street is.
    (B) Nobody can find Elm Street.
    (C) There's no one to ask directions from.
    (D) They've only seen one street that may be Elm Street.

29. (A) It was taken in the union.
    (B) The results are displayed on the bulletin board.
    (C) The poll was postponed.
    (D) The union board members passed the results on.

30. (A) She had to eat breakfast too early.
    (B) She can't have breakfast at this time of day.
    (C) She is always hungry at this time.
    (D) She missed her breakfast.

31. (A) He's looking forward to listening to Gloria's speech.
    (B) He'll miss the presentation to meet Gloria.
    (C) He doesn't want to hear another presentation.
    (D) He doesn't want Gloria to miss the program.

32. (A) He always gives old quizzes.
    (B) There's nothing to study in his class.
    (C) He usually gives tests on Mondays.
    (D) He doesn't usually give exams.

33. (A) They are engaged.
    (B) They are married.
    (C) They are students.
    (D) They are strangers.

34. (A) He only has to do one problem.
    (B) He's finished one list of problems.
    (C) He has more problems to do.
    (D) He has just written a list of his problems.

35. (A) She'd like to go along.
    (B) There is a toll fee along the way.
    (C) The walk will take all evening.
    (D) She knows of a place to buy some rolls.

GO ON TO THE NEXT PAGE

Part C

Directions: In this part of the test, you will hear longer conversations and talks. After each conversation or talk, you will be asked some questions. You will hear the talks and conversations and the questions about them only <u>one</u> time. They will <u>not</u> be written out for you.

After you hear a question, read the four possible answers in your workbook and decide which <u>one</u> is the best answer to the question you heard. Then, on your answer sheet, find the number of the question and fill in the space that corresponds to the letter of the answer you have chosen. Answer all questions on the basis of what is <u>stated</u> or <u>implied</u> by the speakers in the talk or conversation.

Here is an example.

On the recording, you hear: *Listen to a conversation between a professor and a student.*

(Woman)	*Would you please type this paper? I can't read your handwriting.*
(First Man)	*I'm sorry, Professor Mills. I don't have a typewriter, and besides, I can't type.*
(Woman)	*Well, rewrite it then, but be sure to make it clear.*

Now listen to a sample question.

(Second Man) *What does the professor want the man to do?*

In your workbook, you read: (A) Buy a typewriter.
(B) Read his handwriting.
(C) Clear the papers away.
(D) Rewrite the paper.

Sample Answer

The best answer to the question "What does the professor want the man to do?" is (D), "Rewrite the paper." Therefore, the correct choice is (D).

Remember, you are not allowed to take notes or write in your workbook.

NOW WE WILL BEGIN PART C.

36. (A) At the registration desk.
    (B) At the student loan office.
    (C) In Mr. Schultz's office.
    (D) At the bank.

37. (A) His registration has been canceled.
    (B) His emergency loan will be late.
    (C) He doesn't understand the application form.
    (D) He can't pay his university tuition fees.

38. (A) Two weeks.
    (B) September 11th.
    (C) Within a month.
    (D) The same day.

39. (A) After he gets his student loan.
    (B) After he pays back his emergency loan.
    (C) The same day he's granted an emergency loan.
    (D) Before he returns the application on September 11th.

40. (A) How to use the library.
    (B) How libraries purchase materials.
    (C) How libraries meet users' needs.
    (D) How libraries use modern technology.

41. (A) Libraries have limited funds and space.
    (B) Libraries must purchase computers.
    (C) Libraries contain everything the user needs.
    (D) Libraries are no longer needed by students and professors.

42. (A) They use the interlibrary loan system.
    (B) Professors make suggestions.
    (C) They contact other libraries.
    (D) They buy everything in print.

43. (A) Purchase it at the bookstore.
    (B) Borrow it from the professor.
    (C) Contact the publisher.
    (D) Have the librarian do a computer search.

44. (A) At the recreation center.
    (B) At the bus stop.
    (C) At the music complex.
    (D) At family housing.

45. (A) They are acquaintances.
    (B) They are members of a family.
    (C) They are in the same university class.
    (D) They are strangers.

46. (A) The man is married.
    (B) The woman is going toward the recreation center.
    (C) The man is going to the music center.
    (D) The woman enjoys sports.

GO ON TO THE NEXT PAGE

47. (A) She usually walks to the recreation center.
    (B) She has an expensive car.
    (C) She doesn't drive during rush hour.
    (D) She's not used to taking the university shuttle bus.

48. (A) Produces films.
    (B) Reforms prisoners.
    (C) Studies acting.
    (D) Writes plays.

49. (A) Because it took nearly 15 years to complete her bachelor degree.
    (B) Because an author was born.
    (C) Because she didn't intend to take the playwriting seminar.
    (D) Because she had experience on speaking tours.

50. (A) Completing her university bachelor degree.
    (B) Starting student groups dedicated to racial progress and black unity.
    (C) Transposing numbers at the University of Minnesota.
    (D) Acting on stage in Chicago, Los Angeles, and Washington.

THIS IS THE END OF THE LISTENING COMPREHENSION SECTION OF PRACTICE TEST 1.

THE NEXT PART OF THE TEST IS SECTION 2. TURN TO THE
DIRECTIONS FOR SECTION 2 IN YOUR WORKBOOK,
READ THEM, AND BEGIN WORK.
DO NOT READ OR WORK ON ANY OTHER SECTION OF THE TEST.

SECTION 2
STRUCTURE AND WRITTEN EXPRESSION

Time – 25 minutes

This section is designed to measure your ability to recognize language that is appropriate for standard written English. There are two types of questions in this section, with special directions for each type.

Directions: Questions 1–15 are incomplete sentences. Beneath each sentence you will see four words or phrases marked (A), (B), (C), and (D). Choose the one word or phrase that best completes the sentence. Then, on your answer sheet, find the number of the question and fill in the space that corresponds to the letter of the answer you have chosen. Fill in the space so that the letter inside the oval cannot be seen.

Example   John Le Carré ----- for his novels concerning espionage.

     (A) famous
     (B) has fame
     (C) is famous
     (D) famed for

Sample Answer
Ⓐ Ⓑ ⬤ Ⓓ

The sentence should read, "John Le Carré is famous for his novels concerning espionage." Therefore, you should choose answer (C).

After you read the directions, begin work on the questions.

1. It is now known that Saturn ----- not the only planet in our solar system with rings.
   (A) which
   (B) be
   (C) so
   (D) is

2. ----- is essential for the plant life of the Amazon Basin.
   (A) It is an adequate rainfall
   (B) An adequate rainfall
   (C) Though an adequate rainfall
   (D) Although an adequate rainfall

3. The Mediterranean monk seal is distinguished from the more familiar gray seal by -----.
   (A) is a size
   (B) its size
   (C) is its size
   (D) is size

4. ----- places which attract so many art lovers as Florence, Italy.
   (A) Fewer
   (B) As few
   (C) There are few
   (D) That fewer

5. ----- numerous at the turn of the century, the number of tigers in India had fallen to 2,500 by 1969.
   (A) They were
   (B) It was
   (C) Although
   (D) Not only

6. ----- that F. W. Frohawk made his greatest contribution to the field of natural history during the Victorian period.
   (A) It was as a butterfly illustrator
   (B) He was as a butterfly illustrator
   (C) A butterfly illustrator
   (D) When he was a butterfly illustrator

7. Anthony Burgess, ----- as a novelist, was originally a student of music.
   (A) because of being famous
   (B) who has achieved fame
   (C) who because he was famous
   (D) he achieved fame

GO ON TO THE NEXT PAGE ➤

8. Not until Edward Jenner developed the first anti-smallpox serum in 1796 ----- against this terrible disease.
   (A) protection was
   (B) protection was given
   (C) it was protected
   (D) was there protection

9. A fine tomb, -----, marks the grave of the poet Chaucer.
   (A) which in the fifteenth century was erecting
   (B) erected in the fifteenth century
   (C) erecting in the fifteenth century
   (D) being erected in the fifteenth century

10. Not every plan that was presented -----.
    (A) of suitability
    (B) was suitable
    (C) to be suited
    (D) suitable

11. Today the cotton textile industry is ----- important for the economy as it was a century ago.
    (A) so
    (B) more
    (C) as
    (D) an

12. ----- first three years of the war with Germany and Austria-Hungary left 1.8 million Russian soldiers dead.
    (A) The
    (B) In the
    (C) It was the
    (D) When the

13. Grace Kelly was first famous as a Hollywood actress and then ----- Prince Rainier of Monaco.
    (A) to be the wife of
    (B) she was the wife of
    (C) the wife of
    (D) as the wife of

14. ----- Mount Whitney, one of America's highest mountains, is popular with hikers.
    (A) It is high, although
    (B) The height of
    (C) Although its height
    (D) Despite its height,

15. Not only are reindeer used for their hides and milk -----.
    (A) but for pulling sleighs as well
    (B) as well as pulling sleighs
    (C) but they pull sleighs
    (D) also to pull sleighs

Directions: In questions 16–40 each sentence has four underlined words or phrases. The four underlined parts of the sentence are marked (A), (B), (C), and (D). Identify the one underlined word or phrase that must be changed in order for the sentence to be correct. Then, on your answer sheet, find the number of the question and fill in the space that corresponds to the letter of the answer you have chosen.

Example   The balloonists who remained aloft in the air radioed the control center.
           A   B   C   D

Sample Answer
Ⓐ Ⓑ ● Ⓓ

The sentence should read, "The balloonists who remained aloft radioed the control center." Therefore, you should choose answer (C).

After you read the directions, begin work on the questions.

16. It was not until 1937 when the southernmost source of the Nile River was discovered.
              A   B   C   D

17. The highly endangered Waldrapp ibis it is a wading bird related to the stork and flamingo.
        A   B C   D

18. Platinum is a rare and value metal, white in color, and easy to work.
            A   B   C   D

GO ON TO THE NEXT PAGE

19. During the two centuries <u>between</u> Herschel and *Voyager*, <u>relatively</u> little <u>is learned</u>
    A   B   C   D
about the planet Uranus.

20. Some conservationists <u>attempt</u> to <u>save</u> rare domestic farm animals, <u>such the</u>
    A   B   C   D
Tamworth pig.

21. <u>Prior to the race</u> the horses <u>were</u> stabled <u>near the track</u> the night before <u>the race</u>.
         A   B   C   D

22. The head proctor tells the students when they should <u>begin</u> the exam, how long
                                                  A
<u>they have</u> to complete it, and what <u>the procedures</u> are for <u>turning in</u>.
   B   C   D

23. The Charles Dickens character Wilkins Micawber lived in <u>optimistic</u> <u>expectation</u> of
    A   B   C
a <u>best</u> fortune.
    D

24. Passive smoking is <u>defined</u> as the <u>exposure</u> of <u>nonsmoker</u> to <u>environmental</u> tobacco
                     A   B   C   D
smoke.

25. In recent <u>years</u>, sulfur dioxide <u>has</u> disfigured <u>much</u> ancient buildings and <u>monuments</u>.
        A   B   C   D

26. Estimates <u>for</u> scientists <u>suggest</u> that only 1 percent of the world's <u>extinct</u> animals and
          A   B   C
plants have been <u>identified</u>.
               D

27. <u>When</u> a human being walks, he <u>or</u> she exerts a certain <u>number</u> of force <u>on</u> the ground.
    A   B   C   D

28. <u>Many</u> opinions have been <u>voiced</u> on <u>its</u> likely effects of the <u>computer</u>.
    A   B   C   D

29. The <u>oceans</u> contain many <u>forms</u> of life that <u>has</u> not <u>yet</u> been discovered.
        A   B   C   D

30. There have <u>recently</u> been <u>any</u> important <u>findings</u> in medical <u>technology</u>.
            A   B   C   D

31. Sigmund Freud, the <u>founding</u> of psychoanalysis, <u>settled</u> in London <u>at</u> the <u>age</u> of
                  A   B   C   D
eighty-two.

GO ON TO THE NEXT PAGE →

32. Although France is a <u>predominant</u> Catholic country, <u>it has</u> a <u>large</u> Muslim minority.
      A   B   C   D

33. Adult education has become <u>increasingly</u> popular in <u>the</u> United States in <u>recent</u>
    A   B   C
<u>years ago</u>.
   D

34. Many <u>disabled</u> children cannot <u>derive</u> full <u>enjoyment</u> from toys <u>make</u> for
       A   B   C   D
nondisabled children.

35. Before 1992, Bobby Fischer had not <u>played</u> in <u>other</u> chess tournament <u>since</u>
                                 A   B   C
winning the Chess World Championship <u>in</u> 1972.
                                D

36. As medical costs soar, <u>the</u> idea of a complete physical checkup has come <u>under</u> fire
  A   B   C
as both a waste of time <u>or</u> money.
                     D

37. <u>Perhaps was</u> his defiance against <u>his</u> parents' attitude <u>that led</u> Salvatore Ferragamo
       A   B   C
to fame <u>as the</u> shoemaker for the world's most famous women.
         D

38. Queen Elizabeth prefers <u>have</u> her jewels <u>left</u> in <u>their</u> original <u>setting</u>.
                              A   B C   D

39. Married women are <u>twice</u> <u>so</u> likely as married <u>men</u> to be <u>depressed</u>.
                    A B   C   D

40. Broken <u>tapes</u> from a cassette <u>can</u> be joined <u>with touch</u> of nail <u>polish</u>.
        A   B   C   D

THIS IS THE END OF SECTION 2 OF PRACTICE TEST 1.

IF YOU FINISH BEFORE TIME IS UP, CHECK YOUR WORK
ON SECTION 2 ONLY.
DO NOT READ OR WORK ON ANY OTHER SECTION OF THE TEST.

SECTION 3
VOCABULARY AND READING COMPREHENSION

Time – 45 minutes

This section is designed to measure your comprehension of standard written English. There are two types of questions in this section, with special directions for each type.

Directions: In questions 1–30 each sentence has an underlined word or phrase. Below each sentence are four other words or phrases, marked (A), (B), (C), and (D). You are to choose the one word or phrase that best keeps the meaning of the original sentence if it is substituted for the underlined word or phrase. Then, on your answer sheet, find the number of the question and fill in the space that corresponds to the letter you have chosen. Fill in the space so that the letter inside the oval cannot be seen.

Example   Many women have made a mark on American art since the early 1800s.
    (A) target for
    (B) dedication to
    (C) contribution to
    (D) degree of

The best answer is (C) because "Many women have made a contribution to American art since the early 1800s" is closest in meaning to the original sentence. Therefore, you should choose answer (C).

After you read the directions, begin work on the questions.

1. Rachmaninoff's stirring music was strongly influenced by his friend Tchaikovsky.
    (A) melodic
    (B) variable
    (C) dramatic
    (D) flexible

2. This type of balloon is made from fibers which can retain helium.
    (A) nets
    (B) fringes
    (C) threads
    (D) pockets

3. Twenty sixteenth-century schooners were moored in the bay the day before the race.
    (A) anchored
    (B) stopped
    (C) launched
    (D) tugged

4. Lead contamination occurs with very high frequency.
    (A) casting
    (B) construction
    (C) solidification
    (D) poisoning

5. Smallpox has been universally eradicated.
    (A) eliminated
    (B) pushed over
    (C) assimilated
    (D) verified

6. The thermographic foil is a heat-sensitive device.
    (A) feature
    (B) drill
    (C) instrument
    (D) service

7. The collapse of the Mesopotamian civilization may have been accelerated by irrigation practices.
    (A) charged
    (B) hastened
    (C) moistened
    (D) spurned

8. The need for adequate housing is very acute in areas where catastrophes have occurred.
    (A) faults
    (B) disasters
    (C) dangers
    (D) tornadoes

GO ON TO THE NEXT PAGE

9. Dot-matrix printers construct characters by using assemblies of dots.
   (A) alphabets
   (B) signatures
   (C) points
   (D) symbols

10. For centuries people have exploited the ability of certain herbs to improve stamina.
    (A) taken advantage of
    (B) searched for
    (C) improved on
    (D) argued for

11. The great land masses are moving perpetually.
    (A) chronically
    (B) incessantly
    (C) perniciously
    (D) perversely

12. Natural sponges are considered indispensable for cleaning certain scientific instruments.
    (A) essential
    (B) impossible
    (C) irresolute
    (D) indicative

13. One way in which children learn to read is by sounding out each letter and piecing the sounds together to form words.
    (A) shouting
    (B) envisioning
    (C) enunciating
    (D) clarifying

14. Standard IQ tests have been denounced by many educators as being culturally biased.
    (A) hailed
    (B) condemned
    (C) exemplified
    (D) endorsed

15. Space ventures require a judicious balance of safety and practicality.
    (A) legal
    (B) maximum
    (C) wishful
    (D) wise

16. Beekeeping has become a sophisticated operation.
    (A) feasible
    (B) complex
    (C) confident
    (D) profitable

17. Barnacles and algae attached to a ship's hull create friction that impedes its movement.
    (A) hinders
    (B) implies
    (C) enforces
    (D) denies

18. Bamboo has certain qualities that are important in the papermaking process.
    (A) viewpoints
    (B) descriptions
    (C) characteristics
    (D) components

19. Elephants are known to eat rocks from mineral-rich strata to get needed sodium and potassium in their diet.
    (A) stripes
    (B) columns
    (C) layers
    (D) mountains

20. The tropical rain forest canopy shelters 40 percent of all life species on Earth.
    (A) provides
    (B) harbors
    (C) includes
    (D) maintains

21. The question of when humans first inhabited the North American continent is intriguing.
    (A) fascinating
    (B) invigorating
    (C) entertaining
    (D) improbable

22. Large carnivorous aquatic creatures have been seen in Loch Ness since the Middle Ages.
    (A) acrobatic
    (B) muscular
    (C) marine
    (D) ancient

23. Pagan, the ancient capital of Burma, was widely renowned for its 5,000 Buddhist temples, pagodas, and monasteries.
    (A) discussed
    (B) worshipped
    (C) acclaimed
    (D) visited

GO ON TO THE NEXT PAGE

24. New chemicals are not always tested to determine if they will cause cancer or genetic <u>mutations</u>.
    (A) traits
    (B) implants
    (C) regularities
    (D) alterations

25. Black slaves were <u>hidden</u> in certain houses along the Underground Railroad.
    (A) assisted
    (B) fabled
    (C) concealed
    (D) reputed

26. The <u>buoyant</u> leaf of the Amazon water lily is the world's largest leaf.
    (A) fragrant
    (B) climbing
    (C) delicate
    (D) floating

27. The Egyptian climate has helped to preserve papyrus in the <u>soil</u> for thousands of years.
    (A) dune
    (B) waste
    (C) earth
    (D) site

28. One of the most <u>peculiar</u> of small mammals is the aye-aye, a Madagascar lemur.
    (A) enjoyable
    (B) curious
    (C) enviable
    (D) surprising

29. Vultures prevent the spread of diseases by disposing of animal <u>carcasses.</u>
    (A) corpses
    (B) bacteria
    (C) habitats
    (D) flesh

30. The most <u>damaging</u> solar radiation is ultraviolet light that is reflected from water, sand, and snow.
    (A) punishing
    (B) painful
    (C) misused
    (D) harmful

<u>Directions</u>: In the rest of this section you will read several passages. Each one is followed by several questions about it. For questions 31–60, you are to choose the best answer, (A), (B), (C), or (D), to each question. Then, on your answer sheet, find the number of the question and fill in the space that corresponds to the letter of the answer you have chosen.

Answer all questions following a passage on the basis of what is <u>stated</u> or <u>implied</u> in that passage.

Read the following passage.

The horse has played a little-known but very important role in the field of medicine. Horses were injected with toxins of diseases until their blood built up immunities. Then a serum was made from their blood. Serums to fight both diphtheria and tetanus were developed in this way.

Example   According to the passage, horses were given
    (A) poisons from illnesses
    (B) immunities to diseases
    (C) diphtheria and tetanus serums
    (D) medicines to fight toxins

Sample Answer
● (B) (C) (D)

The passage states that "horses were injected with toxins of diseases." Therefore, you should choose answer (A).

After you read the directions, begin work on the questions.

GO ON TO THE NEXT PAGE ➤

Questions 31–38

1   Diamond value is based on four characteristics: carat, color, clarity, and cut. A
2   diamond's size is measured by carat weight. There are 100 points in a carat and
3   142 carats in an ounce. Each point above 1 carat is more valuable than each point
4   below 1 carat. Thus, a stone that weighs more than 1 carat is more valuable per
5   point than a stone that is smaller than 1 carat.
6   The scale used for rating a diamond's color begins with "D," which means the
7   stone is absolutely colorless and therefore most valuable. "E" and "F" are almost
8   colorless. All three are good for investments. A stone rated between "G" and "J" is
9   good for jewelry. After that the stones take on a slightly yellowish color, which
10 gets deeper as the grade declines.
11   The clarity of a stone is determined by its lack of carbon spots, inner flaws, and
12 surface blemishes. While most of these are invisible to the unaided eye, they do
13 affect the diamond's brilliance. For jewelry, a diamond rated VVS1 (very very
14 slight imperfections) is as close to flawless as one will find. After that the scale
15 goes to VVS2, VS1, VS2, SI1, SI2, I1, I2, and so on.
16   The final characteristic is cut. When shaped (round, oval, emerald, marquise,
17 pear, or heart), the diamond should be faceted so that light is directed into the
18 depths of the prism and then reflected outward again. A well-cut diamond will
19 separate the light into different colors when reflected. Only stones of similar shape
20 should have their reflective qualities compared, as some shapes are more reflective
21 than others. For example, the round shape is the most reflective.

31. The passage is mainly about
   (A) the cost of diamonds
   (B) qualities affecting diamond value
   (C) how to judge an expensive diamond
   (D) buying diamonds for jewelry

32. What can be said about a 1-carat diamond?
   (A) It has 100 points.
   (B) It weighs an ounce.
   (C) It costs twice as much as a smaller one.
   (D) It has the same quality as a half-carat diamond.

33. A stone that has no color at all is rated
   (A) A
   (B) Z
   (C) D
   (D) J

34. It can be inferred from the passage that a stone rated "H" is
   (A) good for jewelry
   (B) good for investment
   (C) very colorful
   (D) deep yellow

35. Clarity of a stone
   (A) is invisible to the unaided eye
   (B) affects the diamond's brilliance
   (C) has spots, flaws, and blemishes
   (D) is determined by imperfections

36. It can be inferred from the passage that a diamond which is flawless
   (A) is not used for jewelry
   (B) is rated VVS1
   (C) is very large
   (D) is invisible to the unaided eye

37. Diamonds reflect
   (A) the prism
   (B) the depths
   (C) the facets
   (D) light

38. Two diamonds of the same shape
   (A) have the same value
   (B) can be compared for reflective quality
   (C) are usually the same weight
   (D) are equally brilliant

GO ON TO THE NEXT PAGE

Questions 39– 46

1   It was once believed that being overweight was healthy, but nowadays few
2 people subscribe to this viewpoint. While many people are fighting the battle
3 to reduce weight, studies are being conducted concerning the appetite and how it is
4 controlled by both emotional and biochemical factors. Some of the conclusions of
5 these studies may give insights into how to deal with weight problems. For
6 example, when several hundred people were asked about their eating habits in
7 times of stress, 44 percent said they reacted to stressful situations by eating.
8 Further investigations with both humans and animals indicated that it is not food
9 which relieves tension but rather the act of chewing.
10   A test in which subjects were blindfolded showed that obese people have a
11 keener sense of taste and crave more flavorful food than nonobese people. When
12 deprived of the variety and intensity of tastes, obese people are not satisfied and
13 consequently eat more to fulfill this need. Blood samples taken from people after
14 they were shown a picture of food revealed that overweight people reacted with an
15 increase in blood insulin, a chemical associated with appetite. This did not happen
16 to average-weight people.
17   In another experiment, results showed that certain people have a specific,
18 biologically induced hunger for carbohydrates. Eating carbohydrates raises the
19 level of serotonin, a neurotransmitter in the brain. Enough serotonin produces a
20 sense of satiation, and hunger for carbohydrates subsides.
21   Exercise has been recommended as an important part of a weight-loss program.
22 However, it has been found that mild exercise, such as using the stairs instead of
23 the elevator, is better in the long run than taking on a strenuous program, such as
24 jogging, which many people find difficult to continue over long periods of time and
25 which also increases appetite.

39. The word "crave" in line 11, can best be replaced with
    (A) devour
    (B) absorb
    (C) season
    (D) desire

40. It can be inferred from the passage that
    (A) overweight people are tense
    (B) thin people don't eat when under stress
    (C) weight watchers should chew on something inedible when tense
    (D) 56 percent of the population isn't overweight

41. It can be inferred from the passage that
    (A) thin people don't enjoy food
    (B) a variety of foods and strong flavors satisfies heavy people
    (C) overweight people have an abnormal sense of taste
    (D) deprivation of food makes people fat

42. According to the passage, insulin
    (A) increases in the bloodstream when people eat large amounts of food
    (B) can be used to lessen the appetite
    (C) causes a chemical reaction when food is seen
    (D) levels don't change in average-weight people who see food

GO ON TO THE NEXT PAGE

43. It can be inferred that for certain people
    (A) eating carbohydrates eliminates hunger
    (B) carbohydrates biologically induce hunger
    (C) carbohydrates don't satisfy a hungry person
    (D) carbohydrates subside when serotonin is produced

44. What can be said about serotonin?
    (A) It is a chemical that increases the appetite.
    (B) Only certain people produce it in their brains.
    (C) It tells the brain when a person is full.
    (D) It neurotransmits carbohydrates to the brain.

45. In order to lose weight, it would be a good idea for heavy people to
    (A) jog 3 miles daily and chew on carrot sticks
    (B) walk up stairs and look at pictures of food
    (C) eat plenty of chewy carbohydrates
    (D) avoid stressful situations and eat spicy foods

46. Which one of the following exercises might be best for an overweight person to engage in daily?
    (A) an evening walk
    (B) a long swim
    (C) cross-country skiing
    (D) 10-mile bicycle rides

GO ON TO THE NEXT PAGE

Questions 47–53

1   In some rural agricultural societies, the collection of available fuel such as
2   firewood, dung cake, and agricultural waste can take 200 to 300 person-days per
3   year. As well as being time consuming, the typical patterns of collection lead to
4   deforestation, soil erosion, and ecological imbalances. In the future, experts predict
5   that even if food supplies are adequate for rural populations, fuel supplies for
6   domestic use may not be.
7   In the light of such considerations, a team in India has developed a solar oven
8   for home use. The oven is cheaply constructed, easily operated, and extremely
9   energy efficient. The device consists of an inner and outer metal box, a top cover,
10   and two panes of plain glass. The inner box is painted black to absorb maximum
11   solar radiation. The space between the two boxes is filled with an insulating
12   material, such as rice husks, which are easily available and which, because of their
13   high silicon content, neither attract insects nor rot easily. Other easily available
14   materials for insulation are ground nutshells or coconut shells. An adjustable
15   mirror mounted on one side of the oven box reflects the sunlight into the interior,
16   boosting the temperatures by 15–30 degrees Celsius. This is most useful during the
17   winter when the sun is lower. Inside the oven, a temperature between 80 and 120
18   degrees Celsius above ambient temperature can be maintained. This is
19   sufficient to cook food gradually but surely. Trials have shown that all typical food
20   dishes can be prepared in this solar device without loss of taste or nutrition.

47. This passage is mainly about
(A) deforestation in the rural agricultural societies
(B) use of rice husks in an insulation material
(C) design and use of a solar oven
(D) maintenance of temperature in a solar oven

48. Which one of the following reasons is NOT mentioned for using rice husks as insulating material?
(A) They are easily available.
(B) They don't attract insects.
(C) They don't rot easily.
(D) They reflect sunlight.

49. According to the passage, the use of an adjustable mirror increases the oven temperature by
(A) 80–120 degrees Celsius
(B) at least 80 degrees Celsius
(C) up to 30 degrees Celsius
(D) up to 15 degrees Celsius

50. Where would this kind of oven be most useful?
(A) on a camping trip
(B) in a busy restaurant
(C) in a rural community
(D) in a cold wintery climate

51. Which of the following is NOT mentioned as a typical fuel in parts of rural agricultural societies?
(A) firewood
(B) dung cake
(C) solar power
(D) agricultural waste

52. According to the passage, the adjustable mirror is most useful
(A) at midday
(B) during the winter
(C) when firewood is lacking
(D) to improve taste and nutrition

53. It can be inferred from the passage that the solar oven might prove most useful to a family in an agricultural society because
(A) it will save time
(B) it is easy to construct
(C) it does not attract insects
(D) it cooks all kinds of food

GO ON TO THE NEXT PAGE

Questions 54–60

1   Many folk cures which have been around for centuries may be more therapeutic
2   than previously suspected. A case in point is that of penicillin. Alexander Fleming
3   did not just randomly choose cheese molds to study when he discovered this very
4   important bacteria-killing substance. Moldy cheese was frequently given to
5   patients as a remedy for illness at one time. Fleming just isolated what it was about
6   the cheese which cured the patients.
7   In parts of South America, a powder obtained from grinding sugar cane is used
8   for healing infections in wounds and ulcers. This usage may date back to
9   pre-Colombian times. Experiments carried out on several hundred patients indicate
10   that ordinary sugar in high concentrations is lethal to bacteria. Its suction effect
11   eliminates dead cells, and it generates a glasslike layer which protects the wound
12   and ensures healing.
13   Another example of folk medicine which scientists are investigating is that of
14   Arab fishermen who rub their wounds with a venomous catfish to quicken healing.
15   This catfish excretes a gellike slime which scientists have found to contain
16   antibiotics, a coagulant that helps close injured blood vessels, anti-inflammatory
17   agents, and a chemical that directs production of a gluelike material that aids
18   healing.
19   It is hoped that by documenting these folk remedies and experimenting to see if
20   results are indeed beneficial, an analysis of the substances can be made, and
21   synthetic substances can be developed for human consumption.

54. This passage is mainly about
    (A) using folk medicines in place of modern medicines
    (B) antibiotics in the field of medicine
    (C) the validity of folk remedies and their use for advances in modern medicine
    (D) isolating antibiotics in cheese, sugar, and slime

55. It can be inferred from the passage that Alexander Fleming
    (A) discovered moldy cheese
    (B) isolated infectious patients
    (C) suspected medicinal properties of mold
    (D) enjoyed eating cheese

56. According to the passage,
    (A) bacteria feed on sugar
    (B) sugar kills unhealthy cells
    (C) glass is formed from sugar
    (D) sugar promotes healing

57. The gellike substance which promotes healing comes from
    (A) catfish bodies
    (B) Arab fishermen
    (C) coagulants
    (D) catfish venom

58. Which one of the following is NOT an important quality of the catfish slime?
    (A) It prohibits inflammation.
    (B) It fights bacteria.
    (C) It stops bleeding.
    (D) It produces mold.

GO ON TO THE NEXT PAGE

59. According to the passage, why is it important to study folk medicine?
    (A) to document cultural heritages
    (B) to perpetuate superstitions
    (C) to experiment with synthetic substances
    (D) to advance modern medical practices

60. In what way are cheese molds, sugar, and catfish slime similar?
    (A) They cause blood clots.
    (B) They fight bacteria.
    (C) They heal wounds.
    (D) They eliminate dead cells.

THIS IS THE END OF SECTION 3 OF PRACTICE TEST 1.

IF YOU FINISH BEFORE TIME IS UP, CHECK YOUR WORK
ON SECTION 3 ONLY.
DO NOT READ OR WORK ON ANY OTHER SECTION OF THE TEST.

PRACTICE TEST 2

TEST OF WRITTEN ENGLISH (TWE)
ESSAY QUESTION

Time – 30 minutes

DO NOT TURN THE PAGE UNTIL THE SUPERVISOR TELLS YOU TO DO SO.

The TWE essay question follows. You will have 30 minutes to plan, write, and correct your essay. Your essay will be graded on its overall quality.

1. When the Supervisor tells you to begin, turn the page and read the Essay Question carefully.
2. Think before you write. Making notes may help you to organize your essay. Below the Essay Question is a space for notes. Use only this area to outline your essay or make notes.
3. Write only on this topic. If you write an essay on a different topic, it will not be scored. Write clearly and precisely. Use examples to support your ideas. How well you write is much more important than how much you write, but to cover the topic adequately, you may want to write more than one paragraph.
4. Start writing your essay on the first line of Essay Page Side 3. Use Side 4 if you need more space. Extra paper will not be provided. Write neatly and legibly. Do not skip lines. Do not write in very large letters or leave large margins.
5. Check your work. Allow a few minutes before time is called to read over your essay and make small changes.
6. After 30 minutes, the Supervisor will tell you to stop. You must stop writing and put your pencil down. If you continue to write, it will be considered cheating.

STOP! WAIT FOR THE SUPERVISOR'S INSTRUCTIONS.

COMPOSITION

Time – 30 minutes

Directions: Write a composition on a separate sheet of paper.

It has been said that "if the earth is to be saved from an environmental catastrophe, we shall all have to make major changes in our life-styles." Discuss at least three measures individuals can take to help prevent damage to our world.

THIS SPACE MAY BE USED FOR NOTES.

SECTION 1
LISTENING COMPREHENSION

In this section of the test, you will have an opportunity to demonstrate your ability to understand spoken English. There are three parts to this section, with special directions for each part. Do <u>not</u> read ahead or turn the pages while the directions are being read. Do <u>not</u> take notes or write in your workbook at any time.

Part A

<u>Directions</u>: For each question in Part A, you will hear a short sentence. Each sentence will be spoken just once. The sentences you hear will <u>not</u> be written out for you.

After you hear a sentence, read the four choices in your workbook, marked (A), (B), (C), and (D), and decide which <u>one</u> is closest in meaning to the sentence you heard. Then, on your answer sheet, find the number of the question and fill in the space that corresponds to the letter of the answer you have chosen. Fill in the space completely so that the letter inside the oval cannot be seen.

Listen to an example.

On the recording, you hear: *The new observatory is nothing less than outstanding.*

In your workbook, you read: (A) The new observatory is excellent.
(B) There is nothing outstanding to observe.
(C) You must stand outside to make the observance.
(D) His new observations are more outstanding than usual.

Sample Answer
● Ⓑ Ⓒ Ⓓ

The man said, "The new observatory is nothing less than outstanding." Sentence (A), "The new observatory is excellent," is closest in meaning to what the man said. Therefore, the correct choice is (A).

NOW WE WILL BEGIN PART A WITH QUESTION 1.

GO ON TO THE NEXT PAGE ➤

1. (A) Peter asked the waiter to bring in his friend.
   (B) Peter asked the waiter for the bill.
   (C) Bill and Peter asked the waiter for a table.
   (D) Peter ordered a meal from the waiter.

2. (A) David had a good solution for his friend.
   (B) David solved his friend's problems.
   (C) A good friend of David's showed him the problems.
   (D) A good friend found an answer to David's problems.

3. (A) We couldn't finish on time for Joyce.
   (B) Joyce enabled us to meet her in time.
   (C) We were capable of meeting Joyce's train.
   (D) Joyce wasn't able to save our place in line.

4. (A) If Diana wants to wash the car, she will.
   (B) Let Diana wash the car, since she is willing.
   (C) Since you asked Diana to wash the car, she will.
   (D) Why don't you ask Diana to wash the car?

5. (A) Lisa's wallet must be at my place.
   (B) Lisa doesn't know where her billfold is.
   (C) Lisa's billfold was lost on the bus.
   (D) Lisa was put in the wrong place.

6. (A) Since you were in New York, you must have visited the Statue of Liberty.
   (B) If you go to New York, you should visit the Statue of Liberty.
   (C) I think you should have visited the Statue of Liberty while you were in New York.
   (D) Did you visit the Statue of Liberty while you were in New York?

7. (A) We don't have to buy a new Ford.
   (B) We don't have enough money to buy a new car.
   (C) We shouldn't offer to buy a new car.
   (D) We can't buy four new cars!

8. (A) If you can't see the point, tell me.
   (B) If you don't understand, you should ask.
   (C) If you're unable to come, please let me know.
   (D) You should shake the ointment, if you ask me.

9. (A) Has she really earned that many points?
   (B) I didn't realize she'd put on so much weight.
   (C) It is true that she can sell grain?
   (D) She really needs to gain weight.

10. (A) People are cheerful at our house when they return from the stadium.
    (B) The stadium has clouds over it on most days.
    (C) The noise from the stadium is too loud.
    (D) The stadium is near enough to our house that you can hear the people shouting.

11. (A) The flight attendant and the passengers got on the airplane.
    (B) The flight attendant greeted the passengers as they boarded the plane.
    (C) The flight attendant thanked the passengers for getting on board.
    (D) The bored passengers were met by the flight attendant of the plane.

GO ON TO THE NEXT PAGE

12. (A) There's nothing certain about Jane's success.
    (B) Jane's determination has nothing to do with her success.
    (C) Jane certainly is determined to be successful.
    (D) Jane's success has never been determined for certain.

13. (A) Mary only passed this test because she scored higher than the others.
    (B) Mary's score was barely enough to pass.
    (C) Only on this test was Mary's score high enough.
    (D) Mary was the only one to pass this test.

14. (A) Susan, like Scott, finds it difficult to study mathematics.
    (B) Mathematics is harder for Susan than for Scott.
    (C) Susan studied less than Scott for the math class.
    (D) The math class was harder for Susan than for Scott.

15. (A) The newspaper that came is mine!
    (B) Shouldn't the newspaper be here by now?
    (C) Please come and check the newspaper.
    (D) Please find out whether or not the newspaper is here.

16. (A) They didn't want to stay home or go to the movies.
    (B) They prefer staying home to going to the movies.
    (C) They don't like to go to the movies.
    (D) They prefer watching movies at home to going out.

17. (A) Betty was very late.
    (B) It was a two-hour wait for Betty.
    (C) Betty was over at Elliott's for two hours.
    (D) Elliott hates to be at Betty's for more than two hours.

18. (A) William sold three of them.
    (B) William isn't very well yet.
    (C) William's language is advanced.
    (D) William was not quiet when he was younger.

19. (A) We were used to playing tennis.
    (B) Now we like to play tennis.
    (C) We've been playing tennis longer than we've been watching it.
    (D) We stopped playing tennis when we got injured.

20. (A) They forgot to charge for breakfast.
    (B) Guests at the hotel must pay additionally for breakfast.
    (C) Breakfast is not served at the hotel.
    (D) Do not pay for breakfast at that hotel.

GO ON TO THE NEXT PAGE

Part B

<u>Directions</u>: In Part B you will hear short conversations between two people. After each conversation, a third person will ask a question about what was said. You will hear each conversation and question about it only <u>one</u> time. After you hear a conversation and the question about it, read the four possible answers in your workbook and decide which <u>one</u> is the best answer to the question you heard. Then, on your answer sheet, find the number of the question and fill in the space that corresponds to the letter of the answer you have chosen.

Listen to an example.

On the recording, you hear: (Man)   *I think I'll have the curtains changed.*
                            (First Woman)   *They are a bit worn.*

                            (Second Woman) *What does the woman mean?*

In your workbook, you read: (A) She thinks every bit of change is important.

Sample Answer

                              (B) She wants to wear them.
                              (C) She thinks they've been worn enough.
                              (D) She thinks they are in bad condition.

You learn from the conversation that the woman thinks the curtains are worn. The best answer to the question "What does the woman mean?" is (D), "She thinks they are in bad condition." Therefore, the correct choice is (D).

NOW WE WILL BEGIN PART B WITH THE FIRST CONVERSATION.

GO ON TO THE NEXT PAGE ➡

21. (A) The students asked people to make them.
    (B) The students asked people to buy them.
    (C) The students asked people to post them.
    (D) The students asked people to contribute them.

22. (A) Making salad.
    (B) Tossing balls.
    (C) Playing a board game.
    (D) Designing squares.

23. (A) He couldn't get a ticket.
    (B) He bought a ticket weeks ago.
    (C) He reserved a ticket for tomorrow.
    (D) The concert has been canceled.

24. (A) Mr. Brown isn't good at repairing TVs.
    (B) The TV doesn't need fixing.
    (C) The TV cannot be fixed.
    (D) He can repair the TV himself.

25. (A) She's always hungry.
    (B) She's full of apples.
    (C) She's on a diet.
    (D) She's pleased he packed them.

26. (A) Nancy will want to write her own notes.
    (B) She can't imagine Nancy writing notes.
    (C) She doesn't want to lend her notes to Nancy.
    (D) She thinks Nancy won't be able to read the notes.

27. (A) Tom and Lucy getting standing-room-only tickets.
    (B) Tom and Lucy stopping traffic.
    (C) Tom and Lucy being stuck in traffic.
    (D) Tom and Lucy standing outside in the snow.

28. (A) Jennifer has to look for a spring.
    (B) Jennifer must learn those facts in order to graduate.
    (C) Jennifer has faced many problems this spring.
    (D) Jennifer must accept not being able to graduate.

29. (A) She set the pail on the flowers.
    (B) She bought light blue writing paper.
    (C) She had to water the flowers.
    (D) She got the blue flowers behind the station.

30. (A) He is indifferent about the chemistry class.
    (B) He doesn't mind the chemistry class.
    (C) He isn't careful in chemistry class.
    (D) He doesn't like his chemistry lessons.

31. (A) Her mother likes the potato salad.
    (B) Her mother makes better potato salad.
    (C) Her mother says there's never enough potato salad.
    (D) Her mother has never tasted the potato salad.

32. (A) Sam doesn't like parties.
    (B) Sam wishes he weren't at the party.
    (C) Sam's personality makes parties more enjoyable.
    (D) Sam lives above the place where the party is.

33. (A) During Christmas.
    (B) The last week before Christmas.
    (C) About two weeks ago.
    (D) Last week.

34. (A) The man is blind.
    (B) It is snowing very hard.
    (C) She doesn't know if it's snowing.
    (D) She can't get across the street.

35. (A) He called for the string.
    (B) He cut his finger.
    (C) He fingered the tie.
    (D) He remembered the box.

GO ON TO THE NEXT PAGE

405

Part C

Directions: In this part of the test, you will hear longer conversations and talks. After each conversation or talk, you will be asked some questions. You will hear the talks and conversations and the questions about them only <u>one</u> time. They will <u>not</u> be written out for you.

After you hear a question, read the four possible answers in your workbook and decide which <u>one</u> is the best answer to the question you heard. Then, on your answer sheet, find the number of the question and fill in the space that corresponds to the letter of the answer you have chosen. Answer all questions on the basis of what is <u>stated</u> or <u>implied</u> by the speakers in the talk or conversation.

Here is an example.

On the recording, you hear: *Listen to a conversation between a professor and a student.*

(First Woman)	*Would you please type this paper? I can't read your handwriting.*
(Man)	*I'm sorry, Professor Mills. I don't have a typewriter, and besides, I can't type.*
(First Woman)	*Well, rewrite it then, but be sure to make it clear.*

Now listen to a sample question.

(Second Woman) *What does the professor want the man to do?*

In your workbook, you read: (A) Buy a typewriter.
(B) Read his handwriting.
(C) Clear the papers away.
(D) Rewrite the paper.

Sample Answer

The best answer to the question "What does the professor want the man to do?" is (D), "Rewrite the paper." Therefore, the correct choice is (D).

Remember, you are not allowed to take notes or write in your workbook.

NOW WE WILL BEGIN PART C.

36. (A) The library.
    (B) A university classroom.
    (C) The reserve desk.
    (D) The microfiche room.

37. (A) They are no longer published.
    (B) They're on microfiche.
    (C) They cannot be found in the library.
    (D) They must be purchased at the bookstore.

38. (A) They cannot be taken out of the library.
    (B) They are out of print.
    (C) They have an asterisk.
    (D) They must be read before the following class.

39. (A) The librarian can teach her.
    (B) She can read the microfiche.
    (C) The instructions are on the folder.
    (D) There are instruction pamphlets in the machine room.

40. (A) 100 monkeys on an island.
    (B) Islands off the coast of Japan.
    (C) A study showing the interconnectedness of life.
    (D) The Japanese sweet potato monkey.

41. (A) Copy the behavior of other monkeys.
    (B) Eat sweet potatoes in a particular way.
    (C) Contact monkeys 200 miles away.
    (D) Teach monkeys on other islands.

42. (A) Japan.
    (B) 200 miles from Japan.
    (C) An island off Japan.
    (D) A sweet potato farm.

43. (A) It was not typical of monkeys.
    (B) The other monkeys refused to learn it.
    (C) It was difficult to learn.
    (D) Monkeys learned it at different rates.

44. (A) At Mary's.
    (B) At Jeff's.
    (C) At Mary's parents'.
    (D) At Jennifer and Lisa's.

45. (A) Lisa.
    (B) Jennifer.
    (C) Mary's parents.
    (D) Jeff.

46. (A) They've never met each other.
    (B) They knew Mary's parents.
    (C) They live together.
    (D) They need Jeff's help.

GO ON TO THE NEXT PAGE

47. (A) They are roommates.
    (B) They are married.
    (C) They are classmates.
    (D) They are friends.

48. (A) Improving your ability to perform sports skills.
    (B) Carrying through a sport-specific motion.
    (C) Ingraining patterns in your subconscious movement memory.
    (D) Improving arm muscles for better performance.

49. (A) Repeating the movement.
    (B) Memorizing the pattern.
    (C) Performing with less effort.
    (D) Applying greater speed.

50. (A) It is less important than strengthening the larger muscles.
    (B) It is time consuming.
    (C) It reduces your risk of injury.
    (D) It is not part of most athletes' fitness program.

THIS IS THE END OF THE LISTENING COMPREHENSION SECTION OF PRACTICE TEST 2.

THE NEXT PART OF THE TEST IS SECTION 2. TURN TO THE
DIRECTIONS FOR SECTION 2 IN YOUR WORKBOOK,
READ THEM, AND BEGIN WORK.
DO NOT READ OR WORK ON ANY OTHER SECTION OF THE TEST.

SECTION 2
STRUCTURE AND WRITTEN EXPRESSION

Time – 25 minutes

This section is designed to measure your ability to recognize language that is appropriate for standard written English. There are two types of questions in this section, with special directions for each type.

Directions: Questions 1–15 are incomplete sentences. Beneath each sentence you will see four words or phrases marked (A), (B), (C), and (D). Choose the <u>one</u> word or phrase that best completes the sentence. Then, on your answer sheet, find the number of the question and fill in the space that corresponds to the letter of the answer you have chosen. Fill in the space so that the letter inside the oval cannot be seen.

Example   John Le Carré ----- for his novels concerning espionage.

   (A) famous
   (B) has fame
   (C) is famous
   (D) famed for

Sample Answer
Ⓐ Ⓑ ● Ⓓ

The sentence should read, "John Le Carré is famous for his novels concerning espionage." Therefore, you should choose answer (C).

After you read the directions, begin work on the questions.

1. ----- infinitely large number of undiscovered galaxies.
   (A) An
   (B) There are an
   (C) From an
   (D) Since there are

2. The Great Wall of China is perhaps the most awe inspiring ----- the great structures of the world.
   (A) that
   (B) with
   (C) among
   (D) alone

3. No matter -----, Mozart was an accomplished composer while still a child.
   (A) how remarkable it seems
   (B) how it seems remarkable
   (C) how seems it remarkable
   (D) how it remarkable seems

4. Novelist Jane Austen ----- the first twenty-six years of her life in the village of Steventon, Hampshire.
   (A) living
   (B) was lived
   (C) lived
   (D) who lived

5. By far ----- of Saudi Arabia is oil.
   (A) it is the most important export
   (B) the most important export is
   (C) that is the most important export
   (D) the most important export

6. Yellowstone National Park's attractions include the famous Old Faithful geyser, vast forests, plentiful wildlife, and -----.
   (A) campgrounds are well maintained
   (B) well-maintained campgrounds
   (C) campgrounds are maintained well
   (D) maintains campgrounds well

7. ----- the Dartmoor ewe and the Dumpy hen, the Tamworth pig is a rare breed of farm animal.
   (A) How
   (B) Like
   (C) The
   (D) Even

GO ON TO THE NEXT PAGE

8. ----- often serve as places of public entertainment and festivals, they can also be places where people can find peace and solitude.
(A) Even though city parks
(B) City parks
(C) City parks that
(D) There are city parks which

9. ----- in the planet Uranus dates from its discovery in 1781 is not surprising.
(A) That scientific interest
(B) It was scientific interest
(C) Though scientific interest
(D) Scientific interest

10. The Himalaya Mountains are the -----.
(A) height of world extensive ranges
(B) ranges of the most extensive world
(C) world's most extensive ranges
(D) extensive ranges of the world

11. -----, Luxor did not reach preeminence until about 2,000 B.C.
(A) Many centuries earlier it was founded
(B) The city founded centuries earlier
(C) Although founded many centuries earlier
(D) Founding the city centuries earlier

12. Early sailing ships, ----- sometimes in uncharted seas, faced many hazards in reaching their destination.
(A) navigating
(B) were navigated
(C) navigate
(D) and navigates

13. Not until about a century after Julius Caesar landed in Britain ----- actually conquer the island.
(A) the Romans did
(B) did the Romans
(C) the Romans
(D) Romans that

14. ----- is as simple as it looks.
(A) Adobe houses building
(B) Adobe houses which are built
(C) Building adobe houses
(D) Adobe houses built

15. Square-rigged ships, ----- high speeds only when traveling with the trade winds, are not used commercially nowadays.
(A) can attain
(B) when attaining
(C) they can attain
(D) which can attain

Directions: In questions 16–40 each sentence has four underlined words or phrases. The four underlined parts of the sentence are marked (A), (B), (C), and (D). Identify the one underlined word or phrase that must be changed in order for the sentence to be correct. Then, on your answer sheet, find the number of the question and fill in the space that corresponds to the letter of the answer you have chosen.

Example   The balloonists who remained aloft in the air radioed the control center.
                         A   B   C   D

Sample Answer
(A)(B)●(D)

The sentence should read, "The balloonists who remained aloft radioed the control center."
Therefore, you should choose answer (C).

After you read the directions, begin work on the questions.

16. Drying food by means of solar energy is a ancient process applied wherever food
    A   B   C   D
and climatic conditions make it possible.

17. An itch resulting when a nerve that can carry pain is only slightly stimulated.
              A   B   C   D

18. A healthy person snores most because the membrane in the nose becomes dry.
       A   B   C   D

GO ON TO THE NEXT PAGE

19. For they, the most rewarding shipwreck found was the HMS Associated.
     A   B   C   D

20. America's first satellites exploded before it had risen three and a half feet off the
                 A   B   C   D
ground.

21. The Concorde can fly across the Atlantic without refueling and carrying 11 tons
                A   B   C
of freight.
D

22. Most babies will grow up to be as cleverer as their parents.
   A   B   C   D

23. With animals both humans, chewing helps relieve tension.
 A   B   C   D

24. Diane Arbus's unusual and controversial work includes photograph of sixties
          A   B   C   D
celebrities.

25. It should not be assume that the lower the price, the happier the buyer.
         A   B   C   D

26. To help policymakers and another, the U.S. government spends as much as
 A   B   C
$1.4 billion a year in collecting statistics.
D

27. The Victorian constructions of Haight-Ashbury are among the fewer architectural
                               A   B
survivors of the San Francisco earthquake in 1906.
C   D

28. One out of every eight balloons in the world are launched at Albuquerque, New
 A   B   C   D
Mexico.

29. At space camp, youngsters go through concentrated astronaut training but shuttle
A   B   C   D
simulations.

30. Sprinkler system have proven to be the most effective means of fighting hotel fires.
     A   B   C   D

31. For more than 450 years, Mexico City has been the economic, culture, and political
    A   B
center of the Mexican people.
   C   D

GO ON TO THE NEXT PAGE ➤

32. The rings of Saturn are so distant to be seen from Earth without a telescope.
         A   B   C   D

33. In 1927, Charles Lindbergh completed a solo crossing of the Atlantic Ocean in its
    A   B   C   D
    aircraft, the *Spirit of St. Louis.*

34. There is estimated that the Orion nebula contains enough matter to form 10,000
        A   B   C
    stars.
    D

35. Lack of animal protein in the human diet is a serious cause of the malnutrition.
        A   B   C   D

36. Measle has not yet been eradicated because of controversy concerning
        A   B   C   D
    immunization.

37. The firing of bricks and tiles for use in the build industry requires large amounts
            A   B   C   D
    of fuel.

38. The cinecamera has fastly become obsolete with the invention of video recording
    A   B   C   D
    technology.

39. Plants known so adaptogens improve human vitality, eliminate stress, and sustain
                  A   B   C
    life in the most arduous conditions.
                            D

40. A new battery for domestic appliances in the house is as thin and flexible as paper.
                  A   B   C   D

THIS IS THE END OF SECTION 2 OF PRACTICE TEST 2.

IF YOU FINISH BEFORE TIME IS UP, CHECK YOUR WORK
ON SECTION 2 ONLY.
DO NOT READ OR WORK ON ANY OTHER SECTION OF THE TEST.

STOP STOP STOP STOP STOP STOP STOP

SECTION 3
VOCABULARY AND READING COMPREHENSION

Time – 45 minutes

This section is designed to measure your comprehension of standard written English. There are two types of questions in this section, with special directions for each type.

Directions: In questions 1–30 each sentence has an underlined word or phrase. Below each sentence are four other words or phrases, marked (A), (B), (C), and (D). You are to choose the one word or phrase that best keeps the meaning of the original sentence if it is substituted for the underlined word or phrase. Then, on your answer sheet, find the number of the question and fill in the space that corresponds to the letter you have chosen. Fill in the space so that the letter inside the oval cannot be seen.

Example   Many women have made a mark on American art since the early 1800s.
    (A) target for
    (B) dedication to
    (C) contribution to
    (D) degree of

Sample Answer

The best answer is (C) because "Many women have made a contribution to American art since the early 1800s" is closest in meaning to the original sentence. Therefore, you should choose answer (C).

After you read the directions, begin work on the questions.

1. Cast iron covers for street holes were originally decorated to provide sure footing for horses.
    (A) real
    (B) firm
    (C) kind
    (D) fine

2. Coral needs strong currents that keep the water temperature around it ideal for its growth.
    (A) waves
    (B) tides
    (C) pressures
    (D) streams

3. In Venice even the buildings of the common quarters are often beautified with small carvings.
    (A) created
    (B) described
    (C) adorned
    (D) engineered

4. Snake venom can be vacuum dried and used for the production of antivenin serum.
    (A) potion
    (B) saliva
    (C) poison
    (D) flesh

5. The root system of the water hyacinth acts as a filter by removing suspended specks from the water.
    (A) portions
    (B) beams
    (C) debris
    (D) particles

6. The whale's inexplicable predilection for beaching itself is the second greatest threat to its survival.
    (A) unexplainable
    (B) unusual
    (C) unforgettable
    (D) essential

7. The use of flags as symbols of national identity began to develop a thousand years ago.
    (A) signs
    (B) plans
    (C) codes
    (D) goals

8. The problem was caused by a malfunction in the mechanism used to release the parachute.
    (A) disengage
    (B) relent
    (C) liberate
    (D) rescue

GO ON TO THE NEXT PAGE ▶

9. The microtelephone is a miniaturized telephone transmitter and receiver that can be <u>inserted</u> in the ear.
   (A) attached
   (B) impaled
   (C) heard
   (D) placed

10. Because animals such as hedgehogs, shrews and moles live on insects, they are very <u>beneficial</u> to humans.
    (A) distressing
    (B) helpful
    (C) forgiving
    (D) careful

11. Charles Wheatstone invented the <u>concept</u> of three-dimensional drawing in 1838.
    (A) model
    (B) condition
    (C) notion
    (D) thought

12. The <u>task</u> of note taking in Braille is fatiguing and time consuming.
    (A) reading
    (B) chore
    (C) stroke
    (D) practicing

13. Wheezing is thought to occur when there is a <u>narrowing</u> of airways within the lungs.
    (A) enveloping
    (B) respiration
    (C) agitation
    (D) constricting

14. When a magnet is <u>immersed</u> in liquid oxygen, its pulling power is intensified.
    (A) exposed
    (B) submerged
    (C) dropped
    (D) dissolved

15. George Gershwin gathered <u>motifs</u> for his opera *Porgy and Bess* while living in Charleston.
    (A) themes
    (B) support
    (C) talent
    (D) money

16. Bivalve mollusks are widely <u>distributed</u> in both marine and fresh water.
    (A) invested
    (B) detailed
    (C) dispersed
    (D) located

17. The arms race, conducted in the <u>quest</u> for security, has itself become a greater source of insecurity.
    (A) need
    (B) program
    (C) perception
    (D) search

18. Chromosomes usually <u>adhere</u> to each other in most cell stages.
    (A) adjust
    (B) move
    (C) cling
    (D) come

19. In today's technical world, language needs to be <u>compatible with</u> both humans and machines.
    (A) in accord with
    (B) translated to
    (C) compared with
    (D) disclosed to

20. Cellulose is the most <u>abundant</u> organic compound in nature.
    (A) varied
    (B) plentiful
    (C) discrete
    (D) disruptive

21. Many survivors of airplane crashes <u>subsequently</u> die because rescue teams have difficulty in locating the plane.
    (A) unfortunately
    (B) necessarily
    (C) usually
    (D) later

22. Milk production may have been the first purpose for which sheep were <u>domesticated</u>.
    (A) herded
    (B) housed
    (C) fenced
    (D) tamed

23. The polar bear's adaptation to its environment may have been achieved by combining a <u>state</u> of hibernation with one of physical activity.
    (A) system
    (B) condition
    (C) portion
    (D) position

GO ON TO THE NEXT PAGE

24. The main routes used by the pony express were equipped with stops for food and lodging.
(A) stables
(B) shelter
(C) drinks
(D) sleep

25. Architects must take noise levels into consideration when designing an auditorium.
(A) into account
(B) into view
(C) seriously
(D) positively

26. Many dangerous areas had to be reconnoitered by pioneers crossing the Western plains.
(A) set aside
(B) entered into
(C) scouted out
(D) sorted out

27. Light hovercrafts can traverse very effectively virtually any surface.
(A) cross
(B) dig
(C) detour
(D) elevate

28. Legend has it that people known as the Mongulala were the forebears of the Incas.
(A) dependents
(B) enemies
(C) destroyers
(D) predecessors

29. The Florida Power and Light Company serves more than two million customers.
(A) visitors
(B) clients
(C) tourists
(D) settlers

30. Feelings of ambivalence are common during courtship.
(A) cowardliness
(B) recognition
(C) adoration
(D) uncertainty

Directions: In the rest of this section you will read several passages. Each one is followed by several questions about it. For questions 31–60, you are to choose the best answer, (A), (B), (C), or (D), to each question. Then, on your answer sheet, find the number of the question and fill in the space that corresponds to the letter of the answer you have chosen.

Answer all questions following a passage on the basis of what is stated or implied in that passage.

Read the following passage.

The horse has played a little-known but very important role in the field of medicine. Horses were injected with toxins of diseases until their blood built up immunities. Then a serum was made from their blood. Serums to fight both diphtheria and tetanus were developed in this way.

Example   According to the passage, horses were given
(A) poisons from illnesses
(B) immunities to diseases
(C) diphtheria and tetanus serums
(D) medicines to fight toxins

Sample Answer
● Ⓑ Ⓒ Ⓓ

The passage states that "horses were injected with toxins of diseases." Therefore, you should choose answer (A).

After you read the directions, begin work on the questions.

GO ON TO THE NEXT PAGE

Questions 31–35

1   The debt of lawn tennis to its French origins is illustrated in the unusual scoring
2   system. This system probably stems from the habit of betting on individual points
3   by the players or supporters. A game was worth one *denier*, so the points were
4   worth the most convenient divisions of a *denier*. These were 15, 30, and 45 *sous*.
5   In time, the latter became 40.
6   Deuce, when both players have reached 40 in a game, is a corruption of the
7   French *à deux*, meaning "both." This may refer to both players having the same
8   score – or to the fact that a player will need to take both the next two points to win.
9   The term (as *dewce*) was first known in England in 1598.
10   The word "love," which means nil, may well come from the French word *l'oeuf*,
11   meaning egg. The explanation for the use of the word *l'oeuf* is said to be the
12   similarity of the shape of an egg to a zero. Modern player slang for a 6 – 0 6 – 0
13   result is "egg and egg."

31. What is the main topic of this passage?
    (A) betting and its effect on the game of tennis
    (B) the corruption of the French terminology for tennis
    (C) differences in terminology for the game of tennis in England and France
    (D) the influence of the French language on the scoring system of tennis

32. It can be inferred that the word "denier" in line 3 was
    (A) a monetary unit
    (B) a point system
    (C) a division
    (D) a score

33. The term "deuce"
    (A) comes from the English word "dewce"
    (B) means that the player scored two points
    (C) is used when both players have reached a score of 40
    (D) is a corruption of the French word meaning "two"

34. In line 10, the word "love" is used to refer to
    (A) tennis fans
    (B) two points
    (C) a score of zero
    (D) a winning point

35. An example of the corruption of French in the game of tennis is the word
    (A) love
    (B) nil
    (C) both
    (D) egg

GO ON TO THE NEXT PAGE

416

Questions 36–41

1   One of the major hazards for deep-sea divers is the "bends." This condition is
2   caused by gas bubbles forming in the bloodstream if the diver ascends too rapidly.
3   The reason for this condition has to do with the saturation and desaturation of body
4   tissues with various gases. At increasingly greater depths, the diver breathes air at
5   higher pressures. This results in an increased quantity of air being dissolved in the
6   bloodstream. Different body tissues are saturated with different gases from the air
7   at different rates. When the diver ascends, oxygen is used by the body tissues,
8   carbon dioxide is released quickly, and nitrogen remains. The nitrogen needs to be
9   released gradually from the bloodstream and body tissues. If nitrogen is subjected
10 to a too rapid pressure reduction, it forms gas bubbles in the blood vessels. The
11 bubbles become trapped in the capillaries. This prevents blood and oxygen from
12 supplying necessary nutrients to body tissues, which consequently begin to die.
13   Saturation and desaturation are affected by various factors such as the depth,
14 length of time, and amount of exertion under water. There are other factors that a
15 diver must take into account when determining a safe ascent rate. These include
16 the diver's sex and body build, the number of dives undertaken within the previous
17 12 hours, the time spent at the dive location before the dive, and the composition
18 of the respiration gas.

36. The passage is mainly about
    (A) how to calculate a safe depth when diving
    (B) how to determine saturation and desaturation rates
    (C) instructions for diving safely
    (D) the factors causing the bends in divers

37. It can be inferred from the passage that
    (A) a woman is more likely to get the bends
    (B) men and women may ascend at different rates
    (C) men and women of certain athletic builds shouldn't dive
    (D) men are better divers than women

38. According to the passage, gas bubbles
    (A) trap the capillaries
    (B) are gradually released from the tissues and bloodstream
    (C) block the supply of nutrients to body tissues
    (D) are formed from compressed air

39. Which of the following does NOT affect the desaturation of body tissues?
    (A) the location of the dive
    (B) the number of previous dives
    (C) the composition of the gas being used
    (D) the amount of activity under water

40. According to the passage, the bends
    (A) is the major diving hazard
    (B) reduces pressure in the bloodstream
    (C) is a condition caused by diving too quickly
    (D) is a direct result of dying body tissues

41. According to the passage, which of the following is NOT true?
    (A) Air at higher pressure is taken in at greater depths.
    (B) More air is dissolved into the bloodstream at increasing depths.
    (C) Carbon dioxide stays in the body when the diver ascends.
    (D) Body tissues are saturated at different rates.

GO ON TO THE NEXT PAGE

Questions 42–47

1   Water scarcity is fast becoming one of the major limiting factors in world crop
2   production. In many areas, poor agricultural practices have led to increasing
3   desertification and the loss of formerly arable lands. Consequently, those plant
4   species that are well adapted to survival in dry climates are being looked at for an
5   answer in developing more efficient crops to grow on marginally arable lands.
6   Plants use several mechanisms to ensure their survival in desert environments.
7   Some involve purely mechanical and physical adaptations, such as the shape of
8   the plant's surface, smaller leaf size, and extensive root systems. Some of the
9   adaptations are related to chemical mechanisms. Many plants, such as cacti, have
10   internal gums and mucilages which give them water-retaining properties. Another
11   chemical mechanism is that of the epicuticular wax layer. This wax layer acts as
12   an impervious cover to protect the plant. It prevents excessive loss of internal
13   moisture. It also protects the plant from external aggression, which can come from
14   inorganic agents such as gases, or organic agents which include bacteria and plant
15   pests.
16   Researchers have proposed that synthetic waxes with similar protective abilities
17   could be prepared based on knowledge of desert plants. If successfully developed,
18   such a compound could be used to greatly increase a plant's ability to maintain
19   health in such adverse situations as inadequate water supply, limited fertilizer
20   availability, attack by pests, and poor storage after harvesting.

42. This passage deals mainly with
(A) desertification
(B) decreasing water supplies
(C) factors limiting crop production
(D) developing efficient plants

43. Which of the following is a mechanical or physical mechanism desert plants use?
(A) the plant's shape
(B) the small root system
(C) the vast leaf size
(D) the high water consumption

44. Which is one of the ways the epicuticular wax protects the plant?
(A) It helps the plant to avoid excessive moisture intake.
(B) It helps the plant to attack aggressors.
(C) It releases gases against plant pests.
(D) It guards against bacteria.

45. It can be inferred that synthetic simulated waxes have
(A) not been developed yet
(B) not succeeded
(C) been determined to be impervious to organic and inorganic agents
(D) the quality of causing bacteria

46. What is an example of an inorganic agent that may attack plants?
(A) bacteria
(B) insects
(C) gas
(D) pests

47. What is NOT an example of an adverse situation for crops?
(A) inadequate water
(B) insufficient fertilizer
(C) pest aggression
(D) proper storage

GO ON TO THE NEXT PAGE

Questions 48–53

1   Every year about two million people visit Mount Rushmore, where the faces of
2   four U.S. presidents were carved in granite by sculptor Gutzon Borglum and his
3   son, the late Lincoln Borglum. The creation of the Mount Rushmore monument
4   took 14 years – from 1927 to 1941 – and nearly a million dollars. These were
5   times when money was difficult to come by and many people were jobless. To
6   move the more than 400,000 tons of rock, Borglum hired laid-off workers from the
7   closed-down mines in the Black Hills area. He taught these men to dynamite, drill,
8   carve, and finish the granite as they were hanging in midair in his specially devised
9   chairs, which had many safety features. Borglum was proud of the fact that no
10 workers were killed or severely injured during the years of blasting and carving.
11   During the carving, many changes in the original design had to be made to keep
12 the carved heads free of large fissures that were uncovered. However, not all the
13 cracks could be avoided, so Borglum concocted a mixture of granite dust, white
14 lead, and linseed oil to fill them.
15   Every winter, water from melting snows gets into the fissures and expands as it
16 freezes, making the fissures bigger. Consequently, every autumn maintenance work
17 is done to refill the cracks. The repairers swing out in space over a 500-foot drop
18 and fix the monument with the same mixture that Borglum used to preserve this
19 national monument for future generations.

48. In line 12, the word "fissures" refers to
    (A) designs
    (B) cracks
    (C) heads
    (D) carvings

49. According to the passage, Borglum's son
    (A) is dead
    (B) was a president
    (C) did maintenance work
    (D) spent a million dollars

50. The men who Borglum hired were
    (A) trained sculptors
    (B) laid-off stone masons
    (C) Black Hills volunteers
    (D) unemployed miners

51. It can be inferred from the passage that
    (A) the heads are not as originally planned
    (B) the workers made mistakes when blasting
    (C) the cracks caused serious injuries
    (D) the designs had large fissures in them

52. Borglum's mixture for filling cracks was
    (A) very expensive
    (B) bought at the Black Hills mines
    (C) invented by the sculptor himself
    (D) uncovered during carving

53. Today Mount Rushmore needs
    (A) to be protected from air pollution
    (B) to be polished for tourists
    (C) to be restored during the winter
    (D) to be repaired periodically

GO ON TO THE NEXT PAGE

Questions 54–60

1 History books record that the first film with sound was *The Jazz Singer* in 1927.
2 But sound films, or "talkies," did not suddenly appear after years of silent
3 screenings. From the earliest public performances in 1896, films were
4 accompanied by music and sound effects. These were produced by a single
5 pianist, a small band, or a full-scale orchestra; large movie theaters could buy
6 sound-effects machines. Research into sound that was reproduced at exactly the
7 same time as the pictures – called "synchronized sound" – began soon after the
8 very first films were shown. With synchronized sound, characters on the movie
9 screen could sing and speak. As early as 1896, the newly invented gramophone,
10 which played a large disc carrying music and dialogue, was used as a sound
11 system. The biggest disadvantage was that the sound and pictures could become
12 unsynchronized if, for example, the gramophone needle jumped or if the speed of
13 the projector changed. This system was only effective for a single song or dialogue
14 sequence.
15   In the "sound-on-film" system, sounds were recorded as a series of marks on
16 celluloid which could be read by an optical sensor. These signals would be placed
17 on the film alongside the image, guaranteeing synchronization. Short feature films
18 were produced in this way as early as 1922. This system eventually brought us
19 "talking pictures."

54. The passage is mainly about
    (A) the history of silent movies
    (B) the disadvantages of synchronized sound
    (C) the development of sound with movies
    (D) the research into sound reproduction

55. According to the passage, films using sound effects were screened
    (A) before 1896
    (B) as early as 1896
    (C) as early as 1922
    (D) in 1927

56. It can be inferred that
    (A) most movie theaters had a pianist
    (B) sound-effects machines were not common because they were expensive
    (C) orchestras couldn't synchronize sound with the pictures
    (D) gramophones were developed about the same time as moving pictures

57. Which of the following is NOT mentioned as a producer of sound to accompany movies?
    (A) a jazz singer
    (B) a single pianist
    (C) a small band
    (D) a gramophone

58. According to the passage, gramophones were ineffective because they
    (A) got out of synchronization with the picture
    (B) were too large for most movie theaters
    (C) were newly invented and still had imperfections
    (D) changed speeds when the needle jumped

GO ON TO THE NEXT PAGE

59. According to the passage, sound-on-film guaranteed synchronization because the recording was
    (A) made during the filming of the picture
    (B) read by an optical sensor
    (C) placed beside the image on the film
    (D) marked on the gramophone

60. Short feature films produced as early as 1922
    (A) were recorded by optical sensors
    (B) put musicians out of work
    (C) were only effective for dialogue sequences
    (D) preceded talking pictures

THIS IS THE END OF SECTION 3 OF PRACTICE TEST 2.

IF YOU FINISH BEFORE TIME IS UP, CHECK YOUR WORK
ON SECTION 3 ONLY.
DO NOT READ OR WORK ON ANY OTHER SECTION OF THE TEST.

ANSWER
•KEYS•

When explanations are given for all possible answers to a question, an asterisk (*) will be used to indicate the correct answer.

DIAGNOSTIC TEST (p. 6, transcript on p. 511)

Note: If you answer an item incorrectly, complete the exercises following the letter you chose and those following the explanation of the correct answer.

Section 1 Listening Comprehension

Part A

1. (A), (B), and (D) See Exercises L1 and L4–L6.
   * (C) In this sentence "nice" means "kind" and a "gesture" is something someone does as a courtesy. See Exercises L1 and L4–L6.
2. (A) See Exercise L1.
   (B), (C) See Exercises L4–L6.
   * (D) "Chip in" means donate a small sum of money or amount of time to help someone. See Exercises L9–L11.
3. * (A) The expression "have a knack for something" means "to have a special ability." See Exercises L9–L11.
   (B) See Exercise L1.
   (C) See Exercises L1 and L4–L6.
   (D) See Exercises L4–L6.
4. (A), (C) See Exercises L7–L8 and L13–L18.
   (B) See Exercises L13–L18.
   * (D) In this sentence, "avoid" means "to keep from doing something" (to make an effort not to do something). See Exercises L13–L18.
5. * (A) The two ideas are contrasted: (1) Janet doesn't watch TV often (seldom) and (2) Janet has watched TV every night this week (nightly). See Exercises L13–L18.
   (B), (C) See Exercises L13–L18.
   (D) See Exercises L7–L8.
6. (A) See Exercise L1.
   (B) See Exercises L13–L18.
   * (C) The action of playing the piano has not taken place (has stopped) for a length of time (15 years). See Exercises L13–L18.
   (D) See Exercises L7–L8.

7. (A) See Exercise L1.
   * (B) The expression "see eye to eye" means "to think the same about something." See Exercises L9–L11.
   (C) See Exercises L4–L6.
   (D) See Exercises L9–L11.
8. * (A) "Costs" means the same as "price," "twice as much" means the same as "double," and "in three years" indicates "three years before now." See Exercises L7–L8.
   (B), (C) See Exercises L7–L8.
   (D) See Exercise L1.
9. (A), (B), (D) See Exercises L7–L8.
   * (C) "As easy as" means that the subjects are equally easy for the speaker. See Exercises L7–L8.
10. * (A) The expression "keep in touch" means "to be in contact" (through letters, phone calls, or mutual friends). See Exercises L9–L11.
    (B), (C), (D) See Exercises L9–L11.
11. (A), (B), (D) See Exercises L13–L18.
    * (C) "It doesn't seem possible" means "it is hard to believe." See Exercises L13–L18.
12. (A), (C) See Exercises L13–L18.
    * (B) The facts are that "the cupboard is full" and "I cannot find the jam." See Exercises L13–L18.
    (D) See Exercises L4–L6.
13. (A) See Exercise L3.
    (B), (C) See Exercises L4–L6.
    * (D) Since Carmen "serves" on the "board" (the committee) of directors, she is one of the directors. See Exercises L4–L6.
14. (A) See Exercises L4–L6.
    (B) See Exercises L13–L18.
    (C) See Exercise L1.
    * (D) "To be speechless" (to be left speechless) means "unable to say anything in response." We were unable to speak because we were shocked by his accusations (charges that someone had done something wrong), which were false (not true). See Exercises L9–L11.
15. (A), (B) See Exercises L13–L18.
    * (C) If two people don't get together very often, they don't see each other much. See Exercises L13–L18.
    (D) See Exercises L4–L6.

16. (A), (C) See Exercises L4–L6.
   *(B) It was a long drive (a trip by car), and the children became restless (unable to sit still). See Exercises L13–L18.
   (D) See Exercise L1.
17.*(A) The expression "close call" is used when a person has had a narrow escape (has just barely managed to avoid an accident). See Exercises L9–L11.
   (B) See Exercises L1, L2, and L4–L6.
   (C), (D) See Exercises L4–L6.
18. (A) See Exercise L1.
   (B) See Exercises L4–L6.
   *(C) The expression "catch someone's eye" means "get someone's attention." See Exercises L9–L11.
   (D) See Exercises L9–L11.
19. (A), (B) See Exercise L2.
   (C) See Exercises L13–L18.
   *(D) The fact that Alice wrote the paper in one night surprised the speaker. See Exercises L13–L18.
20. (A), (C) See Exercise L1.
   *(B) The length of time of the lecture (far longer than usual) and the usual lectures (one class hour) are being compared. See Exercises L7–L8.
   (D) See Exercises L7–L8.

Part B
21. (A), (D) See Exercises L50–L51.
   *(B) Michael is related to the man through marriage to the man's sister. See Exercises L50–L51.
   (C) See Exercises L22–L24.
22. (A) See Exercises L20–L21.
   *(B) The woman says, ". . . I've found an eyewitness . . ." An eyewitness is someone who has observed the incident and can make a statement (testify) about it. See Exercises L47–L49.
   (C), (D) See Exercise L1.
23. (A), (C), (D) See Exercises L41–L46.
   *(B) The man says, "at the third stop sign, turn left . . ." See Exercises L41–L46.
24.*(A) The man makes an excuse ("I just went caving"). The woman tries to convince him to go by saying that's not a good reason for not going again. See Exercises L39–L40.
   (B) See Exercise L1.
   (C) See Exercises L22–L24 and L50–L51.
   (D) See Exercises L32–L37.
25. (A), (D) See Exercises L26–L27.
   (B) See Exercises L28–L30.
   *(C) When the man asks, "how long?" the woman replies, "at least that long," meaning five years or more. See Exercises L26–L27.
26. (A) See Exercises L39–L40.
   (B), (D) See Exercises L32–L37.
   *(C) The woman suggests taking the bus to the movies so going by bus is fine with her. See Exercises L39–L40.

27. (A) See Exercises L32–L37.
   (B) See Exercise L1.
   *(C) In this case, "a professional" refers to the professional carpenter who made the cabinets (a kind of cupboard) for Peter. See Exercises L32–L37.
   (D) See Exercise L3 and L20–L21.
28. (A) See Exercises L32–L37.
   *(B) By saying that he wouldn't want to drive in it, the man is agreeing with the woman that the fog is very heavy (making driving difficult). See Exercises L32 –L37.
   (C), (D) See Exercises L50–L51.
29. (A) See Exercises L50–L51.
   *(B) The woman is responding to the man's complaint of not understanding the map by suggesting that they pull in to the gas station. It can be inferred that this is to ask for directions. See Exercises L50–L51.
   (C), (D) See Exercises L28–L30.
30. (A), (C) See Exercises L22–L24.
   (B) See Exercise L1.
   *(D) A barber is a person who cuts hair. Since Rob is going to the barber's, he is probably going to have his hair cut. See Exercises L47–L49.
31. (A), (B), (D) See Exercises L47–L49.
   *(C) It can be inferred that they are in a car because the first man asks about "exiting" (in this case, getting off the highway), and the second man wants to read the "road" signs. See Exercises L47–L49.
32.*(A) The woman needs help with her yard (lawn care and trimming the trees). The man suggests getting advice from Mrs. Brown at the Green Thumb Nursery (a place where plants are grown in order to be sold). See Exercises L47–L49.
   (B) See Exercises L47–L49.
   (C) See Exercises L22–L24.
   (D) See Exercise L1.
33.*(A) The woman says the van is more spacious (roomy), so it's bigger. See Exercises L41–L46.
   (B), (D) See Exercises L26–L27.
   (C) See Exercises L41–L46.
34. (A), (C), (D) See Exercises L26–L27 and L33.
   *(B) The woman is surprised that an exam which took her "no time" to finish (which she finished quickly) took the man a long time to finish. See Exercises L26–L27 and L33.
35. (A), (B), (C) See Exercises L28–L30.
   *(D) In this sentence, the expression "turn green" means "be envious about something." See Exercises L28–L30.

Part C
36.*(A) The talk is about saffron in general. Therefore, it includes many facts about saffron. See Exercises L53–L56.
   (B), (C), (D) See Exercises L60–L66.

37. (A), (B), (D) See Exercises L58–L59.
   *(C) Saffron is referred to as the "king of spices" because it is one of the world's most prized and expensive foodstuffs. See Exercises L58–L59.
38.*(A) In the lecture, it is stated that "India and Iran [are] the only other producers of note (of importance)." See Exercises L60–L66.
   (B), (C), (D) See Exercises L60–L66.
39. (A), (B), (D) See Exercises L60–L66.
   *(C) It is stated in the lecture that "Not only is Spain the largest producer . . . but it is also the largest consumer." See Exercises L60–L66.
40. (A), (C), (D) See Exercises L67–L69.
   *(B) The woman asks about the items in the museum. Since she is referring to paintings, the museum is probably an art museum. See Exercises L67–L69.
41. (A), (B), (C) See Exercises L67–L69.
   *(D) The man points out the Rembrandt in the first line of conversation and asks for questions. He probably gives tours in the museum. See Exercises L67–L69.
42.*(A) The man says the painting has been out on "unauthorized loan for three years." "Unauthorized loan" is a humorous way of saying it was stolen. See Exercises L60–L66.
   (B), (C), (D) See Exercises L60–L66.
43. (A), (B), (C) See Exercises L71–L73.
   *(D) Its small size makes it easy to conceal and take out of the museum. See Exercises L71–L73.
44. (A), (D) See Exercises L67–L69.
   *(B) The woman is discussing her lost luggage with the man. See Exercises L67–L69.
   (C) See Exercises L60–L66.
45. (A), (B), (C) See Exercises L67–L69.
   *(D) The man is getting information about the luggage in order to help the woman locate the missing items. See Exercises L67–L69.
46. (A), (B), (D) See Exercises L60–L66.
   *(C) The woman tells the man that she has her name and address (identification) inside the luggage. See Exercises L60–L66.
47. (A), (B), (C) See Exercises L71–L73.
   *(D) The man states, "We'll . . . contact you . . ." See Exercises L71–L73.
48.*(A) It is stated that the wall imitates a variety of elements found on real cliffs. See Exercises L71–L73.
   (B), (C), (D) See Exercises L71–L73.
49. (A), (C), (D) See Exercises L60–L66.
   *(B) It is stated that students participated in a two-day festival. See Exercises L60–L66.
50. (A), (B), (D) See Exercises L60–L66.
   *(C) It is stated that Cornell's outdoor education department sponsored the festival. See Exercises L60– L66.

Section 2 Structure and Written Expression

1. A verb is missing (the word "flow" is a noun used as a subject in this sentence). The phrase "by the heart" indicates that the verb should be passive: "is controlled."
   (A) See Exercises S62–S67.
   (B), (C) See Exercises S26–S32.
   * (D) See Exercises S26–S32.
2. The sentence is complete. Therefore, a phrase or adverb clause giving more information is needed to fill in the blank. "When he was fifteen" tells when the decision was made.
   (A), (B) See Exercises S53–S54.
   *(C) See Exercises S73–S77.
   (D) See Exercises S1–S5.
3. A verb is needed to complete the sentence: "fly."
   *(A) See Exercises S26–S32.
   (B), (C), (D) See Exercises S26–S32.
4. The adjective clause "that can be" is incomplete. A verb "fitted" can complete the clause. "Together" tells how the parts fit.
   (A) See Exercises S53–S54.
   (B) See Exercises S11–S15 and S68–S71.
   *(C) See Exercises S26–S32.
   (D) See Exercises S26–S32.
5. The infinitive "to obtain" is needed to complete the sentence.
   (A), (B), (D) See Exercises S26–S32.
   *(C) See Exercises S26–S32.
6. An aux-word "does" is needed to complete the sentence.
   *(A) See Exercises S33–S36.
   (B), (D) See Exercises S11–S15 and S92–S95.
   (C) See Exercises S92–S95.
7. "Like," meaning "similar to," is a preposition that indicates a comparison between "porpoises and dolphins" and "whales."
   (A), (B) See Exercises S92–S95.
   *(C) See Exercises S92–S95.
   (D) See Exercises S73–S77.
8. A subject "coffeehouses" and a verb "were used" are needed to complete the sentence. The phrase "by literary figures" indicates that the verb should be in the passive form.
   *(A) See Exercises S53–S54.
   (B) See Exercises S62–S67.
   (C) See Exercises S73–S77.
   (D) See Exercises S17–S23.
9. The word "like" indicates that a comparison is being made. The word "those" refers to the "central heating systems" of today.
   *(A) See Exercises S44–S51.
   (B) See Exercises S11–S15 and S73–S77.
   (C) See Exercises S92–S95.
   (D) See Exercises S83–S88.

10. A past-tense verb is needed for the dependent clause. (The verb in the main sentence "was shaped" indicates that the action took place in the past.)
    (A), (B), (D)   See Exercises S26–S32.
    *(C)   See Exercises S62–S67.

11. A subject and verb are needed to complete the sentence. The word "it" fills the subject position, and the verb "was" fills the verb position. An adverb is needed to introduce the adverb phrase "living in Birmingham, England."
    (A)   See Exercises S17–S23.
    (B), (D)   See Exercises S73–S77.
    *(C)   See Exercises S17–S23.

12. A preposition indicating a contrast is needed to complete the sentence. The "lack of success and financial reward" is in contrast to the action of persevering.
    (A)   See Exercises S92–S95.
    *(B)   See Exercises S92–S95.
    (C)   See Exercises S53–S54.
    (D)   See Exercises S73–S77.

13. The verb "influenced" needs a subject. The noun group "James Joyce's *Ulysses*" can take the subject position and correctly completes the sentence.
    (A)   See Exercises S26–S32.
    *(B)   See Exercises S17–S23.
    (C)   See Exercises S17–S23.
    (D)   See Exercises S55–S60.

14. The verb "has never been determined" needs a subject. The noun clause "who built the stone circle known as Stonehenge" can fill the subject position.
    *(A)   See Exercises S55–S60.
    (B)   See Exercises S55–S60.
    (C), (D)   See Exercises S53–S54.

15. An adjective clause or adjective phrase is needed to modify the noun "terms." The phrase "indicating the location of their discovery" describes "what kind" of terms.
    (A), (B), (C)   See Exercises S62–S67.
    *(D)   See Exercises S68–S71.

16. (B) The correct form for making this comparison is "as fast as." See Exercises S83–S88.

17. (A) The infinitive with "to" cannot follow the modal "can." The correct form is "can reach." See Exercises S26–S32.

18. (A) The nouns "predators" and "pollution" are used as subjects. Therefore, the word "disturbing" needs to be in the noun form "disturbances" to be a part of the parallel subject. See Exercises S38–S43 and S89–S91.

19. (B) The relative pronoun "which" refers to things, not people. "Who" should be used to refer to people. See Exercises S62–S67.

20. (A) The superlative form "oldest" should be used because Soay are being compared to all other breeds of sheep. See Exercises S83–S88.

21. (C) The pronoun "ours" cannot be used in an adjective position. "Our" is the correct possessive to use before a noun. See Exercises S11–S15.

22. (B) The pronoun "others" cannot be used before a noun. "Other" is the correct adjective to use. See Exercises S44–S51.

23. (C) The verb form "be" cannot follow the aux-word "are." "Are (being) explored" is the correct form. See Exercises S26–S32.

24. (A) The article "an" should be used before a vowel sound. See Exercise S6–S10.

25. (B) The adjective "easy" cannot modify the verb "worked." The adverb form "easily" should be used to indicate "how" metal is worked. See Exercises S38–S43.

26. (C) "Two times" means the same as "twice," so it is redundant. See Exercises S96–S97.

27. (A) "Nor" is used for negative sentences. "Or" is correct, because "Asian camel" is another name for the "Bactrian." See Exercises S44–S51.

28. (A) The word "first" is used as an adjective to indicate an ordinal number, so the article "the" is needed. See Exercises S6–S10.

29. (C) "The most" is a superlative form, but a comparison is not being made. "Most," meaning "the majority," should be used. See Exercises S83–S88.

30. (B) The verb "refer" is in plural form and does not agree with the singular subject "the term." The correct form is "refers." See Exercises S26–S32.

31. (D) The solution consists of venom. Therefore, the active form of the adjective phrase "consisting of snake venom" should be used. See Exercises S68–S71.

32. (C) "Brought about" is a phrasal verb that takes an object. "Collapse" is in the object position, so the object "it" is incorrect. See Exercises S1–S5.

33. (A) "Agile" is an adjective. "Agility" is the noun form that should be used to be parallel with the nouns "cunning" and "strength." See Exercises S38–S43 and S89–S91.

34. (A) "Alone" cannot be used before a noun. "Only" is the correct word to use in this position. See Exercises S44–S51.

35. (C) The superlative form "greatest" should be used because Shakespeare is being compared to all writers in the English language. See Exercises S83–S88.

36. (A) "Much" should be used with noncount nouns but "nutritionists" is a count noun. "Many" is the correct word to use. See Exercises S1–S5 and S44–S51.

37. (D) The object pronoun "it" and not the possessive form should be used. See Exercises S11–S15.

38. (C) The two-word verb "take care" should be followed by "of." See Exercises S92–S95.

39. (C) The plural noun "novelists" needs a plural verb "reside." See Exercises S26–S32.

40. (C) The adverb "previously" indicates a time in the past. However, the verb "are considered" indicates a present time. The word "now" is the correct adverb to indicate a present time. See Exercises S44–S51.

Section 3 Vocabulary and Reading Comprehension

Note: The definitions given in the answers for questions 1–30 are not necessarily appropriate in contexts different from those of the test sentences.

1. (B) A "refuge" or "sanctuary" is a place where people can go for safety or protection. See Exercises V1–V12.

2. (B) An object that "commemorates" a person or an event has been made or built in order to make people remember that person or event. If you "honor" someone, you give him or her public praise or a symbol of that praise. See Exercises V1–V12 and V14–V27.

3. (C) If things are "clustered" together, they are found or are "grouped" together, especially around a central point. See Exercises V1–V12.

4. (C) Animals that are "shy" or "timid" avoid humans and are easily frightened by them. See Exercises V1–V12.

5. (D) Schliemann "found" or "discovered" the ruins as a result of searching for them. See Exercises V1–V12 and V14–V27.

6. (A) Things that are "petty" or "insignificant" are small and unimportant. See Exercises V1–V12 and V14–V27.

7. (D) "Slain" means "killed" in a violent way. See Exercises V1–V12.

8. (B) A "rigid" or "strict" rule or order is very precise and must be obeyed absolutely. See Exercises V1–V12.

9. (D) If something is "reputedly" or "supposedly" true, it is generally believed to be true. See Exercises V14–V27.

10. (A) To "destroy" or "ruin" something means to cause it so much damage that it cannot be repaired. See Exercises V1–V12 and V14–V27.

11. (A) "Tremendous" or "huge" means a very large amount. See Exercises V1–V12 and V14–V27.

12. (B) "Primarily" or "mainly" is used to indicate the most important or significant use of the corn. See Exercises V14–V27.

13. (C) To "mention" or "name" someone is to refer to them by name. See Exercises V1–V12. ·

14. (A) To "warrant" or "justify" an action means to provide a good reason for doing something. See Exercises V1–V12 and V14–V27.

15. (A) Here "false" means mistaken or based on a wrong understanding. "Incorrect" means wrong or inaccurate. See Exercises V14–V27.

16. (B) If something "survives" or "persists," it continues to exist. See Exercises V14–V27.

17. (D) If you "deliver" or "give" a lecture or speech, you present it in public. See Exercises V1–V12 and V14 –V27.

18. (C) Something that is "sacred" or "holy" is believed to have a special connection with a god or gods. See Exercises V1–V12 and V14–V27.

19. (B) "Profound" and "deep" can be used to emphasize the seriousness or intensity of something. See Exercises V1–V12 and V14–V27.

20. (B) Something that is "extensive" is something that covers a large area. "Widely" means over a great range. (See Exercises V1–V12 and V14–V27.

21. (D) Having "fame" or a "reputation" is the condition of being well known for having done something memorable. See Exercises V1–V12 and V14–V27.

22. (D) To be "existing" or "living" is to continue surviving. See Exercises V1–V12 and V14–V27.

23. (B) If something is "unearthed" or "excavated," it is dug out of the ground. See Exercises V1–V12 and V14–V27.

24. (C) A galaxy that "consists of" a hundred million stars "contains" those stars. See Exercises V14–V27.

25. (D) An "activity" or "pursuit" is something that you spend time doing because you enjoy it. See Exercises V14–V27.

26. (A) A "concentration" of something is a large amount or a large number of it in a given space or area. An "accumulation" is a collection of something. See Exercises V1–V12 and V14–V27.

27. (A) To "budget" money means to plan how much you can spend. To "allocate" money means to set aside a certain amount to use for a special purpose (in this case, a film). See Exercises V1–V12 and V14–V27.

28. (D) A "tale" is a kind of "story" (a narrative) which frequently involves adventure or magic. See Exercises V1–V12.

29. (C) Something that is "impressive" or "awesome" causes people to admire it because of its size, importance, or quality. See Exercises V14–V27.

30. (D) If something is "anchored" or "secured," it is linked firmly with something that is fixed in one place. See Exercises V14–V27.

31. (D) Since cryptozoologists research mysterious, unclassified beasts, they would be most interested in a giant octopus, which is not known to exist. See Exercises R15–R19.

32. (A) While many people "claim" they have seen Bigfoot, it is stated in the passage that "others argue that Bigfoot is just an elaborate hoax." See Exercises R10–R13.

33. (B) The giant squid was classified when it was washed up on a beach. See Exercises R10–R13.

34. (C) This passage discusses "unclassified creatures" which were found to exist and those which have not yet been proven to exist. See Exercises R5–R8.

35. (D) The author points out the example of the pygmy hippopotamus because its existence proved skeptics to be mistaken. See Exercises R15–R19.

36. (B) This passages gives information about the various creatures that some scientists are trying to research. See Exercises R15–R19.

37. (C) It is stated in the passage that "local inhabitants of the mountains are convinced of its existence." See Exercises R10–R13.

38. (D) In the passage it is stated that there are "estimates" but "no reliable data" concerning the number of narcoleptics. See Exercises R10–R13.

39. (D) It is stated that "narcoleptics may fall asleep at unusual or embarrassing times." See Exercises R10–R13.

40. (B) An illness which incapacitates a person while, for example, driving a car can be considered serious. See Exercises R15–R19.

41. (A) It is stated that "the problem may stem from an immune system reacting abnormally to the brain's chemical processes." See Exercises R10–R13.

42. (D) It is stated that there are no reliable data showing how many people have narcolepsy. See Exercises R10–R13.

43. (B) Only a person with narcolepsy would be likely to fall asleep while eating. See Exercises R15–R19.

44. (A) The topic "aspects" covers all the supporting ideas discussed in the passage. See Exercises R5–R8.

45. (C) The main topic is stated in the sentence "passengers can increase their chances of survival by learning and following certain tips." These tips or guidelines are discussed in the passage. See Exercises R5–R8.

46. (A) It is stated that if smoke is present, you should keep your head low. See Exercises R15–R19.

47. (B) It is suggested that passengers locate two exits– the nearest one and an alternative. See Exercises R10–R13.

48. (C) The passage states that passengers can increase their chances of surviving an accident by following certain safety tips. The remainder of the passage gives and explains those tips. See Exercises R15–R19.

49. (B) It is stated that feet should be flat on the floor during takeoffs and landings. See Exercises R10–R13.

50. (D) It is stated, "read and listen to safety instructions before takeoff." See Exercises R10–R13.

51. (D) Passengers are specifically told not to carry personal belongings in an emergency. See Exercises R10–R13.

52. (A) It is stated in the passage that many researchers believe that apes can understand spoken language. See Exercises R10–R13.

53. (D) It is stated that Washoe is an adult chimpanzee and that she uses American Sign Language. See Exercises R10–R13.

54. (C) "The skeptics" are the ones who severely criticize the research. See Exercises R10–R13.

55. (D) It can be inferred from the phrase "subhuman primates" that humans are also primates and that there are primates that are not human. See Exercises R15–R19.

56. (A) It is stated that "subhuman primates have not been taught to speak." See Exercises R10–R13.

57. (A) Proponents are those scientist at the forefront of the research who believe that apes can communicate. See Exercises R2–R4.

58. (C) The tone is instructive because it gives facts and information. See Exercises R15–R19.

59. (B) A baby needs to respond in order to develop its potential. See Exercises R10–R13.

60. (C) There are 600 species. See Exercises R10–R13.

SECTION 1 LISTENING COMPREHENSION

Part A Short sentences

Exercise L1 (p. 29, transcript on p. 513)

1. B (ship/sheep)	5. B (pan/pen)
2. A (bell/bill)	6. A (cup/cap)
3. A (clue/glue)	7. B (dye/tie)
4. B (major/mayor)	8. B (cat/cart)

Exercise L2 (p. 30, transcript on p. 513)

1. Q	3. Q	5. S	7. S
2. S	4. S	6. Q	8. S

Exercise L3 (p. 30, transcript on p. 514)

1. right	5. heir
2. feat	6. four
3. wait	7. way
4. hour	8. fare

Exercise L4 (p. 31, transcript on p. 514))

1. B	3. C	5. C	7. D
2. A	4. A	6. A	8. B

Exercise L5 (p. 31, transcript on p. 514)

1. (A) "Light" in sentence (B) means "not heavy."
2. (A) "Strike" in sentence (B) means to "ignite."
3. (B) "Box" in sentence (A) means to "package."
4. (A) "Space" in sentence (B) means "a blank line."
5. (A) "Note" in sentence (B) means "a musical tone."
6. (B) "Shower" in sentence (A) means "a light rain."
7. (B) "A spring" in sentence (A) is "a place where water comes up from the ground."
8. (A) "Exercise" in sentence (B) means "do physical activities."

Exercise L6 (p. 32, transcript on p. 514)

1. A	3. A	5. A	7. B
2. B	4. A	6. B	8. A

Exercise L7 (p. 33, transcript on p. 514)

1. (B) The speaker wants to know if the person is coming. This information is needed tomorrow at the latest. When the person is coming cannot be inferred.
2. (A) Quarter to two is fifteen minutes before two, or one forty-five (1:45).
3. (A) The word "still" indicates that Connie's father is in the hospital now.
4. (B) The expression "week after next" means one week after the coming week.
5. (B) "Until" indicates that Tom was not studying and at midnight he began to study.
6. (A) "A couple" means "two" or "few."
7. (B) "A single" means "one," but Dick hasn't sold one (a dictionary) yet.
8. (B) "Up to thirty" can mean thirty or nearly thirty, but not more than thirty.
9. (A) "Tripled in value" means "three times as valuable."
10. (B) "A dozen" is twelve, and "half a dozen" is six.
11. (B) "Not any more than" implies the same amount or less than.
12. (A) "Far more" means "a lot more" or "many more." Since Tim has many more responsibilities than the other staff members, they don't have as many responsibilities as Tim.
13. (B) "Much cheaper" means "less expensive." Since the bus is less expensive, it is more expensive to go by train.
14. (B) "Even" is used to emphasize how high Emma's salary is in comparison to Frank's. Emma's salary is higher than Frank's which is already very high.
15. (A) When Irene types fast, she doesn't make as many mistakes as she does when she types slowly.

Exercise L8 (p. 35, transcript on p. 514)

1. (A) "One more time" indicates that the action occurred before.
2. (B) "No later than tomorrow" means "not after tomorrow."
3. (A) "As many as" means "the same amount" and "and then some" means "more"; in other words, more than the same amount.
4. (A) Only half the number expected showed up.
5. (B) The amount she bought divided by three (one third) is all that she needed.
6. (A) Someone who has more skill should have the lead.
7. (B) Every time Carol goes to class, she likes it more.
8. (B) The music started immediately after our arrival.

9. (B) The new regulation will go into effect. At that time no more extensions will be given.
10. (B) "At least a dozen" means no fewer than a dozen (twelve) and maybe more than a dozen.

Exercise L9 (p. 36, transcript on p. 515)

1. (B) "To her heart's content" means "as much as she wants."
2. (A) "Beside oneself with worry" means "be very worried."
3. (A) "Fly into a rage" means "to show extreme anger."
4. (B) "To see someone off" means "to say good-bye to someone who is leaving."
5. (A) "To catch cold" means "to get sick with a cold."
6. (A) "To cross that bridge when I come to it" means "to take care of that situation when it arises" (usually at a later date).
7. (B) "To not lift a finger" means "to not help."
8. (B) "To have something in one's head" means "to have a plan to do something or an idea about something."
9. (A) Something that "makes one's hair stand on end" is something that is very frightening.
10. (B) "To be getting on" means "to be aging."

Exercise L10 (p. 37, transcript on p. 515)

1. (A) If you had to put up with the idea, you had to tolerate it.
   (B) If you had to put the idea together, you had to compose it.
   *(C) If you had to put the idea across, you had to make it understood (convey it).
   (D) If you had to put away the idea, you had to store it or remove it.
2. *(A) If Rita helped Emma see the light, she helped her understand something.
   (B) If Rita helped Emma see the light at the end of the tunnel, she helped her see the end of a difficult situation.
   (C) If Rita helped Emma light up, she helped her either to become happy or ignite a cigarette.
   (D) If Rita helped Emma go out like a light, she helped her go to sleep quickly.
3. (A) If Stephen was in over his head, he was beyond his understanding or in too deep.
   (B) If Stephen was head over heels in love, he was very much in love.
   *(C) If Stephen lost his head, he couldn't control himself – he panicked.
   (D) If Stephen had a big head, he was conceited.
4. (A) If my brother is footing the bills, he is paying for everything.
   (B) If my brother is on his toes, he is well prepared.
   *(C) If my brother is pulling my leg, he is joking with me.
   (D) If my brother is underfoot, he is getting in my way.

5. (A) If we want the money come rain or shine, we want it under any condition – no matter what happens.

   (B) If we want the money for a rain check, we want to be assured that an offer can be taken up at a later date.

   (C) If we want the money at the end of the rainbow, we want something that we hope to get.

   *(D) If we want the money for a rainy day, we want it to use in an emergency.

6. *(A) If I'm going to put that bicycle together, I'm going to take the parts and join them to make a bicycle – to assemble it.

   (B) If I put that bicycle aside, I am moving it out of the way.

   (C) If I put that bicycle down, I am laying it on the floor or ground.

   (D) If I put that bicycle out, I am taking it outside.

7. (A) If they are laying into workers, they are physically or verbally attacking the workers.

   *(B) If they are laying off workers, they are discharging or firing the workers.

   (C) If they are laying the blame on workers, they are accusing the workers of something.

   (D) If they are laying their eyes on workers, they are taking notice of the workers.

8. (A) If the romance tests the waters, it is a situation which will make people's views and opinions clear.

   (B) If the romance is a test case, it is one which establishes an important principle that can afterwards be applied.

   (C) If the romance is put to the test, some new event will put a strain on it and thus give an indication of how strong the romance is.

   *(D) If the romance stands the test of time, it is strong enough to last for a very long time.

9. (A) If she held something against her son, she didn't forgive him.

   *(B) If she held onto her son, she wouldn't let go of him – she clung to him.

   (C) If she got hold of her son, she contacted him by telephone or some other means of communication.

   (D) If she held her son up, she either supported him or stopped or delayed him from doing something.

10. (A) If the children give me a run for my money, they force me to use all my skills to succeed with them.

    (B) If the children make my blood run cold, they frighten me.

    *(C) If the children run me ragged, they tire me – exhaust me.

    (D) If the children put me in the running, they enter me into a contest.

Exercise L11 (p. 37, transcript on p. 515)

1. *(A) "Little by little" means "gradually."

   (B) Jeff and Mike were not friendly at first, but they grew friendly over the years.

   (C) Jeff and Mike weren't friends, but they became friends. The use of "even when" here suggests that they are still not friends.

   (D) This is contrary to the facts. Jeff and Mike did not like each other when they were boys.

2. (A) The expression "run into" can mean "meet unexpectedly" or "collide." This meeting or collision took place in the mall, not in the parking lot.

   (B) The expression "ran into" is confused with "ran" (jogged).

   *(C) The expression "run into" means "meet unexpectedly" in this sentence.

   (D) The expression "run into" can mean "enter in a hurry." However, Sue did not run into the *mall*, she ran into *Mary* (that is, she met her unexpectedly).

3. (A) The expression "doesn't stand a chance" means "hasn't a possibility of succeeding," so John will probably not win.

   (B) The expression "does his best" (does the best job that he can do) is confused with "has the best chance" (is the most likely).

   *(C) "Does his best" means "does the best job that he can do" and "doesn't stand a chance" means "has no possibility of succeeding."

   (D) The expression "doesn't stand a chance" (has no possibility of succeeding) is confused with "can't stand" (cannot tolerate).

4. (A), (B), (D) "Run" in the expression "in the long run" (meaning eventually) is confused with "run" (jog), and "work out" (resolve) is confused with "work out" (which means do physical exercises).

   *(C) "In the long run" means "eventually," and "work out" (resolve) means "turn out."

5. (A) The expression "right away" (immediately) is confused with "all right" (a good job).

   (B) "Entrance" in the term "entrance exam" (an exam necessary to take in order to enter a university or college) is confused with "entrance" (the door used to enter an area), and "right away" (meaning immediately) is confused with "on the right" (the right-hand side).

   (C) The expression "right away" (immediately) is confused with "everything" (all) "correctly" (right).

   *(D) "Notified" means "let someone know," "mother and father" are "parents," and "right away" means "immediately."

6. (A) The expression "time after time" (repeatedly) is confused with "on time" (punctual).
  *(B) The expression "time after time" means "repeatedly" (with frequency).
  (C) Max did not "wait" (spend time doing nothing) while Pete locked the door. He repeatedly told Pete to always lock the door.
  (D) If Pete always locks the door, Max probably wouldn't have to remind him repeatedly to do so.

7. (A) The expression "on the other hand" (by contrast) is confused with "in the other hand" (held in the opposite hand).
  *(B) The expression "on the other hand" means "by contrast." Amy needs gloves in contrast to a new coat.
  (C) The expression "on the other hand" (by contrast) is confused with "handed" (pass something over to someone).
  (D) The expression "on the other hand" (by contrast) is confused with "difficulty getting something" (getting hands on something).

8. (A) The expression "on time" (punctual) is confused with "time" (a specific point in time). Bill didn't take the test because he didn't have his identification card, not because of the time the test was held.
  *(B) The expression "on time" means "punctual" (not late), and Bill didn't take the test because he couldn't. He didn't have his identification card.
  (C) The expression "on time" (punctual) is confused with "short time" (a small duration of time). "Check something out" is confused with "take something."
  (D) Bill could not have used his identification card to take the test because he had forgotten the card.

Exercise L12 (p. 38, transcript on p. 515)
1.*(A) The expression "as much as" is used to emphasize a fact which makes the other part of the sentence rather surprising. Mary hates (dislikes) her job. But in contrast to her disliking the work, she does an adequate job (she's good at her job).
  (B) The statement tells us she dislikes her work, but does not tell us why.
  (C) In this sentence, "as much as" is used to compare homework with work.
  (D) The statement said "she does a very adequate job," whereas this statement means "she would do a better job (but doesn't), if she liked her work."

2.*(A) The intonation of this statement indicates that this is an exclamation which means: Peter is good at making cakes. The word "ever" emphasizes how good a cook he is.
  (B), (C), (D) These are all questions concerning Peter's ability in baking or the possibility of his doing the baking, whereas the statement heard is making a comment concerning how well he cooks.

3. (A) The expression "take care of" may mean "watch over someone or something" or "attend to something that needs to be done." The similar sounds of "brother" and "bother" are confused.
  *(B) "Let me know" means "tell me," and in this sentence "I'll take care of him" means "I'll make him stop."
  (C) "Be careful" (take care) is confused with "take care of" (attend to something that needs to be done).
  (D) The similar sound of "brother" and "bother" are confused. Also, there is a confusion about who is taking care of whom ("I" will take care of "him"). "Him" is not "my brother" but the person that is being bothersome.

4. (A) The similar sound of "might earn" and "my turn" are confused.
  (B) The meanings of "turn" are confused. The verb "turn" means "change directions," and the noun "turn" means "a chance to do what others are doing."
  (C) The similar sounds of "return" and "turn" are confused.
  *(D) "Have a turn" means "have a chance to do what others have had the opportunity to do."

5. (A) "At least twenty-five guests" means "no less than twenty-five guests, and possibly more." Nothing is stated concerning what Jim wants.
  (B) "As many guests as possible" means "an unlimited number of guests." Bob gave Jim a limit of twenty-five names.
  *(C) "As many as twenty-five names" means "up to twenty-five and no more."
  (D) Nothing is stated concerning what Jim wants.

6. (A) The sounds of "night train" and "night rain" are confused.
  (B) The sounds of "train" and "rain" are confused.
  *(C) A "downpour" is a heavy rain. The noise of the rain woke the speaker up (disturbed the speaker's sleep).
  (D) If the rain disturbed my sleep, it woke me up. Therefore, I didn't sleep through it.

7.*(A) "To book a flight" means "to make a plane reservation."
  (B) "Book" can mean "a bound volume of printed material" or "to schedule a time for a flight."
  (C) The similar sounds of "have looked" (have seen) and "have booked" are confused, as are the similar sounds of "fight" and "flight."
  (D) The similar sounds of "light" and "flight" are confused, and the wrong meaning for "book" is used (see B).

8. (A) "At most two" means "no more than two, and possibly less than two."
  (B) David likes sugar in his tea because he uses "at most" two spoonfuls (see A).
  (C) There is no comparison between how much sugar David uses and how much others use.
  *(D) See (A).

9. (A) From the phrase "everyone she meets" we cannot infer that "everyone" is "a lot of people" or that Peggy knows them all.
    (B) The similar sounds of "fault" and "malt" are confused.
    (C) It is Peggy who is complaining about other people. No one is complaining about the food.
  * (D) In this sentence "to find fault with" means "to criticize."

10. (A) The similar sounds of "iced tea" and "eyes sting" are confused.
    (B) The similar sound of "mice" and "my eyes" are confused. Also the meanings of "sting" are confused; "sting" can mean "bite" or "a burning pain."
    (C) The similar sounds of "icing" and "eyes sting" are confused.
  * (D) In this sentence "sting" means "a burning pain."

11. (A) The meanings of "board" are confused. "Board" can mean "a committee" or "meals." The similar sounds of "fee" and "free" are also confused.
  * (B) Since "board" (meals) is not included in the fee, people participating in the conference will have to pay for it.
    (C) A "board" can be "a chalkboard to write on."
    (D) A "board" can be "a board to display notices on" (such as a bulletin board).

12.* (A) "To rush" means "to be in a hurry." Since Roger forgot his belongings (his umbrella and scarf), he left without them (did not take them).
    (B) The similar sounds of "hurry" and "worry" are confused.
    (C) In this sentence "left" means "leave something for someone else." The similar sounds of "hurry" and "Murray" are confused.
    (D) The confusion occurs because of the similar sounds of "leave" and "live" from the idiom "can't live without" (very attached to).

13. (A) The similar sounds of "Beth" and "beef" are confused.
    (B) The similar sounds of "Beth over" and "leftover" are confused.
  * (C) "To have someone over" means "to invite someone to your house."
    (D) "To have someone over" (entertain someone) is confused with "to go over to someone's place" (to visit someone).

14. (A) "Put into" (insert) is confused with "put in two hours" (spend two hours of time doing something).
    (B) "Put in two hours" is confused with "put in (returned) two books."
    (C) The similar sounds of "walk" and "work" are confused.
  * (D) "A couple" means "two," and the idiom "to put in" means "to spend time."

15. (A) The similar sounds of "cat" and "got" are confused.
    (B) The similar sounds of "cat" and "card" are confused.
  * (C) "Cats" are pets, and having "fleas" is a problem.
    (D) The similar sounds of "cap" and "cat" as well as "fleas" and "fleece" are confused.

16. (A) "To head" (go in the direction of) is confused with "head out" (to begin a journey). The similar sounds of "before" and "four" are confused. "Dawn" is the name of a woman and a time of day (sunrise).
    (B) "To head out" (to begin a journey) is confused with "to put one's head out of something" such as a door or window. "Dawn" (a woman's name) and "dawn" (sunrise) are confused.
  * (C) "Dawn" means "sunrise," and "headed out" means "left on a journey."
    (D) The similar sounds of "yawn" and "dawn" are confused.

17.* (A) "To leave" means "to forget to take something along" (Jill forgot to take her lunch with her when she got off the bus), and "lunch" consists of food.
    (B) In this statement "to leave" means "to depart."
    (C) The similar sounds of "left" and "laughed" as well as "much" and "lunch" are confused.
    (D) "To leave" means "to forget to take something along." It was not that Jill forgot to take her lunch onto the bus, but that she forgot to take her lunch with her when she got off the bus.

18. (A) "To be handed" (given) and "to hand in" (submit) are confused. "Half past twelve" (the time) is confused with "half the questionnaire" (one part of the questionnaire).
    (B) "A handful" (a small number of, in this case, students) and "hand in" (submit) are confused.
    (C) "Half past twelve" (the time) is confused with "half a dozen" (six).
  * (D) "To turn in" means "to hand in" (submit), and "half past twelve" is another way to say "twelve thirty" (the time).

19. (A) "To overeat" (eat too much) is confused with "to eat over at" (eat at someone else's house), and the similar sound of "Pat" and "fat" are confused.
  * (B) "To be afraid" means "to be worried or concerned about something," and "to get fat" means "to put on weight."
    (C) "To overeat" means "to eat too much." However, it isn't that Ted eats too much when he is afraid, but that he's afraid to eat too much.
    (D) We only know from the statement that Ted is concerned about eating too much. The statement doesn't tell us if he likes or dislikes fattening foods.

20.*(A) "Used to do something" means "to have had the habit of doing something." "Always" means "all the time."

(B) "Too much time" (more time than needed or necessary) is confused with "all the time" (the number of occasions).

(C) "On time" (not late) is confused with "all the time" (the number of occasions).

(D) "A lot of time" (a large amount of time) is confused with "all the time" (the number of occasions).

Exercise L13 (p. 43, transcript on p. 515)

| 1. B | 3. B | 5. A | 7. A | 9. A |
| 2. A | 4. B | 6. A | 8. B | 10. B |

Exercise L14 (p. 43, transcript on p. 516)

| 1. A | 3. A | 5. B | 7. A | 9. B |
| 2. A | 4. A | 6. B | 8. A | 10. A |

Exercise L15 (p. 44, transcript on p. 516)

| 1. A | 3. B | 5. A | 7. B | 9. B |
| 2. B | 4. B | 6. B | 8. B | 10. A |

Exercise L16 (p. 45, transcript on p. 516)

| 1. B | 3. B | 5. B | 7. A | 9. A |
| 2. A | 4. A | 6. B | 8. B | 10. B |

Exercise L17 (p. 45, transcript on p. 516)

| 1. C | 3. C | 5. R | 7. R | 9. R |
| 2. R | 4. R | 6. C | 8. C | 10. C |

Exercise L18 (p. 46, transcript on p. 516)

| 1. A | 3. B | 5. B | 7. A |
| 2. B | 4. A | 6. B | 8. A |

Exercise L19 (p. 47, transcript on p. 516)

1. (A) The negative "didn't" is confused with the negative "wouldn't."

(B) It is true that Ted married Ann, but the reason was because she was so beautiful not because she was ugly.

(C) According to this statement, Ted did not marry Ann, which is the opposite of the original statement.

*(D) The information in the spoken statement has been restated using affirmative (rather than negative) language.

2. (A) "Julie can't remember" means that she doesn't know if she signed the paper or not.

(B) The similar sounds of "uniform" and "form" and the similar spelling of "sign" and "signal" are confused.

(C) The meanings of "sign" (to write one's name) and "sign" (a posted announcement) are confused.

*(D) "Julie forgot to sign" (write her name) means she didn't put her name on the form.

3. (A) Andy gave the newsletter to Sue, not Mr. Roberts. There is no information concerning whose newsletter it was.

*(B) Andy gave the newsletter to Sue. Mr. Roberts asked him to do this.

(C) Andy did not give the newsletter to Mr. Roberts. Mr. Roberts gave it to him and he gave it to Sue. There is no information concerning whose newsletter it was.

(D) Sue was given the newsletter at Mr. Robert's request.

4. (A), (D) "Should have been taken" (the action of taking the test was a desirable thing to do in the past, but it was not taken) is confused with "must have been taken" (indicating a belief that the test was already taken sometime in the past).

*(B) "Was probably" means "must have been" and "harder than any other" means "the most difficult."

(C) "Must take" implies "to take in the future," but the spoken statement says "must have been taken," which implies that the action has already taken place.

5. (A) We are not told how Jim knocked over the juice, only that he did so.

(B) Jim knocked only the grape juice over.

*(C) Jim spilled (knocked over) the juice and didn't ("failed to") clean it up (mop it up).

(D) We are not told that Jim picked up a mop, only that he didn't mop up the juice.

6. (A) David does have a serious problem (a serious handicap).

(B) "Never miss classes" means "always go to classes," and "hardly ever makes it to classes" means "seldom goes to classes."

(C) The meanings of "serious" (to be earnest about something) and "serious" (severe) are confused.

*(D) "A serious handicap" may suggest a "physical condition" and "not keep from" means "not prevent."

7. (A) "To call off" (cancel) and "to call" (contact by phone) are confused.

*(B) "To call off" means "to cancel" and "a cloudy day" describes the weather.

(C) The similar sounds in "outing" and "cloudy" are confused.

(D) This is contrary to the facts. If Kim had wanted the picnic on a cloudy day, she wouldn't have called it off because of the clouds.

8. (A) The similar sounds of "assignment" and "sign" and the meanings of "line" (a line of people) and "line" (a space to write something on) are confused.

*(B) "To go ahead" means "to proceed," and "seat assignment" means "a seat number."

(C) The similar sounds of "assignment" and "sign up" and "time" and "line" are confused.

(D) The similar meanings of "sit" and "seat" are confused, as are meanings of "grandstand" (bleachers) and "stand" (remain on foot).

9. (A) It was the student who left the testing center because the professor required him to do so.

  *(B) The professor did not allow the student to come into the center because the student forgot to bring his identification.

  (C) We are told that the student went to get his card, but that he left because he didn't bring his card.

  (D) It was the student who forgot to bring his card.

10.*(A) First Donna finished art school, and then she got a job at the gallery.

  (B) "She hopes to get a job" refers to the future; "she got a job" means that it has already happened.

  (C) The position was at the Town Gallery, not the Art Academy.

  (D) We are not given any information concerning how Donna has financed her studies.

11. (A) The similar sounds of "Will" (a man's name) and "we'll" (we will) are confused, as are the meanings of "report" (a weather prediction) and "report" (a class paper).

  (B) The meanings of "report" as a noun (a weather prediction) and as a verb (to inform) are confused.

  (C) A report *for* snow suggests a weather report. A report *on* snow suggests a class paper.

  *(D) The weather report predicts snow, which is necessary for skiing.

12. (A) Mrs. Davis told her son something – he didn't tell her anything. There is a difference between disliking dogs in general and avoiding stray (homeless) dogs in particular.

  (B) The meaning of "stray" as an adjective (homeless) and as a verb (wander off) are confused.

  *(C) Mrs. Davis wants her son to stay away from (avoid) stray (homeless) dogs.

  (D) Mrs. Davis's son should (ought to) avoid dogs, not get a dog.

13. (A) The speaker wants to look at the classified ads, not place an ad.

  (B) "Could you buy the newspaper" is a request for someone to purchase a newspaper. "Could I have the classified ads" is a request to look at one section of the newspaper (in the event that a newspaper is purchased).

  (C) "Could I have" implies the future and "did you see" is in the past.

  *(D) The speaker is asking for the classified ads from the paper the listener might buy.

14. (A) Marie wrote Rick's speech, she didn't give it.

  (B) Rick didn't give Marie his speech, but instead he asked her to write it.

  (C) "To get someone to do something" is confused with "to get something for someone."

  *(D) Rick persuaded Marie to write the speech for him.

15. (A) "To be used to" (to be accustomed to) is confused with "used to do something" (a past habit).

  *(B) The negative "not" used with "so much" means "less" (see A).

  (C) Since Nancy isn't used to dancing so much, she may find it difficult to dance.

  (D) "As much as" is confused with "so much," and "used to" is confused with "be used to" (see A).

16. (A) This answer is wrong because there is a way to finish, and that is with Jerry's help.

  (B) It is not that Jerry "will never" help, but that you "will never" finish without his help.

  *(C) "Unless" is used to introduce the only circumstance in which you can finish. That circumstance is if Jerry helps you.

  (D) It is *you* that needs Jerry's help, not Jerry who needs *your* help.

17.*(A) "Before" means "first" and "check with the committee" means "to discuss the report with the committee."

  (B) "Must" (to have to) and "should" (ought to), as well as "check" (a note of payment) and "check with" (to discuss points with someone) are confused.

  (C) This statement confuses who did what and implies that the report has already been submitted.

  (D) This statement confuses who did what and confuses "check" (a note of payment) and "check with" (discuss).

18. (A) "To stop to make" (stop in order to make something) is confused with "to finish making" (stop or end one's doing something).

  (B) This confuses your being asked to leave with the phrase "before we leave" (prior to our leaving).

  (C) "To go" means "to leave," but the noun "stop" (where a bus picks up passengers) is confused with the verb "stop" (to halt).

  *(D) "As soon as" introduces the action (use the telephone) that must be completed before the second action (leave) can take place. First I need to use the telephone, and then we can leave.

19. (A) "Worn out" means "exhausted," but "must have been" (probably was) is confused with "must do something" (have to do something).

  *(B) "Was probably tired" means "must have been exhausted," and swimming was what caused Rebecca to be tired.

  (C) "Must have been" implies that the swimming was done in the past, whereas "always swims" implies that it is done with frequency.

  (D) The spoken statement does not mention other swimmers – only Rebecca.

20.*(A) "To try doing something" means "to test an action." Simon tried closing the door, but that action didn't stop him from hearing the music.

(B) The word "but" shows a relationship between the door's being closed and the music's still being heard. Consequently, Simon was able to close the door.

(C) The door was closed, but the music could still be heard.

(D) "Trying to hear" is confused with "try closing." Simon closed the door because he didn't want to hear the music.

Part B Short conversations

Exercise L20 (p. 50, transcript on p. 517)
1. dye   3. won   5. hole
2. brakes   4. loan

Exercise L21 (p. 50, transcript on p. 517)
1. A (meet, not meat)
2. B (sail, not sale)
3. B (cruise, not crews)
4. B (weak, not week)
5. A (mail, not male)

Exercise L22 (p. 51, transcript on p. 517)
1. B   2. D   3. D   4. A   5. C

Exercise L23 (p. 52, transcript on p. 517)
1. B   2. A   3. B   4. A   5. A   6. A

Exercise L24 (p. 52, transcript on p. 517)
1. B   2. A   3. A   4. B   5. B

Exercise L25 (p. 53, transcript on p. 518)
1. (A) The similar sounds of "means" and "cream" are confused.
(B) "Plain" (without anything) and "plane" (an airplane) are confused.
*(C) "To take" can mean "to use or put."
(D) The woman wants her tea plain. The man doesn't ask if it is *too* plain.

2. (A) Although the woman doesn't want to go to the people's house, it is not because she doesn't like their house.
*(B) "Fighting," in this context, means "arguing."
(C) The arguing concerns "little things" (unimportant matters). It is the arguing, not the little things, that bothers the woman.
(D) The meanings of "fight" (a boxing match) and "fight" (argue) are confused.

3. (A) The meanings of "miss" (fail to notice something) and "miss" (get left behind) are confused. Also, "travel" is confused with "trip." "Travel" can mean "take a trip," but in this case, it is an adjective indicating the kind of book being discussed.
(B) The meanings of "book" (to reserve) and "book" (a bound volume of printed material) are confused.
(C) The meanings of "return" (come back) and "return" (give back) are confused.
*(D) The woman says that it didn't matter to Bill whether he had the book this month; therefore, it won't matter to him next month. Thus, she is probably going to keep the book.

4.*(A) "To put on" means "to wear." They are discussing what to wear.
(B) The meanings of "check" (a note of payment) and "checked" (a pattern of squares) are confused.
(C), (D) The similar sounds of "pants" and "paints" are confused.

5. (A) "Weak" and "week" are confused because they are pronounced the same.
*(B) "To be weak" means "to be lacking strength."
(C) "Timing" (the selection of a moment to do something) and "time" (duration) are confused.
(D) "For" and "four" are confused because they are pronounced the same.

6.*(A) "Snoring" is a noise made when sleeping.
(B) The woman said he didn't hear the professor.
(C) The similar sounds of "boring" and "snoring" are confused.
(D) The similar sounds of "wonder" and "wander" are confused.

7. (A) The meanings of "space" (room) and "space" (the region beyond the earth's atmosphere) are confused.
(B) The similar sounds of "class" and "glass" are confused, as are the meanings of "backpack" and "back."
*(C) The man wants to know if there is room in the backpack for a glass.
(D) The man is not offering to carry the woman's pack, but is asking if there is room in her pack for his glass.

8. (A) The similar sounds of "coin" and "join" are confused.
*(B) "A coin" and "change" are terms for money.
(C) The similar sounds of "clean" and "coin" are confused. Also, an engine is a kind of machine, but not the kind that would use a coin.
(D) The meanings of "change" (money) and "change" (replace) are confused.

9. (A) The meanings of "play" (a drama) and "play" (to have fun with) are confused.
   *(B) "To have a role" in theatrical drama is "to act a part."
   (C) "Roll" and "role" are confused because they are pronounced the same.
   (D) One "plays" (amuses oneself) with a game, but "plays" (acts) a part on stage.

10. (A) The meanings of "spare" (an extra tire) and "spare" (anything extra) are confused.
    *(B) A sink has a drain and "blocked" can mean "stopped-up."
    (C) The meanings of "plug" (a device to put in the drain to stop the water from getting out) and "plugged-up" (stopped-up) are confused.
    (D) The similar sounds of "sink" (a basin) and "stink" (an odor) are confused.

11. (A) The meanings of "pool" (a billiard game) and "pool" (a swimming pool) are confused.
    (B) The similar sounds of "cab" and "cap" are confused.
    (C) The similar sounds of "cool" and "pool" as well as "car" and "cap" are confused.
    *(D) The woman is getting her swimming cap to go to the pool with the man.

12. (A) "To climb stairs" is confused with "to go climbing" (climb mountains).
    (B) The meanings of "flight" (an airplane trip) and "flight" (a set of stairs) are confused.
    *(C) "The stairs" are made up of "steps."
    (D) The meanings of "fly" (to take an airplane trip) and "flight" (a set of stairs) are confused.

13. (A) The similar sounds of "replace" and "place" are confused, and the similar vocabulary "shop" and "shopping" is used.
    (B) The similar sound of "glass" and "class" are confused.
    (C) A painting can be called a picture, and it too, can be put in a "frame," but the man is talking about the glass in the picture frame.
    *(D) In order to replace the glass, the people will have to buy some glass.

14. (A) "Twice" means "two times" and "couple" means "two," but the similar sounds of "mistake" and "steak" are confused.
    (B) The similar sounds of "correcting" and "collecting" are confused.
    (C) The similar sounds of "proof" and "prove" as well as "mistake" and "state" are confused.
    *(D) "To proofread" something means "to look for mistakes"; "mistakes" are "errors."

15.*(A) The truck was parked in a place that blocked the driveway so that the woman couldn't get out.
    (B) The meanings of "block" (obstruct) and "block" (a rectangular space in a city) are confused.
    (C) "To back out" means "to reverse," but it is the woman who cannot back out.
    (D) The meanings of "block" (obstruct) and "block" (a solid piece of cement or wood) as well as the similar sounds of "back" and "pack" are confused.

Exercise L26 (p. 54, transcript on p. 518)

1. (B) The expression "at least three years" means "three years or more."
2. (B) The woman's statement "when I see him" indicates that she has not seen him, but will be seeing him in the future.
3. (B) The woman's answer "the following week" means "the week following next week" (the week after next week).
4. (A) According to the woman, Mr. Green's store is open until 9:00 (it closes at 9:00).
5. (A) The man took piano lessons from sometime in the past until six years ago, at which time he stopped taking lessons.
6. (B) "Several" means "more than two, but not many more than two."
7. (A) The woman means that Sam has completed at least 60 credit hours. Here, "at least" means 60 is the minimum number and that the actual number is 60 or more.
8. (B) The use of "either" implies that there are two examples. The people cannot understand either one of the two examples.
9. (B) "Quite a few" means "a large number," whereas "a few" means "not many."
10. (B) "Both" indicates "two."
11. (A) If the man has studied more for geology than for calculus and is still not passing geology, he is probably having more difficulty understanding geology than calculus.
12. (A) The woman is not discussing the quality of a box, but the size of the box. She means that a big box is a better box for her purposes.
13. (A) Both people give reasons why schedules with more flexible hours are beneficial.
14. (B) The woman didn't write as much as she intended to write. She wrote less than half of what she intended to write.
15. (A) The scenic route is more interesting, but it takes longer. Therefore, Interstate 90 is less interesting but takes less time (in other words, is faster).

Exercise L27 (p. 56, transcript on p. 519)

1. (B) "Could you?" means "Is it possible for you to bring over some extra chairs?" The woman's response, which is a polite way of accepting his offer, is used because she wants more chairs.

2. (A) "A lot more books this semester" means the man bought fewer books last semester; in other words, he didn't buy as many last semester.

3. (B) "A couple of hours at least" means "a minimum of two, but probably more than two."

4. (A) The man bought two boxes of candy.

5. (A) "A full week" is one complete week.

6. (B) The man's question indicates that he is surprised that 1,500 students are employed. His response to the woman's comment about the number having doubled indicates that he must have known that there were 750 employed students before.

Exercise L28 (p. 57, transcript on p. 519)

1. (A) "To stand someone up" means "to not meet that person at the prearranged time."

2. (B) "To have a crack at something" means "to have the opportunity to try doing something."

3. (B) "To blow up" means "to suddenly lose one's temper."

4. (A) "To put something off" means "to postpone it." The man says he can't put it off, so he will register for the music course.

5. (A) "To ring a bell" means "to sound familiar." The woman has heard the name before, so she might know Cindy.

6. (B) "To be given the runaround" means "to be given incorrect information or evasive answers to a request."

Exercise L29 (p. 57, transcript on p. 519)

1. *(A) In this sentence, "fall behind" means "fail to do something on time."
   (B) "Fall asleep" means "go to sleep."
   (C) "Fall in love" means "feel love for."
   (D) "Fall apart" means "break down."

2. (A) "Weigh one's words" means "think carefully before speaking."
   (B) "Gain weight" means "add pounds."
   (C) "Throw one's weight around" means "use one's influence."
   *(D) "Pull one's weight" means "do one's share of the work."

3. (A) "Have a night out" means "go somewhere for an evening."
   (B) "Make a night of it" means "do an activity for the entire night."
   (C) "Turn day into night" means "be active during the night and sleep during the day."
   *(D) "Have a bad night" means "be unable to sleep."

4. (A) "On the off chance" means "there's a small possibility."
   *(B) "Stand a good chance" means "there's a good possibility of achieving success."
   (C) "Chance upon something" means "accidentally find something."
   (D) "Chance something" means "take a risk."

5. (A) "Call it a day" means "stop working for the day."
   (B) "Call a halt to something" means "order somebody to stop doing something."
   (C) "Call someone's bluff" means "test to see if someone is being serious about something."
   *(D) "Call someone's attention to something" means "point something out to someone."

6. (A) "Turn the other cheek" means "ignore or decide not to get angry when someone treats you badly."
   (B) "Speak tongue in cheek" means "say something as a joke."
   *(C) "Dance cheek to cheek" means "dance very closely."
   (D) "Be cheeky" means "be disrespectful."

7. (A) "See the last of something" means "it will never be seen again."
   *(B) "See things" means "imagine that things are there."
   (C) "See one's way clear" means "decide to do something that one had not intended to do previously."
   (D) "See the daylight" means "suddenly understand or finish an overwhelming job."

8. *(A) "Throw cold water on something" means "to discourage something."
   (B) "Throw a party" means "have a party."
   (C) "Throw in the towel" means "give up or stop trying."
   (D) "Throw something away" means "get rid of something."

9. (A) "Might as well" means "see no reason not to do something."
   (B) "Come off well" means "be successful."
   *(C) "Leave well enough alone" means "don't tamper with what is already in good shape."
   (D) "It's just as well" means "it is fortunate that it happened the way it did."

10. *(A) A "wild goose chase" is a "search for something that you have little chance of finding."
    (B) "Sow one's wild oats" means "behave in an uncontrolled way when young, before settling down to a career or family life."
    (C) "Be wild about something" means "like something very much."
    (D) "Spread like wildfire" means "move very quickly."

Exercise L30 (p. 59, transcript on p. 519)

1. (A) "Laundry" (the washing) is confused with "Washington."
   (B) "Wash" is confused with "Washington."
   *(C) "Keep in touch" means "stay in contact through writing letters or making phone calls."
   (D) The woman wants the man to be certain to keep in touch (see C), not to be certain about which day he is leaving.

2. (A), (B) The expression "be a stone's throw" (be nearby) is confused with "toss stones" (throw rocks).
   *(C) The expression "a stone's throw" means "very close by."
   (D) She doesn't want to drive because it is so close (a stone's throw), not because of "stony roads" (roads which are rough because of rocks).

3. *(A) "Set up" means "get something ready" (organize it).
   (B) The concession "stands" (where food is sold) is confused with "stands" (where observers sit). "Set up" (get something ready) is confused with "seat" (a place to sit).
   (C) "Set up" (get something ready) is confused with "upset" (unhappy). The noun "stand" (where food is sold) is confused with the verb "stand" (remain on foot).
   (D) "Set up" (get something ready) is confused with "set" (a television set).

4. (A) The phrasal verb "to wrap up" (to cover with paper or to package) is confused with "to be wrapped up in" (to be completely involved in).
   *(B) "To be wrapped up in" means "to be completely involved or engrossed in something."
   (C) The phrasal verb "to wrap up" (to complete something) is confused with "to be wrapped up in" (see B).
   (D) If you "cover for someone," you take his or her position until the person returns. "Cover" is confused with "wrap."

5. (A) "Miss" (make a mistake) is confused with "miss" in the expression "missed the point" (see D).
   (B) The expression "missed the point" (see D) is taken literally as "miss the point" (get the point wrong).
   (C) "Miss" (fail to attend) is confused with "miss" in the expression "missed the point" (see D).
   *(D) The expression "missed the point" means "failed to understand the argument." The woman failed to understand the argument presented in the lecture.

6. (A) "Run" (move quickly) is confused with "run" in the expression "run across something" (see C).
   (B) The similar sounds of "panting" (breathing hard) and "pamphlet" (a small brochure) are confused. "Run" (move quickly) is confused with "run" in the expression "run across something" (see C).
   *(C) The expression "run across something" means "find (discover) something by chance."
   (D) "Cross" (annoyed) is confused with "cross" in the expression "run across something" (see C).

7. (A) Rebecca refuses to speak to the man. She isn't refusing to return his watch (for telling the time).
   (B) The expression "not give the time of day" (see D) is taken literally as "not tell someone what time it is."
   (C) The similar sounds of "the time of the play" and "the time of day" are confused.
   *(D) The expression "not give the time of day" means "ignore or refuse to speak to someone."

8. (A) It is the speakers who are going to vote, not Mary.
   *(B) The expression "have what it takes" means "have the ability or skills to do something."
   (C) The expressions "have what it takes" (see B) and "takes what one can" (tolerates as much as possible) are confused.
   (D) The original statement concerns "seriously" voting for Mary, not "seriousness" about elections.

9. (A) "Set up" (get something ready, in this case, a business) is confused with "upset" (distressed).
   *(B) In this sentence "mind your own business" means "pay attention to your own affairs and not to mine."
   (C) The expression "mind your own business" is taken literally as "take care of one's business" (see B).
   (D) "Mind" in the expression "on one's mind" (what one is thinking about) is confused with "mind" in the expression "mind your own business" (see B).

10. *(A) "The go-ahead" is the approval or permission to proceed.
    (B) "Ahead" (in advance) is confused with "go-ahead" (see A).
    (C) "Head" (leader) and "go" (leave) are confused with "go-ahead" (see A).
    (D) "Ahead" (in advance) is confused with "go-ahead" (see A).

Exercise L31 (p. 60, transcript on p. 520)

1. (A) The expression "shut-eye" (sleep) is confused with "closing one's eyes."
   *(B) "Get some shut-eye" means "get some sleep."
   (C) "Shut-eye" is confused with "shut off" (turn off).
   (D) "Shut-eye" is confused with "shut" (close).

2. (A) The similar sounds of "pack" and "back" are confused.
   (B) "Back out of" (withdraw from an engagement) is confused with "come back" (return).
   *(C) The expression "back out of" means "to withdraw from an engagement." The man doesn't want to go to the party.
   (D) "Back out of" is confused with "out back" (in the yard behind the house).

3.*(A) The expression "make light of" means "to treat as unimportant." The woman thinks that the man is not being serious about his bad exam grade.

(B) The meaning of "light" in the expression "make light of" (treat as unimportant) is confused with "light" (not hard).

(C) The meaning of "light" in the expression "make light of" is confused with "light" (lamp).

(D) The meaning of "light" in the expression "make light of" is confused with "light" (not dark).

4. (A) The similar sounds of "brush up" (to review) and "hush up" (keep silent) are confused.

(B) The similar sounds of "rush" (in a hurry) and "hush" (be quiet) are confused.

*(C) The expression "hush something up" means "keep others from finding out about something." The woman understands why the man doesn't want people to know (find out) about the accident.

(D) The woman understands why the man doesn't want people to know about the accident. It cannot be inferred by her statement whether or not she knows why the accident occurred.

5.*(A) The man says Bill has been "lying down on the job" which means Bill has "not been working as hard as he should."

(B), (C) "Lying down on the job" (see A) is confused with "napping" (sleeping) at work.

(D) The meanings of "down" (depressed) and "down" in the expression "lying down on the job" are confused (see A).

6. (A) The meanings of "TV screen" (a TV monitor) and "screen out" (eliminate) are confused.

(B) The similar sounds of "screen" and "scream" are confused.

(C) The similar sounds of "screen" and "ice cream" are confused.

*(D) The expression "screen out" means "to eliminate." The people are disqualified and cannot continue in the experiment.

7. (A) The similar sounds of "yoke" and "joke" are confused.

*(B) The expression "sink in" means "to become understood slowly." The woman means that Ted understands the jokes after he has had time to think about them.

(C) Eggs have yokes (see A). The similar sounds of "sink" and "stink" are confused.

(D) The meanings of "sink in" (to become understood) and "sink" (a basin for washing) are confused.

8.*(A) The expression "make short work of" means "do something quickly." The children ate the cookies quickly.

(B) The meanings of "make" in the expression "make short work of" (see A) and "make" (bake something) are confused as are the similar sounds of "make" and "bake."

(C) The meanings of "short work" (work done quickly) and "little work" (not much work) are confused.

(D) The meanings of "short" (quick) and "shorts" (short pants) are confused.

9. (A) The expression "stick around" (stay) is confused with "sticky" (gooey, like glue).

(B) The similar sounds of "stick" and "Rick" are confused.

(C) The expressions "stuck up" (have too high an opinion of oneself) and "stick around" are confused.

*(D) The expression "stick around" means "stay." Neil usually stays after class has ended.

10.*(A) The expression "water something down" means "make something less difficult." The professor made his course easier or simplified it.

(B) The similar sounds of "course" and "horse" are confused.

(C) The university has changed its requirements, so the professor has changed aspects of his course to make it easier. He has not required a change to another course.

(D) The professor has simplified his course because of the change in university requirements, but that doesn't mean he has dropped the requirements for this particular course.

11. (A) The expressions "pass something out" (distribute) and "pass out" (lose consciousness) are confused.

*(B) The expression "pass out" means "lose consciousness."

(C) "Pass" (give a mark of adequate completion) and "pass out" (lose consciousness) are confused.

(D) "Past" and "passed" are confused because they are pronounced the same.

12. (A) The meanings of "stumble" (trip over) and "stumble across" (discover by chance) are confused.

(B) The similar sounds of "tumble" and "stumble" are confused.

*(C) If the woman discovered the shop by chance, she "stumbled across it."

(D) The similar sounds of "shop" and "hop" are confused.

13. (A) "Take something up" (pursue a new interest) is the opposite of "swearing off something" (decide not to do something anymore).

(B) The similar sounds of "sworn" and "has worn" are confused.

*(C) The expression "swear off something" means "to decide against doing something, or give it up."

(D) The expression "swear by something" (place great confidence in something) is confused with "swear off something" (see C).

14. (A) The expression "tag along" (accompany) is confused with "tag" (a label).

(B) The expressions "tag along" (accompany) and "get along" (be friendly with) are confused.

(C) "A price" is put on a "tag" and attached to an article for sale. The meaning of "tag" (a label) is confused with the expression "tag along" (accompany).

*(D) The woman thought that the man did not want them to go (tag along) with him.

15. (A) A tailor doesn't clean clothing, but makes or alters clothing.

*(B) The expression "take something in," in this case, means "make something smaller."

(C) Although the jacket doesn't fit, it is not being returned to the store where it was bought. It is being taken to someone who can alter it.

(D) Although a tailor may be asked to mend clothing, the problem is not that the jacket is torn, but that it needs to be made smaller.

Exercise L32 (p. 62, transcript on p. 520)
1. B	3. A	5. B	7. A
2. B	4. A	6. A	8. B

Exercise L33 (p. 62, transcript on p. 521)
1. B	3. B	5. A	7. B
2. A	4. A	6. B	8. B

Exercise L34 (p. 63, transcript on p. 521)
1. A	3. B	5. A	7. B
2. A	4. B	6. B	8. A

Exercise L35 (p. 64, transcript on p. 521)
1. A	3. B	5. B	7. B
2. A	4. A	6. A	8. B

Exercise L36 (p. 64, transcript on p. 521)
1. C	3. C	5. R	7. C
2. R	4. R	6. R	8. C

Exercise L37 (p. 65, transcript on p. 521)
1. A	3. B	5. A	7. A
2. B	4. B	6. B	8. B

Exercise L38 (p. 66, transcript on p. 522)

1. (A), (B) The man already has a car.

(C) Whether or not he gives her a ride does not depend on his having a car but rather when she must be on campus.

*(D) The man implies that he will give the woman a ride if she is going at a convenient time for him.

2.*(A) "He almost didn't pass" means that while he came close to failing, he did pass and this is the stated reason for his being happy.

(B) "Must not have passed" (probably didn't pass) is confused with "almost didn't pass" (came close to failing, but didn't).

(C) "Almost didn't pass" (came close to failing, but didn't) is confused with "didn't pass" (failed).

(D) "Almost didn't pass" means "barely passed" and, therefore, he did not do very well.

3. (A) Tom, not the woman, is in the hospital.

(B) She wants Tom to receive the card.

*(C) The expression "can't make it" means "unable to do something" (in this case, get to the hospital).

(D) "Make" in the expression "can't make it" is confused with "make" (construct).

4. (A) The man doesn't like sports (see D).

(B) "To be contrary" (behave in an unreasonable way) is confused with "on the contrary" (an expression used to indicate that the opposite of something just said is true).

(C) The preferences concern sports and reading, not brothers.

*(D) The woman thinks he likes sports and his brother likes reading, but he tells her that the truth is the opposite of this: He likes reading and his brother likes sports.

5. (A) "Stopped giving" (no longer give) is confused with "quit taking" (no longer take).

(B) It is not Mary who has quit (stopped attending); it is the woman who has stopped giving the class.

(C) It is not Mary's class, but the woman's.

*(D) The woman has postponed (delayed giving) her class, but only for a month. After a month the class will resume.

6.*(A) The man's exclaiming "have I!" means that "yes, he has gone over the results." The expression "you won't believe them" indicates that "they are very surprising."

(B) It's not that he "wouldn't go over" (examine) the statistics, but that he thinks the statistics are so surprising that the woman "wouldn't believe" them.

(C) The expression "you won't believe them" means that the statistics are very surprising.

(D) "Have I!" is an exclamation meaning "Yes, I have."

7. (A) The woman is referring to how readable his handwriting is. She is not referring to how well he writes.

*(B) If the man's handwriting is "difficult to read" (not legible), she cannot type his report by Wednesday.

(C) The question does not concern how fast the report is written, but how fast it can be typed.

(D) The question of how fast it can be typed depends on how easily the handwriting can be read.

8.*(A) If Bob won't let the man touch his recorder, it is probably because he doesn't trust him to use it correctly.
  (B) It is the woman who is recording this lecture.
  (C) The similar sounds of "yet" and "bet" are confused.
  (D) The man "bets" (speculates) that Bob won't let him use the recorder.

9. (A) "Not only" is confused with "only."
  (B) It is not the department head who is complaining. Rather, Dan and Maria are complaining to the department head.
  (C) Maria is one of the people who may be exaggerating the problem.
  *(D) Both Dan and Maria are complaining about a problem that the man thinks they are exaggerating.

10. (A) The man doesn't want to go to the shopping mall, so they probably won't go there.
  *(B) The street bazaar is the only place that neither person objects to, so they will probably go there.
  (C) The woman doesn't want to go downtown, so they probably won't go there.
  (D) "Downtown" and "mall" are confused with "town hall."

11.*(A) If Joan leaves the room every time Andrew comes in, she probably doesn't want to see him.
  (B) Walking in to or out of a room is confused with taking a walk together.
  (C) Andrew and Joan had an argument, but it didn't necessarily occur while they were going for a walk.
  (D) "To go for a walk" (take a stroll) is confused with "walk in (enter) and walk out" (leave).

12. (A) "You know Roger" means "You know what Roger is like." They are discussing his being late, which is typical of Roger. He probably didn't forget. He's just late.
  (B) Roger is probably usually late as opposed to usually being early (see A).
  (C) If Roger is already one hour late and it will be another hour before he comes, than he is not on time (see A).
  *(D) Roger is an hour late, but the man tells the woman that Roger will come even later.

13. (A) "Had no problems" means that it was not difficult for her to sell her car.
  (B) It is not that Nancy wouldn't sell her car, but rather that the woman wouldn't have bought it.
  (C) "No problems" refers to "no problems in selling the car," not to "no problems with the car."
  *(D) Since Nancy had no problems selling her car, she sold it easily.

14. (A) "Had to finish by Monday" (last Monday) is confused with "will have finished by Monday" (next Monday).
  (B) "Finished last Monday" is confused with "will have finished by Monday" (next Monday).
  *(C) "Will have finished by Monday" means that on Monday all her exams will be done.
  (D) "Finished by Monday" (a Monday in the past) is confused with "will have finished by Monday" (next Monday).

15. (A) The woman does not want to talk. She wants to study.
  (B) The woman doesn't want to go to the library; the man wants her to go there.
  *(C) The woman is trying to study, but she is having difficulty because the man is talking too much.
  (D) It is the man who wants the woman to go to the library to study. The woman doesn't want to get a book.

Exercise L39 (p. 68, transcript on p. 522)
1. (B) In this case, the expression "how about" is used informally to mean "Would you like . . . ?"
  (D) "What a good idea" expresses the woman's opinion of having a cup of coffee. In other words, she would like one and is accepting the man's offer.

2. (B) The woman is describing an exam. She is making a complaint (stating what she found unsatisfactory) about its difficulty.
  (D) The man uses the expression "cheer up" to try to help her feel better.

3. (A) The man is explaining the reason he wasn't in class. He is giving an excuse.
  (D) Although "I'm sorry" can be used to introduce an apology, it is also used to express regret when you hear sad news. The woman is expressing her feelings of sympathy.

4. (B) When the man uses the expression "fit me in," he means "find a time to make an appointment" (arrange a time for a meeting).
  (C) The woman wants to know if 11:45 is a convenient time for the man to come. She suggests a time.

5. (B) The woman uses the idiom "give me a hand" to ask for help in doing something.
  (C) Although "which" is used to indicate a choice, the man is asking her whether she wants his left hand or his right hand. He is making a joke by taking her words "give me a hand" literally.

6. (A) The man's question "Don't you think so?" means that he is asking if the woman has the same opinion as he does.
  (C) "You sure would" indicates that the woman agrees that the man would look better with a mustache.

7. (B) "I don't understand" and "mix-up" (change in order, disorder) indicate that the man is confused.

   (C) The woman is advising the man (telling him what she thinks he should do). In this case, she thinks the man shouldn't worry (be concerned).

8. (A) The man's problem is that he needs to have his watch fixed.

   (D) The woman suggests that he take it to the jewelry store where it can be fixed.

Exercise L40 (p. 69, transcript on p. 523)

1. (B) The woman says "You can, can you" to tease the man about his boastfulness.

2. (B) The woman uses the expression "sick of" to mean that she is annoyed. She is making a complaint (stating what she finds unsatisfactory) about busywork (work she feels is not useful).

3. (B) The man's apology ("I'm sorry") and excuse ("I've got a headache") imply that he is refusing the invitation.

4. (B) The man says "he doesn't know," not because he actually doesn't know, but because he is politely disagreeing with the woman.

5. (B) The man is declining dessert by stating the reason he doesn't want any.

6. (A) The woman is explaining where the car keys can be found because she is agreeing to the man's request to use the car.

7. (B) The man criticizes the paintings by saying they look like a child's work. This indicates that he dislikes them. The woman disagrees with his opinion (she likes the paintings).

8. (A) The woman says "help yourself," meaning "you're welcome to take as many cookies as you want."

Exercise L41 (p. 70, transcript on p. 523)

1. B, C, D   4. A, B, D
2. B, C   5. B, C, D
3. A, C, D

Exercise L42 (p. 71, transcript on p. 523)

1. C   2. B   3. A   4. C   5. A

Exercise L43 (p. 71, transcript on p. 523)

1. A   2. C   3. C   4. B   5. A

Exercise L44 (p. 72, transcript on p. 523)

1. A   2. C   3. A   4. A   5. B

Exercise L45 (p. 73, transcript on p. 523)

1. A   2. B   3. C   4. C   5. B

Exercise L46 (p. 73, transcript on p. 524)

1. B   2. A   3. B   4. A   5. C

Exercise L47 (p. 74, transcript on p. 524)

1. (B) Identifying vocabulary words are "ace," "king," "suit," and "trump."

2. (C) Identifying vocabulary words and phrases are "ball," "tee," "club," "swing," "hole in one," and "the green."

3. (B) Identifying vocabulary words and phrases are "my turn," "roll the dice," and "land on (collect $200) square."

4. (A) Identifying vocabulary words are "front" and "lawn mower."

5. (D) Identifying vocabulary words are "pail," "soapy water," "mud," "fenders," and "tires."

Exercise L48 (p. 75, transcript on p. 524)

1. (D) Identifying vocabulary words are "turkey," "rye," "drink," and "sandwich."

2. (C) Identifying vocabulary words are "biography," "card catalog," and "subject."

3. (A) Identifying vocabulary words and phrases are "soups," "aisle 10," and "canned fruits and vegetables."

4. (B) Identifying vocabulary words are "makeup," "performance," and "season."

5. (B) Identifying vocabulary words are "radiator," "brake shoes," "fix," and "hole."

Exercise L49 (p. 76, transcript on p. 524)

1. (B) Identifying vocabulary words are "account," "savings," and "checking."

2. (A) Identifying vocabulary words are "suntan lotion" and "sand."

3. (B) Identifying vocabulary words and phrases are "return the car" and "extra charge if you don't bring it back with a full tank."

4. (D) Identifying vocabulary words and phrases are "report a missing van," "chief," and "Officer."

5. (A) Identifying vocabulary words are "dive," "breast stroke," and "team."

Exercise L50 (p. 77, transcript on p. 524)

1. (B) The man's question "What's the matter?" indicates that something may be troubling Lisa. She answers that she has "failed" (not passed) Spanish again. Therefore, she is probably "depressed" (feeling sad).

2. (D) The woman offers to help the man study for an exam. He doesn't accept her offer. He says that it is useless because he cannot understand anyway. This indicates that he is "discouraged" (he has lost his enthusiasm).

3. (C) A "defiant" person is one who shows independence by refusing to behave in the expected way. The woman thinks the man shouldn't go to class dressed in a particular outfit. He defies her by doing it anyway.

4. (A) The expression "win hands down" means "win very easily." The man's use of that expression shows his "confidence" (his certainty of winning).

5. (C) The man shows "indecisiveness" (inability to decide) by not being able to decide about summer school and by asking for the woman's opinion.

6. (B) The woman mentions Cindy's failure to turn in an assignment and the man mentions her sleeping through class. The man's statement indicates that this is typical behavior for Cindy. Although she may be tired for other reasons, "laziness" is the only reason in the set of answers which would describe this kind of behavior.

7. (D) The woman indicates that Stephanie types well and gets things done on time. These are characteristics of someone who is "efficient" (competent).

8. (C) The woman states that she is allergic to cats. A person with an allergy will become sick when coming in contact with a particular substance (in this case, a cat) which does not normally bother people.

Exercise L51 (p. 77, transcript on p. 525)

1. (B) The man is suggesting they go get a drink. The woman rejects the suggestion by pointing out that they might miss the end of the game. Because the woman strongly opposes leaving before the end, the man will probably wait for his friend.

2. (B) Although the woman doesn't say that she broke the glass, her mentioning a "crash" implies that the woman dropped or knocked over the glass of milk and that's why it is no longer on the table.

3. (A) The woman is asking the man if she can come over for help. Therefore, the man is probably good at math.

4. (A) If the woman keeps advising Chris to study harder, it is probably because he needs to improve his grades. Therefore, he isn't doing well in his studies.

5. (B) Since Tim and Dave don't get along, and Dave is definitely coming, the man probably won't invite Tim.

6. (B) Although the man says that the party will be over, the woman's response that he is being silly indicates that the man is just complaining about their being late and that the party, in fact, will not be over.

7. (B) If the man is encouraged by the fact that Linda got the job without experience, it is probably because he wants a similar job and doesn't have experience either.

8. (A) The man's saying "nothing that you would want to read" indicates that what he wrote would not interest the woman.

Exercise L52 (p. 78, transcript on p. 525)

1. (A), (B) The meanings of "I'm afraid" (I'm frightened) and "I'm afraid" (an expression used to show regret or concern) are confused.

 *(C) The woman uses the phrase "I'm afraid" to show regret that she can't go with the man because she will be busy writing the report.

 (D) The woman gives no indication of willingness to go out after the report has been written.

2. (A) A bank teller doesn't sell train tickets.
 (B) A flight attendant works on a plane, not a train.
 (C) An engineer doesn't sell the tickets.
 *(D) The ticket seller is giving the man his tickets and information concerning the departure times and place of the train.

3. (A) Tim was upset because he didn't get to Boston.
 *(B) Washington, D.C., and New York City are the two places the woman says that Tim visited.
 (C) The similar sounds of "New Orleans" and "New York" are confused.
 (D) "Denver" is not mentioned.

4.*(A) The woman states that the concert begins at 8:15.
 (B) The similar sounds of "8:50" and "8:15" are confused.
 (C) 10:30 is when the concert ends.
 (D) 12:00 (midnight) is the time the speakers will get home.

5. (A) The similar sounds of "$20.95" and "$29.95" are confused.
 (B) Although the sale price for two is half as much as the regular price for two, the price given has already been halved.
 *(C) This is the price of one jogging outfit, but the sale price is two for the same price as one outfit.
 (D) The two outfits together would have cost "$59.90," if they hadn't been on sale.

6. (A) The woman's remark suggests that *she* doesn't enjoy taking the children on the bus. Nothing is stated about how the children feel about taking the bus.
 (B) The mother must be able to get the children to the lesson by bus because her remark indicates that she doesn't like taking the children by bus.
 (C) If the man did his own maintenance work, he would not be taking the car in for an oil change.
 *(D) If the family had two cars, the woman could take the children in the second car while the man takes the first car in for an oil change.

7. (A) No vocabulary is used that indicates horseback riding.
 *(B) When people go camping, they would probably take "a tent," "a cooler for food," "some blankets," and "a first aid kit."
 (C) The need for a tent means that the people will be sleeping outside. Therefore, they probably are not going skiing.
 (D) A tent is not used in a boat.

8. (A) Bookstores do not have card catalogs.
 (B) The meanings of "check" (a bank voucher) and "check out" (to officially take a book out of the library) are confused.
 *(C) The vocabulary "check out a book" and "card catalog" suggest that the conversation takes place in a library.
 (D) Cards and books can be found in a gift shop and purchased at the checkout counter. However, a gift shop would not have a card catalog, and the book is being checked out, not purchased.

9. (A) "See a film" is what people do when they go to the movies.
   (B) The woman suggests that they go to the theater.
   (C) The man wants to watch a football game on TV.
   *(D) The man is not going to attend a football game but watch one on TV.

10. (A) The fact that the man is now studying for final exams makes this a false statement.
    *(B) The fact that the man has begun his studying only a week before the final exams suggests that he probably doesn't study very often.
    (C) The final exams are next week and he is studying for them now.
    (D) There is nothing stated that suggests the man is studying in the library.

11. (A) If the man thought there was little to worry about, he would not be so worried about it.
    *(B) If the interview is the most important event in the man's life, it is very important to him.
    (C) The woman calls the interview "little," meaning "unimportant," not "short."
    (D) It cannot be inferred from the conversation whether or not this is the man's first interview.

12. (A) "An order form from the book" is confused with "ordering a book."
    (B) "Tearing out the order form" is confused with "tearing up a book."
    (C) "Fill in the spaces with numbers" (put numbers in the blanks) is confused with "black out the numbers in the spaces" (cover the numbers written in the blanks with black).
    *(D) The man wants to order shoes from a catalog and the woman is showing him how to do that.

13. *(A) If the man had seen Lynn's dog, he wouldn't have thought she had a new cat.
    (B) Lynn has a new dog. There is no information concerning whether or not the man has a dog.
    (C) Lynn has a new dog, but there is no information concerning whether or not she has a cat.
    (D) It is not a new cat, but a new dog that the man hasn't seen.

14. (A) She hasn't forgotten the book, but she wants the man to forget it.
    *(B) Since the woman was hoping that the man would forget about the book, it can be inferred that she probably wants to keep it.
    (C) Had the woman returned the book, she wouldn't have wanted the man to forget it.
    (D) It is the man who lent the woman the book.

15. *(A) If Rita does not thank people for "their time and trouble" (the time and effort they have spent doing things for her), then she hasn't shown that she appreciates what they have done for her.
    (B) "Trouble" (problems) is confused with the expression "their time and trouble" (see A).
    (C) It's not that she wastes people's time, but that she doesn't thank them for the time they spend doing things for her.
    (D) It was the man who was helpful to Rita.

Part C Short talks and conversations

Exercise L53 (p. 81, transcript on p. 526)
1. warts (A second speaker will probably continue the conversation by answering the first speaker's question about the wart.)
2. Persian carpets (The first speaker wants a Persian carpet but knows little about them. The second speaker may give him some information about Persian carpets or give him the name of someone who can give advice about buying them.)
3. the United Kingdom (The speaker will probably go on to give more facts about the United Kingdom.)
4. the Award for Architecture (The speaker will probably continue his talk by giving more information about the award. He may discuss the qualities an architect must have in order to be considered for the award.)
5. patterns of Irish linen (The speaker will probably continue to talk about the patterns as he displays the Irish linen.)

Exercise L54 (p. 82, transcript on p. 526)
1. (A) Although the discussion may develop into the uses of acupuncture in the West, the talk will probably concentrate on the practice of acupuncture.
   (B) The topic sentence concerns acupuncture in China 5,000 years ago, not modern China.
   *(C) The talk has begun with the topic of the practice of acupuncture and will probably continue to discuss the development of acupuncture throughout the centuries.
   (D) There is no mention of arthritis or cures.
2. (A) Although fabric is made up of threads called fibers, the fibers in the topic sentence concern those of muscles.
   *(B) The talk begins with a description of muscles and will probably continue with more information about them.
   (C) Muscle fiber is measured in millimeters. The talk will probably not continue with details about millimeters.
   (D) The length of muscle fiber is mentioned. The talk will probably not continue with details about lengths in general.
3. (A) The shelves at the hardware store will probably be discussed, but hardware in general probably won't be.
   (B) The hardware store may be discussed, but stores in general probably won't be.
   (C) The shelves at the hardware store are metal, but that is only a detail about the shelves.
   *(D) The shelves are being discussed. The speaker may continue discussing the merits of metal shelves.

4. (A) There is no mention of skiing techniques.
   (B) The competition took place in Sun Valley, not the Alps.
   (C) Jim said something about a skiing competition, not skiing in general.
   *(D) The next speaker in the conversation will probably answer the first speaker's question concerning the competition.
5. (A) The talk mentions satellite communications technology, not communications technology in general.
   (B) The challenges mentioned are those in education, not in communication.
   (C) The satellites are those of communication, not education.
   *(D) The talk will probably expand on the possibilities and challenges in education that satellites have opened up.

Exercise L55 (p. 83, transcript on p. 526)
1. yes (topic = magic squares)
2. no (topic = the Pony Express)
3. no (topic = a part-time job)
4. yes (topic = an apartment close to campus)
5. no (topic = zoos)

Exercise L56 (p. 83, transcript on p. 526)
1. B   2. A   3. D   4. D   5. B

Exercise L57 (p. 84, transcript on p. 526)
These are sample answers. If possible, check your answers with a native speaker of English.
1. (B) gems *or* rocks
2. (B) test *or* trial
3. (B) records *or* report *or* diary
4. (B) charm *or* magical charm
5. (B) amount *or* quantity
6. (B) sighted *or* seen *or* observed
7. (B) attack
8. (B) part of a meal

Exercise L58 (p. 85, transcript on p. 527)
1. surnames   4. volunteers
2. bodies   5. pilgrims
3. mosses

Exercise L59 (p. 86, transcript on p. 527)
1. (A) elderly people
   (B) no home and no one to help
   (C) delegates
2. (A) the washing machine
   (B) a peculiar noise
   (C) a load
3. (A) a fire
   (B) the police
   (C) an arsonist started the fire
4. (A) climb of Mount Everest
   (B) a club
   (C) permits
5. (A) the East Coast
   (B) Mrs. Pickford
   (C) teaching position

Exercise L60 (p. 87, transcript on p. 527)
1. (B) It is not that the people in Homer's time used words from the Kárpathos dialect, but that the Kárpathos dialect uses words from the time of Homer.
2. (A) It is not the first hot-air balloon, but the first hot-air balloon which was piloted by a person on board.
3. (B) It is not that the word for "beautiful bird" means "tail feather," but that "quetzal," which is the name of a beautiful bird, means "tail feather."
4. (A) It wasn't the areas that set up the centers; the centers were set up in the areas.
5. (B) It is not our past which has been revolutionized, but our concepts which have been revolutionized.

Exercise L61 (p. 88, transcript on p. 527)
1. A, B, D   4. A, B
2. A, B   5. D
3. A, B, C, D

Exercise L62 (p. 88, transcript on p. 527)
1. C   2. C   3. B   4. B

Exercise L63 (p. 89, transcript on p. 528)
1. C   2. B   3. C   4. A

Exercise L64 (p. 90, transcript on p. 528)
1. C   2. B   3. C   4. A

Exercise L65 (p. 90, transcript on p. 529)
1. B   2. A   3. A   4. C

Exercise L66 (p. 91, transcript on p. 529)
1. B   2. C   3. A   4. B

Exercise L67 (p. 92, transcript on p. 529)
1. (C) Identifying vocabulary words are "arrows," "bull's-eye," "target," "shoot," and "bow."
2. (A) Identifying vocabulary words and phrases are "wrench," "tool box," "car," "change spark plugs," "change the oil," and "engine."
3. (B) Identifying vocabulary words and phrases are "Can I have a light," "matches," and "lighter."
4. (A) Identifying vocabulary words and phrases are "check," "move a queen any direction," "take a queen with a bishop," "take a bishop with a knight," and "loss."

Exercise L68 (p. 92, transcript on p. 530)
1. (B) Identifying vocabulary words and phrases are "save a person," "certified," "swimming tests," "get drowning people safely to shore," "life-saving classes," and "training."
2. (A) Identifying vocabulary words and phrases are "a haircut," "a permanent," "a trim," "cut short," "come to the sink," and "shampoo."
3. (D) Identifying vocabulary words and phrases are "collect call," "name and number," "area code," "busy," and "try later."
4. (D) Identifying vocabulary words and phrases are "organ," "wind instrument," "pull knob," "a stop," "pump air," "play with feet and hands," and "practice."

Exercise L69 (p. 93, transcript on p. 530)
1. (A) Identifying vocabulary words and phrases are "overcooked carrots," "canned peas," "cheaper than restaurants," "cook for 3,000 students," and "keep food hot for two hours."
2. (C) Identifying vocabulary words and phrases are "binoculars," "smoke over near the campground," "[fire] out of control," "fire in the trees," and "radio headquarters."
3. (C) Identifying vocabulary words and phrases are "report a stolen car," "check records," and "officer."
4. (D) Identifying vocabulary words and phrases are "ring," "rubies," "diamonds," "sapphire," "set," and "gold band."

Exercise L70 (p. 94, transcript on p. 531)
1. (C) The woman is envious because she also wants to get a car. The man gives an example of her being envious on a previous occasion.
2. (D) The woman is boasting about the condition of her teeth because she is pleased about the dentist's comment.
3. (A) The woman was not looking forward to the coming semester. The man "lifted her spirits" (made her feel better) by suggesting a way she can improve the semester.
4. (A) The man is describing why he wouldn't be able to work in a hospital (fainting, feeling sick to his stomach). His reasons indicate that he is squeamish (sensitive to unpleasant sights).
5. (B) The woman is accusing Pete of boasting about his sports abilities. A person who boasts a lot is a braggart.

Exercise L71 (p. 95, transcript on p. 531)
The best answer is given for each question; other possible answers are in parentheses.
1. (A) Mata Hari (French accusers)
    (B) at her trial (First World War)
    (C) a spy (eight charges, spying)
2. (A) play
    (B) last night
    (C) comedy about life in a small town
3. (A) this morning
    (B) elevator
    (C) didn't want to attend staff meeting
4. (A) Professor Adams
    (B) schedule (chemistry lab)
    (C) every week (on Wednesday)
5. (A) Leaning Tower of Pisa (base, landmark)
    (B) architects
    (C) stop or slow movement
6. (A) time of the Great Flood
    (B) Manx cat (tail, Ark, the door)
    (C) the Ark

Exercise L72 (p. 96, transcript on p. 531)
The information that answers the question is in parentheses.
1. B (at the Meridian Arena)
    D (from six to seventeen years old)
    E (daredevil acts)
2. A (which flying bird is the largest in the world)
    B (the albatross)
    D (the South American vulture)
3. B (build mud houses)
    C (New Mexico)
    E (They are mild.)
4. A (on a ship at sea)
    B (diving instructor)
    F (in 45 minutes)
5. A (fox hunting)
    C (Great Britain)
    D (animal rights campaigners)

Exercise L73 (p. 97, transcript on p. 532)
1. (A) Metropolitan Museum of Art, Manhattan
    (C) October 29th to January 18th (about three months)
    (E) Sunday
    (F) three
2. (A) communication disorders
    (B) disorder of speech or hearing mechanisms, abnormal functioning of the brain, unusual emotional or psychological problems
    (D) he or she may have difficulty communicating
    (F) a speech pathologist
3. (A) official languages of the United States
    (C) English
    (F) none
4. (A) doctor's office
    (B) doctor
    (D) bronchitis
    (E) how much she smokes (How much is "a lot"?)
5. (A) registration (registrar's) office
    (B) registers students
    (D) Monday, Wednesday, and Friday
    (E) College of Arts

Exercise L74 (p. 100, transcript on p. 532)
1. (D) The man states that he is eliminating starches so that he "can lose weight."
2. (B) The woman states that he should "cut down on his intake of fats."
3. (C) The woman gives examples of how to prepare meat.
4. (B) The man says he especially liked the gargoyles. Gargoyles are then defined by the referent "those grotesque heads."
5. (A) The man asks if gargoyles were used to frighten away bad spirits and the woman says "no."
6. (B) The woman states that the joke of gargoyles is that the ugly faces represent the stoneworkers' friends.

7. (D) The man states that he wonders if they (the stoneworkers and the friends) were friends afterwards.

8. (D) In the talk it is stated that the world's largest butterfly farm is both a sanctuary and breeding center. The remainder of the talk discusses why it was needed and what is being done there.

9. (D) In the talk it is stated that studies are being conducted. Examples of the research are given.

10. (D) Marketing butterflies is not mentioned in the talk.

11. (A) In the talk it is stated that research is being done to see how the ecological balance would be affected if foreign butterflies were to be imported.

12. (C) It is stated in the talk that these portraits were called shades.

13. (B) The mentioned materials are ivory, plaster, porcelain, and glass.

14. (C) It is stated in the talk that Étienne de Silhouette was an eighteenth-century French finance minister who was infamous for his stringent economics.

15. (A) Because the phrase "á la silhouette" meant "cheap," the term was used for this art form which was inexpensive to produce.

Exercise L75 (p. 102, transcript on p. 534)
Part A

1. (C) "Be finished" means "be over," and "in two weeks time" can be used to mean "the week after next."

2. (D) Since he caused the accident, it was not my fault.

3. (C) "Put up with" means "tolerate," and in this sentence the expression "ranting and raving" means "complaining."

4. (A) To sign up for a course means to enroll in a course. A crash course is a course in which one learns a large amount of information in a short period of time; in other words, it's intensive.

5. (B) The idiom "get mixed up" means "to be confused."

6. (B) If Mr. Simmons prefers walking in the rain to staying at home, he doesn't like to stay at home when it is raining.

7. (A) Rebecca missed the connecting flight to Chicago, and therefore she couldn't get on flight 219.

8. (C) "Is used to using" means "is accustomed to using." Since Virginia isn't used to using electric stoves, she has probably been accustomed to gas stoves.

9. (A) Sam was rich; therefore, Lisa married him.

10. (B) Mark took a trip to Indiana after he arrived in New York.

11. (B) The women had to "talk over" (discuss) a problem. The problem is having the car "worked on" (repaired).

12. (B) "Had better" means "should," and "apologize" means "say you are sorry for something." It was Margaret who lost Mrs. Morris's necklace, so Margaret should say she is sorry for losing it.

13. (C) "Get information" means "find out."

14. (B) "Irritated" means "upset," and "brought up" means "mentioned."

15. (D) In this sentence, "It's all right" means "she doesn't care."

16. (A) The expression "what about" is a way to make a suggestion, and the suggestion is to go to a different restaurant (new for them).

17. (A) The speaker cannot pay back the money owed until next week. "Yet" means "not now."

18. (C) If Kim doesn't object to the food, he thinks it is all right.

19. (B) "Jason's lines" are "his part of the script," and to memorize them "backwards and forwards" (thoroughly) means that he knows them extremely well.

20. (B) "Must have" means "probably," and "catch cold" means "get sick."

Part B

21. (B) The woman uses the expression "twist his arm" to imply that she had to pressure Peter because he didn't want to help. His not wanting to help can also be understood from her saying "It wasn't easy" in response to the man's question.

22. (D) The vocabulary for putting jigsaw puzzles together are "pieces fit," "interlock," "picture on the box," and "green pieces."

23. (C) The expression "That's not a minute too soon for me" means "Classes cannot be over soon enough to please me." In other words, the man is extremely eager for classes to be over.

24. (C) The woman had a flat tire, and the tire to replace it was flat too. Therefore, she had two flat tires.

25. (B) Robert promised to help solve students' problems that concerned housing.

26. (A) Because Sam has allergies, he had Barbara cut the bushes. Because bushes are plants, we can infer that Sam has allergies to plants.

27. (C) If someone "has a mind for something" (gain knowledge about something easily), that person is probably "good at it" (competent at doing it).

28. (B) The man is sorry (regrets) that she can't take the photograph because there is no film in the camera.

29. (D) The man didn't go to the review, didn't do his homework, didn't read the books, and he didn't pass the test.

30. (C) The woman is expressing her opinion of why the man keeps meeting Carol.

31. (D) The expression "go halves" means "share the cost." Because the woman does not have the money to buy gasoline for the trip, the man is suggesting that they share the cost of gas. Perhaps in that way she can afford the trip.

32. (B) The vocabulary words and phrases that refer to a ball game are "dribble the ball," "the court," "pass the ball," and "make a basket."
33. (A) The woman states that she is worried, and the man states that it will be the first time that a president will listen to her play in the concert.
34. (B) The vocabulary phrase that refers to car repairs is "scraping sound when the ignition is on."
35. (C) The man states that what the woman says about the traffic is said every day. This implies that he thinks the traffic is no different than usual.

Part C

36. (C) The woman states that she drives to New Orleans for this parade every year. The identifying vocabulary words are "parade," "pass by," and "float." Clowns and musicians can pass in a parade.
37. (B) The woman says she drives from Birmingham for the parade every year.
38. (B) The man says he thinks he'll come back next year.
39. (D) "Spectators" are people who watch an event, and the man and woman are watching a parade.
40. (A) The passage states that the Boston Tea Party was the first major act of defiance on the part of the American colonists.
41. (B) The "Boston Tea Party of 1773" means that 1773 is the date that the party took place.
42. (C) The colonists were defiant because the tax was imposed without their having a representative in the British Parliament to represent their interests ("taxation without representation").
43. (D) Prominent citizens dressed as Indians threw the cargo overboard.
44. (D) It can be inferred that Boston is where it took place because the party was called the "Boston Tea Party."
45. (B) Betty and Peter are living in Kenya and that is where the package is from.
46. (D) It can be inferred that Rachel opened the package because she describes what Betty sent her.
47. (A) The lions were in the package to Rachel and therefore were probably a gift to her.
48. (A) The interactive computer system is a way of training nursing students to make critical decisions without endangering the lives of patients.
49. (D) Students can make critical decisions and the computer will inform them whether or not the decision was correct.
50. (B) The professor states that one particularly helpful aspect of the program is that it can simulate body parts. This enables students to touch the body and even listen to the lungs.

SECTION 2   STRUCTURE AND WRITTEN EXPRESSION

Exercise S1 (p. 116)
1. N   3. C   5. C   7. C
2. N   4. N   6. N   8. C

Extended practice: The nouns in items 2, 7, and 8 can be either count or noncount.

Exercise S2 (p. 117)
1. people/persons
2. life
3. series
4. tooth
5. child
6. men
7. sheep
8. leaves
9. mice
10. geese

Exercise S3 (p. 117)
1. wave (The noun "wave" should be in its plural form "waves." The article "a" is needed for "wave" to be in its singular form.)
2. wildlives ("Wildlife" is a noncount noun and has no plural form.)
3. gram (The plural form is needed: there are "650 grams of gold.")
4. saint ("Saints" should be in its singular form because there was only one "first saint.")
5. This sentence is correct.
6. century ("Century" should be in its plural form: there are "two centuries.")
7. informations ("Information" is a noncount noun and takes the singular form.)
8. This sentence is correct.

Exercise S4 (p. 118)
1. This sentence is correct.
2. colony
3. disturbance
4. This sentence is correct.
5. This sentence is correct.
6. This sentence is correct.
7. importance
8. activity
9. arrival(s)
10. situation

Exercise S5 (p. 119)
1. "Politician" is the correct form for a person in the profession of politics.
2. "Motivation" is the correct noun form.
3. The use of "that kind" indicates that the noun "genes" should be in its singular form, "gene."
4. "Metalworker" should be in the plural form, "metalworkers," because there is a comparison between Yellin and all the other metalworkers in America.
5. "Children" is the plural form. An "s" should not be added.

6. The use of the plural verb "are" indicates that the noun "wolf" should be in its plural form, "wolves."
7. "Advice" does not have a plural form.
8. "Book" should be in its plural form, "books," because there are several books in a series.

Exercise S6 (p. 122)
1. an herb (see 1C, page 119)
2. Ø Mars (see 3F, page 120)
3. Ø school (see 4B, page 121)
4. the rich (see 3C, page 120)
5. An untold number (see 4A, page 121)
6. the only actor (see 3D, page 120)
7. an hour (see 2C, page 120)

Exercise S7 (p. 122)
1. This article is correct. (see 3F, page 120)
2. This article is correct. (see 3B, page 120)
3. the eighteenth century (see 3D, page 120)
4. An hour (see 1C, page 119)
5. Ø Russia (see 3G and 3H, page 121)
6. This article is correct. (see 1B, page 119)
7. Ø advice (see 4D, page 121)

Exercise S8 (p. 123)
1. (A) See Practice with Nouns, 1, page 114.
2. (A) See Practice with Articles and Demonstratives, 5B, page 122.
3. (A) See Practice with Nouns, 3D, page 115.
4. (B) See Practice with Articles and Demonstratives, 5A, page 122.
5. (A) See Practice with Nouns, 3D, page 115.
6. (B) See Practice with Articles and Demonstratives, 5B, page 122.
7. (B) See Practice with Nouns, 3D, page 115.
8. (B) See Practice with Articles and Demonstratives, 5A, page 122.

Exercise S9 (p.124)
1. This sentence is correct. (see 3A and 3D, page 120)
2. twice a year (see 2C, page 120)
3. For the first time ever (see 3D, page 120)
4. to find work (see 4D, page 121)
5. This sentence is correct. (see 4D, page 121)
6. Since the beginning (see 3D, page 120)
7. of improvisation (see 4D, page 121)
8. This sentence is correct. (see 3E, page 120)

Exercise S10 (p. 124)
1. (That) dissertations have to be completed within a four-year time limit.
   "That" should be "Those" or "These" (see 5B, page 122); "a" is correct.
2. The good Dr. Sneider began his first year at Arizona State University after having been appointed (a) associate professor.
   "The" is correct ("the" can be used before adjectives preceding names for emphasis); "a" should be "an" (see 1A, page 119).

3. At (a) height of the tourist season, the small seaside community boasts a population of 15,000.
   The first "a" should be "the" (see 3D, page 120); the other articles are correct.
4. Since (the) beginning the research, Dr. Ahmedi has collected 70 different kinds of plant rocks.
   The first "the" is incorrect (an article is not used before a verb); the second "the" is correct.
5. In a famous book by Daniel Defoe, the hero, Robinson Crusoe, spent 20 years on (a) island.
   The first two articles are correct; the last "a" should be "an" (see 1A, page 119).
6. (Those) child's computer was installed with added features for the blind.
   "Those" should be "That" (see 5B, page 122); "the" is correct.
7. The tourists on the bus witnessed the beauty of (the) Mount Rushmore.
   The first three articles are correct; the last "the" should be omitted (see 3F, page 120).
8. The kangaroo travels at speeds up to 20 miles (the) hour by jumping on (the) powerful hind legs.
   The first "the" is correct; the second "the" should be "a" (see 2C, page 120); the third "the" should be "its" (see 3E, page 120).

Exercise S11 (p. 126)
1. his, their
2. his, they, their, they
3. themselves
4. its
5. it, her
6. itself, us
7. their
8. its, its

Exercise S12 (p. 126)
1. "Them" is an object pronoun that is used incorrectly in the possessive adjective position. "Their" is the correct form.
2. "Their" is a possessive adjective, but it is used in the subject position. "They" is the correct form.
3. "Yourself" is a reflexive pronoun and is used in the correct position. However, "yourself" refers to only "you." "Yourselves" refers to "you and other people" and is the correct pronoun to use.
4. "Their" is a possessive adjective and is used correctly.
5. "They" is a subject pronoun, but here it is used in the object position. "Them" is the correct object of the preposition "of."
6. "Theirselves" is an incorrect form of "themselves."
7. "His" is a possessive pronoun used correctly in a noun position.
8. "Their" is a possessive adjective. However, "days" does not belong to anyone. The object pronoun "them" should be used in this position because the meaning is "it took days for them to reach the lower regions."

Exercise S13 (p. 127)
1. their: Vikings
   his: chief
   his: chief

2. them: creatures
3. they: people
   it: symbol
4. its: the English House of Lords
   they: members
   it: something
   they: members
5. his: the dean
   it: university
6. This: place
   its: ship
7. his: Charles d'Orléans
   his: Charles d'Orléans
   this: Charles d'Orléans smuggled out rhyming love
       letters to his wife
8. its: nutmeg
   their: kernels

Exercise S14 (p. 127)
1. "They" should refer to "site" which is singular. Therefore, the correct pronoun is "it."
2. "Us" should refer to "risks." Therefore, the correct pronoun is "them."
3. "Themselves" refers to the "Tayronas" and is used correctly.
4. "Their" should refer to "gun," which is singular. Therefore, the correct pronoun is "its."
5. "Their" refers to "people" and is correct.
6. "It" should refer to "books." Therefore, the correct pronoun is "them."
7. "Themselves" should refer to "Colonel Shelly." Therefore, the correct pronoun is either "himself" or "herself."
8. "It" should refer to "properties," which is plural. Therefore, the correct pronoun is "them."

Exercise S15 (p. 128)
1. Does the pronoun "others" refer to "other records" or "other travelers"?
2. Does the word "it" refer to "the process" or to "the result"?
3. The word "them" can refer only to "hieroglyphics."
4. The word "their" can refer only to "idols."
5. Does the word "they" refer to "seals" or "biologists"?
6. Does the word "it" refer to "waste," "industry," or "environment"?
7. The word "they" can refer only to "snowflakes."
8. Does the word "they" refer to "needs" or to "resources"?
9. The word "them" refers to both "dew point" and "ambient temperature."
10. The word "they" refers to "botanists."

Exercise S16 (p. 129)
1.*(A) A possessive adjective is usually used with body parts. Therefore, "the" should be "their."
   (B) "Together" is an adverb indicating "how" crickets rub their legs.
   (C) "Their" refers to the plural noun "crickets."
   (D) In this case, "sound" is a noncount noun meaning that which one hears.

2. (A) "Progressive" is an adjective that describes Constantinople.
   (B) "Its" is a possessive adjective that refers to Constantinople.
   (C) "Care" is a noncount noun.
  *(D) "The" is used with adjectives that represent the group. "The destitute" means "destitute people."
3. (A) "A" is used with a singular count noun mentioned for the first time.
  *(B) "Wolves" is the plural form of "wolf."
   (C) "Encircled" is the correct past tense verb form.
   (D) Since "moose" has the same form for singular and plural, the number of moose cannot be determined.
4.*(A) The possessive adjective "their" should be used to refer to "divers."
   (B) "Thrown" is a verb that is used as an adjective to indicate which money.
   (C) "The" is used when it is clear in the situation which thing is being referred to: the river that pilgrims throw money into.
   (D) The word "pilgrim" indicates that more pilgrims throw money into the river.
5. (A) The verb "hope" agrees with its subject, "conservationists."
   (B) "Someday" indicates "when" the conservationists hope the wildlife will be reestablished.
   (C) "Populations" is used because there are many populations: a population of lions, a population of pandas, etc.
  *(D) "The" is used with adjectives that represent a group. "The wild" means "wild areas."
6. (A) "The" is used when it is clear in the situation which thing is being referred to: here it's the institute.
  *(B) "Participation" is a noncount noun and, therefore, has no plural form.
   (C) "Them" is an object pronoun and refers to "teachers."
   (D) Both the singular and plural form of "lodging" are acceptable.
7. (A) The plural verb "are" indicates that the plural subject "dogs" is correct.
   (B) "Are trained" is the passive voice.
  *(C) "The" is used with adjectives that represent a group. "The blind" means "blind people."
   (D) "Loyal" is an adjective. It is parallel to the adjectives "intelligent" and "calm."
8. (A) "The" is used because the noun "sale" is identified by the phrase "of turtles."
   (B) The plural form "turtles" indicates that more than one turtle was on sale.
   (C) "They" refers to "turtles" and is the subject of the verb "posed."
  *(D) "Children" is the plural form of "child." Turtles were a disease risk to more than one child.

9. (A) "Inevitably" is an adverb that indicates "how" certain it is that scholars disagree.
 *(B) "The" should be used before a noun when it is clear in the situation which thing is being referred to: the authenticity of many objects.
 (C) "Origins" refers to many objects.
 (D) "Unknown" is the adjective describing "origins."

10. (A), (B) "The fruit bat" refers to a particular type of bat.
 (C) "To have" is an infinitive phrase used with the verb "to have found."
 *(D) The singular form "system" should be used with the article "a."

11. (A) "The" is used when it is clear in the situation which thing is being referred to: lines of American poetry.
 (B) "Poetry" is a noncount noun.
 (C) The aux-word "were" agrees with the subject "seven."
 *(D) The possessive adjective "her" should be used with the noun "lifetime" to refer to Emily Dickinson.

12.*(A) "Chinese" has the same singular and plural form.
 (B) "The" is used when it is clear in the situation which thing is being referred to: the word "happiness."
 (C) "White" refers to "white color."
 (D) "Tree" refers to the concept of tree, not to a particular tree.

13. (A) The plural noun "strikes," meaning "discoveries," indicates that more than one strike has provided fuel.
 *(B) "The" is not used with the names of states.
 (C) "Its" is a possessive adjective and refers to "Alaska."
 (D) "Growth" is a noncount noun.

14. (A) "Totem" is an adjective that describes the kind of poles.
 (B) The plural noun "records" indicates that more than one record is provided.
 (C) The article "a" indicates that "lineage" is singular.
 *(D) "Its" should be used as the possessive adjective referring to "tribe."

15. (A) The verb "serve" indicates that the plural subject "hot springs" is correct.
 (B) The article "a" is used because "bathhouse" is mentioned for the first time.
 *(C) "Them" is an object pronoun and cannot be used to show possession. Either the possessive adjective "their" referring to "the people" of the town, or the article "the" referring to that particular town, could be used here.
 (D) The singular for "town" indicates that there is only one town.

16. (A) The singular form "capital" refers to one town, "Sitka."
 (B) "The" is used when it is clear in the situation which thing is being referred to: the town named Sitka.
 *(C) The article "the" should be used with the plural noun form "legacies."
 (D) "Its" is a possessive adjective and refers to Sitka.

17. (A) The verb "remain" indicates that the plural subject "scars" is correct.
 (B) "The" is used when it is clear in the situation which thing is being referred to: the earthquake that left scars.
 (C) In this case, "rock" is a noncount noun.
 *(D) "Its" is the possessive adjective that should be used to refer to "earthquake."

18.*(A) The verb "allow" indicates that the subject "ligament" should be in the plural form.
 (B) "Whale" may refer to the class of whales or to a specific whale. In either case, the article "the" is used.
 (C) The "jaws" consist of a set, an upper jaw and a lower jaw.
 (D) "Its" is a possessive adjective and refers to whale.

19. (A) The article "a" indicates that "stronghold" is singular.
 *(B) The plural noun "forces" indicates that the article "an" is incorrect. Either the article "the," indicating particular forces, or no article, indicating forces in general, would be correct.
 (C), (D) "The" is used when there is only one of something. In this case, there has been only one "war" called the Spanish civil war.

20. (A) The verb "dissolves" indicates that the singular subject "limestone" is correct.
 (B) "The" is used because the noun "surface" is identified by the word "ground," and it is clear that "surface" is being referred to.
 *(C) The verb "collapses" indicates that the singular form "land" should be used.
 (D) The verb "forms" is parallel with the verb "collapses."

21.*(A) The noun "fish" is both plural and singular.
 (B) "That" is the relative pronoun which refers to "algae and mosses."
 (C) "The" is used when it is clear in the situation which thing is being referred to: the waters of Australia.
 (D) The plural form "waters" indicates that there are various water areas.

22. (A) The verb "show" indicates that the plural form "sculptures" is correct.
 *(B) "Him" should be used as the object pronoun for the verb "show."
 (C), (D) Borglum is one specific person and, therefore, can be only one in a group of artists.

23.*(A) The verb "have" indicates that the plural form "historians" should be used.
   (B) "The" is used because there is only one Frenchman named Clement Ader.
   (C) The article "a" indicates that the singular form "leap" is correct.
   (D) The article "a" indicates that the singular form "flight" is correct.
24. (A) "A" is used with a singular count noun mentioned for the first time.
   (B) The plural form "sailplanes" indicates that more than one sailplane was designed.
   *(C) The singular form "inventor" should be used because the doctor can only be one inventor.
   (D) "Bicycle" is singular because it refers to one type of bicycle invented.
25.*(A) "Craftsmen" should be used to refer to "Finns."
   (B) In this case, "rule" is a noncount noun.
   (C) "The" is used because the noun "cabin" is identified by the word "log."
   (D) "Cabin" is singular because it refers to log cabins as a type of cabin.

Exercise S17 (p. 134)
1. "Fishermen" is the complete subject of the verb "thought."
2. "Sam" is the complete subject of the verb "plans." The phrase "along with other students" is not part of the subject and does not affect the verb.
3. The complete subject is "St. John's Cathedral." The subject noun which agrees with the verb "is" is "Cathedral." The word order of this sentence has been changed from "St. John's Cathedral is pictured on the one-dollar stamp."
4. The complete subject is "birds, mammals, reptiles, and fish that are not hunted, fished, or trapped." The subject nouns which agree with the verb "need" are "birds, mammals, reptiles, and fish."
5. "Scientists" is the complete subject of the verb "can measure."
6. The complete subject is "Far too many preservation programs in too many states." The subject noun which agrees with the verb "rely" is "programs."
7. "It" is the complete subject of the verb "causes."
8. The complete subject is "Pesticide residues in livestock." The subject noun which agrees with the verb "are" is "residues."

Exercise S18 (p. 135)
1. "How wildlife has adapted to life along the road systems" is a clause used as a subject.
2. "To be among 200-foot-high towering rocks" is an infinitive phrase used as a subject.
3. "Isolating the insects" is a gerund phrase used as a subject.
4. "What was decided during the meeting" is a clause used as a subject.

5. "Whispering in class" is a gerund phrase used as a subject.
6. "To create and produce new combinations of line and color" is an infinitive phrase used as a subject.
7. "What caused the most damage to Michelangelo's works in the Sistine Chapel" is a clause used as a subject.
8. "Rolling dice, buying property, and accumulating play money" are gerund phrases used as a plural subject.

Exercise S19 (p. 135)
1. C See Practice with Nouns, 3D, page 115.
2. I "Physics" is singular and takes the verb "is." See Practice with Nouns, 3G, page 115.
3. C See Practice with Subjects, 3E, page 133.
4. I The subject "crossing Puget Sound in ferries" is a gerund phrase and takes the singular verb "is." See Practice with Subjects, 3H, page 133.
5. I "Each" indicates that all rivers and ravines are being discussed as individual units. Therefore, it takes the verb "creates." See Practice with Nouns, 2D, page 114.
6. I The subject "president" is singular and takes the verb "is meeting." See Practice with Subjects, 3B, page 132.
7. C "Two weeks" is considered a single unit and takes the verb "is." See Practice with Nouns, 3F, page 115.
8. I "Lion and lioness" are two nouns that together make a plural subject, which takes the verb "are." See Practice with Subjects, 3C, page 133.

Exercise S20 (p. 136)
1. (C) (C) has an infinitive with the subject preceded by "for." This structure can take a subject position. (A) is incorrect because it contains both a subject and a verb. (B) is incorrect because it implies that "the fact (that nutmeg yields fruit) takes eight years" rather than "it takes eight years for nutmeg to yield fruit. (D) is incorrect because it is a prepositional phrase, which cannot take the subject position.
2. (C) The sentence needs a simple subject that agrees with the singular verb.
   (A) is an infinitive but is illogical because of the redundant verb "use." (B) is not a complete clause and, therefore, cannot be used as a subject. (D) is a prepositional phrase and cannot be used as a subject.
3. (B) "Clenching the teeth" is a gerund phrase and can take the subject position.
   (A) and (D) are simple subjects, but are not logical because teeth do not clench themselves. Rather, something else (the jaw) clenches the teeth. (C) is not a complete clause and, therefore, cannot be used as a subject.

4. (D) The sentence needs a simple subject that agrees with the verb "do."
   (A) is not a complete clause and, therefore, cannot be used as a subject. (B) is incorrect because it implies that 6 percent, rather than the stated 26 percent, is the total. (C) is a prepositional phrase and cannot be used as a subject.

5. (D) The sentence needs a subject that is the name of the sport.
   (A), an infinitive, is not the name of the sport. (B) is not a complete clause and, therefore, cannot be used as a subject. (C) is a piece of equipment used in the sport.

6. (A) (A) completes the clause that is used as a subject.
   (B) added to the sentence makes a complete independent clause, which cannot be used as a subject. Neither an infinitive phrase (C) nor a gerund phrase (D) can be used to complete the clause.

7. (A) (A) is a list of nouns, which can be used as a plural subject and agrees with the plural verb "are."
   (B) is not a complete clause and, therefore, cannot be used as a subject. (C) and (D) use phrases that take a singular verb.

8. (D) The sentence needs a simple subject that agrees with the verb "began."
   (A) is not a complete clause and, therefore, cannot be used as a subject. (B) is illogical because an infinitive phrase cannot perform an activity such as beginning to set up a business. (C) needs an article to be correct.

9. (B) (B) completes the clause that is used as a subject.
   (A) or (C) added to the sentence makes a complete independent clause, which cannot be used as a subject. (D) is an infinitive subject and takes a singular verb.

10. (B) In (B) the gerund phrase is used as a subject and takes the singular verb "makes."
    (A) and (C) are independent clauses and, therefore, cannot be used as subjects. In (D) the subject "climbers and trekkers" is plural and needs a plural verb.

Exercise S21 (p. 137)
1. the castle of Neuschwanstein
2. Ross Island
3. true
4. believed
5. hoped
6. coronary heart disease
7. disputed
8. stuttering

Exercise S22 (p. 137)
1. females
2. lines
3. Cricket St. Thomas Wildlife Park
4. services
5. the southern states
6. a renaissance
7. special troughs
8. Australia

Exercise S23 (p. 138)
1. (B) A subject and verb are needed to complete the sentence. (A) and (B) have subjects and verbs. However, since the incomplete sentence does not indicate the existence of something, (A) cannot complete the sentence. "It" in (B) is used at the beginning of the sentence to emphasize the object – the fact that the invention of the camera changed how artists painted horses.

2. (A) Only a subject is needed to complete the sentence. (A) and (C) have only subjects. However, since the incomplete sentence does not contain a noun group which indicates existence, (C) does not complete the sentence. The pronoun "it," in (A) can be used as a subject to complete the sentence and can refer to "crocodile."

3. (D) Only a subject is needed to complete this sentence. (B) and (D) have only subjects. However, the incomplete sentence does not contain a noun group which indicates existence, so (B) does not complete this sentence. The pronoun "it" in (D) can be used as a subject to complete the sentence and can refer to "arrangement."

4. (B) A subject and verb are needed to complete the sentence. (B) and (C) have subjects and verbs. However, the incomplete sentence contains a noun group which indicates existence (nutrition and adult literacy classes), so only (B) can complete the sentence.

5. (D) A subject and verb are needed to complete the sentence. (B) and (D) have subjects and verbs. However, the incomplete sentence contains a noun group which indicates existence (noisy market stalls), so only (D) can complete the sentence.

6. (A) A subject and verb are needed to complete the sentence. (A) and (B) have subjects and verbs. However, the incomplete sentence contains a noun group which indicates existence (a growing demand), so only (A) can complete the sentence.

7. (C) The sentence is complete and cannot take another subject and verb as in (A) and (B) or a pronoun as in (D). However, the adverb "there" in (C) can be used to emphasize the place, "the center of old Sanaa."

8. (D) A subject and verb are needed to complete the sentence. Both (C) and (D) have subjects and verbs. The phrase "there is" in (C) needs to be followed by a noun. The phrase "it is" (D) can be followed by an adjective. "Impossible" is an adjective so (D) completes the sentence.

Exercise S24 (p. 139)

1. (A) "Surprises" is the main verb and "are" is the verb for a clause used as a subject. A subject is needed to complete the dependent clause.
   (B) added to the sentence makes a complete independent clause which cannot be used as a subject. (C) and (D) have both a subject and a verb, so they cannot be used as subjects.

2. (B) A subject and verb are needed to complete the sentence. (B) has both a subject "drops" and a verb "drip."
   (A) and (C) have no verbs. (D) is a clause that can be used as a subject but not as a verb.

3. (D) The independent clause is complete. Therefore, either a clause or phrase is needed in the blank. (D) is a phrase.
   (A) has verbs that need a subject. The use of (B) makes a complete independent clause. (C) is a dependent clause that takes a subject position in an independent clause.

4. (B) A subject is needed to complete the sentence. (A) and (C) contain both a verb and a subject. (D) is an incomplete clause and, therefore, cannot be used as a subject.

5. (B) A singular subject is needed to complete the sentence.
   (A), (C), and (D) all contain both a subject and a verb.

6. (A) "Has come" is the main verb and "is" is the verb for the dependent clause used as a subject. Only a subject is needed to complete the dependent clause.
   The use of (B) makes an independent clause that cannot be used as a subject. (C) and (D) contain a subject and a verb.

7. (D) Only a subject is needed for the verb "explains." The phrase "by its previous owner" indicates a passive voice. (D) is a gerund that can be used as a subject, and it is in the passive voice.
   (B) and (C) contain both a subject and a verb. (A) is in the active voice.

8. (B) A subject and a verb are needed to complete the sentence. (B) has both a subject "it" and a verb "was."
   (A) is a clause that can only take the position of a subject in the sentence. (C) and (D) do not contain verbs.

9. (A) The plural verb "were" indicates a plural subject. The infinitive form of (A) is parallel to the infinitive "promote" and makes a plural subject that agrees with the verb.
   (B) is an incomplete clause that does not complete the subject. The simple subject in (C) and the gerund subject in (D) are not parallel to the second subject "promote," which is the infinitive form.

10. (C) A singular subject is needed to complete the sentence and agree with the singular verb "was." The plural subject "pigments" in (A) does not agree with the singular verb "was." (B) contains a subject and a verb. (D) is an incomplete clause that does not complete the subject.

11. (D) A subject that agrees with the singular verb is needed to complete the sentence.
    (A) contains a verb. In (B) the subject is plural and does not agree with the singular verb "has." (C) is an incomplete clause and, therefore, cannot be used as a subject.

12. (A) Both a subject and a verb are needed to complete the sentence.
    (C) does not contain a verb. In (B) and (D) the phrase "the cotton textile industry" takes the object position, but the sentence already has the object "the single largest organized industry in India."

13. (B) A singular subject is needed to complete the sentence.
    (A) contains both a subject and a verb. Although (C) is a subject, it does not fit into the sentence because its verb "translated" cannot be modified by the prepositional phrase "of the 'Rubaiyat of Omar Khayyam.'" (D) is a prepositional phrase and cannot be used as a subject.

14. (A) (A) can complete the sentence with the subject "it," the verb "is," and a noun in the object position. The relative clause in the given sentence indicates the structure used to emphasize the noun and clause.
    (B) and (C) do not have verbs. (D) completes the sentence but is illogical because the article "the" indicates specific "air." However, air in general keeps out the cold.

15. (D) Only a subject is needed to complete the sentence. (D) is an infinitive that can be used as a subject.
    (A) is a verb. (B) contains both a verb and a subject. (C) is an incomplete clause. It needs to be complete to be used as a subject.

Exercise S25 (p. 141)

1. (B) The noun "rest" refers to the remaining areas of Africa. Therefore, the article "the" should be used.

2. (A) "Physicists" is the noun form, but it is used to refer to people. "Physics" is the correct noun form to refer to a course.

3. (C) The verb "try" doesn't agree with its subject, "everyone." The singular form "tries" should be used.

4. (B) The pronoun "they" and the noun "treasures" cannot be used together in a subject position. "They" is not needed.

5. (A) The singular verb "was" and the word "every" indicate that the subject "recruits" should be in the singular form "recruit."

6. (B) The article "a" indicates that the word "times" should be in the singular form "time."

7. (A) The singular form of the verb "was" and the name of one newspaper indicate that only one newspaper is being discussed. Therefore, the word "some" (meaning "more than one") should be changed to "one."

8. (A) The words "and photographs" in the subject position indicate that another subject is needed here. Therefore, the noun form "illustrations" should be used.

9. (A) The article "a" should be used with "number of" to indicate several battles.

10. (B) The subject "The Enchanted Horse" is a single story. Therefore, the verb form "is" should be used.

11. (B) The plural subject "ships" indicates that the verb form "were" should be used.

12. (A) The plural noun "installations" indicates that the article "a" is incorrect. No article or the article "the" should be used.

13. (A) The object pronoun "them" cannot be used in a subject position. In this sentence, "those" is the correct word.

14. (C) The possessive "her" should be used with the noun "ships." The possessive "hers" cannot be used with a noun.

15. (B) The other subjects in the sentence are in the gerund form. To be parallel, the gerund form "interpreting" should be used.

16. (D) There is only one universe. The article "the" is needed before this noun.

17. (C) A noun clause in the subject position takes a singular verb. Therefore, the singular verb "is" should be used.

18. (C) The singular form "citizen" needs an article. The absence of an article before "U.S." indicates that the plural form "citizens" should be used.

19. (A) The article "the" and the prepositional phrase "of Cyprus" indicate that the noun form "beauty" should be used.

20. (B) The plural form "flies" should be used to be parallel with the other plural forms, "mosquitoes" and "pests."

21. (A) The word "many" should be used with the count noun "people."

22. (D) The article "the" and the prepositional phrase "of these actions" indicate that the noun form "significance" should be used.

23. (C) The plural subject "differences" indicates that the plural verb "are" should be used.

24. (B) The singular count noun "period" needs an article. Either the article "a" should be used before "long period" or the plural form "periods" should be used.

25. (C) The pronouns "they" and "themselves" indicate that the plural noun "men" should be used.

Exercise S26 (p. 150)

1. "Bounce," "toss," and "roll" are all actions that the subject "actors" performs.

2. "Caused" is the past tense verb indicating the action of the plural subject "swells" and "winds."

3. This sentence has two independent clauses joined by "and." "Dropped" is the past tense verb indicating the action of the subject "temperature," and "blew" is the past tense verb indicating the action of the subject "wind."

4. "It" is followed by the verb "would have been," the conditional perfect of "be." (See Practice with Subjects, 4A, page 133.) The infinitive phrases "to postpone" and "to continue" are used as nouns, not as verbs, in this sentence.

5. "Might have proved" is the verb of the independent clause and indicates the action of the subject "fingerprints."

6. This sentence has two independent clauses joined by "and." "Was" indicates the state of being of the subject "father," and "wrote" indicates the action of the subject "mother."

7. "Grasp," "fasten," and "paint" are the verbs of the independent clause and indicate the action of the subject "robots."

8. "Is being financed" is the passive of the present progressive verb. The receiver of this action is the noun clause "what can be done for the refugees." "Can be done" is the passive form of "can do."

Exercise S27 (p. 151)

1. A   The "situation" is doing the action of "becoming difficult."

2. P   "Horatio Alger Jr." is not doing the action of "associating." Others are "associating" him with hardworking poor boys achieving success.

3. A   The "ditches" are in the state of "danger" and the "plains" are in the state of being "vulnerable."

4. A   The "men" did the action of "living longer."

5. P   "J. Paul Getty" could not bury himself after he had died. Others did the action of "burying him."

6. A   The "members" did the action of "finishing the discussion."

7. P   The "restaurants" could not establish themselves. Others have done the action of "establishing them."

8. P   The "spacecraft" could not design, build, and equip itself. Others did the action.

Exercise S28 (p. 152)

1. The verb is used correctly. The action took place in the past and the verb is in the passive form because someone or something caused the people to resettle.

2. The word "since" indicates that this is an action that began in the past and is continuing. Therefore, the verb should be in a present perfect tense. Either "have harbored" or "have been harboring" could be used correctly.

3. The word "recently" indicates a recent past action. Therefore, the verb should be either "has revealed" or "revealed."
4. The verb is used correctly. It indicates the electricity's present ability to travel.
5. The word "now" indicates that the verb should be in the present tense: "are."
6. The verb is used correctly. The word "today" indicates that a present tense should be used. "Are being designed" is in the present progressive tense and indicates that the action is ongoing.
7. The phrase "in the future" indicates that a future tense should be used. "May have been measuring" indicates possibility in an undefined past time. "May be measuring" would be correct.
8. The verb is used correctly. "Have been grown" is the passive voice of the present perfect and indicates that someone has done this action in an undefined past time.

Exercise S29 (p. 152)
1. C   The verb "has been eliminated" agrees with the subject "difference." See Practice with Subjects, 3A, page 132.
2. C   The verb "occurs" agrees with the subject "reorganization." See Practice with Subjects, 3A, page 132.
3. I   The verb "is" should be "are" to agree with the plural subject "levels." See Practice with Subjects, 3A, page 132.
4. C   The verb "were transferred" agrees with the subject "fish." See Practice with Nouns, 3D, page 115.
5. I   The verb "are" should be "is" to agree with the subject "mathematics." See Practice with Nouns, 3G, page 115.
6. C   The verb "is taking" agrees with the noncount noun "pollution." See Practice with Subjects, 3B, page 132.
7. I   The verb "is planned" should be "are planned" to agree with the plural subject "picnic and visit." See Practice with Subjects, 3C, page 133.
8. I   The verb "are seen" should be "is seen" to agree with the subject "species." The demonstrative "that" indicates that the singular form of the subject is being used. See Practice with Nouns, 3D, page 115, and Practice with Articles and Demonstratives, 5B, page 122.

Exercise S30 (p. 153)
1. "comes" is correct
2. "haunted" is correct
3. are
4. spoke
5. makes
6. "longed" is correct
7. had begun or began
8. are held
9. "lies" is correct
10. "dates" is correct

Exercise S31 (p. 153)
If you have difficulty with any of these items, see Practice with Verbs, 8 and 9, pages 148–149.
1. A   3. B   5. B   7. B
2. A   4. B   6. A   8. B

Exercise S32 (p. 154)
1. (A)   The phrase "in 1970" shows that a past tense is required.
   (C) and (D) are present tenses. (B) is an incomplete verb.
2. (A)   Since the subject "rebuilding" cannot begin itself, the voice is passive. A past participle is needed: "begun."
   (C) and (D) are complete verbs. (B) is the continuous verb in the active voice.
3. (D)   Since the agreement is reached by people, the voice is passive. A past participle is needed: "reached."
   (A) is the present tense. (B) is an infinitive. (C) is the continuous verb in the active voice.
4. (B)   Since the subject "people" is doing the action, the voice is active. The verb "be" (in this case, "have been") is used as an aux-word. It precedes a continuous verb in the active voice.
   (C) and (D) are complete verbs. (A) is the past participle for the passive voice.
5. (B)   Since the subject "company" is doing the action, the voice is active. The aux-word "has" is used for the perfect tense.
   (A) is a continuous verb. (D) is a complete verb. (C) is the passive form.
6. (A)   The sentence needs a complete verb.
   (D) is not a complete verb. (B) and (C) are complete verbs but are incorrect because they indicate that platinum is no longer rare and valuable (which is not true).
7. (C)   "Has" indicates that a present perfect tense (D) or an infinitive meaning "must have" (C) is needed.
   (D) is in the passive voice, but "a great deal of thought" is doing the action. (A) and (B) are verb forms that cannot be used with "has."
8. (D)   The verb "have" can indicate a perfect tense. The subject "properties" is not doing the action. Therefore, a passive voice is needed.
   (B) and (C) are not perfect tenses or passive forms. (A) is used for a perfect tense, but does not make a passive voice.
9. (D)   The verb "sank" indicates that the action took place in the past. (D) indicates a past possibility.
   (A) indicates a present time. (B) indicates a present passive. (C) indicates a future time.
10. (B)   The phrase "in 1609" indicates a past tense.
   (B) is a past tense in the active voice.
   (A) is a present tense. (C) is incomplete. (D) indicates a passive voice, but Galileo did the action of building.

Exercise S33 (p. 156)

1. Rarely
2. On no account
3. Only
4. Not until
5. Not only . . . as well
6. No sooner . . . than
7. Nowhere
8. So

Exercise S34 (p. 157)

    AUX   **SUBJ**   **V**
1. Had the drought not lowered

    AUX   **SUBJ**
2. should the staff members' telephone numbers
       V
  be given out

    AUX SUBJ
3. does tea

    AUX SUBJ V
4. should you start

    AUX SUBJ _____**V**_____
5. will they be able to continue

    AUX   **SUBJ**
6. was the package

    AUX   **SUBJ**   **V**
7. Should an emergency arise

      V   **SUBJ**
8. remains the only representation

Exercise S35 (p. 157)

1. This sentence is correct.
2. Not only before exercising should one stretch . . . (see Practice with Subject/Aux-Word Inversions, 5, page 156)
3. This sentence is correct.
4. This sentence is correct.
5. . . . neither is a hot climate. (see Practice with Subject/Aux-Word Inversions, 2, page 155)
6. This sentence is correct.
7. Not only do swallows build their nests inside farm buildings, but sparrows do as well. (see Practice with Subject/Aux-Word Inversions, 5, page 156)
8. This sentence is correct.

Exercise S36 (p. 158)

1. (B) "Only" in this sentence means that "nothing" got underway until after years of planning.
2. (B) The use of "nor" implies that in addition to something else, the expense should not be considered a problem.
3. (A) "No sooner" means that "as soon as" and "not before" the restaurant opened the people went there.
4. (A) "Under no circumstances" means "never."
5. (B) "Not only" is used with "but also" to join two related ideas.
6. (A) "Not once" means that the penguin never leaves its nest.
7. (B) "Only through" is a preposition and needs to be followed by a noun.

8. (B) "Nowhere" means "no other place" has such splendid autumn colors.

Exercise S37 (p. 159)

1. (C) A verb is missing. The phrase "by a new technology using radiation" indicates a passive voice. (C) is a passive and completes the sentence.
2. (A) The "if" clause needs a subject and a verb. The word "only" affects the word order of the main clause, and not the "if" clause. (A) has both a subject and verb in the correct word order. (B) and (C) have word order changes. The verb in (D) is incomplete.
3. (C) A verb is missing. Since the subject "sulky" cannot believe anything, a passive form is needed. (C) is a passive and completes the sentence.
4. (A) A subject and verb are needed to complete the sentence. (A) has a subject and a verb. The verb in (B) is not complete. (C) and (D) are dependent clause forms that cannot complete both a subject and verb position.
5. (A) The verb is incomplete. Since the subject "lack" cannot know anything, a passive form is needed. In the passive, the verb "be" comes before the past participle. The word order in (A) is correct.
6. (C) The words "but also" indicate that a "not only" phrase is needed. (C) uses the "not only" phrase after the subject, not at the beginning, so a subject/aux-word inversion is not needed. If the "not only" phrase begins the sentence as in (A) and (D), a subject/aux-word inversion should be used. (B) is incorrect because the verb "keep" should follow the subject "habits."
7. (C) A subject and verb are needed to complete the sentence. The phrase "not until" indicates that a subject/aux-word inversion is needed. (C) has a subject and verb and uses the subject/aux-word inversion needed to complete the sentence.
8. (C) The prepositional phrase indicating place at the beginning of the sentence requires a subject/aux-word inversion. (C) has the needed subject/aux-word inversion. (A) has the inversion but includes the adverb "there," which is an unnecessary redundancy because the place is being emphasized by the prepositional phrase at the beginning of the sentence.
9. (D) A subject and verb are needed to complete the dependent clause. Since llamas did not bring themselves, a passive form is necessary. (D) has a subject and verb in the correct order and its verb is in the passive form. The word order in (B) is incorrect because no inversion is needed.
10. (B) An article is needed with the subject noun "source." (A) and (C) do not have articles. In this sentence, the word "only" is used as an adjective meaning "sole." The article should precede the adjective, as in (B).

11. (A) The blank before the subject "air pollution" indicates that the subject/aux-word have been inverted to avoid repetition. (A) is the aux-word that precedes the subject "air pollution." (B) and (D) use "it" as a subject, which is redundant because "air pollution" is already the subject.

12. (D) The words "but also" indicate the need for the words "not only."

13. (D) A verb is needed to complete the sentence. The phrase "by bacteria" indicates the use of a passive form. The verb in (D) is in the passive form. (A) and (B) are not complete verbs. The verb in (C) is in the active form.

14. (D) A subject and verb are needed to complete the sentence. The prepositional phrase of location at the beginning of the sentence indicates that a change in the word order of the subject and verb is needed. (D) has a word order change and completes the sentence.

15. (A) A verb is needed to complete the sentence. The verbs in (B) and (D) are incomplete. (C) is an infinitive, not a verb.

Exercise S38 (p. 164)

1. N   (-ist)
2. ADJ   (-ic)
3. N   (-hood)
4. V   (-ize)
5. ADJ   (-ful)
6. ADV   (-ly)
7. N   (-ance)
8. ADJ   (-able)
9. N   (-ity)
10. V   (-en)
11. N   (-ship)
12. ADJ (-ial)
13. V   (-ate)
14. ADV (-ly)
15. N   (-ness)

Exercise S39 (p. 164)

1. ADV   3. V   5. ADJ   7. V   9. ADJ
2. ADJ   4. N   6. N   8. ADV   10. ADV

Exercise S40 (p. 165)

1. (correct)
2. restoration
3. (correct)
4. tranquility
5. excitement
6. varieties
7. impediment
8. (correct)
9. Immigrants
10. employment

Exercise S41 (p. 165)

1. tolerate
2. (correct)
3. (correct)
4. establish
5. (correct)
6. symbolizes
7. explained
8. (correct)
9. verbalize
10. (correct)

Exercise S42 (p. 166)

1. (correct)
2. cooperative
3. (correct)
4. historical
5. beautiful
6. famous/famed
7. (correct)
8. traditional
9. (correct)
10. burial

Exercise S43 (p. 166)

1. (correct)
2. yearly
3. reasonably
4. collectively
5. (correct)
6. virtually
7. undeniably
8. (correct)
9. frequently
10. (correct)

Exercise S44 (p. 170)

1. (correct)
2. and
3. Either "and" or "or" can be used here. "And" would indicate that the tomatoes can resist high and low temperatures alike. "Or" would indicate the tomatoes can resist either high temperatures or low temperatures, but not both.
4. (correct)
5. (correct)
6. but
7. and
8. but

Exercise S45 (p. 170)

1. (correct)
2. nor
3. and
4. either
5. or
6. and
7. both
8. neither

Exercise S46 (p. 171)

1. such as
2. (correct)
3. (correct)
4. As
5. such as
6. (correct)
7. as
8. so

Exercise S47 (p. 171)

1. (correct)
2. so
3. enough
4. enough
5. so
6. (correct)
7. too
8. too

Exercise S48 (p. 172)

1. much
2. Few
3. (correct)
4. many
5. (correct)
6. (correct)
7. little
8. much

Exercise S49 (p. 172)

1. (correct)
2. alike
3. like
4. alike
5. (correct)
6. Unlike
7. (correct)
8. (correct)

Exercise S50 (p. 173)

1. other
2. the other
3. (correct)
4. (correct)
5. another
6. (correct)
7. others
8. other

Exercise S51 (p. 173)

1. enable
   A verb is needed. "Enable" is a verb, whereas "able" is an adjective.
2. alive
   An adjective is needed. "Alive" is an adjective, whereas "life" is a noun.
3. somewhat
   An adverb is needed. "Somewhat" is an adverb. "Some" is a quantifier – a word that indicates a quantity.
4. people
   A plural noun is needed. "People" is plural, whereas "person" is singular.
5. number
   "Number" is used with count nouns. Buffalo can be counted. "Amount" is used with noncount nouns.
6. have made
   The general meaning of "do" is connected with activity. The general meaning of "make" is to produce something that did not exist before.
7. alive
   An adjective is needed. Although both "alive" and "live" are adjectives, "live" must be used before a noun and "alive" cannot be used before a noun. It is always used after a verb.
8. aside
   "Aside" is used to indicate a movement. "Beside" is used to indicate a position.
9. observation
   "Observation" is the action of carefully watching someone or something. "Observance" is the practice of obeying or following a law or custom.
10. number
    "Number" is used with a count noun. "Peaks" can be counted. "Quantity" is used with a noncount noun.

Exercise S52 (p. 174)

1. (B) "So" cannot be used as a preposition. The correct word is "as."
2. (A) "Much" is used with noncount nouns, but plants and animals can be counted. "Many" is the correct word.
3. (A) The correct form in the subject position is "wood." "Wooden" is the adjective form.
4. (C) The word order is incorrect. "Enough" should follow the word it modifies: "strong enough."
5. (A) The correct form in the subject position is "clouds." "Cloudy" is the adjective form.
6. (C) "Every" indicates that "mountaineers" should be in the singular form "mountaineer."
7. (D) "Adventurously" is an adverb and cannot modify a noun. The adjective "adventurous" should be used to modify the noun "aspect."
8. (B) "Controversial" is an adjective. The noun "controversy" should be used in the object position.

9. (D) "Impassably" is an adverb. The adjective "impassable" should be used to modify the noun "barrier."
10. (B) "Hastily" is an adverb. The verb "hastened" should be used in the verb position.
11. (C) "Enough" follows an adjective or adverb. "Hillside" is a noun. "So" can follow a noun and is the correct word to introduce a "that" clause.
12. (B) The main sentence is "weapons and stable gear were placed upon the grave." That means that the prepositional phrase introducing the sentence is "in ancient Greek traditional." Since a prepositional phrase needs a noun, "traditional" should be changed from an adjective form to the noun form "tradition."
13. (B) "So" should be used in clauses of cause/result before the adjective – in this case, "scarce."
14. (B) "Heart" and "kidneys" are examples of "organs." Examples are introduced by the words "such as."
15. (A) "Do" is generally used to indicate an activity. "Make" is generally used to indicate the production of something that didn't exist before. In this case, "made" indicates that the grenade has been constructed.
16. (C) "Others" is the pronoun form. The adjective "other" should be used before the noun "subspecies."
17. (C) "Develop" is the verb form. The article "the" indicates that the noun "development" should be used.
18. (B) "To" indicates that the infinitive form "to keep" should be used.
19. (B) "Some" indicates an indefinite quantity. "Somewhere" is an adverb indicating a place. In this case, the place is "between $8 million and $10 million."
20. (B) A verb cannot be used in a prepositional phrase. Since "unlike a tractor" is a prepositional phrase, the verb "is" should be omitted from the sentence.
21. (B) "Able" is an adjective, but there is no noun for it to modify. The verb "enable" should be used to complete the infinitive form "to enable."
22. (A) "Faint" is an adjective. The noun form "fainting" should be used in the subject position.
23. (B) "Joy" is an adjective. The verb form "enjoy" should be used in the verb position.
24. (A) "Attend" means "to be present." "Intend," meaning "have the intention," is the correct verb to use.
25. (C) "Alike" is an adverb or adjective and cannot be used to introduce a clause. "Like" is the correct word to use.

Exercise S53 (p. 177)

1. I	3. I	5. I	7. D
2. D	4. D	6. I	8. I

Exercise S54 (p. 178)

1. C	3. I	5. I	7. C
2. C	4. C	6. I	8. I

Exercise S55 (p. 181)

1. noun clause
2. noun clause
3. noun clause/independent clause
4. independent clause
5. noun clause/independent clause
6. noun clause
7. independent clause
8. noun clause/independent clause

Exercise S56 (p. 181)

1. S   How the buildings are constructed to keep their inhabitants cool
2. S   What the doctor advised
3. S   When the city of Rome was actually founded
4. O   that a woman can be just as good a scientist as a man can be
5. O   which troops were to be moved
6. S   what really occurred during the fight
7. O   that their journey was a noteworthy achievement
8. S   That the city has lost its charm in its zeal to modernize

Exercise S57 (p. 182)

1. That rent control laws inhibit landlords from repairing properties is
2. Sophia realized
3. How glass is blown in a cylinder was demonstrated
4. A top architect lamented
5. Why consumers hesitated to buy the controversial digital audiotape players is
6. Whom the late Dr. Bishopstone left his fortune to will be revealed
7. Richards claimed
8. What the manufacturer does to syrup results

Exercise S58 (p. 182)

1. that is
2. no alcohol or chemicals are included
3. a disaster had struck
4. many nonsmokers find
5. radioactive antibodies can help locate
6. far too little is being done
7. the poverty action group was set up
8. witch doctors cure

Exercise S59 (p. 183)

1. In 1776, the U.S. Congress resolved that the authority

   would

   of the British crown will be suppressed.
   (The action in the independent clause took place in the past, in 1776, so the verb in the noun clause must be in past form.)

2. This sentence is correct.

   be

3. Peter fears that he might not have been able to master the intricacies of the craft.
   (Peter fears something now, so the verb in the noun clause should indicate either a present or future possibility.)

   proved

4. What will prove to be a mistaken identity caused him many problems.
   (The past tense "caused" indicates that the mistaken identity happened in the past. Therefore, a past tense is needed in the noun clause.)

   have   made

5. What you will already make is sufficient to buy the house.
   (The word "already" indicates that the action took place in the recent past.)

6. This sentence is correct.
7. This sentence is correct.

   was

8. Many people believed that space exploration is impossible.
   (The past tense "believed" means that a past tense is needed in the noun clause as well.)

Exercise S60 (p. 183)

1. (C) "what" is used to focus on specific information.
2. (A) "where" is used to indicate a place.
3. (A) "That" is used to indicate a fact.
4. (C) "who" is used to indicate a person.
5. (C) "that" is used to indicate a fact.
6. (B) "which" is used to specify an alternative.
7. (D) "how" is used to indicate the manner in which something is done.
8. (D) "why" is used to indicate the reason.

Exercise S61 (p. 184)

1. (D) The noun clause needs a clause marker. (A) and (C) do not contain clause markers. In (B) the information indicated by the clause marker "what" is mentioned in the sentence and, therefore, is incorrect. In (D), the clause marker "that" completes the sentence by indicating a fact.

2. (C) The verb in the noun clause is incomplete. The verb form in (A) cannot be used with the aux-word "would." (B) and (D) indicate that the action has already occurred, but the verb in the independent clause indicates that the action is something that may occur in the future. The verb in (C) indicates a future action and completes the sentence.

3. (B) The noun clause used as a subject needs a clause marker. (A) and (C) are not clause markers. In (D) the clause marker "which" indicates a choice. However, there is no choice between Latin speakers. (B), "whether," is correct and indicates an alternative. Either Latin speakers borrowed the word "caupo" from Germanic speakers or Germanic speakers borrowed the word from Latin speakers.

4. (B) An article or demonstrative adjective is needed with the noun "temples." (C) and (D) are clause markers. (A) is a demonstrative that is used with singular nouns. (B) is a demonstrative that is used with plural nouns and completes the sentence.

5. (A) An object is needed to complete the sentence. A noun clause can take the object position. (C) and (D) do not use a clause marker to introduce the clause. (B) uses the word order for a question. (A) is a noun clause with a clause marker and completes the sentence.

6. (A) A verb is needed to complete the noun clause used as a subject. A passive voice is indicated by the phrase "by daily consumption." (B) and (D) are not in the passive voice. The future perfect in (C) indicates that the action has not taken place. However, it is that the action has taken place, as in (A), that "gives the encouragement."

7. (C) A clause marker is needed to complete the sentence. (A) indicates a fact. (B) indicates a reason. (D) indicates a place. However, it is specific information that is being emphasized. Therefore, the clause marker in (C), "what," is used to focus on the information concerning the treasure.

8. (D) A subject and verb are needed to complete the sentence. The clause marker "that" should introduce the noun clause. The clause marker does not introduce the clause in (A) and (B). In (C) the verb is incomplete. In (D) there is a subject, "doctors," and a verb, "agree." The clause marker "that" introduces the noun clause.

9. (D) A subject, verb, and clause marker are needed to complete the sentence. (A) does not have a subject. (C) does not have a verb. (B) is in the question word order. (D) has a subject, verb, and clause marker in the correct word order.

10. (A) A subject, verb, and clause marker are needed to complete the sentence. The clause marker "that" should introduce the noun clause. The clause marker does not introduce the clause in (C) and (D). In (B) the verb is incomplete. In (A) there is a subject, "World Wildlife Fund," and a verb, "show." The clause marker "that" introduces the noun clause.

11. (C) A subject and aux-word for the noun clause are needed to complete the sentence. The word "longer" should follow the clause marker "how much." (A), (B), and (D) are incorrect because of the word order. (C) uses the correct word order.

12. (C) A clause marker is needed to complete the sentence. (B) and (D) are not clause markers. In (A) the information indicated by the clause marker "what" is mentioned in the sentence and, therefore, is incorrect. In (C) the clause marker "that" indicates a fact.

13. (A) A subject is needed to complete the sentence. (B) is an incomplete noun clause and, therefore, cannot take the subject position. (C) and (D) are plural forms and do not agree with the singular verb "has." (A) is a singular noun.

14. (D) A clause marker is needed to complete the sentence. (A), (B), and (C) are not clause markers. In (D) the clause marker "that" indicates a fact.

15. (B) A clause marker is needed to complete the sentence. In (A) "where" indicates a place. In (C) "which" indicates a choice. In (D) "when" indicates a time. In (B) "what" focuses on the specific thing – the act of tying shoes.

Exercise S62 (p. 189)

1. who	3. who	5. which	7. whom
2. which	4. where	6. that	8. where

Exercise S63 (p. 189)

1. (date) on which Romulus founded Rome
2. (description) that has puzzled playgoers, directors and even critics
3. (Those) who flip through this brochure
4. (hedgehog) which has outlived the mammoth and the sabre-toothed tiger
5. (plays) people have enjoyed for four centuries
6. (impression) he gave
7. (enclosure) where children can play with baby goats
8. (balance) which will safeguard succeeding generations

Exercise S64 (p. 190)

1. IC "Which" is the correct pronoun for the subject position. "Where" cannot fill a subject position.
2. IC "who" is the correct pronoun in the subject position.
3. C
4. C
5. IC "who" is the correct pronoun in the subject position.
6. C
7. IC "which" is the correct pronoun referring to civilization.
8. IC "who" is the correct pronoun in the subject position.

Exercise S65 (p. 190)

1. (D) The missing clause marker refers to "city." (D) is a clause marker which refers to a location and takes the adverb position in the clause.

2. (B) The missing clause marker is the subject of the clause and refers to "job." (B) is the clause marker that refers to things and can be used in the subject position.

3. (D) The missing clause marker takes the possessive position before the noun "works" and refers to "Monteverdi." (D) is the clause marker that is used in clauses showing possession.

4. (B) The missing clause marker is in the adverb position of the clause and refers to a place, "Death Valley." (B) is the clause marker that takes an adverb position and refers to a place.

5. (B) The missing clause marker is the subject of the clause and refers to "looters." Looters are people. (B) is the clause marker that can be used in the subject position and refers to people.

6. (C) The missing clause marker is the object of the preposition "for" and refers to "those." "Those" refers to people who are obsessed with skiing. (C) is the clause marker that can take the object of the preposition position and refers to people.

7. (A) The missing clause marker is the subject of the clause and refers to "inventors." Inventors are people. (A) is the clause marker that takes the subject position and refers to people.

8. (C) The missing clause marker is the subject of the clause and refers to "glaucoma." (C) is the clause marker that can be used in the subject position and refers to a thing.

Exercise S66 (p. 191)

1. (who) was
2. (people) use
3. (population growth) is
4. (bees) carry
5. (they) go
6. (which) is
7. (the doctors) found
8. (whose appetites) are

Exercise S67 (p. 192)

1. Bicyclists pedal through the countryside during a

   held

   week-long ride which is ~~holding~~ every summer in Iowa.

2. This sentence is correct.

   makes

3. It is Earth's magnetic field that ~~made~~ a compass work.

4. A vending machine is a kind of robot salesperson

   gives

   which automatically ~~gave~~ out candy or other items when the money is inserted.

5. This sentence is correct.

6. A laser cane, which the blind find useful, sends out

   detect

   beams that ~~detecting~~ obstacles.

   supplies/is supplying

7. For the foreign buyers to whom Canada ~~supplying~~ furs, the industry has never been healthier.

8. Lucid dreamers are those people who recognize when

   control/can control

   they are dreaming and thus ~~controlling~~ the plot of their dreams.

Exercise S68 (p. 195)

1. suffering from the heat on warm summer days
2. on display
3. first revived in 1951 in York
4. giving full details of the program
5. used in the street-sweeping machines
6. consenting to help erect the building
7. in remote areas
8. lucky enough to be wealthy and male; composed exclusively of men; born on the same day

Exercise S69 (p. 195)

1. C   which historians call the Renaissance
2. P/C leading into the city; which create a green tunnel
3. P   exiled to Siberia in czarist Russia
4. P   linking the southwestern corner of France to the Mediterranean
5. C   the first of whom pedaled off in September
6. P   found in the Andes
7. P   flowing over weaker ones
8. C   where they give birth to their calves

Exercise S70 (p. 196)

1. The letter "M" may have originated as a hieroglyphic symbol representing the crests of waves and meaning "water."
2. There are still people dying from diseases that are preventable and controllable.
3. Before the age of steam, hemp, used for ropes on ships, was an important commodity.
4. No change is possible.
5. No change is possible.
6. Rings, probably invented by the Egyptians, were an easy way to display authority.
7. Wind deflected down the face of tall buildings causes gusty swirling winds in the streets.
8. Pain is the body's warning signal calling attention to a potentially harmful condition.

Exercise S71 (p. 197)

1. Ambroise Paré, known as the father of modern surgery, brought medicine out of the Dark Ages.
2. Each child entering the school is individually screened.
3. This sentence is correct.
4. Scissors, a Bronze Age invention remaining basically unchanged to this day, consist of two blades linked by a C-shaped spring.
5. This sentence is correct.
6. Butterfly wings have iridescent scales consisting of thin, interlaced layers.

7. Glacier National Park is impressive with its mountain peaks towering over splendid lakes.
8. The medicine found in the cabinet had expired.

Exercise S72 (p. 197)

1. (C) An adjective clause or phrase is needed. (A) is incorrect because the clause marker "where" cannot take the subject position. (B) and (D) are complete verbs that cannot take an adjective clause or phrase position. (C) is a complete adjective clause.

2. (B) A clause marker is needed. (A) and (C) each contain a verb, but the clause already has a verb. The clause marker in (D) is a relative pronoun and, therefore, cannot take an adverb position. The clause marker in (B) is an adverb and refers to the place "sandhills."

3. (C) An independent clause containing a noun which the adjective clause can refer to is needed. (C) contains a subject and verb and the noun "park," which the possessive clause marker "whose" can refer to.

4. (B) A subject for the independent clause is needed. (C) is an incomplete clause and cannot take the subject position. (D) contains a verb which is incorrect because the independent clause already has a verb. (A) has a subject but is incorrect because the clause marker "which" cannot be used with the verb "found" without the aux-word "were." (B) completes the sentence with a noun that can be used in the subject position.

5. (C) An adjective clause or phrase is needed. (A) and (B) are neither adjective clauses nor adjective phrases. The relative pronoun "that" in the object position in (D) is incorrect because the phrase "international telephone transmissions" is already in the object position. (C) is an adjective clause.

6. (A) An adjective clause or phrase is needed. (C) is incorrect because it is an independent clause. In (B) the verb form indicates a passive, which is incorrect because the "dealer" was not returned to the museum. (D) is an adjective clause but is illogical because the items could not come into the hands of the dealer at the same time that he or she was returning them. (A) is an adjective clause.

7. (C) A verb is needed. (C) is a verb.

8. (A) An adjective clause or phrase is needed. All four choices are adjective phrases, but the word order in (B), (C), and (D) is incorrect. (A) completes the sentence correctly.

9. (C) An adjective clause or phrase is needed. (A) has a clause marker but no verb. (B) is not an adjective clause or phrase. In (D) the clause marker "where" cannot be used to refer to people. In (C) the adjective "unable" completes the adjective phrase.

10. (D) The passive verb form for the independent clause is needed. (A) is the passive form for an adjective phrase. (B) is a complete independent clause. (C) is an adjective clause. (D) has a passive verb.

11. (B) An adjective clause or phrase is needed. The passive voice is indicated because someone forced the Indians west. (C) and (D) are verbs, not adjective clauses or phrases. The verb form in (A) indicates the active voice. The verb form in (B) indicates the passive voice.

12. (D) An adjective clause or phrase in the active voice is needed. (A) is an adjective phrase but the verb form indicates a passive voice. (B) is not an adjective clause or phrase. The word "those" in (C) is not an adjective clause marker. The relative pronoun "who" in (D) is the clause marker introducing a clause that refers to "people."

13. (A) An adjective clause or phrase is needed. (B) is an independent clause. (C) is incorrect because the verb "is" is dropped when the adjective clause pattern "subject + to be + noun" is reduced. (D) is an incomplete adjective clause because the verb is missing. (A) is an adjective phrase, reduced from the clause "which was the famous endangered snaildarter."

14. (D) An adjective clause or phrase in the active voice is needed. (A) and (C) are not adjective clauses or phrases. The passive form in (B) is incorrect because the moths are doing the action of surviving. The active voice of the adjective phrase in (D) indicates that the moths are surviving.

15. (C) An adjective clause or phrase referring to the word "shoes" is needed. (A) is incorrect because the relative pronoun "who" is the clause marker referring to people. The clause marker "when" in (B) refers to a time. The possessive "whose" in (D) is the clause marker referring to the possessor. The relative pronoun "which" in (C) is the clause marker used to refer to things.

Exercise S73 (p. 203)

1. so that pedestrians would not get their feet muddy
2. Although the existence of germs was verified in about 1600
3. If you should step on a stingray
4. While the men were arguing
5. as soon as the hunter entered the jungle
6. whereas fired clay does not
7. When an Easterner in 1886 described St. Paul, Minnesota, as another Siberia
8. Since the search to find and document sites of Indian cave paintings was first begun

Exercise S74 (p. 203)

1. There is no adverb clause in this sentence. The adjective phrase "related to 'month'" describes the word "word."

2. Even though it contains no fish
3. As traders mill about in the New York Stock Exchange
4. There is no adverb clause. The prepositional phrases "on Negit Island" and "in one day" are used as adverbs to indicate place and time.
5. There is no adverb clause. This sentence has a gerund phrase used as a subject, and the phrase "not only. . . but also" is used to join the two verbs.
6. until violent earthquakes and invasions brought its prosperity to an end
7. There is no adverb clause. The prepositional phrase "from the blazing fire" comes from the reduced adjective clause and describes the word "smoke."
8. There is no adverb clause. "To combat damaging impurities" is a phrase. "That have penetrated the marble" is an adjective clause describing the word "impurities."

Exercise S75 (p. 204)

1. (monitoring earthquakes) is
2. (one of the species of bamboo on which they feed) died out
3. (oceans) cover
4. (the Chinese sage Confucius) lived
5. (less than four percent of the land) is
6. (the world population) continues to grow
7. (some Eskimos) migrate
8. (the father) repaired

Exercise S76 (p. 204)

1. As dusk ~~settling~~ *settles*, fireflies begin to signal.
2. If the Italian authorities hadn't ~~took~~ *taken* measures to control the smuggling of national treasures, many Roman artifacts would have been lost.
3. Sixteenth-century mariners called Bermuda the "Isle of Devils" partly because breeding seabirds ~~are making~~ *made* horrid sounds in the night.
4. This sentence is correct.
5. This sentence is correct.
6. Whenever privateering ~~falls~~ *fell* off, the natives rearranged beacons to lure ships onto the reefs.
7. This sentence is correct.
8. When a key ~~pressed~~ *is pressed*, a series of levers opens the hole in the pipe and air is pumped through.

Exercise S77 (p. 205)

1. (D) A clause marker that indicates a time sequence is needed. "After" indicates that first the wasp deposits the egg, and then the flower grows the covering.
2. (B) A clause marker that indicates a cause and effect (reason) is needed. "Because" introduces the reason the region is referred to as the "Land of Fruit."

3. (A) A clause marker that indicates a purpose is needed. "So that" introduces the purpose of having seat belt laws.
4. (A) A clause marker that indicates a time is needed. "As soon as" indicates that the skewers were tilted toward the flames immediately after the fires began to blaze.
5. (C) A clause marker that indicates a time is needed. "Until" indicates that the city flourished and then fell. (A) also indicates time, but "as soon as" introduces a time sequence of one action happening almost immediately after the other.
6. (B) A clause marker that indicates a cause and effect (reason) is needed. "So" introduces the reason fire fighters must enter skyscrapers dressed in suits designed to supply oxygen and reflect heat.
7. (C) A clause marker that indicates a time sequence is needed. "When" indicates that the myth was shattered at the time the elephants were destroyed. (B) is incorrect because "until" indicates that the action occurred up to a point in time.
8. (D) A clause marker that indicates a concession is needed. "Even though" indicates that the thriving cultivation of the poppy is contrary to the government's approval.

Exercise S78 (p. 208)

1. C   until a multihued design is complete
2. P   While staying at the Greyfield Inn
3. C   Before migrating whales head for Baja California's lagoons
4. P   When photographing the set
5. C   because holding the reins in one hand frees the other hand for roping
6. P   After harpooning the walruses
7. P   Before Disneyland's opening in 1955
8. P   After having convinced himself that the Hudson was only a river and not the Northwest Passage

Exercise S79 (p. 209)

1. The adverb clause "so you have to learn by experience" cannot be reduced.
2. The adverb clause "when Cartier first discovered them" cannot be reduced.
3. While waiting for the tide to come in, the crew checked all their equipment.
4. After ending their larval period, the worms suddenly grow sluggish and enter the stage of metamorphosing into adults.
5. The adverb clause "by the time the permit was ready" cannot be reduced.
6. The adverb clause "While knowledge about the brain is growing" cannot be reduced.
7. When building the wall, the Romans also erected forts every mile.
8. The Hutterites had fled persecution in central Europe and Russia before coming to settle in the United States.

Exercise S80 (p. 209)

chipping
1. While chipped away with a long-handled ax, the woodsman tore his coat.
2. This sentence is correct.

been
3. Having ∧bitten by the snake, the farmer quickly tied a tourniquet above the wound.

having
4. After ∧reconstructed the newly found skull, the anthropologist found it to be similar to human skulls.
or After reconstructing the . . .

coming
5. Since came to the area, the company has brought many new jobs to the community.
6. This sentence is correct.

bumping
7. After bump our way over dirt tracks, we were relieved to reach a paved road.
or After having bumped our . . .
8. This sentence is correct.

Exercise S81 (p. 210)

1. (B) A clause marker that indicates concession is needed. "Through" indicates the contrast between the Australopithecus's capability of walking and its walking only for short periods of time.

2. (A) A clause marker that indicates a time sequence is needed. "After" indicates that intermittent eruptions occurred following the first eruption in May 1980. (C) is incorrect because when a clause introduced by "since" is used, the verb in the independent clause is usually either in the present perfect or the past perfect.

3. (D) A clause marker that indicates a time sequence is needed. "After" indicates that first the boys may have been frightened by the ghost story and then they were challenged to enter the house.
(A) "Until" is incorrect because it suggests that the boys were challenged up to the point of being told the story. (C) "Since" is illogical because it is used to indicate when a situation began.

4. (B) A clause marker that indicates a time sequence is needed. "When" indicates that at the time the horse was entering, it reared.

5. (C) A clause marker that indicates a time sequence is needed. "While" indicates that the people were cheering the bullfighter on at the same time they were watching the bullfight. (A) is incorrect because clauses introduced by "as soon as" cannot be reduced. (B) "Since" is illogical because it indicates that the crowds cheered the bullfighter on after the bullfight was finished.

6. (B) A clause marker that indicates a time sequence is needed. "When" indicates that at the time Daniel Webster declared the area useless, it was not possible for him to know the importance of irrigation for the valley.

7. (B) A clause marker that indicates a time sequence is needed. "While" indicates that the farmer uncovered the jawbone during the time that he or she was plowing. (C) "Since" is incorrect because it indicates that the farmer uncovered the jawbone after plowing the field. (D) "Until" is incorrect because it indicates that the farmer uncovered the jawbone up to the point of time that he or she plowed the field.

8. (D) A clause marker that indicates a concession is needed. "Although" indicates that contrary to one's expectation that the tree would die after being struck by lightning, it thrived.

Exercise S82 (p. 210)

1. (C) An adverb clause or phrase of concession is needed. (A) and (D) are not adverb clauses or phrases. The clause marker "when" in (B) is illogical because the relationship between the clauses is not one of time. The clause marker "while" in (C) indicates a contrast between the flower's strength and its fragility.

2. (D) A clause marker that indicates a concession is needed. (A) "not only" is not a clause marker. (B) "Until" and (C) "As soon as" indicate a time sequence. (D) "Although" indicates a contrast between the pandas' eating bamboo and their being carnivorous.

3. (C) A subject for the adverb clause is needed. (A) is incorrect because it includes an unnecessary clause marker ("when"). (B) is incorrect because it includes a verb, and there is already a verb in the clause. (D) is incorrect because it is the verb form for an adverb phrase. (C) is the subject that is needed (the gerund is used as a subject of the adverb clause).

4. (B) A clause marker that indicates a time sequence is needed. (A) "Because" indicates a reason. (C) "That" is not a clause marker. (D) "As if" indicates a manner. (B) "Until" indicates that the condor glides up to the point in time when it needs to flap its wings to reach updrafts.

5. (D) A clause marker that indicates a time sequence is needed. (A) and (C) are illogical because "instead of" indicates an alternative. (B) is illogical because a driver cannot slow down and speed up at the same time. In (D) the prepositional phrase "instead of slowing down" begins the sentence, and the clause marker "when" introduces the adverb phrase "sighting an approaching car."

6. (A) A clause marker that indicates a concession and a subject for the adverb clause are needed. In (B) the verb "tied" cannot take the subject position. (D) does not include a clause marker or a subject. (C) has a clause marker and subject, but the clause marker "before" is incorrect because the verb tense in the clause indicates that the actions occurred at the same time. In (A) the noun "ties" fills the subject position, and the clause marker

"although" indicates a contrast between keeping strong ties and escaping taxes.

7. (C) An adverb clause or phrase is needed. (A) is a noun clause. The clause marker "as soon as" in (B) does not introduce clauses that can be reduced. (D) is an independent clause. (C) is a prepositional phrase used as an adverb to indicate where the travelers found out the information.

8. (B) A subject and verb for the independent clause are needed. (A) is a noun clause and can only fill the subject position. (C) has an incomplete verb and, therefore, does not fill the verb position. (D) is an adverb clause and cannot fill a subject and verb position. (B) includes a subject and verb.

9. (D) A clause marker that indicates a concession is needed. (A) "Since" indicates a time sequence or cause and effect (reason). (B) "Because" indicates a cause and effect (reason). (C) "So that" indicates a purpose. (D) "While" indicates a contrast between the increase in mechanization and the fact that human and animal power still produce much of the world's food.

10. (C) An adverb clause indicating a concession is needed. (A) is incorrect because it is an incomplete adverb clause. (B) is a noun clause. (D) is an independent clause. (C) is an adverb clause introduced by the clause marker "even though" and indicates a contrast between the campaign against smoking and the fact that the farmers had not felt the effect.

11. (A) An adverb clause indicating a cause and effect (reason) is needed. (B) and (C) indicate a time sequence. (D) is a noun or adjective clause. (A) includes a clause marker, a subject, and a verb, and completes the sentence by giving the reason there were few settlements.

12. (C) An independent clause is needed. (A), (B), and (D) are not complete independent clauses. (C) includes a subject and a verb which completes the sentence.

13. (B) An adverb clause or phrase indicating a time sequence is needed. (A) and (C) are independent clauses. (D) "As if" indicates a manner. (B) is an adverb phrase indicating that first the people bargained and then they came to an agreement.

14. (C) An adverb clause or phrase indicating a time sequence is needed. In (A) and (D) the verb is missing. In (B) the verb is incomplete and the subject is in the wrong position. (C) is an adverb clause.

15. (A) An adverb clause or phrase indicating a reason is needed. The verb "fail" in (B) should be followed by the infinitive form, not the *-ing* form. (C) is an independent clause. (D) is a noun clause or adjective clause. (A) is a phrase that indicates the reason the runner gave up. The verb tenses also indicate that the failure to reach the finish line occurred first and the runner's giving up occurred next.

Exercise S83 (p. 214)
1. The largest
2. as much as
3. As recently as
4. bigger
5. the rarest
6. the world's largest
7. the more isolated; the happier
8. as well as

Exercise S84 (p. 215)
1. C	3. E	5. S	7. C
2. S	4. S	6. C	8. E

Exercise S85 (p. 215)
1. "Best than" is incorrect because two things are being compared.
2. "The flatter and drier" is incorrect because there are more than two continents.
3. "The more feed corn than" is incorrect because the words "the" and "than" are not used together in a comparative structure.
4. This sentence is correct.
5. This sentence is correct.
6. "Smaller" is incorrect because the word "the" is used with the comparative that takes a noun position.
7. This sentence is correct.
8. "Heavy" is incorrect because it is not in the comparative form.

Exercise S86 (p. 216)
1. This sentence is correct.
2. This sentence is correct.
3. "The fast" is incorrect because "fast" is not in the comparative form.
4. "Harder" is incorrect because the word "the" is missing from the phrase.
5. "Tough" is incorrect because it is not in the comparative form.
6. This sentence is correct.
7. This sentence is correct.
8. "Likelier" is incorrect because the word "less" is used to indicate the comparative form.

Exercise S87 (p. 216)
1. "The largest city" is incorrect because the word "the" is not used with the possessive "Turkey's."
2. This sentence is correct.
3. This sentence is correct.
4. "Greater" is incorrect because it is not in the superlative form.
5. "The most early" is incorrect because the word "most" should not be used with "early" and "early" should be in the superlative form.
6. This sentence is correct.
7. "A" is incorrect because the article "the" is used with the superlative.
8. This sentence is correct.

Exercise S88 (p. 217)

1. "Many pounds of peanuts are grown as sweet potatoes" is incorrect because the word "as" is missing from the beginning of the phrase.
2. This sentence is correct.
3. "As many ice skaters take part in the games" is incorrect because the word "as" is missing from the end of the phrase.
4. "As not severe as" is incorrect because the word "not" should not be within the phrase.
5. This sentence is correct.
6. "As larger as" is incorrect because the comparative form "larger" should not be used in a phrase of equality.
7. This sentence is correct.
8. This sentence is correct.

Exercise S89 (p. 218)

1. gnomes, sprites, elves
2. Warm ocean conditions, regulation of foreign catches within the U.S. 200-mile limit, international agreements reducing fishing fleets
3. tapestries, rugs, clothes, accessories
4. aqueducts, cisterns, drains; water, sanitation
5. insects, weeds, disease, hunger; cancer, birth defects, genetic mutations, sterility
6. Lashed by storms, violated by opportunists plundering its resources, struggling against today's economic pressures
7. the instability of the economy, the high inflation, the exchange-rate fluctuations
8. a den for thieves, a hideout for guerrillas, a tomb for unwary explorers

Exercise S90 (p. 219)

1. Y   breed, multiply, and injure crops
2. Y   pageantry, ritual, and fanfare
3. N
4. Y   freedom and land; Swedes, Dutch, and English
5. Y   public murals, free art instruction, and special exhibitions
6. N
7. Y   pollen, cornmeal, and ground-up stones
8. Y   bathe, touch her skin, or drink from a glass

Exercise S91 (p. 219)

1. "Were paying homage to pagan gods" is incorrect because the verb is in the past progressive form and the other verbs are in the simple past form.
2. This sentence is correct.
3. "Across Death Valley" is incorrect because it is a prepositional phrase and the other phrases are subjects.
4. "Most importantly medical supplies" is incorrect because it is a noun phrase and the other phrases are gerund phrases.
5. "The small bitter apples make the best cider" is incorrect because it is an independent clause and the other clauses are noun clauses.
6. This sentence is correct.
7. This sentence is correct.
8. "One must be courageous" is incorrect because it is an independent clause and the other phrases are nouns.

Exercise S92 (p. 222)

1. Y	3. N	5. N	7. N
2. Y	4. Y	6. Y	8. Y

Exercise S93 (p. 222)

1. In the aftermath, of the explosion
2. to the park, on several occasions, through the range
3. For several weeks, to Earth
4. with the laundry, into the washing machine
5. by accident, for the billiard ball
6. about the various legal aspects
7. after midnight, in the French quarter, of New Orleans, for a taxi
8. in Europe, as a pastime, of the upper classes, by the bustle, of servants

Exercise S94 (p. 223)

1. (A) A preposition that indicates the movement of time from one year to another year is needed. "To" can be used to indicate movement and takes a position between the given years: "1804 to 1806."
2. (C) A preposition that indicates that two things accompany each other is needed. "With" indicates that the two objects were together. (B) is incorrect because "from" can be used to indicate a source; it is illogical because the burners were not likely to be made from the lids.
3. (A) A preposition that indicates a position is needed. "Behind" indicates a position and can follow the word "from." (B) is incorrect because "out" indicates an outward movement and would need the word "of" to indicate an outward movement from a place (out of the tent).
4. (D) A preposition that indicates a movement toward or a movement above is needed. "Over" indicates a movement above or at a higher level.
5. (D) A preposition that indicates a position higher than another position is needed. "Above" indicates a position higher than another position. (A) is incorrect because "up" indicates movement toward a higher position ("The climbers went up the mountain").
6. (B) A preposition that indicates a given point is needed. "Up to" indicates to a given point and no further. In this case, the given point is 16 feet and no deeper.
7. (B) A preposition that indicates duration is needed. "On" indicates a duration, in this case "during the time of a visit to Georgia."
8. (D) A preposition that indicates a position is needed. In this sentence, "on" indicates a position touching the surface.

Exercise S95 (p. 223)

1. (A) "As" is a clause marker but there is no verb to complete a clause.
   *(B) "Through" indicates from one point in time to another point in time.

2.*(A) "Full" is the adjective describing the region and "of" is used in the sense of containing.
   (B) "Filled" makes the sentence a passive, so the preposition "with" is needed to complete the sentence correctly.

3.*(A) "That" is a clause marker, "the report" is the subject of the clause, and "would cause" is the verb.
   (B) The object of the preposition "from" is the noun "report," which cannot also serve as the subject for the verb "would cause."

4. (A) "Because" is a clause marker, but there is no verb to complete the clause.
   *(B) "Because of" is the preposition and "response" is the object of the preposition.

5. (A) "That" is a clause marker, but there is no verb to complete the clause.
   *(B) "For" is a preposition. The noun "names" completes the prepositional phrase.

6. (A) "Was" cannot be used with "were."
   *(B) "Of" indicates pertaining to the carnival.

7.*(A) "For" expresses the object or purpose of the need.
   (B) "Being a new attitude" suggests a reduced adverbial clause which does not fill the position of describing the noun "need."

8.*(A) "From" indicates the source of the statue.
   (B) "That" is a clause marker, but there is no verb to complete a clause.

Exercise S96 (p. 225)

1. Cross out "and grew."
2. Cross out "and injured."
3. (correct)
4. (correct)
5. (correct)
6. Cross out "and guard."
7. (correct)
8. Cross out "and first."

Exercise S97 (p. 225)

1. Cross out "and timid."
2. Cross out "and needed."
3. Cross out "and contents."
4. (correct)
5. Cross out "and drinking a lot of wine."
6. (correct)
7. Cross out "and enchanting."
8. Cross out "ancient."

Exercise S98 (p. 225)

1. (C) The choices indicate that a comparison is made. (A) indicates a superlative, but the word "second" indicates that there are only two rooms. (B) indicates an expression of equality, but the word order is incorrect. (D) indicates a comparison but uses the incorrect form. (C) indicates a comparison and uses the correct form.

2. (D) The list of nouns indicates that a parallel structure is needed. In (B) the word "forming" is in a verb position. (A) and (C) are independent clauses. (D) is a noun with adjective modifiers.

3. (B) The choices indicate that a comparison is being made. (A) is ungrammatical because the adjective "long term" cannot be modified by the prepositional phrase "to Africa's elephants." (C) is ungrammatical because the word order is wrong. (D) is ungrammatical because a second threat is not mentioned. (B) completes the sentence with the correct word order for the superlative form.

4. (B) A phrase is needed. (A) is an independent clause. (C) is ungrammatical because "alike" cannot be used as a preposition. (D) is ungrammatical because "alike" used as an adjective must follow the verb form of "be." (B) is a prepositional phrase that can be used in an adverb position.

5. (A) An adverb clause or phrase is needed. (B) is an adverb clause but is incorrect because the verb "may be" needs an object to complete the clause. (C) and (D) are not adverb clauses or phrases. (A) is an adverb clause; the object of "may be" is the word "isolated."

6. (C) Since the sentence is complete without filling in the blank, a phrase that adds information is needed. (A) is incorrect because it indicates a past time, whereas the verb "have been trying" indicates a time spanning from the past up to the present. (B) and (D) are ungrammatical because the clause markers "that" and "because" cannot follow another clause marker, in this case "how." (C) is a prepositional phrase which gives extra information and indicates a time spanning from the past up to the present.

7. (B) An adverb clause or phrase is needed. (A) and (C) are independent clauses. (D) is a noun phrase that must take a noun position. (B) is a prepositional phrase correctly used in the adverb position.

8. (D) A list of verbs + objects in the sentence indicates that a verb + object is needed to complete a parallel structure. (A) is an adverb phrase. (B) is an independent clause. (C) is a prepositional phrase. (D) is a verb + object.

9. (B) A preposition is needed. (A) and (D) are incorrect because "alike" and "as if" are not prepositions. In (C), "like" is a preposition which indicates a manner or comparison. However, the shire horses are not similar to work horses, but are work horses. (B) is correct because "as" is a preposition used to indicate the function of the horses.

10. (A) A parallel comparison is needed. (B) is a noun modified by a comparison. (C) is a noun modified by an adjective. (D) is a superlative. (A) is the parallel comparison form.

11. (C) A noun object is needed. The word "ever" indicates that the noun is modified by a superlative. (A) is incorrect because the article "the" is missing. (B) and (D) use an incorrect word order. (C) uses the correct word order – article + number + superlative + a noun used as an adjective + a noun.

12. (D) An adverb clause or phrase is needed. (A) is ungrammatical because a prepositional phrase does not include a verb. (B) is an independent clause. (C) is incorrect because there is no position for the adjective "grizzly." (D) is a prepositional phrase which indicates a contrast between grizzly bears and black bears.

13. (A) A preposition indicating source is needed. (B) is illogical because "by" indicates that the marble did the carving. (C) is illogical because "about" is used to introduce a topic or to indicate position. (D) is illogical because "at" is used to indicate a position. (A) is correct because "from" indicates that the source of the bottle was the material called marble.

14. (A) A prepositional phrase modifying the noun "collection" is needed. (C) is not a prepositional phrase. In (B) and (D), "about" is used to introduce the topic "6,000 drawings and paintings." However, the topic is the collection. In (A) the prepositional phrase "of some 6,000 drawings and paintings" describes the collection.

15. (D) A prepositional phrase indicating a position is needed. (A) "by the yard" and (C) "in yards" are illogical because the measurement "yard" cannot belong to a hand. (B) is illogical because "between" indicates the presence of two objects. (D) is correct because "within a yard" means not more than a yard away (distance).

Exercise S99 (p.227)

1. (C) An independent clause is needed. The prepositional phrase which states location at the beginning of the sentence indicates that the subject and verb should be inverted. (C) uses the correct subject/verb inversion.

2. (D) A noun used as the object of the preposition "in" is needed. The possible answers indicate that the tense is present perfect. The verb should agree with the plural subject "architecture and pottery." (D) completes the sentence with the demonstrative before the noun and the verb which agrees with the subject.

3. (A) A noun object is needed. (A) uses the correct superlative form.

4. (C) A verb is needed. (C) completes the sentence with a verb and an adverb.

5. (B) A clause marker indicating a contrast is needed. (B) "whereas" is a clause marker that indicates a contrast between "carpets" and "rugs."

6. (A) The list of parallel adjectives in the sentence are in an infinitive phrase. (A) correctly uses the infinitive "to double," which is parallel to the infinitive "to be."

7. (B) A subject is needed. (B) is a noun clause which can take the subject position.

8. (D) The word "and" indicates that the last verb completes the parallel structure. The missing part of the sentence is, therefore, something that modifies the verb. (D) has an infinitive phrase used as an adverb explaining that the tiger "crouched down in the grass" in order "to ready itself for the attack."

9. (B) An independent clause is needed. (B) completes the sentence with a subject, verb, and object.

10. (A) Only a verb is needed. (A) is a verb.

11. (B) The sentence has all the necessary parts to be complete. This indicates that a phrase that adds information is needed. (B) is a prepositional phrase that indicates Napoleon's function in England.

12. (A) The verb "considered" takes an object or an infinitive. (A) completes the sentence with an infinitive phrase.

13. (C) A verb is needed to complete the noun clause. (C) uses the correct word order "aux-word + verb + preposition."

14. (D) An adverb clause or phrase is needed. (D) is a prepositional phrase that can take the position of an adverb at the beginning of the sentence.

15. (C) A verb is needed. (C) is a simple verb and agrees with the subject "sailors."

16. (A) "Can" is followed by the base form of the verb, not the infinitive form (*to* + verb).

17. (B) The preposition "by" is illogical because it indicates that the reduction is the way the laws are credited. The correct preposition "for" indicates that reduction is the purpose the laws exist.

18. (C) The relative pronoun "which" cannot refer to people. "Who" is the correct pronoun.

19. (D) A superlative is required because Belgian chocolate is being compared to all chocolates in the world.

20. (C) "May" is followed by the base form of the verb, not the infinitive form (*to* + verb).

21. (A) The adjective form of "know" is "known."

22. (B) The verb "attempted" is followed by the infinitive form.

23. (D) The noun "Earth" can be used with the word "the" because it is a specific place or without an article because "Earth" is the name of the planet.

24. (B) The preposition "at" indicates a specific place. Its use here is illogical because there are two places. "Within" is the correct preposition and indicates being inside a certain area.

25. (D) The preposition "without" is frequently followed by an -ing form + noun. The correct form of the word "add" is "adding."

26. (B) "Increasingly" means the same as "going up" and, therefore, is redundant.

27. (D) "Such as" introduces examples, but "Marilyn Monroe" is not an example. "As" is the correct preposition used to indicate that "Marilyn Monroe" was "the famous Hollywood actress" whose real name was Norma Jean Baker.

28. (C) The capital cannot perform the action of situating. Therefore, "situated," the passive form of the verb, is correct.

29. (C) The superlative form "most controversial" indicates that more than one novel was written. Therefore, the noun "novel" should be in the plural form, "novels."

30. (B) The preposition "of" indicates possession, but the famines do not possess Egypt. The preposition "from" can be used to show separation. Here, "from" should be used because Egypt is separated from famines.

31. (D) The superlative form "smallest" should be used because there are more than two particles in the world.

32. (C) The verb "helped" is followed by the infinitive form (to + verb).

33. (C) The subject "it" is missing from the noun clause.

34. (D) The pronoun form "ours" cannot be used before a noun. The form "our" is used with a noun.

35. (C) "Founded" is the past tense of the verb "found" meaning "established."

36. (C) "Setting" is an incomplete verb. The date 1841 indicates a completed past action, so the verb should be in the simple past tense form, "set."

37. (D) "Attentive" is the adjective form. The noun form "attention" should be used in the object position.

38. (B) The word "some" indicates more than one civilization. However, the word "civilization," which agrees with the singular verb "was," indicates that the correct word is "one."

39. (A) The relative pronoun "which" does not refer to people. "Who" is the correct pronoun.

40. (B) The number "several hundred" indicates that the word "particle" should be plural.

SECTION 3   VOCABULARY AND READING COMPREHENSION

Vocabulary

Exercise V1 (p. 236)

Correct words are preceded by an asterisk (*).

1. A gem and *jewel are precious *stones. Boulders, sand, and pebbles are not precious stones.

2. "Eradicate" means get rid of something by *exterminating or *destroying it. "Consume" and "devour" mean to use something up. "Devastate" means to reduce something to chaos or disorder.

3. To liberate something or someone means to *release or *free them from captivity. To *rescue something or someone means to free them from a dangerous situation. To redeem means to get back or recover. To salvage something means to extract something thought to be useful or valuable.

4. To provoke someone is to incite or *arouse a feeling or action in someone. To *offend someone is to insult them and hurt their feelings. To *incense someone means to make them very angry. To explode is to burst physically or emotionally. To irritate is to cause an annoyance.

5. To be guilty means to be responsible for something bad that has happened. It can also be said that the person is *to blame and is *at fault for what happened. A bad or offensive (obnoxious) person may not be the one who is responsible for what has happened. The action of the guilty person may not be shameful.

6. The motive is the *reason or the *cause of someone's doing something. The motive may urge, push, or induce the person to do something.

7. A scent usually refers to an agreeable *odor or *smell such as a *perfume or a *fragrance. Something that stinks has a disagreeable smell.

8. To stare is to look at something for an extended period of time. To *gaze means to look at something for an extended period of time, and to *gape means to stare with astonishment. To glance and to glimpse mean to have a short look. To blink means to close and open one's eyes quickly.

9. To wander means to travel without any particular goal in mind. To *rove, *ramble, and *meander also mean to travel without heading in a particular direction. When one travels or tours, one usually has a set goal or direction.

10. An inn is a place where someone pays to spend the night. People also pay to stay in a *hotel and a *lodge. A dwelling is a place where someone lives, a tent is a portable dwelling, and a hovel is a hut which is in need of repair.

Exercise V2 (p. 238)

1. _____ train – a means of transportation on land
   _____ plane – a means of transportation in the air
   _____ bus – a means of transportation on land
   _S_ vessel
   _S_ boat

2. _____ indiscreet – unwary
   _____ ambiguous – obscure
   _S_ absurd
   _S_ ridiculous
   _____ rude – insulting

3. _S_ caverns
   _____ mines – holes in the earth made for the extraction of minerals
   _____ shafts – vertical openings made for ventilating underground spaces
   _S_ grottos
   _____ tunnels – underground passageways

4. _____ angry – in a bad temper. Anger is a component of ferocious, but someone or something can be angry without being ferocious.
   _____ irritating – bothersome
   __S__ fierce
   _____ annoying – bothersome
   __S__ savage

5. _____ viciously – brutally
   _____ naturally – logically
   __S__ heartily
   __S__ energetically
   _____ haughtily – disdainfully

6. __S__ prohibit
   _____ discontinue – stop doing something
   _____ complete – finish doing something
   __S__ forbid
   _____ antagonize – provoke hostility

7. __S__ observe
   _____ predict – foretell
   _____ spy – to watch secretly
   _____ foresee – to predict something in the future
   __S__ see

8. __S__ a plentiful
   _____ an exuberant – without restraint
   __S__ an ample
   _____ an extreme – too much
   _____ a varied – different kinds

9. _____ proposal – suggestion
   __S__ speech
   __S__ talk
   _____ chatter – idle talk
   _____ utterance – a statement

10. __S__ hidden
    __S__ covered
    _____ prevented – stopped
    _____ deposited – placed
    _____ ruined – destroyed

11. __S__ weary
    _____ misled – sent in the wrong direction
    __S__ exhausted
    _____ collapsed – broken down
    _____ wasted – misused, improperly used

12. __S__ children
    _____ progenitors – ancestors
    _____ forefathers – ancestors
    _____ predecessors – ancestors
    __S__ descendants

Exercise V3 (p. 239)

1. pilot
   __√__ test
   _____ landing
   _____ fault
   _____ restrain
   __√__ navigate

2. gain
   __√__ profit
   _____ gallows
   __√__ win
   __√__ acquire
   _____ distort

3. annual
   _____ crowd
   _____ endure
   __√__ yearbook
   _____ holiday
   __√__ yearly

4. foundation
   __√__ endowment
   _____ hinder
   _____ installation
   __√__ justification
   __√__ base

5. list
   __√__ lean
   _____ garb
   _____ brag
   __√__ enumerate
   _____ mediocrity

6. range
   __√__ vary
   __√__ extent
   _____ attic
   _____ breathe
   __√__ grazing lands

7. loose
   _____ decorate
   __√__ limp
   __√__ unfastened
   _____ vacant
   __√__ free

8. border
   _____ barrier
   __√__ frontier
   __√__ boundary
   __√__ edge
   _____ projection

9. absorb
   _____ jeer
   __√__ take in
   _____ effect
   __√__ consume
   _____ monopolize

10. shed
    __√__ hut
    _____ shelf
    __√__ emit
    _____ filter
    __√__ cast off

Exercise V4 (p. 241)

1. lot
   _____ exact
   __√__ fate
   __√__ portion of land
   _____ direction

2. stock
   __√__ inventory
   __√__ ancestor
   _____ character
   _____ trial

3. pelt
   _____ composition
   _____ variety
   __√__ skin
   __√__ bombard

4. stage
   _____ grain
   __√__ part
   __√__ perform
   __√__ period

5. mean
   __√__ intend
   __√__ average
   __√__ vicious
   _____ deal

6. word
   __√__ term
   __√__ promise
   __√__ oath
   _____ legend

7. yield
   __√__ output
   __√__ give way
   _____ deduce
   __√__ produce

8. bore
   __√__ diameter
   __√__ drill
   __√__ tire
   _____ desire

9. pen
   __√__ enclosure
   __√__ write
   __√__ confine
   _____ swallow

10. peer
    __√__ equal
    _____ escape
    _____ itch
    __√__ look

Exercise V5 (p. 242)

1. S
2. S
3. S
4. A
5. A
6. S
7. A
8. S
9. A
10.
11. A
12.
13. S
14. A
15.

Exercise V6 (p. 243)

These are possible synonyms and antonyms. Your answers may differ.

1. synonym: base
   antonym: superstructure
2. synonym: advancements
   antonym: setbacks
3. synonym: guiding
   antonym: following
4. synonym: one-time, previous
   antonym: subsequent
5. synonym: wonderful
   antonym: insignificant
6. synonym: disappeared
   antonym: materialized, appeared
7. synonym: reciprocal
   antonym: one-sided
8. synonym: naivete
   antonym: sophistication
9. synonym: unwilling
   antonym: inclined
10. synonym: stale
    antonym: fresh

Exercise V7 (p. 244)

These are possible synonyms. Your answers may differ.

1. (A) rotten
   (B) pampered
   (C) loot
2. (A) shore
   (B) inclined
   (C) mass
3. (A) swayed
   (B) stones
   (C) support
4. (A) thumbing
   (B) calling
   (C) attendant
5. (A) locomotive
   (B) taught
   (C) line
6. (A) path
   (B) scent (or tracks)
   (C) dragging
7. (A) media
   (B) ironed
   (C) pushed
8. (A) blast
   (B) injection
   (C) photograph, picture
9. (A) match
   (B) animals
   (C) scheme, plan
10. (A) slid
    (B) sneaked
    (C) undergarment

Exercise V8 (p. 245)

The possible correct answers are so variable that you may find it helpful to discuss your choices with a fluent English speaker. The following charts give possible answers.

1. grant
   Nouns sanction: concession
                    charter
          gift: award
               offering
               present
        subsidy: allowance
                  stipend
                  aid
                  assistance

   Verbs allow for: concede

   acknowledge: accept
                     recognize
   permit: allow
         let
         consent
         vouchsafe
   give: donate
        bestow
        allot
        present

   Expressions grant amnesty to: pardon
             take for granted: accept without
                             question

2. spread
   Nouns expanse: area
                 ranch
        covering: bedspread
                   counterpane
                   comforter
                   quilt
        feast: food
               provisions

   Verbs expand: enlarge
                  increase
                  multiply
        extend: stretch
        apply: cover
             butter
             overlay
             set
        make known: inform
                     disseminate
        disperse: sow
                scatter
                distribute
        separate: push apart

   Expressions spread one's wings: gain independence
             spread oneself thin: engage in too
                             many activities

3. bump
   Nouns swelling: lump
                  bulge
                  rise
                  knot
        push: nudge
               jolt
               jostle
        collision: crash
                   smashup
                   impact
        thud: thump
             bang
   Verbs push: jog
               nudge
               jolt
               jostle

collide: hit
    strike
    run into
    knock into
discharge: dismiss
    lay off
    fire
    retire
    sack
shake: bounce
    joggle
    jar
demote: reduce
    lower
    downgrade

Expressions bump into: meet by chance
    bump off: assassinate, kill

4. match
Nouns counterpart: duplicate
    double
    twin
    partner
    equal: equivalent
    peer
    rival
    two: pair
    couple
    twosome
    mates
    contest: competition
    encounter
    engagement
    game: bout
    meet
    marriage: union
    wedlock
    matrimony

Verbs coincide: correspond
    tally
    be alike: resemble
    look alike
    take after
    correspond: agree
    accord
    harmonize
    equal: amount to
    measure up to
    rival
    pair: couple
    team up
    size: sort
    group
    rank
    oppose: confront
    contrast

compare: check
    liken
    assimilate
    draw a parallel
marry: wed
    unite
    join together

5. act
Nouns process: motion
    procedure
    action: deed
    feat
    stunt
    performance
    law: statute
    ordinance
    rule
    dictate
    decree
    bill

Verbs function: perform
    do
    impersonate: characterize
    portray
    pose as
    pass for
    masquerade as
    portray: perform
    star
    play
    pretend: feign
    make believe
    affect
    officiate: serve
    do duty
    perform the duties
    behave: do
    conduct oneself
    manage oneself
    bear oneself

Expressions catch in the act or catch red-handed:
    catch someone committing a crime or
    misdeed
    in the act of: in the middle of doing
    something
    put on an act: make a show of
    something
    act a part: impersonate
    act for: substitute for
    act of grace: favor, blessing, courtesy,
    good turn, kind deed
    act on: follow or affect
    act one's part: do one's duty
    act out: enact
    act the part of: pose as
    act up: misbehave or malfunction

act one's age: behave in a way
appropriate to one's age

6. leave
Nouns departure: parting
leave-taking
farewell
vacation: holidays
leave of absence
furlough
sabbatical
permission: consent
license

Verbs depart: go
cease: stop
give up
abandon: vacate
evacuate
forsake
jilt
quit
discard
resign: give up
retire
quit
abdicate
bequeath: bequest
will to
pass on
hand down

Expressions by one's leave: with permission
give leave: give permission
on leave: on vacation
leave in the cold: ignore, snub
leave in the lurch: desert, abandon
leave no stone unturned: search
thoroughly
leave no trace: disappear
leave off: cease
leave one cold: bore
leave out: omit
leave the beaten path: not conform
leave the door open: allow freedom
leave well enough alone: let things take
their course
leave word: make known

7. change
Nouns alteration: modification
variation
transformation
metamorphosis
mutation
substitution: exchange
switch
replacement

money: cash
coins
bills
currency

Verbs alter: modify
diversify
deviate
transform
convert
substitute: exchange
replace
put in the place of
switch
interchange
move: shift
stir
trade: swap
barter
deal

Expressions change back: return to original
change hands: change ownership
change one's mind: decide on another
idea
change one's ways: reform

8. end
Nouns cessation: stop
discontinuation
completion: conclusion
result
finish
termination
finale
close
tip: point
extremity
death: expiration
passing away
decease
extinction
annihilation
limit: border
edge
remainder: remnant
rest
balance
fate: fortune
destiny
ruin: destruction
doom

Verbs terminate: complete
conclude
finish up
stop: cease
discontinue
quit
desist

kill: slay
murder
destroy
perish: be destroyed
expire
succumb
die
pass away

Expressions at loose ends: uncertain
at the end of one's rope: dying or
extremely
irritated
dead end: cul-de-sac
end of the line: last stop on the train
route
end on that note: stop at this last point
end to end: adjoining
make both ends meet: manage to
support oneself
financially
no end: without ceasing
on end: continuously or upright
put an end to: stop or kill
to that end: for that motive
end up in smoke: fail
end-all: the clincher
odds and ends: scraps
the end: the ultimate

9. top
Nouns summit: peak
crest
point
acme
apex
lid: cover
cap
shirt: pullover
blouse

Verbs dominate: excel
surpass
exceed
rise above
tower over
crown: cap
surmount
adorn

Adjectives supreme: leading
chief
greatest
topmost
uppermost
maximum

Expressions at the top of the ladder: the highest
position
on top: triumphant

on top of: additionally or in control of
on top of the heap: prosperous
top off: perfect or add the finishing
touches, fill to the top
go to the top: reach or be the person in
the highest position
on top of the world: in a position of
success, happiness,
or fame
off the top of one's head: in an
impromptu
fashion,
spontaneously

10. part
Nouns share: interest
cut
lot
allotment
proportion
percentage
quota
region: area
zone
district
quarter
plot
piece: segment
fragment
fraction
portion
section
role: character (in a play)
capacity
position
function
component: content
element
feature
function: duty
job
responsibility

Verbs separate: disjoin
disconnect
detach
remove
cut off
divorce
die: decease
succumb
expire
perish
depart
pass away
disband: part company
disperse
break up
go separate ways

open: split
       spread
       slit
       divide
share: divide up
       split up
       parcel out

Expressions   do one's part: do one's duty, share
                               the responsibility
           in part: to a degree
           on the part of: in regard to or on
                               behalf of
           take the part of: take up the cause for or
                               stand behind
           part company with: separate
           part with: discard, give away, or
                               relinquish
           part ways: go in separate directions
           for the most part: in general

Exercise V9 (p. 255)

These are possible answers. Your answers may differ.

1. exclusive: singular, unique, select
2. stole: took, robbed, appropriated
3. trap: cage, snare, net
4. endear: enamor, charm, captivate
5. store: business, market, shop
6. reserve: cache, stash, stockpile
7. minute: small, tiny, insignificant
8. brash: rude, brazen, disrespectful
9. expire: die, cease, perish
10. intermittently: occasionally, sporadically, periodically
11. flabby: limp, slack, weak
12. definitely: absolutely, positively, unquestionably
13. fickleness: arbitrariness, capriciousness, inconsistency
14. dampen: wet, moisten, sprinkle
15. territory: realm, domain, dominion
16. enable: empower, entitle, permit
17. prompting: impelling, inducing, provoking
18. contingent: group, delegation, organization
19. sieve: sift, strain, filter
20. spacious: commodious, roomy, deserted

Exercise V10 (p. 256)

These are possible synonyms. Your answers may differ.

1. ~~erudite~~   submissive
2. chaos
3. ~~apportioned~~   dispersed
4. ~~ample~~   cursory
5. ~~sublimity~~   enormity
6. ~~thriving~~   catastrophic
7. benign
8. ~~courageously~~   obstinately
9. ~~hospitable~~   neighboring
10. widespread

Exercise V11 (p. 257)

1. Both "carve" and "cut" mean to open something with a sharp instrument. However, the word "carve" is used when one is cutting a cooked piece of meat into servings or cutting a piece of wood or stone into a figure. "Cut" means to slit or slash something with a knife or scissors.
2. Both "smolder" and "blaze" mean to burn. However, "smolder" means to burn slowly without flames, whereas "blaze" means to burn strongly with high flames.
3. Both emblems and symbols are shapes or designs that represent something. However, an emblem is a special symbol that can be used to represent an organization. A symbol can be any shape or sign used to represent a word, function, or idea.
4. Both "glance" and "stare" mean to look at something. However, "glance" means to look quickly, whereas "stare" means to look intently.
5. Both "evade" and "escape" mean to elude someone. However, "evade" means to keep from getting caught by avoiding someone, whereas "escape" means to get away after being caught.
6. Both letters and cards are written messages. However, a letter is a message written down on paper, whereas a card is usually a printed greeting.
7. Both a band and a quartet are a group of musicians. However, a band can have any number of musicians, whereas a quartet can have only four.
8. Both "chuckle" and "snicker" refer to laughter. However, "chuckle" has a positive meaning (laugh quietly to oneself), whereas "snicker" has a negative meaning (laugh quietly and disrespectfully).
9. Both "bizarre" and "strange" refer to things that are out of the ordinary. However, "bizarre" is used to describe things that are extremely strange, whereas "strange" is used to describe things that are just odd.
10. Both "exiled" and "expelled" mean to be thrown out. However, one is exiled from a country, whereas one is expelled from school or an organization.
11. Both "tease" and "mock" mean to make fun of someone. However, "tease" means to disturb or annoy by persistent irritating or provoking, whereas "mock" means to treat someone with contempt or ridicule.
12. Both "gaudy" and "colorful" mean to have many colors. However, "gaudy" has a negative meaning (e.g., cheap, tasteless), whereas "colorful" has a positive meaning (e.g., cheerful, attractive).
13. Both "gossip" and "talk" mean to speak. However, gossip is frequently unkind rumors, whereas talk can be any kind of conversation.
14. A vow and a promise are pledges. However, a vow is a more formal pledge (such as a wedding vow), whereas a promise can be any statement of intention, formal or informal.
15. Both "skeptical" and "cynical" mean doubtful. However, a person who is skeptical has a questioning attitude, whereas a person who is cynical thinks everyone acts out of selfish motives.

Exercise V12 (p. 259)

Correct words are preceded by an asterisk (*).

1. *"Slept" usually indicates a rest for a period of several hours, whereas "napped" usually indicates a rest for a very short period of time.

2. Both *"site" and "spot" mean a location. However, "site" usually refers to a piece of ground that is used or will be used for a particular purpose, such as erecting a building. "Spot" refers to a particular place or area (e.g., "This is the spot where General Custer fell"; or "This is a beautiful spot for a picnic").

3. Both "prophesy" and *"prediction" refer to foretelling the future. However, "prophesy" refers only to foretelling future events, whereas "prediction" refers to both foretelling future events and forecasting the weather.

4. Both "lecture" and *"speech" refer to a talk given to a group of people. However, a lecture is a talk on a particular subject that is given in order to teach a group of people about that subject. A speech is a formal talk given to thank people or to inform them of something that is happening, or to introduce a ceremony.

5. Both "leap" and *"hop" mean to jump. However, to leap is to make a high jump into the air or a long jump. To hop is to make a small jump. Since the children in this sentence were holding one foot behind them, their jumps were more likely to be small ones.

6. Both "kings" and *"aristocrats" are people of high social rank. In some countries aristocrats hold a title such as "lord," "lady," "count," "countess." A king is the aristocrat that leads a country. In this sentence the word "all" indicates that the correct word is "aristocrats" because many aristocrats can live in a kingdom, but there can be only one king.

7. "Abundant amount" indicates a quantity greater than the need, whereas a *"sufficient amount" indicates a quantity that is as much as necessary and no more. Since the word "just" indicates that there was enough and no more, the amount of food was sufficient.

8. Both *"proud" and "vain" indicate a feeling that something one has done or possesses is a good thing. However, "proud" indicates a sense of being glad about an achievement, whereas "vain" indicates a sense of feeling superior to other people.

9. Both *"acquaintances" and "friends" refer to people one knows. An acquaintance is someone whom one has met but does not know well, whereas a friend is someone with whom one has established a relationship.

10. Both "wise" and *"clever" indicate a mental proficiency. However, a wise person is someone who uses experience and knowledge in order to make good decisions or judgments, whereas a clever person is someone who can learn and understand things easily.

Exercise V13 (p. 260)

1. (B) A myriad or variety of activities is a large number of different things to choose from.

2. (D) A trinket or bauble is a pretty piece of jewelry or small ornament that is inexpensive.

3. (A) Something or someone that is aloof or distant remains detached or far away from others.

4. (A) "Permeate" and "penetrate" mean to spread through a place.

5. (C) A prank or a trick is a mischievous deed played on someone in order to make that person seem foolish.

6. (A) Something that is precarious or hazardous is dangerous to people's health or safety.

7. (B) "Upheaval" and "unrest" indicate turmoil in society or in family life.

8. (C) Something that is pliant or yielding is flexible and can be bent when pressure is applied to it.

9. (B) To endure or to bear (the past tense is "bore") something is to survive a pressure or a difficult situation.

10. (D) Haughtiness or arrogance is an unpleasant manner someone has when the person believes that he or she is better than other people.

11. (A) "Sort" and "sift through" mean to separate things into a useful order.

12. (B) "Mull over" and "ponder" mean to consider something very carefully.

13. (A) "Novel" and "unique" mean original.

14. (B) Talons are the hooked claws of a bird of prey. Claws are the "toenails" of an animal or bird.

15. (C) "Usurp" and "supplant" mean to remove someone from power.

16. (B) "Shard" and "sliver" mean fragment.

17. (A) "Quarry" and "prey" refer to that which is being hunted.

18. (D) "Grinding" and "pulverizing" mean to crush something into a fine powder.

19. (D) Wit or humor is a talent for amusing others.

20. (D) "Ostracized" and "excluded" mean shut out from friendship or membership.

21. (B) "Scarred" and "disfigured" mean badly marked as the result of an injury.

22. (B) A canister and a container are objects used for storage. A canister is a container with a lid.

23. (A) "Skid" and "slide" (the past tense is "slid") mean to continue moving while trying to slow down or stop.

24. (D) "Finicky" and "fastidious" mean too particular or difficult to please.

25. (B) "Fetch" and "retrieve" mean to bring back something.

26. (C) "Serenity" and "tranquility" mean peacefulness.

27. (B) "Embellish" and "enhance" mean to add details that improve something.

28. (A) Something that is extraneous or irrelevant is unconnected with or concerned with things outside the situation or subject being dealt with.

29. (C) "Ominous" and "menacing" mean threatening that something unpleasant will happen.
30. (A) "Ephemeral" and "fleeting" mean lasting only a short time.

Exercise V14 (p. 263)
1. (C) "Expelled" comes from the words meaning "push out" or "drive or force away." Someone who is expelled or dismissed from an organization is told that he or she no longer belongs to it (the person is pushed away from the organization).
2. (A) "Resolved" comes from the words meaning "loosen again." To resolve a problem, one looks at the aspects of the problem and untangles (or loosens) them and, thus, "takes care of" (finds a remedy for) the problem.
3. (B) "Disposed of" comes from the words meaning "put apart or remove." To dispose of something unwanted means to "get rid of" it (or remove it to a place for unwanted objects).
4. (D) "Impulse" comes from the words meaning "inner drive." When someone has an impulse to do something, that person has an inner drive (a strong and constant feeling) to do it. A whim is a sudden urge or drive to do something.
5. (A) "Aspects" comes from the words meaning "look toward." An aspect of something is one of its considered (looked at) parts. A facet is a single feature or part.
6. (D) "Repels" comes from the words meaning "drive or push back." The material pushes away the water. If something sheds water, it causes it to run off its surface (repels it) instead of letting it soak through.
7. (A) "Event" comes from the words meaning "come out." An event is something that happens (a happening) or a social occasion.
8. (C) "Invent" comes from the words meaning "come into being." An invention or creation is something that someone has brought into existence.
9. (A) "Dissolve" comes from the words meaning "loosen away." When something dissolves or disbands, its parts or members break away and go in separate directions.
10. (D) "Inquiry" comes from the words meaning "seek into." An inquiry or investigation takes place when something happens that people must examine or ask questions about.

Exercise V15 (p. 264)
1. (A) "Conduct" comes from the words meaning "lead together." Someone who conducts a survey puts this survey together and leads or runs it. In other words, the person organizes it and carries it through.
2. (D) "Consumes" comes from the words meaning "use." The prefix *con-* is used to emphasize the meaning. When something or someone consumes something, they use it up.

3. (C) "Dejected" comes from the words meaning "throw down." "Discouraged" means lose one's enthusiasm. A person who is dejected or discouraged feels low or has lost enthusiasm because of some unhappy experience.
4. (A) "Interjected" comes from the words meaning "throw between." "Inserted" comes from the words meaning "put into." In this sentence, the speaker has interjected (thrown between) or inserted (put into) anecdotes concerning the football team into the talk.
5. (B) "Subversive" comes from the words meaning "turn under." It means "done in a way that is intended to weaken or destroy a system." Someone who does a subversive thing does it secretly (turned under so as to be out of sight) in order to overturn (turn under) a system. Someone involved in a rebellious activity is involved in an action against an authority figure.
6. (B) "Coherence" comes from the words meaning "stick together." When something has coherence, its parts fit together well so that it is clear and easy to understand. The professor wants Jan's ideas to fit together logically. Something that is consistent is organized or presented so that each part of it agrees with all the other parts. Jan needs to work on the consistency of his term paper.
7. (D) "Projected" comes from the words meaning "thrown before." When something is projected, it is thrown outward. "Hurled" means to throw something violently. In this case, the explosion threw something violently outward.
8. (A) "Deduced" comes from the words meaning "lead from." A person who deduces something is led from the facts to a conclusion about it. "Surmise" comes from the words meaning "send beyond." Someone who surmises something goes beyond the evidence to arrive at a conclusion.
9. (C) "Introverted" comes from the words meaning "turn into." People who are introverted turn their thoughts in toward themselves and are reluctant to interact with others. "Reserved" comes from the words meaning "keep back." People who are reserved keep their feelings hidden.
10. (C) "Subjected" comes from the words meaning "thrown under." Someone who is subject to something is forced into experiencing it (thrown under the control of someone else). "Exposed" comes from the words meaning "put out." Someone who is exposed to something is placed in a situation (although not necessarily by force) where something is experienced.

Exercise V16 (p. 265)
1. (C) "Retroactive" comes from the words meaning "made back to." If a decision is retroactive, it is intended to take effect from a date in the past (made back to that date). An agreement is back-dated when it is considered valid from a date prior to the date when the agreement was made.

2. (B) "Seceded from" comes from the words meaning "come/go apart." A group that secedes from the larger group to which it belongs formally ends its membership or withdraws (goes apart) from that group.

3. (A) "Transferred" comes from the words meaning "carried across." When someone or something is transferred, that person or thing is moved or relocated to a different place or position.

4. (A) "Superseded" comes from the words meaning "to go/come over." Something that is superseded is replaced by something else because it has become unacceptable or out of date. "Supplanted" means to be replaced.

5. (C) "Retroflexed" comes from the words meaning "bend backward." In this case, the tongue is bent in a backward position.

6. (A) "Transactions" comes from the words meaning "act across." A transaction is an act of negotiating or making a deal (an arrangement) about something.

7. (C) "Circumference" comes from the words meaning "carry around." The circumference is the distance around the edge of something. The perimeter is the length of the boundary.

8. (B) "Antecedent" comes from the words meaning "come before." The antecedent of something is something else that existed before (came before) it and that is related to it in some way. A predecessor is something that came before in a process of development.

9. (D) "Retrogressed" comes from the words meaning "moved backward." If something retrogresses, it goes or moves back to an earlier and less efficient state in its development. If something regresses, it returns to a worse condition.

10. (D) "Offered" comes from the words meaning "bring toward." Someone who offers something brings that thing forward to be accepted. To offer one's services indicates bringing forward an intention of performing that service. A person who volunteers to do something is offering to do it without expectation of payment.

Exercise V17 (p. 267)

These are possible meanings. Your wording may be different.

1. "Adapt" means "make fit for a new use or situation."
2. "Accede" means "give agreement."
3. "Affluent" means "flowing with abundance, or wealthy."
4. "Aggression" means "a forceful action or attack (step forward) with the intention to dominate."
5. "Adhere" means "stick to as if glued."
6. "Allocate" means "place or set apart something for a specific purpose."
7. "Announce" means "make known (proclaim) publicly."
8. "Appetite" means "a desire for something (usually for food and drink)."

9. "Ascend" means "move or climb gradually upward."
10. "Assign" means "give a task, or appoint to a post or duty."
11. "Assume" means "take upon oneself."
12. "Attract" means "pull to or toward oneself."

Exercise V18 (p. 267)

1. *Con-* means "together" and *-fer* means "bring." To confer is for two or more persons to get together and discuss something.
2. *De-* means "off" and *-fer* means "carry." To defer means to respectfully yield (give way) to the opinion of another.
3. *In-* means "into" and *-fer* means "bring." To infer means to derive as a conclusion from facts or premises.
4. *Pre-* means "before" and *-fer* means "carry." To prefer means to like something better than something else.
5. *Re-* means "back" and *-fer* means "carry." To refer means to send or direct to someone or something.
6. *Trans-* means "across" and *-fer* means "carry." To transfer means to convey (carry across) from one person, place, or situation to another.

Exercise V19 (p. 268)

1. "Aggression" comes from the prefix *ad-* (toward), the root gress (step), and the suffix *-ion* (the condition of). It means a forceful action.
2. "Ascension" comes from the prefix *ad-* (toward), the root scend (climb), and the suffix *-ion* (the condition of). It means being raised.
3. "Convention" comes from the prefix *con-* (together), the root vent (come), and the suffix *-ion* (the condition of). It can mean a meeting of people having common interests.
4. "Distraction" comes from the prefix *dis-* (away), the root tract (draw away), and the suffix *-ion* (the condition of). It means an action that draws one's attention away from something.
5. "Expulsion" comes from the prefix *ex-* (out), the root pulse (push), and the suffix *-ion* (the condition of). It means being pushed out of an organization or country.
6. "Induction" comes from the prefix *in-* (into), the root duct (lead), and the suffix *-ion* (the condition of). It refers to a way of reasoning in which facts lead to or give a result.
7. "Introspection" comes from the prefix *intro-* (into), the root spect (look at), and the suffix *-ion* (the condition of). It means an examination of (looking into) a person's own thoughts and feelings.
8. "Reflection" comes from the prefix *re-* (back), the root flex (bend), and the suffix *-ion* (the condition of). It refers to the process in which light bounces back from surfaces.
9. "Resolution" comes from the prefix *re-* (again), the root solve (loosen), and the suffix *-ion* (the condition of). It refers to the final untangling or solving of a problem.

10. "Subtraction" comes from the prefix *sub-* (under), the root tract (draw away), and the suffix *-ion* (the condition of). In math, it refers to the act of taking one amount away from another.

Exercise V20 (p. 268)

1. "Aggressive" comes from the prefix *ad-* (toward), the root gress (step), and the suffix *-ive* (having the nature of). It means having a forceful nature.
2. "Attractive" comes from the prefix *ad-* (toward), the root tract (draw away), and the suffix *-ive* (having the nature of). It means having an appealing nature (one that draws others toward it).
3. "Deductive" comes from the prefix *de-* (from), the root duct (lead), and the suffix *-ive* (having the nature of). It describes a method or reasoning where known facts lead a person to a logical conclusion.
4. "Distractive" comes from the prefix *dis-* (away), the root tract (draw away), and the suffix *-ive* (having the nature of). It means having the nature of drawing away one's attention.
5. "Excessive" comes from the prefix *ex-* (out), the root cess (come), and the suffix *-ive* (having the nature of). It is used to describe things that are considered to be too great or too extreme (coming out too much).
6. "Impulsive" comes from the prefix *im-* (in), the root pulse (push), and the suffix *-ive* (having the nature of). It describes someone who is pushed into doing something by a strong desire which the person cannot control.
7. "Inventive" comes from the prefix *in-* (into), the root vent (come), and the suffix *-ive* (having the nature of). It is used to describe someone who brings things into existence.
8. "Objective" comes from the prefix *ob-* (toward), the root ject (throw), and the suffix *-ive* (having the nature of). It refers to a person's opinion as fair or based on facts (thrown toward the truth).
9. "Respective" comes from the prefix *re-* (back), the root spect (look at), and the suffix *-ive* (having the nature of). It means "in the order mentioned," and refers back to previously mentioned information.
10. "Subjective" comes from the prefix *sub-* (under), the root ject (throw), and the suffix *-ive* (having the nature of). It refers to a person's point of view or opinion.

Exercise V21 (p. 268)

These are possible answers. Your answers may differ.

1. ambiguous: Something that is ambiguous is unclear because it can be understood in more than one way.
2. contradictory: If two statements are contradictory, they are incompatible. Either one or the other is true.
3. enchant: If something enchants you, it puts a spell on you.
   embitter: Someone who is embittered is angry or feels despair because of unpleasant or unfair things that have happened to that person.
4. extraordinary: If something is extraordinary it has exceptional qualities. It is out of the ordinary.

5. infrastructure: The infrastructure of something is the basic structure on which it is built, such as the facilities or services needed for it to function.
6. malocclusion: "Malocclusion" refers to the condition of teeth not coming together properly.
7. multipurpose: "Multipurpose" refers to the condition of something having many purposes.
8. pernicious: If something is considered pernicious, it is considered harmful.
9. postmortem: A postmortem is a medical examination of a dead person's body in order to find out the cause of death.
10. preternatural: If something is preternatural it is exceptional in a way that leads you to believe that superhuman forces are involved.
11. synchronized: If two people or things are synchronized, they do things at the same moment or together.
12. ultrasonic: "Ultrasonic" is used to describe a sound of such a high frequency that people cannot hear it.

Exercise V22 (p. 269)

These are possible answers. Your answers may differ.

1. amiss: If something is amiss, there is something wrong or it is not as you expected it should be.
2. disinterested: Someone who is disinterested in something is not involved in it or unlikely to benefit from it and, therefore, is able to act in a fair and unselfish way.
3. misinterpretation: Someone who misinterprets something understands it wrongly. The misinterpretation is the person's incorrect understanding or explanation of it.
4. indecisive: Someone who is indecisive finds it difficult to make decisions.
5. impractical: Something that is impractical is not sensible or realistic.
6. illiterate: Someone who is illiterate does not know how to read or write.
7. irreverent: Someone who is irreverent does not show respect toward others or another.
8. nondescript: Something that is nondescript has no interesting or noticeable characteristics.
9. uninspiring: Something that is uninspiring does not cause interest or excitement.

Exercise V23 (p. 269)

1. *ambula* means walk
2. *ami, amo* mean love
3. *aque, aqua* mean water
4. *anthropo, anthrop* mean human
5. *carni, carna* mean flesh
6. *cide, cid* mean kill
7. *frag, frac* mean break
8. *fuge, fug* mean flee
9. *herbi* means grass
10. *lumin* means light
11. *magni, magna* mean large
12. *omni* means all

13. *pater, patri* mean father
14. *fidel, fid* mean trust
15. *pend* means hang

Exercise V24 (p. 270)

1. The state of being first in importance, order, or rank.
2. An interval of eight (especially in music).
3. A vehicle that has a single wheel and is propelled by pedals.
4. A shape having three sides.
5. A musical composition for two performers.
6. An insect with many feet.
7. A 100th anniversary.
8. Five offspring born at one birth.
9. A system based on the number ten.
10. The school following primary school.

Exercises V25, V26, and V27 (pp. 271–274)

There are no answer keys for these exercises.

Exercise V28 (p. 276)

1. (B) "Corresponds" comes from the words meaning "answer together." In this sentence, "correspond" means "be similar." "Coincides" comes from the words meaning "together unchanged" and means "occurring at a similar time."

2. (A) "Conference" comes from the words meaning "carry or bring together." A conference is a meeting among people who have a similar interest. "Symposium" comes from the words meaning "drink together" and refers to a conference in which experts or scholars discuss a particular subject.

3. (D) "Incurable" comes from the words meaning "without a cure." "Irreparable" comes from the words meaning "not able to repair."

4. (B) "Compulsory" comes from the words meaning "with a push." When something is compulsory, an authority insists that it be done. "Mandatory" comes from the words meaning "hand given." When something is mandatory, there is a legal obligation to do it.

5. (A) "Impeded" comes from the words meaning "without feet." When something is impeded, its development, progress, or movement is made difficult. "Hamper" means "restrict or obstruct movement."

6. (A) "Assumed" comes from the words meaning "take before." Someone who assumes responsibility or control of something accepts responsibility for it. If you take on responsibility for something, you accept responsibility for it.

7. (C) "Assuring" comes from the words meaning "safe before." If you are assured of something, you are made to feel less worried about it. "Promise" comes from the words meaning "put before." If

you are promised something, you are told before that something will definitely happen or be given.

8. (B) "Impending" comes from the words meaning "over hang." If something is impending, it is about to happen. "Imminent" comes from the words meaning "jut over." If something is imminent, it is almost certain to happen soon.

9. (C) "Predominant" comes from the words meaning "dominate over." Something that is predominant is more important or more noticeable. "Principle" comes from the word meaning "the first." A principle form is the most important form.

10. (A) "Variation" comes from the words meaning "vary." A variation is something that is different from others of the same group. "Modification" comes from the word meaning "measure." A modification is a limited change.

11. (D) "Indispensable" comes from the words meaning "not able to dispense of." If something is indispensable, it is essential and you cannot do without it. "Vital" comes from the words meaning "life." If something is vital, it is extremely important or necessary.

12. (D) "Diversification" comes from the words meaning "turn in different directions." Someone who diversifies something increases the variety of something. "Variegation" comes from the words meaning "vary." If something is variegated, it consists of a lot of different types.

13. (B) "Sequence" comes from the words meaning "follow." A sequence is a series. "Succession" comes from the words meaning "undergo." A succession of the same kind of things is a number of them coming one after another.

14. (A) "Proclaimed" comes from the words meaning "cry out for." If something is proclaimed, it is announced publicly. "Declared" comes from the words meaning "clear." If something is declared, it is made known.

15. (B) "Recognition" comes from the words meaning "learn again." "Recognition" can mean the understanding and acceptance of a fact or situation. "Prestige" comes from the words meaning "bind before." If you have prestige, others admire you because of the high quality of your work or your position or status in society. In this sentence, there is a status based on the recognition of the high quality or work.

16. (C) "Exclusively" comes from the words meaning "shut out of." Something that is exclusive is limited to a certain group of people. "Uniquely" comes from the words meaning "one." If something is unique to one thing, person, or group, it concerns or belongs to this thing, person, or group only.

17. (C) "Conciliation" comes from the word meaning "council." If you conciliate, you try to end a disagreement with someone by saying something to please that person or by changing your attitude or demands. "Appeasement" comes from the words meaning "toward peace." Appeasement is the act of trying to prevent others from being angry with you by giving them what they want.

18. (D) "Inaccessible" comes from the words meaning "not come toward." If something is inaccessible, it is difficult or impossible to get at. "Unreachable" comes from the words meaning "not in reach." If something is unreachable, it is not in a position where it can be grasped or contacted.

19. (A) "Persist" comes from the words meaning "stand through." If something persists, it continues to exist. "Survive" comes from the words meaning "over life." If something survives, it continues to exist in spite of being in a situation where it could be made extinct.

20. (C) "Invaluable" comes from the words meaning "without value." If something is invaluable, it is so useful or important that a value cannot be placed on it. "Irreplaceable" comes from the words meaning "not able to place back." If something is irreplaceable, it is so special that nothing else can take its place. In this sentence, Marco Polo's account is so valuable that it cannot be replaced.

21. (A) "Misdemeanor" comes from the words meaning "lead wrongly." A misdemeanor is an action that is considered unacceptable. "Crime" comes from the words meaning "judgment, offense." A crime is an action that is against the law.

22. (D) "Symmetrical" comes from the words meaning "measured together." When something is symmetrical, it has two sides that are mirror images of each other. "Balanced" comes from the words meaning "two scales." Something that is balanced is pleasing or beneficial because its parts are arranged or exist in the correct amounts.

23. (D) "Implanted" comes from the words meaning "plant in." Someone who implants something in a person's body puts it there, usually by operating on the person. "Inserted" comes from the words meaning "join in." Someone who inserts an object in something puts the object inside it.

24. (A) "Benefactor" comes from the words meaning "make well." A benefactor is a person who helps others by giving them money. "Patron" comes from the words meaning "father." A patron is someone who supports and gives money to a particular charity, group, or individual.

25. (D) "Compensate" comes from the words meaning "weigh together." To compensate for something that has a bad effect means to do something that cancels out this effect. "Adjust" comes from the words meaning "to be near." If you adjust something, you change it so that it is more effective. In this sentence, the lenses compensate for an error through an adjustment.

26. (A) "Prominent" comes from the words meaning "jut out before." Someone who is prominent is well known and important. "Significant" comes from the words meaning "sign or mark." Something that is significant has a marked effect on other things or people, usually because it is large in quantity or degree.

27. (C) "Coordination" comes from the words meaning "with order." To coordinate the movements of parts of your body means to make the parts work together in order to perform particular actions. "Synchronization" comes from the words meaning "time together." Things that are synchronized occur at the same time.

28. (A) "Lauded" comes from the words meaning "praised." Someone who is lauded is praised or admired. "Acclaimed" comes from the words meaning "shout out." Someone who is acclaimed has the approval of others because of something that person has accomplished.

29. (B) "Permanently" comes from the words meaning "remain before." If something is permanent, it remains the same for a very long time. "Irrevocably" comes from the words meaning "not voiced again." If something is irrevocable, it cannot be stopped or changed.

30. (B) "Internal" comes from the words meaning "turn in." "Internal" is used to describe something that exists inside a person, place, or object. "Interior" also comes from the words meaning "turn in." "Interior" is used to describe the inside part which is surrounded by the main part that you usually see.

Reading Comprehension

Exercise R1 (p. 281)
1. an illness
2. a rodent
3. the smallest part of a chemical element
4. a falling star
5. a (male) bee
6. a fish
7. electrical devices
8. a goddess
9. a system of signals
10. explosions of dying stars
11. loudness or softness
12. carved birds
13. a slender person

14. inscriptions (writing) in stones
15. taped interviews
16. height above sea level
17. evening worship
18. an American Indian woman
19. groups of nerve cells
20. the fear of being enclosed
21. large fish
22. creatures (animals)
23. plants
24. camping equipment
25. the process of an area becoming a desert
26. a compound used for burns
27. a structure used as a place for ceremonies
28. the succession of sounds
29. not deadly
30. descended from
31. insects
32. poisons
33. variety
34. kinds of clothes
35. a basket
36. not deadly
37. flourishes, grows easily, does well
38. decreases
39. friendly, sociable, outgoing
40. inexpensive items
41. a flower
42. part of a bagpipe
43. stopped, lessened
44. part of a ship
45. creative

Exercise R2 (p. 286)

1. who: Noah Webster
   that: English
2. they: bubbles
3. who: individuals
   their: political prisoners
4. it: Alaska
5. their: Royal Canadian Mounted Police
6. his: every person
   her: every person
7. when: 1863
   he: a Hungarian count
   the first European variety: wine grapes
   there: California
8. it: the human mind
9. her: Willa Cather
   subject matter: frontier life
10. themselves: Arctic people
    they: Arctic people
    these natural resources: the environment and wild
                                                animals

Exercise R3 (p. 288)

1. (D) "But" is used to qualify a statement. The statement concerning the value of glass in Egyptian times is qualified by (D) concerning the value of glass today.
   (A) is added information. (B) and (C) are not related to the fact that glass was valued in Egyptian times.

2. (C) "Such as" is used to introduce examples. An example of "behavior" is (C), sucking a thumb. (A) development, (B) the sex, and (C) structures are not examples of behavior.

3. (D) "Although" is used to qualify a statement. In (D) the fact that desert wildlife is similar is qualified by the contrasting fact that their ancestry is different.
   (A) gives information that one might assume to be true. However, "although" indicates that the information is not as one might expect. In (B) the wildlife's not adapting to jungles is not related to their coming from different ancestral stocks. (C) is a repetition of the phrase "the world's various deserts."

4. (C) "In contrast" is used to contrast statements. The informality of Halloween is contrasted with (C), the formality of Thanksgiving.
   (A) doesn't make a contrast but gives another example of a traditional holiday. (B) and (D) don't make contrasts but instead give information that is not related to the topic of Halloween.

5. (C) The main point of the statement is the *uses* of bamboo in general. "Equally important" introduces another way bamboo is used. In this case, (C), the food that can be made from bamboo and the items that can be made from bamboo are both important.
   In (A) the reason why the grass growing in warm climates is important is not clear. In (B) the longer cooking time seems to be more of a disadvantage than an aspect of equal importance. (D) does not relate to the importance of making something.

6. (A) "In conclusion" is used to indicate that something is true because the facts lead to this belief. All the facts about satellites lead to the belief that, (A), the lives of humankind have been enriched by their existence.
   (B) The facts given do not lead to any conclusion about the difficulties of satellites. (C) The facts given do not lead to any conclusion about how many TV channels can be picked up. (D) The facts given do not lead to any conclusion about orbital placement.

7. (B) "In addition" is used to add more information. The lasers and two-way wrist TV in (B) are two additional items Dick Tracy used besides the atomic-powered space vehicle.
   (A) gives new information about today's astronauts, not added information about space items introduced in a comic strip. In (C) Dick Tracy's popularity is not an addition to his devices. (D) gives new information about space items of today's astronauts. These items do not relate to items Dick Tracy used.

8. (B) "As a result" is used to show a consequence. The consequences of the infection's being difficult to detect is (B), that it is rarely diagnosed.
   (A) The number of students afflicted with the infection is not a result of its difficulty to detect. It is a result of the infection's spreading. (C) The fact that there are few centers which offer the test and the test takes up to seven days to be completed suggests that the infection is not treated promptly and in many cases is not even diagnosed. (D) The doctors would not prescribe a medicine for the infection as a consequence of the infection's being difficult to detect.

9. (A) "In some cases" is used to explain. The information in (A) is used to give information which explains the advantages of the nonsurgical method of treating heart disease.
   In (B) the nonsurgical method cannot replace an artery. In (C) the fact that coronary bypass operations are underused does not explain the nonsurgical method. In (D) the fact that the chest is opened up indicates that this information does not relate to the "nonsurgical method."

10. (A) "Indeed" is used to emphasize a fact. In (A) the fact that Einstein's brain contained more glial cells than other people's brains is being emphasized.
    (B) is added information concerning scientists' studies of brains. (C) is added information concerning where scientists looked for glial cells. (D) is a conclusion concerning the development of Einstein's intellectual processing.

Exercise R4 (p. 290)

The following are possible ways to break down the sentences into ideas. Your answers may be different.

1. Critics separate Charles Dickens's novels. They are separated according to their structural complexity. His mature works are more complex than his earlier novels. Both his mature works and his earlier novels are masterpieces of narrative.

2. Car tires are thrown away. Rubber from these tires can be reused. It can be reused in a process where it reacts with hot asphalt. This process gives the asphalt elasticity. The elasticity prevents the asphalt from breaking. It is used for certain surfaces. These surfaces are ones that suffer great stresses. An example of this kind of surface is that of airport runways.

3. In 1785, two men from France tried to cross the English Channel. Their names were Pilatre de Rozier and Pierre Romain. They tried to cross the Channel in a balloon. Their balloon was filled with a mixture of hot air and hydrogen. This balloon caught fire and fell to the ground.

4. The Royal Canadian Mounted Police are informally called Mounties. They were first formed to stop trade in whiskey. This trade was against the law. Now the Mounties enforce all federal laws everywhere in Canada.

5. Savannah and Charleston are sister cities. They have historic centers. These centers have been saved from destruction and neglect. These historic centers attract tourists. The tourists are eager to view the gracious old houses there.

Exercise R5 (p. 292)

1. the Japanese macaque
2. robots
3. parade (This is implied by the phrases "streets lined with people," "shopkeepers locking their doors and joining the crowds," and "the first float.")
4. parsley
5. mud
6. Hay-on-Wye
7. foster grandparents
8. The koto
9. bicycle race (This is implied by the words "starting gate," "bicycle racers," "classes," "sponsors," and "racers.")
10. thinking

Exercise R6 (p. 294)

1. (B) The passage explains information derived from dinosaur tracks, and (B) states "dinosaur tracks are giving important information about dinosaurs."
   (A) gives details about the dinosaur tracks.
   (C) gives details about dinosaurs.

2. (A) The passage tells how the spider is different, and (A) states this spider is different from other spiders.
   (B) and (C) give details about the spider.

3. (C) The passage discusses how the trees communicate, and (C) states what scientists believe about trees communicating.
   (A) is a restatement of information in the passage.
   (B) could be inferred as a logical use of this information.

4. (A) The passage discusses how satellites will be used and the importance of this use. (A) introduces the topic that satellites will be used.
   (B) is a restatement of the first detail. (C) is a conclusion based on the information given in the passage.

5. (C) The passage mainly discusses what the conclusion about animal screams is. (C) states that conclusions have been drawn.
   (A) gives examples of predators. (B) gives details of how the research took place.

6. (A) The kind of pottery that is discussed in the passage is introduced in (A).
   (B) and (C) are details about pottery.

7. (A) The passage discusses the details of the vaccine, and (A) introduces the topic of a cavity-preventing vaccine.
   (B) is a detail about vaccines. (C) tells of the research.

8. (B) The passage discusses each type of cloud, and (B) states that there are four basic cloud types.
   (A) gives more information about stratus clouds. (C) could be the topic of the following paragraph.

9. (B) All the people mentioned in the passage are famous people from the past, and (B) states that the name William was the name of many famous people in the past.
   (A) and (C) may be details concerning the name William today.

10. (A) The passage discusses three ways to deal with oil spills, and (A) states that there are ways to deal with oil spills.
    (B) states only that oil spills are a problem. (C) tells how oil spills spread, but the passage does not discuss that problem.

Exercise R7 (p. 296)

1. (A) and (E) are the only choices that concern the relationship between vitamin D and the sun.

2. (B), (C), (D), and (E) all concern recycling waste products. Choice (A) concerns garbage (waste) but not the recycling of it.

3. (B) and (E) concern where edelweiss is found.

4. (A) and (B) concern the qualities of steel frames which make skyscrapers possible.

5. (C) and (E) concern the snake's jaws. Although (D) mentions the snake's jaw, it really concerns the snake's teeth.

6. (B), (C), and (D) describe aspects of Pennsylvania Avenue.

7. (A), (B), and (C) describe the act of bending the longbow.

8. (B) and (D) concern the location of the Aleutian Islands.

Exercise R8 (p. 297)

1. (4) The main idea of the passage concerns domestic turkeys. Sentence 4 concerns wild turkeys.

2. (3) The main idea of the passage concerns rice as a food crop. Sentence 3 concerns the origins of rice.

3. (2) The main idea of the passage concerns nicotine addiction. Sentence 2 concerns smoking and cancer.

4. (4) The main idea of the passage concerns meteorites reaching Earth. Sentence 4 concerns the implications of a fossil being found in a meteorite.

5. (1) The main idea of the passage concerns the advantages of underground homes. Sentence 1 concerns the disadvantages of underground homes.

6. (4) The main idea of the passage concerns dust clouds from China. Sentence 4 concerns the composition of the Hawaiian soil.

7. (2) The main idea of the passage concerns the disappearance of birds from Christmas Island. Sentence 2 concerns the discovery of Christmas Island.

8. (4) The main idea of the passage concerns the cross between the hairy potato and the common potato. Sentence 4 is a definition of the potato.

9. (3) The main idea of the passage is Caroline and William Herschel's common interest in astronomy. Sentence 3 concerns Caroline's upbringing.

10. (4) The main idea of the passage is the importance of clothing in winning a skiing race. Sentence 4 concerns skiing equipment in general.

Exercise R9 (p. 299)

1. (A) It is not the Kimono design that dates from the seventeenth century but the dyeing that dates from the seventeenth century.
   *(B) The passage consists of step-by-step instructions for Yuzen dyeing.
   (C) There is no information on how kimonos are made but rather on how the design is made on kimonos.
   (D) The elaborate embroidery is one detail in the passage.

2.*(A) The passage states the different ways a flashlight fish can use bioluminescence.
   (B) The way a flashlight fish saves its life is only one of the ways it uses bioluminescence.
   (C) How bioluminescence works is a detail introducing the main topic – its uses.
   (D) The flashlight fish is the only fish discussed in the passage.

3. (A) The passage states that the songwriter Cole Porter was not regarded as socially conscious in his lifetime.
   (B) Porter's being rich and famous is a detail.
   *(C) The passage contains various details of the life of the songwriter Cole Porter.
   (D) Porter's making sophistication popular is a detail.

4. (A) How the beaver's tail looks is only one detail in the passage.

   *(B) The passage discusses each of the uses that a beaver's tail has.

   (C) A lesson in nature studies is too broad a topic to be the main idea.

   (D) A reader cannot use a beaver's tail; only a beaver can use its tail.

5. (A) The passage is not about how earthquakes affect tree rings but how tree rings can be used to obtain information about earthquakes.

   (B) Once the tree has recorded an earthquake, it has already occurred and therefore cannot warn people of its coming.

   *(C) Although the passage doesn't explain how this information is gained, it lists the kind of information that can be gained from tree rings.

   (D) The passage tells us that tree rings can be used to obtain this information but it does not explain why.

Exercise R10 (p. 301)

1. S	3. S	5. S	7. D	9. D
2. S	4. D	6. D	8. S	10. S

Exercise R11 (p. 302)

1.*(B)
   (A) and (D) It is not the brain that faints.
   (C) It is not the brain that causes the drop in the blood supply.

2.*(D)
   (A) It is not vegetarians that treat gorillas and small animals gently, but gorillas that treat small animals gently.
   (B) All gorillas are vegetarians, not just some.
   (C) Gorillas have been observed behaving in a gentle manner, not the small creatures.

3.*(C)
   (A) The crews do not dig a fire; they dig a fire line.
   (B) It is not the fire that varies the fire line but the crews who vary the fire line according to the strength and nature of the fire.
   (D) "Depend on " means "rely on." Crews do not rely on fighting fires to dig a line. The result of the fire line is determined by the strength and nature of the fire.

4.*(B)
   (A) It is not the well educated who promise cures, but the medical quacks.
   (C) All people are promised cures, not only the well educated.
   (D) It is not the medical profession that has appealed to the well educated but the promise of cures that has appeal for even the well educated.

5.*(D)
   (A) It is not the tsetse fly that kills the parasitic protozoa, but the tsetse fly that carries the parasitic protozoa.
   (B) The tsetse fly carries the parasitic protozoa, not the silver compound.
   (C) Parasitic protozoa cause the sleeping sickness, not the tsetse fly.

6.*(A)
   (B) Six out of 37 stories were published, not written.
   (C) Only six stories were published.
   (D) There is no information concerning the topic of the six accepted stories.

7.*(B)
   (A) It is the convection currents that behave like conveyor belts driving the plates, not the plates.
   (C) It is the convection currents that are in the hot magma and that behave as conveyor belts.
   (D) The Earth's crustal plates cannot propose a theory.

8.*(C)
   (A) Medical authorities are reluctant to support the views.
   (B) This statement might be inferred, but it is not a restatement of the sentence that medical authorities are reluctant to support the nutritionists' findings.
   (D) Medical authorities have not supported the findings that vitamin C may prevent the common cold.

9.*(A)
   (B), (C), and (D) Female cowbirds can teach songs by responding to certain chirps.

10.*(A)
   (B) The conflict is of interest not only to those who want to abolish the last remnants of wilderness but to those who want to save it as well.
   (C) There is no information about lawyers' involvement in this conflict.
   (D) The conflict is not about abolishing industry but about abolishing or maintaining wilderness areas.

Exercise R12 (p. 304)

1. Europa, one of Jupiter's moons, is the only place in the solar system (unequaled in the solar system) – outside of Earth (with one exception) – where enormous quantities of water (vast oceans) are known to exist . . . .

2. . . . A single discharge (a lightning bolt) can actually (it is possible) contain 20 or more successive strokes (a series of bolts) . . .

3. . . . . they (porpoises) leap out of the water (travel through the air) to escape the pull of surface drag (air, which creates less drag than water). At that point, leaping out of the water (travel through the air) actually requires less energy (conserve energy) than swimming . . . .

4. . . . During the flare-up, <u>strong winds</u> blowing off the surface of the star <u>disperse the surrounding</u> dust (scatter the dust particles) <u>and expose the newborn star</u> (allow the birth of a star to be seen) <u>to observers on Earth</u> (people who see).

5. Perhaps <u>the greatest navigators</u> (expert sailors) in history <u>were the Vikings</u> (the Vikings were) . . . .

6. . . . Today, dolphins do such dangerous and <u>necessary work</u> (important task) as <u>locating explosives</u> (find mines) hidden in the sea. . .

7. . . . First, <u>it</u> (a city tree) <u>must be</u> (has to be) <u>able to withstand</u> (survive/be tough). . . .

8. . . . trained <u>them</u> (Saint Bernards) to <u>search for travelers lost in snowstorms or avalanches</u> (aided travelers) in the Alps. <u>For hundreds of years,</u> (for centuries) <u>Saint Bernards served this purpose</u> (aided travelers). . . .

9. . . . Out on Lake Biwa, <u>participants</u> attempt to break records <u>by flying</u> (fly) <u>their own inventions</u> (crafts they have designed themselves) . . . .

10. . . . . the <u>mineral constituent of the pearl being dissolved</u> (damage to a pearl) by weak acids. . . . . The acidic nature of <u>perspiration</u> (sweating) is one such acid . . .

Exercise R13 (p. 306)

1. (A) T
   (B) F The third time the plan was proposed it was accepted.
   (C) T
   (D) T
   (E) F We are not given any information concerning where the tunneling began.
   (F) F We are not told why the plan was rejected in 1883. ("Bore" has two meanings: "to drill" and "to tire.")
   (G) F It was not the construction itself but other reasons which led to the tunnel's rejection.
   (H) F The tunnel was not made in 1930.
   (I) F The passage does not mention a wonderful engineer (a person who plans how to build structures) but that the tunnel was to be an engineering wonder (a structure that would cause wonder).
   (J) T

2. (A) F There are thousands of varieties of cheese.
   (B) F All cheeses are made with curd.
   (C) T
   (D) T
   (E) F Blue-veined cheese is not molded (a form which is used to give food a shape), but a mold (a fungus) is put into the cheese.
   (F) T
   (G) F Penicillin mold is injected into cheese, and Roquefort is an example of such a cheese.
   (H) T
   (I) F Blue-veined cheeses are treated with penicillin.
   (J) F Cheddar cheese, unlike Gruyère, is not cooked.

3. (A) F Their homing instinct has made them popular for racing.
   (B) F Their instinct is what makes it possible to train them.
   (C) T
   (D) T
   (E) F The training begins when the bird is seven weeks old (a little under two months).
   (F) F A pigeon should be able to fly at least 100 miles before it is ready to race.
   (G) T
   (H) F No information is given about the distance of the races.
   (I) F A bird has not completed the race until it has entered its cote and the owner has removed the tag and recorded the arrival time.
   (J) F A bird with a shorter distance to fly between the release point and its home may arrive first but may not be flying as fast as another bird that must fly a longer distance. The bird making the best flying time is the winner.

4. (A) F Information on how to be popular in ancient Egypt is not given.
   (B) F To play marbles, one has to flick a marble at a target.
   (C) F The target is usually a marble, but it can be something else, such as a hole.
   (D) T
   (E) F The players try to shoot marbles out of the circle.
   (F) T
   (G) T
   (H) F There is no information about whether the players are only shooting to get their marbles into the holes or if they are trying to hit marbles that are already in the holes.
   (I) T
   (J) F Although the passage only discusses these three games, it does not state that they are the only games. It states that they are popular ways to play marbles.

5. (A) F The three methods could be used in an attempt to control people's minds, and how far people's minds can be influenced against their wills is a disturbing question.
   (B) T
   (C) F Subception is not a new observation; it's a technique.
   (D) F No information is given about whether the people of New York were upset about the experiment.
   (E) T
   (F) F The suggestion for a person to do something is made during the hypnotic trance.
   (G) F The passage states it is still uncertain whether a person can be made to carry out an action against his or her will while under a posthypnotic suggestion.
   (H) T

(I) F It is not the brainwashed people who force others to look at evidence, but those who are doing the brainwashing who force those being brainwashed to look at evidence that is supposedly true.

(J) T

6. (A) T

(B) T

(C) F The artists used the lens to make the image clearer. It was not possible to preserve the image.

(D) F There is no information concerning the light-sensitive chemical that Niepce used. The article "a" is frequently used when first mentioning an object. Its use in the phrase "a light-sensitive chemical" implies that the chemical was not the same as the one previously mentioned.

(E) F Schulze made his mixture almost 100 years before Niepce made the first permanent photographic image.

(F) T

(G) T

(H) T

(I) F No information is given concerning who was responsible for the development of color film.

(J) F The images from a camera obscura are not permanent and therefore could not be used for taking photographs of the earth.

Exercise R14 (p. 310)

1. (A) It is not the fossils that are 6 to 8 feet long and 350 pounds but the animal itself.

(B) The fossils cannot be descended from an animal. They are the remains of one.

(C) It is not that the foothills were under water, but that the whale was on land.

  *(D) The first line of the passage states that the fossils are of an ancient whale. The second sentence states that "the fossils consist of . . . the well-preserved middle ear."

2.*(A) The passage states that eardrums do not work in water.

(B) Marine means "of the sea." The presence of eardrums suggests that the ancient whales lived on land.

(C) Since eardrums do not work in water, whales with eardrums could not distinguish underwater sounds.

(D) It is their having eardrums which suggests that they did live on land.

3.*(A) It is stated in the passage that the separation of the right and left ear bones enables marine whales to detect the direction of underwater sounds.

(B) A middle ear suggests eardrums, which do not work in water.

(C) It is not because it lives under water that a whale can hear.

(D) It is the fossils that have a well preserved middle ear.

4. (A) Cornmeal was introduced to the early colonists by the Indians.

(B) New England is mentioned only as a place where visitors can get johnnycakes.

  *(C) It is stated that cornmeal began as an Indian staple.

(D) The people of the south are mentioned as using cornmeal to make spoonbread. Nothing is stated about their using it originally.

5. (A) This is a description of a "hushpuppy."

  *(B) The passage mentions "mush, leftover cornmeal porridge cut and fried."

(C) Succotash is a dish in which cornmeal is added, not mush.

(D) Mush is one of two meals developed by the colonists.

6. (A) These forms would not be eaten nationwide if they were unpopular.

(B) The common forms are eaten nationwide, not restricted to regions.

  *(C) The passage mentions "the most common forms of cornmeal nationwide."

(D) The corn the Indians grew was multicolored.

7. (A) Age and number are not qualities but reasons why they are expensive.

(B) Violinists and collectors are not qualities but people who want them.

  *(C) It is stated that the Stradivarius is unmatched in tonal quality and responds more quickly and easily than any other violin.

(D) The color is not a quality.

8. (A) 1737 was the year that Stradivari died.

  *(B) It is stated that "650" Stradivarius violins are believed to be in existence today.

(C) A quarter million dollars is how much a cheap Stradivarius costs.

(D) Hundreds of thousands is the approximate price of any Stradivarius.

9. (A) All Stradivarius violins are rare.

(B) A price is not given for the most expensive one.

(C) Cheap reproductions are not mentioned in the passage.

  *(D) It is stated that a cheap Stradivarius costs a quarter million dollars.

10. (A) It is stated that filling wall space with materials absorbs noise.

(B) Using thick carpets and heavy curtains is an example of the techniques used to reduce noise.

(C) Air conditioners and furnaces were designed to filter air through soundproofing materials.

  *(D) Air filters themselves are not mentioned in the passage.

11. (A) There is no mention of new techniques being designed.

(B) See (C).

  *(C) Architects are designing structures that have the right kind of noise.

(D) Architects are designing buildings which are desirable, not adverse.

12. (A) A noisy furnace is not stated as one of the noises people need.
    (B) It is stated that people react adversely to the lack of sound.
    (C) It is not reduced noise in general but reduced undesirable noise that people need.
  *(D) It is stated that there is a "kind of noise that people seem to need."

13. (A) The computer printer produces the dots per inch, not measures them.
    (B) The density of the dots are changed to make the image look like a photograph.
    (C) The graphics, not the printer, look almost photographic.
  *(D) The printer can produce graphics (images) which look photographic (like photographs).

14. (A), (B) These are ways graphics are *unlike* photographs.
  *(C) Although the gray shade is made differently, in both photographs and graphics the colors are seen as different shades of gray.
    (D) The different dot patterns on graphics create an individual effect but not on photographs.

15. (A), (B) The graphics look *almost* photographic. They are not an exact reproduction or of the same quality.
  *(C) The image is less lifelike when you are looking at it closely.
    (D) The graphics image is made through changes of dot density.

Exercise R15 (p. 314)

1. (A) Private individuals must be able to submit reports because two reports came from private individuals.
    (B) The reports were already published. This is understood from the phrase "three of the published reports."
  *(C) Three reports from official investigations and two from private individuals equals a total of five reports.
    (D) There is no information given on what the investigations covered.

2. (A) No information is given concerning how the villages were destroyed.
  *(B) Information must have been collected for the Institute of Anthropology to computerize it, and the villages must be in ruins if the plans are to restore them.
    (C) It is not the Indians who have the computers to store data but the Institute of Anthropology.
    (D) It is not the plans that need to be restored but the villages.

3. (A) This statement is contrary to the information given in the statement, which suggests that the

European bees will make the African bees gentler. This may be an advantage.
  *(B) If the bees have "devastated" the beekeeping industry, they must be destructive, and if it is believed that the interbreeding might make them "gentler," they must not be gentle now.
    (C) The question of becoming gentler refers to the bees, not the industry.
  *(D) Both kinds of bees must live in Latin America if they are interbreeding there.

4. (A) While people who think nobody likes them might own a pet, it cannot be inferred that all pet owners feel unloved.
  *(B) This is one way a person frustrated in feeling love may express the need.
    (C) Appropriate ways in which to show love cannot be inferred from the statement.
  *(D) Collecting stamps could be one of the substitutes that a person frustrated by the need for love may choose.

5.*(A) If the condition of the rider were as important as the condition of the horse, the contestants would give as much attention to themselves as to their horses.
    (B) It cannot be inferred that the riders like their horses better; they would probably give more attention to their horses in order to win the race.
    (C) The statement does not concern the horses' giving attention to themselves but the riders' giving attention to the horses.
    (D) What happens after a race is not mentioned. Race contestants may continue to give attention to their horses in preparation for the next race.

6.*(A) If "no partner" helps the male, then the female does not help him.
  *(B) If the nest is floating, it must be on water, and this suggests that the jacana is an aquatic bird.
    (C) The male protects and nurtures its chicks, but whether or not it protects its partner cannot be inferred. A partner probably doesn't need to be nurtured.
    (D) Mating is not mentioned.

7. (A) Elephants are being trapped as a result of farmers' clearing land, not by hunters.
  *(B) It can be inferred by the elephants being trapped in forest enclaves that these must be their habitat, and these forests are being cleared away for agriculture or farming.
  *(C) Since the land cleared of forests is being used for agriculture, these farms would have to be crossed for an elephant to reach another forest.
    (D) People are not trapping elephants for use. The elephants are unintentionally being trapped through the process of making space for more cropland.

8. (A) Since it is sunken ships that are being safeguarded, it is understood that they were already sunken and not made to sink by thieves.

 *(B) Sunken shops must contain something valuable to someone for thieves to be interested in plundering them.

 (C) It is not the salvagers who are caught but the salvagers who are trying to protect the ships from adventurers or thieves.

 *(D) There must be more ways than electronic means to protect a ship because "other" means are also used.

9.*(A) The weeds known as gopher plants have been given the name (renamed) gasoline plant.

 *(B) The hydrocarbons in latex can be refined into substitutes for crude oil and gasoline. Therefore, hydrocarbons must contain something that can be made into a substitute for crude oil and gasoline.

 (C) Although gasoline can be refined from the gasoline plant, there is no mention of replacing other sources of gasoline.

 (D) It is the "milky latex" which contains hydrocarbons. It cannot be inferred that milk contains hydrocarbons.

10. (A) Since morphine is still being scraped from the poppy plant and since it has not been profitably synthesized, it must still be profitable to cultivate.

 *(B) If morphine is unsurpassed for controlling pain, it must be more effective than any other drug, including cocaine.

 (C) Although morphine has been used for at least 5,000 years, it cannot be inferred that its use was for controlling pain.

 (D) If morphine is not yet profitably synthesized, then artificial morphine cannot be made economically.

Exercise R16 (p. 316)

1. "Unlike other toads, the male golden toad is nearly voiceless"; "which is as effective as croaking in luring females during the mating season."
2. "Besides earthquakes and volcanos, torrential rains, encroaching tropical vegetation, and time have all taken their toll."
3. "medical authorities are skeptical of the treatment"
4. "powerful legs"; "lacks the barbules that are needed to lock feathers into a flat vane"; "head is crowned by a leathery helmet that protects it when it is charging through the jungle."
5. "Away from the master carver who dictated what was to be carved"
6. "Members of both sexes . . . learn the art of sword fighting in mock combat"
7. "Computer-generated motion pictures allow the viewer to see the meaning of data and complex relationships instantly and are a new aid to human understanding"
8. "not recommended for beginners"

9. "Nowhere else, except perhaps in tropical coral reefs, is nature so great in its diversity of organisms"
10. "Champion athletes combine new heights of athleticism with the elegance of dance"

Exercise R17 (p. 318)

1. yes If communities are discovering that they are living near toxic waste dumps, then they must not have known it in the first place because no one told them.
2. yes E. B. White must have been well known if his death was cause for sadness in millions of homes.
3. no The Richter scale was not named for an earthquake but probably for Charles F. Richter, the man who helped devise it.
4. no Although a firestorm may have caused the dinosaurs to disappear, it was not *necessarily* the actual cause of their disappearance. Some other catastrophe may have been responsible for the dinosaurs' extinction.
5. yes There were twelve deaths and three were not linked to fresh fruits and vegetables. The rest (nine) were linked to fresh foods. The deaths were sulfite associated and, therefore, the fresh foods must have been contaminated with sulfite.
6. no The women do not want their cosmetics to smear. It is not a matter of laziness.
7. no If data is being received from *Vega I* and if people had expected this object to encounter dust, it is probably not an "unidentified" object.
8. no Other antibiotics may still be useful for other kinds of illnesses.
9. no It may be possible that bifocal lens wearers can use contact lenses that don't take advantage of the way the eye reacts to light.
10. yes If actions such as walking and grasping may be impossible for those people who have had nerves damaged, then the nervous system must be important for muscle control.

Exercise R18 (p. 320)

1. (A) _I_ Individuals who have shown outstanding talents in a field must be known. Since these awards are given to such people, it can be inferred that those who are not already known will not receive an award.

 (B) _I_ The last sentence in the passage implies that some people might attain success because they worry about money.

 (C) ____ The freedom from financial worries gives individuals more time, but that does not mean that time can be bought with money.

 (D) _R_ $300,000 is the maximum amount of money given to individuals to allow them time to devote to creative "thinking."

2. (A) __I__ The phrase "attempting to solve" suggests that the CDC is not always successful.

   (B) __R__ "To crisscross the country" means "to travel back and forth across the nation."

   (C) __I__ If patterns and common links among the victims are found during epidemics, it can be inferred that it is through the extra data collected that the patterns emerge.

   (D) __I__ The examples of activities given of the epidemiologists' research imply that a lot of research needs to be done to solve medical mysteries.

3. (A) __R__ On the basis of the amount of light absorbed and reflected, astronomers determined that comets contain frozen water.

   (B) __I__ It can be inferred that since the ice content in Comet Bowell was determined by measuring the light it absorbed and reflected, the ice content in other comets can also be determined.

   (C) ____ This statement may be true, but from the information in the passage we can only infer that they study comets.

   (D) __R__ The name given for the comet that astronomers were observing was Comet Bowell.

4. (A) ____ It is the corpse (the body of a dead bee) that emits a chemical, not the dying bee that emits the chemical.

   (B) __R__ "Must be removed" means "not left" and "prevent the spread of disease" means "stop other bees from being sick."

   (C) __R__ If the corpses emit a chemical that signals death, then the chemical that is emitted signals the honeybees that a death has occurred.

   (D) __R__ "Within an hour" means "in less than one hour."

5. (A) __R__ If the seals once thrived off the coast of California, then there used to be a large number of them there.

   (B) __I__ If the availability of petroleum products is a factor in the reduced demand for seal oil, the implication is that products that were made from seal oil are now made from petroleum.

   (C) __I__ Because petroleum products are more available, we can infer that the petroleum to make those products is probably easier to obtain than seal oil.

   (D) ____ Although the northern elephant seal has made a dramatic comeback, there is no information concerning how numerous they are.

6. (A) __I__ The months of prolonged sunlight may be the summer months in contrast to the winter months when the sun disappears.

   (B) __R__ More than the severe cold (the harsh climate), it's the lack (the scarcity) of resources for food, clothing, and shelter that define (influence) the life-styles (living conditions).

   (C) __I__ It can be inferred from the words "probably descended from" that their ancestry is not known for certain.

   (D) ____ One cannot make any inference from the information in this passage whether there is more or less sunshine the further north one is.

7. (A) __I__ If scientists could tell whether an astronaut who suffers from car sickness will suffer from space sickness, they would not be attempting to find a way to predict who was susceptible.

   (B) __R__ It (space sickness) interferes with (causes problems or makes difficult) the important work that must be done (work the astronauts do).

   (C) __R__ "Akin" means "related to."

   (D) ____ It is believed that the zero gravity and its effect on the inner ear causes space sickness, but that doesn't mean that gravity and its effect on the inner ear causes car sickness.

8. (A) __I__ If there are remains of victims, then white sharks do kill people.

   (B) __I__ If the white shark did not attack people, it would not have a terrifying reputation.

   (C) __I__ If the shark does not eat people as the evidence suggests, it must kill them for other reasons. Also, "mindless ferocity" implies that the shark attacks for no discernible reason.

   (D) __R__ It is stated in the passage that the white shark is a kind of mackerel shark, and it doesn't eat people.

9. (A) __R__ An inchworm is a geometrid. "Extends itself forward" means "stretching forward," "draws its back end up to its front legs" means "moving its back to its front," and "repeats the sequence" means "repeating this process."

   (B) __I__ If only some caterpillars are called earth measurers or inchworms, it can be inferred that not all caterpillars are inchworms.

   (C) __I__ It can be inferred from "looping stride" that a loop is formed when the inchworm moves. A loop cannot be made when the caterpillar is extending itself, so it must be when the back legs are drawn up to its front legs.

   (D) __R__ The caterpillars that are called geometrids, or earth measurers, are commonly named inchworms.

10. (A) __I__ The Merlin must be a kind of aircraft because it is compared with a helicopter or small plane and it "takes off and hovers."

(B) __I__ If the Merlin is safer than a helicopter or small plane because it has no exposed blades, it must be the exposed blades that make some aircraft unsafe.

(C) ____ There is no information given concerning the production of the Merlin. The passage could simply be describing the "design" or a "model" of the Merlin, not a Merlin that has actually been produced.

(D) ____ No information is given concerning how the Merlin is controlled. For example, it could be controlled by remote control devices or through automatic pilots.

Exercise R19 (p. 323)

1.*(A) Along the coast would be at sea level, where the races must be slower if racing is faster at high altitudes.

(B) An indoor track could be in an area at sea level or at a higher altitude.

(C) and (D) A high plateau and the snowline of a volcano are both high-altitude areas, where the racing would be faster, not slower.

2. (A) While an owner may think it amusing to trick an expert, there would be no need for the owner to do so.

*(B) An owner could hang a copy of a valuable painting so that in the case of a theft, the real painting would not be taken.

(C) If owners want to encourage talented artists, they would do so through other means, such as buying an original work by those artists or encouraging them to paint something special.

(D) If owners enjoyed buying fake paintings, they would probably do this instead of spending a lot of money on valuable paintings.

3. (A), (B), and (C) These are all places where a law enforcement official could use a dog for detecting drugs, but only if suspicious that drugs were in use.

*(D) A law enforcement official would always be on the lookout for possible smuggling of drugs into a country and might, therefore, use such a trained dog.

4. (A) There is no information that implies that a Steiner school does not include academic subjects.

(B) A game which is not competitive could be played in a coeducational (boys and girls together) school.

*(C) A contest suggests a competition, and this kind of activity is discouraged in a Steiner school.

(D) A school that is practicing mixed-ability teaching is teaching children with different abilities; therefore, the children are probably at different levels.

5.*(A) If the bacteria can destroy the cyanide, a toxic waste dumped into rivers, then the bacteria can save the water life by getting rid of this poison.

(B) The bacteria destroys cyanide, not fish.

(C) Cyanide is not put into swimming pools; therefore, the bacteria would not serve a purpose there.

(D) The bacteria were exposed to increasing levels of cyanide. An increase of cyanide in the chemical plants is not desirable.

Exercise R20 (p. 324)

1. (A) Being blind to the humanity of their members does not mean that the people are actually blind.

*(B) It may be difficult for a person who is more concerned with schedules to deal with a person who is not so concerned and vice versa.

(C) Monochronic cultures are linear cultures.

(D) In monochronic cultures, schedules take precedence over all people, and in polychronic cultures all people take precedence over schedules.

2.*(A) If people are more important than schedules, a person may skip an appointment for another person.

(B) In a monochronic society a person might be blind to the needs of a friend.

(C) A person from a polychronic society might be on time for an appointment with a person from a monochronic society only if no other person needs attention.

(D) Since schedules are important in a monochronic society, people will probably do everything possible to keep an appointment.

3.*(A) Since monochronic and polychronic cultures are at opposing ends of the spectrum, it can be inferred that there are other cultures between the two opposing ones.

(B) A monochronic culture is linear, and a polychronic culture is simultaneous.

(C) According to the passage, time can be regarded not as a physical absolute but as a cultural invention.

(D) It is not biological or physical absolutes that a culture invents but a way to regard time.

4. (A) and (B) The essential point is that those areas which have heavy crop production are most affected by land erosion. Those areas may or may not have been prairies and grasslands.

*(C) If soil erosion is accelerating in the areas where new demands placed on the land by heavy crop production exist, then the areas which produce many crops probably suffer more land erosion.

(D) Petroleum is mentioned as a critical natural resource problem. Nothing is stated about areas where it is produced.

5.*(A) The passage implies that soil erosion was worse in the 1930s than in the nineteenth century. Furthermore, it states that the erosion has accelerated in the past 40 years. Thus, erosion is probably worse today than it was in the nineteenth century.

(B) After 282 million acres were damaged, the conservation efforts began.

(C) It cannot be inferred that nineteenth century farmers had less land erosion than those of the 1930s because of better environmental practices. Probably they put fewer demands on the land.

(D) Heavy crop production may be necessary to meet the demands of the nation, but it may *cause* a critical disaster, not divert one.

6. (A) If soil erosion and pollution problems are going to replace petroleum scarcity as the most critical problem, petroleum cannot be the most critical problem of the future.

(B) Perhaps the drilling of petroleum or the refining of it can cause soil erosion and pollution problems, but petroleum itself cannot cause these problems.

(C) It is the new demands on the land by heavy crop production that has caused soil erosion.

*(D) If soil erosion and pollution problems may replace the problem of petroleum scarcity as the most critical, all three of these problems must be critical problems faced by the nation.

7.*(A) The phrase "carries about 5 gallons of fuel" implies that ultralights have an engine that uses fuel.

(B) If human energy were used, then there would be no need for fuel.

(C) If an ultralight were powered by remote control, there would be no need for a pilot.

(D) No mention is made of solar energy in the passage.

8.*(A) If ultralights are sold as kits and take about 40 hours to assemble, people can probably buy their own kit and assemble it.

(B) There is no information given as to where the kits can be bought.

(C) Although a person without experience can fly an ultralight, it doesn't mean that people in general who fly ultralights have no experience.

(D) If a person can buy a kit and assemble it, there is probably no need to have training in aviation to do this.

9. (A) There is no information given as to whether or not ultralights are registered.

(B) "Rarely fatal" means that they are "not frequently fatal."

*(C) If an accident is rarely fatal or even serious, the pilots can probably walk away from most of the accidents.

(D) Fatal accidents rarely occur.

10. (A) The rivers from two Canadian provinces drain into the Mississippi River. Drainage areas in Canada are not mentioned.

(B) Only 31 states out of all the states in the United States have rivers that drain into the Mississippi.

(C) If only parts of some states have rivers that drain into the Mississippi, there are probably other rivers in other parts of those states that drain elsewhere.

*(D) If the Mississippi extends to Canada and flows down to the sea carrying sand, silt, and clay, probably some of the silt the river is carrying comes from Canada.

11.*(A) Since the delta system provides shelter and nutrients for the continent's most fertile marine nursery, it must be very important to marine life.

(B) "Nursery" in the passage means a place where marine life grows, not a nursery for children.

(C) There is no information about diseases caused by mosquitoes and other insects in the passage.

(D) There is no information about the United States' establishing nurseries.

12. (A) It is not being destroyed but being built up.

*(B) If the delta is constantly being built up by the river deposits of sand, silt, and clay, it is probably always changing.

(C) It is not the sea movement but the river deposits that are building up the delta.

(D) The delta is being built on the continental shelf. The continental shelf is already there.

13. (A) The term "chicks" can refer to any baby bird, not just chickens.

(B) Seals do not build nests in trees.

*(C) The words "nests," "molts," "chicks," "hatch," and "plumage" all refer to birds.

(D) Bears do not build nests in trees.

14.*(A) Since the female molts (loses her feathers) inside the nest, the nest is probably lined with those feathers.

(B) The female probably loses her feathers in order to make the nest, not because the nest is too warm.

(C) After the female molts, she seals herself into the nest; she does not break it up.

(D) To lose feathers by molting is different than to lose feathers by plucking them out. The female probably uses her feathers to make the nest warm. The passage states she uses mud and dung to seal the nest.

15.*(A) The female probably seals herself in on purpose for laying her eggs and hatching the chicks.

(B) There is no information to indicate that the male forces the female into the nest. Both birds seal the opening.

(C) If sealing the nest happened by accident, it would be exceptional rather than the typical behavior of the species.

(D) There is no information to indicate that the female is protecting her eggs from the male as opposed to other predators.

16. (A) The baby chicks can be fed but eggs cannot.
    (B) The male helps seal in the female.
    (C) It is not plumage that keeps the chicks safe but sealing the nest that keeps the chicks safe.
  *(D) Since the male is outside of the sealed nest, it cannot hatch the eggs by keeping them warm.

Exercise R21 (p. 328)

1. C	3. A	5. D	7. A	9. D
2. C	4. B	6. C	8. A	10. C

Exercise R22 (p. 329)

1. C	17. D	33. A	49. D
2. B	18. B	34. D	50. A
3. B	19. B	35. C	51. C
4. D	20. A	36. C	52. C
5. A	21. A	37. B	53. B
6. A	22. C	38. D	54. D
7. C	23. A	39. C	55. B
8. D	24. A	40. B	56. A
9. C	25. C	41. A	57. A
10. B	26. B	42. D	58. C
11. D	27. B	43. A	59. C
12. B	28. D	44. B	60. C
13. B	29. C	45. D	61. A
14. D	30. A	46. A	62. D
15. A	31. A	47. C	63. C
16. B	32. B	48. B	64. B

Exercise R23 (p. 333)

1. D	15. B	29. B	43. A	57. D
2. C	16. D	30. D	44. D	58. B
3. A	17. B	31. A	45. B	59. C
4. D	18. A	32. D	46. C	60. D
5. A	19. A	33. A	47. C	61. D
6. B	20. D	34. C	48. D	62. A
7. D	21. D	35. C	49. A	63. C
8. A	22. C	36. B	50. B	64. B
9. C	23. D	37. C	51. B	65. B
10. C	24. A	38. A	52. C	66. B
11. A	25. C	39. B	53. B	67. A
12. A	26. B	40. D	54. D	68. D
13. B	27. A	41. C	55. A	69. C
14. B	28. A	42. A	56. A	70. C

Exercise R24 (p. 338)

1. (C) The name of something is the word that is used to identify (specify) it. When something is identified, it is named (given a name).
2. (B) If you carve a design or name onto an object, you cut the design or name into the surface. If you scratch something, you make cuts on it, which mark its appearance.
3. (D) If you attain or achieve something, you reach or gain it. In this case, a bear reaches the speed of 35 miles an hour.
4. (A) If something puts forth or exerts pressure, it uses great strength, which produces an effect.
5. (C) If something contains or includes something else, it has that something else in it.
6. (D) The contents of a particular thing is everything that is contained in it (its insides).
7. (D) Acclaim is praise for someone or for something that they have done. If you hail a person as important, you praise them publicly.
8. (B) If you make a rough or approximate calculation, it is more or less correct but is not exact.
9. (B) If something is discharged or released from inside a place, it is sent out or allowed to come out.
10. (A) Someone or something that is regarded or considered to have a particular quality is believed to have that quality.
11. (C) The chief or principal symptom of something is that one which is most important or significant.
12. (D) To eliminate or eradicate something means to remove or destroy it completely.
13. (C) If you acquire or gain a skill, you develop or learn that skill.
14. (C) If you trace or track the history of something, you find out how it began and how it has developed.
15. (B) A temperate or moderate climate is one that is never extremely hot nor extremely cold.
16. (B) Something that is incredible or unbelievable is so amazing that you find it difficult to imagine.
17. (B) Proof of something is evidence or facts that show that it is true or that it exists.
18. (C) Settlements or colonies are places where people have come to live and have built homes.
19. (A) A link or connection is a relationship between two things or situations in which one causes the other to exist or happen.
20. (D) Relatively or comparatively means to some extent or degree.
21. (D) If something afflicts or troubles someone, it causes them physical or mental suffering.
22. (C) Something or someone that is celebrated for a particular quality or achievement is famous for it.
23. (A) Animals that roam wild are untamed rather than kept by people.
24. (B) If something cures or heals an injury or illness, it causes the injury or illness to disappear.
25. (D) Something that is modified or altered is changed.
26. (C) Something that is stylish is fashionable in a distinctive way that attracts people's attention and impresses them.
27. (A) The peak or summit is the top of a mountain.
28. (B) Something that is extended or stretched is straightened out to reach over a distance.
29. (B) Something that is permanent lasts for a long time or forever. Something that is irreparable cannot be fixed. In this case, the deformities cannot be fixed. They will remain throughout one's lifetime.
30. (C) A plague is an infectious and usually fatal disease.
31. (D) The passage mainly discusses how the arcs of light are formed.
32. (B) It is stated in the passage that the light is bent by the gravitational pull of another galaxy.

33. (C) It is stated in the passage that the pull is from invisible or dark matter, so it is not visible.
34. (B) It is theorized that dark matter accounts for the pull, which is not produced by the stars in the galaxy.
35. (C) The dark matter may cause the universe to collapse.
36. (A) The arcs are thought to be optical illusions.
37. (A) It can be inferred that astronomers are not certain about the properties of dark matter because dark matter itself is only a theory.
38. (C) Epstein was born in the United States.
39. (C) This restates the sentence "He moved to Paris in his youth."
40. (D) The author states that artists and critics praised his works, that it now receives the recognition it deserves, and that Epstein is considered one of the major sculptors of the twentieth century.
41. (A) It is stated in the passage that Epstein is considered one of the major sculptors of the twentieth century.
42. (A) "While the general public condenmed his work, many artists and critics praised it," means the same as "While the general public denounced his work, many artists and critics praised it."
43. (C) It is stated in the passage that the sculptures offended the public.
44. (D) It is stated in the passage that critics noted the influence of "primitive and ancient sculptural motifs from Africa."
45. (C) Because the work has received the recognition it deserves, it would probably be well received.
46. (A) "Then, several hundred powerful pumps, operating for more than a year, would draw out the sea water from within the dam," means the same as "Then, several hundred powerful pumps, operating for more than a year, would suck out the sea water from within the dam."
47. (D) "The city" refers to "Marinnation" a city to be completed by the end of the second decade of the twenty-first century.
48. (B) By questioning whether anyone would want to live there, the author implies that people might refuse to live there.
49. (C) It will be a marine city because it will be constructed in the sea.
50. (D) The author gives information concerning the project.
51. (B) Most of the passage describes the engineering feats that would have to be done.
52. (B) Both Marinnation and Atlantis can be called cities in the ocean.
53. (A) It is stated in the passage that the hormone was linked to a brain disease.
54. (B) This is the group that needs it to grow properly and will gain direct benefits from it.

55. (B) A cautious tone can be seen from the statement that implications of the use must be thoroughly understood before widespread distribution is undertaken.
56. (D) It is stated that it is claimed that the drug "has no dangerous side effects."
57. (B) The passage is mainly about the new synthetic growth hormone, which is a medical breakthrough.
58. (D) The specific children who need the drug are those with the hormone deficiency.
59. (C) With the various people who may want it, it could be in great demand.
60. (A) It is stated in the passage that Somatrem is an important medical advance for children who do not produce enough of their own growth hormone.

THE TEST OF WRITTEN ENGLISH

Exercise W1 (p. 347)
Two examples are given for each item. The controlling idea is underlined. Your controlling ideas may be different.

1. Owning a large car has many advantages.
   The disadvantages of owning a large car are many.
2. The reason a person lives in a remote area may be one of the following.
   A person who lives in a remote area may face many problems.
3. Before applying to a foreign university, one should consider the disadvantages of studying abroad.
   The advantages of studying abroad outweigh the disadvantages.
4. Car accidents can be avoided or minimized if the driver takes certain precautions.
   Although a person thinks it is safe at home, many different kinds of accidents occur there.
5. An international airport is divided into different sections.
   There are several kinds of airports.
6. Teachers can list many reasons why students are absent from their classes.
   Absenteeism causes the employer many problems.
7. Taking exams is required of all students, and to do their best, students should use the following methods to prepare themselves.
   One should follow these procedures when taking an exam.
8. Computers have brought many changes to our way of life.
   Many educational games can be played on computers.
9. Rice can be prepared in many ways.
   Rice can be put to many uses.
10. Preparing to go camping is easy when you organize your trip using these steps.
    Camping has changed in many ways.

Exercise W2 (p. 348)
The following topic sentences are only examples. Your sentences may be different.
1. This is a strong topic sentence.
2. This is a weak topic sentence because the rest of the paragraph describes what the writer does when he or she goes to the beach. A better topic sentence would be: "Whenever I have the opportunity to go to the beach, I always follow the same routine."
3. This is a weak topic sentence because the rest of the paragraph describes the various ways students can get to class. A better topic sentence would be: "For the many students who cannot afford a car, there are several alternative ways of getting to class."

Exercise W3 (p. 349)
These are only examples. Your topic sentences may be different.
1. A dormitory room is cold and impersonal until several changes have been made to make it more inviting.
2. American telephone books are divided into several sections.
3. The fast-food restaurant has become popular for various reasons.

Exercise W4 (p. 350)
1. D   2. B   3. D   4. A   5. C

Exercise W5 (p. 351)
1. Students who need extra money can hold down a full-time temporary job during their summer vacation.
2. A person can also meet other people by going to parties.
3. In my opinion, people should write clearly.

Note: The possible correct answers for Exercises W6–W25 are so varied that you might wish to discuss your answers with a fluent English speaker.

Exercise W6 (p. 352)
These supporting ideas are based on the examples given in the answer key for Exercise W1. Yours may be different.
1. I. disadvantages of large cars
    A. expensive to buy
    B. expensive to maintain
    C. use more gasoline
    D. difficult to park
2. I. reasons for living in a remote area
    A. get away from city noise
    B. live in unpolluted area
    C. remaining where one has been born
    D. be closer to nature
3. I. disadvantages of studying abroad
    A. far from family and friends
    B. difficulty in understanding a foreign language
    C. more expensive
    D. hard to get home in an emergency
4. I. kinds of home accidents
    A. falls
    B. poisoning
    C. burns
    D. cuts
5. I. kinds of airports
    A. international
    B. national
    C. rural
    D. private
6. I. problems caused by absenteeism
    A. lost production
    B. missed deadlines
    C. mistakes made by substitutes
    D. expenses for training substitutes
7. I. methods to prepare for taking exams
    A. study on a regular basis
    B. review appropriate material
    C. anticipate questions
    D. get good night's sleep the night before
8. I. changes brought by computers
    A. better telephone services
    B. information easier to obtain
    C. easier inventory procedures in businesses
    D. helpful in education
9. I. ways to prepare rice
    A. rice with vegetables
    B. fried rice
    C. curried rice
    D. rice salad
10. I. steps to organize a camping trip
    A. make list of necessary items to take
    B. get maps of area
    C. have car in good condition
    D. check weather report

Exercise W7 (p. 353)
These are only a few examples. Your paragraphs will be different. Have a fluent English speaker check your paragraphs.
1. The disadvantages of owning a large car are many. First, they are much more expensive to buy. After having purchased a large car, the owner is then faced with the expense of maintaining it. It uses more gasoline than a small car. Also, it is frequently hard to find a parking place for large cars.
2. The reasons a person lives in a remote area may be one of the following. Cities are usually very noisy, and a person may want to get away from the noise. Another attraction of a remote area might be that it is unpolluted. If a person was born and raised in a remote area, he or she may want to remain in the place that is best known. Finally, some people like to be closer to nature, and this is easier away from a city.
3. Before applying to a foreign university, one should consider these disadvantages of studying abroad. First, a student may feel alone by being far from family and friends. Also, difficulty in understanding a foreign language can be very frustrating and can affect the student's grades. It can be very expensive to pay the costs of travel and housing in a different country. Finally, if there is an emergency at home, it is hard to get home in a hurry.

4. Although a person thinks it is safe at home, many different kinds of accidents occur there. Falls are perhaps the most common accident among both young children and older adults. Poisoning is a danger, especially if an adult leaves medicines or cleaning chemicals within the reach of a small child. Burns frequently occur in the kitchen area during meal preparation. Finally, people cut themselves when using kitchen knives, trimming equipment in the yard, and power tools in the workshop or garage.

5. There are several kinds of airports. From an international airport, flights go to other countries as well as to cities in the same country. A national airport usually only serves the cities within its nation. Rural airports usually link a town with a nearby national airport. Private airports are those on a military base or a hospital. Individuals and companies can own their own private airports.

Exercise W8 (p. 354)

These are only examples. Your answers may differ greatly.

1. It is the largest and most interesting city in the country.
2. I read on the bus on my way to class, while I'm waiting for my friends, and before I go to sleep.
3. People can choose the movie they want and watch it in the comfort of their own homes.
4. The university that I want to attend requires that I get a score of at least 500.
5. The sound of the water along the shore calms one's nerves.
6. They can be both psychologically and physically addictive.
7. Had my brother been paying attention instead of changing the tape in the tape deck while he was driving, he wouldn't have crashed into the tree and broken his leg.
8. A building such as the Pompidou Center in Paris has had as many people criticize its design as it has had people praise its modern features.
9. In fact, it's still possible to find ancient relics in parks and other undeveloped spaces.
10. Many city centers are not bustling with shoppers anymore. Instead, the streets are empty except when workers are leaving or returning to their offices.

Exercise W9 (p. 355)

The following answers are only one way that you could add details. Your answers may be different.

1. When you plant a tree, you are helping your environment in many ways. Your tree will provide a home and food for other creatures. Birds may build nests in the branches. The flowers will provide honey for insects and the fruits or nuts may feed squirrels or other small animals. Your tree will hold the soil in place. This will help stop erosion. In addition, your tree will provide shade in the summer. This will provide welcome relief on hot days. You can watch your tree grow and someday show your children or even grandchildren the tree you planted.

2. Airplanes and helicopters can be used to save people's lives. Helicopters can be used for rescuing people in trouble. For example, when a tall building is on fire, people sometimes escape to the roof, where a helicopter can pick them up. Passengers on a sinking ship could also be rescued by helicopter. Planes can transport food and supplies when disasters strike. This is very important when there is an earthquake, flood, or drought. Getting a victim of an accident or heart attack to a hospital quickly could save the person's life. Helicopters and airplanes can be used to provide medical services to people who live in remote areas. They can be used as a kind of ambulance service in cases where getting to the hospital by car would take too long.

3. Studying in another country is advantageous in many ways. A student is exposed to a new culture. This exposure teaches him or her about other people and other ways of thinking, which can promote friendships among countries. Sometimes students can learn a new language. This language may be beneficial for keeping up with research after the student has finished studying. Students can often have learning experiences not available in their own countries. For example, an art history student studying in Rome would get to see works of art that can only be seen in Italian museums and churches. A student may get the opportunity to study at a university where a leading expert in his or her field may be teaching. A leading expert can introduce the student to the most up-to-date findings of the top researchers in the field. Exposure to such valuable knowledge and insights into the field can aid the student in becoming an expert as well.

Exercise W10 (p. 356)

The following are possible questions to stimulate details.

1. What kind of scenery do you like?
   Why would you want to stop along the road?
   Where and when have you met interesting people on your travels?
   How much luggage can you carry on airplanes?
   Why don't you have to worry about missing flights?
2. What are the poor and inhumane conditions?
   Why don't the animals get exercise?
   What is an example of neurotic behavior?
   Why is it a problem for animals not to breed?
   Why is it a problem for animals to breed with a related animal?
3. Why is knowing the material important?
   Why should teachers be able to explain their knowledge?
   Why are patience and understanding important?
   What should teachers do to show their patience and understanding?
   How can teachers make the subject matter interesting?

Note: There is no Answer Key for Exercises W11–W18 and W21.

Exercises W19, W20, and W22 (pp. 365–368)
The following are completed student essays using the questions in W19. There are several other ways these essays could be written. As long as the arguments are well reasoned, it does not matter whether or not the examiner agrees with their content.

1.   Our world today is faced with many major threats. The most dangerous threat of all is war. Everyone in the world fears the outbreak of a war, especially another world war in which nuclear weapons may be used. With the use of nuclear weapons there is the possibility of the destruction of our entire planet. Each war starts for a particular reason, but there are a number of steps countries can take to prevent its outbreak.

    One main reason for war is a difference in ideology. For example, nations have engaged in struggles over the merits of communist and capitalist systems of government. They frequently aided other countries in wars in order to topple governments that have not agreed with their principles.

    Land ownership is also a reason that countries declare wars on their neighbors. Frequently, these conflicts are economic in nature. For example, if oil is found on land in one country and that land can be claimed by another country for historical reasons, that country may declare war in order to recover the land containing oil. A landlocked country needing access to the sea may claim the territory between itself and the sea. When a border between two countries lies in an important food growing area such as, for example, a border formed by rivers, disputes over the water rights and the fertile land can turn into war.

    To prevent the destruction of our Earth in a nuclear catastrophe, countries should try to resolve their differences through international organizations such as the United Nations. All countries need to educate their citizens to be more tolerant of other ideologies. After all, no ideology is worth total annihilation of the planet. In addition, the countries that are better off need to give more assistance to those countries that suffer severe economic troubles, so that those countries will not try to solve their problems through violence. In conclusion, there are solutions to the world's problems, and they should be put into practice now before it is too late.

2.   For centuries, the roles of women and men in any particular country remained unchanged. However, modern technology has spread into most societies. This has made it possible for men and women to enter into new roles. Some of these changes in roles have been very beneficial.

    The role of women has shifted from the homemaker/nurturer to the outside working world. This change has widened women's point of view. Women can now better understand men and the problems they face every day in their jobs. Because women are more knowledgeable about the world, they are now more prepared to take on decision-making roles. Their solutions to problems may be very different from those of men.

    Men's roles have changed dramatically as well. It is no longer a man's world. Husbands find that with their wives helping to support the family, they are helping to do many chores that were not considered manly before. However, in activities such as taking care of children, men have learned more nurturing habits. Men also no longer view women as helpless, mindless grown children, but as adults with decision-making abilities. Such experiences have helped men acquire a different, more positive attitude toward women and children.

    In conclusion, these changes have been very beneficial. The two sexes are able to understand each other better and, therefore, help each other as a team. However, as with all change, there are conflicts. Some men resent the intrusion of women into their domain, and some women resent being forced out of their homemaking role. But it is with the raising of new generations accustomed to these roles that these conflicts will eventually smooth themselves out for the benefit of all.

3.   Nowadays, we have many conveniences in our society which have been brought about through technology and science. However, these same advancements in technology and science have caused some very dangerous problems. These problems won't go away easily because people don't want to give up the conveniences of a modern life-style. The most critical problems which should be dealt with immediately are those of pollution.

    Pollution caused by chemicals is a very serious problem because it causes the loss of the ozone layer. Without our ozone, not only we ourselves but all plant and animal life are exposed to dangerous rays from the sun. Aerosol cans emit chemicals which break down our ozone layer. Refrigeration and air-conditioning systems and cars also have dangerous emissions.

    Perhaps the most serious threat to the planet is the warming of the earth's atmosphere, primarily through carbon dioxide emissions. Many scientists think that the warming could be sufficient to melt the polar ice caps, thus raising the sea levels. This would mean that many parts of the world would be submerged below sea level.

    There are other problems caused by pollution. Factories which make our modern conveniences emit poisonous gases into the air we breathe. The chemicals we use for cleaning and wastes from factories go into our water systems and pollute the water we drink and the fish we eat. They also kill much of the wildlife we depend on for food. Some of the pesticides we have sprayed on our crops have been found to be dangerous. This kind of pollution may stay in the ground for a very long period of time.

In conclusion, the problems created by pollution are growing daily. Because people do not want to change their life-styles, we must invent a way to neutralize the pollutants we are putting into our environment. People need to be educated so they will stop damaging the planet. Furthermore, governments must take action to prevent individuals and companies from harming their environment.

Exercise W23 (p. 369)

Question A

1. no   An introductory paragraph consists of more than one sentence.
2. no   The restated problem should be in different words, not the same words as the question.
3. yes The thesis statement gives the controlling idea as *advantages and disadvantages* of small and large cars.
4. yes In the topic sentence of the first developmental paragraph, the topic is "large cars" and the controlling idea is "advantages." In the topic sentence of the second developmental paragraph, the topic is "small cars" and the controlling idea is "advantages and disadvantages."
5. no   According to the first developmental paragraph, only *advantages* of large cars will be discussed.
6. no   The first developmental paragraph discusses both advantages and disadvantages. This supports the thesis statement but not the topic sentence of the paragraph.
7. yes However, more details could be added. For example, how are large cars good for big families? Why is strength important in a bad accident? Has the student had any experiences of crashes in big or small cars?
8. no   A concluding paragraph is more than one sentence.
9. no   The topic and controlling idea are not restated. It is not clear what "for this" refers to or why the student has this preference.
10. no A concluding statement should sum up the essay.
11. no The reasons the writer likes small cars are not included.
12. no There are some minor grammatical mistakes, which may cause confusion.

Question B

1. yes
2. yes
3. yes The controlling idea is "pollution problems."
4. yes
5. yes
6. no   The statements "Public safety does not concern the factory owners, who must know that people don't want to live in pollution that is dangerous for their health." and "Nobody in this world wants to breathe dirty air" are irrelevant.
7. yes
8. yes
9. yes It gives solutions.
10. yes However, it is weak. A better concluding statement might be "In conclusion, the pollution of our air and seas is a major problem which we must work together to solve now."
11. yes
12. yes

Exercise W24 (p. 370)

1. Score _3_   This essay demonstrates some development, but the writer focuses on people who read instead of supporting his or her agreement or disagreement with the given statement. There are insufficient details and a noticeably inappropriate choice of words or word forms (e.g., "emphasize," "imagines," "the read").
2. Score _6_   This essay demonstrates competence in writing. It gives a thesis statement which all the paragraphs support. It uses details to illustrate ideas. There is unity, coherence, and progression. Syntactic variety and appropriate word choices are demonstrated.
3. Score _2_   This essay contains serious errors in sentence structure. It states an opinion but does not give enough information to support that opinion. There are few details. The specifics are irrelevant (e.g., Helen of Troy).
4. Score _4_   This paper demonstrates minimal competence. It lacks a strong thesis statement to give it a direction. The first developmental paragraph supports the opinion that reading nonfictional works is beneficial. The second developmental paragraph supports (with only one detail) an implied opinion that reading novels is no longer beneficial. That detail is unnecessarily repeated (TV has taken the place of the novel). There are a number of mistakes in syntax and usage.
5. Score _1_   This is not an essay. There is no development of ideas. There are writing errors that make the meaning difficult to understand.
6. Score _5_   This paper demonstrates a generally well-organized and well-developed essay. The paper shows unity, coherence, and progression. There are some grammatical errors, but they do not impede understanding. Although the essay is well developed, it does not have the details and the syntactic variety seen on a score 6 paper.

Note: There is no Answer Key for Exercise W25.

PRACTICE TEST 1 (p. 377, transcript on p. 532)

Note: If you answer an item incorrectly, complete the exercises following the letter you chose and those following the explanation of the correct answer.

Section 1   *Listening Comprehension*

Part A

1. (A) See Exercise L3.
  *(B) "To serve oneself" means "to give oneself something," in this case food. "A lot" could be "too much." See Exercises L7–L11.
   (C) See Exercises L1 and L3.
   (D) See Exercise L1.
2.*(A) If the windows needed washing, they were probably dirty. See Exercises L13–L18.
   (B) See Exercises L13–L18.
   (C), (D) See Exercise L1.
3. (A), (C), (D) See Exercise L1.
  *(B) When one is practicing a musical instrument, one is playing music. See Exercises L4–L6.
4. (A) See Exercise L3.
   (B) See Exercises L4–L6.
   (C) See Exercises L13–L18.
  *(D) When you tell someone to leave you alone, you want that person to stop bothering you. See Exercises L9–L11.
5.*(A) John remembered to do something. He didn't forget to lock the door. See Exercises L13–L18.
   (B), (D) See Exercises L13–L18.
   (C) See Exercise L1.
6. (A), (B), (C) See Exercise L1.
  *(D) If you have to go to work for someone, that person probably needs you to work. See Exercises L13–L18.
7. (A) See Exercises L9–L11.
  *(B) "Used to" means that something was a habit in the past but is not anymore. See Exercises L13–L18.
   (C) See Exercise L1.
   (D) See Exercise L4–L6.
8. (A) See Exercise L1.
   (B), (D) See Exercises L13–L18.
  *(C) The spoken statement indicates that I was angry because he was late. See Exercises L13–L18.
9. (A), (C) See Exercise L1.
  *(B) The expression "off a diet" means "not following rules about what food to eat." See Exercises L9–L11.
   (D) See Exercises L4–L6.
10. (A), (C) See Exercise L1.
   (B) See Exercises L13–L18.
  *(D) The word "never" in the spoken statement indicates that she has never in the past been as entertained (amused) as now. In other words, she is more entertained now than ever before. See Exercises L13–L18.

11. (A), (B), (D) See Exercises L13–L18.
   *(C) You turn right at the traffic signal (stoplight). See Exercises L13–L18.
12. (A) See Exercise L1.
    (B), (C) See Exercises L7–L8 and L13–L18.
   *(D) First I left, and then my friends returned. See Exercises L7–L8 and L13–L18.
13.*(A) "Not permitted" means you cannot do something. See Exercises L13–L18.
    (B) See Exercises L4–L6.
    (C), (D) See Exercises L13–L18.
14. (A) See Exercises L4–L6.
    (B), (D) See Exercises L13–L18.
   *(C) The speaker likes the ideas and asks for a confirmation from the person spoken to. See Exercises L13–L18.
15. (A) See Exercises L9–L11.
   *(B) "To forward something" means "to send it on." See Exercises L9–L11.
    (C) See Exercise L3.
    (D) See Exercise L1.
16. (A), (B), (C) See Exercises L13–L18.
   *(D) "The forecast is rain" means that "it may rain." The question "should we" indicates that the speaker is asking for an opinion. See Exercises L13–L18.
17. (A), (C), (D) See Exercises L13–L18.
   *(B) The facts are that Jane had a long vacation, and Bill didn't. See Exercises L13–L18.
18.*(A) "Couldn't have" indicates that something is contrary to expectation. The intonation of the sentence indicates surprise because the speaker thinks it is impossible that he has returned. See Exercises L2 and L13–L18.
    (B) See Exercises L2 and L13–L18.
    (C) See Exercises L4–L6.
    (D) See Exercise L1.
19. (A), (D) See Exercises L13–L18.
   *(B) The word "let" means the same as "allow." See Exercises L13–L18.
    (C) See Exercise L1.
20. (A), (B), (C) See Exercises L13–L18.
   *(D) The politician was the person being questioned, and the interviewer was the person asking the questions. See Exercises L13–L18.

Part B
21. (A) See Exercises L47–L49.
    (B), (D) See Exercises L22–L24.
   *(C) Vocabulary words and phrases identifying a dentist's office are "hurt," "pulled," and "replace the filling." See Exercises L47–L49.
22.*(A) The expression "give a piece of one's mind" means "let someone know that one is angry about something that person has done." See Exercises L28–L30.
    (B) See Exercises L28–L30.
    (C) See Exercise L1.
    (D) See Exercises L22–L24.

23. (A) See Exercises L32–L37.
    (B) See Exercises L22–L24.
    *(C) He's getting an application form for a student loan (financial aid). See Exercises L41–L46.
    (D) See Exercises L50–L51.
24. (A), (B), (D) See Exercises L32–L37.
    *(C) The club members caused the carpenter (through payment or asking a favor) to design the scenery which they built. See Exercises L32–L37.
25.*(A) He keeps changing his major because he can't decide what he wants to study. See Exercises L50–L51.
    (B) See Exercise L1.
    (C), (D) See Exercises L50–L51.
26. (A) See Exercise L1.
    *(B) The phrase "take in" can mean "decrease the size of something." See Exercises L28–L30.
    (C), (D) See Exercises L28–L30.
27. (A) See Exercises L32–L37 and L50–L51.
    *(B) The expression "come what may" means "no matter what happens." Even if it rains, he's still going camping (not changing his plans). See Exercises L28–L30.
    (C) See Exercises L22–L24.
    (D) See Exercises L32–L37.
28. (A), (D) See Exercises L32–L37.
    (B) See Exercises L50–L51.
    *(C) The expression "not a single soul" means "no one." See Exercises L28–L30.
29. (A) See Exercises L50–L51.
    *(B) "Posted" means "displayed." See Exercises L22–L24.
    (C) See Exercises L1 and L58–L59.
    (D) See Exercises L22–L24.
30. (A) See Exercises L41–L46.
    (B), (C) See Exercises L50–L51.
    *(D) The woman missed her breakfast because it was not ready before she had to leave. See Exercises L41–L46.
31.*(A) The man's not wanting to miss the presentation means that he wants to hear it. See Exercises L39–L40.
    (B), (C), (D) See Exercises L32–L37.
32. (A), (D) See Exercises L39–L40.
    (B) See Exercise L1.
    *(C) The idea that there's nothing new about his giving quizzes on Monday means he usually does this. See Exercises L39–L40.
33. (A), (B), (D) See Exercises L47–L49.
    *(C) It can be inferred that the two people study together from the vocabulary phrase "term project" and the arrangement of a time to discuss it. See Exercises L47–L49.
34. (A) See Exercises L26–L27.
    (B) See Exercises L41–L46 and L58–L59.
    *(C) "Just one on a list of many" means there are more problems to do. See Exercises L39–L40.
    (D) See Exercises L41–L46.

35.*(A) By expressing that she likes the idea, the woman shows that she wants to go with them. See Exercises L39–L40.
    (B), (D) See Exercise L1.
    (C) See Exercises L50–L51.

Part C
36. (A), (C) See Exercises L60–L66.
    *(B) The vocabulary words and phrases identifying a student loan office are "student loan," "money won't be available," "money for late applicants," "emergency loan," and "forms." See Exercises L67–L69.
    (D) See Exercises L71–L73.
37. (A), (B) See Exercises L60–L66.
    (C) See Exercises L71–L73.
    *(D) The man's concern about paying his fees can be seen in his question "How will I complete my registration?" and the statement "The registrar drops students if they fail to pay their fees." See Exercises L67–L69.
38.*(A) The woman says the money won't be ready for another two weeks. See Exercises L60–L66.
    (B), (C), (D) See Exercises L60–L66.
39. (A), (B), or (D) See Exercises L71–L73.
    *(C) The woman tells the man that he could get an emergency loan the same day he applied for one and complete his registration that day. See Exercises L60–L66.
40. (A), (B), (D) See Exercises L53–L56.
    *(C) The talk discusses three ways libraries meet users' needs. See Exercises L53–L56.
41.*(A) If libraries had sufficient funds and space, they would not need to use microfilm, microfiche, and computers, because they could purchase and house all materials. See Exercises L71–L73.
    (B), (C), (D) See Exercises L71–L73.
42. (A), (C), (D) See Exercises L60–L66.
    *(B) It is stated in the talk that professors make recommendations for the purchase of books and journals. See Exercises L60–L66.
43. (A), (B), (C) See Exercises L60–L66.
    *(D) It is stated in the talk that students can ask their librarian to use a computer search. See Exercises L60–L66.
44. (A), (C), (D) See Exercises L67–L69.
    *(B) The woman asks "Is this where the university shuttle bus stops?" See Exercises L67–L69.
45. (A), (B), (C) See Exercises L67–L69.
    *(D) The woman approaches the man by saying "Excuse me," and asks questions concerning the bus. See Exercises L67–L69.
46. (A), (C), (D) See Exercises L67–L69.
    *(B) While it cannot be inferred that the woman is going directly to the recreation center, she is going in the vicinity of the center or else she wouldn't be taking that particular bus. See Exercises L67–L69.

47. (A), (B), (C) See Exercises L67–L69.
   *(D) It can be inferred by the woman's ignorance of bus schedules and bus stop locations that she is unaccustomed to taking these particular buses. See Exercises L67–L69.
48. (A), (B), (C) See Exercises L60–L66.
   *(D) Ms. Holland got involved in writing plays after inadvertently signing up for an advanced playwriting seminar. See Exercises L60–L66.
49. (A), (B), (D) See Exercises L71–L73.
   *(C) A twist of fate is something that happens that changes one's destiny. Ms. Holland didn't intend to take the seminar. She took it because of a mistake she made in registration. This mistake resulted in her becoming a playwright. See Exercises L71–L73.
50. (A), (C), (D) See Exercises L71–L73.
   *(B) It is stated that Ms. Holland was consumed by activities other than academics. One of these types of activities was starting student groups dedicated to racial progress and black unity. See Exercises L60–L66.

Section 2   Structure and Written Expression

1. A verb is needed to complete the noun clause. "Is" agrees with the subject "Saturn."
   (A), (C) See Exercises S62–S67 and S73–S77.
   (B) See Exercises S26–S32.
   *(D) See Exercises S55–S60.
2. A subject is needed to complete the independent clause: "an adequate rainfall."
   (A) See Exercises S17–S23.
   *(B) See Exercises S17–S23.
   (C) See Exercises S73–S77.
   (D) See Exercises S73–S77.
3. The preposition "by" needs a noun to fill the object position. The noun phrase "its size" can fill the object position.
   (A), (C), (D) See Exercises S92–S95.
   *(B) See Exercises S1–S5.
4. A verb (are) is needed to complete the independent clause.
   (A), (B), (D) See Exercises S53–S54.
   *(C) See Exercises S53–S54.
5. A clause marker (although) is needed to complete the sentence.
   (A), (B) See Exercises S53–S54.
   *(C) See Exercises S73–S77.
   (D) See Exercises S44–S51.
6. A subject (it) and a verb (was) are needed to complete the independent clause.
   *(A) See Exercises S17–S23.
   (B) See Exercises S17–S23.
   (C) See Exercises S53–S54.
   (D) See Exercises S73–S77.

7. An adjective clause or phrase is needed to identify the noun "Anthony Burgess." "Who has achieved fame" completes the sentence.
   (A), (C) See Exercises S73–S77.
   *(B) See Exercises S62–S67.
   (D) See Exercises S53–S54.
8. A subject (protection) and verb (was) are needed to complete the sentence. The negative phrase "not until" indicates that the positions of the subject and aux-word or verb will be inverted.
   (A), (B), (C) See Exercises S33–S36.
   *(D) See Exercises S17–S23 and S33–S36.
9. An adjective clause or phrase identifying the noun "tomb" is needed to complete the sentence. The passive voice is needed because someone erected the tomb.
   (A), (D) See Exercises S26–S32.
   *(B) See Exercises S68–S71.
   (C) See Exercises S68–S71.
10. A verb and an adjective or noun phrase are needed. "Was suitable" completes the sentence.
   (A), (D) See Exercises S53–S54.
   *(B) See Exercises S53–S54.
   (C) See Exercises S26–S32.
11. The structure "adjective (important) + as" indicates that a comparison of equality is being made. The rest of the phrase of equality (as) is needed to complete the sentence.
   (A) See Exercises S44–S51.
   (B) See Exercises S83–S88.
   *(C) See Exercises S83–S88.
   (D) See Exercises S1–S5.
12. An article (the) is needed to complete the noun phrase used as the subject.
   *(A) See Exercises S6–S10.
   (B) See Exercises S92–S95.
   (C) See Exercises S26–S32.
   (D) See Exercises S53–S54.
13. A prepositional phrase (as the wife) is needed to be parallel with the prepositional phrase "as a Hollywood actress."
   (A), (B), (C) See Exercises S89–S91.
   *(D) See Exercises S89–S91.
14. The sentence is complete. Therefore, a phrase or clause giving more information is needed to fill the blank. "Despite its height" provides the information.
   (A) See Exercises S53–S54.
   (B) See Exercises S11–S15.
   (C) See Exercises S73–S77.
   *(D) See Exercises S92–S95.
15. "Not only" indicates that a phrase or clause introduced by "but" or "but also" is needed to complete the sentence. The prepositional phrase "for their hides and milk" indicates that a prepositional phrase (for pulling sleighs) is needed to complete a parallel structure.
   *(A) See Exercises S44–S51 and S89–S91.
   (B), (C), (D) See Exercises S89–S91.

16. (B) The clause marker "that" should be used to introduce the adjective clause because the emphasis is on the event. The clause marker "when" emphasizes the time. See Exercises S62–S67.

17. (B) The subject of the sentence is "ibis." The pronoun "it" cannot be used to fill the same subject position. See Exercises S17–S23.

18. (B) "Value" is a noun. The adjective form "valuable" should be used to describe "what kind" of metal. See Exercises S38–S43.

19. (D) The time "between Herschel and *Voyager*" is "two centuries." This indicates that the verb tense should either be in the past, "was learned," or in the present perfect, "has been learned." The passive voice is used because people are the ones learning about Uranus. See Exercises S26–S32.

20. (D) The word "such" is followed by the word "as" when used to indicate an example. See Exercises S44–S51.

21. (A) The night before the race is prior to the race. Therefore, "A" is redundant. The sentence is correct without this phrase. See Exercises S96–S97.

22. (D) When the phrasal verb "turn in" means "hand something in," it needs an object. The phrase should be "turning it in." The object "it" refers to the exam. See Exercises S11–S15.

23. (D) The "fortune" is not being compared to all fortunes so the superlative form should not be used. The comparative form "better" should be used because the fortune he expects is better than the one he has. See Exercises S83–S88.

24. (C) The noun "nonsmoker" should be used in its plural form, "nonsmokers," or with the article "the" or "a." See Exercises S1–S10.

25. (C) "Much" is used with noncount nouns. Because buildings and monuments can be counted, the word "many" should be used. See Exercises S44–S51.

26. (A) The preposition "by" should be used because scientists ordinarily make these estimates, not receive them. See Exercises S92–S95.

27. (C) "A number of" is used with count nouns. Because "force" cannot be counted, the word "amount" should be used. See Exercises S1–S5.

28. (C) The possessive "its" refers to computers. Because the prepositional phrase "of the computer" is used to indicate possession, "its" is redundant. The article "the" should be used when the prepositional phrase shows possession. See Exercises S96–S97.

29. (C) The subject of the adjective clause "that" refers to "forms," a plural noun. Therefore, the verb of the clause should be the plural form "have." See Exercises S26–S32.

30. (B) "Any" is used with "not." Either "some" or "many" would be grammatically correct in this sentence. See Exercises S44–S51.

31. (A) The suffix *-ing* can be used to indicate a noun. However, the suffix *-er* should be used with this noun to indicate a person. See Exercises S38–S43.

32. (B) "Predominant" is an adjective. The adverb "predominantly" should be used to modify the adjective "Catholic." See Exercises S38–S43.

33. (D) "Ago" indicates an action completed in the past. The present perfect tense "has become" indicates an ongoing action. Therefore, "ago" is illogical and should be deleted. See Exercises S26–S32.

34. (D) "Make" is the active form of the verb in the adjective phrase. The passive form "made" should be used because toys do not make themselves. Someone makes them. See Exercises S26–S32.

35. (B) "Other" is used with plural nouns. "Another" should be used with the singular noun "tournament." See Exercises S44–S51.

36. (D) "Or" is used for alternatives. The word "both" indicates that the word "and" should be used. See Exercises S44–S51.

37. (A) A subject is needed to complete the sentence. The word "it" should be used in the phrase "perhaps was" in order to complete the sentence ("perhaps it was"). See Exercises S17–S23.

38. (A) "Have" is the base form of the verb. The infinitive "to have" or the gerund "having" should be used after the verb "prefers." See Exercises S26–S32.

39. (B) The word "so" is used before adjectives or adverbs that precede a "that" clause. However, the adverb "likely" precedes the word "as." This indicates a comparison of equality. The word "as" should be used to complete the comparison of equality phrase. See Exercises S83–S88.

40. (C) The article "a" should be used before "touch" because it is a count noun in this sentence. See Exercises S6–S10.

Section 3   Vocabulary and Reading Comprehension

1. (C) When something is done in a "stirring" or "dramatic" way, it causes people to feel strong emotions. See Exercises V1–V12 and V14–V27.

2. (C) A "fiber" is a thin "thread" (a long, thin piece of cotton, silk, nylon, etc.) of a natural or artificial substance that is usually used to make cloth or rope. See Exercises V1–V12.

3. (A) When a boat is "moored" or "anchored," it is secured by a rope or cable so that it cannot drift away. See Exercises V1–V12.

4. (D) If something is "contaminated" or "poisonous," it is polluted in such a way as to be harmful or deadly. See Exercises V1–V12 and V14–V27.

5. (A) When something is "eradicated" or "eliminated," it is completely removed or wiped out. See Exercises V14–V27.

6. (C) A "device" or "instrument" is an object that has been invented for a particular purpose. See Exercises V14–V27.

7. (B) When a process or the rate of something is "accelerated" or "hastened," it is speeded up and the results come about sooner than they would have otherwise. See Exercises V1–V12 and V14–V27.

8. (B) A "catastrophe" or "disaster" is a terrible occurrence which frequently involves great destruction, injury, or loss of life. See Exercises V14–V27.

9. (D) A "character" is a letter, number, or "symbol" (a design or shape that is used to represent something) that is written or printed. See Exercises V14–V27.

10. (A) If something is "exploited" or "taken advantage of," it is used in such a way that its users gain something from it. See Exercises V14–V27.

11. (B) Something that is "perpetual" or "incessant" never stops or changes. See Exercises V14–V27.

12. (A) When something is "indispensable," it is absolutely essential. See Exercises V14–V27.

13. (C) If you "sound out" or "enunciate" a particular letter or sound, you pronounce it or say it. See Exercises V1–V12 and V14–V27.

14. (B) If someone "denounces" or "condemns" something, they criticize it severely and publicly because they feel strongly that it is wrong or evil. See Exercises V14–V27.

15. (D) An action or decision that is "judicious" or "wise" shows good judgment and common sense. See Exercises V14–V27.

16. (B) A "sophisticated" or "complex" device or operation is one which uses advanced methods or technology. See Exercises V14–V27.

17. (A) If something is "impeded" or "hindered," its movements, development, or progress are made difficult. See Exercises V1–V12 and V14–V27.

18. (C) A "quality" or "characteristic" is a physical feature of a substance or object. See Exercises V14–V27.

19. (C) A "layer" of a substance is a piece of it that exists in a flat strip underneath or on top of other similar strips. "Strata" are "layers" of rock, earth, or other material that lie between layers of other kinds of material. See Exercises V1–V12 and V14–V27.

20. (B) When something or someone is "sheltered" or "harbored," they are being protected and provided with a place to stay or live. See Exercises V1–V12.

21. (A) If something is "intriguing" or "fascinating," people are interested or curious about it. See Exercises V1–V12 and V14–V27.

22. (C) "Aquatic" or "marine" means involving, relating to, or occurring in the water. See Exercises V1–V12 and V14–V27.

23. (C) When something is "renowned" or "acclaimed" for a particular quality or thing, it is well known or admired because of it. See Exercises V1–V12 and V14–V27.

24. (D) A "mutation" or "alteration" in a genetic structure is a change which causes a new sort of animal or plant to develop. See Exercises V14–V27.

25. (C) Something or someone that is "hidden" or "concealed" is in a place that cannot easily be seen or found. See Exercises V1–V12 and V14–V27.

26. (D) Something that is "buoyant" has the ability to "float" or remain on the top of a liquid. See Exercises V1–V12.

27. (C) "Soil" is the top layer of earth in which plants grow. "Earth" is the substance on the land surface of the earth, such as clay, sand, or soil. See Exercises V1–V12.

28. (B) Something that is "peculiar" or "curious" is unusual and interesting or unique. See Exercises V1–V12 and V14–V27.

29. (A) A "carcass" is the body of a dead animal. A "corpse" is the body of a dead animal or person. See Exercises V14–V27.

30. (D) Something that is "damaging" or "harmful" spoils something physically so that it doesn't work properly or look as good as it did before. See Exercises V1–V12 and V14–V27.

31. (B) All the supporting ideas in the passage concern the "qualities" of diamonds that affect their value. See Exercises R5–R8.

32. (A) It is stated in the passage that "there are 100 points in a carat." See Exercises R10–R13.

33. (C) It is stated that "D" means the stone is absolutely colorless. See Exercises R10–R13.

34. (A) Because "H" is between "G" and "J," it is good for jewelry. See Exercises R15–R19.

35. (D) Clarity is rated according to whether imperfections are present. See Exercises R10–R13.

36. (A) Since the most flawless diamonds for jewelry are rated VVS1 (very very slight imperfections), it can be inferred that a perfect diamond is not used for jewelry. See Exercises R15–R19.

37. (D) It is stated in the passage that "a well-cut diamond will separate the light into different colors when reflected." See Exercises R10–R13.

38. (B) It is stated that reflective quality should only be compared between diamonds of the same shape. See Exercises R10–R13.

39. (D) The phrase "obese people have a keener sense of taste and desire more flavorful food" means the same as the original phrase. See Exercises R1–R4 and R21–R22.

40. (C) Since the act of chewing relieves tension, a weight watcher could avoid eating by chewing on something inedible. See Exercises R15–R19.

41. (B) Because the lack of variety and flavor leaves heavy people dissatisfied, it can be inferred that eating a variety of food with strong flavors will satisfy them. See Exercises R15–R19.

42. (D) It is stated in the passage that "this (an increase in blood insulin) did not happen to people of average weight." See Exercises R10–R13.

43. (A) It is stated in the passage that "eating carbohydrates raises the level of serotonin . . . [which] produces a sense of satiation." See Exercises R15–R19.

44. (C) It is stated that serotonin is a neurotransmitter that produces a sense of satiation or feeling full. See Exercises R10–R13.

45. (D) If people avoid stressful situations, they would not have to eat to relieve tension, and if they eat spicy foods, they will satisfy the need for the intensity of tastes and will not continue eating more to fulfill this need. See Exercises R15–R19.

46. (A) An evening walk is a mild exercise and this is the kind of exercise recommended. See Exercises R15–R19.

47. (C) The passage is mainly about an alternative for fuel supplies—the solar oven. See Exercises R5–R8.

48. (D) The reflection of sunlight is not mentioned as a reason for using rice husks as an insulating material. See Exercises R10–R13.

49. (C) The passage states that the temperature is boosted by 15 to 30 degrees Celsius. Since 30 degrees is the maximum, the temperature increases "up to" 30 degrees. See Exercises R10–R13.

50. (C) Since the collection of fuel in a rural agricultural community takes 200 to 300 person-days a year, it is probably most useful in a rural community. See Exercises R15–R19.

51. (C) The passage mentions firewood, dung cake, and agricultural waste. Solar power is not mentioned as a typical fuel. See Exercises R10–R13.

52. (B) It is stated in the passage that the mirror "is most useful during the winter when the sun is lower." See Exercises R10–R13.

53. (A) Because the family won't need to use 200 to 300 person-days per year for fuel collection, it should save them time. See Exercises R15–R19.

54. (C) The passage gives three examples of useful folk medicines and the last paragraph summarizes the passage with this idea. See Exercises R5–R8.

55. (C) From the statement "Fleming did not just randomly choose cheese molds to study," it can be inferred that there was something about cheese molds that he suspected was medicinal. See Exercises R15–R19.

56. (D) It is stated in the passage that sugar generates a glasslike layer that ensures healing. See Exercises R10–R13.

57. (A) It is stated that the "catfish excretes a gellike slime." See Exercises R10–R13.

58. (D) This is a property of cheese. See Exercises R10–R13.

59. (D) The passage mentions the possibility of developing synthetic substances for human consumption, which would advance modern medical practices. See Exercises R10–R13.

60. (B) All are mentioned as fighting bacteria. See Exercises R10–R13.

PRACTICE TEST 2 (p. 399, transcript on p. 539)

Note: If you answer an item incorrectly, complete the exercises following the letter you chose and those following the explanation of the correct answer.

Section 1   Listening Comprehension

Part A

1. (A), (C) See Exercises L4–L6.
   *(B) Peter caused the waiter to bring the bill. See Exercises L13–L18.
   (D) See Exercises L13–L18.

2. (A), (B), (C) See Exercises L13–L18.
   *(D) David had the problems. David's friend solved the problems. See Exercises L13–L18.

3.*(A) "To meet a deadline" means "to finish on time." See Exercises L9–L11.
   (B) See Exercise L1.
   (C), (D) See Exercises L4–L6.

4. (A), (C), (D) See Exercises L13–L18.
   *(B) "Why don't you" introduces a suggestion. The suggestion is to "let" (allow) Diana wash the car, because Diana wants to wash it. See Exercises L13–L18.

5. (A), (C) See Exercise L1.
   *(B) "To misplace something" means "to put it in the wrong place and subsequently not be able to find it." See Exercises L9–L11.
   (D) See Exercises L13–L18.

6. (A), (B), (D) See Exercises L13–L18.
   *(C) The use of the negative question "Why didn't you?" implies that the speaker believes the person he or she is speaking to should have visited the Statue of Liberty. See Exercises L13–L18.

7. (A), (C), (D) See Exercise L1.
   *(B) "Can't afford" means "to not have enough money for something." See Exercises L9–L11.

8. (A), (D) See Exercise L1.
   (B) See Exercises L9–L11.
   *(C) You "can't make an appointment," means "you're unable to come." "Calling" is one way of "letting someone know." See Exercises L13–L18.

9. (A) See Exercises L1 and L4–L6.
   *(B) The question "Has she really . . . ?" indicates surprise. The speaker didn't know or realize she gained twenty pounds. See Exercises L39–L40.
   (C) See Exercise L1.
   (D) See Exercises L39–L40.

10. (A) See Exercises L4–L6.
    (B) See Exercise L1.
    (C) See Exercises L13–L18.   *
    (D) Being able to hear the people indicates that the stadium is near enough to the house. See Exercises L13–L18.
11. (A), (C) See Exercises L4–L6.
   *(B) When people are welcomed, they are being greeted. See Exercises L4–L6.
    (D) See Exercise L3.
12. (A), (B), (D) See Exercises L13–L18.
   *(C) "Certainly" means the same as "nothing is more certain," and "determined to be successful" refers to "determination to succeed." See Exercises L13–L18.
13. (A) See Exercises L7–L8 and L13–L18.
    (B), (C) See Exercises L13–L18.
   *(D) "Only Mary" means that "she was the only one." See Exercises L13–L18.
14. (A) See Exercises L4–L6.
    (B), (D) See Exercises L7–L8 and L13–L18.
   *(C) It can be inferred that this is true, since Scott studied harder than Susan. See Exercises L7–L8 and L13 –L18.
15. (A) See Exercise L2.
    (B) See Exercise L1.
    (C) See Exercises L13–L18.
   *(D) "Check" means "find out." See Exercises L4–L6.
16. (A), (C), (D) See Exercises L13–L18.
   *(B) The people want to stay home. See Exercises L13–L18.
17.*(A) It can be assumed that Betty was very late if Elliott was waiting more than two hours for her. See Exercises L13–L18.
    (B) See Exercises L13–L18.
    (C) See Exercises L4–L6.
    (D) See Exercise L1.
18. (A), (D) See Exercise L1.
    (B) See Exercises L4–L6.
   *(C) If William speaks quite well for his age, his language is advanced. See Exercises L13–L18.
19. (A), (C), (D) See Exercises L13–L18.
   *(B) "We enjoy playing tennis" means the same as "we like to play tennis." See Exercises L13–L18.
20. (A), (C), (D) See Exercises L13–L18.
   *(B) Because the charge does not include breakfast, guests must pay additionally for it. See Exercises L13– L18.

Part B
21. (A), (B), (C) See Exercises L32–L37.
   *(D) "To contribute something" means "to give something to help others." People contributed or donated the props to help the students. See Exercises L32–L37.
22. (A), (B), (D) See Exercises L47–L49.
   *(C) The vocabulary words and phrases that indicate a board game are "dice," "token," and "move to the blue square." See Exercises L47–L49.

23.*(A) "To be sold out" means "there are no tickets left because they were all sold." Consequently, he could not get a ticket. See Exercises L28–L30.
    (B), (C) See Exercises L26–L27.
    (D) See Exercises L28–L30.
24. (A) See Exercises L39–L40.
    (B) See Exercises L50–L51.
   *(C) "To be beyond repair" means "it is not possible to fix." See Exercises L28–L30.
    (D) See Exercises L28–L30.
25. (A) See Exercises L32–L37.
    (B) See Exercises L20–L21.
    (C) See Exercises L50–L51.
   *(D) By saying "how thoughtful," the woman is showing that she's pleased that he packed them. See Exercises L39 –L40.
26. (A) See Exercises L50–L51.
    (B) See Exercises L39–L40.
    (C) See Exercises L32–L37.
   *(D) The woman is criticizing the way the man writes. She doesn't think that Nancy will want the notes because his handwriting is hard to read. See Exercises L39– L40.
27. (A) See Exercises L28–L30.
    (B) See Exercises L32–L37.
   *(C) She is worried that they will be stuck in a traffic jam caused by the snowstorm. See Exercises L50–L51.
    (D) See Exercises L47–L49.
28. (A) See Exercises L22–L24.
    (B), (C) See Exercises L32–L37.
   *(D) The expression "face a fact" means "accept that fact." See Exercises L28–L30.
29. (A) See Exercises L1 and L20–L21.
   *(B) "Pale blue" means "light blue" and "stationery" means "writing paper." The expression "to settle for" means "to reconcile oneself to something." The woman bought the writing paper, even though it wasn't exactly what she wanted. See Exercises L28– L30.
    (C) See Exercises L20–L21.
    (D) See Exercise L1.
30. (A), (B), (C) See Exercises L28–L30.
   *(D) "To not care for something" means "to not like something." See Exercises L28–L30.
31.*(A) The mother thinks the same as the man. See Exercises L39–L40.
    (B) See Exercises L39–L40.
    (C) See Exercises L26–L27.
    (D) See Exercise L1.
32. (A) See Exercises L50–L51.
    (B) See Exercises L41–L46.
   *(C) "To liven up" means "to make more lively or exciting." Sam has an enthusiastic personality which makes parties more enjoyable. See Exercises L39–L40.
    (D) See Exercises L28–L30.

33. (A), (B), (D) See Exercises L26–L27.
 *(C) Last week was one week ago, and the week before that was two weeks ago. See Exercises L26–L27.

34. (A) See Exercises L32–L37.
 *(B) The woman means that there is so much snow falling that it is blocking the view; therefore, it must be snowing very hard." See Exercises L39–L40.
 (C), (D) See Exercises L39–L40.

35. (A) See Exercises L41–L46.
 (B) See Exercises L50–L51.
 (C) See Exercises L22–L24.
 *(D) It can be inferred that the man remembered the box because he answered "yes" when the woman asked him if he would have remembered it without her calling to remind him. See Exercises L50–L51.

Part C

36. (A) See Exercises L58–L59 and L60–66.
 *(B) The man discusses the required reading list and tells the students to be prepared to discuss the first assignment for the next class meeting. See Exercises L67–L69.
 (C), (D) See Exercises L60–L66.

37.*(A) The man says that these books are "out of print" (no longer published). See Exercises L60–L66.
 (B), (C), (D) See Exercises L60–L66.

38.*(A) Because the articles are on microfiche and microfiche cannot be taken from the library, it can be inferred the articles cannot be taken out. See Exercises L58–L59 and L71–L73.
 (B), (C) See Exercises L71–L73.
 (D) See Exercises L60–L66.

39. (A), (B), (C) See Exercises L60–L66.
 *(D) The instructor states that "there are pamphlets beside each machine explaining how to insert the microfiche." See Exercises L60–L66.

40. (A) See Exercises L53–L56.
 (B), (D) See Exercises L60–L66.
 *(C) The experiment on monkeys was done to show the interconnectedness of life. See Exercises L53–L56.

41. (A), (C), (D) See Exercises L60–L66.
 *(B) The monkeys were taught to eat sweet potatoes in a special way. See Exercises L60–L66.

42. (A), (B) See Exercises L60–L66.
 *(C) It is stated that the monkeys inhabited "an island off the coast of Japan." See Exercises L60–L66.
 (D) See Exercises L71–L73.

43.*(A) It is stated "the taught behavior" (eating sweet potatoes in a particular way) was "not typical of monkeys." See Exercises L60–L66.
 (B) See Exercises L60–L66.
 (C), (D) See Exercises L71–L73.

44. (A), (B), (C) See Exercises L60–L66.
 *(D) The woman answers the man's question about where the party will take place by saying "at Lisa and Jennifer's place." See Exercises L60–L66.

45.*(A) The man says "I thought Lisa's surprise birthday party . . . ." See Exercises L60–L66.
 (B), (C), (D) See Exercises L60–L66.

46. (A), (B) See Exercises L71–L73.
 *(C) It can be inferred that they live together because the party will be "at Lisa and Jennifer's place." See Exercises L71–L73.
 (D) See Exercises L60–L66.

47. (A), (B), (C) See Exercises L67–L69.
 *(D) They are probably friends, since they are discussing a surprise party of a third person and the man is offering to help. See Exercises L67–L69.

48. (A), (B), (C) See Exercises L53–L56.
 *(D) The importance of arm muscles is introduced followed by ways for improving arm motions and reasons for strengthening arm muscles. See Exercises L53–L56.

49.*(A) It is stated that the motion needs to be repeated thousands of times. See Exercises L60–L66.
 (B), (C), (D) See Exercises L60–L66.

50. (A) See Exercises L58–L66.
 (B) See Exercises L60–L66.
 *(C) This is one of the stated goals of arm strength training. See Exercises L60–L66.
 (D) See Exercises L71–L73.

Section 2 Structure and Written Expression

1. A verb ("are") is needed to complete the independent clause.
 (A), (C) See Exercises S17–S23 and S26–S32.
 *(B) See Exercises S17–S23 and S26–S32.
 (D) See Exercises S73–S77.

2. A preposition is needed to complete the sentence. "Among" is the correct preposition because the Great Wall is being compared to a number of other structures.
 (A) See Exercises S62–S67.
 (B) See Exercises S92–S95.
 *(C) See Exercises S92–S95.
 (D) See Exercises S44–S51.

3. An adverb clause is needed to complete the sentence. The word order for an adverb clause introduced by the clause marker "how" is how + adjective + subject + verb.
 *(A) See Exercises S73–S77.
 (B), (C), (D) See Exercises S73–S77.

4. A verb in the simple past tense (lived) is needed to complete the sentence.
 (A), (B) See Exercises S26–S32.
 *(C) See Exercises S26–S32.
 (D) See Exercises S62–S67.

5. A subject is needed. The noun phrase "the most important export" completes the sentence.
   (A), (C) See Exercises S53–S54.
   (B) See Exercises S17–S23.
   *(D) See Exercises S1–S5 and S17–S23.

6. The list of nouns in the object position indicates that a parallel structure using a noun is needed to complete the sentence.
   (A), (C) See Exercises S53–S54.
   *(B) See Exercises S89–S91.
   (D) See Exercises S89–S91.

7. A preposition that introduces the phrase and indicates a comparison is needed. "Like" completes the sentence.
   (A), (D) See Exercises S73–S77.
   *(B) See Exercises S92–S95.
   (C) See Exercises S6–S10 and S92–S95.

8. A clause marker (even though) and subject (city parks) are needed to complete the adverb clause.
   *(A) See Exercises S73–S77.
   (B), (D) See Exercises S53–S54.
   (C) See Exercises S62–S67 and S73–S77.

9. A clause marker (that) and a subject (interest) for the verb "dates" are needed to complete the noun clause which is used as a subject for the verb "is."
   *(A) See Exercises S55–S60.
   (B), (D) See Exercises S55–S60.
   (D) See Exercises S53–S54.

10. A noun is needed to fill the object position. "World's most extensive ranges" uses the correct word order and is logical.
    (A), (B), (D) See Exercises S83–S88.
    *(C) See Exercises S83–S88.

11. The sentence is complete. This indicates that a clause or phrase could be added to the sentence. "Although" introduces the adverb phrase "founded many centuries earlier."
    (A) See Exercises S53–S54.
    (B) See Exercises S53–S54.
    *(C) See Exercises S73–S77.
    (D) See Exercises S68–S71.

12. An adjective clause or phrase is needed to describe the noun "ships." "Navigating sometimes in uncharted seas" is an adjective phrase.
    *(A) See Exercises S68–S71.
    (B), (C), (D) See Exercises S68–S71.

13. A subject is needed to complete the independent clause. The use of the phrase "not until" at the beginning of the sentence indicates that the subject and an aux-word will be inverted. "Did the Romans" completes the sentence.
    (A), (C) See Exercises S33–S36.
    *(B) See Exercises S33–S36.
    (D) See Exercises S62–S67.

14. A subject is needed to complete the sentence. The gerund phrase "building adobe houses" can be used in the subject position.
    (A) See Exercises S38–S43.
    (B), (D) See Exercises S17–S23.
    *(C) See Exercises S17–S23.

15. An adjective clause or phrase is needed to describe the noun "ships." "Which can attain" is an adjective phrase.
    (A) See Exercises S68–S71.
    (B) See Exercises S62–S67 and S73–S77.
    (C) See Exercises S17–S23.
    *(D) See Exercises S62–S67.

16. (C) The article "an" should precede a word that begins with a vowel sound. See Exercises S6–S10.

17. (A) Because the action happens each time a nerve is stimulated, it is a recurring action. Therefore, the verb "resulting" should be in the present tense form, "results." See Exercises S26–S32.

18. (B) The adverb form "mostly" should be used when indicating that the statement is true most of the time. See Exercises S38–S43.

19. (A) The pronoun "them" is the correct form when used as the object of a preposition. See Exercises S11–S15.

20. (A) The pronoun "it" refers to the noun "satellites." Because "it" is a singular form, the noun should also take the singular form, "satellite." See Exercises S1–S5.

21. (C) The -ing form of the verb, "carrying," is not parallel with the simple verb form "fly." The verb form should be "carry." — "The Concorde can fly and carry." See Exercises S89–S91.

22. (C) The comparative form "cleverer" should not be used in a comparison showing equality ("as . . . as"). The adjective form "clever" is the correct form. See Exercises S83–S88.

23. (B) "Both" precedes two nouns as in "both animals and humans." "As well as" meaning "in addition to" should be used here. See Exercises S44–S51.

24. (C) "Photograph" should be preceded by the article "a" if there is only one. The absence of "a" indicates that the plural form, "photographs," should be used. See Exercises S1–S10.

25. (A) The passive form "assumed" should be used because "it" (the lower the price, the happier the buyer) doesn't assume itself. Somebody assumes this. See Exercises S26–S32.

26. (B) "Another" is singular in number. The plural form "others" should be used in order to be parallel with the plural noun "policymakers." See Exercises S44–S51.

27. (B) Because the Victorian constructions are not being compared, the adjective "few" should be used. See Exercises S38–S43 and S83–S88.

28. (D) The plural verb form "are" doesn't agree with the singular subject "one." The singular verb form "is" should be used. See Exercises S26–S32.

29. (D) "Simulations" is not being contrasted with "training." Therefore, the two nouns should be joined by the word "and." See Exercises S44–S51.

30. (A) The singular subject form "system" does not agree with the plural verb form "have." The plural form "systems" should be used. See Exercises S17–S23.

31. (B) The adjective form "cultural" is needed in order to be parallel with the other adjectives "economic" and "political." See Exercises S38–S43 and S89–S91.

32. (B) "So" introduces an adverb clause. The word "too" should be used to indicate more than enough. See Exercises S44–S51.

33. (D) The possessive adjective "his" should be used to refer to "Charles Lindbergh's aircraft." See Exercises S11–S15.

34. (A) "There" indicates the existence of something. "It" should be used when a clause has been moved from the subject position. See Exercises S17–S23.

35. (D) The article "the" should not be used. A noncount noun ("malnutrition") used in a general sense does not take an article. See Exercises S6–S10.

36. (A) The singular noun form for this illness is "measles." See Exercises S1–S5.

37. (C) The adjective form "building" should be used to describe the "kind of" industry. See Exercises S38–S43.

38. (B) The word "fast" does not use -ly in its adverb form. See Exercises S38–S43.

39. (A) "So" introduces an adverb clause. The preposition "as" meaning " in this way" should be used here. See Exercises S44–S51 and S92–S95.

40. (B) The prepositional phrase "in the house" is redundant because it means the same as "domestic." It should be omitted. See Exercises S96–S97.

Section 3   Vocabulary and Reading Comprehension

1. (B) Something is "sure" when it is certain. Something is "firm" when it is fixed so that it cannot move easily. In this case, the horse can step with certainty or put down its feet without slipping. See Exercises V1–V12.

2. (D) A "current" or "stream" is a steady and continuous flowing movement of water or air. See Exercises V1–V12 and V14–V27.

3. (C) To "beautify" something means "to cause it to look more attractive." To "adorn" something means "to make something more beautiful or attractive by adding decorations or ornaments." See Exercises V14–V27.

4. (C) "Venom" is the "poison" (a substance that harms or kills another being) that some snakes and other creatures produce and use when biting or stinging their enemy or prey. See Exercises V14–V27.

5. (D) A "speck" or "particle" is a very small piece or amount of a substance. See Exercises V1–V12 and V14–V27.

6. (A) Something that is "inexplicable" or "unexplainable" is something that people cannot comprehend. See Exercises V14–V27.

7. (A) A "symbol" is a shape or design that is used to represent something. A "sign" is a mark or shape that always has a particular meaning. See Exercises V14–V27.

8. (A) To "release" or "disengage" something means to separate it from that to which it is attached. See Exercises V14–V27.

9. (D) If you "insert" or "place" an object into something, you put the object inside it. See Exercises V1–V12 and V14–V27.

10. (B) Something that is "beneficial" or "helpful" is something that aids someone or something. See Exercises V1–V12 and V14–S27.

11. (C) A "concept" or "notion" is an idea or abstract principle that relates to a particular subject or to a particular view of that subject. See Exercises V14–V27.

12. (B) A "task" or "chore" is work to be done. See Exercises V1–V12.

13. (D) If something is "narrowed," it is reduced in extent, range, or scope. If something is "constricted," it is squeezed so that it becomes narrower. See Exercises V1–V12 and V14–V27.

14. (B) If you "immerse" or "submerge" something in a liquid, you put it into the liquid so that it is completely covered. See Exercises V14–V27.

15. (A) A "motif" or "theme" is an idea that is frequently repeated throughout a piece of music or literature. See Exercises V1–V12 and V14–V27.

16. (C) Something that is "distributed" or "dispersed" is spread or scattered over an area. See Exercises V14–V27.

17. (D) A "quest" is a long and difficult "search" (hunt) for something that is valued. See Exercises V1–V12.

18. (C) To "adhere" or "cling" to something means to stick to it. See Exercises V1–V12 and V14–V27.

19. (A) Two things that are "compatible" or "in accord" can exist in the same place and at the same time without harming each other. See Exercises V14–V27.

20. (B) Something that is "abundant" or "plentiful" is present in large quantities. See Exercises V1–V12 and V14–V27.

21. (D) Something that happens "subsequently" or "later" is something that happens following something else. See Exercises V1–V12 and V14–V27.

22. (D) If someone "domesticates" or "tames" a wild animal, he or she brings it under control and uses it to produce food or as a pet. See Exercises V1–V12 and V14–V27.

23. (B) If you say that people, animals, or things are in a particular "state" or "condition," you describe an aspect of them, such as their physical appearance, behavior, feelings, or the way that they are functioning. See Exercises V1–V12 and V14–V27.

24. (B) "Lodging" or "shelter" is a place to stay for a period of time. See Exercises V1–V12.

25. (A) If you take something "into consideration" or "into account," you think about it because it is important or relevant to something that you are doing. See Exercises V14–V27.

26. (C) To "reconnoiter" or "scout out" means to obtain information about the size and position of an army or about the geographical features of an area by sending a small group of people to explore it or by using planes or satellites. See Exercises V1–V12 and V14–V27.

27. (A) If you "traverse" or "cross" a river, area of land, etc., you move or travel to the other side of it. See Exercises V1–V12 and V14–V27.

28. (D) Your "forebears" (ancestors) or "predecessors" are those who were born and died before you. See Exercises V14–V27.

29. (B) A "customer" or "client" is someone who pays to receive a service or an object. See Exercises V1–V12 and V14–V27.

30. (D) To be in a state of "ambivalence" or "uncertainty" about something is to be unsure about it. See Exercises V14–V27.

31. (D) The first sentence introduces the topic — the French origins of lawn tennis as reflected in its scoring system. The rest of the passage discusses details of that system and the development of the terminology. See Exercises R5–R8.

32. (A) The phrases "betting on points," "worth one denier," and "divisions of a denier" indicate that this was the money used for betting on tennis matches. See Exercises R15–R18.

33. (C) It is stated that deuce is when both players have reached 40 (the score of 40) in a game. See Exercises R10–R13.

34. (C) "Love" refers to "nil" (zero). See Exercises R1–R4.

35. (A) "Love" is a corruption of the French word "l'oeuf." See Exercises R15–R18.

36. (D) This topic covers the major details in the passage. See Exercises R5–R8.

37. (B) Since sex is a factor which must be taken into account when determining safe ascent rates, it can be inferred that ascent rates for men and women may be different. See Exercises R15–R19.

38. (C) The passage states that trapped gas bubbles prevent blood and oxygen from supplying necessary nutrients to body tissues. See Exercises R10–R13.

39. (A) It is not the location of the dive that affects desaturation but the time spent at the location before the dive. See Exercises R10–R13.

40. (D) The passage states that the condition is caused by gas bubbles and explains how bubbles cause body tissues to die. See Exercises R10–R13.

41. (C) The passage states that "when the diver ascends . . . carbon dioxide is *released*." See Exercises R10–R13.

42. (D) The passage is mainly concerned with ways in which plants are efficient so that crops could be developed that would grow on marginally arable lands. See Exercises R5–R8.

43. (A) The shape of the plant's surface is given as an example of a survival mechanism. See Exercises R10–R13.

44. (D) The passage states that bacteria is an example of an organic agent that attacks plants. See Exercises R10–R13

45. (A) Because they have been proposed, it can be assumed that they have not been developed. See Exercises R15–R19.

46. (C) Gas is an example of an inorganic agent. See Exercises R10–R13.

47. (D) Poor storage, not proper storage, is an example of an adverse situation for crops. See Exercises R10–R13.

48. (B) The phrase "the carved heads free of large cracks that were uncovered" means the same as the original phrase. The use of the word "cracks" in the sentence following this one shows the meaning of "fissure." See Exercises R1 and R21–R22.

49. (A) It can be understood from the words "the late Lincoln Borglum" that he is dead. See Exercises R10–R13.

50. (D) The passage states that Borglum hired "laid-off workers from the closed-down mines." See Exercises R10–R13.

51. (A) The passage states that changes in the original design had to be made. So it can be inferred that the heads are not as originally planned. See Exercises R15–R19.

52. (C) It is stated that Borglum "concocted a mixture. . . to fill them (the fissures)." See Exercises R10–R13.

53. (D) Mount Rushmore is repaired every autumn, or "periodically." See Exercises R10–R13.

54. (C) The passage discusses the development of sound from the earliest performances with live musicians to the "sound-on-film" system. See Exercises R5–R8.

55. (B) It is stated that sound effects accompanied films from the earliest public performances in 1896. See Exercises R10–R13.

56. (D) It is stated that the newly invented gramophone was used as early as 1896 and the earliest public performances of films were in 1896. Therefore, it can be inferred that they were developed about the same time. See Exercises R15–R19.

57. (A) *The Jazz Singer* is mentioned as the name of a film, not as a producer of sound to accompany movies. See Exercises R10–R13.

58. (A) Two ways the gramophone got out of synchronization with the picture are discussed — the jumping of the needle and the speeding up of the projector. See Exercises R10–R13.

59. (C) With the sound recording beside the image, a synchronized sound could be guaranteed. See Exercises R10–R13.

60. (D) It is stated that this system (the system used for short feature films) eventually brought us "talking pictures." This indicates that short feature films came before "talking pictures." See Exercises R15–R19.

• TRANSCRIPTS •

DIAGNOSTIC TEST

Section 1   Listening Comprehension

In this section of the test, you will have an opportunity to demonstrate your ability to understand spoken English. There are three parts to this section, with special directions for each part. Do not read ahead or turn the pages while the directions are being read. Do not take notes or write in your workbook at any time.

Part A

Directions: For each question in Part A, you will hear a short sentence. Each sentence will be spoken just once. The sentences you hear will not be written out for you.

After you hear a sentence, read the four choices in your workbook, marked (A), (B), (C), and (D), and decide which one is closest in meaning to the sentence you heard. Then, on your answer sheet, find the number of the question and fill in the space that corresponds to the letter of the answer you have chosen. Fill in the space completely so that the letter inside the oval cannot be seen.

Listen to an example.

On the recording, you hear:
The new observatory is nothing less than outstanding.

In your workbook, you read:
(A) The new observatory is excellent.
(B) There is nothing outstanding to observe.
(C) You must stand outside to make the observance.
(D) His new observations are more outstanding than usual.

The woman said, "The new observatory is nothing less than outstanding." Sentence (A), "The new observatory is excellent," is closest in meaning to what the woman said. Therefore, the correct choice is (A).

Go on to the next page.

Now we will begin Part A with question number 1.

1. That was a nice gesture on Tom's part.
2. We all chipped in for the going away present.
3. Sue has a knack for getting people to donate their time and money.
4. Mark avoids driving on Friday nights because there's too much traffic.
5. Even though Janet doesn't watch TV often, she's watched it every night this week.

6. It's been 15 years since Bill stopped playing the piano.
7. Peter and I seldom see eye to eye on politicians.
8. The price of tuna fish has doubled in three years.
9. Botany is as easy for me as zoology.
10. Keep in touch while you're gone.
11. I couldn't believe you didn't go to the rally.
12. If this cupboard weren't so full, I could find the jam.
13. Carmen serves on the board of directors of the Yacht Club.
14. Dan's false accusations left us speechless.
15. Although Diane and Barbara have been friends since childhood, they don't see each other much.
16. The children were restless after the long drive.
17. What a close call!
18. Sam caught the waitress's eye.
19. How Alice was able to write that paper overnight, I'll never know.
20. The professor lectured far longer than her usual class hour.

This is the end of Part A. Go on to the next page.

Now read along with me as I read the directions for Part B. Remember, you may NOT read ahead or turn the pages while the directions for this part are being read.

Part B

Directions: In Part B you will hear short conversations between two people. After each conversation, a third person will ask a question about what was said. You will hear each conversation and question about it only one time. After you hear a conversation and the question about it, read the four possible answers in your workbook and decide which one is the best answer to the question you heard. Then, on your answer sheet, find the number of the question and fill in the space that corresponds to the letter of the answer you have chosen.

Listen to an example.

On the recording, you hear:
(First Man)   I think I'll have the curtains changed.
(Woman)   They are a bit worn.

(Second Man)   What does the woman mean?

In your workbook, you read:
(A) She thinks every bit of change is important.
(B) She wants to wear them.

(C) She thinks they've been worn enough.
(D) She thinks they are in bad condition.

You learn from the conversation that the woman thinks the curtains are worn. The best answer to the question "What does the woman mean?" is (D), "She thinks they are in bad condition." Therefore, the correct choice is (D).

Now we will begin Part B with the first conversation.

21. W: Do you know Michael Jones?
    M: Know him! Why, he's my brother-in-law.
    What do we learn about Michael?
22. M: How do you think your court case will turn out?
    W: Fine, now that I've found an eyewitness to the incident.
    What does the woman say about her case?
23. W: Can you explain to me how to get to your house?
    M: Sure. Go past the light by the library, and at the third stop sign, turn left. Continue straight to the dead end, and it's the last house on the right.
    Where does the man say to turn left?
24. M: I just went caving with the Grotto Club last weekend.
    W: That's not a good reason for not joining us this coming weekend.
    What does the woman mean?
25. M: How long has Scott been restoring furniture – five years?
    W: At least that long.
    What is the woman saying about Scott?
26. M: I'd like to drive to the movies, but my father is using the car tonight.
    W: Who needs a car? If we leave a little earlier, we can go by bus.
    What does the woman mean?
27. M: Peter does carpentry, doesn't he?
    M: Yes, but he had a professional make the cabinets according to his design.
    What do we learn from this conversation?
28. W: This fog is so heavy that you can't see the other side of the street.
    M: I wouldn't want to drive in it.
    What does the man mean?
29. M: I can't make head nor tail of this map.
    W: Let's pull in at the next gas station.
    What does the woman mean?
30. W: Where are you headed, Rob?
    M: To the barber's.
    What is the man probably going to do?
31. M: Do I take this exit?
    M: I'm not sure. Slow down so I can read the road signs.
    Where are the people?
32. W: My trees need trimming, and something must be done about that lawn.
    M: Mrs. Brown at the Green Thumb Nursery can give you some advice.
    What does Mrs. Brown do?

33. W: The station wagon was a nicer color and style, but the van was more spacious for our family.
    M: Yes, but it would cost more to run.
    What does the woman prefer about the van?
34. M: I hardly had time to finish the exam.
    W: Really? I finished in no time.
    What does the woman mean?
35. M: I turned green when I saw Ann's new car.
    W: I can understand why.
    What do we learn about the man?

This is the end of Part B. Go on to the next page.

Now read along with me as I read the directions for Part C. Remember, you may NOT read ahead or turn the pages while the directions for this part are being read.

Part C

Directions: In this part of the test, you will hear longer conversations and talks. After each conversation or talk, you will be asked some questions. You will hear the talks and conversations and the questions about them only one time. They will not be written out for you.

After you hear a question, read the four possible answers in your workbook and decide which one is the best answer to the question you heard. Then, on your answer sheet, find the number of the question and fill in the space that corresponds to the letter of the answer you have chosen. Answer all questions on the basis of what is stated or implied by the speakers in the talk or conversation.

Here is an example.

On the recording, you hear:
Listen to a conversation between a professor and a student.
(Woman)   Would you please type this paper? I can't read your handwriting.
(First Man) I'm sorry, Professor Mills. I don't have a typewriter, and besides, I can't type.
(Woman)   Well, rewrite it then, but be sure to make it clear.

Now listen to a sample question.
(Second Man) What does the professor want the man to do?

In your workbook you read:
(A) Buy a typewriter.
(B) Read his handwriting.
(C) Clear the papers away.
(D) Rewrite the paper.

The best answer to the question "What does the professor want the man to do?" is (D), "Rewrite the paper." Therefore, the correct choice is (D).

Remember, you are not allowed to take notes or write in your workbook.

Now we will begin Part C.

Questions 36 through 39. Listen to a talk.

Treasured since ancient times, saffron is obtained from the autumn-flowering crocus sativus. It is the dried flower stigmas – the three slender threads in the center of each flower – which are the source of saffron. In New York, this "king of spices" can fetch up to $15 a gram, making it one of the world's most prized and expensive foodstuffs. The finest variety is grown in La Mancha in the central plateau of Spain. Spain is by far the biggest producer. It contributes 70% of the world's output, with India and Iran the only other producers of note. The cultivation of saffron in Spain goes back to the Moorish invasion of the eighth century, when the crocuses were first introduced from the Middle East. Not only is Spain the largest producer of saffron, but it is also the largest consumer. Up to one-third of the crop is bought in Spain, and the remainder is exported. The biggest buyers are Saudi Arabia and Bahrain, followed by the United States, Italy, and France.

36. What is the lecture about?
37. What reason is given for saffron being known as the "king of spices"?
38. Besides Spain, which countries export saffron?
39. Which country is the biggest consumer of saffron?

Questions 40 through 43. Listen to a conversation about art.
M: Now this Rembrandt has just recently been returned to this museum after being out on unauthorized loan for three years. Do you have a question?
W: Yes, why was that particular painting stolen when there are more valuable items in the museum?
M: Actually this painting is favored by thieves. It's been taken four times in the last twenty years. We believe it may have something to do with its size – nine by eleven inches.
W: That would make it easier to steal and hide, wouldn't it? By the way, what is its value?
M: It's been appraised at five million dollars, but I don't know what a thief can sell it for.
W: This painting is quite well known, isn't it? It seems that no one would want a stolen picture that's so easily recognized.
M: It seems that way, but we've had to take extra security precautions because of its popularity with thieves.

40. Where does this conversation probably take place?
41. What does the man do?
42. How long had the Rembrandt been missing?
43. What reason is given for the painting's popularity among thieves?

Questions 44 through 47. Listen to a conversation about luggage.
M: May I help you?
W: Yes. I couldn't find my luggage at the baggage pickup. I waited until everything had been claimed.
M: What flight were you on?
W: Transcontinental flight 526 arriving from Chicago.
M: Could I see your baggage claim tickets, please?
W: Yes, of course. I have two suitcases: a large brown one with straps and a medium-sized black one.

M: Do you have identification tags on them?
W: Yes, I do. I also have my name and address on the inside.
M: Good. Can you please fill out this form with your name and where you can be reached? We'll put a search on them and contact you as soon as they're recovered.

44. Where does this conversation take place?
45. What is the man's job?
46. What does the woman have in her luggage?
47. What will the man do when the luggage is found?

Questions 48 through 50. Listen to a talk.
The largest artificial rock-climbing wall in the United States is located on the campus of Cornell University. This thirty-foot-high climbing wall is made of natural rock that's embedded into concrete blocks, and is sculpted to imitate a variety of elements found on real cliffs. Cornell recently hosted the nation's largest intercollegiate rock-climbing event. Nearly one hundred students from fifteen universities participated in the two-day festival, sponsored by Cornell's Outdoor Education Department.

48. Why is Cornell a good place for climbing?
49. What recently happened at Cornell University?
50. Who sponsored the event?

This is the end of the Listening Comprehension section of the Diagnostic Test.

SECTION 1 LISTENING COMPREHENSION

Read the directions to each exercise. When you understand what to do, start the recording. You will hear the exercise title and then the question number. The directions and the example are not on the recording.

Start the recording where you see the 📼 symbol. Stop or pause the recording when you see the 📼 symbol and the word "stop" or "pause."

Part A   Short sentences

Exercise L1   Identifying the correct sound
1. Did you see the sheep?
2. He gave me the bell.
3. I didn't have any clue.
4. The mayor was sitting at his desk.
5. Where did she put the pen?
6. John bought a new cup.
7. Can you help me tie this belt?
8. Please put the cart in the garage.

Exercise L2   Recognizing questions and statements
1. Ann's from San Francisco?
2. What an impossible teacher!
3. Read anything good recently?
4. Can Tom ever cook!
5. What a terrible mistake that was!
6. Why should I?
7. He asked where the library was.
8. Is it ever raining hard!

Exercise L3   Identifying words that are pronounced the same but have different meanings

1. At the corner turn right.
2. It was a difficult feat to climb that mountain.
3. Please, wait your turn.
4. It's one hour before the movie starts.
5. Bill is an heir to a fortune.
6. There were four buses parked at the terminal.
7. Do you know your way home from here?
8. What's the fare to Brooklyn?

Exercise L4   Identifying which meaning is correct

1. I will exhaust all means of finding the answer.
2. That's a very simple cake to make.
3. Rita pays a reasonable rate for room and board there.
4. At the end of the fast, there is a feast.
5. Please don't kid me about such a serious matter.
6. That police officer's beat covers this entire neighborhood.
7. Nancy and I have a common interest in horses.
8. Dan's new car has a lot of class.

Exercise L5   Identifying multiple meanings in sentences

1. (A) New evidence came to light after the investigation.
   (B) Because of the heat she wore a light summer dress.
2. (A) Did you read about the military strike in the newspaper?
   (B) These matches are damp and won't light when you strike them.
3. (A) Tom will box some food to send to the flood victims.
   (B) I bought some new gloves to use when I box.
4. (A) Mary wants to be an astronaut and travel in space.
   (B) This needs to be typed with a double space between the lines.
5. (A) Please note that the times for the concert have been changed.
   (B) Fred can sing the lowest note of anybody in the choir.
6. (A) The spring shower freshened the air.
   (B) Kathy's friends surprised her with a baby shower.
7. (A) There's a freshwater spring near the park.
   (B) The cat waited patiently to spring on the mouse.
8. (A) If you don't agree with the decision, you can exercise your rights to a new trial.
   (B) The doctor has advised me to exercise more and eat less.

Exercise L6   Matching words in sentences

1. (A) The pass through those mountains is treacherous.
   (B) Do you need a pass to get into the conference?
2. (A) Patty's just an ordinary looking girl.
   (B) She was famous for being a just leader.
3. (A) I like to visit the fruit stall in the open market.
   (B) The little girl didn't want to go to bed, so she started to stall for time.
4. (A) Those kinds of chairs tip easily, so be careful.
   (B) She left the waiter a large tip.
5. (A) The angry protesters filed past the armed guards.
   (B) I filed down the rough edges of the wood.
6. (A) I wrote a check to pay for the furniture.
   (B) Put a check in front of the items you wish to order.
7. (A) The airplane will bank when turning to make its landing.
   (B) My grandfather doesn't trust the bank, so he keeps his money under the mattress.
8. (A) The tree branch broke in the storm and blocked the road.
   (B) Cindy is a cousin from my father's branch of the family.

Exercise L7   Listening for time, quantity, and comparison

Time

1. Let me know by tomorrow if you're coming.
2. Jane's due at quarter to two.
3. Connie just told me that her father was still in the hospital.
4. Jeff's leaving the week after next.
5. Tom didn't start studying until midnight.

Quantity

6. Alice only needs a couple more credits to graduate.
7. Dick hasn't sold a single dictionary.
8. Professor Merrill has written up to thirty articles on art history.
9. My coin collection has tripled in value since I started it.
10. This cake recipe calls for half a dozen eggs.

Comparisons

11. I haven't eaten any more cookies than you have.
12. Tim has far more responsibilities than the other staff members.
13. It's much cheaper to go by bus than train.
14. Frank's salary is high, but Emma's is even higher.
15. The faster Irene types, the fewer mistakes she makes.

Exercise L8   More practice with time, quantity, and comparisons

1. If Tom touches that cake one more time, I won't let him have any after supper.
2. Can you let me know no later than tomorrow?
3. Steve has taken as many semester hours as Linda has, and then some.
4. Half the members we expected showed up at the last meeting.
5. Jane only needed a third of the food she bought for the picnic.
6. A person with far greater acting skills than I have should be the lead in the play.
7. The more Carol attends that class, the better she likes it.
8. No sooner did we arrive than the music started.

9. When the new regulation goes into effect, no more extensions will be given.
10. I think I'll buy at least a dozen file folders.

Exercise L9 Understanding idiomatic expressions

1. During the summer, Marsha swims to her heart's content.
2. Jim was beside himself with worry.
3. Bob flew into a rage.
4. Ann is going to see me off.
5. Gordon catches colds easily.
6. I'll cross that bridge when I come to it.
7. Sue didn't lift a finger during the cleanup.
8. Janet has it in her head to go camping.
9. That movie will make your hair stand on end.
10. My grandfather is really getting on in years.

Exercise L10 Identifying the correct idiom or phrasal verb

1. It was hard to convey the idea.
2. Only Rita was able to help Emma understand.
3. Stephen panicked at the interview.
4. My brother is always teasing me.
5. We want the money in case of an emergency.
6. Tonight I'm going to assemble that bicycle.
7. They are discharging good workers from the factory.
8. Do you think their romance will last?
9. The old woman clung to her son.
10. Those children exhaust me.

Exercise L11 Identifying the correct meaning of expressions

1. Even though Jeff and Mike hated each other at first, they became friends little by little.
2. Sue ran into Mary in the mall.
3. Even though John is doing his best, he doesn't stand a chance of winning the medal.
4. In the long run, things will work out for the best.
5. When Rebecca failed to pass the entrance exams, she notified her mother and father right away.
6. Max has told Pete time after time to keep the door locked.
7. Ellen could buy a new coat for Amy, but on the other hand, Amy does need gloves.
8. Even though Bill was on time to take the test, he couldn't because he had forgotten his identification card.

Exercise L12 Mini-test

Directions: For each question you will hear a short sentence. Each sentence will be spoken just once. The sentences you hear will not be written out for you. Therefore, you must listen carefully to understand what the speaker says.

After you hear a sentence, read the four choices in your book marked (A), (B), (C), and (D), and decide which one is closest in meaning to the sentence you heard. Then circle the letter that corresponds to the answer you have chosen.

Listen to an example.

On the recording, you hear:
If you can't finish this research, please let me know no later than Wednesday.

In your workbook, you read:
(A) Tell me by Wednesday if you're unable to finish.
(B) Please help me find the ladder.
(C) You'll need more than a liter of varnish.
(D) Don't tell me about the research until after Wednesday.

The woman said, "If you can't finish this research, please let me know no later than Wednesday." Sentence (A), "Tell me by Wednesday if you're unable to finish," is closest in meaning to what the woman said. Therefore, the correct choice is (A).

1. As much as Mary hates her work, she does a very adequate job.
2. Can Peter ever make cakes!
3. Let me know if he's bothering you, and I'll take care of him.
4. When is it my turn?
5. Bob told Jim that he could put as many as twenty-five names on the guest list.
6. The night rain disturbed my sleep.
7. Have you booked the flight?
8. David puts at most two spoonfuls of sugar in his tea.
9. Peggy finds fault with everyone she meets in the cafeteria.
10. My eyes sting.
11. Board isn't included in the conference fee.
12. Roger was in such a hurry that he left without his umbrella and scarf.
13. Dan is having Beth over for dinner.
14. Rick put in two hours working at the library last night.
15. Ron's cat has fleas.
16. I headed out before dawn.
17. Jill left her lunch on the bus.
18. It was half past twelve when the students handed in the questionnaire.
19. Ted is afraid to overeat and get fat.
20. We used to take the bus all the time.

Exercise L13 Understanding causatives

1. M: I would consult Mrs. Jones, if I were you, Bob.
   Who needs advice?
2. W: Kathy got John to give her a ride.
   Who needed a ride?
3. M: Vicky let Ann take the blame.
   Who took the blame?
4. M: Mary made Dan leave the room.
   Who left the room?
5. W: Nancy caused Jeff to have an accident.
   Whose fault was the accident?
6. M: Debbie made Jim replace her watch.
   Who received a new watch?

7. W: Ellen had Fred cut her hair.
    Whose hair was cut?
8. M: Sue let Don leave the meeting early.
    Who left the meeting?
9. W: Liz wished Ms. Nelson had let her have the day off.
    Who wanted a free day?
10. M: Mr. Jones wondered if Tom had gotten the plumbing fixed.
    Who was supposed to take care of the plumbing?

Exercise L14   Understanding negative meaning
1. I don't always catch the 7:45 train.
2. Motivation, not experience, often determines success.
3. Not a single student came to class.
4. Seldom have my suggestions been taken seriously.
5. There is barely enough bread for lunch.
6. I've read nothing you would like.
7. That wasn't a bad-looking car.
8. Not once has Rita invited Sarah to one of her parties.
9. On no occasion should Ben's friends call after 11:00.
10. I'll never know how Dan was able to finish on time.

Exercise L15   Understanding modals
1. Sam must be out of town.
2. We'd better meet once a week to discuss our project.
3. Lynn ought to study more.
4. Ben couldn't have heard the lecture.
5. Ricky would rather go to the beach than the park.
6. I'd prefer that you not call me tomorrow.
7. Jill must have returned to the dorm.
8. John might have gotten the job.
9. Sharon will have left by this time next week.
10. We should get together more often.

Exercise L16   Identifying conditions
1. If Sarah had gotten the raise, she would have bought a car.
2. If it's raining on Friday nights, William goes to the movies.
3. She'll buy the car if the dealer gives her a discount.
4. Mary wouldn't have gone to Spain if her mother hadn't been there.
5. If Sam were rich, he'd have quit his job.
6. If she had bought the dress, she would have had to lower the hem.
7. If I even smell cake, I gain five pounds.
8. I wouldn't pay cash, even if I had it.
9. I wouldn't be nervous if I hadn't drunk so much coffee.
10. If Ted doesn't bring the sandwiches, Cindy will make some.

Exercise L17   Identifying causes and results
1. It was such a boring lecture that I fell asleep.
2. Because the weather was nice, everyone was at the lake.
3. Now that Mike has a car, we never see him.
4. The pizza was so hot that Bob burned his tongue.
5. As long as you have a pen, could you take notes?
6. I need to cash this check so that I'll have some money for the weekend.
7. It was such a difficult exam that Paul didn't finish it.
8. Since you are a math major, maybe you could help me with this equation.
9. Due to the heat, we stayed at home and watched TV.
10. The instructor didn't come, so we left the classroom.

Exercise L18   Understanding other structures
1. Professor Silva is always stopping to smoke.
2. Bill used to ski.
3. I'm used to jogging before breakfast.
4. Sue remembers watering the plants.
5. Carol took the photograph herself.
6. Barbara used to work for an art dealer.
7. Mark remembered not to turn off the lights.
8. Alison stopped to light a match.

Exercise L19   Mini-test
Directions: For each question you will hear a short sentence. Each sentence will be spoken just once. The sentences you hear will <u>not</u> be written out for you.

After you hear a sentence, read the four choices in your book, marked (A), (B), (C), and (D), and decide which <u>one</u> is closest in meaning to the sentence you heard. Then circle the letter that corresponds to the answer you have chosen.

Listen to an example.

On the recording, you hear:
I couldn't have done a better job than Sam.

In your workbook, you read:
(A) I couldn't do the job and neither could Sam.
(B) I did a better job than Sam did.
(C) Sam did a job that I couldn't have done so well.
(D) Sam couldn't do the job that I did.

The man said, "I couldn't have done a better job than Sam." Sentence (C), "Sam did a job that I couldn't have done so well," is closest in meaning to what the man said. Therefore, the correct choice is (C).

1. If Ann hadn't been so beautiful, Ted wouldn't have married her.
2. Julie forgot to sign her name on the application form.
3. Mr. Roberts had Andy give Sue the newsletter.
4. It must have been the most difficult test you've ever taken.
5. Not only did Jim knock over the grape juice, but he failed to mop it up.
6. David never misses a day of classes, even though he has a serious handicap.
7. It was such a cloudy day that Kim decided to call off the picnic.
8. If you have your seat assignment, there's no need to stand in line.
9. The professor made the student who didn't bring his identification card leave the testing center.

10. Donna graduated from the Art Academy and then got a good position at the Town Gallery.
11. If the weather report is correct, we'll have the needed snow for cross-country skiing.
12. Mrs. Davis told her son he ought to avoid stray dogs.
13. If you get the newspaper, could I have the classified ads section?
14. Rick got Marie to write his speech.
15. Nancy isn't used to dancing so much.
16. You'll never finish on time unless you get Jerry's help.
17. Amy should check with the committee before she submits that report.
18. I'd like to stop to make a phone call before we leave, please.
19. Rebecca must have been exhausted after swimming all those laps.
20. Simon tried closing the door, but he could still hear the loud music.

Part B   Short conversations

Exercise L20   Identifying words that are pronounced the same but have different meanings
1. W: I want to dye my hair.
   M: Why do that? It's already a nice color.
2. M: My brakes failed on the freeway last night.
   W: That must have been very frightening.
3. W: Who won the motorcycle race?
   M: Albert Jackson did.
4. M: Did you have enough money for tuition and books?
   W: No, I had to take out a loan.
5. M: I've just torn a hole in my sweater.
   W: Too bad. It was such a nice sweater.

Exercise L21   Identifying the meaning of the word in the conversation
1. meet
   W: What time did you tell Ann we would meet her?
   M: At 6:00 at the Bay Leaf Restaurant.
2. sail
   M: Did Michael replace the torn sail for his boat?
   W: No. He thinks he can mend it.
3. cruise
   M: Sue is going on a cruise to the Bahamas.
   W: Is she? I wish I could go, too.
4. weak
   W: I felt very weak when I came home from the hospital.
   M: How long were you there?
5. mail
   M: Has the mail been delivered yet?
   W: Yes. But it was all junk.

Exercise L22   Identifying which meaning is correct
1. W: Where did Jack earn his degree?
   M: At Colorado State Teachers College.
2. M: I thought your major was economics.
   W: It was. But I changed to business last semester.

3. W: Why are you getting rid of that easy chair?
   M: It has a broken spring.
4. M: Could you turn up the volume on the radio?
   W: That's as loud as it can go.
5. M: Are you sure that it's a sound deal?
   W: Not really. You can't believe everything Tim says.

Exercise L23   Identifying multiple meanings in conversations
1. (A) M: I heard Steve's father is in the hospital.
       W: Yes. He had a stroke.
   (B) W: Are you a good swimmer?
       M: Well, I know all the strokes, but I don't have much stamina.
2. (A) M: I recommend the curried rice.
       W: Oh, that's too hot for me. I can't eat it.
   (B) W: I've just made coffee. Would you like some?
       M: A nice hot cup of coffee sounds great.
3. (A) M: I want to mount this oil painting.
       W: Why don't you ask Amy to do it? She does excellent work.
   (B) W: What did you learn in your first riding class?
       M: How to mount a horse properly.
4. (A) M: How did your sister get a concussion?
       W: She got a blow on the head when she fell off her bicycle.
   (B) M: I live near the railway station.
       W: Do you wake up at night when the train whistles blow?
5. (A) M: If you want to catch any fish, you'll have to cast the line out further.
       W: Will I? You haven't caught any fish either.
   (B) W: The doctor will take off my cast tomorrow.
       M: Great. Just make sure you take it easy for a while.
6. (A) W: Why were you so cross with Sue?
       M: Because she forgot to return my typewriter again.
   (B) W: That man was driving too fast.
       M: I know. We hardly had time to cross the street.

Exercise L24   Matching words in conversations
1. (A) M: Did you get a birthday card for Susan?
       W: Oh, I'm sorry. I completely forgot.
   (B) W: Jack invited us over to play cards next Friday.
       M: Great. We haven't done that for a long time.
2. (A) W: This food is so rich, I can't eat very much.
       M: Hmm. I'm really enjoying it.
   (B) M: When I'm rich, I'll buy a cattle ranch in Colorado.
       W: You don't even know what a cow looks like.
3. (A) W: Why are you doing all those exercises?
       M: I want my body to be in good shape for the ski season.
   (B) M: Is Lake Tahoe a good recreation area?
       W: Yes. It's a very large body of water with good boating facilities.

4. (A) M: Jane isn't in good form for the race
          tomorrow.
       W: Does she plan on participating anyway?
   (B) M: I really hate filling out these tax forms.
       W: Let me help you. I like to do them.
5. (A) W: How did you break your arm?
       M: I tripped on the stair and fell against the
          railing.
   (B) M: Are you going anywhere special for spring
          break?
       W: Yes. We're going to take a cruise to the
          Virgin Islands.

Exercise L25   Mini-test

Directions: In Part B you will hear short conversations
between two people. After each conversation, a third
person will ask a question about what was said. You will
hear each conversation and question about it only <u>one</u>
time.

After you hear a conversation and the question about it,
read the four possible answers in your book and decide
which <u>one</u> is the best answer to the question you heard.
Then circle the letter that corresponds to the answer you
have chosen.

Listen to an example.

On the recording, you hear:
(First Man)   Nick broke the window pane while
                 cleaning it.
(Woman)   Did he hurt himself?
(Second Man) What did Nick do?

In your workbook, you read:
(A) He hurt himself.
(B) He cleaned the wound.
(C) He broke the glass.
(D) He got soaked.

You learn from the conversation that Nick broke the
window pane while he was cleaning it. The best answer to
the question "What did Nick do?" is (C), "He broke the
glass." Therefore, the correct choice is (C).

1. M: Do you take cream in your tea?
   W: No, thank you. I'll have it plain.
   What does the man want to know?
2. M: Why don't you want to go to Judy and David's?
   W: Because they are always fighting over little
      things.
   What doesn't the woman like?
3. M: Are you ever going to return that travel book?
   W: If Bill didn't miss it this month, he won't miss it
      next month.
   What are the people talking about?
4. W: Why don't you wear the striped shirt?
   M: Because it doesn't match my checked pants.
   What is the man doing?
5. W: You sure were sick for a long time.
   M: Yes. And I'm still very weak.
   What is the man's problem?

6. W: Tom didn't hear Dr. Matthew's assignment.
   M: No wonder. I heard him snoring in class.
   What was Tom doing?
7. M: Is there space in your backpack for this glass?
   W: What do you want to take that for?
   What does the man want to do?
8. M: Do you have a coin for this machine?
   W: Sorry, I don't have any change at all.
   What can't the woman do?
9. M: What role did you get in the play?
   W: Would you believe the daughter?
   What is the woman going to do?
10. M: Which sink is blocked?
    W: The one in the spare bathroom.
    What are the people discussing?
11. M: I'm going to the pool. Would you care to join me?
    W: Sure. Let me grab my cap.
    What are the people going to do?
12. W: Let's take the stairs.
    M: Let's not. There are too many flights to climb.
    What does the man not want to do?
13. M: We need to replace the glass in that picture
       frame.
    W: We can go to the shop and have it done now.
    What are the people discussing?
14. M: I proofread that essay twice.
    W: Well, I still had to correct a couple of mistakes.
    What are the people doing?
15. W: Would you move your truck so I can back out?
    M: I'm sorry. I didn't realize I'd blocked the
       driveway.
    What had the man done?

**Exercise L26   Listening for time, quantity, and
comparisons**

Time
1. W: I haven't seen Mary for at least three years.
   M: Did you know that she's head of a big
      engineering firm?
2. W: What did you want me to tell Tom when I see
      him?
   M: That the book he ordered has arrived.
3. M: Is the dog show next week?
   W: It's the following week.
4. W: Mr. Green's grocery store stays open until nine
      o'clock on Fridays.
   M: Good. I forgot to buy cheese for the pizzas.
5. M: It's been six years since I took piano lessons.
   W: You still play very well.

Quantity
6. W: Did you buy a cassette tape?
   M: Yes. In fact, I bought several.
7. M: Sam's completed sixty credit hours, hasn't he?
   W: At least.
8. M: I don't understand either example.
   W: Neither do I.
9. W: I couldn't get a student loan this semester.
   M: Quite a few students haven't been able to get
      loans

10. M: Your brother is a lawyer, isn't he?
    W: Both are lawyers.

Comparisons

11. M: I've studied harder in that geology class than for my calculus class, and I'm still not passing.
    W: Why don't you discuss it with the professor?
12. M: What size box do you need for all those books?
    W: The bigger the better.
13. W: Schedules with more flexible hours would be beneficial for working parents.
    M: Also, there would be fewer traffic problems if people were commuting at different hours of the day.
14. W: I didn't get half as much written as I intended.
    M: Maybe you can write more later.
15. M: The scenic route takes longer, but it's more interesting than Interstate 90.
    W: Let's take it.

Exercise L27   Understanding the meaning in expressions of time, quantity, and comparison

1. M: Would you like me to bring over some extra chairs?
   W: Oh, could you?
2. M: I had to buy a lot more books this semester.
   W: You should have gone to the used book store.
3. W: How much time did you spend preparing that speech?
   M: A couple of hours at least.
4. W: Did you buy the box of candy I asked for?
   M: I did better than that. I bought you two boxes.
5. M: When is the last day I can drop a class?
   W: Thursday. You have a full week.
6. W: The number of students working part-time has doubled.
   M: You mean fifteen hundred students on this campus have jobs?

Exercise L28   Understanding idiomatic expressions

1. W: Tom stood me up last Saturday.
   M: So that's why you're so angry.
   What does the woman mean?
2. M: I just can't uncork this bottle.
   W: Can I have a crack at it?
   What does the woman mean?
3. M: I heard that your chemistry instructor blew up in class.
   W: That's right. None of us had done the assignment.
   What happened in the chemistry class?
4. W: Are you going to sign up for Music 319?
   M: Well, I can't put it off any longer.
   What are the man's plans?
5. M: Do you know Cindy Wilson?
   W: That name rings a bell.
   What does the woman mean?
6. M: They sure gave me the runaround at registration.
   W: I know what you mean. That's happened to me.
   What happened to the man?

Exercise L29   Identifying the correct expressions

1. W: Why are you studying so hard these days?
   M: Because the class is five units ahead of me.
2. M: Why don't you ask Tim to join the committee?
   W: That's a good idea. He always does his share of the work.
3. W: You look blurry-eyed this morning.
   M: Yeah. I had insomnia last night.
4. M: Wendy may well win the election for student body president.
   W: She does have a good chance.
5. W: I was so embarrassed when the professor showed everyone my mistake.
   M: I'll bet that you don't make that mistake again.
6. M: Janet and Mike were dancing close together at Bill's party.
   W: Did you know that they're engaged?
7. W: I saw a snake in the kitchen.
   M: You just imagined it.
8. W: My roommate was really critical of my project.
   M: Don't let her discourage you.
9. M: I'm going to rewrite my essay.
   W: Again? Don't do that. It's fine the way it is.
10. W: Why are you so upset?
    M: Mrs. Becker sent me to six different offices to do something she knew couldn't be done.

Exercise L30   Identifying the correct meaning of expressions

1. M: Tomorrow's the day I leave for Washington.
   W: Well, be sure to keep in touch.
   What does the woman want the man to do?
2. M: Why don't we drive to the park?
   W: Why drive? It's within a stone's throw.
   What does the woman mean?
3. W: Why are you going to the game so early?
   M: I'm working and have to set up the concession stand.
   Why is the man going to the game early?
4. W: I haven't seen Pete for weeks.
   M: That's because he's wrapped up in his job.
   What can be said about Pete?
5. W: Professor Martin's talk on ethics was very boring.
   M: You must have missed the point. It was fantastic.
   What does the man mean?
6. M: Where did you find out about this diet?
   W: I ran across it in a pamphlet in the doctor's office.
   What happened to the woman?
7. M: Rebecca won't give me the time of day.
   W: I'm not surprised, after the way you criticized her paper.
   What does the man say about Rebecca?
8. W: Are you seriously going to vote for Mary in the election?
   M: Well, I think she has what it takes.
   What is the man's opinion of Mary?
9. W: Would you mind your own business?
   M: I'm sorry. I didn't mean to upset you.
   What does the woman want the man to do?

10. W: Haven't you started your project yet?
    M: No. I still haven't been given the committee's go-ahead.
    What is the man's problem?

Exercise L31   Mini-test

<u>Directions</u>: You will hear short conversations between two people. After each conversation, a third person will ask a question about what was said. You will hear each conversation and the question about it only one time.

After you hear a conversation and the question about it, read the four possible answers in your book and decide which one is the best answer to the question you heard. Then circle the letter that corresponds to the answer you have chosen.

Listen to an example.

On the recording, you hear:
(Man)   Have you followed up on Michael's recommendations?
(First Woman)   Sally has. And her report looks very promising.
(Second Woman)   What did Sally do?

In your workbook, you read:
(A) Followed Michael.
(B) Promised a report.
(C) Recommended Michael.
(D) Submitted a report.

You infer from the conversation that Sally wrote a report concerning the recommendations she "followed up on." The best answer to the question "What did Sally do?" is (D), "Submitted a report." Therefore, the correct choice is (D).

1. W: I studied all night long.
   M: Why don't you go home and get some shut-eye?
   What does the man mean?
2. M: Do you think we could back out of the dinner party gracefully?
   W: That may be difficult.
   What does the man want to do?
3. W: You sure are making light of that bad exam grade in sociology.
   M: Well, I can't let it ruin my life.
   What does the woman mean?
4. M: Don't let anyone know about the car accident.
   W: I understand why you want to hush it up.
   What does the woman understand?
5. M: Recently Bill has been lying down on the job.
   W: I think he's a bit lazy myself.
   What does the man say about Bill?
6. W: Why do they insist on the test?
   M: To screen out those who shouldn't be in the experiment.
   What is done to some of the people?

7. M: Ted never understands my jokes.
   W: Yes he does. It just takes a while for them to sink in.
   What does the woman mean?
8. W: Those children made short work of eating the cookies.
   M: Children always do.
   What did the children do?
9. M: Neil usually sticks around after class.
   W: Today he rushed off to the cafeteria.
   What does the man mean?
10. M: Professor Higgins has watered down his course.
    W: That's because of the change in university requirements.
    What has the instructor done?
11. W: Professor Jenson passed out in class.
    M: Did they discover the reason for it?
    What happened to Professor Jenson?
12. W: I stumbled across an interesting shop near the fish market.
    M: Really? What was special about it?
    What does the woman mean?
13. M: Steve has sworn off smoking.
    W: I don't believe he'll be able to for very long.
    What has Steve done?
14. M: Are you and Cindy ready to go to the bookstore with me?
    W: I thought you didn't want us to tag along.
    What did the woman think?
15. M: I need to have my jacket taken in.
    W: The tailor on Third Avenue is very good.
    What needs to be done to the jacket?

Exercise L32   Understanding causatives

1. M: What a nice hairstyle. Did you have it done professionally?
   W: No. I had my sister do it.
   Who did the woman's hair?
2. W: Did Joe cut those dead branches from the tree himself?
   M: He got Fred to cut them because he doesn't like to climb ladders.
   Who cut the dead branches?
3. M: Mike consulted Steve about the overcharge.
   W: I would have consulted Tom myself.
   Who consulted Steve?
4. M: Ms. Jones admitted Mary into the testing center without an I.D.
   W: Dr. Welsh would have too.
   Who admitted the student?
5. W: Ellen's mother wouldn't permit her to use the family car.
   M: I know. But her father did.
   Who let Ellen use the car?
6. W: Rebecca asked both Amy and Barbara to take her home.
   M: Actually, Amy was the one who took her.
   Who needed a ride home?

7. M: It's Mary's fault that Alex cut his finger.
   W: Still, Alex should have been more careful.
   Who caused the accident?

8. M: Sue wished that Jane had told her the travel plans.
   W: Why didn't she call and ask?
   Who knew the travel plans?

Exercise L33   Understanding negative meaning

1. W: I heard you had a little problem with the calculus exercises.
   M: Are you joking? Never have I had so much trouble in my life.

2. W: Who you know, not what you know, will get you that job.
   M: I guess I'd better not apply then.

3. W: I didn't see a single blouse I liked.
   M: What are you going to do?

4. M: I've never seen Mark so tense about an exam.
   W: I can understand why. It's an important one.

5. W: There was hardly enough equipment to go around.
   M: You're lucky some students were absent.

6. M: Beth isn't half bad looking.
   W: That's true.

7. W: Seldom has Robert gone to so much trouble to please his parents.
   M: Why is he doing that now?

8. W: I'll never understand why Steve isn't more ambitious.
   M: Neither will I.

Exercise L34   Understanding modals

1. W: When we lived in the country, we'd take long walks.
   M: I'd like to do that.

2. W: Are you going to the cafeteria with us?
   M: I really must finish this report before anything else.

3. M: Will you be attending the graduation ceremonies this year?
   W: Only if I graduate.

4. M: Did Jim call a plumber to fix the leaking faucet?
   W: That would have been a waste of money. It only needed a new washer.

5. W: You should have been at the soccer match on Friday.
   M: So it was a good game, was it?

6. M: You might get Professor Roth for biology.
   W: By the time I take that course, he will have retired.

7. W: We will have been married ten years on our next anniversary.
   M: How are you going to celebrate?

8. W: Can Henry really be taking up skiing?
   M: That's what I heard.

Exercise L35   Identifying conditions

1. W: I wouldn't have studied so hard if I'd known the test only covered Unit 10.
   M: Now you don't have to study as hard for the final.

2. W: If you had come to the meeting, you would have met Helen Martin.
   M: She's the famous poet, isn't she?

3. M: If Sue gets another low grade, she'll be put on probation.
   W: She'd better start studying.

4. M: Marion would have attended the protest march if her father hadn't come for a visit.
   M: She should have brought him.

5. M: Had Marvin had the money, he could have gone with Larry.
   W: Larry could have offered to pay.

6. W: What shall we do if our experiment doesn't work?
   M: We'll think about that if it happens.

7. W: I wonder what would have happened if Peggy had told Bruce to leave her alone.
   M: I don't think it would have mattered.

8. M: No matter how hard I try to solve this problem, I just can't seem to get it.
   W: If you took a walk to clear your mind, it might help.

Exercise L36   Identifying causes and results

1. M: As long as the movie at the Student Union is free, why don't we go there?
   W: That's a good idea.

2. M: Now that I live in an apartment, I do my own cooking.
   W: Maybe you'd cook dinner for me sometime!

3. M: Since Monday is a national holiday, all the banks will be closed.
   W: I'd better get some cash out today.

4. W: It was such a beautiful day, I skipped class.
   M: You shouldn't have. Professor Gordon gave a pop quiz.

5. M: I went into the office because I needed to get some work done.
   W: Did you finish everything?

6. M: Did you buy Linda's car?
   W: No, it was so expensive, we had to decline.

7. M: My parents are going to call tonight, so I am staying home.
   W: Give them my regards.

8. M: As long as the coffee is ready, I think I'll have some.
   W: Do you take sugar?

Exercise L37   Understanding other structures

1. M: Mary stopped to buy jam.
   W: Oh, I hope she remembered to pick up bread, too.

2. M: I asked Ralph to wait before signing the contract.
   W: He took your advice and will see a lawyer tomorrow.

3. W: Chris remembered not to lock the door.
    M: We really should get an extra key made.
4. M: I'd better apply for a student loan next semester.
    W: Why don't you apply for the work-study program?
5. M: Ms. Stevenson is used to working late at the geology lab.
    W: I hope she doesn't expect me to.
6. W: I was to have turned in that report yesterday.
    M: Well, don't put it off any longer.
7. M: John forgot to get the theater tickets.
    W: I hope they aren't sold out.
8. M: I wonder if that's the correct date and time for the test.
    W: Well, Pamela herself said that date and time.

Exercise L38   Mini-test

Directions: You will hear short conversations between two people. After each conversation, a third person will ask a question about what was said. You will hear each conversation and the question about it only <u>one</u> time.

After you hear a conversation and the question about it, read the four possible answers in your book and decide which <u>one</u> is the best answer to the question you heard. Then circle the letter that corresponds to the answer you have chosen.

Listen to an example.

On the recording, you hear:
(First Man)   Lee wanted Mary to tell Ann about his accident.
(Woman)   Mary is good at breaking bad news.
(Second Man) What happened to Lee?

In your workbook, you read:
(A) He was told the news.
(B) He had an accident.
(C) He got a lucky break.
(D) He broke his back.

You learn from the conversation that Lee had an accident. The best answer to the question "What happened to Lee?" is (B), "He had an accident." Therefore, the correct choice is (B).

1. W: Now that you have a new car, are you going to give me a ride to campus?
    M: Well, that depends on when you have to be there.
    What does the man mean?
2. M: Peter must be very happy to have passed the French exam.
    W: Yes, but he almost didn't pass.
    What happened to Peter?
3. W: I can't make it to the hospital, so can you give Tom this get-well card?
    M: Sure. Is there anything you want me to tell him?
    What is the woman's problem?
4. W: I thought you liked sports whereas your older brother preferred reading.
    M: No. On the contrary.
    What does the man mean?

5. M: Mary mentioned that you've stopped giving the aerobics class.
    W: Yes. But only until next month.
    What does the woman mean?
6. W: Have you been going over the computer results?
    M: Have I! And you won't believe the statistics.
    What does the man mean?
7. M: If I get this report to you by Tuesday, could you have it typed by Wednesday?
    W: That depends on how legibly you write.
    What does the woman mean?
8. W: Bob let me use his new cassette recorder to record the geography lecture.
    M: I bet he wouldn't let me touch it.
    What does the man mean?
9. W: Not only did Dan complain to the department head, but Maria did as well.
    M: I think they're exaggerating the problem somewhat.
    Who is exaggerating the problem?
10. W: I would rather go to the mall or the street bazaar than go shopping downtown.
    M: Well, the mall is definitely not where I want to go.
    Where will the man and woman probably go?
11. W: Whenever Andrew walks into the room, Joan walks out.
    M: They really had a big argument, didn't they?
    What is the problem?
12. W: Roger was to have been here an hour ago.
    M: Well, you know Roger. He'll be here in an another hour.
    What does the man mean?
13. M: Nancy had no problems selling her car.
    W: I wouldn't have bought it.
    What does the man mean?
14. M: My last final is on Wednesday.
    W: I will have finished my finals by Monday.
    What does the woman mean?
15. W: I can't get any studying done with all your talking.
    M: Why don't you try going to the library?
    What does the woman want to do?

Exercise L39   Identifying what people are doing
1. M: How about a cup of coffee?
    W: What a good idea.
2. W: The chemistry exam was much more difficult than necessary.
    M: Cheer up. You probably did all right.
3. M: I missed your class last week, Professor Blair, because my uncle died.
    W: I'm sorry to hear that.
4. M: Can you fit me in during the morning?
    W: Well, there is a cancellation at 11:45. Is that too late?
5. W: Would you give me a hand with these boxes?
    M: Which hand would you like?

6. M: I'd look better with a mustache. Don't you think so?
   W: You sure would.
7. M: I don't understand all this mix up.
   W: Well, don't worry yourself about it.
8. M: My watch needs fixing.
   W: Why don't you take it to the jewelry store?

Exercise L40   Understanding responses

1. M: I can write better essays than Paul.
   W: Oh you can, can you?
2. M: Professor Davis assigned another three books in class today.
   W: I sure am sick of his busywork.
3. W: How about going to the movies tonight?
   M: I'm sorry. I've got a headache.
4. W: That was a very interesting lecture Dr. Elliot gave, wasn't it?
   M: Oh, I don't know.
5. W: Shall we have dessert?
   M: I'm on a diet.
6. M: May I use the car to run down to the grocery store?
   W: The keys are on the table.
7. M: The paintings in the exhibition look like the work of a child.
   W: Personally, I like them.
8. M: Those cookies look fresh from the oven.
   W: Help yourself.

Exercise L41   Getting all the facts

1. W: My sandals would be easier to pack, and I could wear my high heels.
   M: Just don't pack your climbing boots.
2. W: How about picking up some coffee on your way home?
   M: O.K. I'll get some more of these crackers, too.
3. W: Where were you? The plane's boarding.
   M: I was waiting for you at the check-in desk. It's lucky I thought to look for you at the gate.
4. W: Did you graduate in 1983 or 1985?
   M: Neither. I graduated in 1982.
5. W: First, I'm stopping at the photographer's and then the flower shop.
   M: Could you drop me off at the health club?

Exercise L42   Identifying who

1. M: Cathy, did you invite Sue to Jim's party?
   W: Of course I invited her.
   Who's having a party?
2. W: Robert, do you know Ted's phone number?
   M: No, but Frank surely has it.
   Whose number does the woman want?
3. M: Mary did an excellent job of singing.
   W: John and Sara backed her up nicely on the guitars, too.
   Who did the singing?
4. W: Max is taller than either Ned or Ben.
   M: But Ben is short for his age, don't forget.
   Who is short for his age?

5. W: Shall we stop at Donna's on the way home?
   M: Oh, I promised Jackie and Liz that I'd be home by nine.
   Who does the woman want to visit?

Exercise L43   Identifying where

1. M: Have you made an itinerary for your trip to Europe yet?
   W: Yes. I'm spending three weeks in France, one week in Spain, and two weeks in Italy.
   Where is the woman spending three weeks?
2. W: Are you going to the boxing match or the football game?
   M: To be truthful, I'm going to the movies for a change.
   Where is the man going?
3. W: I need to pick up my suit at the dry cleaner's on my way to the clinic.
   M: Would you have time to drop me off at the bookstore?
   Where does the man want to go?
4. M: I can't identify Victoria's accent.
   W: She was born in the Midwest, raised in Texas, studied in Boston, and now lives in New York.
   Where did Victoria study?
5. M: I turn at the stop sign, don't I?
   W: No, you pass the school and turn at the light.
   Where does the man think he should turn?

Exercise L44   Identifying what

1. W: I'm really enjoying this bestseller. Have you read it yet?
   M: I don't have enough time to read short stories or poetry, let alone a novel like that one.
   What is the woman doing?
2. W: Not only is there a mountain climbing expedition planned for the weekend after next, but a skiing trip as well.
   M: Oh, no! That's the weekend I planned on rafting down the Colorado River.
   What was the man planning to do?
3. M: Joan doesn't go to parties, does she?
   W: No, she prefers reading and listening to classical music.
   What doesn't Joan do?
4. W: I'd really like to watch that documentary on channel 10.
   M: But there's a golf tournament on channel 8 followed by an old Woody Allen movie.
   What does the woman want to watch?
5. M: While you pay the bill, I'm going to get the car.
   W: Okay. I'll wait for you in front.
   What is the man going to do?

Exercise L45   Identifying when

1. W: What days do you work at the snack bar, Pat?
   M: Friday and Saturday afternoon and Thursday evening.
   What night does Pat work?

2. W: The ballet starts at 8:30.
   M: It's 6:15 now. If we left on the 6:30 train, we'd have time for a coffee before the show.
   What time is it now?
3. W: We have two morning flights; Flight 620 departing at 10:00 and flight 340 at 11:45.
   M: Do you have any flights that leave after 4:30 in the afternoon?
   When does the man want to leave?
4. M: Will you be arriving in the morning or afternoon?
   W: I'm sorry, Dad. My bus doesn't get in until evening. Will that cause a problem?
   When will the woman arrive?
5. M: Bill's surgery the day before yesterday went so well that he was released from the hospital last night.
   W: I thought his operation was scheduled for this morning.
   When was Bill able to leave the hospital?

Exercise L46   Identifying how much and how many

1. M: I want to exchange this striped shirt for the plaid one.
   W: Let's see. The striped shirt cost $26.53 and the plaid, $24.49. That's a difference of $2.04.
   How much did the plaid shirt cost?
2. M: Fewer than a dozen people came to the meeting.
   M: Really? I expected twice that many to come.
   How many people were at the meeting?
3. W: It's only three more weeks until final exams.
   M: That means fifteen more chemistry classes and only six more math classes.
   How many more times will the man have chemistry classes?
4. M: Fifty percent of the students failed the exam.
   W: That doesn't surprise me. More than half don't attend regularly.
   How many students failed?
5. W: Do you sell hiking boots here?
   M: Yes, we do. They're on special this week. Only $49.95 a pair, which is a savings of $6.00, or two for $96.99.
   How much money can be saved?

Exercise L47   Inferring activities through vocabulary

1. W: My ace takes your king.
   M: Just a minute. Which suit is trump?
   What are the people doing?
2. W: O.K., so I put the ball on the tee, hold the club this way, and swing like this.
   M: Wow! You almost got a hole in one. See your ball on the green?
   What is the woman learning?
3. M: Is it my turn to roll the dice?
   W: No. You just landed on the "collect $200" square.
   What are these people doing?
4. M: You certainly finished the front quickly.
   W: Yes, that new lawn mower is really efficient.
   What was the woman doing?

5. M: Here's a pail of soapy water.
   W: Thanks, Dennis. I'll really need it to get the mud off the fenders and tires.
   What is the woman going to do?

Exercise L48   Inferring professions through vocabulary

1. M: I'd like turkey on rye, please.
   W: Would you like anything to drink with your sandwich, sir?
   What is the woman's job?
2. W: I'm looking for a biography of T. E. Lawrence.
   M: Have you checked the card catalog under "subject"?
   What is the man's profession?
3. W: Could you tell me where the soups are?
   M: They're in aisle 10 next to the canned fruits and vegetables.
   What is the man's job?
4. M: I really hate all this sticky makeup.
   W: Well, tonight is your last performance of the season.
   What is the man's profession?
5. W: The hole in the radiator couldn't be fixed so I had to replace it.
   M: Okay. I see you checked all the brake shoes, too.
   What is the woman's profession?

Exercise L49   Inferring locations through vocabulary

1. W: Who do I see about opening an account?
   M: Would you like a savings account or a checking account?
   Where does this conversation take place?
2. M: Could you please hand me the suntan lotion?
   W: Sure. But it's covered with sand.
   Where does this conversation take place?
3. W: When is the latest I can return the car?
   M: At this time tomorrow. And remember there's an extra charge if you don't bring it back with a full tank of gas.
   Where does this conversation take place?
4. M: I've come to report a missing van.
   W: The chief is busy right now. You can give the details to Officer Jacobs.
   Where does this conversation take place?
5. W: Did you see that? Carol sure can dive!
   M: She's also got the strongest breast stroke of anyone on the team.
   Where does this conversation take place?

Exercise L50   Identifying feelings, attitudes, and personality traits

1. M: What's the matter, Lisa?
   W: Oh, I just failed Spanish again.
   How does Lisa probably feel?
2. W: Would you like me to explain those formulas before the test?
   M: What's the use? I can't understand a thing.
   How does the man feel?

3. W: You really can't go to class in that outfit.
   M: Just watch me.
   What do we learn about the man?

4. W: How do you think you'll do in the final play-offs?
   M: We'll win hands down.
   How does the man feel?

5. W: Have you decided whether or not you're going to summer school?
   M: Not yet. What would you do if you were me?
   How can the man be described?

6. W: Cindy hasn't turned in her assignment.
   M: That's nothing new. She always sleeps through class, too.
   What is Cindy like?

7. W: If you want that report typed accurately and punctually, give it to Stephanie.
   M: I'll take your advice on that.
   What is Stephanie like?

8. W: Is there a cat in the house? I'm allergic to them.
   M: Yes, there is.
   Why is the woman concerned about cats?

Exercise L51   Drawing conclusions

1. M: Let's go get a nice cold drink.
   W: And miss the final inning?

2. M: Where's the glass of milk I set on the table?
   W: Oh, didn't you hear that crash a little while ago?

3. M: I heard you were having a little trouble with the math assignment.
   W: No kidding! Could I come over for some help tonight?

4. W: I've told Chris time after time to study harder.
   M: He never listens.

5. W: Since Dave is bringing his friend, why don't you invite Tim?
   M: Tim and Dave don't get along.

6. M: The party will be over by the time we get there.
   W: Don't be silly. We aren't that late.

7. W: Until Linda started working at the department store, she didn't have any sales experience.
   M: That's encouraging. Maybe they'll hire me.

8. W: What have you written recently?
   M: Nothing that you would want to read.

Exercise L52   Mini-test

Directions: You will hear short conversations between two people. After each conversation, a third person will ask a question about what was said. You will hear each conversation and the question about it only one time.

After you hear a conversation and the question about it, read the four possible answers in your book and decide which one is the best answer to the question you heard. Then circle the letter that corresponds to the answer you have chosen.

Listen to an example.

On the recording, you hear:
(Man)   Where did you put the leftover pizza?

(First Woman)   I threw it out.
(Second Woman) What can we say about the woman?

In your workbook, you read:
(A) She left the pizza out.
(B) She got sick.
(C) She doesn't like cold pizza.
(D) She forgot the pizza.

You learn from the conversation that the woman threw out the leftover (cold) pizza. The best answer to the question "What can we say about the woman?" is (C), "She doesn't like cold pizza." Therefore, the correct choice is (C).

1. M: How about going out to eat this evening?
   W: I'm afraid I have to write this accident report.
   What does the woman mean?

2. W: Here are your tickets, sir. The train will depart from platform 6 at two o'clock.
   M: Thank you. And could you tell me if there's a dining car on this train?
   What is the woman's job?

3. W: Tim was upset because he didn't get to Boston.
   M: He shouldn't be that upset. After all, he did get to Washington, D.C., and New York City.
   Where did Tim go?

4. W: The concert starts at 8:15 and ends at about 10:30.
   M: That means we'll be home around midnight.
   What time does the concert begin?

5. W: Where did you get those fancy jogging outfits?
   M: They were on sale. Two for the price of one at $29.95.
   How much did the two outfits cost?

6. M: I'm going to take the car in for an oil change.
   W: And leave me to take the children to their music lesson by bus?
   What do we learn from this conversation?

7. W: Have you already packed the tent and the cooler?
   M: Yes. I've thrown in some extra blankets and the first aid kit, too.
   Where are the people going?

8. M: I have to check this book out and then I'll be ready to go.
   W: I'll wait for you by the card catalog.
   Where does this conversation take place?

9. W: Would you prefer to go to the movies or the theater?
   M: Neither. I want to stay home and watch football on TV.
   Which activity is not mentioned?

10. W: This is the first time I've seen you studying.
    M: I have to study. Final exams are next week.
    What can be said about the man?

11. W: How can you be so worried about a little interview?
    M: Little? This is the most important event in my life.
    What does the man mean?

12. M: Could you show me how to order these black
shoes from this catalog?
   W: Sure. Tear the order form out of the book. Now
fill in these numbers in this space.
   What are the people doing?

13. W: Have you seen Lynn's new dog?
   M: Oh, I heard she'd gotten a cat.
   What do we learn from this conversation?

14. M: When are you going to return my book?
   W: Oh, I was hoping you'd forgotten about it.
   What can be said about the woman?

15. M: That's the last time I'm helping Rita.
   W: She never thanks anyone for their time and
trouble.
   What do we learn about Rita?

Part C   Short talks and conversations

Exercise L53   Predicting the topic from the first statement

1. W: What did the doctor tell you about that wart?
2. M: I would like to purchase a Persian carpet, but I
don't know much about them.
3. W: The United Kingdom is made up of four countries
– England, Northern Ireland, Scotland, and
Wales.
4. M: Architects from around the world vote for the
architect they believe should receive their Award
for Architecture.
5. M: Let me show you our selection of Irish linen to
help you get a better idea of the various patterns
available.

Exercise L54   Identifying the topic from the first statement

1. W: The practice of acupuncture was started in China
about five thousand years ago.
2. M: Muscles are made of many fine fibers about
twenty-five millimeters long.
3. W: The metal shelves at the hardware store are good
quality and not very expensive.
4. W: What did Jim tell you about the skiing
competition in Sun Valley last week?
5. M: A whole new world of possibilities and
challenges in education has been opened up by
satellite communications technology.

Exercise L55   Determining if the topic is stated in the first sentence of a passage

1. M: A magic square is a square-shaped arrangement
of numbers. The numbers are arranged so that
the horizontal, vertical, and diagonal groups of
numbers all add up to the same figure. The
largest magic square ever devised had 578,865
boxes.
2. W: In the mid-1800s, the Overland Mail stagecoach
carried the mail across the American continent.

Because this service was unsatisfactory, a
freighting firm established a new service called
the Pony Express. The Pony Express used relays
of pony riders. These daring young riders made
weekly treks across the rough and dangerous
terrain between St. Joseph, Missouri, and
Sacramento, California. Although very
successful, the Pony Express was short lived.
After only sixteen months of service, it was
replaced by the telegraph.

3. M: I was supposed to buy a lot more books but I
didn't have enough money.
   W: You are always short of money. Why don't you
look for a part-time job?
   M: I'm afraid a job would interfere with my studies.
   W: I don't think so. They're always looking for
people to work at the concession stands during
the sports events and concerts.
   M: Hey, I could see the games and concerts for free
while I earned money!
   W: That's right. And it would not take that much
time away from your studying.

4. W: I've managed to find an apartment close to
campus.
   M: That was lucky. They are not very easy to get.
Everyone seems to want one.
   W: Yeah. It's more expensive than one further away,
but I will save on commuting expenses.

5. W: The wealthy have kept their own private
collections of animals for thousands of years. The
first public zoo, however, was not opened until
1793, at the Jardin des Plantes in Paris. Zoos have
not only protected endangered species but have
allowed people to see exotic animals without
having to travel to distant countries.

Exercise L56   Predicting what will logically follow the topic sentence

1. There are a number of human and animal-shaped
figures carved in hillsides around the world.
2. Hello, the Dover Temporary Employment Service sent
me.
3. Would anybody like another turkey sandwich?
4. Goethe was not the only German of his time to be
attracted to Italy.
5. How are you feeling this morning?

Exercise L57   Multiple meanings

1. The notorious pirate known as Blackbeard is rumored
to have buried treasures of gold, silver, and precious
stones at many sites along the Atlantic seaboard.
2. Archaeologists believe that a pilot excavation at the
fabled tomb of China's first emperor would require
financing from the state.
3. Recent explorers have been unable to locate the island
that was vividly described in the captain's log in
March of 1783.

4. Some people believe that the Voodoo Lily casts a spell on its insect visitors in order to achieve cross-pollination.

5. By the time Mozart was eight years old, he had already composed a great deal of music.

6. The executive secretary of the Protection of the Marine Environment Organization has reported that a large number of dead fish, dolphins, and whales have been spotted off the east coast.

7. Twenty-two men from the Red Army had to storm the Luding Bridge after an all-night march to capture a needed escape route for Mao Tse-tung's forces.

8. Steamed spinach, chopped and lightly sauteed with butter and garlic, was the choice for the first course.

Exercise L58   Understanding referents in a statement

1. When surnames first came into use, they generally referred to occupations or places of residence.

2. The ancient Egyptians mummified the bodies of distinguished people as well as those of sacred animals.

3. Most mosses live in moist habitats, but there are some that have adapted to living on rocks.

4. Although they are not trained for specific jobs, hospital volunteers give valuable help to patients.

5. To escape persecution in their own country, the pilgrims set sail for America.

Exercise L59   Understanding referents in a passage

1. Because of the breakdown of the traditional family in some countries, many elderly people have no home and no one to help them in an emergency. In order to address these problems, delegates to the United Nations Symposium on Population met to pool their ideas and make recommendations.

2. M: I've come about the washing machine.
   W: Oh, good. It has been broken for a week. The water isn't draining and there's a peculiar noise.
   M: When is that? When you start a load or while one is being washed?

3. M: I heard there was a fire in your neighborhood last night.
   W: Yes. An abandoned warehouse caught fire. The police suspect an arsonist started it.
   M: Why do they think that?
   W: Because an empty can of gasoline and a box of matches were found nearby.

4. To climb Mount Everest is the dream of every mountaineer. In order for an alpine club to make this climb, it must apply to the Nepalese Tourism Ministry for a permit. Normally these are granted to only three groups per season.

5. W: Did you know that the Pickfords are moving to the East Coast? Mr. Pickford has a new job there.
   M: Mrs. Pickford won't want to give up her teaching position.
   W: I'm sure she'll find a new one there.

Exercise L60   Understanding restatements

1. The dialect spoken in Kárpathos is so old that many words date back to the time of Homer.

2. A Frenchman's twenty-five-minute flight in a hot-air balloon in 1783 was the first manned flight.

3. One of the most beautiful birds in the world, the quetzal, takes its name from the Aztec word meaning "tail feather."

4. Many relief centers were set up in the drought-stricken areas.

5. Recently discovered fossils have revolutionized our concept of the human past.

Exercise L61   Getting all the facts

1. M: I think I'm going to sell my car and get a bicycle.
   W: Why not take the bus? The service here is very good.
   M: It's not that good. Besides, riding bicycles is healthy, and they're cheap and easy to maintain.

2. M: What kind of house were you thinking of buying?
   W: We'd like to have a small one in a quiet suburb near the downtown area.
   M: The Los Altos district is quiet and it's within a ten-minute drive from downtown.

3. Arthritis is one of the oldest complaints that has tormented not only the human race but animals as well. Even dinosaurs suffered from it millions of years ago. The earliest known example of one with arthritis is the platycarpus.

4. Some people were nervous about the restoration of Michelangelo's frescoes on the ceiling of the Sistine Chapel. Painted there at the height of the Renaissance, they are Italian national treasures which could have been damaged as other treasures have been in the past due to restorers' blunders.

5. Every year game manufacturers introduce many new games to the public. These are designed to puzzle, preoccupy, frustrate, and delight millions of fun seekers around the world who roll the dice, pick a card, guess a quote, or buy a property according to the game. Very popular on the market in recent years have been the ones which test a player's general knowledge.

Exercise L62   Identifying who

1. W: Do you know who Carl picked for the lead part?
   M: Angela.
   W: Angela? I thought that Terry did a much better job of acting.
   M: Perhaps, but she doesn't sing as well.
   According to the woman, who does the best acting?

2. W: I saw a very good movie about Agatha Christie.
   M: Was that the one with Vanessa Redgrave as Agatha?
   W: Yes, and Dustin Hoffman played a reporter. Did you see it?
   M: No, but I read the reviews.
   Who played the reporter?

3. William Cody, more widely known as Buffalo Bill, was an American showman who founded the great "Wild West Show" in 1883. He traveled around Europe with other famous people such as the sharpshooter Annie Oakley and the Indian "Chief Sitting Bull" to perform for many heads of state, like the Czar of Russia and the King of England.
Who was a famous sharpshooter?

4. Just before the turn of the twentieth century, a new musical form captivated America: ragtime. Although ragtime had its start in 1897 with William Krell's "Mississippi Rag," it was Scott Joplin who popularized the form with his "Maple Leaf Rag." John Philip Sousa began to feature rags in his band concerts in America and Europe. By the early 1900s, ragtime was the most popular art form in America.
Who popularized ragtime?

Exercise L63   Identifying where

1. M: Have you decided whether you'll spend the winter break in California or Arizona?
   W: Well, we had decided to go to Arizona, but our plans have suddenly changed.
   M: Why? What happened?
   W: My brother called. He's being transferred to Alaska and he's asked us to help him move.
   M: So instead of escaping the cold, you're going where it's even colder?
   W: Yes. But I'm looking forward to it. I've never been there before.
   Where is the woman going?

2. W: Are you going to meet me at the club?
   M: Yes. I think that would be the easiest place to meet. Then we can share a taxi to the theater.
   W: What time shall I be there?
   M: I usually leave the office at six o'clock, so I can be at the club by seven o'clock at the latest.
   W: Good. We'll plan on seven o'clock then.
   Where are the people going after they meet?

3. W: The proposed Fine Arts building would serve the university drama and music majors as well as the art majors. The building would contain several stages – a main stage for visiting groups and major productions and two smaller stages for experimental theater classes. For the music majors, a large concert hall and many practice rooms are planned. Finally, for the art majors, the building would provide an exhibition hall with a permanent collection and space for students' temporary shows as well as many work rooms and classrooms.
   Where will the art students show their work?

4. M: Walls built to serve as barriers against attacks can be found in several countries. The Romans built two walls in the north of England, Hadrian's Wall and the Antonine Wall. Both of these were many miles long and were built as a defense against invaders from Scotland. Another well-known wall is the Great Wall of China. This was also built as a means to protect people from invaders.
In which country is Hadrian's Wall?

Exercise L64   Identifying what

1. W: How is your job at the library working out?
   M: Very well. I've been working in the acquisitions department.
   W: What do you do there?
   M: Log in new books. The best part of the job is opening the boxes of newly purchased books. It's like getting presents.
   W: That does sound like fun.
   M: Later I have to enter each book into the computer. I don't mind that so much, but I don't like having to paste the checkout sheet into the front cover.
   What does the man like to do?

2. M: I think I'll buy Phil a cassette for his birthday.
   W: I'm going downtown to pick up my new contact lenses. Would you like a ride to the store?
   M: What time would you be going?
   W: About one o'clock.
   M: I have a fencing class then.
   W: I can wait until later if you'd like.
   M: Can you? That would be great.
   What is the woman going to do?

3. Folk dances have been passed on from one dancer to another over the years without the movements being written down. Since this system is not always very accurate, choreographers invented ways of writing down the movements. At first, they drew little pictures under the music. Later a new system which uses dots on lines to represent hands, feet, and heads was invented.
What do choreographers do?

4. It was during his search for a new route to India, that Columbus reached America. Although he made his discovery in 1492, it took a little over 100 years for people to finally settle in the New World. Some settlers hoped to escape from the problems of the Old World by emigrating to the New. Reports that excellent crops could be produced in Virginia induced many more people to make the long journey. America was not the searched-for India but, it offered its settlers a new and potentially rich life.
What did the settlers do?

Exercise L65   Identifying when

1. W: I thought you only had classes from nine o'clock to twelve o'clock.

   M: I did. But my ten o'clock history class was cancelled and the only other class open that would fulfill my course requirements was at two.

   W: I know you prefer classes in the morning, but two o'clock isn't so bad, is it?

   M: Well, I suppose it's better than an evening class.

   What time was the history class to have been held?

2. M: Is Valentine's Day on a Friday or Saturday this year?

   W: I'm almost certain it's on a Thursday.

   M: Darn. I thought it was on the weekend. I was going to invite Karen to that new French restaurant.

   W: Why can't you invite her on Thursday?

   M: Because I have an exam on Friday.

   W: Well, you could invite her out on the weekend to celebrate a late Valentine's Day.

   M: It's not quite the same, but I guess I'll have to do that.

   According to the woman, what day is Valentine's Day?

3. W: The first machine to replace the abacus for calculating was invented by a French mathematician in 1642. In 1671, a German mathematician improved this calculator. Then, in the 1830s, an English mathematician devised another mechanical one that had most of the features of modern computers. This machine was outdated in 1946 when an American developed the electronic computer.

   When was the first calculator invented?

4. M: Pioneers wanting to reach the west coast of America arrived by riverboat at Missouri River towns in the early spring. They hoped to cross the plains and the Rocky Mountains during the summer while the prairie grass would provide food for their animals. They also wanted to arrive in California before the winter snows closed the mountain passes. Those who didn't make it were stranded in the mountains without sufficient provisions for the entire winter.

   When did the pioneers try to reach the Missouri River?

Exercise L66   Identifying how much and how many

1. M: Twenty people are coming to the party, so we'd better get some plastic cups.

   W: There are a dozen cups in this package. We could buy two of them.

   M: Hmm. That would be only four cups extra. Do you think we might need more than that?

   W: They aren't very expensive. Why not get three packages, just in case?

   M: Okay. We can always use any that are left over.

   How many cups are in a package?

2. M: The tickets for the best seats in the concert hall cost $60.00.

   W: That's much more than I meant to pay.

   M: The least expensive ones are $15.00.

   W: Where are the $15.00 seats located?

   M: In the top balcony.

   W: That's too far away. We wouldn't be able to see anything.

   M: The middle balcony costs $25.00, and the first balcony costs $45.00.

   W: Well, the $45.00 seats are still too expensive, but I guess if we really want to enjoy the concert, we'd better get them.

   How much are the tickets the woman decides to buy?

3. W: Since the seventh century, large bells have been used in cathedrals, churches, and monasteries. The greatest bell in the world is in Moscow. This famous "King of Bells" weighs about 198 tons. The next two largest bells are also located in Russia. One near St. Petersburg weighs 171 tons, and another in Moscow weighs 110 tons. Great Paul, the bell at St. Paul's in London, is the largest bell in England, but weighs a mere 17 tons.

   How many tons does the "King of Bells" weigh?

4. M: Hygiene was almost unheard of in Europe during the Middle Ages. Consequently, millions of people died during various epidemics which raged through Europe. The worst outbreak of plague, called the Black Death, struck between the years 1347 and 1351. The populations of thousands of villages were wiped out. In fact, it is thought that about one-third of all the people in Europe perished during the Black Death.

   How many villages were left empty of people?

Exercise L67   Inferring activities through vocabulary

1. M: How many arrows did you get into the bull's-eye?

   W: Are you joking? I hit the target once.

   M: Let me see you shoot.

   W: Okay. There it goes again – way off to the left.

   M: Try holding your bow like this. I think that'll help you hit the target.

   What sport are the people practicing?

2. M: Could you hand me the wrench, please?

   W: Sure. Where is it?

   M: In the toolbox next to the car.

   W: Here you are. Do you need any help under there?

   M: No thanks. As soon as I change these spark plugs, the engine should run smoothly.

   W: Are you going to change the oil, too?

   M: I already have.

   What is the man doing?

3. M: Can I have a light?
    W: I'm sorry. I don't have any matches.
    M: What? I thought you always carried matches or a lighter.
    W: Not anymore. I gave up smoking.
    M: Really? How did you manage that?
    W: I just threw my last pack of cigarettes into the wastebasket and I haven't had one since.
    M: I wish I could do that, but right now I think I'll go crazy if I don't have a smoke.
    What is the man doing?
4. M: Check.
    W: You don't want to do that.
    M: Why not? Can't I move a queen in any direction I want.?
    W: Yes, but I can take your queen with my bishop.
    M: But then I can take your bishop with my knight.
    W: I think your queen would be more of a loss to you than my bishop would be to me.
    M: I see what you mean. Can I change my mind or is it too late?
    W: I'll let you change your mind since you're new at this.
    What are the people doing?

Exercise L68   Inferring professions through vocabulary

1. M: Have you ever had to save a person?
    W: Fortunately not. But I always have to be prepared.
    M: How do you get certified?
    W: You have to pass some swimming tests to prove your proficiency. Then you have to take a course in how to get drowning people safely to shore. And you also have to take life-saving classes.
    M: That sure seems like a lot of training.
    W: Yes, but someone's life may depend on it.
    What is the woman's job?
2. M: What can I do for you?
    W: I'd like a haircut and a permanent.
    M: Just a trim?
    W: No, I want it cut short.
    M: Are you sure? Your hair is so long and in such good condition.
    W: Well, I've been letting it grow for five years now and I'm getting tired of it.
    M: Okay. Come over here to the sink and we'll shampoo your hair first.
    What is the man's profession?
3. M: I'd like to place a collect call to Laramie, Wyoming, please.
    W: What is your name?
    M: Kevin Roberts.
    W: And the number, please?
    M: Area code 307-742-4637.
    W: Just a minute. It's busy, sir. Would you like me to try again?
    M: No, thank you. I'll try later.
    What is the woman's profession?

4. W: This instrument is over two hundred years old.
    M: How exactly does it work?
    W: The organ is actually a wind instrument. When I pull this knob, called a stop, air is pumped through the pipes that correspond to the keys I press.
    M: And the air going through the pipes would be the same as if a person were blowing on an instrument?
    W: That's right.
    M: It must be very difficult to play with your feet and hands at the same time.
    W: Not really. It just takes practice, like playing football or riding a bicycle.
    What does the woman do?

Exercise L69   Inferring locations through vocabulary

1. M1: These carrots look overcooked, and the peas came from a can.
    M2: You don't have to eat them, you know.
    M1: I sure hate eating here.
    M2: It's better than cooking your own meals, and it's a lot cheaper than eating in restaurants.
    M1: But why is the food always so bad?
    M2: Well, it can't be easy to cook for three thousand students and keep the food hot for two hours.
    M1: Still, I sure miss Mom's cooking.
    Where does this conversation take place?
2. M: Could you hand me the binoculars, please?
    W: What do you see?
    M: There's smoke over near the West Bend campground.
    W: A camper may have made a bonfire.
    M: Well, if that's the case, it's out of control. The fire is in the trees.
    W: I'll radio the forest ranger's headquarters so they can send in some fire fighters.
    Where does this conversation take place?
3. M: I want to report a stolen car.
    W: Can you describe it, please?
    M: It's a 1982, four-wheel-drive Subaru.
    W: Where did you last see it?
    M: I went on a weekend outing with a friend and I left it in front of his house on Elm Street.
    W: Let me check our records. Yes, Elm Street was resurfaced on Saturday. Your car was probably towed away.
    M: Where would it have been towed?
    W: The City Roads Department usually has Jim's Wrecker Service do the towing. You can call them from here if you like.
    M: Thank you, officer.
    Where does this conversation take place?

4. M: How do you like this ring?
    W: It's very nice the way the rubies are arranged in a circle around the diamond, but I don't want anything so showy. I'd like something more delicate.
    M: I have a lovely sapphire set in a plain gold band. Here it is.
    W: Yes. That's more like what I was looking for. Only it's too small.
    M: Don't worry about that. It can be made to fit.
    Where does this conversation take place?

Exercise L70   Inferring feelings, attitudes, and personality traits
1. W: I wish I were getting a new car as a graduation present.
    M: Oh, you always want to have what I'm getting.
    W: That's not true.
    M: Yes, it is. Remember when Dad bought me ice skates? You wanted a pair too.
    W: That's different. We were children.
    M: Besides, it's a graduation present, and you're not graduating yet.
    How does the woman feel?
2. W: My dentist said my teeth are in excellent condition.
    M: It's no wonder. You take very good care of them.
    W: It's been worth it, too. I've never had a cavity.
    M: I wish I could say the same thing.
    How does the woman feel about her teeth?
3. W: I just can't get excited about this coming semester.
    M: Once classes start, you'll feel differently.
    W: I hope so. But what if I don't?
    M: Maybe you should drop one of your required courses and add one to take just for fun.
    W: That's a good idea. I'm feeling better about classes already.
    What has the man done?
4. M: I could never work in a hospital. I'd faint at the first sight of blood.
    W: You'd get used to it.
    M: I don't think so. I can't even imagine seeing an accident victim without feeling sick to my stomach.
    W: It's a good thing not everyone feels like you do or there wouldn't be any doctors or nurses.
    How does the man feel?
5. M: When I was a boy, I could run faster and jump higher than anyone else in the school.
    W: Yes, Pete. You've told us more than once how great you are.
    M: That's not true. I've never told you I'm great.
    W: Not in so many words. But we've heard all about your football touchdowns and baseball home runs and . . .
    M: Okay. Okay. I get your point.
    What does the woman think of Pete?

Exercise L71   Remembering details
1. W: At her trial Mata Hari was dubbed the greatest spy of the First World War. Her French accusers brought eight charges of spying against her. However, new research suggests Mata Hari was not really a spy at all.
2. M: Did you end up going to the movies last night?
    W: No, we didn't. We went to a play instead.
    M: What did you see?
    W: A marvelous comedy about life in a small mid-western town. Rosie May Smith was the leading lady.
    M: She's really good, isn't she?
3. W: Where were you when we had the blackout this morning?
    M: In an elevator on my way to a staff meeting.
    W: Were you stuck in an elevator? What did you do?
    M: Well, the alarm didn't work so I just waited.
    W: That must have been awful.
    M: No, not really. I wasn't looking forward to the meeting, and I had a perfect excuse for missing it.
4. W: I always enjoy my first day back to classes.
    M: Do you have a good schedule this term?
    W: Yes, except for a late afternoon chemistry lab on Wednesdays.
    M: I bet that's with Professor Adams. He usually gives that class.
    W: Yes, it is. Is he a good instructor?
    M: I've never had him, but I've heard he gives a quiz every week.
5. M: Every year the Leaning Tower of Pisa lists more perilously. A team of architects plan to cut into the base of this 55-meter high medieval landmark in hopes of stopping or slowing down this movement. If that doesn't work, the architects will consider building a foundation underneath the tower.
6. W: The Manx is the only domestic cat that doesn't have a tail. Legend has it that at the time of the Great Flood the Manx cat was so late in getting to the Ark that Noah closed the door before it was completely inside and cut off its tail.

Exercise L72   Focusing on details
1. W: I saw a marvelous show at the Meridian Arena last night.
    M: Was that the motorcycle stunt show advertised in the Daily Reporter last week?
    W: Yes, it was. Do you know those kids were from six to seventeen years old and they jumped through hoops of fire, sped over cars, and balanced in pyramid formation, all on their motorcycles?
    M: I should have gone. Daredevil acts usually don't interest me, but it sounds like that was a good show.
2. W: The answer to the question of which flying bird is the largest in the world depends on whether birds

are measured by weight, wingspan, or wing area. The South African bustard is the heaviest. The average male weighs about forty pounds. The bird with the longest wingspan is the albatross. The longest measured was 3.4 meters, but there are sure to be others with a span of 3.6 meters. The bird with the largest wings is the South American vulture, commonly called the condor.

3. W: I heard you took an interesting course in New Mexico last summer. What was it?
   M: A course on building mud houses.
   W: Are you joking?
   M: No. First, we studied about the styles of traditional adobe homes in different parts of the world. We learned the techniques to mix sand and water. Then, we dried the mud in molds and built a structure of our own.
   W: Is it true that adobe structures are cool during the day and warm at night?
   M: Yes, it is.

4. W: The coral reef is only fifty feet below us. Now, before we dive, check all your equipment.
   M: Do we need our gloves?
   W: Yes, some of the coral is sharp and can be dangerous.
   M: How long will we be underwater?
   W: About forty-five minutes. Remember to watch me as we're returning to the ship. We need to make our ascent slowly.

5. M: Fox hunting, the "blood sport" enjoyed by Great Britain's landed gentry for centuries, has come under much criticism. The activities of animal rights campaigners such as the Hunt Saboteurs Association have brought media attention to an area which previously excited little interest. The sight of scores of horses, hounds, and red-coated riders setting off across the English countryside in search of a fox may be a thing of the past within a few years.

Exercise L73   Writing details

1. M: The Turkish architecture exhibition at the Metropolitan Museum of Art in Manhattan will run from October twenty-ninth to January eighteenth. There will be a number of events to complement the exhibition. These will include three lectures. Also, there will be an evening of Turkish singing. Gallery opening times are ten o'clock to five o'clock Tuesday through Saturday and twelve o'clock to five o'clock Sundays. The gallery is closed on Mondays.

2. W: Since people communicate mostly through speech, a defect in speaking or hearing abilities can be an enormous handicap. Communication disorders can result from something going wrong with the speech or hearing mechanisms, abnormal functioning of the brain, or an unusual emotional or psychological problem. Fortunately, most communication disorders can be modified with the help of a speech pathologist.

3. W: Even though snatches of Spanish, French, Russian, Chinese, and a dozen other languages besides English can be heard on the streets of major cities in America, the vast majority of people living in the United States communicate in English. Therefore, the United States is considered an English-speaking country. The fact is, however, that no single language is recognized as an official language in the United States Constitution. Most state constitutions don't recognize an official language, although Nebraska made English its official state language early in the twentieth century, and the Louisiana state constitution recognizes both English and French as official languages.

4. W: Whenever anyone near me comes down with a cold, I always catch it and develop a very painful cough.
   M: Did you have bronchitis as a child?
   W: Yes, frequently when I was very young. But, I seem to have outgrown that.
   M: Hmm. Do you cough during the day even when you don't have a cold?
   W: Yes, but I smoke quite a lot.
   M: How much is "a lot?"
   W: Almost a pack a day.
   M: Mmm. OK. Let me listen to your chest now. Breathe deeply.

5. W: I saw in the course catalogue that the university is offering a batik class this semester. Is it still open?
   M: Do you have the course number?
   W: 309.
   M: Yes, it's open. It meets Monday, Wednesday and Friday at nine o'clock.
   W: Do you know if it can be used to meet undergraduate course requirements for art majors?
   M: Yes, it fulfills course requirements for both art and home economics majors.
   W: Good. I'd like to register for it, please.

Exercise L74 Mini-test

Directions: You will hear conversations and talks. After each conversation or talk, you will be asked some questions. You will hear the conversations and talks and the questions about them only <u>one</u> time. They will not be written out for you.

After you hear a question, read the four possible answers in your workbook and decide which <u>one</u> is the best answer to the question you heard. Then circle the letter of the answer you have chosen. Answer all questions on the basis of what is <u>stated</u> or <u>implied</u> by the speakers in the talk or conversation.

Here is an example.

On the recording, you hear:
Listen to a conversation between two friends.

(Woman)	The way David was going on about that terrible virus, I thought that Mary was deathly ill.
(First Man)	What was the matter with her?
(Woman)	It wasn't her at all. He was talking about her computer.
(First Man)	Oh no, that is serious. I hope that program they lent me wasn't contaminated.
(Woman)	Contaminated? Now you're talking nonsense too.
(First Man)	No, I'm not. Did David say whether they have a vaccine yet?
(Woman)	A vaccine? For a computer? I don't believe it!

Now listen to a sample question.

(Second Man) What doesn't the woman believe?

In your workbook, you read:
(A) That her friend is seriously ill.
(B) That the illness is contagious.
(C) That the man is being serious.
(D) That the vaccine is safe.

The best answer to the question "What doesn't the woman believe?" is (C), "That the man is being serious." Therefore, the correct choice is (C).

Remember, you are not allowed to take notes or write in your workbook.

Questions 1 through 3. Listen to a conversation between two friends.

M: I am eliminating all the starches from my diet so I can lose weight.
W: Don't do that. Carbohydrates provide important nutrients, and they actually help you lose weight.
M: How's that?
W: They take longer to digest, so you're not hungry for a longer period of time. Consequently, you eat less.
M: What do you suggest I do then?
W: Cut down on your intake of fats. Animal products contain large amounts of fats.
M: You mean I should become a vegetarian?
W: Oh, no. You need the protein. Just trim the fat off your meat, broil it instead of frying it, and drink low fat milk.
M: So I need to change my cooking habits as well as my eating habits.

1. What is the man's problem?
2. What does the woman suggest?
3. What can be said about eating animal products?

Questions 4 through 7. Listen to a conversation between two friends.

W: Did you enjoy your visit to Saint Martin's Cathedral?
M: Yes. I enjoyed it very much. I especially like the gargoyles. Why did stoneworkers put those grotesque heads on cathedrals anyway? To frighten away bad spirits?

W: No, they're designed to catch the water that runs off the roof when it rains or the snow melts.
M: I see. The water collects in the gargoyle's mouth and is spit out onto the street.
W: That's right. That protects the walls from moisture dripping down and causing erosion. They were also a practical joke.
M: What do you mean?
W: Those ugly faces represent the stoneworkers' friends.
M: Really? I wonder if they stayed friends afterwards.

4. What about St. Martin's particularly impressed the man?
5. Which statement is not true of gargoyles?
6. Why are gargoyles a joke?
7. What does the man think about the joke?

Questions 8 through 11. Listen to a talk.

Penang, Malaysia, is the home of the world's largest butterfly farm. The farm is both a sanctuary and breeding center for the two thousand recorded species of Malaysian butterflies, which are being driven away from populated areas by pollution and industrialization. Studies into tropical butterflies' habitat, diseases that attack caterpillars, and pest control are being conducted there, as is research into how the ecological balance would be affected if foreign butterflies were to be imported and bred on the farm.

8. What is the main idea of the talk?
9. What is being conducted on the farm at Penang, Malaysia?
10. Which activity is not being done on the farm?
11. Whether or not foreign butterflies will be imported depends on what problem?

Questions 12 through 15. Listen to a talk about silhouettes.

The silhouette portrait, in which the shadow of a sitter's profile is captured on paper, is a popular art form at fairs and school carnivals. Originally this kind of portrait was called a "shade." Once the artist captured the shade on paper, it could be transferred onto ivory, plaster, porcelain, or glass. It could also be reduced to fit into brooches, lockets, or rings.

   The name silhouette was taken from the surname of Étienne de Silhouette, an eighteenth-century French finance minister who was infamous for his cost-cutting policies. In ridiculing these policies, opponents coined the term "à la silhouette" to mean "cheap." This phrase was passed on to the art form of profile drawings because it was so inexpensive. However cheap they may have been in the eighteenth century, these curiosities which might be mistaken for junk could be worth large sums of money depending on the date they were made and the artist. The record price paid for an eighteenth-century silhouette is six thousand dollars.

12. What were silhouettes originally called?
13. What is not mentioned as one of the materials artists transferred portraits onto?

14. Who was Étienne de Silhouette?
15. Why are the discussed art forms known as silhouettes?

Exercise L75   Listening Comprehension Practice Test

Section 1   Listening Comprehension

In this section of the test, you will have an opportunity to demonstrate your ability to understand spoken English. There are three parts to this section, with special directions for each part. Do not read ahead or turn the pages while the directions are being read. Do not take notes or write in your workbook at any time.

Part A

Directions: For each question in Part A, you will hear a short sentence. Each sentence will be spoken just once. The sentences you hear will <u>not</u> be written out for you.

After you hear a sentence, read the four choices in your workbook, marked (A), (B), (C), and (D), and decide which <u>one</u> is closest in meaning to the sentence you heard. Then, on your answer sheet, find the number of the question and fill in the space that corresponds to the letter of the answer you have chosen. Fill in the space completely so that the letter inside the oval cannot be seen.

Listen to an example.

On the recording, you hear:
The new observatory is nothing less than outstanding.

In your workbook, you read:
(A) The new observatory is excellent.
(B) There is nothing outstanding to observe.
(C) You must stand outside to make the observance.
(D) His new observations are more outstanding than usual.

The man said, "The new observatory is nothing less than outstanding." Sentence (A), "The new observatory is excellent," is closest in meaning to what the man said. Therefore, the correct choice is (A).

Go on to the next page.

Now we will begin Part A with question number 1.

1. Our exams are over the week after next.
2. He caused me to have an accident.
3. How Robert puts up with Judy's ranting and raving, I'll never know.
4. Sue signed up for a crash course in German.
5. Maria got mixed up and dressed the salad with gravy.
6. Mr. Simmons would prefer walking in the rain to staying at home.
7. Rebecca would have gotten on flight two nineteen at Chicago had she not missed the connecting flight.
8. Virginia still isn't used to cooking on an electric stove.
9. In fact, if Sam hadn't been so rich, Lisa wouldn't have married him.
10. Just after arriving in New York, Mark took a trip to Indiana.
11. Nancy and Ann had to talk over the problem of having the car worked on.

12. Margaret had better apologize to Mrs. Morris for having lost her pearl necklace.
13. Nicky couldn't find out whether the check was good.
14. Fred became irritated when David brought up the problem of students' being late.
15. It's all right with Martha if we skip dessert tonight.
16. What about going to a different restaurant from the Roadside Cafe for a change?
17. As for the money I owe you, you'll have to wait another week.
18. Kim doesn't object to American fast food.
19. Jason has memorized his lines backwards and forwards.
20. Lee must have caught cold.

This is the end of Part A. Go on to the next page.

Now read along with me as I read the directions for Part B. Remember, you may not read ahead or turn the pages while the directions for this part are being read.

Part B

Directions: In Part B you will hear short conversations between two people. After each conversation, a third person will ask a question about what was said. You will hear each conversation and question about it only <u>one</u> time. After you hear a conversation and the question about it, read the four possible answers in your workbook and decide which <u>one</u> is the best answer to the question you heard. Then, on your answer sheet, find the number of the question and fill in the space that corresponds to the letter of the answer you have chosen.

Listen to an example.

On the recording, you hear:
(Man)   I think I'll have the curtains changed.
(First Woman)   They are a bit worn.

(Second Woman)   What does the woman mean?

In your workbook, you read:
(A) She thinks every bit of change is important.
(B) She wants to wear them.
(C) She thinks they've been worn enough.
(D) She thinks they are in bad condition.

You learn from the conversation that the woman thinks the curtains are worn. The best answer to the question "What does the woman mean?" is (D), "She thinks they are in bad condition." Therefore, the correct choice is (D).

Now we will begin Part B with the first conversation.

21. M: How did you ever get Peter to help out at the convention center?
    W: It wasn't easy – I had to twist his arm.
    What does the woman mean?
22. W: That piece doesn't fit there. The pieces don't interlock properly.
    M: Let me see the picture on the box to see where the green pieces go.
    What are the people doing?

23. W: Classes will be over the week after next.
    M: And that's not a minute too soon for me.
    What does the man mean?
24. W: I had a flat tire on the freeway, and my spare was flat too.
    M: You really should buy a whole new set for your car.
    What happened to the woman?
25. W: Was Robert elected student body president?
    M: Of course he was. He promised to help students with housing problems.
    What did Robert do?
26. W: Did Sam trim the hedge himself?
    M: No, he had Barbara do it because of his allergies.
    What do we learn about Sam?
27. M: Jane had no problems passing calculus.
    W: She sure has a mind for it, doesn't she?
    What do we learn about Jane?
28. W: Quick. Hand me the camera. I want to get a shot of that deer.
    M: Sorry. We're out of film.
    Why is the man sorry?
29. M: I wouldn't have failed that test if I'd gone to the review.
    W: And if you had read the books and done the homework.
    What did the man do?
30. M: Wherever I go, I run into Carol.
    W: Did you ever stop to think she may be following you?
    What does the woman mean?
31. W: I don't have enough money to buy gas for the trip.
    M: We could go halves.
    What does the man mean?
32. M: Watch how Jim dribbles the ball down the court.
    W: I know. But he should pass it because he never makes a basket.
    Where does this conversation take place?
33. W: Never have I been more anxious about playing in a concert.
    M: Never have you been heard by a president either.
    What is the woman's problem?
34. W: The car makes a scraping sound when I turn on the ignition.
    M: Why don't you take it in to Mr. Perkins this afternoon?
    What does Mr. Perkins do?
35. W: I've never seen so much traffic on the freeway.
    M: You say that every day.
    What does the man mean?

This is the end of Part B. Go on to the next page.

Now read along with me as I read the directions for Part C. Remember, you may NOT read ahead or turn the pages while the directions for this part are being read.

Part C

Directions: In this part of the test, you will hear longer conversations and talks. After each conversation or talk, you will be asked some questions. You will hear the talks and conversations and the questions about them only one time. They will not be written out for you.

After you hear a question, read the four possible answers in your workbook and decide which one is the best answer to the question you heard. Then, on your answer sheet, find the number of the question and fill in the space that corresponds to the letter of the answer you have chosen. Answer all questions on the basis of what is stated or implied by the speakers in the talk or conversation.

Here is an example.

On the recording, you hear:
Listen to a conversation between a professor and a student.

(First Woman)   Would you please type this paper? I can't read your handwriting.
(Man)   I'm sorry, Professor Mills. I don't have a typewriter, and besides, I can't type.
(First Woman)   Well, rewrite it then, but be sure to make it clear.

Now listen to a sample question.
(Second Woman) What does the professor want the man to do?

In your workbook, you read:
(A) Buy a typewriter.
(B) Read his handwriting.
(C) Clear the papers away.
(D) Rewrite the paper.

The best answer to the question "What does the professor want the man to do?" is (D), "Rewrite the paper." Therefore, the correct choice is (D).

Remember, you are not allowed to take notes or write in your workbook.

Now we will begin Part C.

Questions 36 through 39. Listen to a conversation.
M: I'm really enjoying the Mardi Gras, aren't you?
W: Yes, I drive to New Orleans from Birmingham for this parade every year. I wouldn't miss it.
M: How did you like those French clowns that just passed by? They had clever costumes, didn't they?
W: Yes. They were great. One of the clowns gave me this bracelet.
M: Look at that float coming with all those dancers.
W: And listen to the marvelous Caribbean musicians.
M: I sure can understand why you come here every year. I think I'll come back next year myself.

36. Where does this conversation take place?
37. Where has the woman come from?
38. What does the man want to do next year?
39. What can we infer about the man and woman?

Questions 40 through 44. Listen to a talk about the Boston Tea Party.

The Boston Tea Party of 1773 was not a tea party at all, but the first major act of defiance on the part of the American colonists against their British rulers. The British Parliament under King George the Third had imposed high taxation without representation on the British colonies. A party of prominent citizens disguised themselves as Indians and secretly boarded ships which were laden with tea. These Indians threw the entire cargo of tea overboard. This incident was a prelude to the American War of Independence and perhaps the beginning of a nation of coffee drinkers.

40. What was the Boston Tea Party?
41. According to the passage, when did the Tea Party take place?
42. Why did the Boston Tea Party take place?
43. Who threw the cargo overboard?
44. Where can it be inferred that the Tea Party took place?

Questions 45 through 47. Listen to a conversation between a husband and wife.

M: Rachel, the mail carrier just brought a registered package to the door for you.
W: I haven't ordered anything. Did you sign for it?
M: Yes. It's from Kenya.
W: Oh! It must be from my cousin Betty. Mother wrote that she's moved to Nairobi.
M: What is she doing there?
W: Her husband, Peter, is doing some research for the University of Pennsylvania's Biology Department.
M: That sounds interesting? What's in the package?
W: A family of lions carved in wood.

45. Who sent the package?
46. What did Rachel do?
47. What can be said about the lions?

Questions 48 through 50. Listen to a talk given by a professor to nursing students.

Today I want to show you a new educational tool that we've just acquired. It's an interactive computer system that allows you to make critical health care decisions without endangering patients' lives. The system uses a computer with a touch screen and a videodisc, and it takes you step by step through simulated emergency situations. For instance, on the computer screen you might see a picture of an elderly man being wheeled into the emergency room, complaining that he can't breathe. He shows signs of chronic pulmonary disease. Then you have to decide what to do. If you make the right decision, the computer answers, "Correct."

You can take this pulmonary patient through the entire care process, from emergency admission, initial stabilization, and crisis management to discharge. One particularly helpful aspect of this computer program is that it can simulate body parts onscreen. For example, it can simulate a chest, and you can touch different parts of the chest on the screen or even listen to the lungs, as if you're listening through a stethoscope. At the end of the program, you receive a grade for the work you've done.

48. What is the talk about?
49. In what way is the interactive computer system important?
50. What aspect of the program is mentioned as being particularly helpful?

This is the end of the Listening Comprehension Practice Test.

PRACTICE TEST 1

Section 1   Listening Comprehension

In this section of the test, you will have an opportunity to demonstrate your ability to understand spoken English. There are three parts to this section, with special directions for each part. Do not read ahead or turn the pages while the directions are being read. Do not take notes or write in your workbook at any time.

Part A

Directions: For each question in Part A, you will hear a short sentence. Each sentence will be spoken just once. The sentences you hear will not be written out for you.

After you hear a sentence, read the four choices in your workbook, marked (A), (B), (C), and (D), and decide which one is closest in meaning to the sentence you heard. Then, on your answer sheet, find the number of the question and fill in the space that corresponds to the letter of the answer you have chosen. Fill in the space completely so that the letter inside the oval cannot be seen.

Listen to an example.

On the recording, you hear:
The new observatory is nothing less than outstanding.

In your workbook, you read:
(A) The new observatory is excellent.
(B) There is nothing outstanding to observe.
(C) You must stand outside to make the observance.
(D) His new observations are more outstanding than usual.

The woman said, "The new observatory is nothing less than outstanding." Sentence (A), "The new observatory is excellent," is closest in meaning to what the woman said. Therefore, the correct choice is (A).

Go on to the next page.

Now we will begin Part A with question number 1.

1. He put too much food on his plate.
2. The windows needed washing.
3. Mary is practicing the piano.
4. Leave me alone!
5. John remembered to lock the door.
6. Do you have to go to work for Lee tomorrow?
7. I used to go to evening classes.

8. If he had arrived on time, I wouldn't have been angry.
9. Bob is off his diet.
10. Never has she been so entertained.
11. At the stoplight turn right.
12. I started out before my friends returned.
13. Fishing is not permitted.
14. Her ideas for the party sound great, don't you agree?
15. Dawn had the post office forward her letters.
16. Should we cancel our picnic since the forecast is rain?
17. Jean took a long vacation, and Bill should have, too.
18. He couldn't have returned from the store already!
19. Peter let Robert use the car.
20. The politician was questioned by the interviewer.

This is the end of Part A. Go on to the next page.

Now read along with me as I read the directions for Part B. Remember, you may not read ahead or turn the pages while the directions for this part are being read.

Part B

Directions: In Part B you will hear short conversations between two people. After each conversation, a third person will ask a question about what was said. You will hear each conversation and question about it only one time. After you hear a conversation and the question about it, read the four possible answers in your workbook and decide which one is the best answer to the question you heard. Then, on your answer sheet, find the number of the question and fill in the space that corresponds to the letter of the answer you have chosen.

Listen to an example.

On the recording, you hear:
(First Man)   I think I'll have the curtains changed.
(Woman)   They are a bit worn.

(Second Man) What does the woman mean?

In your workbook, you read:
(A) She thinks every bit of change is important.
(B) She wants to wear them.
(C) She thinks they've been worn enough.
(D) She thinks they are in bad condition.

You learn from the conversation that the woman thinks the curtains are worn. The best answer to the question, "What does the woman mean?" is (D), "She thinks they are in bad condition." Therefore, the correct choice is (D).

Now we will begin Part B with the first conversation.

21. W: It hurts a lot when I drink cold liquids. Do you think it needs to be pulled?
    M: No. I just need to replace the filling.
    Where does this conversation take place?
22. M: Did Jill return your notes last night?
    W: No, and when I see her I'm going to give her a piece of my mind.
    What does the woman mean?

23. M: Where was Bob going in such a hurry?
    W: He was going to pick up his application for a student loan.
    What was Bob going to do?
24. W: Did the drama club members make all the scenery for the play?
    M: Yes, but they had a carpenter design it for them.
    Where did the scenery come from?
25. W: Why hasn't Alex finished his degree yet?
    M: He keeps changing majors.
    What can be said about Alex?
26. M: Your new skirt looks better now.
    W: Thanks. I had the tailor take it in.
    What was done to the skirt?
27. W: Rain has been forecast for the weekend.
    M: Come what may, I'm going camping.
    What does the man mean?
28. M: I've been driving around for an hour and I can't find Elm Street.
    W: There's not a single soul to ask, is there?
    What does the woman mean?
29. W: Did you see the results of the poll?
    M: Yes, they were posted on the bulletin board in the union.
    What did the man say about the poll?
30. M: Why are you eating at this time of day?
    W: I had to leave before breakfast was ready.
    What is the woman's reason for eating now?
31. W: Gloria's giving her presentation this afternoon.
    M: Oh, I don't want to miss that.
    What does the man mean?
32. W: Professor Wilson said we'd have a quiz on Monday.
    M: That's nothing new.
    What do we learn about Professor Wilson?
33. M: We should meet once a week to discuss our term project.
    W: Wednesday afternoons would be a good time for me.
    What can be said about the people?
34. W: You sure have spent a long time on that calculus assignment.
    M: And that's just one on a list of many!
    What does the man mean?
35. M: Would you like to join us for a stroll along the river?
    W: What a pleasant way to spend a warm evening!
    What does the woman imply?

This is the end of Part B. Go on to the next page.

Now read along with me as I read the directions for Part C. Remember, you may NOT read ahead or turn the pages while the directions for this part are being read.

Part C
Directions: In this part of the test, you will hear longer conversations and talks. After each conversation or talk, you will be asked some questions. You will hear the talks and conversations and the questions about them only one time. They will not be written out for you.

After you hear a question, read the four possible answers in your workbook and decide which one is the best answer to the question you heard. Then, on your answer sheet, find the number of the question and fill in the space that corresponds to the letter of the answer you have chosen. Answer all questions on the basis of what is stated or implied by the speakers in the talk or conversation.

Here is an example. On the recording, you hear:

Listen to a conversation between a professor and a student.

(Woman)	Would you please type this paper? I can't read your handwriting.
(First Man)	I'm sorry Professor Mills. I don't have a typewriter, and besides, I can't type.
(Woman)	Well, rewrite it then, but be sure to make it clear.

Now listen to a sample question.
(Second Man) What does the professor want the man to do?

In your workbook you read:
(A) Buy a typewriter.
(B) Read his handwriting.
(C) Clear the papers away.
(D) Rewrite the paper.

The best answer to the question "What does the professor want the man to do?" is (D), "Rewrite the paper." Therefore, the correct choice is (D).

Remember, you are not allowed to take notes or write in your workbook.

Now we will begin Part C.

Questions 36 through 39. Listen to a conversation between a student and a clerk.
W: I'm afraid your student loan money won't be available for another two weeks.
M: Two weeks! Oh, no! Why is that?
W: It appears that your application arrived a few days after the deadline.
M: Does that mean I might not get a loan?
W: No. It means that we had to wait until those who met the deadline were processed before we knew if there was enough money for late applicants.
M: How will I complete my registration without my loan money? The registrar drops students if they fail to pay their tuition fees by September 11th.
W: Students in your situation usually apply for an emergency loan. An emergency loan must be paid back within a month or a very high interest rate will be charged. As soon as you receive your student loan, you use it to pay back your emergency loan.

M: How long does the procedure take?
W: Emergency loans are usually granted on the same day as you apply for them, so you could get one and complete your registration today. Here are the forms.
M: All right. Where do I return the forms?
W: To Mr. Schultz in the office next door.
M: Thank you very much.

36. Where does this conversation take place?
37. What is the student's problem?
38. How long will it be before the student loan is ready?
39. When could the student complete his registration?

Questions 40 through 43. Listen to a talk given by a university librarian.

It is simply not feasible for every university library in the nation to contain all the books and journals that university students and professors need for their research. To meet the needs of their users, libraries have made many innovations. While some money is used for the yearly purchasing of hardbound books and current journals which are recommended by professors, other funds are used to obtain materials which have been put on microfilm and microfiche. These techniques have proved extremely useful for adding informative materials to a library's collection at a low cost and without taking much space. Most libraries now have computers which connect with other libraries. Professors and students can ask their librarian to use a computer search to find a library that has the material they need. The material is then ordered and checked out through this interlibrary loan system, which costs the user a nominal shipping fee.

40. What is the main idea of the talk?
41. What can be inferred from the talk?
42. How do librarians decide what to purchase?
43. According to the talk, what can students do if they can't find a book in the library?

Questions 44 through 47. Listen to a conversation between two people.
W: Excuse me. Is this where the University Shuttle bus stops?
M: Well, that depends on which bus you want. Both the Family Housing bus and the Student Recreation Center bus stop here, but the bus to the Music Complex stops around the corner.
W: Oh, good. How can I tell which one is the Recreation Center bus?
M: It has the letters RC in the window above the windshield.
W: Okay. Do you know when the bus comes by?
M: Every 20 minutes during daytime hours – from 8 a.m. till 5 p.m. After 5, it runs every hour until midnight.
W: Is it usually on schedule?
M: Yes. Except during rush hour. Here comes my bus now. There's the RC right behind it.
W: Well, thanks.
M: Not at all. Goodbye.
W: Bye.

44. Where does this conversation take place?
45. What is the relationship between the man and the woman?
46. What can be inferred from the conversation?
47. What can be said about the woman?

Questions 48 through 50. Listen to a talk about a playwright.

Endesha Ida Mae Holland became a playwright by a mere twist of fate. While studying at the University of Minnesota, Ms. Holland was consumed by activities other than academics. She helped start student groups dedicated to racial progress and black unity. Off the campus, she formed an organization to get former prisoners back on their feet. So diverted, it took her nearly 15 years to earn her bachelor's degree. When she found herself four credit hours short of a degree, she enrolled in an acting course, which she thought would be easy because of her experiences on speaking tours. But by transposing two numbers, Ms. Holland had accidentally signed up for an advanced playwriting seminar. An author was born. Ms. Holland's latest play, *From the Mississippi Delta*, has been staged at major regional theaters in Chicago, Los Angeles, and Washington.

48. What does Ms. Holland do?
49. Why is her career a twist of fate?
50. What did Ms. Holland devote herself to?

This is the end of the Listening Comprehension Section of Practice Test 1.

PRACTICE TEST 2

Section 1   Listening Comprehension

In this section of the test, you will have an opportunity to demonstrate your ability to understand spoken English. There are three parts to this section, with special directions for each part. Do not read ahead or turn the pages while the directions are being read. Do not take notes or write in your workbook at any time.

Part A

Directions: For each question in Part A, you will hear a short sentence. Each sentence will be spoken just once. The sentences you hear will not be written out for you.

After you hear a sentence, read the four choices in your workbook, marked (A), (B), (C), and (D), and decide which one is closest in meaning to the sentence you heard. Then, on your answer sheet, find the number of the question and fill in the space that corresponds to the letter of the answer you have chosen. Fill in the space completely so that the letter inside the oval cannot be seen.

Listen to an example.

On the recording, you hear:
The new observatory is nothing less than outstanding.

In your workbook, you read:
(A) The new observatory is excellent.
(B) There is nothing outstanding to observe.
(C) You must stand outside to make the observance.
(D) His new observations are more outstanding than usual.

The man said, "The new observatory is nothing less than outstanding." Sentence (A), "The new observatory is excellent," is closest in meaning to what the man said. Therefore, the correct choice is (A).

Go on to the next page.

Now we will begin Part A with question number 1.

1. Peter got the waiter to bring the bill.
2. David's problems were solved by a good friend.
3. We were unable to meet Joyce's deadline.
4. Since Diana wants to wash the car, why don't you let her?
5. Lisa has just misplaced her billfold.
6. Why didn't you visit the Statue of Liberty while you were in New York?
7. We can't afford to buy a new car.
8. If you can't make the appointment, please call me.
9. Has she really gained twenty pounds?
10. From our house, you can hear the crowds cheering in the stadium.
11. The flight attendant welcomed the passengers aboard the airplane.
12. Nothing is more certain than Jane's determination to succeed.
13. Only Mary scored high enough to pass this test.
14. Scott studied harder than Susan for the math class.
15. Would you check if my newspaper has come yet?
16. They would rather stay home than go to the movies.
17. Elliot waited over two hours for Betty.
18. William is three years old and speaks quite well for his age.
19. We used to watch tennis, but now we enjoy playing it.
20. The charge for the hotel room does not include breakfast.

This is the end of Part A. Go on to the next page.

Now read along with me as I read the directions for Part B. Remember, you may NOT read ahead or turn the pages while the directions for this part are being read.

Part B

Directions: In Part B you will hear short conversations between two people. After each conversation, a third person will ask a question about what was said. You will hear each conversation and question about it only one time. After you hear a conversation and the question about it, read the four possible answers in your workbook and decide which one is the best answer to the question you heard. Then, on your answer sheet, find the number of the question and fill in the space that corresponds to the letter of the answer you have chosen.

Listen to an example

On the recording, you hear:
(Man)   I think I'll have the curtains changed.
(First Woman)   They are a bit worn.

(Second Woman) What does the woman mean?

In your workbook, you read:
(A) She thinks every bit of change is important.
(B) She wants to wear them.
(C) She thinks they've been worn enough.
(D) She thinks they are in bad condition.

You learn from the conversation that the woman thinks the curtains are worn. The best answer to the question, "What does the woman mean?" is (D), "She thinks they are in bad condition." Therefore, the correct choice is (D).

Now we will begin Part B with the first conversation.

21. W: Did the drama students make all the props for the show?
    M: No, they posted an announcement asking for donations.
        Where did the props come form?
22. M: Who tossed the dice last? I think it's my turn.
    W: No, Sara just moved her token to the blue square.
        What are the people doing?
23. W: Did you get a ticket for the concert tomorrow?
    M: They were sold out weeks ago.
        What does the man mean?
24. W: We need to call Mr. Brown about the television.
    M: I think it's beyond repair.
        What does the man mean?
25. M: Should you get hungry, I packed some apples.
    W: Oh, how thoughtful.
        What does the woman mean?
26. M: I don't imagine Nancy will want to borrow my notes, will she?
    W: Not the way you write.
        What does the woman mean?
27. M: The snowstorm has brought traffic to a standstill.
    W: I hope Tom and Lucy didn't get caught in it.
        What is the woman worried about?
28. W: Jennifer is very close to finishing but won't graduate this spring.
    M: She has to face that fact.
        What does the man mean?
29. M: Did you find the flowered stationery you wanted?
    W: No, I had to settle for the pale blue.
        What does the woman mean?
30. W: You don't care for your chemistry class, do you?
    M: I'll say I don't.
        What does the man mean?
31. M: You make by far the best potato salad I've ever tasted.
    W: Thank you. Even my own mother says that.
        What does the woman mean?
32. W: I sure wish Sam were here.
    M: So do I. His enthusiasm always livens up a dull party.
        What does the man mean?

33. M: When did Susie pay you back?
    W: The week before last, when she got her Christmas bonus.
        When did the woman get her money?
34. M: Is it snowing out?
    W: Is it snowing? You can't even see across the street.
        What does the woman mean?
35. W: Would you have remembered the box if I hadn't called?
    M: Yes, because I tied a string around my finger.
        What did the man do?

This is the end of Part B. Go on to the next page.

Now read along with me as I read the directions for Part C. Remember, you may NOT read ahead or turn the pages while the directions for this part are being read.

Part C

Directions: In this part of the test, you will hear longer conversations and talks. After each conversation or talk, you will be asked some questions. You will hear the talks and conversations and the questions about them only one time. They will not be written out for you.

After you hear a question, read the four possible answers in your workbook and decide which one is the best answer to the question you heard. Then, on your answer sheet, find the number of the question and fill in the space that corresponds to the letter of the answer you have chosen. Answer all questions on the basis of what is stated or implied by the speakers in the talk or conversation.

Here is an example.

On the recording, you hear:
Listen to a conversation between a professor and a student.
(First Woman)   Would you please type this paper? I can't read your handwriting.
(Man)   I'm sorry Professor Mills. I don't have a typewriter, and besides, I can't type.
(First Woman)   Well, rewrite it then, but be sure to make it clear.

Now listen to a sample question.
(Second Woman) What does the professor want the man to do?

In your workbook you read:
(A) Buy a typewriter.
(B) Read his handwriting.
(C) Clear the papers away.
(D) Rewrite the paper.

The best answer to the question "What does the professor want the man to do?" is (D), "Rewrite the paper." Therefore, the correct choice is (D).

Remember, you are not allowed to take notes or write in your workbook.

Now we will begin Part C.

Questions 36 through 39. Listen to a conversation between a professor and a student.

M: Are there any questions concerning the required reading list I've just passed out?

W: Yes, sir. I see that some of the book titles have an asterisk by them.

M: Yes. Those books are out of print and cannot be purchased, so I've put my personal copies on reserve at the library. You'll have to read them there.

W: Okay. Also, I was wondering about the list on the second page. I don't understand the numbers.

M: Oh. These articles are on microfiche. Have you ever used microfiche?

W: No. I'm afraid I haven't.

M: Give that number to the librarian at the reserve desk and he will give you a small folder containing the articles on microfiche. Then, go to the room directly across from the desk where the microfiche machines are. There are pamphlets beside each machine explaining how to insert the microfiche. It's really very easy.

W: Okay. Thank you.

M: That's all for today. Now be prepared to discuss the first reading for our next class.

36. Where does the conversation take place?
37. Why are some book titles marked by asterisks?
38. What can be inferred about the articles?
39. According to the man, how can the woman learn to use the machine?

Questions 40 through 43. Listen to a talk.

In an attempt by researchers to show the interconnectedness of life some intriguing studies have been made. One such study involved a group of monkeys inhabiting an island off the coast of Japan. The monkeys were shown how to eat sweet potatoes in a particular way. The taught behavior was not typical of monkeys. Other monkeys living on the island began to copy this behavior and soon one hundred monkeys were eating sweet potatoes in the new way. At this point monkeys on another island about two hundred miles away began performing the new sweet potato eating behavior. These monkeys had never had contact with the monkeys on the first island. This phenomenon has been called the "hundredth monkey" phenomenon.

40. What is the lecture mainly about?
41. What were the original monkeys taught to do?
42. Where did the original monkeys live?
43. What was said about the taught behavior?

Questions 44 through 47. Listen to a conversation between two friends.

M: Mary, I thought Lisa's surprise birthday party was supposed to be at your place.

W: It was, Jeff, but my parents decided to come for a visit that week.

M: So where will the party be?

W: At Lisa and Jennifer's place.

M: At Lisa and Jennifer's? How will you manage that?

W: I'm going to invite Lisa over to meet my parents, and that will give Jennifer time to decorate their apartment and get everything ready.

M: I hope it works. Is there anything I can do to help?

W: Thanks for the offer, Jeff. I'm sure Jennifer could use some help organizing the food and refreshments.

44. Where will the party be held?
45. Who is the party for?
46. What can be inferred about Lisa and Jennifer?
47. What is the relationship between the people talking?

Questions 48 through 50. Listen to a talk.

The largest, strongest muscles in the body are in the hips, legs and torso, and they're the ones that give the most power to your total body movements. Most athletes work these muscles hard in their fitness program. But arms are at least as important when it comes to carrying through a sport-specific motion, such as swinging a golf club or tennis racket, or throwing a softball or controlling a sailboard.

There are two ways to become more efficient at these motions: practice and gaining strength. You have to repeat the motion literally thousands of times to ingrain its neuromuscular pattern in your subconscious movement memory. And you have to strengthen the muscles so that they can perform the movement with less effort, more power and, often, greater speed. Arm strength training is not time consuming, and its goals are very practical: to reduce your risk of injury and improve your ability to perform sports skills by strengthening muscles, bones, joints and connective tissue.

48. What is the talk about?
49. What was one of the ways to improve efficiency of movement?
50. What is said of arm strength training?

This is the end of the Listening Comprehension Section of Practice Test 2.

ANSWER SHEET FOR THE DIAGNOSTIC TEST

SECTION 1	SECTION 2	SECTION 3

SECTION 1

1. Ⓐ Ⓑ Ⓒ Ⓓ
2. Ⓐ Ⓑ Ⓒ Ⓓ
3. Ⓐ Ⓑ Ⓒ Ⓓ
4. Ⓐ Ⓑ Ⓒ Ⓓ
5. Ⓐ Ⓑ Ⓒ Ⓓ
6. Ⓐ Ⓑ Ⓒ Ⓓ
7. Ⓐ Ⓑ Ⓒ Ⓓ
8. Ⓐ Ⓑ Ⓒ Ⓓ
9. Ⓐ Ⓑ Ⓒ Ⓓ
10. Ⓐ Ⓑ Ⓒ Ⓓ
11. Ⓐ Ⓑ Ⓒ Ⓓ
12. Ⓐ Ⓑ Ⓒ Ⓓ
13. Ⓐ Ⓑ Ⓒ Ⓓ
14. Ⓐ Ⓑ Ⓒ Ⓓ
15. Ⓐ Ⓑ Ⓒ Ⓓ
16. Ⓐ Ⓑ Ⓒ Ⓓ
17. Ⓐ Ⓑ Ⓒ Ⓓ
18. Ⓐ Ⓑ Ⓒ Ⓓ
19. Ⓐ Ⓑ Ⓒ Ⓓ
20. Ⓐ Ⓑ Ⓒ Ⓓ
21. Ⓐ Ⓑ Ⓒ Ⓓ
22. Ⓐ Ⓑ Ⓒ Ⓓ
23. Ⓐ Ⓑ Ⓒ Ⓓ
24. Ⓐ Ⓑ Ⓒ Ⓓ
25. Ⓐ Ⓑ Ⓒ Ⓓ
26. Ⓐ Ⓑ Ⓒ Ⓓ
27. Ⓐ Ⓑ Ⓒ Ⓓ
28. Ⓐ Ⓑ Ⓒ Ⓓ
29. Ⓐ Ⓑ Ⓒ Ⓓ
30. Ⓐ Ⓑ Ⓒ Ⓓ
31. Ⓐ Ⓑ Ⓒ Ⓓ
32. Ⓐ Ⓑ Ⓒ Ⓓ
33. Ⓐ Ⓑ Ⓒ Ⓓ
34. Ⓐ Ⓑ Ⓒ Ⓓ
35. Ⓐ Ⓑ Ⓒ Ⓓ
36. Ⓐ Ⓑ Ⓒ Ⓓ
37. Ⓐ Ⓑ Ⓒ Ⓓ
38. Ⓐ Ⓑ Ⓒ Ⓓ
39. Ⓐ Ⓑ Ⓒ Ⓓ
40. Ⓐ Ⓑ Ⓒ Ⓓ
41. Ⓐ Ⓑ Ⓒ Ⓓ
42. Ⓐ Ⓑ Ⓒ Ⓓ
43. Ⓐ Ⓑ Ⓒ Ⓓ
44. Ⓐ Ⓑ Ⓒ Ⓓ
45. Ⓐ Ⓑ Ⓒ Ⓓ
46. Ⓐ Ⓑ Ⓒ Ⓓ
47. Ⓐ Ⓑ Ⓒ Ⓓ
48. Ⓐ Ⓑ Ⓒ Ⓓ
49. Ⓐ Ⓑ Ⓒ Ⓓ
50. Ⓐ Ⓑ Ⓒ Ⓓ

SECTION 2

1. Ⓐ Ⓑ Ⓒ Ⓓ
2. Ⓐ Ⓑ Ⓒ Ⓓ
3. Ⓐ Ⓑ Ⓒ Ⓓ
4. Ⓐ Ⓑ Ⓒ Ⓓ
5. Ⓐ Ⓑ Ⓒ Ⓓ
6. Ⓐ Ⓑ Ⓒ Ⓓ
7. Ⓐ Ⓑ Ⓒ Ⓓ
8. Ⓐ Ⓑ Ⓒ Ⓓ
9. Ⓐ Ⓑ Ⓒ Ⓓ
10. Ⓐ Ⓑ Ⓒ Ⓓ
11. Ⓐ Ⓑ Ⓒ Ⓓ
12. Ⓐ Ⓑ Ⓒ Ⓓ
13. Ⓐ Ⓑ Ⓒ Ⓓ
14. Ⓐ Ⓑ Ⓒ Ⓓ
15. Ⓐ Ⓑ Ⓒ Ⓓ
16. Ⓐ Ⓑ Ⓒ Ⓓ
17. Ⓐ Ⓑ Ⓒ Ⓓ
18. Ⓐ Ⓑ Ⓒ Ⓓ
19. Ⓐ Ⓑ Ⓒ Ⓓ
20. Ⓐ Ⓑ Ⓒ Ⓓ
21. Ⓐ Ⓑ Ⓒ Ⓓ
22. Ⓐ Ⓑ Ⓒ Ⓓ
23. Ⓐ Ⓑ Ⓒ Ⓓ
24. Ⓐ Ⓑ Ⓒ Ⓓ
25. Ⓐ Ⓑ Ⓒ Ⓓ
26. Ⓐ Ⓑ Ⓒ Ⓓ
27. Ⓐ Ⓑ Ⓒ Ⓓ
28. Ⓐ Ⓑ Ⓒ Ⓓ
29. Ⓐ Ⓑ Ⓒ Ⓓ
30. Ⓐ Ⓑ Ⓒ Ⓓ
31. Ⓐ Ⓑ Ⓒ Ⓓ
32. Ⓐ Ⓑ Ⓒ Ⓓ
33. Ⓐ Ⓑ Ⓒ Ⓓ
34. Ⓐ Ⓑ Ⓒ Ⓓ
35. Ⓐ Ⓑ Ⓒ Ⓓ
36. Ⓐ Ⓑ Ⓒ Ⓓ
37. Ⓐ Ⓑ Ⓒ Ⓓ
38. Ⓐ Ⓑ Ⓒ Ⓓ
39. Ⓐ Ⓑ Ⓒ Ⓓ
40. Ⓐ Ⓑ Ⓒ Ⓓ

SECTION 3

1. Ⓐ Ⓑ Ⓒ Ⓓ
2. Ⓐ Ⓑ Ⓒ Ⓓ
3. Ⓐ Ⓑ Ⓒ Ⓓ
4. Ⓐ Ⓑ Ⓒ Ⓓ
5. Ⓐ Ⓑ Ⓒ Ⓓ
6. Ⓐ Ⓑ Ⓒ Ⓓ
7. Ⓐ Ⓑ Ⓒ Ⓓ
8. Ⓐ Ⓑ Ⓒ Ⓓ
9. Ⓐ Ⓑ Ⓒ Ⓓ
10. Ⓐ Ⓑ Ⓒ Ⓓ
11. Ⓐ Ⓑ Ⓒ Ⓓ
12. Ⓐ Ⓑ Ⓒ Ⓓ
13. Ⓐ Ⓑ Ⓒ Ⓓ
14. Ⓐ Ⓑ Ⓒ Ⓓ
15. Ⓐ Ⓑ Ⓒ Ⓓ
16. Ⓐ Ⓑ Ⓒ Ⓓ
17. Ⓐ Ⓑ Ⓒ Ⓓ
18. Ⓐ Ⓑ Ⓒ Ⓓ
19. Ⓐ Ⓑ Ⓒ Ⓓ
20. Ⓐ Ⓑ Ⓒ Ⓓ
21. Ⓐ Ⓑ Ⓒ Ⓓ
22. Ⓐ Ⓑ Ⓒ Ⓓ
23. Ⓐ Ⓑ Ⓒ Ⓓ
24. Ⓐ Ⓑ Ⓒ Ⓓ
25. Ⓐ Ⓑ Ⓒ Ⓓ
26. Ⓐ Ⓑ Ⓒ Ⓓ
27. Ⓐ Ⓑ Ⓒ Ⓓ
28. Ⓐ Ⓑ Ⓒ Ⓓ
29. Ⓐ Ⓑ Ⓒ Ⓓ
30. Ⓐ Ⓑ Ⓒ Ⓓ
31. Ⓐ Ⓑ Ⓒ Ⓓ
32. Ⓐ Ⓑ Ⓒ Ⓓ
33. Ⓐ Ⓑ Ⓒ Ⓓ
34. Ⓐ Ⓑ Ⓒ Ⓓ
35. Ⓐ Ⓑ Ⓒ Ⓓ
36. Ⓐ Ⓑ Ⓒ Ⓓ
37. Ⓐ Ⓑ Ⓒ Ⓓ
38. Ⓐ Ⓑ Ⓒ Ⓓ
39. Ⓐ Ⓑ Ⓒ Ⓓ
40. Ⓐ Ⓑ Ⓒ Ⓓ
41. Ⓐ Ⓑ Ⓒ Ⓓ
42. Ⓐ Ⓑ Ⓒ Ⓓ
43. Ⓐ Ⓑ Ⓒ Ⓓ
44. Ⓐ Ⓑ Ⓒ Ⓓ
45. Ⓐ Ⓑ Ⓒ Ⓓ
46. Ⓐ Ⓑ Ⓒ Ⓓ
47. Ⓐ Ⓑ Ⓒ Ⓓ
48. Ⓐ Ⓑ Ⓒ Ⓓ
49. Ⓐ Ⓑ Ⓒ Ⓓ
50. Ⓐ Ⓑ Ⓒ Ⓓ
51. Ⓐ Ⓑ Ⓒ Ⓓ
52. Ⓐ Ⓑ Ⓒ Ⓓ
53. Ⓐ Ⓑ Ⓒ Ⓓ
54. Ⓐ Ⓑ Ⓒ Ⓓ
55. Ⓐ Ⓑ Ⓒ Ⓓ
56. Ⓐ Ⓑ Ⓒ Ⓓ
57. Ⓐ Ⓑ Ⓒ Ⓓ
58. Ⓐ Ⓑ Ⓒ Ⓓ
59. Ⓐ Ⓑ Ⓒ Ⓓ
60. Ⓐ Ⓑ Ⓒ Ⓓ

ANSWER SHEET FOR SECTION PRACTICE TESTS

SECTION 1

1. Ⓐ Ⓑ Ⓒ Ⓓ
2. Ⓐ Ⓑ Ⓒ Ⓓ
3. Ⓐ Ⓑ Ⓒ Ⓓ
4. Ⓐ Ⓑ Ⓒ Ⓓ
5. Ⓐ Ⓑ Ⓒ Ⓓ
6. Ⓐ Ⓑ Ⓒ Ⓓ
7. Ⓐ Ⓑ Ⓒ Ⓓ
8. Ⓐ Ⓑ Ⓒ Ⓓ
9. Ⓐ Ⓑ Ⓒ Ⓓ
10. Ⓐ Ⓑ Ⓒ Ⓓ
11. Ⓐ Ⓑ Ⓒ Ⓓ
12. Ⓐ Ⓑ Ⓒ Ⓓ
13. Ⓐ Ⓑ Ⓒ Ⓓ
14. Ⓐ Ⓑ Ⓒ Ⓓ
15. Ⓐ Ⓑ Ⓒ Ⓓ
16. Ⓐ Ⓑ Ⓒ Ⓓ
17. Ⓐ Ⓑ Ⓒ Ⓓ
18. Ⓐ Ⓑ Ⓒ Ⓓ
19. Ⓐ Ⓑ Ⓒ Ⓓ
20. Ⓐ Ⓑ Ⓒ Ⓓ
21. Ⓐ Ⓑ Ⓒ Ⓓ
22. Ⓐ Ⓑ Ⓒ Ⓓ
23. Ⓐ Ⓑ Ⓒ Ⓓ
24. Ⓐ Ⓑ Ⓒ Ⓓ
25. Ⓐ Ⓑ Ⓒ Ⓓ
26. Ⓐ Ⓑ Ⓒ Ⓓ
27. Ⓐ Ⓑ Ⓒ Ⓓ
28. Ⓐ Ⓑ Ⓒ Ⓓ
29. Ⓐ Ⓑ Ⓒ Ⓓ
30. Ⓐ Ⓑ Ⓒ Ⓓ
31. Ⓐ Ⓑ Ⓒ Ⓓ
32. Ⓐ Ⓑ Ⓒ Ⓓ
33. Ⓐ Ⓑ Ⓒ Ⓓ
34. Ⓐ Ⓑ Ⓒ Ⓓ
35. Ⓐ Ⓑ Ⓒ Ⓓ
36. Ⓐ Ⓑ Ⓒ Ⓓ
37. Ⓐ Ⓑ Ⓒ Ⓓ
38. Ⓐ Ⓑ Ⓒ Ⓓ
39. Ⓐ Ⓑ Ⓒ Ⓓ
40. Ⓐ Ⓑ Ⓒ Ⓓ
41. Ⓐ Ⓑ Ⓒ Ⓓ
42. Ⓐ Ⓑ Ⓒ Ⓓ
43. Ⓐ Ⓑ Ⓒ Ⓓ
44. Ⓐ Ⓑ Ⓒ Ⓓ
45. Ⓐ Ⓑ Ⓒ Ⓓ
46. Ⓐ Ⓑ Ⓒ Ⓓ
47. Ⓐ Ⓑ Ⓒ Ⓓ
48. Ⓐ Ⓑ Ⓒ Ⓓ
49. Ⓐ Ⓑ Ⓒ Ⓓ
50. Ⓐ Ⓑ Ⓒ Ⓓ

SECTION 2

1. Ⓐ Ⓑ Ⓒ Ⓓ
2. Ⓐ Ⓑ Ⓒ Ⓓ
3. Ⓐ Ⓑ Ⓒ Ⓓ
4. Ⓐ Ⓑ Ⓒ Ⓓ
5. Ⓐ Ⓑ Ⓒ Ⓓ
6. Ⓐ Ⓑ Ⓒ Ⓓ
7. Ⓐ Ⓑ Ⓒ Ⓓ
8. Ⓐ Ⓑ Ⓒ Ⓓ
9. Ⓐ Ⓑ Ⓒ Ⓓ
10. Ⓐ Ⓑ Ⓒ Ⓓ
11. Ⓐ Ⓑ Ⓒ Ⓓ
12. Ⓐ Ⓑ Ⓒ Ⓓ
13. Ⓐ Ⓑ Ⓒ Ⓓ
14. Ⓐ Ⓑ Ⓒ Ⓓ
15. Ⓐ Ⓑ Ⓒ Ⓓ
16. Ⓐ Ⓑ Ⓒ Ⓓ
17. Ⓐ Ⓑ Ⓒ Ⓓ
18. Ⓐ Ⓑ Ⓒ Ⓓ
19. Ⓐ Ⓑ Ⓒ Ⓓ
20. Ⓐ Ⓑ Ⓒ Ⓓ
21. Ⓐ Ⓑ Ⓒ Ⓓ
22. Ⓐ Ⓑ Ⓒ Ⓓ
23. Ⓐ Ⓑ Ⓒ Ⓓ
24. Ⓐ Ⓑ Ⓒ Ⓓ
25. Ⓐ Ⓑ Ⓒ Ⓓ
26. Ⓐ Ⓑ Ⓒ Ⓓ
27. Ⓐ Ⓑ Ⓒ Ⓓ
28. Ⓐ Ⓑ Ⓒ Ⓓ
29. Ⓐ Ⓑ Ⓒ Ⓓ
30. Ⓐ Ⓑ Ⓒ Ⓓ
31. Ⓐ Ⓑ Ⓒ Ⓓ
32. Ⓐ Ⓑ Ⓒ Ⓓ
33. Ⓐ Ⓑ Ⓒ Ⓓ
34. Ⓐ Ⓑ Ⓒ Ⓓ
35. Ⓐ Ⓑ Ⓒ Ⓓ
36. Ⓐ Ⓑ Ⓒ Ⓓ
37. Ⓐ Ⓑ Ⓒ Ⓓ
38. Ⓐ Ⓑ Ⓒ Ⓓ
39. Ⓐ Ⓑ Ⓒ Ⓓ
40. Ⓐ Ⓑ Ⓒ Ⓓ

SECTION 3

1. Ⓐ Ⓑ Ⓒ Ⓓ
2. Ⓐ Ⓑ Ⓒ Ⓓ
3. Ⓐ Ⓑ Ⓒ Ⓓ
4. Ⓐ Ⓑ Ⓒ Ⓓ
5. Ⓐ Ⓑ Ⓒ Ⓓ
6. Ⓐ Ⓑ Ⓒ Ⓓ
7. Ⓐ Ⓑ Ⓒ Ⓓ
8. Ⓐ Ⓑ Ⓒ Ⓓ
9. Ⓐ Ⓑ Ⓒ Ⓓ
10. Ⓐ Ⓑ Ⓒ Ⓓ
11. Ⓐ Ⓑ Ⓒ Ⓓ
12. Ⓐ Ⓑ Ⓒ Ⓓ
13. Ⓐ Ⓑ Ⓒ Ⓓ
14. Ⓐ Ⓑ Ⓒ Ⓓ
15. Ⓐ Ⓑ Ⓒ Ⓓ
16. Ⓐ Ⓑ Ⓒ Ⓓ
17. Ⓐ Ⓑ Ⓒ Ⓓ
18. Ⓐ Ⓑ Ⓒ Ⓓ
19. Ⓐ Ⓑ Ⓒ Ⓓ
20. Ⓐ Ⓑ Ⓒ Ⓓ
21. Ⓐ Ⓑ Ⓒ Ⓓ
22. Ⓐ Ⓑ Ⓒ Ⓓ
23. Ⓐ Ⓑ Ⓒ Ⓓ
24. Ⓐ Ⓑ Ⓒ Ⓓ
25. Ⓐ Ⓑ Ⓒ Ⓓ
26. Ⓐ Ⓑ Ⓒ Ⓓ
27. Ⓐ Ⓑ Ⓒ Ⓓ
28. Ⓐ Ⓑ Ⓒ Ⓓ
29. Ⓐ Ⓑ Ⓒ Ⓓ
30. Ⓐ Ⓑ Ⓒ Ⓓ
31. Ⓐ Ⓑ Ⓒ Ⓓ
32. Ⓐ Ⓑ Ⓒ Ⓓ
33. Ⓐ Ⓑ Ⓒ Ⓓ
34. Ⓐ Ⓑ Ⓒ Ⓓ
35. Ⓐ Ⓑ Ⓒ Ⓓ
36. Ⓐ Ⓑ Ⓒ Ⓓ
37. Ⓐ Ⓑ Ⓒ Ⓓ
38. Ⓐ Ⓑ Ⓒ Ⓓ
39. Ⓐ Ⓑ Ⓒ Ⓓ
40. Ⓐ Ⓑ Ⓒ Ⓓ
41. Ⓐ Ⓑ Ⓒ Ⓓ
42. Ⓐ Ⓑ Ⓒ Ⓓ
43. Ⓐ Ⓑ Ⓒ Ⓓ
44. Ⓐ Ⓑ Ⓒ Ⓓ
45. Ⓐ Ⓑ Ⓒ Ⓓ
46. Ⓐ Ⓑ Ⓒ Ⓓ
47. Ⓐ Ⓑ Ⓒ Ⓓ
48. Ⓐ Ⓑ Ⓒ Ⓓ
49. Ⓐ Ⓑ Ⓒ Ⓓ
50. Ⓐ Ⓑ Ⓒ Ⓓ
51. Ⓐ Ⓑ Ⓒ Ⓓ
52. Ⓐ Ⓑ Ⓒ Ⓓ
53. Ⓐ Ⓑ Ⓒ Ⓓ
54. Ⓐ Ⓑ Ⓒ Ⓓ
55. Ⓐ Ⓑ Ⓒ Ⓓ
56. Ⓐ Ⓑ Ⓒ Ⓓ
57. Ⓐ Ⓑ Ⓒ Ⓓ
58. Ⓐ Ⓑ Ⓒ Ⓓ
59. Ⓐ Ⓑ Ⓒ Ⓓ
60. Ⓐ Ⓑ Ⓒ Ⓓ

ANSWER SHEET FOR PRACTICE TEST 1

SECTION 1	SECTION 2	SECTION 3

SECTION 1

1. Ⓐ Ⓑ Ⓒ Ⓓ
2. Ⓐ Ⓑ Ⓒ Ⓓ
3. Ⓐ Ⓑ Ⓒ Ⓓ
4. Ⓐ Ⓑ Ⓒ Ⓓ
5. Ⓐ Ⓑ Ⓒ Ⓓ
6. Ⓐ Ⓑ Ⓒ Ⓓ
7. Ⓐ Ⓑ Ⓒ Ⓓ
8. Ⓐ Ⓑ Ⓒ Ⓓ
9. Ⓐ Ⓑ Ⓒ Ⓓ
10. Ⓐ Ⓑ Ⓒ Ⓓ
11. Ⓐ Ⓑ Ⓒ Ⓓ
12. Ⓐ Ⓑ Ⓒ Ⓓ
13. Ⓐ Ⓑ Ⓒ Ⓓ
14. Ⓐ Ⓑ Ⓒ Ⓓ
15. Ⓐ Ⓑ Ⓒ Ⓓ
16. Ⓐ Ⓑ Ⓒ Ⓓ
17. Ⓐ Ⓑ Ⓒ Ⓓ
18. Ⓐ Ⓑ Ⓒ Ⓓ
19. Ⓐ Ⓑ Ⓒ Ⓓ
20. Ⓐ Ⓑ Ⓒ Ⓓ
21. Ⓐ Ⓑ Ⓒ Ⓓ
22. Ⓐ Ⓑ Ⓒ Ⓓ
23. Ⓐ Ⓑ Ⓒ Ⓓ
24. Ⓐ Ⓑ Ⓒ Ⓓ
25. Ⓐ Ⓑ Ⓒ Ⓓ
26. Ⓐ Ⓑ Ⓒ Ⓓ
27. Ⓐ Ⓑ Ⓒ Ⓓ
28. Ⓐ Ⓑ Ⓒ Ⓓ
29. Ⓐ Ⓑ Ⓒ Ⓓ
30. Ⓐ Ⓑ Ⓒ Ⓓ
31. Ⓐ Ⓑ Ⓒ Ⓓ
32. Ⓐ Ⓑ Ⓒ Ⓓ
33. Ⓐ Ⓑ Ⓒ Ⓓ
34. Ⓐ Ⓑ Ⓒ Ⓓ
35. Ⓐ Ⓑ Ⓒ Ⓓ
36. Ⓐ Ⓑ Ⓒ Ⓓ
37. Ⓐ Ⓑ Ⓒ Ⓓ
38. Ⓐ Ⓑ Ⓒ Ⓓ
39. Ⓐ Ⓑ Ⓒ Ⓓ
40. Ⓐ Ⓑ Ⓒ Ⓓ
41. Ⓐ Ⓑ Ⓒ Ⓓ
42. Ⓐ Ⓑ Ⓒ Ⓓ
43. Ⓐ Ⓑ Ⓒ Ⓓ
44. Ⓐ Ⓑ Ⓒ Ⓓ
45. Ⓐ Ⓑ Ⓒ Ⓓ
46. Ⓐ Ⓑ Ⓒ Ⓓ
47. Ⓐ Ⓑ Ⓒ Ⓓ
48. Ⓐ Ⓑ Ⓒ Ⓓ
49. Ⓐ Ⓑ Ⓒ Ⓓ
50. Ⓐ Ⓑ Ⓒ Ⓓ

SECTION 2

1. Ⓐ Ⓑ Ⓒ Ⓓ
2. Ⓐ Ⓑ Ⓒ Ⓓ
3. Ⓐ Ⓑ Ⓒ Ⓓ
4. Ⓐ Ⓑ Ⓒ Ⓓ
5. Ⓐ Ⓑ Ⓒ Ⓓ
6. Ⓐ Ⓑ Ⓒ Ⓓ
7. Ⓐ Ⓑ Ⓒ Ⓓ
8. Ⓐ Ⓑ Ⓒ Ⓓ
9. Ⓐ Ⓑ Ⓒ Ⓓ
10. Ⓐ Ⓑ Ⓒ Ⓓ
11. Ⓐ Ⓑ Ⓒ Ⓓ
12. Ⓐ Ⓑ Ⓒ Ⓓ
13. Ⓐ Ⓑ Ⓒ Ⓓ
14. Ⓐ Ⓑ Ⓒ Ⓓ
15. Ⓐ Ⓑ Ⓒ Ⓓ
16. Ⓐ Ⓑ Ⓒ Ⓓ
17. Ⓐ Ⓑ Ⓒ Ⓓ
18. Ⓐ Ⓑ Ⓒ Ⓓ
19. Ⓐ Ⓑ Ⓒ Ⓓ
20. Ⓐ Ⓑ Ⓒ Ⓓ
21. Ⓐ Ⓑ Ⓒ Ⓓ
22. Ⓐ Ⓑ Ⓒ Ⓓ
23. Ⓐ Ⓑ Ⓒ Ⓓ
24. Ⓐ Ⓑ Ⓒ Ⓓ
25. Ⓐ Ⓑ Ⓒ Ⓓ
26. Ⓐ Ⓑ Ⓒ Ⓓ
27. Ⓐ Ⓑ Ⓒ Ⓓ
28. Ⓐ Ⓑ Ⓒ Ⓓ
29. Ⓐ Ⓑ Ⓒ Ⓓ
30. Ⓐ Ⓑ Ⓒ Ⓓ
31. Ⓐ Ⓑ Ⓒ Ⓓ
32. Ⓐ Ⓑ Ⓒ Ⓓ
33. Ⓐ Ⓑ Ⓒ Ⓓ
34. Ⓐ Ⓑ Ⓒ Ⓓ
35. Ⓐ Ⓑ Ⓒ Ⓓ
36. Ⓐ Ⓑ Ⓒ Ⓓ
37. Ⓐ Ⓑ Ⓒ Ⓓ
38. Ⓐ Ⓑ Ⓒ Ⓓ
39. Ⓐ Ⓑ Ⓒ Ⓓ
40. Ⓐ Ⓑ Ⓒ Ⓓ

SECTION 3

1. Ⓐ Ⓑ Ⓒ Ⓓ
2. Ⓐ Ⓑ Ⓒ Ⓓ
3. Ⓐ Ⓑ Ⓒ Ⓓ
4. Ⓐ Ⓑ Ⓒ Ⓓ
5. Ⓐ Ⓑ Ⓒ Ⓓ
6. Ⓐ Ⓑ Ⓒ Ⓓ
7. Ⓐ Ⓑ Ⓒ Ⓓ
8. Ⓐ Ⓑ Ⓒ Ⓓ
9. Ⓐ Ⓑ Ⓒ Ⓓ
10. Ⓐ Ⓑ Ⓒ Ⓓ
11. Ⓐ Ⓑ Ⓒ Ⓓ
12. Ⓐ Ⓑ Ⓒ Ⓓ
13. Ⓐ Ⓑ Ⓒ Ⓓ
14. Ⓐ Ⓑ Ⓒ Ⓓ
15. Ⓐ Ⓑ Ⓒ Ⓓ
16. Ⓐ Ⓑ Ⓒ Ⓓ
17. Ⓐ Ⓑ Ⓒ Ⓓ
18. Ⓐ Ⓑ Ⓒ Ⓓ
19. Ⓐ Ⓑ Ⓒ Ⓓ
20. Ⓐ Ⓑ Ⓒ Ⓓ
21. Ⓐ Ⓑ Ⓒ Ⓓ
22. Ⓐ Ⓑ Ⓒ Ⓓ
23. Ⓐ Ⓑ Ⓒ Ⓓ
24. Ⓐ Ⓑ Ⓒ Ⓓ
25. Ⓐ Ⓑ Ⓒ Ⓓ
26. Ⓐ Ⓑ Ⓒ Ⓓ
27. Ⓐ Ⓑ Ⓒ Ⓓ
28. Ⓐ Ⓑ Ⓒ Ⓓ
29. Ⓐ Ⓑ Ⓒ Ⓓ
30. Ⓐ Ⓑ Ⓒ Ⓓ
31. Ⓐ Ⓑ Ⓒ Ⓓ
32. Ⓐ Ⓑ Ⓒ Ⓓ
33. Ⓐ Ⓑ Ⓒ Ⓓ
34. Ⓐ Ⓑ Ⓒ Ⓓ
35. Ⓐ Ⓑ Ⓒ Ⓓ
36. Ⓐ Ⓑ Ⓒ Ⓓ
37. Ⓐ Ⓑ Ⓒ Ⓓ
38. Ⓐ Ⓑ Ⓒ Ⓓ
39. Ⓐ Ⓑ Ⓒ Ⓓ
40. Ⓐ Ⓑ Ⓒ Ⓓ
41. Ⓐ Ⓑ Ⓒ Ⓓ
42. Ⓐ Ⓑ Ⓒ Ⓓ
43. Ⓐ Ⓑ Ⓒ Ⓓ
44. Ⓐ Ⓑ Ⓒ Ⓓ
45. Ⓐ Ⓑ Ⓒ Ⓓ
46. Ⓐ Ⓑ Ⓒ Ⓓ
47. Ⓐ Ⓑ Ⓒ Ⓓ
48. Ⓐ Ⓑ Ⓒ Ⓓ
49. Ⓐ Ⓑ Ⓒ Ⓓ
50. Ⓐ Ⓑ Ⓒ Ⓓ
51. Ⓐ Ⓑ Ⓒ Ⓓ
52. Ⓐ Ⓑ Ⓒ Ⓓ
53. Ⓐ Ⓑ Ⓒ Ⓓ
54. Ⓐ Ⓑ Ⓒ Ⓓ
55. Ⓐ Ⓑ Ⓒ Ⓓ
56. Ⓐ Ⓑ Ⓒ Ⓓ
57. Ⓐ Ⓑ Ⓒ Ⓓ
58. Ⓐ Ⓑ Ⓒ Ⓓ
59. Ⓐ Ⓑ Ⓒ Ⓓ
60. Ⓐ Ⓑ Ⓒ Ⓓ

ANSWER SHEET FOR PRACTICE TEST 2

SECTION 1	SECTION 2	SECTION 3

SECTION 1

1. Ⓐ Ⓑ Ⓒ Ⓓ
2. Ⓐ Ⓑ Ⓒ Ⓓ
3. Ⓐ Ⓑ Ⓒ Ⓓ
4. Ⓐ Ⓑ Ⓒ Ⓓ
5. Ⓐ Ⓑ Ⓒ Ⓓ
6. Ⓐ Ⓑ Ⓒ Ⓓ
7. Ⓐ Ⓑ Ⓒ Ⓓ
8. Ⓐ Ⓑ Ⓒ Ⓓ
9. Ⓐ Ⓑ Ⓒ Ⓓ
10. Ⓐ Ⓑ Ⓒ Ⓓ
11. Ⓐ Ⓑ Ⓒ Ⓓ
12. Ⓐ Ⓑ Ⓒ Ⓓ
13. Ⓐ Ⓑ Ⓒ Ⓓ
14. Ⓐ Ⓑ Ⓒ Ⓓ
15. Ⓐ Ⓑ Ⓒ Ⓓ
16. Ⓐ Ⓑ Ⓒ Ⓓ
17. Ⓐ Ⓑ Ⓒ Ⓓ
18. Ⓐ Ⓑ Ⓒ Ⓓ
19. Ⓐ Ⓑ Ⓒ Ⓓ
20. Ⓐ Ⓑ Ⓒ Ⓓ
21. Ⓐ Ⓑ Ⓒ Ⓓ
22. Ⓐ Ⓑ Ⓒ Ⓓ
23. Ⓐ Ⓑ Ⓒ Ⓓ
24. Ⓐ Ⓑ Ⓒ Ⓓ
25. Ⓐ Ⓑ Ⓒ Ⓓ
26. Ⓐ Ⓑ Ⓒ Ⓓ
27. Ⓐ Ⓑ Ⓒ Ⓓ
28. Ⓐ Ⓑ Ⓒ Ⓓ
29. Ⓐ Ⓑ Ⓒ Ⓓ
30. Ⓐ Ⓑ Ⓒ Ⓓ
31. Ⓐ Ⓑ Ⓒ Ⓓ
32. Ⓐ Ⓑ Ⓒ Ⓓ
33. Ⓐ Ⓑ Ⓒ Ⓓ
34. Ⓐ Ⓑ Ⓒ Ⓓ
35. Ⓐ Ⓑ Ⓒ Ⓓ
36. Ⓐ Ⓑ Ⓒ Ⓓ
37. Ⓐ Ⓑ Ⓒ Ⓓ
38. Ⓐ Ⓑ Ⓒ Ⓓ
39. Ⓐ Ⓑ Ⓒ Ⓓ
40. Ⓐ Ⓑ Ⓒ Ⓓ
41. Ⓐ Ⓑ Ⓒ Ⓓ
42. Ⓐ Ⓑ Ⓒ Ⓓ
43. Ⓐ Ⓑ Ⓒ Ⓓ
44. Ⓐ Ⓑ Ⓒ Ⓓ
45. Ⓐ Ⓑ Ⓒ Ⓓ
46. Ⓐ Ⓑ Ⓒ Ⓓ
47. Ⓐ Ⓑ Ⓒ Ⓓ
48. Ⓐ Ⓑ Ⓒ Ⓓ
49. Ⓐ Ⓑ Ⓒ Ⓓ
50. Ⓐ Ⓑ Ⓒ Ⓓ

SECTION 2

1. Ⓐ Ⓑ Ⓒ Ⓓ
2. Ⓐ Ⓑ Ⓒ Ⓓ
3. Ⓐ Ⓑ Ⓒ Ⓓ
4. Ⓐ Ⓑ Ⓒ Ⓓ
5. Ⓐ Ⓑ Ⓒ Ⓓ
6. Ⓐ Ⓑ Ⓒ Ⓓ
7. Ⓐ Ⓑ Ⓒ Ⓓ
8. Ⓐ Ⓑ Ⓒ Ⓓ
9. Ⓐ Ⓑ Ⓒ Ⓓ
10. Ⓐ Ⓑ Ⓒ Ⓓ
11. Ⓐ Ⓑ Ⓒ Ⓓ
12. Ⓐ Ⓑ Ⓒ Ⓓ
13. Ⓐ Ⓑ Ⓒ Ⓓ
14. Ⓐ Ⓑ Ⓒ Ⓓ
15. Ⓐ Ⓑ Ⓒ Ⓓ
16. Ⓐ Ⓑ Ⓒ Ⓓ
17. Ⓐ Ⓑ Ⓒ Ⓓ
18. Ⓐ Ⓑ Ⓒ Ⓓ
19. Ⓐ Ⓑ Ⓒ Ⓓ
20. Ⓐ Ⓑ Ⓒ Ⓓ
21. Ⓐ Ⓑ Ⓒ Ⓓ
22. Ⓐ Ⓑ Ⓒ Ⓓ
23. Ⓐ Ⓑ Ⓒ Ⓓ
24. Ⓐ Ⓑ Ⓒ Ⓓ
25. Ⓐ Ⓑ Ⓒ Ⓓ
26. Ⓐ Ⓑ Ⓒ Ⓓ
27. Ⓐ Ⓑ Ⓒ Ⓓ
28. Ⓐ Ⓑ Ⓒ Ⓓ
29. Ⓐ Ⓑ Ⓒ Ⓓ
30. Ⓐ Ⓑ Ⓒ Ⓓ
31. Ⓐ Ⓑ Ⓒ Ⓓ
32. Ⓐ Ⓑ Ⓒ Ⓓ
33. Ⓐ Ⓑ Ⓒ Ⓓ
34. Ⓐ Ⓑ Ⓒ Ⓓ
35. Ⓐ Ⓑ Ⓒ Ⓓ
36. Ⓐ Ⓑ Ⓒ Ⓓ
37. Ⓐ Ⓑ Ⓒ Ⓓ
38. Ⓐ Ⓑ Ⓒ Ⓓ
39. Ⓐ Ⓑ Ⓒ Ⓓ
40. Ⓐ Ⓑ Ⓒ Ⓓ

SECTION 3

1. Ⓐ Ⓑ Ⓒ Ⓓ   31. Ⓐ Ⓑ Ⓒ Ⓓ
2. Ⓐ Ⓑ Ⓒ Ⓓ   32. Ⓐ Ⓑ Ⓒ Ⓓ
3. Ⓐ Ⓑ Ⓒ Ⓓ   33. Ⓐ Ⓑ Ⓒ Ⓓ
4. Ⓐ Ⓑ Ⓒ Ⓓ   34. Ⓐ Ⓑ Ⓒ Ⓓ
5. Ⓐ Ⓑ Ⓒ Ⓓ   35. Ⓐ Ⓑ Ⓒ Ⓓ
6. Ⓐ Ⓑ Ⓒ Ⓓ   36. Ⓐ Ⓑ Ⓒ Ⓓ
7. Ⓐ Ⓑ Ⓒ Ⓓ   37. Ⓐ Ⓑ Ⓒ Ⓓ
8. Ⓐ Ⓑ Ⓒ Ⓓ   38. Ⓐ Ⓑ Ⓒ Ⓓ
9. Ⓐ Ⓑ Ⓒ Ⓓ   39. Ⓐ Ⓑ Ⓒ Ⓓ
10. Ⓐ Ⓑ Ⓒ Ⓓ   40. Ⓐ Ⓑ Ⓒ Ⓓ
11. Ⓐ Ⓑ Ⓒ Ⓓ   41. Ⓐ Ⓑ Ⓒ Ⓓ
12. Ⓐ Ⓑ Ⓒ Ⓓ   42. Ⓐ Ⓑ Ⓒ Ⓓ
13. Ⓐ Ⓑ Ⓒ Ⓓ   43. Ⓐ Ⓑ Ⓒ Ⓓ
14. Ⓐ Ⓑ Ⓒ Ⓓ   44. Ⓐ Ⓑ Ⓒ Ⓓ
15. Ⓐ Ⓑ Ⓒ Ⓓ   45. Ⓐ Ⓑ Ⓒ Ⓓ
16. Ⓐ Ⓑ Ⓒ Ⓓ   46. Ⓐ Ⓑ Ⓒ Ⓓ
17. Ⓐ Ⓑ Ⓒ Ⓓ   47. Ⓐ Ⓑ Ⓒ Ⓓ
18. Ⓐ Ⓑ Ⓒ Ⓓ   48. Ⓐ Ⓑ Ⓒ Ⓓ
19. Ⓐ Ⓑ Ⓒ Ⓓ   49. Ⓐ Ⓑ Ⓒ Ⓓ
20. Ⓐ Ⓑ Ⓒ Ⓓ   50. Ⓐ Ⓑ Ⓒ Ⓓ
21. Ⓐ Ⓑ Ⓒ Ⓓ   51. Ⓐ Ⓑ Ⓒ Ⓓ
22. Ⓐ Ⓑ Ⓒ Ⓓ   52. Ⓐ Ⓑ Ⓒ Ⓓ
23. Ⓐ Ⓑ Ⓒ Ⓓ   53. Ⓐ Ⓑ Ⓒ Ⓓ
24. Ⓐ Ⓑ Ⓒ Ⓓ   54. Ⓐ Ⓑ Ⓒ Ⓓ
25. Ⓐ Ⓑ Ⓒ Ⓓ   55. Ⓐ Ⓑ Ⓒ Ⓓ
26. Ⓐ Ⓑ Ⓒ Ⓓ   56. Ⓐ Ⓑ Ⓒ Ⓓ
27. Ⓐ Ⓑ Ⓒ Ⓓ   57. Ⓐ Ⓑ Ⓒ Ⓓ
28. Ⓐ Ⓑ Ⓒ Ⓓ   58. Ⓐ Ⓑ Ⓒ Ⓓ
29. Ⓐ Ⓑ Ⓒ Ⓓ   59. Ⓐ Ⓑ Ⓒ Ⓓ
30. Ⓐ Ⓑ Ⓒ Ⓓ   60. Ⓐ Ⓑ Ⓒ Ⓓ

INDEX